Business Organizations

ASPEN STUDENT TREATISE SERIES

BUSINESS ORGANIZATIONS

J. MARK RAMSEYER
Harvard Law School

Wolters Kluwer
Law & Business

Printed in the United States of America.

1 2 3 4 5 6 7 8 9 0

ISBN 978-1-4548-0672-1

Library of Congress Cataloging-in-Publication Data

Ramseyer, J. Mark, 1954-
  Business organizations / J. Mark Ramseyer.
    p. cm. — (Aspen student treatise series)
  ISBN 978-1-4548-0672-1
  1. Business enterprises — Law and legislation — United States. 2. Commercial law — United States. I. Title.

KF889.R28 2012
343.7307 — dc23

                                                          2012012397

About Wolters Kluwer Law & Business

Wolters Kluwer Law & Business is a leading global provider of intelligent information and digital solutions for legal and business professionals in key specialty areas, and respected educational resources for professors and law students. Wolters Kluwer Law & Business connects legal and business professionals as well as those in the education market with timely, specialized authoritative content and information-enabled solutions to support success through productivity, accuracy and mobility.

Serving customers worldwide, Wolters Kluwer Law & Business products include those under the Aspen Publishers, CCH, Kluwer Law International, Loislaw, Best Case, ftwilliam.com and MediRegs family of products.

CCH products have been a trusted resource since 1913, and are highly regarded resources for legal, securities, antitrust and trade regulation, government contracting, banking, pension, payroll, employment and labor, and healthcare reimbursement and compliance professionals.

Aspen Publishers products provide essential information to attorneys, business professionals and law students. Written by preeminent authorities, the product line offers analytical and practical information in a range of specialty practice areas from securities law and intellectual property to mergers and acquisitions and pension/benefits. Aspen's trusted legal education resources provide professors and students with high-quality, up-to-date and effective resources for successful instruction and study in all areas of the law.

Kluwer Law International products provide the global business community with reliable international legal information in English. Legal practitioners, corporate counsel and business executives around the world rely on Kluwer Law journals, looseleafs, books, and electronic products for comprehensive information in many areas of international legal practice.

Loislaw is a comprehensive online legal research product providing legal content to law firm practitioners of various specializations. Loislaw provides attorneys with the ability to quickly and efficiently find the necessary legal information they need, when and where they need it, by facilitating access to primary law as well as state-specific law, records, forms and treatises.

Best Case Solutions is the leading bankruptcy software product to the bankruptcy industry. It provides software and workflow tools to flawlessly streamline petition preparation and the electronic filing process, while timely incorporating ever-changing court requirements.

ftwilliam.com offers employee benefits professionals the highest quality plan documents (retirement, welfare and non-qualified) and government forms (5500/PBGC, 1099 and IRS) software at highly competitive prices.

MediRegs products provide integrated health care compliance content and software solutions for professionals in healthcare, higher education and life sciences, including professionals in accounting, law and consulting.

Wolters Kluwer Law & Business, a division of Wolters Kluwer, is headquartered in New York. Wolters Kluwer is a market-leading global information services company focused on professionals.

*Dedicated to the kind soul in the UCLA law school class of 1988
who wrote on her (his?) teaching evaluation,
"Ramseyer seems like a nice guy. He obviously tries really hard.
Maybe someday he'll be a good teacher.
I'm just sorry I had to be part of the learning experience."*

Summary of Contents

Contents

CHAPTER 1

Agency

CHAPTER 2

Partnership

Contents

CHAPTER 3

Implications of the Corporate Form

Contents

CHAPTER 4

Corporate Fiduciary Duties

CHAPTER 5

Insider Trading

CHAPTER 6

Corporate Control (I)

CHAPTER 7

Corporate Control (II)

Contents

CHAPTER 8

Mergers and Acquisitions

Contents

APPENDIX

Self-Study

Preface

Consider this a simple guide to the simple course on corporate law. It explains the mostly straightforward doctrine that judges apply to the only superficially subtle disputes they face. It explains the relatively few principles that tie together the only-deceptively disparate opinions in the books. It summarizes cases. It applies statutes. It states the law. And it explains why judges say what they say and do what they do.

Organizationally, the book tracks two of the principal texts on the market: William A. Klein, J. Mark Ramseyer, and Stephen M. Bainbridge, *Business Associations: Cases and Materials on Agency, Partnerships, and Corporations* (8th ed., Foundation Press 2012); and William T. Allen, Reinier Kraakman, and Guhan Subramanian, *Commentaries and Cases on the Law of Business Organizations* (4th ed., Wolters Kluwer 2012). At least for the former, it explains why the editors included the cases they did and what they intended the cases to show. It closes with a set of review questions, and some suggested answers.

The book approaches the field with a modest rule that any decent lawyer would understand instinctively: Judges are people too. To predict the outcome of a case, a lawyer needs to know the law, but he or she needs to know a good bit more besides. Decades into legal realism, this is hardly news. But it does imply several points relevant here. First, some cases make sense only in light of facts not in the opinion. As necessary (and feasible), this book adds the excluded facts that help explain why a judge did what he or she did.

Second, some cases are wrong. A casebook is not an encyclopedia, and neither is this book. A casebook is a pedagogical tool, and this is a book to explain that pedagogical strategy. Some of the cases in the corporate law casebooks are wrong, and — more important — sometimes the editors included them precisely *because* they are wrong. Some are wrong on the law, some are wrong on the welfare analysis, and some are wrong on the logic. The editors included them because they thought a discussion about how the judges went wrong might promote classroom learning. As appropriate, this book discusses why, where, and how the opinions are wrong.

Last, the law is (mostly) simple. At root, the principles that govern complex transactions at firms listed on the New York Stock Exchange stem from the principles that govern the simple transactions in Chapter 1. One person has some spare cash but does not know what to do with it; another person has some ideas about how to get rich but lacks the money needed to indulge them. The law that governs corporate affairs is the law that structures the relations between these two. It is the law that facilitates arrangements where one person advances the funds and the other person uses the funds to make money for both of them.

And all the classic movie references in the book? Look, this is a book to *read*, not to consult 24 hours before the final. The resurrected movie characters and plots are there to help you slog through the law. (All those books you bought last year to help you with your first-year courses — how many of them did you actually read anyway?) If classic movies aren't your thing, ignore the references. It will not matter. But do read the book.

J. Mark Ramseyer
Harvard University
Spring 2012

Acknowledgments

We wish to thank the authors and copyright holders of the following works who permitted their inclusion in this book:

Chapter 1

American Law Institute. Restatement, Second, Agency, © 1958 by The American Law Institute. Reproduced with permission. All rights reserved.

American Law Institute. Restatement, Third, Agency, © 2006 by The American Law Institute. Reproduced with permission. All rights reserved.

Chapter 2

The Hotel Bristol, photo courtesy of the Library of Congress.

500 Fifth Avenue, photo reproduced with permission of Robert B. Thompson.

Chapter 3

Zolt, Eric M., *Tax Deductions for Charitable Contributions: Domestic Activities, Foreign Activities, or None of the Above* (draft of Apr. 6, 2011). Hastings Law Journal, Vol. 63, pp. 361-410, 2012.

Chapter 4

The American Law Institute. Principles of Corporate Governance: Analysis and Recommendations, © 1994 by The American Law Institute. Reproduced with permission. All rights reserved.

Random House. Book Cover, copyright © 1966, 1967 by Random House, Inc., from HELL'S ANGELS by Hunter S. Thompson. Used by permission of Random House, Inc.

DOONESBURY © 1981 G. B. Trudeau. Reprinted with permission of UNIVERSAL UCLICK. All rights reserved.

Chapter 5

American Law Institute. Restatement, Second, Agency, © 1958 by The American Law Institute. Reproduced with permission. All rights reserved.

Excerpt from "WALL STREET" © 1987 Courtesy of Twentieth Century Fox. Written by Stanley Weiser & Oliver Stone. All rights reserved.

Chapter 6

DOONESBURY © 1971 G. B. Trudeau. Reprinted with permission of UNIVERSAL UCLICK. All rights reserved.

Ramseyer, Mark J., The Story of Ringling Bros. v. Ringling: Nepotism and Cycling at the Circus, in Corporate Law Stories 135 (J. Mark Ramseyer ed., Foundation Press 2009). Used with permission of Thomson Reuters.

Arnold Rothstein, 1928, with permission of Transcendental Graphics/Getty Images Sport/Getty Images.

Chapter 7

Courtesy of Professor Eric Gouvin, Western New England College of Law. Printed with permission from The Berkshire Eagle.

Norman, Next to Mother's Victorian Home, © Underwood & Underwood/ Corbis.

Chapter 8

Sorel, Edward. Joseph Flom comic cartoon. Printed with permission of Edward Sorel.

The Unocal Spill, © The Tribune/Photos From the Vault.

CHAPTER 1

Agency

"You're an angel," Sam Spade said.

"I'm going to send you over. The chances are you'll get off with life. That means you'll be out again in twenty years."

But "I'll wait for you," he promised. And "[i]f they hang you, I'll always remember you."[1]

Can he do this? Obviously, he can — and he does. But can he do this *legally*? The "angel" is Brigid O'Shaughnessy, the woman who (as a client) hires him (as a private detective) to tail one Floyd Thursby. She offers him $200 plus expenses, and he agrees. In the process, he becomes her agent and she his principal. He now owes her fiduciary duties. He cannot pocket a payoff from Thursby to let him disappear. Neither can he spend all day at a casino and charge her his usual fee anyway.

Can he "send her over" to hang?

"I don't care who loves who," continued Spade. This was not about love. It was about partnership, and Miles Archer had been his partner. "I'm not going to play the sap for you. . . . You killed Miles, and you're going over for it."[2] Maybe Spade realized partners owe each other fiduciary duties too. "When a man's partner is killed," he tried to explain, "he's supposed to do something about it. It doesn't make any difference what you thought of him. He was your partner and you're supposed to do something about it. It's bad business to let the killer get away with it. It's bad all around . . . bad for every detective everywhere."[3]

Spade gives this speech at the end of *The Maltese Falcon*, a Dashiell Hammett novel and a film noir starring Humphrey Bogart as Spade and Mary Astor as O'Shaughnessy. O'Shaughnessy had hired Spade and his partner to tail Thursby. In fact, however, O'Shaughnessy never wanted Thursby. She wanted a bird — the jewel-encrusted golden falcon that the Knights of Malta had sent Charles V in 1539.

---

[1] Dashiell Hammett, *The Maltese Falcon, The Thin Man, Red Harvest* 219 (Everyman's Library 2000).

[2] *Id.* at 221.

[3] *Id.* at 222.

She wanted Spade to find it and asked him to tail Thursby because she thought Thursby might lead him to it. In the course of events, she shot Spade's partner Archer, and at the end of the film, Spade turned her over to the police.

These principal-agent relations (and the many variations on them) form the heart of this book — and the heart of the basic course in corporate law. By the terms of the "agency law" in this Chapter 1, business firms (as principals) act through "agents." They acquire rights through their agents. They incur contractual liabilities through them. And sometimes they incur tort and criminal liabilities too.

Corporations act through their directors, officers, and other employees — and agency law structures their relations. Partnerships (like Spade & Archer, in the film) act through their partners (Sam Spade, Miles Archer) and employees (their secretary, Effie Perine). Even sole proprietorships (like O'Shaughnessy herself) can act through agents (as when she retained Spade to work on her behalf).

In turn, these men and women who act as agents for their firm owe it a set of legal duties. Most particularly, they owe it the "fiduciary duties" of "loyalty" and "care." These lie at the center of the corporate law in this book. Should these men and women sell the firm their property without disclosing their proprietary interests, they violate their duty of loyalty to the firm — and must disgorge their profits. Should they play blackjack on company time, they violate their duty of care — and must pay damages.

In Chapter 2, this book explores these rules in the context of partnerships. In the rest of the chapters, it explores the rules among corporations. But in Chapter 1, it outlines these rules of agency in a context abstracted from any specific organizational form. It begins by defining the concept of agency (section I), then explores the scope of the authority principals can give their agents (section II). The chapter turns to the liability that agents can impose on their principals (section III) and finally examines the fiduciary duties that agents owe them (section IV).

Joel Cairo eventually offered Spade $5,000 for the falcon. Spade could not have threatened to buy it himself and forced O'Shaughnessy to make a competing bid. He would have violated the duty of loyalty he owed her. But if she shot his partner, Miles Archer, could he — legally — send her over to hang? Consider this question while reading the next several sections and return to it at the close of the chapter.

I. AGENTS

A. Simple Cases

1. Introduction

Agency law matters only when one party is an agent (see Figure 1-1). Among agents, some are servants and others are independent contractors. Both can impose contractual liability on their principals, but only servants can impose tort liability. To complicate matters horribly, however, some parties are

I. Agents

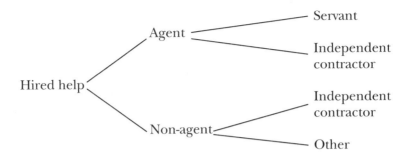

Figure 1-1
Agents, Servants, and Independent Contractors

independent contractors but not agents. Before exploring those complications, consider the more basic line between agents and non-agents.

2. Agents and Non-agents

When O'Shaughnessy hires Spade to tail Thursby, O'Shaughnessy becomes Spade's principal and Spade her agent. Under the terms of their deal, they agree that he will act on her behalf and subject to her control. As the still-classic 1958 Restatement (Second) of Agency (§1) explains the legal implication:

> [Agency results] from the manifestation of consent by one person to another that the other shall act on his behalf and subject to his control, and consent by the other . . . so to act.[4]

The rule includes three components: Spade and O'Shaughnessy must (1) agree that (2) he will act on her behalf and (3) subject to her control. In the process, they create an agency relationship.

Some cases are simple. When O'Shaughnessy hires Spade to tail Thursby, she does not buy his services; rather, she appoints him as her agent. But when Joel Cairo offers to buy the falcon from Spade, he does not become a principal; rather, he becomes a prospective buyer. In the real-life case of *White v. Thomas*,[5] Bradford White Sr. asks part-time secretary Betty Simpson to bid for a piece of land on his behalf at an auction. By agreeing to do so, she becomes his agent. She owes him a set of fiduciary duties, and should she make a bid within the scope of her authorization, he will be bound. In *Dweck v. Nasser*,[6] businessman Albert Nasser hires star

---

[4] Restatement (Second) of Agency §1 (1958). Here and throughout the book, the material from the Second Restatement of Agency is used with permission. Restatement, Second, Agency, © 1958 by The American Law Institute. Reproduced with permission. All rights reserved.
[5] 1991 Lexis 109 (Ark. App. 1991).
[6] 959 A.2d 29 (Del. Ch. 2008).

Israeli lawyer Amnon Shiboleth to settle his case. In agreeing to the arrangement, Shiboleth becomes Nasser's agent. He owes Nasser fiduciary duties, and Nasser becomes bound by his authorized activities.

Other cases are less obvious. If you hire a lawyer (like Shiboleth) or a stockbroker, he or she becomes your agent. But not so, a plumber. Hire him (or her), and he (or she) becomes not your agent but a seller of services (fixing your pipes). And not your paperboy (or -girl), either. Order a paper, and he (or she) simply sells you a product (a newspaper).

Why the distinction? Your broker buys shares for your account; your plumber fixes pipes for your bath. Your paperboy throws the newspaper where you want it; your lawyer negotiates the contractual price you demand. You tell your broker which stocks to buy and what to pay; you tell your plumber which pipes to install and how much you can afford. You tell your paperboy when to bring the paper; you tell your attorney when to deliver the contract.

In truth, many of the legal distinctions make more sense backward. If someone is an agent, certain implications follow. When those implications make sense (business sense, not legal sense), courts tend to declare the person an agent. Take stockbrokers, for instance. They handle large amounts of money. As a result, their industry will not thrive unless customers can trust them with their money. Fiduciary duties help customers trust stockbrokers. By agreeing to those fiduciary duties, brokers commit to treating their customers honestly. By calling brokers agents, courts impose on them exactly those fiduciary duties. A similar dynamic explains why courts call accountants and lawyers agents. By contrast, plumbers and paperboys need not owe their customers fiduciary duties to obtain their business, and courts do not bother calling them agents.

3. Servants and Independent Contractors

Agents come in two flavors: servants ("employees," in the language of the Restatement [Third]), and independent contractors.[7] If a principal can tell an agent not just *what* to do but *how* to do it, the agent is a servant, and the principal is his master. If instead the principal gives the agent substantial discretion about when and how to do his job, the agent is an independent contractor. Again, take the classic Restatement (Second) §2(2):

A servant is an agent . . . whose physical conduct in the performance of the service . . . is subject to the right to control by the master.

Conversely, §2(3) reads:

An independent contractor is a person . . . who is not . . . subject to the other's right to control with respect to his physical conduct. . . .

[7] Restatement (Third) of Agency §§2.04, 7.07 (2006). Here and throughout the book, the material from the Third Restatement of Agency is used with permission. Restatement, Third, Agency, © 2006 by The American Law Institute. Reproduced with permission. All rights reserved.

I. Agents

Again, some cases are easy. Usually, for example, full-time employees are servants, but skilled, irregular workers are not. Kasper Gutman ("the fat man," Spade calls him in the film) hires unemployed thug Wilmer Cook to retrieve the falcon and tells him daily where to go and whom to threaten; Cook becomes his servant. O'Shaughnessy hires licensed detective Spade to tail Thursby but tells him no more; Spade becomes an independent contractor. A firm's vice president is its servant; its outside counsel is an independent contractor. Your chauffer is your servant; your taxi driver is an independent contractor.

The distinction matters because although both types of agents can bind their principals in contract, only servants bind their principals in tort. Spade may shoot someone while tailing Thursby, but O'Shaughnessy will not be liable. Cook may shoot someone while tailing Spade, and Gutman may indeed be liable (more on this below). Your taxi driver may hit a pedestrian while ferrying you to work, but you need not pay. Your chauffer may hit a pedestrian, and you do.

And again, to the extent the distinction makes sense, perhaps it makes sense in reverse. If someone is your servant, you will try to control him — after all, you stand potentially liable for the torts he commits. Courts call someone your servant if it makes sense (business sense, not legal sense) for you to try to control him. It makes sense for you to try to control your chauffer; it makes no sense for you to try to control your taxi driver. It makes sense for a firm to try to control its full-time employees; it makes less sense for it to try to control its outside counsel.

4. Non-agent Independent Contractors

To confuse matters further, some independent contractors are not agents at all. Your stockbroker may be an independent contractor, but he or she is still your agent. Your plumber is an independent contractor and not your agent at all. If you do not control someone's "physical conduct," that someone is not your servant. Depending on the deal you have negotiated, however, an "independent contractor" may or may not be your agent. If you agreed that the person will act on your behalf and subject to your control, the person is an agent-type independent contractor. If you reached no such agreement, the person is a non-agent independent contractor.

B. Not-So-Simple Cases

If *White* and *Dweck* seem simple, other cases seem more complex. In many cases, the apparent complexity results from (frankly) disingenuous judicial manipulation: Sometimes, judges skew otherwise-simple rules to reach politically convenient but legally unwarranted results. Take *Gorton v. Doty*.[8] Charlotte Doty taught at the Soda

---

[8] 69 P.2d 136 (Idaho 1937).

Springs High School. She knew the school's football team had an away game on Friday. Feeling generous, she asked the coach whether he had the cars he needed. When the coach said no, she offered him her own. Lest the high school team members crash it, she asked him to drive it himself. He did, and crashed it anyway. On the theory that the coach had acted as Doty's agent, the father of one of the players sued Doty.

Similarly, take *A. Gay Jenson Farms Co. v. Cargill, Inc.*[9] Warren Grain & Seed Co. bought, sold, and stored grain in tiny Warren, Minnesota (population 1,678). Cargill bought and sold globally, with 2009 sales of more than $116 billion. Occasionally, Warren distributed seeds on Cargill's behalf, but usually it bought grain locally and resold it to multinationals — sometimes Cargill, sometimes other firms.

Warren was crooked. Its employees stole. As Warren borrowed from Cargill, and as its employees stole the money, its debts mounted. To investigate the problem, Cargill sent people to audit Warren's books. It suggested ways for Warren to improve its business. It monitored Warren's daily operations.

Cargill did what it could, but Warren collapsed anyway. It collapsed with debts to Cargill outstanding, of course, but it also owed money to local farmers. On the theory that Warren had acted as Cargill's agent in taking their grain on credit, the local farmers sued Cargill for their money.

The *Doty* and *Cargill* courts let their respective plaintiffs collect. Are you scratching your head? You should be. Both courts roundly ignored the law. Doty had loaned the coach her car. Neither she nor he thought he would act on her behalf, and neither thought she would control how he drove. She simply wanted to be sure none of the high school students drove it.

The court, however, straightforwardly ignored the requirement that an agent agree to act on a principal's behalf and called the coach Doty's agent. To let the injured player's father recover on Doty's insurance policy, it needed to find Doty liable. Toward that end, it needed to call the coach her agent. And to find that agency, it characterized her stipulation that he not let the students drive the car as evidence of her control. Fundamentally, however, Doty never asked the coach to act on her behalf, and he never agreed. She simply offered to lend him her car, and he promised not to let the students drive it.

The *Cargill* court was just as dishonest. To allow the local voters to collect from the out-of-state multinational the money they had lent the fraudulent local elevator, the court needed to call the elevator Cargill's agent. The elevator had indeed acted as Cargill's agent in distributing some seeds, but the plaintiffs were not suing on those transactions. Like the *Doty* court, the court in *Cargill* simply ignored the requirement that an agent act on the principal's behalf and called the elevator Cargill's agent anyway.

Once Warren's debts mounted, Cargill hesitated to "throw good money after bad." It could have cut off Warren's line of credit and thrown it out of business. Instead, it agreed to lend additional funds, but only if Warren agreed to live by its limitations. After all, a creditor will not lend money to a badly performing firm

---

[9] 309 N.W.2d 285 (Minn. 1981).

without setting some controls on what the borrower can do with the funds. In citing those controls as proof of agency, the court ignored a basic premise: that the two parties agree that one will act on behalf of the other. Warren Grain did not think it was acting on Cargill's behalf; it thought it was borrowing money as an independent operation. Cargill did not think Warren was acting on its behalf; it thought it was lending money.

Suppose — counterfactually — that Warren Elevator had been just as crooked but had operated as a Cargill branch office. Although the local thieves would not have intended to act on Cargill's behalf (they planned to steal from it, after all), Cargill still would be liable for their acts. It would be liable because the test turns not on what the parties intended to do but on what they agreed to do. The thieves may have planned to rob Cargill, but as branch-office managers, they agreed to act on its behalf. They became its agents, and it became liable for the debts they incurred in its name.

Note the effect of cases like *Cargill* on a creditor's incentive to rescue a troubled debtor. Some cash-constrained debtors have bad business prospects. A few like Warren are dishonest, but the rest just lack products or services customers want to buy. Other firms are fundamentally healthy operations that hit a spot of bad luck. As a matter of policy, the former should go out of business as quickly as possible. The latter would thrive if only a creditor would lend them a bit more cash.

Creditors need to sort the latter from the former. They can then profitably lend money to the fundamentally healthy and let the bad prospects disappear. Unfortunately, "lender liability" cases like *Cargill* encourage creditors to shut down all troubled firms, good risks or bad. Because lenders can distinguish the good from the bad only with error, they impose controls on troubled firms to prevent the bad risks from consuming more cash. Under lender liability, those controls threaten to turn the debtor into an agent and make the lender liable for the borrower's entire debt. Absent lender liability, a major creditor to a failed firm will lose the amount it has lent. With lender liability, it loses not just what it lent but all the money the failed firm owed to other creditors too. With lender liability, creditors will simply let most troubled firms collapse.

II. AUTHORITY

A. *Introduction*

An agent can impose contractual liability on his principal only when he acts with "authority." If the principal tells the agent to do something, he gives the agent "actual authority" to do it (section B). If the principal tells a third party that the agent has authority, he gives the agent "apparent authority" (whether or not the principal told the agent himself he was authorized; section C). Consider some examples (sections D, E), and then several other sources of authority: inherent agency power (section F), ratification (section G), and estoppel (section H).

B.   Actual Authority

1.   Actual Express

Suppose Brigid O'Shaughnessy tells Sam Spade to find Floyd Thursby and to offer up to $4,000 for the falcon. In so doing, she (the principal) gives him (the agent) "actual express authority" to pay on her behalf $4,000. Provided Spade bids below $4,000, she is bound. As Restatement (Second) §26 explains:

> [A]uthority to do an act can be created by written or spoken words or other conduct of the principal which, reasonably interpreted, causes the agent to believe that the principal desires him so to act on the principal's account.

2.   Actual Implied

Suppose O'Shaughnessy tells Spade to find Thursby and to offer up to $4,000, but Thursby is hard to follow. He drives wildly, and when Spade tells his cab driver to tail him, the cabbie demands an extra $50. Because Spade needs to pay the money to fulfill his assignment, O'Shaughnessy is liable for the $50 by "actual implied authority." Restatement (Second) §35 states:

> [A]uthority to conduct a transaction includes authority to do acts which are incidental to it, usually accompany it, or are reasonably necessary to accomplish it.

C.   Apparent Authority

Now suppose O'Shaughnessy tells Spade to offer Thursby no more than $4,000, but then flatly assures Thursby that Spade speaks on her behalf. Spade has actual express authority to offer $3,999. If he does, O'Shaughnessy will be bound.

Spade does not have express authority to offer $4,001. Should he do so, however, O'Shaughnessy will still be bound—not by actual authority, but by what she told Thursby. Although she limited Spade's actual authority, she did not tell Thursby those limitations. Instead, she simply promised him that Spade spoke on her behalf. By the logic of the law, Thursby can rely on what she told him—and "apparent authority" captures that intuition. According to Restatement (Second) §27:

> [A]pparent authority to do an act is created as to a third person by written or spoken words or any other conduct of the principal which, reasonably interpreted, causes the third person to believe that the principal consents to have the act done on his behalf. . . .

Note the basic distinction: Actual express and actual implied authority arise from what a principal tells an agent; apparent authority arises from what a principal tells a third party.

II. Authority

D. *Examples*

Return to *White v. Thomas*. White sent Simpson to an auction with instructions to bid up to $250,000 on a 220-acre plot of land. Whatever the reason, Simpson bid $327,500. Because of White's limitation, Simpson did not have express authority to bind him at that price. Neither did she have implied authority to do that which her principal expressly prohibited.

Was White bound by apparent authority? He did not say anything to the sellers at the auction about Simpson's authority. He did give her a signed blank check, but the court left open the question of whether that created apparent authority. To be sure, Simpson herself claimed to have authority. An agent can create her own apparent authority, however, only when the statement is truthful when made. Because she did not have actual authority, neither could she create her own apparent authority. White was bound, but only because he concluded that the land was worth $327,500 and ratified (see section G below) the deal after the fact.

When Simpson realized that she had bid far more than her authorized price, she panicked. Rather than deliver the land to White, she decided to sell 45 of the 220 acres first. Distressed as he was about how much Simpson had bid, White was even more distressed by the 45 acres she unloaded. He wanted those acres. He refused to deliver the land, and the court let him refuse. Simpson had no actual or apparent authority to sell the 45 acres, and White did not ratify her sale. He was not bound.

Or return to *Dweck*. After attorney Shiboleth settled a lawsuit against his client Nasser, Nasser refused to sign the settlement. The court found Nasser bound by his lawyer's settlement three different ways. First, when Nasser told Shiboleth he could speak in Nasser's name, he created actual express. Second, when Nasser said things to Shiboleth that reasonably caused Shiboleth to believe he had the authority, Nasser created actual implied. Last, when Nasser told the plaintiff's husband that he planned to follow Shiboleth's advice, he created apparent authority.

Finally, consider *Three-Seventy Leasing*.[10] Ampex sold computer memory. In 1972, through sales agent Thomas Kays, it agreed to sell 3 megabytes of memory to a corporation owned by John Joyce. Under the deal, Joyce's firm would pay $600,000[11] and then lease it to H. Ross Perot's EDS (in 2008, Hewlett-Packard bought EDS for $14 billion).

Ampex tried to cancel the deal. Probably, Kays had extended credit to Joyce. Otherwise, Ampex had little reason to avoid a sale. Although Ampex had not authorized Kays to sell the memory, it did appoint him its sales representative. It let him send a contract (unsigned) detailing the sale to Joyce. It circulated a memorandum about the sale. It let Joyce deal exclusively with Kays. Through all this, the court held, it gave Kays apparent authority to bind the firm. The moral — be careful whom you place in sales.

---

[10] Three-Seventy Leasing Corp. v. Ampex Corp., 528 F.2d 993 (5th Cir. 1976).
[11] Times do change: As of early 2012, 4,000 megabytes of memory went for $18.99.

A digression: If an agent can create his own apparent authority only if the claim is truthful when made, why does anyone care? In effect, an agent can create apparent authority only when he already has actual authority. If the agent has actual authority, who cares about the apparent?

The distinction matters in those cases where a principal cancels an agent's actual authority. Suppose on day one principal Paul authorizes agent Amy to buy a car. Amy tells a car dealer about her authority and begins negotiations. On day two, Paul rescinds Amy's authority. On day three, Amy returns to the dealer and concludes the purchase. Paul is bound. Amy's statement on day one about her authority was true when made. By day three, she no longer had actual authority. The apparent authority she created on day one continues, however, and binds Paul on day three. The moral — if you cancel your authorization to an agent, contact everyone she might have approached on your behalf.

E. Mill Street

The church in *Mill Street Church of Christ v. Hogan*[12] needed its sanctuary painted. Years earlier, it had hired church member Bill Hogan to paint it, and it hired him again. Bill was not one to climb high ladders, though. At the time of the earlier painting, he (like older brothers the world over) had convinced the church to hire his younger brother Sam to paint the high places. Because Sam had since left the church, Bill now talked with a church elder about instead hiring church member Gary Petty to paint those spots. In fact, Bill hired Sam and sent him up the ladder. Within half an hour, Sam fell and broke his arm.

The case turned on whether Bill had authority to hire Sam on behalf of the church. If he did, then Sam was a "subagent," an agent of the church, and — importantly — could collect workman's compensation. If not, then Sam was only an "agent's agent." He was Bill's agent, but not the church's and not, therefore, eligible for workman's compensation.

Bill did not have actual express authority to hire Sam. The church never told him he could hire Sam. Although he did talk with one elder about hiring Petty, they did not reach a conclusion, Petty was not Sam, and the elder did not have authority to speak for the church anyway.

Instead, the church was bound by implied and apparent authority. Bill needed (so he said) someone to help him paint the higher spots — and that need created implied authority. The church had authorized him to hire a helper in the past — and that conduct created apparent authority. For both reasons, Bill had authority to hire Sam on behalf of the church, and Sam could collect workman's compensation.

Note two caveats. First, agents generally lack implied authority to hire another worker in any job that involves substantial discretion. Courts reason that principals should be able to choose the agents who will exercise the discretion. They should

[12] 785 S.W.2d 263 (Ky. 1990).

not find agents thrust on them by other agents. If the first agent does have authority to hire, the hired worker is a subagent and an agent of the principal. If the agent does not have authority, the worker is an agent's agent, an agent of the first agent but not of the principal.

Second, conduct in the past can create apparent authority in the present. Suppose a principal had earlier authorized an agent to hire someone else. That past conduct could constitute a "manifestation" to the world that the agent had authority to hire. If the agent now hires again, the principal might find himself bound by apparent authority.

F.   Inherent Agency Power

"Inherent agency power" routinely bedevils students. The conscientious might sensibly ask: When does it apply, what role does it serve, and when does it differ (if at all) from apparent authority? The less conscientious might ask: Why bother? The Restatement (Second) did not create the doctrine until 1958, after all. Only a minority of state courts ever adopted it, and the Restatement (Third) has now abolished it anyway.

But suppose you (Humble) own and operate a tavern. You sell a range of tap beers, cigars (being outside any politically correct city limits), and a distinctly British pickled-cow-in-a-jar concoction sold as "Bovril" (invented in the pre-Powerbar days as nutrition-on-the-run for the military). Needing cash, you sell the tavern to one Fenwick but offer to continue tending bar. Knowing how personally loyal your customers are to you, Fenwick agrees to keep nearly everything unchanged. You will tend bar, run the tavern, keep your name on the door, and stock beer as you please. Only cigars and Bovril, he tells you, you should now buy from him.

Suppose you order 20 kegs of beer from supplier Watteau. Given that Fenwick (as principal) expressly authorized you (as agent) to order beer on his behalf, Fenwick is liable on your order. Given that Watteau did not realize that anyone owned the tavern but you, Fenwick's liability is arguably a windfall (or arguably not, if he thought you owned the tavern and priced his credit to you accordingly). But, no matter. Fenwick authorized you to buy; you placed the order with Watteau; and Fenwick is liable to Watteau by actual express authority.

Suppose you also order 20 cases of Bovril from Watteau. Given that Fenwick explicitly banned you from ordering it from anyone but him, you had no actual express authority. Given the ban, neither had you actual implied authority. And given that seller Watteau did not know Fenwick existed, Fenwick did not create apparent authority by holding you out to the public as his agent.

Enter the bizarre jurisprudence of *Watteau v. Fenwick*.[13] When Fenwick's lawyer (Finlay, Q.C.) explained to the court that the tavern owner cannot be liable on

---

[13] [1893] 1 Q.B. 346 (1892).

these facts, he correctly stated the classic law of agency. Agency law is a branch of contract law, and contract law would not have held A liable on this deal between B and C. The deal here was indeed purely between B and C: A told B not to buy from C; B never claimed to buy on behalf of A; and C did not even know A existed. Necessarily, under classic contract law, any dispute could concern only B and C.

Nonetheless, the Queen's Bench in 1892 held Fenwick liable for the banned Bovril. Quite what the judges thought they were doing, we will probably never know. Perhaps they simply made a mistake.[14]

At the middle of twentieth century, however, the case presented high-profile U.S. judges and scholars with an opening. These were the decades of seemingly relentless judicially driven expansions in liability—the days of the "death of contract,"[15] the days before prominent judges noted the obvious point that people rarely agree to deals that do not make them better off, the days before judges realized that they can promote social welfare simply by enforcing the actual deals people negotiate. In tort, Benjamin Cardozo and Roger Traynor were inventing products liability to let judges circumvent the agreements between consumers and retailers. In agency, Learned Hand was ridiculing as "archaic" and "factitious" any attempt to limit agency to private agreements,[16] and scholars were expanding the scope of agency in the direction of the broad (but never defined) notion of "enterprise liability."[17] It would, they proclaimed, promote "social insurance."

By 1958, Harvard professor and Restatement (Second) reporter Warren Seavey apparently sensed in *Watteau* an opportunity. By classic agency law, the tavern owner owed nothing. Yet across a broad range of fields, Seavey's peers were freeing liability from the constraints of any actual agreements that the parties might have negotiated. *Watteau* gave Seavey the chance to turn agency law similarly noncontractual. It was a chance Seavey took. He could have declared *Watteau* wrong and walked away. Instead, he invented inherent agency power.

Here is how Seavey articulated his creation in Restatement (Second) §161; *see* §§194-195):

> A general agent . . . subjects his principal to liability for acts done on his account which usually accompany or are incidental to transactions which the agent is authorized to conduct if, although they are forbidden by the principal, the other party reasonably believes that the agent is authorized to do them and has no notice that he is not so authorized.

[14] The only plausible argument in favor of liability in the case is the claim that Humble may have priced his trade credit to Watteau on the assumption that Watteau owned the bar. If Watteau had in fact sold the bar to Fenwick, Humble would have had fewer assets than he expected against which to levy.

[15] This was not, of course, Grant Gilmore's point. See Grant Gilmore, *The Death of Contract* (Ohio State U. Press 1974).

[16] Kidd v. Thomas A. Edison, Inc., 239 F. 405 (S.D.N.Y.), *aff'd*, 242 F. 923 (2d Cir. 1917).

[17] Steven A. Fishman, *Inherent Agency Power—Should Enterprise Liability Apply to Agents' Unauthorized Contracts?*, 19 Rutgers L.J. 1 (1987).

II. Authority

Elsewhere (§3(1)), Seavey explains that a "general agent" is one "authorized to conduct a series of transactions involving a continuity of service" (think vice president, bar tender). All others (think real estate agent, lawyer) were "special agents." Seavey applied his new doctrine of inherent agency power only to general agents.

Put most straightforwardly, Seavey's creation held firms liable for most of the contracts their employees negotiated. Firms were already liable if they authorized a contract or held out an employee as authorized. Under inherent agency power, if they named someone to a position, and if that someone negotiated a deal similar to what they had wanted him to negotiate, they would be liable — actual authorization or no, apparent authority or no.

Conversely, Seavey would not have applied the doctrine in some situations where more recent courts have. In *Gallant Insurance Co. v. Isaac*,[18] for example, a court found an insurer liable on an unauthorized contract modification negotiated by an independent insurance broker. Given that the contract apparently stated that the insurer was not bound by contractual modifications it had not approved, the customer could not claim actual or apparent authority. Given that independent insurance brokers are not general agents, the insurer was not liable on inherent agency power, either. Not to worry — the court declared the insurer liable on inherent agency power anyway.

For all its doctrinal convolutions, however, Seavey's inherent agency power actually changed the law very little. Except where a principal tried to hide his role, inherent agency power almost always coincided with apparent authority. Recall *Three-Seventy Leasing*. In publicly appointing Thomas Kays its "Sales Representative," the firm gave him apparent authority to do that which sales representatives in the industry typically did. Under the Restatement (Second), the firm gave him inherent agency power to do exactly the same.

For all practical purposes, inherent agency power merely extended to undisclosed principals the results that apparent authority already creates for disclosed principals. In *Watteau*, Fenwick was not liable by apparent authority, but only because he hid his identity. If instead he had publicly identified himself as the tavern's owner, he would have held out bartender Humble as his agent, and found himself liable under apparent authority.

Seavey worked hard to argue that inherent agency power has substance beyond the undisclosed principal cases. Consider, however, the example he drafted in Restatement (Second) §161 illus. 3b: Mike works as manager to Foundry Co. CEO Charles tells him to order coal, but not from Coal Co. Mike ignores the order and mails a letter to Coal Co. ordering coal. He writes it on his personal stationery and signs it "Mike, agent of Foundry Co."

Is Foundry bound? Given Charles's explicit instruction not to order coal from Coal Co., Mike has neither express nor implied authority. Had Foundry Co. issued him official stationery, it might have created apparent authority. Here, though, it gave him no such stationery and said nothing to the public about Mike's role. Mike

---

[18] 732 N.E.2d 1262 (Ind. App. 2000).

himself claimed authority, but an agent can create his own apparent authority only when the statement is true. Here, it is false.

According to Seavey's Restatement, however, Foundry is bound. As manager, Mike is a general agent. In that capacity, he routinely orders coal. By the terms of inherent agency power, he binds Foundry even for unauthorized orders.

Note how unreal the example is. Real-world firms give their managers access to stationery, they issue name cards, they list them in their directories, they post their names on their Web sites. In the process, they give these managers apparent authority to bind the firms for responsibilities that typically accompany such positions. Only in examples as unreal as that in the Restatement will *disclosed* principals create inherent agency power without apparent authority.

G. *Ratification*

1. Some Examples

Sometimes, a principal "ratifies" an unauthorized action after the fact. Suppose O'Shaughnessy hires Spade to obtain the bird and authorizes him to pay up to $5,000. Spade discovers that Gutman has the falcon, but finds that he will not sell it for less than $6,000. Reasoning that O'Shaughnessy wants the bird badly enough to pay $6,000, Spade agrees to the price.

Given that O'Shaughnessy has authorized Spade to pay no more than $5,000, Spade has no actual authority. Given that O'Shaughnessy has said nothing to Gutman, Spade has no apparent authority. And given that Spade is not a general agent, he has no inherent agency power. By the law of agency, O'Shaughnessy will not be bound.

In fact, however, suppose Spade is right: O'Shaughnessy does want the bird badly enough to pay $6,000. If she telephones Gutman and tells him that she wants the bird at that price, she will have ratified the contract. Having done so, she will now be bound.

Suppose, though, that Spade negotiates a more complex contract: He tells Gutman that O'Shaughnessy will pay $6,000 for the bird, plus another $2,000 for two "letters of transit" ensuring the bearers' safe passage out of German-occupied Morocco. Spade tells O'Shaughnessy about the $6,000 for the bird but not the $2,000 for the letters. O'Shaughnessy telephones Gutman and tells him that she accepts the contract. Is she now bound on the letters?

If O'Shaughnessy later learns of the $2,000 side deal and then decides that the bird is not worth $6,000 plus another $2,000 for letters of transit she does not want, she is not bound. She did not know all material terms of the contract when she ratified it, and she cannot ratify that which she does not know (Restatement (Second) §91). Upon learning of the $2,000 requirement, she can rescind her ratification. Alternatively, she can accept the contract in whole, pay $8,000, and take the bird and the two letters. What she cannot do is to skip the letters and buy the bird for $6,000. Gutman did not agree to that deal, and a court will not force him to deliver the bird on terms he never accepted.

II. Authority

Turn to Connecticut farms. Walter and Mary Stefanovicz owned a farm as tenants in common.[19] Anthony Botticello offered to buy it for $75,000, but Mary replied that "no way" would she sell it for that price. Botticello and Walter then negotiated a lease with an $85,000 purchase option. When Botticello tried to exercise the option, the Stefanoviczs declined on the grounds that Mary had never agreed to the contract.

The court refused to let Botticello enforce the option. Husbands and wives do not, it explained, necessarily have authority to negotiate sales on each other's behalf. Mary gave Walter neither express nor implied authority to sell her interest in the property. Neither did she do anything to give Walter apparent authority. She did notice Botticello making improvements on the farm and did accept his rental payments. Yet without more, she did not ratify. She could not ratify a contract whose terms she did not know, and those actions did not put her on notice of any purchase option. True, Botticello paid rent—but he might have been paying rent on a simple lease. True, he made improvements to the property—but farmers improve land under long-term leases too.

2. The Law

Still, the doctrine of ratification can generate some odd results. Section 82 of the Restatement (Second) gives the basic doctrine:

> Ratification is the affirmance by a person of a prior act which did not bind him but which was done or professedly done on his account, whereby the act . . . is given effect as if originally authorized by him.

A principal ratifies a contract when (i) someone (who may or may not have been an agent) purports to act on behalf of the principal; (ii) that principal could have authorized the person's actions but did not (§84); and (iii) upon learning of the actions, the principal either (a) indicates that he will treat them as having been authorized or (b) does something that makes sense only if he decided to treat them as authorized (§83).

Posit a contract negotiated purportedly on behalf of a corporation that was not formed until after the contract was signed. Because the principal did not exist at the time of the contract, it could not have authorized it (requirement (ii) above). If it could not have authorized the contract at the time, it cannot ratify it after the fact. Instead, it can only "adopt" the contract.

Although ratification and adoption generally yield similar results, sometimes the distinction can matter. For example, ratification "relates back" to the original contractual date, whereas adoption generates a new contract that dates from the time the principal adopted it. If the date of the contract matters, the two doctrines will yield different results (Restatement (Second) §84 cmt. d). Or suppose the

---

[19] Botticello v. Stefanovicz, 411 A.2d 16 (Conn. 1979).

later-formed corporation wants a slightly modified version of the original contract. If the opposing party to the contract agrees to the modifications, the result will be a "novation" rather than an "adoption" — with yet another set of slightly different consequences.

H.   Estoppel

1.   Introduction

Faced with legally driven results they do not like, judges can take several quite different approaches. In *Doty* and *Cargill*, they disingenuously misapply the law. In other cases, they forthrightly change the law. By inventing the concept of inherent agency power, for instance, Seavey hoped to use the Restatement (Second) to promote such a change. When courts invoke "estoppel" or notions of a "nondelegable duty," they change the law as well. Notwithstanding the law of agency, they declare, the defendants are liable: The defendants either are estopped from denying liability or owe a legal duty they cannot avoid by contract (i.e., a duty they cannot "delegate").

2.   Some Examples

Hoddeson[20] and *Majestic Realty*[21] illustrate ways courts can use concepts like estoppel to change the law. The Hoddesons arrived in the Koos Bros. furniture store in New Jersey in 1956. There — they claimed — they met a tall, dark, and handsome young man who helped them choose a bedroom suite. He promised to deliver the furniture in a month, and Mrs. Hoddeson paid him $168.50 in cash. When the furniture failed to arrive, she contacted the store — only to learn that it had no record of any sale.

Under classic agency law, Mrs. Hoddeson lost. If she had paid anyone, she paid an imposter. The store had not expressly authorized the imposter to sell furniture, impliedly authorized him, or even apparently authorized him. It did not appoint him a general agent with inherent agency power and did not ratify the sale after the fact. In fact, of course, Mrs. Hoddeson may simply have invented the whole story. Given that courts have never done well with he-said-she-said disputes, a rule that bars claims like this makes eminently good administrative sense.

The court held the store liable. Rather than agency or contract (the store had entered no contract, after all), the court turned instead (seemingly) to tort. Suppose Mrs. Hoddeson had slipped on a banana peel, it implied. The store could not escape liability by buying its cleaning services from an independent contractor. It owed customers a "duty of care and precaution for [their] safety," and owed

---

[20] Hoddeson v. Koos Bros., 135 A.2d 702 (N.J. Super. App. Div. 1957).
[21] Majestic Realty Assocs. v. Toti Contracting Co., 153 A.2d 321 (N.J. 1959).

damages whether it cleaned the premises itself or delegated the cleaning to someone not its servant. So too with the risk of fraud. By choosing to sell furniture to the public, the store incurred a duty to protect the public from fraud. More specifically, it incurred a duty on behalf of its customers to use "reasonable care and vigilance to protect [them] from loss occasioned by the deceptions of an apparent salesman."[22] Here, it breached that duty — and was liable.

Similarly, in *Majestic Realty* the court held the City of Patterson, N.J., liable for an accident caused by an independent contractor it had hired. Ordinary rules of agency did not apply, it explained, because the contractor was doing "inherently dangerous" work. The city's parking authority had bought land for a parking lot. The land came with buildings it did not want, so the authority hired a contractor to tear them down. The contractor tried, "goofed" (as the crane operator put it), and smashed the building next door.

The contractor may or may not have been the city's agent, but it was not its servant. Accordingly, by classic agency law the city was not liable. The court would not have it. Demolishing buildings, it explained, was "inherently dangerous." If a principal hires a firm to undertake such activities, it remains liable for the torts that result, servant or no servant, agent or no agent. What is more, if it somehow chooses its contractor negligently (if the process of selecting the contractor constitutes a tort of its own), it can also become liable for damages. And if the contractor's activities are so dangerous as to be "ultra-hazardous," the principal will be liable even without negligence.

III. TORT LIABILITY

A. Introduction

Principals rarely authorize their agents to commit torts, of course. But when an agent does commit a tort, sometimes his principal will be liable (section B). The rule applies only to servants (sections C, D) and only to torts that a servant commits within "the scope of his employment" (section E).

B. Respondeat Superior

Return to the independently wealthy adventurer-at-large Kasper Gutman, the "fat man" who devotes his life to the pursuit of the falcon. Arriving in San Francisco, he hires Wilmer Cook to help him find his way around the city. Cook is conscientious, but imprudent. Cognitively challenged (shall we say), he takes stupid risks.

---

[22] *Hoddeson*, 135 A.2d at 707.

Subject to several exceptions, when Cook harms the people he meets, Gutman is liable. Cook brings no special expertise, works for Gutman full time, and tries to do what Gutman says. Therefore, Cook is Gutman's servant. For the torts servants like Cook commit within the scope of their employment, the law holds principals like Gutman liable.

Perhaps some courts hold masters liable for the torts of their servants (called respondeat superior) because people who work for others often (not always, of course) have less money than the people who hire them. Men like Cook typically lack the resources to pay for the losses they impose. They do not have the cash. Absent respondeat superior, their employers would not have to pay for their harms either and would have an incentive to encourage them to take inefficient risks.

But if so, why not hold principals liable for the torts of their independent contractor agents too? Your chauffer may be judgment proof, but so is your taxi driver. Your secretary may be poor, but your fast-living lawyer may not have much by way of assets either.

As noted earlier, the reason for holding principals liable for the torts only of their servant-agents probably goes to the inefficiency of having principals trying to control some classes of agents. Hold A liable for the torts of B, and A will try to control B. Hold clients liable for the torts of their lawyers, and clients will try to control their lawyers. Lawyers, however, work for multiple clients at once. They work off-site in their private offices. They bring an expertise (we hope) beyond the ken of most clients. Clients could not intelligently control the way they did their work, and nothing good comes from giving them incentives to try.

We can restate the point. Courts do not hold principals liable for the torts of their servants on the ground that principals control their servants. Instead, the logic is backward: Principals control their servants because courts hold them liable for the torts their servants commit. Courts do *not* hold principals liable for the torts of their independent contractors — but the reason does not turn on the fact that principals lack control over their independent contractors. If courts did hold principals liable, those principals would indeed try to control their independent contractors. The courts exempt principals from the torts of their independent contractors because they do not want principals — given what the independent contractors do — trying to control the way independent contractors go about their work.

C. Who Is a Servant?

1. A Simple Example

Begin with a simple case. In *Arguello v. Conoco Inc.*,[23] some Hispanic customers complained of harassment at several Conoco stations. Some of the customers had

---

[23] 207 F.3d 803 (5th Cir. 2000).

III. Tort Liability

bought gas at stations owned and operated by Conoco. The employees worked as Conoco servants. For any torts those employees committed within the scope of their employment (more about this concept later), Conoco was liable.

The other customers bought their gasoline at franchised outlets — at what the court called "Conoco-branded stations." Again, Conoco was liable for any employee torts only if those employees worked as Conoco servants. Because servants are a subset of agents, Conoco was liable for their torts only if they and Conoco had agreed that they would work on Conoco's behalf and subject to its control.

Given that the test turns on the agreement between Conoco and the workers, the court examined the franchise agreement. That contract gave the terms of the agreement between Conoco and the independently owned local station. Those terms — and only those terms — defined the contract to which Conoco and the station had agreed. According to this contract, the Conoco-branded store was

> an independent business and is not, nor are its employees, employees of Conoco. Conoco and [the branded store] are completely separate entitles. They are not . . . agents of each other in any sense whatsoever and neither has the power to obligate or bind the other.

The language was not ambiguous. The gas station was not Conoco's agent. Necessarily, its employees were not Conoco's servants.

2. Contrasting Gas Stations .

If only all franchise cases were so simple. Consider two cases involving gas station accidents. In *Humble Oil*,[24] a driver left her car at a station for repairs. Before a mechanic could examine it, it rolled down the hill and hit the plaintiff and his two daughters. In *Hoover*,[25] the court reports that a fire damaged the plaintiffs' car while an attendant filled the tank. Presumably, the attendant was smoking a cigarette while pumping gas and blew up the car. Both cases involved a franchise contract: A local investor owned the station and bought gasoline and other supplies from the company that provided the brand. In both cases, the plaintiff sued the franchisor gas company. In *Humble*, the plaintiff won; in *Hoover*, they lost.

A reader could justifiably take several different tacks toward the cases. He or she could, for example, simply try to apply classic agency law. The gas company (the franchisor) should be liable only if the local employees are its servants. Those employees are its servants only if the station (the franchisee) and the gas company have agreed that the station will act on the company's behalf. But the Conoco case has it right: They never do. The station operators do not see themselves as working

---

[24] Humble Oil & Refining Co. v. Martin, 222 S.W.2d 995 (Tex. 1949).
[25] Hoover v. Sun Oil Co., 212 A.2d 214 (Del. Super. 1965).

for the gas companies, and the companies do not see them that way either. Both sides see the operators as independent entrepreneurs selling branded gasoline.

A reader inclined toward a more pedantic and "lawyerly" approach might compile a "laundry list." In *Humble*, the gas company set the station's hours; it owned the goods that the operator sold on consignment; it paid a large fraction of the station's operating costs. The only discretion left the operator was to hire and fire workers. In *Hoover*, the operator set his own hours; he took title to what he sold; he sold nonfranchised products as well as franchised ones; he retained what the court called the "overall risk of profit and loss."

The laundry-list approach is troublingly manipulable. One can imagine a second-year law firm associate writing a memo to a partner about the contract terms their gas-company client will need to offer its franchisees to avoid tort liability. The partner will then draft the form contract accordingly. Sometimes (not always) there are multiple ways to accomplish contractual goals. If some terms lead to liability and others do not, clients will generally choose the terms that avoid the liability.

A less cynical reader might ask whether the laundry lists conceal different patterns of financial exposure. Terms like hours, consignment arrangements, and rental clauses do tend to (only "tend to," of course) correlate with the parties' relative financial exposure. In turn, that financial risk tends to (again, only "tends to") correlate with real — substantive — control. If a court wants to hold liable the party with that real control, it could do worse than look to contractual clauses that tend to correlate with financial risk.

Note that imposing liability on franchisors entails real social costs. If franchisors are liable for torts that occur at their franchised outlets, they will demand control. Even if franchisors otherwise might have given the local operators considerable autonomy, if those operators can impose liability on them, they will not. If (as seems likely) social benefits sometimes follow from having locally operated and controlled service establishments, then franchisor liability may generate a net loss.

Franchisor liability is also unnecessary. If judgment-proof gas stations present a social problem, local governments can license them. As a condition for the license, the government can then require would-be operators either to post a bond or to maintain proof of insurance.

D. The Franchise Puzzle

1. Why Control?

As the gas station cases illustrate, in franchise liability disputes, courts focus tightly on "control." Whether a franchisor pays for the torts at a franchised outlet often turns on how closely the franchisor controls the way the outlet operates. To be sure, the courts do not always focus on control. In *Conoco*, the court read the franchise agreement, found that the parties did not intend an agency relation, and let the matter go at that. But *Conoco* may be the exception.

III. Tort Liability

In *Murphy v. Holiday Inns, Inc.*,[26] the court held the franchisor not liable only after exhaustively surveying its controls. The plaintiff had sued Holiday Inns (the franchisor) over a slip-and-fall at a Virginia motel (the franchisee). The Holiday Inns' liability depended on whether the Virginia employees worked as its servants. As in *Conoco*, in the franchise agreement, the parties had declared that they were "not partners, joint adventurers, or agents of the other in any sense." Yet the court did not stop there. It closely reviewed the terms of the franchise agreement and rejected the plaintiff's claims only after finding that Holiday Inns had no "control over the day-to-day operation" of the motel.

Miller v. McDonald's Corp.[27] is more troubling still. Like so many others, the plaintiff argued that she hit something when she bit into a Big Mac — in this case, a sapphire. Plaintiffs have been bringing cases like this for decades, of course. Harry Chapman may have brought the first of the I-found-something-weird-in-my-food suits against a national franchisor. He claimed to have found a mouse in his Coke bottle, sued Coca Cola in 1914, and won.[28] Perhaps foodies think these suits represent moral progress that began with the nadir of Upton Sinclair's *Jungle*, but insurance firms call them fraud. Sometimes the plaintiffs do win, but sometimes they lose spectacularly: A California court in 2006 sentenced a couple who claimed to have found a severed finger in a Wendy's bowl of chili to long prison terms — nine years for the wife, twelve for the husband.[29]

The *Miller* court held McDonald's liable. McDonald's did not own the "offending" restaurant. Instead, it recruited local investors, and the franchise contract they signed explicitly stated that they did not operate as McDonald's agents. Nonetheless, the court first noted that McDonald's dictated the way the restaurant operated. This, it reasoned, made the local employees McDonald's servants. Second, it argued that the local franchisees may have been "apparent agents." When a principal holds out an agent as having more authority than he does, the agent will have apparent authority. When McDonald's holds out a local restaurant as its agent, the restaurant becomes its apparent agent.

In fact, of course, although close control could transform an agent into a servant, it does not prove agency. A local franchisee is McDonald's agent only if it and McDonald's agree that it will run the restaurant on McDonald's behalf. Put otherwise, A does not become B's agent simply because B controls A. A becomes B's agent only if the two also agree that A will act on behalf of B. The courts ignored the requirement in *Doty* and *Cargill*, and they ignore it in these franchise cases as well.

---

[26] 219 S.E.2d 874 (Va. 1975).

[27] 945 P.2d 1107 (Or. App. 1997).

[28] Jan Harold Brunvand, *The Vanishing Hitchhiker: American Urban Legends* 86 (W. W. Norton 1981); Gary Alan Fine, *Cokelore and Coke Law: Urban Belief Tales and the Problem of Multiple Origins*, 92 J. Am. Folklore 477, 479 (1979).

[29] Stephen W. Smith, *Jail for Wendy's Finger Scam Couple*, CBS News (Jan. 18, 2006) (available by searching at http://www.cbsnews.com).

2. Why Franchise?

The cases raise three related puzzles about franchising more generally. First, why does McDonald's not own its restaurants centrally? The answer cannot lie in financial constraints. Should McDonald's want to own the restaurants, it could issue the stock necessary to raise the funds required. Neither does the answer lie in any inability to recruit staff. If McDonald's owned the restaurants, it could readily hire the managers and operators it needed.

Rather, McDonald's recruits local owners because of the hard-edged incentives ownership provides. To a business like McDonald's, service quality is crucial. Customers return to restaurants in the network only if workers are polite, the hamburgers are warm, the coffee is unburned. That quality, however, can only be monitored locally. Executives in McDonald's suburban Chicago headquarters cannot tell whether the fries are crisp at the outlet along the Nevada highway. Only a local manager can. To ensure that the local managers have the strongest possible incentives to maintain quality, McDonald's sells them the restaurant. The local owners invest their life savings in the outlet — and keep any profits it generates.[30]

Second, why do local operators not plan their own restaurants? If they invest their life savings in a restaurant, why not invest it in a restaurant they design themselves, rather than one designed by faceless executives in Oak Brook, Illinois? The answer turns on the information that the brand name conveys.

Picture a family driving from Chicago to Dallas. Passing through Arkansas, they know no restaurants or hotels. Should they see a sign for a McDonald's or Holiday Inn, however, they will immediately know a wide variety of information about quality, price, decor, and cleanliness. They will know how the hamburger in the McDonald's tastes and what it costs. They will know the quality of soap in the Holiday Inn bathroom and the type of painting above the bed.

This reputation for service quality constitutes a collective investment of the franchise network. By joining that network, a local operator can immediately convey information about the quality of his outlet to potential customers — men and women who otherwise would know nothing about the local market. As the court put it in the *Holiday Inn* case: "As from the face of the document, the purpose of those provisions was to achieve system-wide standardization of business identity, uniformity of commercial service, and optimum public good will, all for the benefit of both contracting parties."[31]

Last, why do the local operators agree to such stringent controls over their own operations? Why would a hotel or restaurant operator voluntarily submit to the franchisor's draconian controls? The answer: They agree because they know the franchisor imposes those controls on all *other* outlets and thereby preserves the collective reputation of the franchise.

---

[30] McDonald's Corp., *About McDonald's*, http://www.aboutmcdonalds.com (accessed Feb. 7, 2012).

[31] Murphy v. Holiday Inns, 219 S.E.2d 874, 878 (Va. 1975).

III. Tort Liability

Take a possibly apocryphal story about the barges on the Yangtze River.[32] For centuries, the river flowed rapidly downhill through the steep gorges (alas, now flooded by the Chinese government) that sliced through the southern Chinese mountains. To carry coal and other material upstream, workers loaded it onto barges and pulled those barges upstream by rope from the narrow paths cut into the adjoining mountainside.

According to this tale, sometime in the pre–World War II past, an American missionary lady traveled by boat up the river. As the boat passed a heavy barge pulled upstream by a team of peasants, she watched horrified as an overseer whipped one of the workers who had slipped. "Stop," she yelled at her captain. "Make that horrible man stop whipping the coolie." The captain was incensed. "How could I possibly do that?" he replied. "The coolies hired the man to watch them. They pooled their money and paid him to whip any one of them who sloughed off."

The workers could successfully pull the barge upstream only if every one of them invested his full effort. Absent someone to monitor them and punish the shirkers, they each had an incentive to cheat. By hiring an overseer with a whip, they ensured that they all invested the effort necessary collectively to pull the barge-load of coal upstream.

And so, too, the McDonald's franchise. The outlets maximize profits only if every one of them maintains the service quality captured by the brand name. Absent someone to monitor the outlets and punish anyone who skimps, they each have an incentive to cheat on their collective reputation. By joining a franchise network with strict controls, they ensure that they all invest the resources necessary to maintain that collective reputation for quality.

E. Scope of the Employment

1. The Law

Principals are not liable for all torts their servants commit. Instead, they are liable only for those their servants commit within the "scope of their employment." In the words of the Restatement (Second) §219(1) and (2):

> A master is subject to liability for the torts of his servants committed while acting in the scope of their employment. [Conversely, he is] not subject to liability for the torts of his servants acting outside the scope of their employment.

According to §228(1), conduct is within the "scope of the employment" only if

    (a) it is of the kind [the servant] is employed to perform;
    (b) it occurs substantially within the authorized time and space limits;

---

[32] *See, e.g.*, Steven N. S. Cheung, *The Contractual Nature of the Firm*, 26 J.L. & Econ. 1, 8 (1983).

(c) it is actuated, at least in part, by a purpose to serve the master; and

(d) if force is intentionally used by the servant against another, the use of force is not unexpectable by the master.

Start with the simplest case. Gutman hires Cook to find Thursby and locate the falcon. In the course of tailing Thursby, Cook runs a red light and hits a pedestrian. In driving the car, Cook was doing the kind of work Gutman had hired him to do (clause a) above); he was doing the work when and where Gutman told him to do it (clause b); he was trying to accomplish (find the falcon) what Gutman wanted him to accomplish (clause c); and the tort did not involve the use of force (clause d). Gutman is liable.

Or consider the racist gas station attendants in the Conoco-owned stations in *Arguello v. Conoco*. The attendants harassed the customers while selling gas (clause a); they made the comments while on duty at the gas station (clause b); and the torts did not involve the use of force (clause d). The only question is whether they made the comments "at least in part [out of] a purpose to serve their master" Conoco. The court found that they had and held Conoco (with respect to the Conoco-owned stations) liable.

2. Hard Cases

Ironically, the "scope of the employment" rule makes it hardest for plaintiffs to collect for the most outrageous torts—for intentionally violent behavior. Because Cook ran the red light in order not to lose Thursby, courts would readily hold Gutman liable for any damages Cook inflicted on hapless pedestrians. But what if Cook (while working for Gutman) decided that he did not like the way Spade looked and shot him. Did he shoot Spade out of a purpose of serving his master Gutman? Only if he were so motivated could Spade's heirs collect from Gutman.

To the employer, the rule makes good sense. Most employers do not want their employees committing intentional torts and do not give them incentives to commit those torts. Indeed, many explicitly prohibit their employees from committing them. If they neither want nor encourage the conduct, they might reasonably argue, they should not be held liable for it. But just as intentional torts seem the most outrageous, they generate victims who are among the most sympathetic. Exactly when judges most desperately want to let plaintiffs recover, the "scope of the employment" rule most clearly bars recovery.

Faced with these intentional torts, some judges just pretend that what obviously "is not" in fact "is." *Manning v. Grimsley*[33] involved Baltimore Orioles pitcher Ross Grimsley. While warming up during a game at Boston's Fenway Park, he found himself heckled. Eventually, he "lost it," swung around, and threw the ball directly into the stands. The fastball tore through the wire fence and hit the plaintiff.

---

[33] 643 F.2d 20 (1st Cir. 1981).

III. Tort Liability

To hold the Orioles liable, the judge needed to find that Grimsley threw the ball at the hecklers the better to serve his team. And so the judge did. The heckling prevented Grimsley from preparing to pitch, he reasoned. Grimsley needed to warm up, and toward that end he needed a quieter environment. To stop the heckling, he threw the ball at the hecklers. He wanted to do his job and was simply "respond[ing] to conduct presently affecting his ability to warm up and, if the opportunity came, to play in the game itself."[34]

Nor is the *Manning* case the most egregious. That prize may go to *Lyon v. Carey*.[35] A trucking employee, Michael Carey, arrived at an apartment with a mattress and box spring. Plaintiff Corene Lyon had been waiting for his delivery and let him in. When she asked him to carry the mattress and box spring upstairs to the bedroom, he refused and demanded the unpaid balance. Reluctantly, she went to her bedroom to get a check, and Carey followed her in. Carey demanded cash, Lyon refused, and Carey then threw her on the bed, held a knife to her throat, and raped her. After the rape, he chased her around the apartment, beating her and slashing her with a knife and scissors.

Under agency law, the trucking firm was liable only if Carey raped, beat, and slashed Lyon within the scope of his employment. In turn, he acted within the scope of his employment only if he was motivated, at least in part, by the purpose of serving the trucking company, and if his force was "not unexpectable." The court let Lyon recover.

Other judges simply throw out the law. The most prominent example involves a prominent judge: Henry Friendly. In *Ira S. Bushey & Sons v. United States*,[36] Friendly faced a suit against the Coast Guard. Lane had been a seaman with the Coast Guard and had been stationed on a ship in a drydock. After drinking all evening, he returned stone drunk. Walking along the gangway to the ship, he passed some water intake valves. For no reason other than being drunk, he turned the valves. The drydock flooded, the ship slipped off its blocks, and the drydock owner sued the Coast Guard.

Under agency law, the Coast Guard was liable only if Lane turned the valves to serve the Coast Guard. That being flatly implausible, Friendly simply invented a new rule. He did not claim to invent it for policy reasons. "Policy analysis" he seems to have identified with the new law and economics movement, and he was as eager to display his contempt for Guido Calabresi and Ronald Coase as for the Restatement. Instead, he merely declared it enough if the "risk that seamen going and coming from the [ship] might cause damage to the drydock" was foreseeable. That foreseeability test was obviously as ambiguous as anything it might replace, but Friendly declared himself not worried. If his new approach lacked "sharp contours," so be it.[37]

---

[34] *Id.* at 22.
[35] 533 F.2d 649 (D.C. Cir. 1976).
[36] 398 F.2d 167 (2d Cir. 1968).
[37] *Id.* at 172.

IV.   FIDUCIARY DUTIES

A.   *Introduction*

Return again to our detective Sam Spade. Suppose Brigid O'Shaughnessy walks into his office on Monday and retains him to find the jewel-encrusted sixteenth-century statuette. Suppose Captain Jacobi of the *La Paloma* walks into his office on Tuesday. He hands Spade the statuette and drops dead.

Consider several variations. First, suppose Spade tells O'Shaughnessy that he bought the bird in Istanbul for $10,000 and asks for a reimbursement. Can he legally do this? Of course not.

Second, suppose Spade tells O'Shaughnessy the truth, but says he will not give her the statuette unless she pays him $10,000. Although a non-agent could make such a demand, once Spade has agreed to serve as her agent, he cannot demand the money.

Third, suppose Spade and O'Shaughnessy agree that he will work on her case only Monday through Friday. Jacobi arrives on Saturday with the bird. Even though Spade obtained the bird on his day off, he still cannot demand $10,000. The principle would simply be too manipulable. Take a more realistic variation on the rule: Law firm partners cannot refuse to share revenues from a case with their other partners on the grounds that a client approached them after church on Sunday.

Fourth, suppose Spade declines O'Shaughnessy's work. Instead, he refers her to another detective, Philip Marlowe. Pursuant to their prior (secret) agreement, Marlowe pays Spade 10 percent of his profit from O'Shaughnessy's work as a referral fee. Because Spade never agreed to become O'Shaughnessy's agent, he owes her no obligation. He may keep the money.

Fifth, suppose Spade takes O'Shaughnessy's job, finds the statuette, and (with O'Shaughnessy's permission) asks an antique dealer to check its authenticity. For this service, the dealer charges O'Shaughnessy the market rate of $500 and surreptitiously pays Spade a referral fee of $50. Agents may not make secret profits in the course of their agency. Although O'Shaughnessy has suffered no loss (she obtained competent services at the market price), Spade must pay her his $50 referral fee.

B.   *The Law*

At the level of abstraction, the principle involved in these examples is simple: Agents owe their principals a duty of loyalty and a duty of care. Indeed, these duties lie at the heart of this book, for corporate officers and directors (as agents) owe these duties to the firm or its shareholders (as principals). Restatement (Second) §387 defines the duty of loyalty this way:

> Unless otherwise agreed, an agent is subject to a duty to his principal to act solely for the benefit of the principal in all matters connected with his agency.

IV. Fiduciary Duties

And the duty of care (§379) this way:

> Unless otherwise agreed, a paid agent is subject to a duty to the principal to act with standard care and with the skill which is standard in the locality for the kind of work which he is employed to perform and, in addition, to exercise any special skill that he has.

C. *Further Examples*

Private Reading served with the Royal British Army in Cairo in 1944.[38] On his days off, he worked for some Egyptian truckers: He sat in the cab (in uniform), and they carted material around the city. His presence let them avoid police inspections, and for this advantage they paid him handsomely. The Army discovered the scam and confiscated his money. In return, he sued the Army.

The court (the King's Bench) let the Army keep Reading's earnings. Although Reading violated Army rules in doing what he did, that violation itself did not justify its keeping the funds: Principals are not entitled to confiscate their agents' earnings simply because their agents earned the amounts illegally. Should Ramseyer make $1,000 in Internet gambling, his university cannot take the money just because gambling is illegal.

Instead, the Army could take the money because Reading obtained the chance to earn it through his job: The smugglers paid him to ride in the truck because his job gave him an Army uniform. A principal may confiscate an agent's earnings if the agent earned them through the perquisites of the job. Should Ramseyer earn $1,000 in bribes from students for changing their grades, his employer could indeed take the money.

Note that the Army did not suffer a loss. It could confiscate Reading's bribes — even though he rode in the cab on his days off. Similarly, O'Shaughnessy could take the $50 referral fee Spade obtained from the antique dealer — even though she obtained competent certification services at market rates. If Reading did cause the Army to suffer a loss through his misbehavior, he owed the Army damages — but he owed the Army his profits entirely apart from any damages.

Similarly, in *Tarnowski v. Resop*,[39] the plaintiff hired the defendant to investigate a chain of installed jukeboxes he planned to buy. Rather than do his job, the defendant simply pocketed a bribe from the seller. The plaintiff bought the chain. Upon discovering the payoff, he rescinded the sale, sued the seller, and recovered most of his damages. He then sued the plaintiff for the bribe — and won. As the court put it, "the principle that all profits made by an agent in the course of an agency belong to the principal . . . is firmly established and universally recognized. It matters not that the principal has suffered no damage or even that the transaction has been profitable to him."

---

[38] Reading v. Regem, [1948] 2 K.B. 268.
[39] 51 N.W.2d 801 (Minn. 1952).

Agents do not escape their fiduciary duties by quitting their jobs. The defendants in *Town & Country*[40] worked for a Long Island cleaning service. According to the court, their employer had developed a way to "supersed[e] the drudgery of ordinary house cleaning by mass production methods. The house cleaning is performed by a crew of men who descend upon a home at stated intervals of time, and do the work in a hurry after the manner of an assembly line in a factory. . . . [T]he secrets of the home are kept inviolate, the tastes of the customer are served and each team of workmen is selected as suited to the home to which it is sent." Who could have thought housecleaning so sacrosanct? The "customer relationship is 'impregnated,'" the court continued, "with a 'personal and confidential aspect.'"

The defendants quit their jobs at the firm and then returned to the homes they had been cleaning and solicited their business. Readers who worked for "temp" agencies like Manpower during their college summers will recall the customers who asked them to return the next day, but not through Manpower. Instead, the customers would suggest, why not split the commission Manpower charged?

Town & Country explains "why not." Even though the defendants no longer worked at the firm, they still breached their duties to it. The firm had located its customers only by cold-calling the Long Island telephone book. The resulting customer list represented the yield from a massive investment in time. In using the knowledge they obtained during their tenure at the firm (the identities of the customers), the defendants effectively stole the list. That theft constituted a breach of their duty of loyalty—even though they no longer worked there.

From time to time, courts suggest that the fiduciary duties an agent owes his principal end when the agency relationship ends. Not so. Exactly which of those duties continue beyond the term of the employment, the *Town & Country* court did not explain. At the very least, however, the defendants could not quit their job and contact the customers.

V.   CONCLUSION

Brigid O'Shaughnessy shot Sam Spade's partner Miles Archer. Once Spade learned of the murder, could he "send her over"? In general, employees who report the crimes of their employers earn praise as whistleblowers. They may be agents of their employers, but by most accounts, they do good rather than harm by reporting criminal employers to the police.

The same is not true for lawyers, of course. Instead, the bar goes a long way toward insisting that lawyers defend rather than report criminally guilty clients and hide rather than disclose any secrets they learn about those clients.

[40] Town & Country House & Home Servs. v. Newbery, 147 N.E.2d 724 (N.Y. 1958).

V. Conclusion

But what of private detectives? Of course, movie fans will recall that O'Shaughnessy herself never told Spade she killed Archer. Instead, Spade discovered it on his own. And the social status of private detectives being what it is, courts will not defer to them as broadly as they defer to the bar.

Still, even private detectives owe their clients a duty of loyalty. If Spade turned in O'Shaughnessy to collect a $5,000 reward from Archer's widow, Iva, he could not keep it. Should the result be different just because he turned her in out of spite rather than for money?[41]

---

[41] Several readers of earlier drafts of this book noted that it was terrible policy to ask questions without providing the answers. In truth, however, I confess I have no idea what the answer to this question might be.

CHAPTER 2

Partnership

It was love at first sight.

The first time the Ringling brothers saw a circus they fell madly in love with it. The "sight of the spectacle," brother "Alf T" Ringling recalled, "so affected [them] that they stood riveted to the spot, clasping each other's hands in speechless ecstasy."[1] There, to their Iowa village in 1870, the circus had come.

They were a family of seven boys and one girl. The oldest was brother Al, born in 1852. The youngest was sister Ida, born in 1874. By 1884, five of the brothers had formed a small circus. Six years later, they had loaded it on a train, and soon they dominated the industry.[2]

"[T]he reason of this phenomenal success," Alf T would later claim (continuing with his dubiously historical autobiography), lay in their "harmonious management," in the "absolute harmony [that] prevailed at all times in the management of the Ringling brothers' show." This they managed without a formal agreement. Instead, they treated each other as "an equal owner in the show."[3] By a later account in *Fortune*, they did not even "bother to count profits before dividing them. They were content to fill, haphazardly, five small potato sacks with bank notes of similar denomination."[4]

Were the Ringling brothers partners? And if they were, did it matter? Until the late nineteenth century, partnerships dominated the U.S. business world, and they remain important in several sectors still. Although a distinct subject from agency in most legal discussions, the principles that structure partnership law follow directly

---

[1] Alfred Ringling, *Life Story of the Ringling Brothers* 26 (R. R. Donnelley & Sons 1900). *See generally* J. Mark Ramseyer, Ringling Bros.-Barnum & Bailey Combined Shows v. Ringling: *Bad Appointments and Empty-Core Cycling at the Circus*, in *Corporate Law Stories* 77 (J. Mark Ramseyer ed., Foundation Press 2009). With apologies to Joseph Heller, Catch-22 (Simon & Schuster, 1955).

[2] *See* Robert Lewis Taylor, *Center Ring* 40-42 (Doubleday 1956); David C. Weeks, *Ringling: The Florida Years, 1911-1936*, at 9-11 (University Press of Florida 1993).

[3] Ringling, *supra* note 1, at 239-240.

[4] *Ringling Wrangling*, Fortune 114 (July 1947).

from the principles behind agency law (see Chapter 1). This chapter begins with the way courts decide whether investors have formed a partnership (section I). It continues with an analysis of the consequences of that decision for investor liability (section II). It then turns to transfers of partnership interests (section III), to the fiduciary duties that partners owe each other (section IV), to management (section V), and to dissolution (section VI). The appendix contrasts general partnerships with limited partnerships, limited liability partnerships, and limited liability companies.

I.   WERE THEY PARTNERS?

A.   *Introduction*

The Ringling brothers decided circus policy together (harmoniously, by Alf T's account) and split the profits among themselves (a potato sack for each, according to *Fortune*). Whether intentionally or no, they had organized themselves into a partnership. When entrepreneurs share profits and share control, courts hold that they have formed a partnership.

In the 1930s, the decidedly nonharmonious heirs to the original Ringling brothers would incorporate the circus and nearly destroy it (Chapter 6, section II.B). Through the first decades of the century, however, they ran it still as a partnership. By the language of §6(1) of the Uniform Partnership Act (UPA), "[a] partnership is an association of two or more persons to carry on as co-owners a business for profit." The Ringling brothers "carried on as co-owners" when they shared profits and shared control.

Of course, "the" UPA may be a misnomer. There are at least two, the 1914 Act and the 1997 revision. As of early 2012, 37 states and the District of Columbia have adopted the latter, but 10 states still use the former and Louisiana has never adopted either.[5] The two versions resemble each other on most counts. Crucially, §202(a) of the 1997 Act repeats the "co-owner" prose of §6(1).

If shared profits and shared control lie at the heart of a partnership, they also constitute the default governance rule. Unless partners cut a deal to the contrary, the UPA will assign them equal rights to profits and control. Under §18 of the 1914 Act (to same effect, 1997 Act §401(b), (f)):

> The rights and duties of the partners in relation to the partnership shall be determined, subject to any agreement between them, by the following rules: . . .
> (a) Each partner shall . . . share equality in the profits and surplus remaining after all liabilities . . . are satisfied. . . .
> (e) All partners have equal rights to the management and conduct of the partnership business.

---

[5] Uniform Law Commn., *Partnership Act*, http://www.uniformlaws.org/Act.aspx?title = Partnership%20Act (accessed Feb. 23, 2012).

I. Were They Partners?

It was circularity all over again, as Yogi Berra might have put it. If the Ringling brothers formed a partnership, then (absent an agreement to the contrary) the courts would tell them to share profits and share control. If they shared profits and shared control, the courts would call them a partnership.

Beyond those generalities, the law does not much help. The 1914 Act, for example, specifies at §7 that

> (2) . . . common property, or part ownership does not of itself establish a partnership. . . .
> (3) The sharing of gross returns does not of itself establish a partnership. . . .
> (4) The receipt by a person of a share of the profits of a business is prima facie evidence that he is a partner in the business, but no such inference shall be drawn if such profits were received in payment: . . .
> (b) As wages of an employee. . . .
> (d) As interest on a loan, though the amount of payment vary with the profits of the business. . . .

"Co-owners" are partners (by the definition of §6(1)) — but "part ownership does not of itself establish a partnership." Sharing "profits" is "prima facie evidence" of a partnership — but a share of "gross receipts" is not.

It is what it is, apparently, except when it isn't. Suppose (as in fact happened) that Alf T and his brothers work at the circus. At the end of the day, they pay their bills and divide the rest among their potato sacks. Although they split profits, they obviously intend the profits to compensate themselves for their work. The profit sharing brings them within the "prima facie" language of §7(4), but the labor behind the profit sharing threatens to draw in the "wages" exception in subsection (b). Suppose sister Ida loans her circus brothers some funds. Given the risks involved, she demands 5 percent of the profits rather than 5 percent of the principal. The profits formula brings her within the "prima facie" language of §7(4); the interest takes her to the subsection (d) exception. The 1997 Act is not much better. For all the criticism §7 of the 1914 Act took over the course of the century, §202(b) of the 1997 Act repeats the puzzle all over again.

B. *Partner or Employee?*

The contrast between two cases illustrates the confusion that ensues when facts fall close to the line. In the late 1930s, Arline Chesire went to work for John Fenwick's United Beauty Shoppe at $15 per week.[6] After toiling conscientiously for several months, she asked for a raise. Fenwick replied that he could not afford it. The two negotiated and eventually agreed to a contingent raise: Fenwick would add 20 percent of the year-end profits "if the business warrant[ed] it." To reflect their new arrangement, they signed a partnership agreement.

---

[6] Fenwick v. Unempl. Compen. Commns., 44 A.2d 172 (N.J. 1945).

The agreement ramified in unexpected directions. If Cheshire were an employee, the firm owed the state unemployment insurance premiums; if she were a partner, it did not. Notwithstanding the partnership agreement the two had signed, the court called her an employee. True, she shared the firm's profits. But she did not share its losses. She had invested nothing in it. She held no rights to assets on dissolution, no control over the business. Neither she nor Fenwick had said anything to anyone else about her being a partner. To be sure, context matters. That a court found her an employee for unemployment insurance need not prevent it from finding her a partner for other purposes. But "the principles of law to be applied are the same," insisted the court. Notwithstanding the partnership agreement, she was an employee.

In *Vohland v. Sweet*,[7] the court found a partnership despite the absence of any agreement at all. Norman E. Sweet worked for a nursery. Like Cheshire, he, too, eventually obtained a 20 percent cut of the profits. Yet neither he nor Paul Vohland (son of the nursery's founder) called the business a partnership. On his own tax returns, Vohland treated it as his personal business and deducted Sweet's pay as "commission." On his, Sweet called himself a "self-employed salesman." Vohland handled the books, owned the land under the nursery, and borrowed funds for the business in his own name.

Based primarily on Sweet's 20 percent profit stake, the court found him a partner. Accordingly, he could dissolve the firm and take a share of its assets. He had contributed nothing to the firm's capital. Given his 20 percent profits interest, however, he could take 20 percent of the firm's profits on liquidation. As the official comment to §807 of the 1997 Act explains:

[E]ach partner is entitled to a settlement of all partnership accounts upon winding up. . . . First, the profits and losses resulting from the liquidation of the partnership assets must be credited or charged to the partners' account, according to their respective shares of profits and losses. Then, the partnership must make a final liquidating distribution to those partners with a positive account balance.

If real cases seem confusing, take a simpler hypothetical. Fresh from the University of Minnesota, James Hart lands in an old-line New England law school and the bow-tied Charles Kingsfield's contracts class.

"Go call your mother," Kingsfield told Hart, "and tell her you'll never be a lawyer." Hart "bowed his head and limped back through the 150 students in the class." Finally, "his anger exploded. He screamed: 'You're a son of a bitch, Kingsfield!'"[8]

But Hart also falls for Kingsfield's drop-dead-gorgeous daughter Susan and bags an A in the class. Upon graduating three years later, suppose he cuts his hair. He shaves his Burt Reynolds mustache, ditches his bell-bottoms, and lands a job at a major New York firm.

[7] 433 N.E.2d 800 (Ind. App. 1982).
[8] John Jay Osborn Jr., *The Paper Chase* 3 (Houghton Mifflin 1971).

I. Were They Partners?

Several years later, as a senior associate, Hart will receive a fixed salary. Come December, he will receive a large "Christmas bonus" keyed in part to his work and in part to the firm's profitability. He will have no say, of course, in firm affairs.

A few years more, and Hart will make partner. He will now receive a fixed amount over the course of the year (called a "draw") and a year-end "distribution" keyed in part to his work and in part to the firm's profitability. He still will have no say in firm affairs.

Hart will have no more control over the firm's affairs as a new partner than he had as a senior associate. He will earn no more money, and the money he earns will be no more variable. Should the firm go insolvent, however, he will not likely avoid liability for its debts (see section II below) by claiming to be an employee. In part, the doctrine of "apparent partner" will prevent him from avoiding liability (see section I.D below). Yet in part, simple partnership law may prevent him from avoiding it too.

For despite his having no control over firm business, Hart may well be a partner. Only "may" — courts write contrary opinions, too (see *Davis v. Loftus*, section II.B below). But the issue arose a few years ago when the Equal Employment Opportunity Commission (EEOC) sued the Chicago-based law firm of Sidley & Austin (more on this firm at section V.C below) for forcing 32 senior lawyers to retire.[9] Were the lawyers partners, Sidley was exempt from the age discrimination ban; were they employees, it was not. According to Judge Richard Posner:

> The firm is controlled by a self-perpetuating executive committee. Partners who are not members of the committee . . . are at the committee's mercy. It can fire them, promote them, demote them (as it did to the 32), raise their pay, lower their pay, and so forth. The only firmwide issue on which all partners have voted in the last quarter century was the merger with Brown & Wood and that vote took place after the EEOC began its investigation.[10]

Posner did not ask whether the lawyers were partners under state law, but in his concurring opinion, Judge Frank Easterbrook did:

> Were the 32 lawyers bona fide partners? . . . If this had been a suit under the diversity jurisdiction, . . . we would have acknowledged that all 32 were partners by normal reckoning. We know that all 32 (i) received a percentage of Sidley's profits and had to pony up if Sidley incurred a loss; (ii) had capital accounts that were at risk if the firm foundered; and (iii) were personally liable for the firm's debts and thus put their entire wealth, not just their capital accounts, on the line.

Easterbrook concluded:

> The most important of these is the first (which implies the third): under the Uniform Partnership Act, it is profit-sharing . . . that defines a partnership and

---

[9] EEOC v. Sidley Austin Brown & Wood, 315 F.3d 696 (7th Cir. 2002).
[10] *Id.* at 699.

identifies its partners, all of whom are personally liable for the venture's debts. . . .
The 32 lawyers were real partners and consequently not "employees."[11]

C. *Partner or Creditor?*

Return to the Chapter 1 dispute over Cargill. Although the firm lent money to the
Warren Grain & Seed Company, Warren also borrowed from the local farmers.
According to the court, Warren borrowed from the farmers as Cargill's agent. As a
result, Cargill was liable to the farmers on Warren's debt. Cargill thought it was
creditor to Warren the debtor, but found itself principal to Warren the agent.

A court inclined to shift liability to a deep pocket can use partnership law to
the same effect. After all, creditors (like Cargill) sometimes demand controls over
the debtor so long as the debt remains outstanding. When the debt presents large
risks, they sometimes peg the interest to the firm's profits. They share control and
share profits. Subject to the §7(4)(d) caveat about profit-based interest rates, they
risk finding themselves the debtor's partner — and liable for its debts (on partner
liability, see section II below).

A court will not always call lenders partners. Take the 1927 dispute over the
private banking firm of Knauth, Nachod & Kuhne (KNK).[12] KNK specialized in
German securities. During the First World War and the Weimar instability that
followed, it lost heavily. To recoup its losses, it gambled on the foreign exchange
market and lost even more.

John R. Hall became a KNK partner in 1920. He knew William C. Peyton and
approached him for a loan. Having married into the Du Pont Chemical family,
Peyton had the money. He lent KNK $500,000, but by 1921 the firm needed more.
Hall then approached George W. Perkins Jr. and Edward W. Freeman as well.
Freeman had married Perkins's sister, and Perkins's father had been a partner
to J. P. Morgan. The Peyton-Perkins-Freeman threesome agreed to loan KNK
another $2 million.

KNK had not done well under incumbent management, and the Peyton trio
knew that. They trusted Hall, but not his partners. To minimize their risk, they (like
Cargill) demanded tight controls over the firm so long as the loan remained outstanding. To compensate them for the residual risks they could not avoid, they
demanded a high return.

The trio required regular reports, access to the books, a veto over firm projects, and a ban on all payments to the partners beyond a modest draw. They
insisted that Hall (not his partners) manage the firm and told the other partners
to submit resignation letters for them to accept as they wished. To compensate
themselves, they took 40 percent (up to $500,000) of the profits.

---

[11] *Id.* at 709.

[12] Martin v. Peyton, 158 N.E. 77 (N.Y. 1927). The account below borrows from William A. Klein,
The Story of Martin v. Peyton: *Rich Investors, Risky Investment, and the Line between Lenders and Undisclosed
Partners,* in *Corporate Law Stories* 77 (J. Mark Ramseyer ed., Foundation Press 2009).

I. Were They Partners?

KNK failed, and the creditors sued. Unable to recover from KNK, they sued the Peyton trio. By sharing control and profits with the KNK partners, they argued, the Peyton trio had become partners too. The court disagreed. The trio denominated the arrangement a loan, and the court followed their characterization.

In *Cargill*, the creditor lent extensive funds and demanded substantial controls so long as the debt remained outstanding. Before sending good money after bad, it wanted protection. In *KNK*, the creditors lent extensive funds and demanded substantial controls. Although the plaintiffs sued Cargill in agency and the Peyton trio in partnership, the issue was the same: Do the controls (and, in the *KNK* case, returns) make the creditors liable on the borrowers' other debts? Recognizing that sensible creditors may not save troubled debtors if they assume that liability to the firm's other creditors, the *KNK* court exempted the trio. Perhaps caving to local political pressure, the *Cargill* court did not.[13]

D. Apparent Partner?

1. The Law

Seeing Hart earn an A in contracts, suppose Kingsfield hires him as a research assistant. He owes Aspen Publishers a book on contracts for its student treatise series and asks Hart to place a call:

> "Hart. Here's a dime. Call Aspen. I have serious doubts about my meeting its publication deadline under the current arrangement. I'll meet it only if Aspen raises my royalties by half."

Hart calls Aspen and conveys Kingsfield's threat, Aspen agrees to raise the royalty rate, and Hart assures Aspen that Kingsfield will deliver the manuscript on time. Kingsfield is bound by the actual express authority he gave Hart (Chapter 1, section II.B.1).

Suppose Aspen's representative calls Kingsfield, but Kingsfield cannot be bothered. He tells her that Hart will speak on his behalf. She calls Hart, and they negotiate a new contract. Kingsfield is bound by apparent authority (Chapter 1, section II.C).

Suppose Kingsfield never hires Hart as a research assistant, but learns to like him when Hart starts courting his daughter Susan. Sharing cigars and a single-malt in Kingsfield's walnut-paneled study, the two speculate about whether they can use delay threats to blackmail Aspen into raising the royalty rate. Kingsfield first calls Aspen and tells its representative that Hart speaks for him. Hart calls and negotiates a new contract. Even if Hart never agreed to act on Kingsfield's behalf or to follow Kingsfield's instructions, Kingsfield has made him an apparent agent (Chapter 1, section III.D.1) and imbued him with apparent authority. Kingsfield is bound.

---

[13] A. Gay Jenson Farms Co. v. Cargill, Inc., 309 N.W.2d 285 (Minn. 1981).

Suppose, after the friendly cigars and single-malts, Kingsfield calls Aspen and tells its representative that he and Hart (who is not a research assistant) have formed a partnership to handle his law-related writing. Hart calls Aspen and negotiates a contract. Kingsfield would seem bound by apparent authority. After all, §4(3) of the 1914 UPA (1997 UPA, §104(a)) provides: "The law of agency shall apply under this act."

Given that partners are agents of each other for partnership business (1914 UPA, §9(1); 1997 UPA, §301(1)), when Kingsfield tells Aspen that Hart is his partner, Hart becomes his apparent agent. If Hart negotiates a contract, Kingsfield is bound by the agency principles of Chapter 1.

And so it is under the 1997 Act. According to §308(a):

> If a person . . . purports to be a partner, or consents to being represented by another as a partner . . . the purported partner is liable to a person to whom the representation is made, if that person, relying on the representation, enters into a transaction with the actual or purported partnership.

Even if the third party did not specifically "enter into a transaction" with Kingsfield, the official comment under §308 notes that "[a]part from Section 308, the firm may be bound in other situations under general principles of apparent authority or ratification."

Kingsfield's liability was less clear under the 1914 Act. Section 16 provided:

> When a person . . . represents himself, or consents to another representing him to any one, as a partner . . . he is liable to any such person to whom such represen- tation has been made, who has, on the faith of such representation, given credit to the actual or apparent partnership. . . .

Aspen never lent Kingsfield anything, and the 1914 Act expressly protected only those who extended Kingsfield credit — though the general rule of §4(3) remains.

2. An Illustration

Turn to the 1992 case of *Young v. Jones*.[14] A group of Texas investors deposited $550,000 in a South Carolina bank. The bank forwarded the money to the Swiss firm SAFIG, but SAFIG had cheated on its financial statements, and the money disappeared. The firm that had audited those financials was the Bahamas Price Waterhouse (PW-Bahamas), so, therefore, the investors sued the U.S. Price Water- house (PW-US) firm.

Therefore? In fact, the investors sued both PW-Bahamas and PW-US, but to prevail against PW-US they had to pin PW-Bahamas' misdeeds on the U.S. firm.

---

[14] 816 F. Supp. 1070 (D.S.C. 1992), *aff'd sub nom.* Young v. FDIC, 103 F.3d 1180 (4th Cir.), *cert. denied*, 522 U.S. 928 (1997).

I. Were They Partners?

Preliminarily, they argued that PW-Bahamas and PW-US operated as a partnership. Not so, said the court. The investors had no evidence that they did.

Alternatively, the investors argued that the two firms were "partners by estoppel" (i.e., apparent partners). The two firms did present each other to the public as their partners, argued the investors. Recall from Chapter 1 that courts sometimes hold a central franchisor such as McDonald's liable for the torts of its independently owned franchised outlets. The franchisor, the courts explain, presents the outlets as its agents (impliedly, its servants). If PW-US presented the Bahamas firm as its partner, then (even if they were not partners in fact) PW-US's liability might follow by apparent agency.

The court rejected this argument too. First, PW-US simply did not hold out PW-Bahamas as its partner. Again, the Texas investors had no evidence that it did. Second, the investors did not "give credit" to PW-Bahamas. They deposited funds in SAFIG, but not in any Price Waterhouse entity—and §16 of the 1914 Act expressly held firms liable for the acts of their apparent partners only if the claimant lent those apparent partners money. The 1997 Act holds firms liable for the acts of apparent partners if the claimant "enters into a transaction" with them—but the investors did not enter into transactions with SAFIG either.

Recall, though, that the UPA does not preempt the law of agency. Section 4 of the 1914 Act reminds readers that agency law still applies, and the official comment to §308 of the 1997 Act notes that firms can be liable "under general principles of apparent authority." Suppose PW-Bahamas negligently or fraudulently audited SAFIG books, and the plaintiffs relied on those books in depositing their money. If the two PW firms presented themselves to the world as partners, then PW-US would seem liable under the agency principles of Chapter 1.

Perhaps readers find themselves surprised that the senior accountants in the various Price Waterhouse (now PricewaterhouseCoopers, or PwC) offices are not partners of each other. Most (not all) big law firms are still general partnerships, and the big accounting firms once were too. At the time of this case, PwC seemingly did little to disabuse potential customers of that notion.

No more. In about 2010, the PwC Web site prominently declared:

> "PricewaterhouseCoopers" and "PwC" refer to the network of member firms of PricewaterhouseCoopers International Limited (PwCIL). Each member firm is a separate legal entity and does not act as agent of PwCIL or any other member firm. . . . No member firm is responsible or liable for the acts or omissions of any other member firm nor can it control the exercise of another member firm's professional judgment or bind another member firm or PwCIL in any way.[15]

The modern PwC is a franchise. The "McDonald's Corporation" operates out of Oak Brook, Illinois, but does not itself run most restaurants. Instead, local entrepreneurs own and operate the outlets. The Oak Brook franchisor merely sets

---

[15] Variations on this formula appear from time to time on the Web site (http://www.pwc.com). Apparently, however, PwC changes the exact language occasionally.

the rules (e.g., menus, prices, decor) by which these franchised restaurants operate.

So, too, accounting firms. The central firm sets quality standards. If a local firm agrees to maintain the standards, the central firm licenses it to use the franchise name. The local firms practice the accounting, but practice according to a formula set at the center.

Whether restaurant or accounting firm, the logic to the franchise arrangement is the same: (i) Customers patronize franchisees because of the reputation for quality and price embedded in the brand name. (ii) The network promotes local outlet ownership to give operators high-powered incentives to work hard. (iii) And the central franchisor enforces the quality standards on the local outlets to prevent them from free-riding on the network's collective quality reputation.

II. LIABILITY

A. *The Law*

1. The Principles

Martin Greenstein was one of the top income-producing partners at the Palo Alto office of mega-law-firm Baker & McKenzie.[16] Rena Weeks was a new secretary. After a 1991 lunch, Greenstein sexually harassed Weeks. In fact, he had been harassing women in the office for years — at one point causing a senior partner to warn him that if he generated any more harassment claims, he would "kick his ass to China."

Weeks sued Greenstein and Baker and obtained a jury verdict of $6.9 million in punitive damages against the firm, reduced by the court to $3.5 million. Under the agency principles of Chapter 1, a court would have asked whether Greenstein had acted within the "scope of his employment." Under the UPA (§305(a) of 1997 Act, §13 of the 1914 Act), it asks whether he acted within the "ordinary course of business" of the partnership:

> A partnership is liable for loss or injury caused to a person . . . as a result of a wrongful act or omission . . . of a partner acting in the ordinary course of business of the partnership. . . .

Baker was liable.

---

[16] *When the Biggest Firm Faces Sexual Harassment Suit*, N.Y. Times (July 29, 1994); Kirstin Downey Grimsley, *Sexual Harasser Can Often Prey on Many Victims*, Wash. Post A01 (Dec. 22, 1996); Weeks v. Baker & McKenzie, 63 Cal. App. 4th 1128 (1998).

II. Liability

Given Baker's liability, its 500 partners were potentially liable on the $3.5 million. According to §306(a) of the 1997 Act:

> [A]ll partners are jointly and severally liable for all obligations of the partnership unless otherwise agreed by the claimant or provided by law.

Of course, before Weeks could collect from the partners, she first had to try to collect from the law firm itself. She could collect from the individual partners only if Baker & McKenzie did not pay. By §307(d) of the 1997 Act:

> A judgment creditor of a partner may not levy execution against the assets of the partner to satisfy a judgment based on a claim against the partnership unless . . . a judgment based on the same claim has been obtained against the partnership and a writ of execution on the judgment has been returned unsatisfied in whole or in part. . . .

If Baker could not pay, however, its partners would have been liable.

On the liability of individual partners, the 1997 Act streamlined the 1914 Act. Under §15 of the 1914 Act, partners were "jointly and severally" liable for the partnership's tort liabilities, but only "jointly" liable for its contract liabilities. "The distinction had mainly procedural implications going to questions of joinder and the like," explains law professor Stephen Bainbridge. "Technically, in cases of joint liability, all partners are necessary parties. Suit therefore should be dismissed if plaintiff failed to join all parties. . . ."[17]

Had one Baker partner discharged the firm's liability, he could have obtained indemnity from the others. By the terms of §401(c) of the 1997 Act (§18(b) of 1914 Act):

> A partnership shall reimburse a partner for payments made and indemnify a partner for liabilities incurred by the partner in the ordinary course of business of the partnership or for the preservation of its business or property.

2. Their Significance

Although an investor's personal liability does distinguish the partnership and corporate forms, one can overstate how much it matters. Should a partnership fail to pay its liabilities, its individual partners will find themselves liable. Not only will they lose the amounts they invested in the firm, they will personally owe any amounts the firm does not pay. Should a corporation fail to pay its liabilities, its individual shareholders will lose the amounts they paid for its shares, but nothing more.

---

[17] Stephen M. Bainbridge, *Agency, Partnerships & LLCs* 132 (Foundation Press 2004).

Against most tort liabilities, however, firms can buy insurance. Insurers may hesitate to sell coverage against sexual harassment claims, but against routine torts like traffic accidents they will readily offer coverage. Should investors hope to avoid liability for a firm's torts, they need not incorporate. They can form a partnership and buy insurance.

Against contract liabilities, investors will not avoid personal exposure by incorporating anyway. If a contract creditor is willing to lend to a corporation without a shareholder guarantee, the investors could form a partnership instead and borrow nonrecourse on what are otherwise the same terms. Conversely, if a creditor will not lend to a partnership on a nonrecourse basis, it would not lend on the same terms to an incorporated version of the firm unless the investors personally guaranteed the firm's debt. If a creditor demands investor guarantees, it will demand them whether the investors incorporate or no; if it will lend without the guarantees, it will lend without them even to a partnership.

B. Examples

1. To Third Parties

Contrast Easterbrook's analysis of the Sidley partners (section I.B above) with *Davis v. Loftus.*[18] Several clients of Gottlieb & Schwartz sued the law firm and its partners for malpractice. Among the partners, they sued both "income partners" and "equity partners" (this is not a distinction in either the common law or the UPA). The hard question concerned the liability of the former. The Executive Committee (which included only equity partners) set the compensation that the income partners received. By the terms of the partnership agreement, these income partners shared in neither profits nor losses and had no vote on firm affairs.

The income partners were not true partners, declared the *Davis* court. Easterbrook's Sidley partners had enjoyed no say in firm affairs either, but they did share in the profits and losses of the firm. Not so the *Davis* income partners:

> Here . . . the agreement established that income partners . . . received a fixed salary plus a bonus, and the income partners took no share of the partnership's profit or loss. While income partners paid a "capital contribution" to the firm, the firm would repay the same amount, without regard to the firm's profit or loss from the time of the "capital contribution." The executive committee . . . set the level of compensation for all income partners. Moreover, the income partners had no right to vote on the management or conduct of the partnership business.

Concluded the court:

> [The] income partners under Gottlieb & Schwartz' partnership agreement do not qualify as partners within the meaning of the Act, and therefore the Act

---

[18] 778 N.E.2d 1144 (Ill. App. 2002).

II. Liability

provides no basis for holding income partners liable for the acts of [the other partners.][19]

Left unasked is whether the income partners might have been liable under apparent agency. Illinois has adopted the Revised Uniform Partnership Act. Even the 1914 Act, however, did not displace the general rules of agency law. If the firm represented the income partners to the public as partners, arguably it tied them to the firm by apparent agency.

2.   As Among Partners

Suppose Hart and Kingsfield form a publishing partnership. The literarily stylish Hart will write the articles and books, and the internationally renowned Kingsfield will attach his much more marketable name. Hart will provide the labor, and Kingsfield will invest $100,000 in working capital. Hart will pocket no salary, and Kingsfield will earn no interest. Instead, the two will split profits evenly. Expecting a lucrative enterprise, they do not discuss losses.

At the outset, the two will have the following "capital accounts":

Kingsfield	Hart
$100,000	$0

If during the first year the partnership earns $60,000, the respective capital accounts would increase:

Kingsfield	Hart
$100,000	$0
30,000	30,000
$130,000	$30,000

If the partners then distribute $40,000 of the first year's profits, the capital accounts would fall:

Kingsfield	Hart
$130,000	$30,000
(20,000)	(20,000)
$110,000	$10,000

Suppose instead that the firm loses money during the first year. Hart does not have Kingsfield's authorial touch. The firm spends large sums hiring agents and

---

[19] *Id.* at 1152.

courting publishers, but all in vain. If the losses total $250,000, then the capital accounts become:

Kingsfield	Hart
$100,000	$0
(125,000)	(125,000)
(25,000)	(125,000)

Because Hart and Kingsfield did not discuss how to allocate losses, the UPA allocates losses by their respective profit interests. According to §18(a):

> Each partner . . . must contribute toward the losses, whether capital or otherwise, sustained by the partnership according to his share of the profits.

Although Hart works hard and earns no pay, his services (whether compensated or not) do not generate entries to capital accounts. Hence, he takes a $125,000 deficit to his account.

Suppose that Kingsfield decides to end this money-losing enterprise. He dissolves, winds up, and liquidates the firm. Paraphrased, §40(b) of the 1914 Act requires that the firm distribute its assets in the following order.

1. Amounts owed to nonpartner creditors
2. Amounts owed as debt to partners
3. Capital amounts owed to partners
4. Profits owed to partners

By these rules, the Kingsfield–Hart partnership would repay the debt it owes nonpartners (item 1). Given that the firm started its life with $100,000 in cash and lost $250,000, it must owe someone $150,000. It would repay this amount with the cash about to be contributed by the partners. The firm would also repay the debts it owes partners, but it owes none (item 2). According to item 3, it would repay to the partners their capital accounts, but both partners have a deficit in their accounts. Rather than receive money from the firm, they must pay the amount of their deficits into it. Kingsfield will pay $25,000, and Hart, $125,000. The firm would then use this newly contributed money to repay the $150,000 it owes its outside creditors.

Note the result: The two had thought that Kingsfield would provide capital and Hart would provide services. Hart did indeed supply services, and for them received no compensation. Yet ultimately, he also invested just as much capital as Kingsfield. Kingsfield contributed $100,000 at the outset, and another $25,000 on liquidation. Hart contributed his services, plus the full $125,000 on liquidation.

If the result seems perverse, the California Supreme Court thought so too. In *Kovacik v. Reed*,[20] it ignored the law to avoid exactly this result. In late 1952,

---

[20] 315 P.2d 314 (Cal. 1957).

III. Transfers

Kovacik and Reed had agreed to form a partnership to remodel San Francisco kitchens. Kovacik would invest $10,000 in cash, Reed would do the work, and the two would split profits evenly. After ten months, Kovacik announced that the partnership had lost $8,680, dissolved it, and sued Reed for half of the $8,680.

The statutory formula dictates a result that tracks the Kingsfield–Hart liquidation. At the time they formed the partnership, Kovacik would have had a capital account of $10,000, and Reed, one of $0. Because the opinion details no adjustments to these accounts (e.g., no contributions, distributions, or posted profits or losses), Kovacik's account would have stayed at $10,000, and Reed's at $0. If the firm now posts a loss of $8,680, their capital accounts become:

Kovacik	Reed
$10,000	$0
(4,340)	(4,340)
5,660	(4,340)

The firm would have assets of $10,000 − $8,680 = $1,320. Reed would pay his $4,340 deficit to the firm, and the firm would then distribute to Kovacik $1,320 + $4,340 = $5,660.

The lower court imposed exactly this result, and the California Supreme Court reversed. Reed had invested nothing, but he had worked for the firm and taken no compensation. If Kovacik had lost the bulk of his investment, Reed had lost the value of his services. To the court, sparing Reed the $4,340 was all in a day's work.

Whether the day's work by the *Kovacik* court is a sensible approach, it is not the law. Section 401(b) of the 1997 Act repeats the effect of §18(a):

> Each partner is entitled to an equal share of the partnership profits and is chargeable with a share of the partnership losses in proportion to the partner's share of the profits.

The official comment to the section then explicitly declares *Kovacik* overruled.

III. TRANSFERS

A. *The Law*

Suppose again that Kingsfield and Hart form a partnership to run Kingsfield's authorial ventures. On graduation, Hart takes a job with a pressure-cooker law firm in Manhattan. Finding the Kingsfield partnership a distraction, he sells his position to Franklin Ford III, a friend from his first-year study group.

Kingsfield objects. He picked Hart because he was smart, hungry, in love with his daughter, and the paragon of squeaky-clean midwestern virtues. Had he wanted a dissolute aristocrat like Ford, he could have chosen from among dozens. He does not now want to find himself forced into partnership with Ford.

In fact, Hart cannot transfer his partnership to his friend. According to §18(g) of the 1914 Act (§401(i) of the 1997 Act), new partners are admitted only on the unanimous vote of the existing partners:

> No person can become a member of a partnership without the consent of all the partners.

Should Hart try to sell his interest, he does not sell it. Neither does he dissolve the partnership. He merely assigns to his friend his interest in the firm's profits. By §27(1) of the 1914 Act (§503 of the 1997 Act):

> A conveyance by a partner of his interest in the partnership does not of itself dissolve the partnership, nor, as against the other partners . . . entitle the assignee . . . to interfere in the management or administration of the partnership . . . ; but it merely entitles the assignee to receive in accordance with his contract the profits to which the assigning partner would otherwise be entitled.

B.   Examples

1.   Ringling

Consider again the Ringling brothers. Death came for the first of the brothers (Otto) in 1911. By end of the decade, only three of the original team remained: The autobiographer Alf T (born 1863), Charles (born 1864), and John (born 1866). In the early days, each brother had filled a distinct role. By 1918, Alf T mostly kept the uneasy peace between the quarrelsome Charles and John.[21]

On his death in 1919, Alf T bequeathed his interest in the circus to son Richard.[22] Except that he did not, of course, for heirs do not inherit partnership interests. Instead, the death of a partner dissolves the partnership (§31(a) of the 1914 Act, §601(7)(i) of the 1997 Act):

> Dissolution is caused: . . . (4) By the death of any partner. . . .

Like anyone else, an heir becomes a partner only on the unanimous vote of the others.

When Alf T died, Richard would have had two options. First, he could take the cash value of his father's stake. According to §37 of the 1914 Act (§803 of the 1997 Act):

> Unless otherwise agreed, the partners who have not wrongfully dissolved the partnership . . . [have] the right to wind up the partnership affairs. . . .

---

[21] *See* Jerry Apps, *Tents, Tigers and the Ringling Brothers* ch. 6 (Wisconsin State Historical Society Press 2007); Ringling, *supra* note 1, at 238-242; Richard Thomas, *John Ringling* 61-62 (Pageant Press 1960).

[22] *See* David Lewis Hammarstrom, *Big Top Boss: John Ringling North and the Circus* 35 (U. Ill. Press 1992); Henry Ringling North & Alden Hatch, *The Circus Kings: Our Ringling Family Story* 174 (Doubleday 1960); Thomas, *supra* note 21, at 138.

III. Transfers

As Alf T did not act wrongfully by dying, apparently his heirs could wind up the partnership.[23] Second, under §42 of the 1914 Act (but not the 1997 Act, §701) he could retain an ongoing interest in the circus's profits:

> When any partner retires or dies, and the business is continued . . . , [he or, apparently, his heirs shall have the right to receive] the profits attributable to the use of his right in the property of the dissolved partnership. . . .

Absent John and Charles's consent, Richard could not have participated in management. When brothers Al and Henry died in 1916 and 1918, for example, the others did not admit any heirs to the partnership.[24] When Alf T died in 1919, though, John and Charles seem to have changed tack. Rather than close ranks, they seem to have voted Richard a partner.

In fact, Richard did not help run the circus. As sister Ida's son Henry North put it, "Uncle John and Uncle Charlie simply ignored him." Richard was a "two-bottle man — two bottles of whisky a day."[25] When his father bought him a small circus to run, he ran it into the ground in half a season.[26] He did not want to help run the big Ringling circus, and John and Charles did not want him to try.

When Charles died in 1926, John and Richard Ringling seem to have voted Charles's widow, Edith, into the partnership.[27] Unlike Richard, however, Edith wanted to participate in the control. When Richard died in 1931, John and Edith apparently voted his widow Aubrey (born 1894) a partner too.[28] She wanted a say in the circus as well.

These are the women who would figure so prominently in the dispute over corporate control discussed in Chapter 6.

2. *Putnam v. Shoaf*[29]

Through the early 1970s, four investors owned equal interests in the Frog Jump Gin partnership. Not a moonshine plant, the firm produced cotton in the tiny hamlet of Frog Jump. Carolyn Putnam owned a half interest in the firm, but wanted out. Unfortunately, the firm was insolvent, and as a partner she was liable on its debts. She could not avoid that liability by quitting. By §36(1) of the 1914 Act (§703(a) of the 1997 Act):

> The dissolution of the partnership does not of itself discharge the existing liability of any partner.

---

[23] Subject to dispute in some states. J. Dennis Hynes & Mark J. Loewenstein, *Agency, Partnership, and the LLC* 274 (4th ed., Thomson West 1997).

[24] *See* Thomas, *supra* note 21, at 118, 126.

[25] North & Hatch, *supra* note 22, at 173.

[26] *Id.* at 174.

[27] *Mrs. Ringling, 84, Circus Owner, Dies*, N.Y. Times (Sept. 24, 1953).

[28] *See Aubrey Ringling Haley*, N.Y. Times (Jan. 6, 1976).

[29] 620 S.W.2d 510 (Tenn. App. 1981).

Chapter 2.   Partnership

To escape her liability, she needed the firm's creditors to agree to hold her harmless. To induce them to do so, she needed someone as creditworthy as she to assume her liability. She could find a new partner, but he would not otherwise be liable on the earlier debts. According to §17 of the 1914 Act (§306(b) of the 1997 Act):

> A person admitted as a partner into an existing partnership is liable for all obligations of the partnership arising before his admission, except that this liability shall be satisfied only out of partnership property.

Absent an agreement to the contrary, a new partner could lose the amounts already invested in the partnership, but would not become personally liable on any unpaid debt.

In time, Putnam found John A. and Maurine H. Shoaf. In exchange for her paying $21,000 into the partnership, they agreed to assume her liability. With another couple guarantying her debt, the firm's bank agreed to relieve Putnam of her exposure.

As part of the transaction, Carolyn Putnam executed the following contract:

> For and in consideration of the sum of One Dollar ($1.00), . . . I, Carolyn B. Putnam, . . . hereby sell, transfer, convey and forever quitclaim . . . all the right, title and interest . . . I have in and to the following described real and personal property. . . . [30]

She then listed the assets of the Frog Jump Gin.

A few years later, the firm's bookkeeper discovered that his predecessor had embezzled from the firm. The Gin sued the old bookkeeper and the banks that had honored his forged checks, and obtained a $68,000 judgment. Putnam sued for her half interest in it.

Putnam had no half interest in the judgment, the court declared. As partner, she had owned a half interest in the partnership itself. She had not owned the assets owned by the partnership. One of those partnership assets was a claim against the bookkeeper. When Putnam dissolved the partnership, she abandoned any indirect interest she had in the claim.

In short, Putnam herself never directly had an interest in the claim against the bookkeeper. The Gin did, and she had only an interest in the Gin.[31] Similarly,

---

[30] *Id.* at 512.

[31] All this, however, is a bit misleading. As Professors Stephen Bainbridge and William Klein more precisely explain (in a nonpublic note):

> Under a technically sound application of partnership law, . . . the entity/aggregate distinction is not relevant. If Mrs. Putnam had purported to assign her partnership interest—which is the way the court views the transaction—she would have remained a partner (see Sec. 503(a)(2) of the 1997 Act which codifies prior law that transfer of an interest does not effect a dissolution of the partnership)—which is what she was attempting to avoid. In fact, she and the Charltons [the Putnams' original partners] expressly dissolved the partnership (see the third sentence of

when James Hart eventually becomes a partner in his Manhattan law firm, he will not own the copy machines or computers. The firm will own the machines, and he will own part of the firm. Unfortunately, the 1914 Act buried this issue in a tortured indecision over whether a partnership was an aggregation of investors (the "aggregate theory") or a separate entity in its own right (the "entity theory"). The 1997 Act straightforwardly declares (§201):

> A partnership is an entity distinct from its partners.

It then makes clear that the assets of the partnership are the assets of the firm. They are not the assets of the partners. Section 203 of the 1997 Act states:

> Property acquired by a partnership is property of the partnership and not of the partners individually.

C. Significance

The distinction between corporate and partnership law on the transfer of an investor's interest is basic: Corporate shares are freely transferable, but new partners are admitted only on the unanimous vote of the existing partners. Yet as with limited liability, its importance is easy to exaggerate. Investors in a corporation may transfer their shares, but only if they can find a buyer. With small firms, that may not be easy. What is more, that formal transferability of the corporate shares is but the default term anyway. Should investors want to limit transferability, they may so provide in the corporate charter.

New partners are admitted only by unanimous vote, but this rule too is but the default. Should investors want to eliminate the veto it gives existing partners, they can freely do so. In the large modern law firm, they routinely do.

IV. FIDUCIARY DUTIES

A. Introduction

Return to the Hart–Kingsfield arrangement: Aspen Publishers approaches Kingsfield to write a contracts volume for its student treatise series. Suppose Hart is courting Kingsfield's daughter and working for him as a research assistant.

---

the agreement). Mrs. Putnam then held a half share in the now extinct partnership's assets, presumably as a tenant in common. She then conveyed that interest to the Shoafs. In this view of the transactions, the discussion of the nature of the partnership interests becomes irrelevant (but valuable for pedagogical purposes). Then all that needs to be said is that Mrs. Putnam obviously intended to convey her half of everything that the partnership once held.

Kingsfield tells him about the contract and proposes a deal. Under this proposal, Hart will ghostwrite the book, Kingsfield will add his name, and the two will split the income evenly. Aspen has offered Kingsfield a ten-year contract: five editions on a two-year cycle. Hart and Kingsfield agree that they will work together for the ten-year term. At the end of the decade, they will decide whether (and how) to continue.

Kingsfield signs the contract in his own name. He does not tell Aspen about the side agreement with Hart, as both of them thought it best not to tell Aspen that Hart would be doing all the work. Over the next ten years, Hart writes the book, compiles updates, and revises the treatise every two years. He does a fine job, and the book makes money.

Near the end of the decade, Aspen approaches Kingsfield about another ten-year contract. Kingsfield recognizes that the arrangement with Hart has worked well, but thinks that he can recruit an equally talented writer for a tenth rather than half of the profits. He signs the new contract and does not tell Hart. When Hart learns about the renewal, he becomes apoplectic and sues for half the profits from the second ten-year term. Does he win?

Before addressing the question, consider some easier questions. Suppose Hart and Kingsfield enter into an arrangement to practice law rather than write a book. If Kingsfield handles client business on Saturday and does not split the take with Hart, he breaks the law. According to §21(1) of the 1914 Act (§404(b) of the 1997 Act):

> Every partner must account to the partnership for . . . any profits derived by him without the consent of the other partners from any transaction connected with the formation, conduct, or liquidation of the partnership. . . .

Legal business is a "transaction connected with the . . . conduct . . . of the partnership."

Suppose author John Osborn approaches Kingsfield and asks him to star in a movie about the life of John Houseman. Kingsfield will play the aging Houseman. The transaction is unrelated to Kingsfield's partnership with Hart, and Kingsfield need not share the profits he earns.

But what if Kingsfield is approached by Aspen to produce a new contracts casebook? What if he is approached by Foundation Press to produce a new hornbook? And what if — to return to the original question — he is approached about a renewal of the ten-year contract? Turn to Cardozo's opinion in *Meinhard v. Salmon.*[32]

---

[32] 164 N.E. 545 (N.Y. 1928). For excellent background to the case, see Robert B. Thompson, *The Story of* Meinhard v. Salmon: *Fiduciary Duty's Punctilio*, in *Corporate Law Stories* 105 (J. Mark Ramseyer ed., Foundation Press 2009); Geoffrey P. Miller, *A Glimpse of Society via a Case and Cardozo:* Meinhard v. Salmon, in *The Iconic Cases in Corporate Law* 12 (Jonathan R. Macey ed., Thomson West 2008).

Figure 2-1
The Hotel Bristol

Photo courtesy of the Library of Congress.

B. *Meinhard v. Salmon*

1. The Case

Having inherited a New York real estate fortune, Louisa M. Gerry owned an eight-story residential hotel at the corner of 42nd Street and Fifth Avenue (see the photo showing the Bristol Building). In 1902, she leased the hotel to Walter J. Salmon for 20 years. Without notifying her, Salmon then negotiated a "joint venture" with Morton H. Meinhard to exploit the lease. In time, both Salmon and Meinhard would become successful businessmen, but in 1902 they still lived modestly. They were friends, they sometimes shared an apartment, and they had adjacent opera seats. Shortly after signing the lease, they each married into prominent Jewish families.

Together, Salmon and Meinhard developed the property. Under the terms of their agreement, they each invested half the requisite funds. Private homes were moving north along Fifth Avenue, and Grand Central Station and the New York Public Library were locating nearby. With the value of the area climbing, they planned to exploit the property's commercial potential. Salmon himself would manage the building and take 60 percent of the profits for the first 5 years. For the remaining 15, he and Meinhard would split the profits evenly.

51

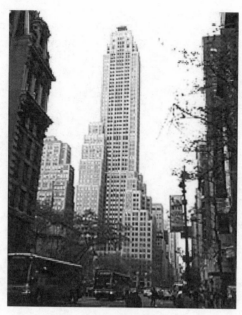

Figure 2-2
500 Fifth Avenue

Reproduced with permission of Robert B. Thompson.

The area boomed, but the friendship faded. On an initial investment of $40,000, Salmon and Meinhard each made more than $500,000. For a variety of reasons, however, by the end of the lease they rarely spoke.

At Louisa Gerry's death, the property went to her son Elbridge. Given the change in the neighborhood, Elbridge wanted to raze the modest building and erect a much larger structure. Unable to find investors who would fund it, he turned to Salmon—the current lessee. Together, he proposed, they could combine several adjacent plots and build something much taller. Salmon agreed. The 59-story tower they eventually built—500 Fifth Avenue—became one of the highest in the world (see the photo showing 500 Fifth Avenue).

On discovering the deal, Meinhard sued. Then still on the New York Court of Appeals, Benjamin Cardozo wrote the appellate opinion. Salmon must offer Meinhard a half interest in the project, he declared, provided Meinhard invested an equal amount. To justify this conclusion, Cardozo indulged in prose as flamboyant as anything by brother Alf T:

> A trustee is held to something stricter than the morals of the market place. Not honesty alone, but the punctilio of an honor the most sensitive, is then the standard of behavior. As to this there has developed a tradition that is unbending and inveterate. Uncompromising rigidity has been the attitude of courts of equity

when petitioned to undermine the rule of undivided loyalty by the "disintegrating erosion" of particular exceptions. . . . Only thus has the level of conduct for fiduciaries been kept at a level higher than that trodden by the crowd. It will not consciously be lowered by any judgment of this court.[33]

In his biography of the justice, Judge Richard Posner suggests that sometimes "the moralistic streak in Cardozo may have led him astray."[34] In fact, Cardozo goes further:

Salmon had put himself in a position in which thought of self was to be renounced, however hard the abnegation. . . . For him and for those like him, the rule of undivided loyalty is relentless and supreme.[35]

The phrase that launch'd a thousand suits; it has been cited relentlessly by plaintiffs ever since.

But is it right? As Justice William Andrews (who famously dissented in *Palsgraf*[36] as well) rightly noted, the case should have turned on what the two friends intended. They might have agreed that Salmon would offer Meinhard a part in any renewal. Or not. They might instead have agreed to share the 20-year lease and no more. Either deal would have been legal. Either deal could have been sensible. In requiring Salmon to share the new lease with Meinhard, Cardozo apparently decided they intended the former — but without any evidence. If the two did plan merely to cooperate for 20 years, then requiring Salmon to share the renewal gave Meinhard a deal he did not negotiate and an option for which he did not pay. But then again, in Posner's words, the typical "characteristic analytic flaw" to Cardozo's opinions "is the substitution of words for thought."[37]

Cardozo may have realized the problem. Crucially, he describes the relationship between the two as a joint venture ("co-adventurers," he calls them) rather than a partnership. A joint venture is an agreement to pursue a particular project.[38] A partnership is one to run an ongoing enterprise. Meinhard and Salmon could have agreed to a deal that extended beyond the 20-year lease. Had they done so, they would have formed a partnership. If they agreed to exploit only a 20-year lease, they would have formed a joint venture. According to Cardozo, they formed a joint venture.

---

[33] 164 N.E. at 546.

[34] Richard A. Posner, *Cardozo: A Study in Reputation* 104 (U. Chi. Press 1990).

[35] 164 N.E. at 548.

[36] Palsgraf v. Long Island R.R., 162 N.E. 99 (N.Y. 1928).

[37] Posner, *supra* note 34, at 119.

[38] Bainbridge, *supra* note 17, at 114-115. And this from a judge whose technique Posner describes as "quintessentially rhetorical in a sense that cannot be taken as wholly complimentary in evaluating a judicial opinion, for one element of the technique is the selection of facts with a freedom bordering on that of a novelist or a short-story writer, and another is outright fictionalizing. . . ." Posner, *supra* note 34, at 47.

2.   Its Reach

In fact, Cardozo never specifies what Salmon needed to do anyway. Presumably, Salmon should have told Meinhard about the chance to renew. But should he have done more? Should he have offered Meinhard a 50 percent stake in his renewal proposal? Should he have offered not just a 50 percent stake, but the right to take the entire lease? If Meinhard wanted the full project, did he have the right to enter a competing bid?

Cardozo's sanctimonious prose — all "thought of self was to be renounced, however hard the abnegation" — implies that Salmon should have offered Meinhard everything. He should have offered Meinhard a 50 percent stake in the renewal. If Meinhard wanted a 100 percent stake, he should have let Meinhard have it all. He should not even have tried to compete against him.

Other passages in the opinion suggest that Cardozo meant nothing so strict. Salmon "might have warned Meinhard that the plan had been submitted, and that either would be free to compete for the award," he writes. Had Salmon done so, "we need not say" whether he should have done more.[39] Yet the notion that Salmon was to renounce all "thought of self . . . however hard the abnegation" does indeed imply that he should have done more. Indeed, he should have done much more.

The case is cited often — Posner counts "653 times, compared to 827 for *McPherson [v. Buick Motor Co.]*, Cardozo's most influential opinion."[40] But that courts quote the purple prose does not mean they apply it. Cardozo himself suggested that "*Meinhard v. Salmon* is one of the cases in which some of my colleagues think that my poetry is better than my law."[41] If he gave Meinhard an option for which he did not pay, then the purple prose is not very good law. But it is decidedly purple.

3.   Its Cost

At root, Cardozo seems oblivious to the price people charge for fiduciary duties. Recall the Hart–Kingsfield partnership: Whiz kid law student Hart will ghostwrite treatises in the name of flamboyantly pedestrian professor Kingsfield. The two could negotiate a fiduciary-duty-lean agreement: They will cooperate on the ten-year contract Aspen offered Kingsfield. Or they could negotiate a fiduciary-duty-rich one: Kingsfield will give Hart a chance to participate in every law-related offer that comes the professor's way.

Should Hart push for a fiduciary-duty-rich agreement, the deal will not come cheap. If Kingsfield routinely receives lucrative consulting arrangements, then any

---

[39] 164 N.E. at 547.

[40] Posner, *supra* note 34, at 105.

[41] Letter to Felix Frankfurter, quoted in Andrew L. Kaufman, *Cardozo* 241 (Harvard U. Press 1998).

requirement that he share his earnings will cost Hart dearly. Before Kingsfield signs the deal, he will raise the price he demands: Cut the percentage Hart can take, or insist that Hart work longer hours and forsake side jobs. Given that rich fiduciary duties are for Kingsfield a costly term, he will not agree to them readily.

Because of the price Kingsfield will charge, Hart will not necessarily prefer a fiduciary-duty-rich agreement. It will all depend on the price. Ex ante, both of the men can walk away from the deal. They will agree to a contract only if it benefits them both. They may rationally opt for a deal that demands extensive fiduciary duties from Kingsfield. Or they may rationally conclude that they are both better off with a deal that demands of Kingsfield only the most minimal fiduciary duties.

Ironically, Salmon may have had the last laugh. Cardozo published his opinion in 1928, the stock market crashed in 1929, and the new building opened in 1931. It opened with few tenants. Rather than give Meinhard access to a stream of revenue, Cardozo mostly made him responsible for half the liabilities. In the end, Meinhard's widow reminisced, the judgment was a "pyrrhic victory. Five Hundred Fifth Avenue has cost [my husband's] estate a fortune."[42]

C. *Meehan v. Shaughnessy*[43]

Whatever Cardozo may have intended, modern courts rarely require partners to "renounce" all "thought of self . . . , however hard the abnegation." Instead, they recognize that more fiduciary duties are not necessarily better than fewer and let parties bargain for the duties they want. They do not even impose Cardozo's formula as a default.

James F. Meehan, Leo V. Boyle, and Cynthia J. Cohen were Boston partners in the plaintiffs' contingency fee law firm of Parker, Coulter, Daley & White. Meehan and Boyle served on its executive committee, but felt underappreciated. In the summer of 1984, they decided to leave.

Of the three, Leo V. Boyle was the most prominent. In the decades since, he has grown more prominent still. In 2000, he negotiated a $4.75 million settlement from MIT for a freshman who drank himself to death at a fraternity party. In 2001-2002, he served as president of the trade association for the plaintiff's bar, the Association of Trial Lawyers of America.[44]

Once the trio decided to leave, rumors began to fly. The three (dishonestly) denied the rumors, but in response to an evasive comment by Boyle on November 30, one of his partners finally guessed the truth. The three announced their plans to leave later the same day. They then immediately (as in, on December 1) began asking clients to come with them. By the time they opened their office on January 1, they had more than 150 of Parker Coulter's 350 contingency fee cases.

---

[42] Thompson, *supra* note 32, at 131.

[43] 535 N.E.2d 1255 (Mass. 1989).

[44] See the Web site for Meehan, Boyle, Black & Bogdanow, P.C., at *http://www.meehanboyle.com/*. The group has been renamed "American Association for Justice."

While still at Parker Coulter, the threesome took several steps:

(1) They discussed the idea of leaving.
(2) They recruited several associates.
(3) They negotiated a lease for their new office.
(4) They scoured their ongoing cases to pick the cases they wanted to take with them (presumably, the highest-value cases).
(5) They contacted the clients they wanted (the clients with the highest value cases) and asked them to move.

None of this bothered the court: Meehan, Boyle, and Cohen did not breach their fiduciary duties to their partners in discussing whether to leave; they did not breach them in recruiting associates; they did not breach them in negotiating a new lease; and they did not breach them by identifying prospective clients. Where the employees in *Town & Country* breached their fiduciary duty when they recruited clients after they had left (see Chapter 1, section IV.C), the Meehan team did not breach it even in recruiting clients while still at the firm.

Instead, concluded the court, the Meehan team breached their fiduciary duties only in three ways. First, they initially lied to their partners about their plans. Second, they stalled for two weeks before giving their partners the list of clients they intended to solicit; by the time those partners knew which clients they wanted, they had already obtained commitments from a majority. Last, they misled their clients by failing to make clear that they could stay at Parker Coulter if they wished.

Note the contrast to *Meinhard.* Rather than act as fiduciaries, the Meehan team behaved as competitors. They planned secretly. They recruited the best associates. They took the most profitable clients. And all this they did before they even left the firm. None of it was illegal.

D. *Lawlis v. Kightlinger & Gray*[45]

1. The Case

Gerald L. Lawlis practiced law with the small Indianapolis firm of Kightlinger & Gray. By 1983, he had become an alcoholic. He told the firm's Finance Committee about his problem, and the firm consulted a physician. It set out a recovery program and warned him that "there is no second chance." A year later, Lawlis started drinking again, and the firm gave him a second chance.

While Lawlis fought his alcoholism, the firm put him on reduced participation (i.e., a smaller fraction of partnership profits). Overcome your addiction, it promised him, and you can return to your earlier status. In time, Lawlis did overcome the alcoholism and asked the Finance Committee for his earlier status.

---

[45] 562 N.E.2d 435 (Ind. App. 1990).

IV. Fiduciary Duties

Rather than give Lawlis the raise, the Committee recommended that the firm fire him. Almost immediately, workers removed his files from his office. To give him continuing insurance coverage and a forum from which to find another job, however, the firm kept him a nominal partner on modest pay for six months.

Lawlis refused to go. The senior partners then voted seven-to-one (only Lawlis voted no) to expel him. He challenged the vote, but the court held for the firm. Crucially, the partnership agreement contained a "guillotine" clause:

> A two-thirds (2/3) majority *of the Senior Partners*, at any time, may expel any partner from the partnership *upon such terms and conditions as set by said Senior Partners.*[46]

The question was whether the firm could validly adopt such a clause. According to the court, it could. Never mind Cardozo's moralizing about sacrificial service. Section 31 of the 1914 Act (§601(3) of the 1997 Act) provided:

> Dissolution is caused: (1) Without violation of the agreement between the partners, . . . (d) By the expulsion of any partner from the business bona fide in accordance with such a power conferred by the agreement between the partners. . . .

The UPA let partners decide how to expel each other, and the Kightlinger partners decided to adopt a quick-and-easy rule: They could vote each other out, at any time, for any reason.

Having agreed to the guillotine clause, Lawlis could not now complain. As the court put it:

> Where the remaining partners in a firm deem it necessary to expel a partner under a no cause expulsion clause in a partnership agreement freely negotiated and entered into, the expelling partners act in "good faith" regardless of motivation if that act does not cause a wrongful withholding of money or property legally due the expelled partner at the time he is expelled.[47]

So long as a firm paid its expelled partner what it promised, it could expel him whenever it wanted, for any reason it wanted.

Recall the contrast to Cardozo. The *Meinhard* court demanded of partners a "punctilio of an honor the most sensitive." The *Kightlinger* court let them expel each other for any reason or no reason. As partners, they owed one another no more than what they put in their contract. Of Cardozo's elaborate apparatus, they owed nothing.

---

[46] *Id.* at 439-440 (italics in original).
[47] *Id.* at 442-443.

2. Alcoholism

Kightlinger raises a harder problem: How should law firms treat alcoholic partners? Law is a stressful job, and one where partners work long hours alone in private offices. It is the kind of job that can lead to alcohol abuse, and it does. Where by some estimates 6 percent of the nation's population is alcoholic, 13 percent of its lawyers are.[48]

Declaring alcoholism a disease (as modern physicians do) does not help. A lawyer does not work for himself; he works for clients. Although some clients may not mind having an alcoholic handle their cases, most probably do. Given that law firms owe fiduciary duties to their clients, they at least owe them the information that their lawyer is an alcoholic. They also owe them the option of demanding someone else.

Suppose most clients ask a firm to reassign the alcoholic partner. Should the firm keep him on the partnership payroll (i.e., the partnership participation, perhaps at a reduced rate) until he recovers? If it does, note the perverse incentives it creates. Paying the partner for doing little, it now has an incentive to return him to service as soon as possible. Yet clients do not want their law firm pushing alcoholic partners back to work prematurely. Any firm that pays alcoholic partners for reduced workloads, however, has exactly that incentive.

Lest law firms push their alcoholic partners back to work, suppose the state requires law firms to cut all pay to alcoholic lawyers immediately. This alternative creates an incentive just as perverse: Deny the problem. Facing such a rule, lawyers like Lawlis will never tell their Finance Committees about their problem. Neither will their friends report it. Instead, both the alcoholic lawyer and his friends will deny it.

The problem is easy to pose. Given the risks to clients, most alcoholic lawyers need to leave work. Given the risks involved in returning a recovering alcoholic to work prematurely, law firms need to avoid any incentive to push their partners back to service. Yet given the way people skirt draconian penalties, any ban on paying alcoholic partners who do no work will simply lead to denial. Easy to pose, the problem is not easy to solve.

V. MANAGEMENT

A. *The Law*

The real-life Ringling brothers ran their partnership informally. They shared profits and shared control — and shared both equally. By contrast, the hypothetical

---

[48] Jen Woods, *Attorneys Kick Addictions with Help from The Other Bar*, LawCrossing, http://www.law crossing.com/article/2583/Attorneys-Kick-Addictions-Kick-Addictions-with-Help-from-The-Other-Bar/ (accessed Feb. 15, 2012).

V. Management

Hart and Kingsfield would never have shared control equally. Charles Kingsfield may have grown fond of the ingenuous Minnesotan who fell in love with his daughter, but would never have given him an equal say in a partnership.

Yet absent an agreement to the contrary, equal say is exactly what Hart will take. According to §18(e) of the 1914 UPA (§401(f) of the 1997 Act):

> The rights and duties of the partners in relation to the partnership shall be determined, subject to any agreement between them, by the following rules: . . . (e) All partners have equal rights in the management and conduct of the partnership business.

A partnership can admit new partners only on the unanimous vote of all existing partners (see section III above), but it will decide all routine matters by majority vote. By §18(h) of the 1914 Act (§401(j) of the 1997 Act):

> Any difference arising as to ordinary matters connected with the partnership business may be decided by a majority of the partners.

Since a majority of two is two, Hart will have a veto over all firm decisions.

B. Simple Partnerships

To explore some of the issues involved, start with a simple partnership. C. N. Stroud and Earl Freeman ran a grocery store together, apparently without a written agreement.[49] In time, they fell out. Stroud called supplier Nabisco and told it he would not pay for more bread. Freeman ordered bread anyway, Nabisco delivered, and Stroud refused to pay.

Consider the actual and apparent authority involved. First, absent a decision to the contrary, partners have actual authority to bind the partnership for conduct within the scope of its business. According to §9(1) of the 1914 Act (§301(1) of the 1997 Act):

> Every partner is an agent of the partnership for the purpose of its business. . . .

Second, partners also have apparent authority to bind the partnership for actions within the scope of its business unless the third party knows they lack actual authority. Section 9(1) continues:

> [T]he act of every partner . . . for apparently carrying on in the usual way the business of the partnership . . . binds the partnership unless the partner so acting has in fact no authority to act for the partnership in the particular matter, and the person with whom he is dealing has knowledge of the fact that he has no such authority.

---

[49] Natl. Biscuit Co. v. Stroud, 106 S.E.2d 692 (N.C. 1959).

Consistent with the latter clause, §9(4) provides:

> No act of a partner in contravention of a restriction on authority shall bind the partnership to persons having knowledge of the restriction.

Suppose the partnership had decided not to order bread from Nabisco. Freeman would have had no actual authority to bind the firm. If Stroud had called Nabisco and told it that the partnership had decided not to order its bread, Freeman would not have had apparent authority either.

Crucially, however, Stroud could not unilaterally decide firm policy. Because the firm had no partnership agreement, it decided policy by majority vote, with each partner having equal say. If two partners have equal say, each has a veto over new policy.

Because the firm had long bought bread from Nabisco, the partners needed a majority vote to change that policy. Because they each held equal stakes, they each held a veto. And because Freeman opposed Stroud's proposal to stop buying bread from Nabisco, he retained his actual authority to buy it anyway. That Nabisco had notice of Stroud's opposition made no difference.

To protect himself from liability for Nabisco bread, all Stroud could do was to dissolve, wind up, and terminate the partnership. He could not change firm policy unless Freeman agreed. If Freeman refused, he had no choice but to leave.

John Summers and E. A. Dooley ran a trash collection business as a partnership.[50] They did most of the work themselves, and when one of them needed help, he hired an assistant out-of-pocket. In 1966, Summers asked Dooley to agree to pay for an assistant with firm funds. Dooley refused, and Summers hired an assistant anyway and sued Dooley for half the cost.

Consider the *Nabisco* logic: Only by majority vote could the partners change firm policy. Summers and Dooley had operated under an arrangement in which each paid individually for any help he needed. To change that policy, they needed a majority vote, and Dooley refused to vote for a change. As a result, Summers had no actual authority to hire anyone at firm expense — and so the court held.

Suppose Summers had not paid his employee, and the employee had sued the partnership. Because the partnership had not authorized its partners to hire employees on its behalf, Summers lacked actual authority to bind the firm. Depending on whether hiring employees constituted "apparently carrying on in the usual way the business of the partnership," however, he might have had apparent authority to do so. If he had, then the employee could still have collected from the partnership.

---

[50] Summers v. Dooley, 481 P.2d 318 (Idaho 1971).

V. Management

C. *Law Firm Partnerships*[51]

Sidley & Austin was not always the "Firm of the Obama Romance." For decades, it was a bastion of the old Chicago upper crust. Dating back to 1866, it had history. With Adlai Stevenson once a partner, it had connections. And in a city famous for its segregated bar, it was very white, very male, and very Protestant.[52]

Much has changed. Sidley & Austin still fills a key place among the Chicago legal elite, but it no longer discriminates by race, sex, or religion. It is no longer even one partnership. Instead, it explains on its Web site that it represents a collection of "affiliated" partnerships. For a brief time, it even employed as an associate one Bernadine Dohrn, resurfaced fugitive Weatherman and wife to Barack Obama acquaintance William Ayers. But that is another story.

Much of the cultural change occurred in the late 1960s and 1970s. During that time, the firm came increasingly under the control of one Howard Trienens. The firm did an enormous amount of work for the telephone monopoly AT&T, and Trienens controlled the AT&T account.

Liebman, Williams, Bennett, Baird & Minow was a very different sort of firm. Largely a post–World War II institution, it was aggressive and innovative. It was profitable like Sidley, but different on a wide range of other dimensions.

Roughly the same age, Trienens and Newton Minow had clerked together at the U.S. Supreme Court and remained friends in the years since. Trienens steadily worked his way up within Sidley's ranks. Minow moved among a variety of posts—positions with Adlai Stevenson, with the Chicago office of what would become the Paul Weiss firm, as commissioner of the Federal Communications Commission (FCC) under Kennedy. In 1965, Minow (still in his 30s) joined Leibman Williams as a name partner.

In 1972, the partners controlling the two firms—including Trienens and Minow—decided to merge. Predictably, given the cultural differences, some partners recoiled. *Day v. Sidley & Austin* was one result.

Consider Sidley's partnership agreement:

> All questions of Firm policy, including determination of salaries, expense, Partner's participation, required balances of Partners, investment of funds, designation of Counsel, and the admission and severance of Partners, shall be decided by an Executive Committee . . . provided, however, that the determination of participation, admission and severance of Partners, shall require the approval of Partners (whether or not members of the Executive Committee) then holding a majority of voting Percentages.[53]

---

[51] Day v. Sidley & Austin, 394 F. Supp. 986 (D.D.C. 1975, *aff'd sub nom.* Day v. Avery, 548 F.2d 1018 (D.C. Cir. 1976), *cert. den'd*, 431 U.S. 908 (1977). *See generally* H. Kogan, *Traditions and Challenges: The Story of Sidley & Austin* (privately printed, 1983).

[52] On religious segregation in the Chicago bar, see John P. Heinz & Edward O. Laumann, *Chicago Lawyers: The Social Structure of the Bar* (rev. ed., Northwestern U. Press 1994). On the absence of Jewish lawyers at Sidley before the 1970s, see Joseph Epstein, *Why I Am Not a Lawyer*, 8 Nexus 3 (2003).

[53] *Sidley & Austin*, 394 F. Supp. at 991 n.8.

Note three things. First, the word "salaries" refers to the compensation of secretaries and associates. Partners do not receive salaries; they receive a "participation." Thus, the Executive Committee decided associate salaries. It also decided partner compensation, but subject to a vote of the partnership. Second, the Executive Committee decided which associates to promote to partnership, with its recommendation subject again to a partnership vote. Associates thus "made partner" only if they passed two hurdles: only if the Committee nominated them and the partners then voted to approve their promotions. Third, partners did not have equal votes. Instead, they had (or did not have) various "voting Percentages."

Today, Sidley has about 1,700 lawyers. The approximately 50 partners on the Executive Committee meet quarterly and hold a monthly telephone meeting. A smaller Management Committee meets by conference call every week for one to two hours. The Executive Committee is self-perpetuating, and in the early 1970s had fewer than 20 members.

By its terms, the partnership agreement implied that the partners met and voted at least annually. The Executive Committee would have presented a list of nominees for partnership, and the partners would have voted to approve. The committee would have presented a list of each partner's "participation," and the partners would have approved that list as well.

"Implied," but only implied. In 1990, I was newly tenured at UCLA and coediting the first edition of my casebook. While editing *Day v. Sidley & Austin*, I called a friend at Sidley. We had once been junior associates together. I had left to teach, while he had stayed and made partner.

Looking for background to the case, I asked my friend how often the partnership voted. I thought he would reply "once a year." Instead, he acted as though I had insulted him — as though I as law professor could celebrate the privilege of voting at faculty meetings while he was "merely" a partner. Taken aback, he replied (as nearly as I can remember):

> "We never have votes."
> "You never vote?" I asked.
> "No. We never vote. Never."
> "Really?"
> "Well, no," he paused. "Supposedly, there've been two votes. Sometime in the late 1940s or '50s, the partners voted on whether the wives of dead partners could come to annual summer outing. They voted no.
> "Then, back in the 1950s, there was another vote. The firm used to pay for free lunches at the Chicago Bar Association every Friday. But the lunches turned into boondoggles for the lawyers who weren't doing any work. They'd go over on Fridays and order steaks and shrimp cocktail on the firm's tab.
> "So the Executive Committee announced at a partnership meeting that it was ending this. Someone piped up and suggested a vote. Apparently lots of partners liked the right to go charge a meal to the firm, even if they were too busy ever to do it. So a majority voted in favor of continuing the free Friday lunch.
> "And the Executive Committee ended it anyway."

V. Management

The firm never voted on new partners, he insisted. It never voted on firm participations. Indeed, my friend had no idea how much other partners earned. The firm used a "closed book" system — such that partners not on the Executive Committee never knew what anyone else made.

When he made partner, my friend continued, the firm invited him and the rest of his cohort to a party at the private club on the top floor of the firm's office building. After lots of drinks, one of the partners came by with the "signature page" of the partnership agreement for him to sign. My friend signed the page, but asked if he could see the partnership agreement. Not to worry, the partner told my friend. He'd get it by interoffice mail the next day. My friend claims he never did.

Much of this has changed, Sidley partners insist. But Sidley partners apparently never voted on the Liebman merger. According to the firm's official history, the "senior partners" voted unanimously in favor of it. Probably, they simply invited the rest to sign the new partnership agreement.

Such is the world of Edward Day's claim. Day joined Sidley in the late 1930s straight out of law school. As a new associate, he did two things of note. First, he fell under the sway of Adlai Stevenson, then a Sidley partner. Second, he married the daughter of Kenneth Burgess, this at a firm that for a time went by the name of Sidley, Austin, Burgess & Smith.

When Stevenson became governor of Illinois Day joined him in Springfield. He retained ties to the Democratic Party (Stevenson would later run for President as the Democratic nominee), and while Minow served as FCC commissioner Day worked as postmaster general. For his service in that post, he eventually earned the Miles Kimball Medallion — given by the Mail Advertising Society of America to the person who makes the greatest contribution to the direct mail industry.

In 1963, Day quit the Post Office and rejoined Sidley to head its Washington office. On the Executive Committee at the time was Kenneth Burgess. By the 1970s, Burgess was dead, and the Executive Committee decided to merge Sidley with the Liebman firm. Day would now have to share the chairmanship of the Washington office with the Republican-connected Liebman partner John Robson. This he could not abide, and he sued.

Day first claimed that he had a contractual right to head the firm's Washington office. The partnership agreement made clear that he had no such right, and the court dismissed the claim. Second, Day argued that the Executive Committee had promised that no Sidley partner would be hurt by the merger. Maybe he was promised, maybe not, the court responded, but the partnership agreement said nothing about his role in the Washington office:

> Plaintiff's allegations of an unwritten understanding cannot now be heard to contravene the provisions of the Partnership Agreement which seemingly embodied the complete intentions of the parties as to the manner in which the firm was to be operated and managed.[54]

---

[54] *Id.* at 991.

The court continued on the fiduciary duties that partners owed each other:

> An examination of the case law on a partner's fiduciary duties . . . reveals that courts have been primarily concerned with partners who make secret profits at the expense of the partnership. Partners have a duty to make a full and fair disclosure to other partners of all information which may be of value to the partnership.[55]

It could hardly present a stronger contrast to *Meinhard*:

> The essence of a breach of fiduciary duty between partners is that one partner has advantaged himself at the expense of the firm. . . . The basic fiduciary duties are: 1) a partner must account for any profit acquired in a manner injurious to the interests of the partnership, such as commissions or purchases on the sale of partnership property; 2) a partner cannot without the consent of the other partners, acquire for himself a partnership asset, nor may he divert to his own use a partnership opportunity; and 3) he must not compete with the partnership within the scope of the business.[56]

Partners owe each other exactly what they promise each other—and no more. They certainly need not renounce "all thought of self." Instead, they should not charge commissions on property they sell the firm (example 1). Neither should they sell legal services on the side without telling their partners (example 2 or 3). Beyond that, the court refused to go.

Day may have a "bruised ego," the court mused, but he is "a knowledgeable, sophisticated and experienced businessman and a responsible member of a large law firm." He chose to sign "a well-defined contractual arrangement" that "clearly provided for management authority in the executive committee."[57] He may have lost a feud with Howard Trienens, but so did most Sidley partners who tried. That loss did not a cause of action make.

As sensible as democracy may be for a country, it tends not to work well for institutions that compete in fast-moving markets. Law firms need to respond quickly to their clients and to allocate and reallocate talent on short notice. Democracy among dozens (or hundreds) of partners does not allow that. Autocracy does. Sidley is not a democracy—but it does run smoothly and profitably. In part, it runs smoothly and profitably precisely because it is not a democracy.

---

[55] *Id.* at 993.
[56] *Id.*
[57] *Id.* at 994.

VI. DISSOLUTION

A. *When Can Partners Dissolve?*

1. Introduction

Partners can dissolve their partnership whenever they wish. Take Hart and Kingsfield. They form a partnership to write and maintain a book for Aspen. Kingsfield values Hart's literary flair. Hart values Kingsfield's name and likes his daughter besides. Given their need for each other, they draft a partnership agreement that gives neither the right to dissolve the firm.

Unfortunately for the enterprise, the two do not work together well. Hart finds Kingsfield incurably autocratic, and his daughter Susan insufferably pedantic. He jettisons them both, takes a job on Wall Street, and moves in with the glamorous Vicki Vale.

Notwithstanding the terms of the agreement, Hart has dissolved the partnership. By §29 of the 1914 Act (but not the 1997 Act):

> The dissolution of a partnership is the change in the relation of the partners caused by any partner ceasing to be associated in the carrying on . . . of the business.

Section 29 does not begin "unless otherwise agreed." Instead, it applies regardless of what the partners may have agreed. If a partner leaves, the partnership dissolves.

2. An Example

Or consider the three physicians in *Adams v. Jarvis*.[58] Together, they ran a medical clinic as a partnership. Reasonably interpreted, their agreement let any of them leave at any time. By its terms, a departing partner would collect his capital account and share of that year's profits, and the others would retain the right to continue the clinic without him. Because the firm was on a cash (rather than accrual) basis, by this formula an exiting partner necessarily forfeited his right to the firm's accounts receivable.

The doctors' arrangement fit nicely within the structure of the UPA. Although §29 does not let partners negotiate away their right to "dissolve" a firm, §37 lets them forfeit their right to "wind it up." Because dissolution marks the end of one legal entity and the beginning of another, it defines the potential

---

[58] 127 N.W.2d 400 (Wis. 1964).

liabilities for which the various partners are responsible. To preserve that line —
crucial to a variety of legal questions — the UPA provides that a partner who
leaves always dissolves the firm. Should his collaborators want the right to continue the firm without him, however, the UPA lets them arrange that deal.
According to §37:

> Unless otherwise agreed, the partners who have not wrongfully dissolved the
> partnership . . . [have] the right to wind up the partnership affairs. . . .

If the partners do not agree otherwise, a (nonwrongful) departing partner has the
right to wind up the firm; if they do agree otherwise, he does not.

One of the *Adams* doctors decided to leave. Unfortunately, their lawyer used
the wrong term in the contract. Rather than require a departing partner to take his
capital account and profit share if the firm was not being "wound up," he wrote
that the formula applied "when said partnership is not *dissolving*" (italics added).
Because a departing partner always dissolves the firm, the exiting doctor argued
that the terms of the partnership agreement did not apply. Instead, he had a right
to a share of the clinic's accounts receivable.

The Wisconsin Supreme Court did the right thing. The doctors intended that
anyone who left would take only his capital accounts and profits share. Had they
hired a better lawyer, they would have said exactly that. Their lawyer made a
mistake, but the court refused to let the departing doctor ignore the deal to
which he had intended to agree.

B.   When Is Dissolution Wrongful?

1.   Introduction

Although a departing partner always dissolves a firm when he leaves, he does
not necessarily dissolve it rightfully. Instead, he may dissolve it wrongfully. If so, his
partners may have a claim for damages.

Suppose again that Hart and Kingsfield form a partnership to produce and
maintain the Aspen contracts book. Strangled by a hairy hand, Hart dies. The
partnership dissolves, but Hart has not acted wrongfully. Killing may be a wrongful
act, but dying is not (§31 of 1914 Act):

> Dissolution is caused: . . . (4) By the death of any partner. . . .

Suppose Hart and Kingsfield define unilateral quitting as wrong. If Hart quits,
he acts wrongfully. Section 31, again:

> Dissolution is caused: . . . (2) In contravention of the agreement between the part-
> ners, where the circumstances do not permit a dissolution under any other
> provision of this section, by the express will of any partner at any time. . . .

VI. Dissolution

Suppose Hart and Kingsfield agree that their partnership (technically, a "joint venture") will last for the ten-year term of the Aspen contract. If Hart quits before its expiration, he acts wrongfully (§31):

> Dissolution is caused: (1) Without violation of the agreement between the partners, . . . (b) By the express will of any partner when no definite term or particular undertaking is specified. . . .

If the partners have not specified a partnership's duration, a partner who quits does not necessarily quit wrongfully. If they do specify a duration, he does.

Suppose Hart and Kingsfield agree that if either of them is convicted of a felony, the felon is automatically expelled from the partnership. After taking a job with a Wall Street law firm, Hart sells information about a client's planned takeover to investment banker Gordon Gecko. His now-estranged wife, Vicki Vale, learns of the tip and reports Hart to the feds, and the judge sends Hart to prison. He is expelled and the partnership is dissolved, but he does not have a claim against Kingsfield (§31):

> Dissolution is caused: (1) Without violation of the agreement between the partners, . . . (d) By the expulsion of any partner from the business bona fide in accordance with such a power conferred by the agreement between the partners. . . .

2. Examples

Owen and Cohen agreed to form a partnership and run a bowling alley in Burbank.[59] Owen lent the firm $6,986, but Cohen played the bully and made collaboration impossible. He "had not worked yet in 47 years and did not intend to start now," he declared. Had the two formed an at-will partnership, Owen could have dissolved the firm without risking damages. In fact, however, the court found it a partnership for an implied term. As a result, Owen could not dissolve it unilaterally without entitling Cohen to damages. To avoid that result, he sued for dissolution under §32 of the 1914 Act (§§601, 801 of the 1997 Act):

> (1) On application by or for a partner the court shall decree a dissolution whenever: . . .
> (b) A partner becomes in any . . . way incapable of performing his part of the partnership contract,
> (c) A partner has been guilty of such conduct as tends to affect prejudicially the carrying on of the business, . . .
> (f) Other circumstances render a dissolution equitable.

The court granted the decree.

---

[59] Owen v. Cohen, 119 P.2d 713 (Cal. 1941).

Another example: The Page brothers formed a partnership to run a linen supply business.[60] Initially, they each invested $43,000, and a few years later one loaned additional funds. The firm lost money for several years, but began to recover. When it did, the brother who had lent the money sued to dissolve the firm.

Writing for the California Supreme Court, Justice Roger Traynor let him dissolve it. Because the partnership was at will, the partners could unilaterally dissolve it when they wished (UPA §31). Traynor found no evidence of bad faith. Although a "partner at will is not bound to remain in a partnership," explained Traynor, he "may not dissolve a partnership to gain the benefits of the business for himself."[61] Partners are fiduciaries of each other and may dissolve a partnership only "in good faith." Here, the partner acted in good faith.

The *Page* case illustrates a crucial aspect of the UPA default rule: Absent an agreement to the contrary, partners have a right to dissolve the firm at any time. Effectively, they have a right to force a sale of the firm. Because the partners sometimes differ widely in how liquid their other investments are (how readily they have access to other cash) and in how heavily they have invested in skills and knowledge specific to the firm (how readily they can find comparable jobs), this right to force a sale can create an incentive for opportunistic games. Against that incentive, Traynor targeted these dicta about good faith.

C. What Is the Result of Dissolution?

1. Dissolution and Windup

Hart abandons Kingsfield and goes to Wall Street. Year in, year out, he toils away at the law firm. Eventually, he makes partner — only to find that partners work harder even than associates. After several months, he cracks — and his partners check him into a hospital, where he shares a ward with an ex-GI named Yossarian.

"They're trying to kill me," Hart announces.
"No one's trying to kill you," Yossarian assures him.
"Then why are they shooting at me?" Hart asks.
"They're shooting at *everyone*," Yossarian answers. "They're trying to kill everyone."
"And what difference does that make?"
"And anyway, who, specifically, do you think is trying to murder you," asks Yossarian.
"Every one of them," replies Hart.
"Every one of whom?"
"Every one of whom do you think?

---

[60] Page v. Page, 359 P.2d 41 (Cal. 1961).
[61] *Id.* at 44.

VI. Dissolution

> "I haven't any idea."
> "Then how do you know they aren't?"[62]

The remaining partners at Hart's Wall Street firm sue for dissolution under §32:

> (1) On application by or for a partner the court shall decree a dissolution whenever:
> (a) A partner has been declared a lunatic in any judicial proceeding or is shown to be of unsound mind.

The court grants the decree.

By the terms of §29, a partnership dissolves whenever any partner quits. It does not, however, necessarily disappear. After checking Hart into the hospital, the law firm's Executive Committee will assign his secretary elsewhere. It will move a senior associate into his office. It will forward his e-mail to Vale. And it will move on.

The firm can do this because dissolution does not terminate the partnership as a business. Instead, it simply identifies the period of time during which a given group of partners (a group that includes Hart) is liable for the firm's debts. The firm itself shuts down only if the other partners "wind up" its business. UPA §30:

> On dissolution the partnership is not terminated, but continues until the winding up of partnership affairs is completed.

2. Wrongful Dissolution

The claim that a partner has on the assets of a dissolved partnership depends on whether he dissolved it wrongfully. Suppose Hart and Kingsfield form a partnership at will, but negotiate no partnership agreement. Hart may quit when he wishes. He will have a right to auction the firm's assets and take his share of the proceeds (after paying firm liabilities). According to §38(1) of the 1914 Act:

> When dissolution is caused in any way, except in contravention of the partnership agreement, each partner . . . , unless otherwise agreed, may have the partnership property applied to discharge its liabilities, and the surplus applied to pay in cash the net amount owing to the respective partners.

Suppose Hart and Kingsfield negotiate a partnership for a term. If Hart quits before the end of the term, as noted above he dissolves the partnership wrongfully. By §38(2)(II), he then owes Kingsfield damages and has no right to force a liquidation of the firm. Instead, Kingsfield has the right to continue the business.

---

[62] This exchange is of course a modified version of the exchange between Yossarian and Clevinger, in Joseph Heller, *Catch-22*, at 25-26 (Simon & Schuster 1955).

(2) When dissolution is caused in contravention of the partnership agreement the rights of the partners shall be as follows:
(a) Each partner who has not caused dissolution wrongfully shall have,
I. All the rights specified in paragraph (1) of this section, and
II. The right, as against each partner who has caused the dissolution wrongfully, to damages for breach of the agreement.
(b) The partners who have not caused the dissolution wrongfully, if they all desire to continue the business in the same name . . . may do so. . . .

3.   Examples

Dreifuerst v. Dreifuerst[63] illustrates a simple, routine windup. In general, when partners wind up a firm, they will auction its assets, pay its liabilities, and distribute the remaining cash among themselves. Because well-run firms will be worth more than the sum of their parts, partners will often find it advantageous to auction a firm as a whole. And because existing owners often control much of the firm's goodwill, those owners may enter higher bids than outside buyers. If the partners wind up a firm by auctioning it intact to a subset of themselves, the "windup" merely represents the process by which one group of partners buys out the others. In *Dreifuerst*, the partners did exactly that.

By contrast, *G&S* and *Pav-Saver* illustrate more complex windups. In *G&S Investments v. Belman*,[64] a limited partnership owned an apartment complex. (For more about limited partnerships, see the appendix at the end of the chapter.) G&S and Thomas N. Nordale served as general partners to the limited partnership, and Gary Gibson and Steven Smith served as the partners to G&S.

Nordale was a problem. Over time, he began snorting cocaine and—put most euphemistically—behaving "erratically." Finding his presence a disaster, Gibson and Smith decided to run the business without him. Perhaps their partnership agreement did not give them the right to continue the business, or perhaps it gave Nordale other rights they did not want him to have. Whatever the reason, they sued for judicial dissolution under §32.

Before the court decided Gibson's and Smith's claim, however, Nordale died. His estate argued that the pair dissolved the firm when they filed their suit; the pair argued that Nordale dissolved it when he died. Gibson and Smith had it right, the court explained. Partners do not dissolve a firm by suing for dissolution; the court dissolves it if it grants their petition. Given that Nordale died before the court had a chance to decide the case, he dissolved the firm on death.

The distinction mattered because it determined the amount Nordale's estate took. If the court dissolved the firm by §32, then Nordale had a right to a proportional interest in the assets of the firm. Given that the partnership owned the apartment complex, that proportional interest could have amounted to a

[63] 280 N.W.2d 335 (Wis. App. 1979).
[64] 700 P.2d 1358 (Ariz. App. 1984).

substantial sum. If Nordale dissolved the firm on death, the continuation term of the partnership agreement applied instead. Under Article 19 of the agreement:

> [I]t is agreed that upon the death . . . of one of the general partners . . . *the surviving or remaining general partners may continue the partnership business. . . .*
>
> (2) In the event the surviving or remaining general partner shall desire to continue the partnership business, *he shall purchase the interest of the retiring or resigning general partner. . . .*[65]

The buyout formula under Article 19 then looked to the dead partner's capital account. Nordale, however, had a negative balance in his account. Had Gibson and Smith dissolved the firm by judicial order, they apparently would have owed Nordale's estate money. Because the court held instead that Nordale dissolved the firm by dying, his estate apparently owed money to Gibson and Smith.

Pav-Saver Corporation (PSC) owned the patents to a concrete paving machine invented by Harry Dale, its majority shareholder.[66] Moss Meersman owned Vasso Corporation. In 1974, Dale and Meersman agreed to form a partnership to manufacture the machines. PSC would provide the technology, Vasso would provide the money, and Dale would do the work.

With business in a slump, PSC terminated the partnership. Meersman responded by throwing Dale out of his office and running the firm himself. PSC had dissolved the partnership and had done so in violation of the agreement. According to the terms of that agreement, it owed Vasso liquidated damages. And so the court held.

The harder legal dispute concerned the technology: whether Meersman could continue to use it after evicting Dale. The partnership agreement stated:

> [PSC] grants to the partnership exclusive license without charge for its patent rights. . . . It [is] understood and agreed that same shall remain the property of [PSC] and all copies shall be returned to [PSC] at the expiration of this partnership. . . .
>
> It is contemplated that this joint venture partnership shall be permanent, and same shall not be terminated or dissolved by either party except upon mutual approval of both parties. If, however, either party shall terminate or dissolve said relationship, the terminating party shall pay to the other party [liquidated damages as specified].[67]

According to the agreement, PSC could retrieve the paving machine technology. According to §38(2)(b) of the UPA, Vasso could continue the business—for which it needed the technology.

The court let Vasso keep the technology. Section 38 trumped the agreement, it impliedly held. To be sure, §38 does not start with the standard "unless otherwise

---

[65] *Id.* at 1362 (italics in original).
[66] Pav-Saver Corp. v. Vasso Corp., 493 N.E.2d 423 (Ill. App. 1986).
[67] *Id.* at 425.

provided" formula. Yet as the dissent noted, except when a dispute touches third parties, the UPA generally lets parties contract around it. Here, they tried to contract around it, and the court ignored the deal they cut. As Professor Bainbridge puts it: "Given the importance freedom of contract plays in partnership law, this holding seems clearly erroneous."[68]

VII.   CONCLUSION

In time, even master impresario John Ringling lost his touch. For more than 50 years, the Barnum & Bailey or Ringling Brothers circus had opened Madison Square Garden. In August 1929, Ringling returned from Europe to find that the Garden had changed the contract terms. When it scheduled a meeting to discuss their differences, he simply skipped it.

Stood up by John Ringling, the Garden offered its location to the American Circus Corporation (ACC). To stiff the Garden was one thing. To let a rival open there in its stead was quite another. Ringling had earlier negotiated an option to buy the ACC. To prevent it from usurping his place at the Garden, he exercised the option and bought it for about $1.8 million. Lacking the cash, he borrowed $1.7 million from the Central Hanover Trust Company. That debt then passed to a group of investors that included his longtime "friend" Samuel Gumpertz.

In ordinary times, the ACC purchase might have made sense. The ACC did own five functioning circuses, 150 railroad cars, and 2,000 animals. To retire the Central Hanover loan, John Ringling planned to incorporate the circus partnership and sell stock to the public. Investment bankers assured him the issue would sell.

Unfortunately, these were not ordinary times. Come October, the stock market crashed. The economy spiraled into depression, and circus revenues plummeted. John Ringling suffered a blood clot and retired to a Coney Island hotel.

But if Gumpertz was ambitious, he was not quite the honorable man John Ringling thought. While Ringling was still recuperating on Coney Island in 1932, an installment came due on the now $1,017,000 debt. Ringling defaulted, and Gumpertz convinced his partners Edith and Aubrey that John had lost his grip. To discuss the crisis and take control, they assembled the creditors and partners.

It was everyone against John Ringling. Ringling having defaulted, the creditors could credibly threaten to repossess the property he had pledged. They would desist, they announced, only if (a) the circus were incorporated as a Delaware corporation, (b) they received one-tenth of the stock (Edith, Aubrey, and John would each receive one-third of the rest), and (c) the $1,017,000 debt were assumed by the corporation and secured by John's personal assets.

John Ringling complied, and the partnership became a corporation. The battle for control of the circus that reappears in Chapter 6 had now begun.

---

[68] Bainbridge, *supra* note 17, at 158.

APPENDIX

Other Organizational Forms

A. INTRODUCTION

This book focuses on partnerships and corporations. And yet, any reader who interns at a law firm will notice limited partnerships, limited liability companies, limited liability partnerships, and — I jest not — limited liability limited partnerships. Reasonable readers will wonder why anyone in his right mind would have invented such a bizarre set of organizational forms and drafted the rules that distinguish them.

The answer, of course, is that no one did. No one canvassed the business world and decided investors needed this specific set of organizational forms. No one thought he could facilitate efficient investment with these options. And only the most ingenuous law professor would ever imagine that the portfolio of options made any sense.

Instead, the organizational forms emerged over time — over a very long time — as lawyers, clients, legislators, judges, and bureaucrats sparred with each other within a shifting legal environment. Mostly, they sparred over taxes. They engineered these organizational forms to capture tax advantages, and the forms in place today represent the accumulated detritus of that historical process. Mostly, the forms in place represent the result of a half century of legal innovation, driven almost entirely by the attempts of legislators to collect revenue and the attempts of entrepreneurs and investors not to pay it.

B. MODEST INDIVIDUAL AND CORPORATE RATES

Begin with a hypothetical framework, not too different from that in 2010. Posit a maximum corporate tax rate (33 percent) equal to the maximum individual tax rate (33 percent) and a capital gains tax on securities at a lower rate. Suppose a corporation earns income of \$100. It will pay a corporate tax of $\$100 \times 0.33 = \$33$. If it distributes the after-tax income of \$67 to shareholders as dividends, they will pay an additional tax on the income of $\$67 \times 0.33 = \$22$. This is the infamous "double tax" on corporate earnings.

If the firm operated as a partnership, it would pay no tax at the firm level. Instead, the partners would recognize personal income equal to their share of the firm's profits. If the firm earned income of \$100, the partners would have personal income of \$100 and pay a tax of \$33.

In this tax regime, partnerships present a modest advantage. Investors who form a corporation that distributes its profits will pay a tax of $\$33 + \$22 = \$55$ on every \$100 earned. If they form a partnership instead, they will pay tax of only \$33. Form a partnership, and voila! they avoid the double tax.

And yet, the investors may not currently need the cash. If content to keep their funds "in corporate solution," they can skip the dividends and pay only the corporate tax. If and when they eventually want the cash, they can sell their stock and pay taxes at the lower capital gains rate. If they bequeath the stock to their children, those children (by another U.S. tax rule) will take the stock with a cost basis equal to the fair market value of the stock at the time of death. Sell the stock immediately upon inheriting it, and they pay a capital gains tax of \$0.

C.   HIGH INDIVIDUAL BUT MODEST CORPORATE RATES

At various times over the past half century, Congress has set the maximum individual tax rate much higher than the maximum corporate tax rate and kept the capital gains rate quite low. Because partners pay a tax on partnership income at the high individual income tax rate, this rate structure can make the partnership form unattractive.

In this environment, rational investors will operate through corporations. They will pay a current corporate-level tax at the modest corporate tax rates. By retaining the earnings in the corporation rather than declaring dividends, they will avoid the high personal income tax rates. If and when they need cash, they will sell their stock and pay the much lower capital gains tax.

D.   TAX SHELTERS

1.   The Shelter

Now suppose that investors organize a firm that buys an asset that falls in value over time. An apartment house, for example, will wear out. An oil well will run dry.

D. Tax Shelters

Because the value of these income-producing assets falls over time, the Internal Revenue Code (IRC) lets firms deduct a portion of their purchase price each year. From the revenue generated by the asset, the firm can deduct a "depreciation" (or "depletion") allowance.

At various times, the Code has allowed firms to depreciate assets at faster rates than economically justified. When a firm does so, it may recognize taxable income substantially less than the actual economic income it earns. If a firm's depreciation allowance sufficiently exceeds the real decline in its assets' value, it may even couple real economic income with a "paper" tax loss.

Firms cannot deduct more than the cost of an asset. If they depreciate an asset on their tax returns at rates faster than real economic depreciation, they will eventually exhaust their allowable deductions. They will then report incomes higher than they would have reported if they had deducted only the real decline in the asset's value. Crucially, however, by depreciating the asset at high rates, they will have deferred the tax to a later year and retained the use of the money in the interim.

During the late 1950s and early 1960s, the maximum marginal rate on individual income reached 91 percent. During these high marginal rate years, investments generating paper losses became extremely valuable. Suppose an apartment complex was an economic wash—it earned no real income. If by virtue of high depreciation allowances it generated substantial tax losses, however, it could become a worthwhile investment.

2. Limited Partnerships

To market investments offering these tax losses, entrepreneurs placed the depreciable asset in a partnership. Because the partnership was not itself a taxable entity, any profits or losses "flowed through" to its investors. For a taxpayer in a 91 percent bracket, a tax loss of $100 saved $91 in taxes on his other income. The "paper losses," in short, let him "shelter" his other income.

Unfortunately for the investors, apartment houses and oil wells could sometimes lose money—real money. Sometimes they generated not just tax losses, but real economic losses. If an investor invested in a general partnership to obtain access to tax losses, he risked becoming personally liable to the firm's other creditors.

Enter the limited partnership. By state law, a limited partner in a limited partnership risked no personal liability. By the practice of Treasury bureaucrats, the limited partnership retained enough of the attributes of a partnership to be taxed as a partnership. Note that the limited partnership had at least one general partner with unlimited personal liability, and the limited partners had no control over the operation of the firm.

3. Limited Liability Limited Partnerships

The truly absurd emerged only with time. State law required that a limited partnership have a general partner who was personally liable for the firm's debts. Eventually, entrepreneurs tried using a corporation as that general partner. Because no one is personally liable for a corporation's debts, a limited partnership with a corporate general partner has no one liable on the limited partnership's debts. Courts approved, and the Treasury continued to tax the firm as a partnership.

With entrepreneurs appointing corporations as general partners, some state legislatures dropped the requirement that a limited partnership have a general partner at all. The limited liability limited partnership was the result: limited partnerships with no partner bearing potentially unlimited personal liability.

4. S Corporations

With limited partnerships, investors coupled the limited liability of the corporate form with partnership taxation. Why not, many observers argued, simply let investors choose whether to pay tax on their firms as corporations or as partnerships? Congress obliged with subchapter S of the IRC. In it, Congress provided that corporations that met various requirements (fewer than a specified number of shareholders, for example) could elect to be taxed as "S corporations." They would pay no tax at the corporate level, and their shareholders would instead report their proportional share of the corporation's income on their personal returns.

E. LIMITED LIABILITY COMPANIES

In the 1980s, the Treasury finally abandoned any pretense of policing whether firms that opted for partnership taxation were "really" partnerships. Instead, it allowed noncorporate firms to "check the box" they wanted: To pay tax as a corporation, check the corporate box; to report income as a partnership, check the partnership box instead.

The result was a proliferation of limited liability companies (LLCs). The firms largely follow corporate organizational law: Investors, for example, have limited liability. Check the "partnership box," however, and they avoid the double tax that has plagued the corporate world for so long.

For small, closely held firms, the LLC is now the organizational form of choice. This book does not separately discuss LLC law. On most issues that matter, note that the organizational law of LLCs tracks that of corporations. Whether on piercing the corporate veil (see Chapter 3) or fiduciary duties, for example, most states apply to LLCs the law of corporations.

F.   LIMITED LIABILITY PARTNERSHIPS

By registering a partnership as a limited liability partnership (LLP), investors can avoid personal liability for many employee torts. Law firms sometimes find this an attractive option — even if they could gain greater limited liability through an LLC. The reason to become an LLP rather than an LLC apparently involves intra-firm politics: To become an LLP, a firm must simply register with the state; to become an LLC, it will need to abandon its partnership agreement and negotiate an entirely new organizational document. For many old law firms, that is more democracy than they want.

CHAPTER 3

Implications of the Corporate Form

From downtown to the sea, through Hollywood and Beverly Hills, Sunset Boulevard snakes its way between rich and poor, chic and clueless. In the 1950s, Billy Wilder placed aging silent-screen goddess Norma Desmond on an estate in the ten-thousand block. He gave her a tennis court, a butler as old as she, and a swimming pool. The net on the court sagged, the lines on the court were faded, and the swimming pool—well, the swimming pool was typically Wilder macabre.[1]

Buy a "star map" at one of the stands by the road, and you learn who lives along the Boulevard today. Paris Hilton, the maps announce, along with Leonardo DiCaprio, Keanu Reeves, Sandra Bullock. Leave Beverly Hills, and you pass UCLA on the left. To the right, you find the faux-gated Bel Air.

But as you near UCLA, the banners from the street lamps begin to advertise the "UCLA Hammer Museum." Before reaching the school, turn left on Hilgard Avenue. You pass between the law school and Holmby Hills. After the university, you enter Westwood Village—if you can call any place with this high a Porsche-to-Caprice ratio a "village."

And at the southern end of this "village," you will find a giant striped-marble cube of a modernist mausoleum. Barely two decades old, the cube has already started to decay. Rust from the bolts holding the facade to the steel frame seeps through the marble. Above the entrance, three-foot-high letters proclaim the man behind the cube: "The Armand Hammer Museum of Art and Cultural Center." To the right of the entrance, an older attached building in the Mies-look-alike steel-and-glass "international" style announces the company that paid for it: the Occidental Petroleum Corporation.

In the 1980s, Holmby Hills was home to a very old Armand Hammer.[2] In 1956 Hammer had married his third wife, the wealthy widow Frances Barrett

---

[1] Billy Wilder, dir., *Sunset Boulevard* (Paramount 1950).

[2] The account that follows is based on Kahn v. Occidental Petro. Corp., 1989 Del. Ch. LEXIS 92; Sullivan v. Hammer, 1990 Del. Ch. LEXIS 119; Kahn v. Sullivan, 594 A.2d 48 (Del. 1991); Kahn v.

Tolman, and this had been her home. With her money, he had then bought a controlling interest in what was still the small Occidental Petroleum firm. As *Forbes* put it, he grew the firm "through bribery, guile and sheer gall."[3] With a share of the gross to an heir-apparent to the king, he bribed his way into an oil concession from pre-Gaddafi Libya. With a $500,000 salary, he bought as corporate vice president the former senator and future vice presidential father Albert Gore Sr.[4]

With a bundle of well-laundered cash, Hammer, a longtime Democrat, even tried to buy his way into the Nixon Whitehouse. Alas, he broke some statutes to do so. He did avoid prison time for the feat, but only after staging a near-death attack and arriving in court in a wheelchair with a troupe of medical assistants. The judge pronounced a trivial sentence, and Hammer returned to work. "I've had a miraculous recovery," he explained.[5]

Born in 1898 to a pharmacist on the left fringe of the fringe-left Socialist Labor Party, Armand Hammer had indeed been named after the symbol of world revolution. When that fringe left the party to form the American Communist Party, Armand's passionate father, Julius, left with it. He worked his way through Columbia medical school, and so did son Armand. The only medicine Armand ever practiced, though, was to sell an illegal abortion to the wife of a czarist diplomat. Given his sheer incompetence, she died. His passionate father also had paternal compassion and then took the blame for his son's mistake. Julius the passionate went to Sing Sing, and Armand the dilettante sailed for the new USSR.

In Moscow, Armand turned his father's revolutionary credentials into business deals. With Lenin's help, he obtained an (ultimately unprofitable) asbestos mining concession. He obtained a license to sell (largely fake or kitsch) Romanoff treasures in the United States. Through these arrangements he gave the Soviets access to the laundered foreign exchange they needed to fund their clandestine activities. Come World War II, he would bribe FDR's son Elliott to obtain military aircraft for them as well.

In time, Hammer would also start to collect art. Initially, he focused on old masters at "bargain prices." He received that for which he paid. "Never have so many major masters been represented in this city by canvasses so poor," declared one critic.[6] Stung, Hammer started to pay more and in time acquired some higher-quality pieces.

Not that Hammer ever liked the art. "Hammer was not an art connoisseur," his publicist recalled. "He just liked wheeling and dealing and using art for

---

Occidental Petro. Corp., 1992 Del. Ch. LEXIS 5; Edward Jay Epstein, *Dossier: The Secret History of Armand Hammer* (Random House 1996); Carl Blumay & Henry Edwards, *The Dark Side of Power: The Real Armand Hammer* (Simon & Schuster 1992); Christie Brown, *The Master Cynic*, Forbes (Oct. 17, 1994); Eric Pace, *Armand Hammer Dies at 92; Executive Forged Soviet Ties*, N.Y. Times A1 (Dec. 11, 1990); Alan Parachini, *Confused Picture at Hammer Museum*, L.A. Times (Jan. 25, 1991).

[3] Brown, *supra* note 2.

[4] Epstein, *supra* note 2, at 303.

[5] Quoted at Brown, *supra* note 2; *see* Epstein, *supra* note 2, at 265.

[6] Quoted in Epstein, *supra* note 2, at 292.

self-promotion."[7] To guide him, he hired his mistress—a freelance writer and estranged wife of a USC professor. By the 1980s, he had amassed works by Rembrandt, da Vinci, Rubens, Goya, Gauguin, and Renoir. Even so, the *Los Angeles Times* would still complain that the collection was "at best sporadic in quality."[8]

Sporadic or no, Hammer promised the collection to the Los Angeles County Museum of Art. To house it, he demanded a special wing named after him and dedicated to his paintings. The museum was happy to take the art, but not to display it as a separate trove. It refused his conditions, and Hammer revoked his pledge. In the County Museum's stead, he built the Armand Hammer Museum of Art and Cultural Center.

Hammer did not pay for the museum with his own money. Instead, he used Occidental's. He may have owned only 1 percent of its stock, but he treated the firm as his own. He traveled the globe in its luxury Boeing 727. He put two mistresses and a grandson on its payroll. And for a museum to house his art collection, he charged Occidental nearly $100 million.

To approve the money it would spend on Hammer's museum, Occidental convened a "special committee." Hammer's advisor-mistress would serve as chief financial officer and museum director. His grandson (no "museum or arts credentials," reported the *Los Angeles Times*)[9] would run it. And Albert Gore Sr. chaired the committee that approved it all.

Shareholders were livid. Several institutional investors (including the state pension fund CalPERS) sued to recover their (i.e., the corporation's) money. On behalf of the corporation, they brought a "shareholders' derivative suit" (suit A). So, too, however, did some other shareholders (suit B). And one of the others was a plaintiff tied to the law firm of Milberg Weiss.

The hyperaggressive Milberg firm specialized in derivative suits and securities class actions. It specialized in ways that, by 2008, would land several of its key partners in prison. The eventually imprisoned partners included the lawyers on the *Hammer* case, David Bershad and Steven Schulman.[10] The *Wall Street Journal* explained how the firm worked:[11]

> In a typical case, [key partner William Lerach] would charge that a company had misled shareholders; he would then sue for damages, claiming to represent a class

---

[7] Quoted in Brown, *supra* note 2.
[8] Quoted in Parachini, *supra* note 2.
[9] Parachini, *supra* note 2.
[10] Michael Parrish, *Leading Class-Action Lawyer Is Sentenced to Two Years in Kickback Scheme*, N.Y. Times (Feb. 12, 2008); *Lawyers Sentenced for Role in Kickback Scheme*, N.Y. Times (Oct. 28, 2008).
[11] Kimberley A. Strassel, *From Bully to Felon: How Bill Lerach Shook Down Corporations, until His Scam Was Uncovered*, Wall St. J. (Mar. 1, 2010). Nor was the criticism unique to the *Journal*. The *New York Times* described the Milberg tactics this way: "The moment a publicly traded company's stock dropped, Milberg Weiss would enlist a shareholder as a plaintiff and rush to court with a lawsuit. Usually the sued company would end up settling rather than risk going to trial." It noted that the firm's partners had donated over $7 million to Democratic candidates since the 1980s. Mike McIntire, *Accused Law Firm Continues Giving to Democrats*, N.Y. Times (Oct. 18, 2007).

of people who had lost money on the company's stock; and, finally, he would bully the company into paying over a settlement.

The firm could extort its payoffs in two ways. Most obviously, it could bring what the *Journal* called "strike suits":

> Mr. Lerach . . . would monitor company stock prices, waiting for one to plunge. Then he would find some prior sunny statement from the chief executive, dig up an inside trade or two, locate a shareholder plaintiff, and scream investor fraud.

It would demand damages the firm could not possibly afford:

> Mr. Lerach would then threaten to bankrupt the firm in court or go away for a hefty sum. "I'll own your f—ing house in Maui and the diamonds on your wife's fingers," he once warned a CEO. Companies rushed to settle. Plaintiffs got modest payouts; Milberg Weiss kept millions in fees.

Alternatively, the Milberg firm could offer to settle legitimate claims for trivial sums, in exchange for large attorneys' fees. Because shareholders bring a derivative suit on behalf of a corporation, a settlement with one plaintiff precludes (res judicata) continued litigation by all others. In *Hammer*, the strike-suit attorneys (i.e., the suit B attorneys) negotiated a settlement that paid nothing to the firm but $1.4 million to themselves. Pay off the lawyers in suit B, and the Occidental officers could kill the legitimate CalPERS claim (suit A). Symptomatic of these tactics, Lerach once bragged that he had "the greatest practice of law in the world. I have no clients."[12]

And settle Occidental did. In its deal with Milberg's plaintiff, Occidental and Hammer promised to cap the amount the firm would pay for the museum.[13] They agreed to name three Occidental directors to the museum board. They agreed to call the building (not the museum) the Occidental Petroleum Cultural Center Building. They agreed that Hammer would donate all his paintings to the museum. They agreed to limit future corporate payments to the museum. And for their service in bringing the suit, they agreed to pay the suit B lawyers $1.4 million.

The institutional investors screamed. But the court merely cut the attorneys' fees to $800,000—and approved the deal. "[T]he settlement in the court's opinion leaves much to be desired,"[14] the court complained. Indeed:

> I increasingly suspect that in some cases plaintiffs' counsel seem to be primarily motivated by the huge counsel fees now being generated in class and stockholder derivative actions and that defendant corporations are often willing to pay the fees to obtain a *res judicata* bar to claims against the corporation.[15]

Fancy that.

[12] Peter J. Henning, *Behind the Rise and Fall of a Class-Action King*, N.Y. Times (Mar. 1, 2010).
[13] *See* Sullivan v. Hammer, 1990 Del. Ch. LEXIS 119, at 11-12.
[14] Sullivan v. Hammer, 1990 Del. Ch. LEXIS 119, at 12.
[15] Kahn v. Occidental Petro. Corp., 1989 Del. Ch. LEXIS 92, at 8-9.

I. Introduction

The court may have "suspected" that Milberg's plaintiffs were selling the firm's claims for a payoff to their lawyers, but it was not about to stop them. It complained — and approved the settlement anyway. The museum stood, Hammer died, and (finding the museum a headache) the firm transferred its operation to UCLA.

Organize a firm as a partnership, and a series of consequences follows. Organize it as a corporation, and a sometimes different series follows. After a short introduction that sets corporate law within the agency principles of Chapter 1 (section I), this chapter turns to the derivative litigation behind the *Hammer* dispute: the consequences that incorporation brings for attempts (by shareholders) to pursue legal claims on behalf of a firm against wayward officers (its agents) (section II). As part of that discussion, it explains the "business judgment rule" so basic to this book and to the corporate law field. It examines the metric by which courts evaluate the strategies adopted by those officers (section III). And it asks when shareholders must pay for the debts of the separately incorporated firm despite having entered into a set of contracts premised on their nonliability (section IV).

Appendix I outlines the legal steps by which one forms a corporation. Readers unfamiliar with corporations may wish to skim Appendix I before reading the rest of the chapter. Appendix II surveys the debate over whether states compete for corporate charters. Appendix III summarizes the law and economics of dividends.

I. INTRODUCTION

A. *Clarity and Ambiguity*

Work together, and entrepreneurs sometimes find themselves in a partnership. Take Norma Desmond from Wilder's *Sunset Boulevard.* Suppose Desmond recruits down-and-out screenwriter Joe Gillis to produce a movie on the life of silent-screen goddess Gloria Swanson. Dialogue did not matter back then, recalled Desmond, wistfully looking in the mirror. We were beautiful. And no one was more beautiful than Swanson. So beautiful was she, added Desmond's butler, that she received 17,000 fan letters in one week. Working from her estate on the Boulevard, Desmond and Gillis package the project, recruit the cast, and produce the film.

Depending on the arrangement Desmond and Gillis negotiate, the two may find that they have formed a partnership. Before the 1997 Uniform Partnership Act, however, it was never quite clear in some jurisdictions whether her partnership was an entity distinct from herself as a partner. As a result, at some times and by the law of some states Desmond could not sue in the name of the collective enterprise.

Neither could she and Gillis be sued as a distinct collective enterprise. As Professors Dennis Hynes and Mark Loewenstein put it:

> [In some states], a partnership cannot sue or be sued because it is not a "person" and only legal persons can be named as parties to litigation. With some exceptions, suits by a partnership had to be brought in the names of all partners and all partners had to be joined as defendants in litigation.[16]

Corporate law eliminates these particular ambiguities. Desmond and Gillis could never "find themselves" in a corporation. They become part of a corporation only if they deliberately "incorporate" their firm and register with the state (see Appendix I). That corporation can sue. And it can be sued.

B. Preliminary Legal Consequences

By incorporating, Desmond and Gillis create a new legal entity. It can borrow money, commit torts, and otherwise incur legal obligations. It can sell property, be wronged, and otherwise obtain legal rights. And when it incurs obligations and obtains rights, it does so as an entity distinct from Desmond and Gillis themselves.

Courts govern the relations among the several (or many) people associated with this new corporation by the agency principles of Chapter 1. In a typical corporation, several (or many) people pool their money. They hire others to use the money in one or more business ventures. They collect the receipts, pay the bills, and split the remainder among themselves. If the firm does well, they earn a high return. If the firm does poorly, they lose their investment. In the language of economics, they agree to be the "residual claimants." In the language of the law, they agree to be the shareholders.

Perhaps the shareholders are too many to supervise the firm effectively, or perhaps they know too little about supervising firms. Whatever the reason, by law these shareholders elect others (or themselves) to look after the firm on their behalf. These others are "directors" or "members of the board." In effect, they serve as direct agents of the corporation and indirect agents of its shareholders.

These directors then hire others (officers, employees, sometimes themselves) to run the firm on a daily basis. Like the directors, these people too work as agents for the firm and its shareholders. Because the shareholders as residual claimants take whatever remains after the firm pays its bills, courts typically reason that the directors, officers, and employees owe shareholders the fiduciary duties specified in Chapter 1.

For the most part (with exceptions noted below), directors, officers, and employees owe fiduciary duties to no one else. They are not themselves entitled to fiduciary duties. After all, they can specify the terms of their own employment by

---

[16] J. Dennis Hynes & Mark J. Loewenstein, *Agency, Partnership, and the LLC* 264 (4th ed., West 1997).

contract as minutely as they want. For the same reason, neither do they owe fiduciary duties to lenders, contract claimants, or local communities. A wide variety of men and women have claims on the firm, but all but one of the groups can specify their rights by contract. Only that other group will take what remains. When courts require the directors, officers, and employees to maximize returns to the shareholders, they do so for a simple reason: Everyone else negotiates specific contractual protections. The job of the officers and directors (a job to which everyone implicitly consents when he chooses to participate in the firm) is (i) to pay the contractual claimants exactly that for which they bargain, and (ii) to leave everything else (namely, as much as possible) for the shareholders.

C. Implications

This chapter focuses on three preliminary implications that follow from the incorporation of the firm. First, if a corporation obtains legal rights, it must enforce them itself. An investor may suffer a loss if his corporation is wronged, but it is not a loss on which the investor can sue. He suffers a "derivative" loss — one that "derives from" the loss to the corporation. Any claim on the loss must be brought by the firm itself (section II).

Second, because a corporation is an entity distinct from its investors, sometimes courts face disputes over the goals it should pursue. Most investors mostly invest in it to make money. May the firm deviate from that goal? And if so, by how much (section III)?

Third, if a corporation incurs legal obligations, it — and only it — is liable on them. Absent more, its investors are not. If the firm's stock becomes worthless, those investors lose their investment. Absent more, they do not become liable for debts left unpaid. Sometimes the courts override these principles — and the chapter concludes by tracing the factors that cause courts sometimes to do so (section IV).

II. SHAREHOLDERS AND LITIGATION

A. The Authority of the Board

When Armand Hammer took $100 million from Occidental to build a shrine to himself, Occidental shareholders suffered a loss. Never mind the salaries Occidental paid to the mistresses Hammer put on the payroll, the funds he used to chase a not-to-be-caught Nobel Peace Prize, or the costs he incurred to jet the globe in Occidental's corporate Boeing 727. Occidental had 290 million shares outstanding, so when Hammer spent $100 million on his museum, he took 35 cents per share from its investors.

As CEO, Hammer worked as agent for Occidental and its shareholders. In that capacity, he abused their trust and stole. By incorporating their firm, however, the investors located the resulting claim against Hammer in the firm itself. The Occidental investors *themselves* had no legal claim against Hammer. They could not sue him for the 35 cents they lost on each share — because legally, Hammer did not take their money. He took the corporation's money, and the corporation was a distinct legal entity. Although Occidental shareholders suffered a loss, their loss was indirect — "derivative" of the loss to the firm.

To recover the $100 million, Occidental itself needed to sue. If a CEO steals from his corporation, only the corporation — not the shareholders — can demand the money back. If the CEO then repays the money, the value of the stock (to simplify matters) will rebound to its earlier value. When Hammer steals $100 million from Occidental, each share falls 35 cents. When he repays the money, each share rises 35 cents, and the shareholders are made whole.

Unfortunately for Occidental shareholders, Hammer did not repay the $100 million, and the board of directors did not demand it of him. Whether to sue was a question for the board, and Hammer controlled the board. Indeed, during the 1960s he had controlled the directors expressly. Upon their election to the board, Hammer demanded a letter of resignation. If and when he found their work unacceptable, he dated the letter and "accepted" their resignation.

In 1972, for example, director and chief financial officer Dorman Commons questioned Hammer's plans to expand into the USSR. Commons explained his objections to Hammer, and Hammer listened. When Commons arrived at work the next day, he found he had resigned. Hammer had retrieved Commons's resignation letter, dated it, and then accepted it.[17]

By his last years, Hammer no longer held resignation letters from his directors. He did not control them directly. But they served him loyally nonetheless.

B. The Business Judgment Rule

1. The Decision to Sue

In general, if a corporate board decides not to sue (or decides to settle a suit already filed), a shareholder cannot file a suit in the firm's stead. Fundamentally, the law entrusts business decisions to the board — and whether to sue (or settle) is a business decision. In the words of the Delaware corporate statute (Gen. Corp. L. §141(a)):

> The business and affairs of every corporation organized under this chapter shall be managed by or under the direction of a board of directors....

Necessarily, to say that the business shall be managed by the board is to say that it will not be managed by the shareholders.

---

[17] Epstein, *supra* note 2, at 206, 323 (SEC forces Hammer to end practice); 271-273 (Commons fired).

II. Shareholders and Litigation

2. The Rule

Whether to sue (and whether to settle) is one of the business decisions the law entrusts to the board — and when the law entrusts, courts rarely intervene. Courts will ask whether the board faced a conflict of interest when it made the decision. They will ask whether the board failed to consider the question carefully. But if the board did neither — if disinterested directors thoughtfully considered a matter — then courts let its decision stand.

Courts call the principle the "business judgment rule" — a fundamental rule, perhaps the most basic rule in the field of corporate law:

> Absent fraud, illegality, a conflict of interest, negligence, or waste, a court will not second-guess the decisions of a board.

That a court lets a board decision stand does not mean that it thought the board right. As an Illinois court explained in *Shlensky v. Wrigley* (discussed below in section III.D):

> [W]e do not mean to say that we have decided that the decision of the directors was a correct one. That is beyond our jurisdiction and ability. We are merely saying that the decision is one properly before directors and the motives alleged in the amended complaint showed no fraud, illegality, or conflict of interest. . . . [18]

The *Shlensky* formula is standard and typically includes negligence and waste as well. Negligence (more accurately, gross negligence) goes to the care the board took in making the decision. Waste goes to whether its decision was "so inadequate in value that no person of ordinary, sound business judgment would deem it worth that which the corporation has paid."[19] Courts ask whether a board decision involved fraud, illegality, conflict of interest, negligence, or waste. If it did not, they invoke the business judgment rule and let the decision stand — right or wrong.

For the most part, judges invoke this business judgment rule for a simple and sensible reason: On their good days, judges know their limits. Judges can spot conflicts of interest. They can spot fraud and illegality. Sometimes, they can even identify gross negligence and waste.

But on their good days, judges also know they cannot run businesses. They went to law school, not business school. Most have no experience running firms. They are lawyers, not executives, and most know the difference.

What is more, judges also know that gambles that almost always go wrong can still be worth taking. A $1,000 investment for a 1 percent chance of $1 million is a good bet, even though the investor will lose his investment 99 percent of the time.

---

[18] Shlensky v. Wrigley, 237 N.E.2d 776, 780 (Ill. App. 1968).
[19] Crobow v. Perot, 539 A.2d 180, 189 (Del. 1988).

Judges realize that a CEO who ran his firm into the ground may have made the right decision every step of the way.

Last, judges realize that executives invest money ex ante, that they as judges review events ex post, and that they will find it enormously hard (if not impossible) to judge the ex ante appropriateness of an investment after it went bad. Maybe a CEO made the right decision. Maybe he did not. But most judges usually understand that they cannot necessarily distinguish the two after the fact.

Judges apply the business judgment rule because they realize they are mortal.

3.   Litigation

In the *Hammer* litigation, the Delaware court rephrased the business judgment rule as a presumption that the directors acted within their legal capacity. Dissatisfied shareholders can overturn the presumption, it wrote, only if they can show

> that a majority of the directors expected to derive personal financial benefit from the transaction, that they lacked independence, that they were grossly negligent in failing to inform themselves, or that the decision of the Board was so irrational that it could not have been the reasonable exercise of the business judgment of the Board.[20]

In *Hammer*, the Delaware court thought the board decision outrageous, but (given that Hammer no longer controlled the board the way he did in the 1970s) let its decision stand anyway.

Shareholders will not want a firm pursuing all legal claims, and courts will not force a firm to pursue them. Instead, courts recognize that decisions about litigation are business decisions. They realize that firms do not promote shareholder welfare by spending $100,000 to recover $10,000, and that estimating costs and recoveries always entails a guess.

Suppose that Desmond and Gillis form a corporation to produce their movie about the life of Gloria Swanson. They hire Raymond Chandler to write the script. He does, but they find it unacceptable — too many split infinitives. They hire a second writer to fix the script, and Chandler explodes:

> By the way, would you convey my compliments to the purist who reads your proofs and tell him or her that I write in a sort of broken-down patois which is something like the way a Swiss-waiter talks, and that when I split an infinitive, God damn it, I split it so it will remain split. . . . [21]

Suppose a shareholder now calls Gillis and explains that the firm should sue Chandler for the cost of the second writer. Gillis raises the issue at the next board

---

[20] Sullivan v. Hammer, 1990 Del. Ch. LEXIS 119, at 16.
[21] Tom Hiney & Frank MacShane, *The Raymond Chandler Papers: Selected Letters and Nonfiction, 1909-1959*, at 77 (Atlantic Monthly Press 2000).

meeting, and the board consults the firm's attorney. It decides not to sue. If a board decides the firm cannot win, a court will not require it to sue anyway. If the board decides the firm would win, but that the victory would cost more in attorneys' fees (or public ridicule) than it would recover, the courts still will not require it to sue. Fundamentally, whether to pursue a claim is a question a court entrusts to the board.

C. Derivative Suit

1. Preliminary Requirements

Matters are not so simple when the man who stole from the firm still runs it. Return to our friend Armand Hammer, who used Occidental resources to pay mistresses, travel the globe, and house his art collection. At least until the 1970s, he could fire directors at will.

If Hammer controls the board and the board decides not to sue him, courts will not (or at least should not) defer. By the end of his life, Hammer no longer formally controlled the board, but in the 1960s he still did. Courts defer to a board by the business judgment rule only when a board exercises its judgment without a conflict of interest. If a shareholder claims the chairman stole from the board, the chairman has a conflict. If the other board members hold their positions at his whim, they have a conflict too. They may decide not to sue him, but given their conflict of interest they have not exercised any independent judgment to which a court would (or at least should) defer.

To enable shareholders to circumvent the reluctance of directors to sue themselves or their friends, corporate statutes provide for "derivative suits." In these suits, (i) shareholders sue the corporation in equity, (ii) to force it to sue the wrongdoer. Procedurally, that makes the corporation both a defendant and a plaintiff. For purposes of federal diversity jurisdiction, it is the defendant, and a "citizen" of both its state of incorporation (see Appendix I) and its principal place of business.

Rule 23.1 of the Delaware Court of Chancery (similarly, Rule 23.1 of the Federal Rules of Civil Procedure) captures several of the procedural anomalies to the derivative suit. First, the suing shareholder must have held stock at the time of the contested event:

> In a derivative action brought by one or more shareholders . . . to enforce a right of a corporation . . . , the complaint shall allege that the plaintiff was a shareholder . . . at the time of the transaction of which the plaintiff complains. . . .

An investor may not watch a CEO steal funds and then buy stock in the firm and file a derivative suit. Only someone who already held stock at the time of the theft may file.

Finding plaintiffs who would meet the contemporaneous ownership requirement of Rule 23.1 takes time. In order to be able to file suits quickly, the Milberg

Weiss firm maintained ties to a variety of large investors — "pet plaintiffs" — whom it paid to serve as plaintiffs. Given that these investors had big portfolios, they often held stock in the very firms Milberg wanted to sue. As a Reuters account described it:

> [The Milberg] firm, once the top U.S. shareholder litigation practice, sought out clients with large stock portfolios and paid them to serve as plaintiffs when negative information surfaced about a company. Having these plaintiffs on the payroll allowed the firm to be the first to the courthouse in order to win lead-counsel status — and thus a higher share of fees.[22]

Paying anyone to serve as a plaintiff is also illegal, and it was for this crime that the firm's main partners eventually went to prison.

Second, a shareholder must generally "demand" that a board file the suit itself. Rule 23.1 continues:

> The complaint shall also allege with particularity the efforts, if any, made by the plaintiff to obtain the action the plaintiff desires from the directors . . . and the reasons for the plaintiff's failure to obtain the action or for not making the effort.

Only if the board faces a conflict of interest will the courts excuse a shareholder from making this demand. Subsection 2 below details the implications of this requirement.

Last, a shareholder may settle a derivative suit only with the approval of the court.

> The action shall not be dismissed or compromised without the approval of the court, and notice by mail, publication or otherwise of the proposed dismissal or compromise shall be given to shareholders . . . in such manner as the court directs. . . .

The reason for the rule, of course, is to prevent corporations and attorneys from cutting exactly the deals Milberg Weiss found so lucrative. Put another way, the reason for the rule is to prevent what happened in *Hammer*. The *Hammer* settlement did survive a courthouse challenge, of course, and that it survived gives some sense of how much the rule actually accomplishes.

2. Demand

Given that (i) litigation is a business decision, and (ii) courts want to leave business decisions to the board, the law requires shareholders to present most

---

[22] Alexandria Sage, *Freed Gadfly Lawyer Lerach Warns of More Wall Street Fraud*, Reuters (Mar. 8, 2010), *available at* http://www.reuters.com/article/idUSTRE6280JM20100309; Henning, *supra* note 12.

II. Shareholders and Litigation

proposed suits to the board (to "demand" that it file suit). Once the shareholder makes this demand, a court judges the board's refusal to sue by the business judgment rule:

> [W]hen stockholders, after making demand and having their suit rejected, attack the board's decision as improper, the board's decision falls under the "business judgment" rule and will be respected if the requirements of the rule are met.[23]

If it finds no conflict or negligence, the refusal stands.

In most cases, this demand requirement kills the derivative suit. After all, the board never wanted to bring the suit. If it had thought litigation a good idea, it would have sued on its own. The shareholder went to the trouble of making demand only because the board did not do so. It will not change its mind because a quarrelsome shareholder decided to quarrel. If a shareholder "makes demand" and the board says no, however, the matter generally ends. Absent a conflict of interest or negligence (or fraud, illegality, or waste), a court will defer to the no.

Sometimes a board faces a conflict, of course. As a result, courts partition derivative suits into those that are "demand required" and those that are "demand excused." If a board faces no conflict of interest in the proposed litigation, then the shareholder must first demand that the board file the suit: Demand is required. If the board refuses the demand, courts will defer. Only if the board faces a conflict can the plaintiff avoid the demand. Demand is excused, and the derivative suit can proceed.

Of course, if per chance the board decides to pursue the claim that the plaintiff proposes, that ends the derivative suit too. After all, the firm is pursuing the claim, and the board controls the firm. The law entrusts litigation to the board, and once the board decides to pursue a claim, the petitioning shareholder — by law — has nothing to do.

3. The Legal Standard

Only when demand is excused can a shareholder pursue a derivative suit, and only where the board lacks the ability independently to evaluate the proposed litigation will courts excuse demand. In those cases — but only those cases — shareholders can bring a derivative suit and litigate a claim on the firm's behalf. The Delaware standard for "excusal" appears in *Aronson v. Lewis*.[24] To determine whether demand is excused, a court

> must decide whether . . . a reasonable doubt is created that: (1) the directors are disinterested and independent, and (2) the challenged transaction was otherwise the product of a valid exercise of business judgment.

---

[23] Zapata v. Maldonado, 430 A.2d 779, 784 n.10 (Del. 1981).
[24] 473 A.2d 805, 814 (Del. 1984).

According again to the Delaware court, though, "[w]here a demand has actually been made, the stockholder making the demand concedes the independence and disinterestedness of a majority of the board to respond."[25] Not surprisingly, according to Professor Stephen Bainbridge, "well-counseled plaintiffs almost never make demand."[26]

Take *Grimes v. Donald.*[27] The plaintiff shareholder contested the employment contract between the firm and its CEO. He "made demand" on the board, it refused to sue, and he contested the refusal. The Delaware Supreme Court dismissed. Demand is futile and therefore excused, it explained, if "a 'reasonable doubt' exists that the board is capable of making an independent decision to assert the claim if demand were made." Here, that doubt did not exist. More specifically:

> The basis for claiming excusal would normally be that: (1) a majority of the board has a material financial or familial interest; (2) a majority of the board is incapable of acting independently for some other reason such as domination or control; or (3) the underlying transaction is not the product of a valid exercise of business judgment.[28]

Suppose a plaintiff makes demand but the firm refuses. The plaintiff can argue wrongful refusal but, the *Grimes* court continued:

> [T]he board rejecting the demand is entitled to the presumption of the business judgment rule unless the stockholder can allege facts with particularity creating a reasonable doubt that the board is entitled to the benefit of the presumption. If there is reason to doubt that the board acted independently or with due care in responding to the demand, the stockholder may have the basis ex post to claim wrongful refusal. The stockholder then has the right to bring the underlying action with the same standing which the stockholder would have had, ex ante, if demand had been excused as futile.[29]

In *Marx v. Akers,*[30] the New York Court of Appeals set out an apparently contrasting standard—though one can wonder how differently the two formulae function in practice. *Marx* concerned executive compensation. The court noted that a plaintiff could not avoid demand merely by naming all the directors as defendants. Instead, the plaintiff faced a three-part test for "demand excusal." As in *Grimes*, he could avoid demand if the board faced a conflict:

> Demand is excused because of futility when a complaint alleges with particularity that a majority of the board of directors is interested in the challenged transaction.

---

[25] Rales v. Blasband, 634 A.2d 927, 935 n.12 (Del. 1993); *see* Spiegel v. Buntrock, 571 A.2d 767, 775 (Del. 1990).

[26] Stephen M. Bainbridge, *Corporate Law* 210 (2d ed., Foundation Press 2009).

[27] 673 A.2d 1207 (Del. Sup. Ct. 1996).

[28] *Id.* at 1216.

[29] *Id.* at 1219.

[30] 666 N.E.2d 1034 (N.Y. 1996).

II. Shareholders and Litigation

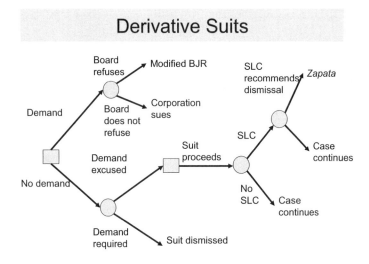

Figure 3-1
Legal Framework for Derivative Suits

Modified from William T. Allen, Reinier Kraakman & Guhan Subramanian, *Notes to Commentaries and Cases on the Law of Business Organization* (3d ed., Aspen Publishers 2009).

> Director interest may either be self-interest in the transaction at issue . . . , or a loss of independence because a director with no direct interest in a transaction is "controlled" by a self-interested director.

Second, the plaintiff could avoid demand if the board violated its duty of care:

> Demand is excused because of futility when a complaint alleges with particularity that the board of directors did not fully inform themselves about the challenged transaction to the extent reasonably appropriate under the circumstances.

Last, the plaintiff could avoid demand if he alleged waste:

> Demand is excused because of futility when a complaint alleges with particularity that the challenged transaction was so egregious on its face that it could not have been the product of sound business judgment of the directors.[31]

The rule obviously parallels the business judgment rule more generally: Conflicts of interest, negligence, and waste each constitutes a reason why a court will not defer to the board.

---

[31] *Id.* at 1041.

D.   Special Litigation Committees

1.   The Practice

Corporations faced with demand-excused claims sometimes respond with a "special litigation committee." Return to Desmond and Gillis's biography of Gloria Swanson. The two form a corporation to handle the project, which they call 77 Sunset Strip, Inc. Desmond will serve as CEO. She, Gillis, and three friends in the movie business will comprise the board.

Rather than hire Chandler to write the script, Desmond convinces the board to give the work to her first husband, Max Von Mayerling. Alas, the assignment is a disaster. Would that Von Mayerling could split an infinitive. In fact, he cannot write at all.

Efrem Zimbalist owns 10 shares of 77 Sunset. He believes that Desmond urged the board to appoint her ex-husband as a ploy to cut the amount she owed him under her divorce settlement. He thinks the board acquiesced under pressure. He files a derivative suit, names all members of the board as defendants, and argues that demand is excused.

In response to Zimbalist's suit, 77 Sunset replaces two of the board members with people who bring long careers in the film industry but no other connection to the firm. It then names them to a special litigation committee. May it delegate the litigation to them? Can they then control the suit? May they exercise that control by recommending (as special litigation committees almost always do) that the firm dismiss the suit?

In *Zapata Corp. v. Maldonado*,[32] the Delaware Supreme Court clarified just how much of a role a special litigation committee could play. The plaintiff claimed fiduciary duty breaches and named all directors as defendants. In response, the firm appointed two new directors and named them to a special litigation committee. The committee then recommended that the firm dismiss the suit.

The court did not just apply the business judgment rule. To be sure, it did ask whether the committee met its duties of loyalty and care: "First, the Court should inquire into the independence and good faith of the committee and the bases supporting its conclusions."[33] But the court did not stop there. In a routine business judgment case, it would have looked for conflicts of interest, negligence, fraud, illegality, or waste. It then would have stopped. The court did look for those elements here, but it asked for more besides:

> [W]e must be mindful that directors are passing judgment on fellow directors in the same corporation and fellow directors, in this instance, who designated them to serve both as directors and committee members. The question naturally arises whether a "there but for the grace of God go I" empathy might not play a role.[34]

---

[32] 430 A.2d 779 (Del. 1981).
[33] *Id.* at 788.
[34] *Id.* at 787.

II. Shareholders and Litigation

Given this risk, explained the court, a judge must inquire into the wisdom of the decision itself: "The Court should determine, applying its own independent business judgment, whether the motion should be granted."[35] A court should exercise its own business judgment, in other words, and second-guess the board itself.

Second Circuit judge (and onetime Yale law professor) Ralph K. Winter Jr. urged closer scrutiny still. A special litigation committee's decision to dismiss a case, he reasoned in *Joy v. North,*[36] depended on the odds it thought the firm might win. Yet those odds involve estimates judges make every day. As a result, "the wide discretion afforded directors under the business judgment rule does not apply when a special litigation committee recommends dismissal of a suit."[37] Instead, "the burden is on the moving party, as in motions for summary judgment generally, to demonstrate that the action is more likely than not to be against the interests of the corporation."[38]

The court, in other words, should make its own judgment. Fundamentally, the question does not involve a business decision. It involves a judicial one, a decision judges routinely make. Accordingly, in this situation, "the function of the court's review is to determine the balance of probabilities as to likely future benefit to the corporation. . . ."[39]

2. Independence

If an Occidental shareholder brings a derivative suit against Hammer for the $100 million he used for his museum, Hammer is not independent. If Hammer's wife, Frances Hammer, serves on the board, she is not independent. Hammer's son Michael would not be independent. If Hammer can (as in the 1960s he could) fire the other directors at will, they are not independent.

But prominent men and women in an industry often attend the same parties. They raise funds for the same charities. They eat at the same restaurants. They play golf on the same courses. Does that social proximity make them less independent?

Consider the remark often attributed to Groucho Marx: Why would I want to belong to a club that would have me for a member?" Marx did in fact say this—about the Hillcrest:

> Hillcrest Country Club was as close to invisible as 142 acres on the south side of Beverly Hills could be. No sign, just a number on the stone entrance gates: 10000 Pico Boulevard. Black Cadillacs slipped inside one by one, the roar of the traffic falling away as they motored toward the club house. . . . Ever since the Depression, this had been the preserve of Hollywood's elite. All the great moguls

---

[35] *Id.* at 789.
[36] 692 F.2d 880 (2d Cir. 1982).
[37] *Id.* at 889.
[38] *Id.* at 892.
[39] *Id.*

had belonged to Hillcrest—Louis B. Mayer and the Warner brothers and Harry Cohn of Columbia and Adolph Zukor of Paramount.[40]

Despite his famous line, Groucho Marx joined the club too. Do movie moguls face a conflict of interest merely because they all lunch at the Hillcrest?

Consider Delaware Chancellor Leo Strine Jr.'s decision in *Oracle*.[41] The plaintiffs had filed a derivative suit against four men on the Oracle board: CEO Lawrence Ellison, Stanford economist Michael Boskin, and two others. They accused the four of trading on inside information (a federal crime, as discussed in Chapter 5) and claimed that the board should have maintained a monitoring mechanism to prevent such trading (a "*Caremark* violation," as discussed in Chapter 4).

In response, Oracle appointed a special litigation committee to decide whether to pursue the case. For the committee, it picked Hector Garcia-Molina and Joseph Grundfest: Garcia-Molina teaches computer science at Stanford, and Grundfest teaches corporate law. It first elected these men to the board and then named them to the committee. Initially, it paid them $250/hour for their work on the committee. The rates fell far below their consulting rates, and the two agreed to surrender any fees if a court thought the money compromised their independence. They then investigated the dispute, wrote a 1,100-page report, and told Oracle to drop the case.

Whether Strine would defer to Garcia-Molina and Grundfest turned on whether he applied the business judgment rule, and whether he applied the rule turned on whether he thought them independent. Under the extant case law, that question would have turned on whether the two were "dominated and controlled" by Ellison. The answer would have been no.

Yet Strine refused to find the pair independent. Boskin had been Grundfest's professor when Grundfest was a Ph.D. candidate. Some of the other defendants had donated to Stanford. Indeed, added Strine, Ellison was "in a position to make—and, in fact, he has made—major charitable contributions to Stanford." At $22.5 billion as of 2010, Ellison was listed by *Forbes* as the fourth richest man in the world. He had even promised Harvard $115 million (though he canceled the gift when the university board refused to back then-president Lawrence Summers during his 2005 women-in-science fiasco).[42]

To Strine, the social ties were just too close. The Stanford Faculty Club, apparently, was the Hillcrest of northern California. Had the two urged Oracle to sue Ellison, their recommendation "would have been, to put it mildly, 'news.'" Had they urged a suit against Boskin—someone they "might see at the faculty club or at interdisciplinary presentations"—it would have been even worse. At stake was

[40] Frank Rose, *The Agency: William Morris and the Hidden History of Show Business* 1 (HarperBusiness 1995).
[41] In re Oracle Corp. Derivative Litig., 824 A.2d 917 (Del. Ch. 2003).
[42] Daniel J. Hemel, *Summers' Comments on Women and Science Draw Ire*, Harv. Crimson (Jan. 14, 2005), *available at* http://www.thecrimson.com/article/2005/1/14/summers-comments-on-women-and-science/.

what Strine called "a general sense of human nature." Grundfest would simply find it too "difficult to assess Boskin's conduct without pondering his own association with Boskin and their mutual affiliations." And those difficulties — those awkward lunches at the Stanford Faculty Club and law and economics workshops — took the case out of the business judgment rule.

E. Derivative versus Direct

1. The Distinction

Abstractly, the distinction between direct and derivative claims is easy to state. If a CEO steals from the shareholders themselves, they have a "direct" claim against the miscreant. If the firm is publicly traded, they can file their direct suit as a "class action." If the CEO steals from the firm, they have only a "derivative" claim. They must sue the firm to induce it to file a claim against the CEO. If a claim is direct, the CEO pays any damages to the investors. If it is derivative, he pays the firm itself.

In the *Hammer* litigation, the investors brought both direct (as a class action) and derivative suits. At root, however, they claimed that Hammer used corporate funds to build a museum for himself. Such claims are derivative, and so the court held:

> The primary claims here . . . relate to the proposed construction and endowment by Occidental of a building to house the art collection of Armand Hammer. These claims are obviously claims for waste which have consistently been held to be . . . stockholder derivative claims.[43]

Suppose Desmond and Gillis form 77 Sunset to produce a movie about the life of Gloria Swanson. Desmond becomes president and Gillis vice president. Both serve on the board, together with several old friends. They own half of the common stock each and sell preferred shares to 50 of their neighbors along the Boulevard (on preferred and common shares, see Appendix III).

Suppose the board pays Desmond and Gillis high salaries. One of the preferred shareholders thinks the salaries excessive. If he sues to recover the amounts, the claim will be derivative: Any harm is to the corporation.

Suppose the board approves a merger (see Chapter 8) of 77 Sunset into MGM. As part of the merger agreement, the board will specify the per-share prices paid for the common and preferred shares. One of the preferred shareholders believes these terms favor the common over the preferred. If the claim be true, the preferred shareholders will have suffered a loss, but the corporation itself will not. The claim will be direct.

---

[43] Kahn v. Occidental Petro. Corp., 1989 Del. Ch. LEXIS 92, at 11.

2. An Example

Other cases are less clear. *Eisenberg v. Flying Tiger Line, Inc.*,[44] is particularly unclear. Apparently to exploit its tax losses and diversify its business, the Flying Tiger Corporation interposed a holding company between itself (the operating company) and its shareholders. The firm needed to engineer a merger and liquidation to do this and successfully obtained the two-thirds shareholder votes it needed under New York law. Max Eisenberg owned a few shares and now found his interest in the operating company replaced by an interest in a holding company. That holding company, in turn, owned all of the shares of the operating company.

Eisenberg complained that he had lost his vote in the operating company and sued to undo the transaction. Flying Tiger replied that the suit was derivative and demanded that he post the bond required (see subsection 3 below) under New York law. Second Circuit Judge Irving Kaufman held the suit direct rather than derivative and let Eisenberg proceed. In doing so, Kaufman followed the case law: For the most part, courts call claims direct when they concern voting rights, preemptive rights, dividends, or the right to inspect corporate books. When claims allege violations of the duties of loyalty or care, courts call them derivative.

Among law students long ago, Kaufman was the stuff of legend. Or nightmares. A law school friend of mine had accepted a one-year clerkship with Kaufman and a job at the Cravath law firm thereafter. When he met a Cravath recruiter at a party, the lawyer assured him that he could start at Cravath "any time." "But I'm committed to clerking for Judge Kaufman for a year," he reminded the lawyer. "That's okay. We know that," the recruiter assured him. "You can start any time."

Among those not in line for clerkships, Kaufman was better known for two cases. In the early 1950s, he sentenced Julius and Ethel Rosenberg to death for passing nuclear bomb technology to the USSR. Later released Soviet files show that Julius Rosenberg and Ethel's brother David Greenglass did indeed pass bomb technology. How heavily Ethel was involved, however, remains unclear.[45] In the 1970s, Kaufman stopped the Immigration and Naturalization Service from deporting John Lennon for smoking pot. Or maybe for opposing Nixon's war in Vietnam. Or then again, maybe not: The FBI's file on Lennon noted that he "appears to be radically oriented, however, he does not give the impression he is a true revolutionist since he is constantly under the influence of narcotics.[46] On his way to his deportation hearing, Lennon blandly remarked to a newsman, "I'm just one of those faces. People never liked my face."[47]

---

[44] 451 F.2d 267 (2d Cir. 1971).

[45] John Earl Haynes & Harvey Klehr, *Venona: Decoding Soviet Espionage in America* ch. 1 (Yale U. Press 1999).

[46] Jon Wiener, *Gimme Some Truth: The John Lennon FBI Files* 215 (U. Cal. Press 1999).

[47] John Wiener, The Nation Blog, *The US vs. John Lennon*, http://www.thenation.com/signup/16290?destination = blog/us-vs-john-lennon (Sept. 12, 2006).

II. Shareholders and Litigation

Although Eisenberg complained about losing his say in the operating company, he never had much say in it anyway. He could vote for the board of directors. After the reorganization, he could vote for the holding company's board of directors, and they in turn selected the operating company board. Earlier, he could vote on mergers and liquidations at the operating company. Yet the very premise of the case, of course, is that he could not even convince shareholders owning a third of the stock to join him in opposing this reorganization.

Eisenberg never claimed that his losing a direct vote in the operating company harmed the value of his investment. He did not argue, for example, that Flying Tiger managers would work harder if shareholders could vote directly on the operating company board. More directly monitored, they might have worked more honestly and industriously. With an extra layer between themselves and their ultimate shareholders, perhaps they now had more scope to indulge their private preferences (and shirk).

Eisenberg never made this argument, and for a simple reason: It would have turned his claim derivative. In effect, Eisenberg would have argued that the new corporate structure — by reducing shareholder oversight — lowered firm value. Yet to claim that firm value fell would be to claim that the corporation was harmed. And to claim that the corporation had been harmed would be to allege a derivative loss.

And yet, if the reorganization did not reduce firm value, how was Eisenberg harmed? If the value of Eisenberg's investment did not fall, he could do little else but argue that he simply liked to vote. He liked to vote. He enjoyed it. And he liked to vote on operating companies more than holding companies. By swapping his operating company shares for holding company shares, Flying Tiger eliminated a pleasure he enjoyed.

To put the argument in these terms illustrates the unreality of it all. Shareholders do not invest in public companies because they like to vote. They invest because they hope to become rich. Ultimately, the reason it is hard to know whether the harm in this case is harm to the corporation or harm to the shareholder is simple: There was no harm. Given that neither the shareholder nor the corporation suffered a harm, asking (as the legal test demands) whether the harm was to the corporation or to the shareholder is akin to asking whether Wookiees are right- or left-handed.

3. Why It Matters

Shareholders like Eisenberg disguise suits for corporate wrongs as direct suits to avoid the bond-posting requirement. The rule began in New York in 1944:

> [i] In any [shareholder derivative] action . . . ,
> [ii] unless the plaintiff or plaintiffs hold five percent or more of any class of the outstanding shares . . . , or the shares . . . have a fair value in excess of fifty thousand dollars,

[iii] the corporation in whose right such action is brought shall be entitled . . . to require the plaintiff or plaintiffs to give security for the reasonable expenses, including attorney's fees, which may be incurred
[a] by it . . . and
[b] by the other parties defendant in connection therewith for which the corporation may become liable under this chapter . . . ,
[iv] to which the corporation shall have recourse in such amount as the court . . . shall determine upon termination of such action.[48]

Take the statute, clause by clause. First, plaintiffs must file a bond only in derivative suits (clause [i]). They need not file it in a shareholder class action (i.e., direct) case. Second, plaintiffs need not file it if they hold more than 5 percent of firm's stock or stock worth more than $50,000 (clause [ii]). Third, if the rule applies, the defendant firm may demand that plaintiffs post a bond for its legal expenses (clause [iii]). Fourth, the bond must cover not just the firm's own expenses (clause [iii.a.], but those of the other defendants for which it will become liable as well (clause [iii.b.]. Corporate statutes typically let firms indemnify their directors for costs they incur in defending themselves against meritless suits (e.g., N.Y. Bus. Corp. Law §722(c)). Fifth, at the end of the litigation, the court will order the bond paid to the firm to cover those costs (clause [iv]).

Many state legislatures (albeit not Delaware) adopted the bond-posting statutes in the wake of the 1930s Depression. Over the course of the decade, derivative suits increased. In response, the New York Chamber of Commerce commissioned one Franklin Wood to study the phenomenon. Wood and his colleagues examined 1,200 Depression-era shareholder suits in the state. Among the suits against exchange-listed firms, they found that only 2 percent of the plaintiffs won at trial and 6 percent of the claims yielded court-approved settlements. Those few plaintiffs who "won" recovered 5 percent of what they alleged; those who settled recovered 3 percent. Concluded Wood, the attorneys involved make "the ambulance-chaser by comparison a paragon of propriety. He at least represents a real client, with usually real injuries, and a legitimate interest in 50% of the recovery."[49]

Some modern studies reach similar conclusions. In her study of shareholder suits, Professor Roberta Romano concluded:

Most lawsuits (83 of 128 resolved suits) settled. Shareholder-plaintiffs . . . have abysmal success in court. Only one suit had a judgment for the plaintiff. . . . This is a success rate of 6 percent of adjudicated cases, but plaintiffs actually won no judgments for damages or equitable relief. The settlements exhibit two striking features. First, only half of all settlements have a monetary recovery (46 of 83).

[48] N.Y. Bus. Corp. Law §627.
[49] Quoted in David A. Skeel Jr., *Shareholder Litigation: The Accidental Elegance of* Aronson v. Lewis, in *The Iconic Cases in Corporate Law* 165, 171 (Jonathan R. Macey ed., Thomson/West 2008).

III. **Shareholders and Corporate Purpose**

Second, awards are paid to attorneys far more frequently than to shareholders (75 of 83). In seven cases (8 percent), the *only* relief was attorneys' fees.[50]

To be sure, the jury is still out. Some studies do suggest that derivative suits improve governance; many, however, find they merely enrich the lawyers.[51]

III. SHAREHOLDERS AND CORPORATE PURPOSE

A. *Introduction*

Entrusted by shareholders to run the firm, a board must set the direction to take. If a shareholder disagrees with its decision, he may sue. He and his shareholder colleagues elected the board to act as their agent, and the board agreed to promote their best interests. Faced with a quarrel between agents and their principals, the court will need to choose a metric by which to evaluate what the agents did.

If a shareholder simply complains that the board pursued the corporate good badly—that it did a poor job—courts invoke the business judgment rule. A shareholder who dislikes a board's decision, they explain, should elect a different board. In the *Hammer* litigation, the court made the point explicitly:

> If the Court [were] a stockholder of Occidental it might vote for new directors, if it [were] on the Board it might vote for new management and if it [were] a member of the Special Committee it might vote against the Museum project.[52]

The Occidental board did indeed do a dreadful job, the court implied. But the shareholders' remedy was to pick a different board.

Suppose Efrem Zimbalist as shareholder in 77 Sunset contests CEO Norma Desmond's decision (and that of the board she dominates) to produce the life of Gloria Swanson. He thinks a movie about Mae ("peel me a grape") West would sell more tickets. Desmond disagrees. Should Zimbalist contest her decision in court, a judge will invoke the business judgment rule and defer to Desmond.

A shareholder could also complain that the firm's directors or officers were using the firm to promote their own private interests. Suppose, for example, that Desmond agrees that West would sell better than Swanson, but focuses on Swanson because her mother wants to play Swanson's part. Courts understand conflicts of interest like this, and when they spot them they do not defer. Should Zimbalist sue,

---

[50] Roberta Romano, *The Shareholder Suit: Litigation Without Foundation*, 7 J.L. Econ. & Org. 55, 60-61 (1991).

[51] *E.g.*, Robert B. Thompson & Randall S. Thomas, *The Public and Private Faces of Derivative Lawsuits*, 57 Vanderbilt L. Rev. 1747 (2004).

[52] Sullivan v. Hammer, 1990 Del. Ch. LEXIS 119, at 12.

a judge would cite Desmond's conflict of interest, refuse to apply the business judgment rule, and evaluate her decision on its own.

Suppose, however, that Desmond flatly declares that she aims for a different goal. She is not trying to maximize 77 Sunset's profits. Instead, she is pursuing a higher good. She agrees that West sells better than Swanson, but wants to focus on Swanson because Swanson embodies the purer cinematic aesthetics that prevailed before the corrupting influence of sound. If Zimbalist sues, should a court defer?

Armand Hammer did not build his museum because he thought it would make money. He built it as a shrine to himself. When asked, however, he claimed he had collected the paintings "for the public — to share the love of art and to promote international peace and goodwill."[53] Should a court defer?

For the most part, shareholders do not buy stock in corporations to celebrate the silent cinema or to promote international peace. Had they wanted to do either, they could have donated to any of a thousand charities. They chose instead to invest in a firm because they wanted to get rich. Should a court defer to an agent who professes not to care whether his or her principals made money? The next sections turn to this question. The answer is decidedly unclear: On the one hand, the logic of the law suggests that the courts should not defer to agents who claim to do good for the world rather than to do well for the shareholders; on the other hand, real-world judges are decidedly reluctant to say that.

B.   Charitable Giving

1.   Introduction

Suppose Desmond decides that joining the Hillcrest would boost her career. Although the club began as a Jewish alternative to old-line Los Angeles clubs that refused Jewish applicants,[54] it no longer limits itself to Jewish members. Neither does it limit itself to men. It does, however, expect large charitable contributions of its applicants. Milton Berle joined in 1932. "It cost me $275 to join in those days," he recalled. "Now the initiation fee is $150,000, if they'll accept you, which all depends on how much money you've given to the United Jewish Appeal [UJA]."[55]

Suppose Desmond gives $200,000 from the 77 Sunset coffers to the UJA. She does so to position herself for the Hillcrest application and wants to join Hillcrest to promote her career. She reasonably believes that in promoting her career, she will also promote the business of 77 Sunset — but she does want to promote her career. Her motives are mixed.

---

[53] Armand Hammer & Neil Lyndon, *Hammer* 447 (G. P. Putnam's Sons 1987).

[54] Regarding the use of its swimming pool, Marx is also alleged to have asked one of these clubs: "My daughter's only half-Jewish. Can she wade in up to her knees?"

[55] Arthur Marx, *Forever Young*, Cigar Aficionado (Mar. 1, 1995), *available at* http://www.cigar-aficionado.com/Cigar/CA_Profiles/People_Profile/0,2540,39,00.html.

III. **Shareholders and Corporate Purpose**

2. **Giving and Social Class**

Charitable preferences are not randomly distributed in the United States. A Methodist shareholder may not want 77 Sunset's funds going to the UJA. A Baptist may not want them going to Episcopal Charities. A Catholic may not want them going to Bob Jones University. And—plausibly—none of them will want its funds going to the Islamic American Relief Agency.

Nominally to avoid this sectarian swamp, most corporations avoid formally religious charities—but in doing so they swap a religious bias for a class bias. Poorer Americans tend to give to churches. Sharing the fashionable upper-middle-class skepticism toward matters religious, richer Americans tend to give to universities and hospitals instead. Table 3-1 describes the social and economic class-driven distinctions in American giving patterns in 2005. Families with income of less than $100,000 made 67 percent of their charitable donations to churches (religious institutions), only 3 percent to hospitals (health institutions), and only 3 percent to universities (educational institutions). Families with income of $1 million or more placed only 17 percent of their gifts with churches. Instead, they gave 25 percent of their gifts to hospitals and 25 percent to universities.

Table 3-1   **U.S. Charitable Giving in 2005, by Income**

Household Income	Religion	Combined	Help meet basic needs	Health	Educa-tion	Arts	Other	Total
$100,000	59.96	7.70	9.34	3.06	2.69	1.01	6.16	89.92
$100,000–$200,000	11.39	2.16	2.46	1.12	1.14	0.44	1.17	19.88
$200,000–$1 million	21.01	10.19	5.3	4.81	29.15	13.57	7.45	91.48
$1 million or more	8.64	2.06	1.93	12.97	12.94	7.88	4.85	51.27
Total	101	22.11	19.03	21.96	45.92	22.9	19.63	252.55

Note: Figures are in billions of dollars.
Source: Eric M. Zolt, *Tax Deductions for Charitable Contributions: Domestic Activities, Foreign Activities, or None of the Above* (draft of Apr. 6, 2011). Hastings Law Journal, Vol. 63, pp. 361-410, 2012.

Corporations may ostensibly shun religious charities to avoid a sectarian bias, but the charities to which they do give reflect the preferences of the highly paid officers who control their money. Put most tactlessly, the rich officers who run large U.S. corporations give the firm's funds to charities favored by their rich friends. They do not give the firm's funds to charities favored by the blue-collar workers whose pension funds invest in the firm's stock. Take the particular nonreligious charities that corporations tend to favor. As of spring 2010, the Metropolitan Opera "salute[d]" the Bank of America, the Deutsche Bank, and Yves Saint Laurent as "leading members of the Corporate Council for Artistic Excellence."[56] The Met, of course, sells entertainment to the upper middle class. The Chicago Lyric similarly celebrated the support of Bank of America and the Deutsche Bank, along with the support of Kraft Foods, Motorola, Boeing, and Accenture.[57] Indeed, the Lyric prominently posted the names of the corporate officers (typically the CEO) who coordinated these corporate gifts.

Support for schools like Princeton similarly tracks class lines. After all, the school sells educational services to the upper middle class. Not only are its alumni rich, but the non-rich seldom succeed in placing their children there. Whatever the reason (and writers propose many theories), elite university students come disproportionately from the upper middle class.

Shareholders do not need agents to give their money away. Zimbalist does not need Desmond to donate to the UJA, or anywhere else. He can choose when to give how much of his savings to whom. A court may claim that

> [w]hen the wealth of the nation was primarily in the hands of individuals they discharged their responsibilities as citizens by donating freely for charitable purposes. With the transfer of most of the wealth to corporate hands and the imposition of heavy burdens of individual taxation, they have been unable to keep pace with increased philanthropic needs.[58]

But its point is simply wrong. Ultimately, all corporations are owned by human beings — always were, and always will be.

To be sure, sometimes charitable giving can sell. Norma Desmond may argue that a gift to the UJA will win her a table at the Hillcrest, and that a table at the Hillcrest will win 77 Sunset lucrative contracts with major studios. Subscribers to the Met and the Lyric probably have funds they could invest in Bank of America and the Deutsche Bank. Perhaps some will park their money with the bank that subsidizes the best performance of *Die Walküre*. Some studies do suggest that firms can increase their profitability by making carefully targeted charitable donations.[59] And even if shareholders do not need their corporate officers to give away their money, they do applaud donations that earn more than offsetting returns. But if only advertising gains can justify corporate charitable donations, should the law

---

[56] Metropolitan Opera, *Corporate Sponsorship*, http://www.metoperafamily.org/metopera/support/corporate_sponsorship/recognition.aspx (accessed Feb. 17, 2012).

[57] Lyric Opera of Chicago, *Corporate Support*, http://www.lyricopera.org/support/annual-corporate-support.aspx (accessed Feb. 17, 2012).

[58] A. P. Smith Mfg. Co. v. Barlow, 98 A.2d 581, 586 (N.J.), *appeal dismissed*, 346 U.S. 861 (1953).

[59] *E.g.*, Baruch Lev, Christine Petrovits & Suresh Radhakrishnan, *Is Doing Good Good for You? How Corporate Charitable Contributions Enhance Revenue Growth* (Sept. 8, 2001), *available at* http://papers.ssrn.com/sol3/papers.cfm?abstract_id = 920502.

III. Shareholders and Corporate Purpose

ban anonymous corporate gifts? That would seem to follow from basic legal principles.

3. A. P. Smith

Even a fire hydrant firm can be on the technological frontier, and at one point in history the A. P. Smith firm was. In the 1890s, the East Orange, New Jersey, firm had patents on several innovative high-pressure hydrants. In 1951, it donated $1,500 to Princeton University. Adjusted for the cost of living, the amount came to $12,000 in 2009.[60]

Shareholder Barlow sued to stop the gift.[61] Charitable contributions were beyond the scope of the firm's authorized activities, he explained. Preposterous, replied a variety of high-profile witnesses. "Capitalism and free enterprise owe their survival in no small degree to the existence of our private, independent universities," the retired CEO of U.S. Steel assured the court. Absent private universities, declared the Princeton president, "freedom as we know it, I submit, is at an end."[62]

Stuff and nonsense, suggests Professor Geoffrey Miller.[63] Fire hydrant companies do not give money to Princeton, but if they did, shareholders would not care. No one would parade the presidents of U.S. Steel and Princeton over a $1,500 gift. As theater, the whole thing was just too good to be true:

[T]he old-line, traditional manufacturing firm, paragon of integrity and virtue, wishing to make a small contribution to a valuable cause, motivated by a benign mix of idealism, patriotism, and enlightened self-interest, and the state's most elite university . . . all played out against the backdrop of an insidious threat of subversion at home and danger abroad.[64]

The case was plain "collusive," concludes Miller. New Jersey did not pass a statute authorizing corporate charitable gifts until 1930, but many companies (like A. P. Smith) had charters that dated from earlier years (the current Del. Gen. Corp. L. §122(9) allows charitable gifts). These firms needed assurance that the 1930 law applied to them too. They colluded to obtain the imprimatur of the New Jersey Supreme Court and engineered the A. P. Smith case to that end.

---

[60] American Institute for Economic Research, *Cost-of-Living Calculator*, http://www.aier.org/research/resources/cost-of-living-calculator (accessed Feb. 17, 2012).

[61] *A. P. Smith Mfg. Co. v. Barlow*, 98 A.2d 581 (N.J. 1953).

[62] *Id.* at 583.

[63] Geoffrey P. Miller, *Narrative and Truth in Judicial Opinions: Corporate Charitable Giving Cases*. N.Y.U. School of Law, Public Law & Legal Theory Res. Paper 09-56 (Oct. 27, 2009), *available at* http://papers.ssrn.com/sol3/papers.cfm?abstract_id = 1495069.

[64] *Id.* at 14.

As Professor Jeremy Telman summarizes the case:

> If your business supports democracy,
> Don't give in to hypocrisy.
> Send your donations
> To the private locations
> That train the future plutocracy.[65]

C. Corporate Purpose

1. The Ford Litigation

In fact, however, on the question of what goals a corporation may pursue, the classic precedent is not a charitable-giving case at all. It is a dividend case (see Appendix III). In 1916, the Ford Motor Company decided to slash its dividends and plow its funds back into what would become the giant, vertically integrated River Rouge manufacturing complex. Henry Ford owned 58 percent of the firm's stock and controlled the company. The Dodge brothers, John and Horace, together owned 10 percent and sued to force Ford to continue its more generous dividends and enjoin the new River Rouge complex.

The Michigan Supreme Court ordered the dividends but denied the injunction. As explained in Chapter 4 (section II.A.2), courts generally evaluate dividends by the business judgment rule. Absent fraud, illegality, conflicts, negligence, or waste, they approve whatever a board decides. Not so the Michigan court in *Dodge v. Ford.* "[The] refusal to declare and pay further dividends appears to be not an exercise of discretion on the part of the directors, but an arbitrary refusal to do what the circumstances required to be done."[66]

This is odd. To be sure, the firm had become massively successful. In 1906, it had earned profits of $100,000 on sales of $1.5 million. In 1909 it introduced the Model T, and in 1913 the assembly line.[67] By 1916, it earned profits of $60 million on sales of $207 million. But CEO Henry Ford had clear plans for the money. He had been distributing 40 to 70 percent of its profits as dividends. Now he wanted to invest them in a plant that would let him capitalize on the firm's revolutionary manufacturing technique.[68]

---

[65] Jeremy Telman, ContractProfs Blog, *Business Associations Limerick of the Week: Barlow,* http://lawprofessors.typepad.com/contractsprof_blog/2008/08/business-associ.html (Aug. 25, 2008).

[66] Dodge v. Ford Motor Co. 170 N.W. 668, 683 (Mich. 1919).

[67] M. Todd Henderson, *The Story of* Dodge v. Ford Motor Company: *Everything Old Is New Again,* in *Corporate Law Stories* 37, 49 (J. Mark Ramseyer ed., Foundation Press 2009).

[68] *Id.* at 59. Internally, the company distinguished between "regular" and "special" dividends. This is not a distinction in the law.

III. Shareholders and Corporate Purpose

2. The Opinion

According to the court, though, Henry Ford was doing two things wrong. First, he was raising quality and slashing prices:

> It had been the policy of the corporation for a considerable time to annually reduce the selling price of cars, while keeping up, or improving, their quality. . . . The plan, as affecting the profits of the business for the year beginning August 1, 1916, and thereafter, calls for a reduction in the selling price of the cars.[69]

Necessarily, the court reasoned, he must be cutting profits intentionally. He was deliberately trying not "to produce immediately a more profitable business, but a less profitable one."[70]

Second, Henry Ford was raising wages. In early 1914, he had doubled wages from $2.34 to $5.00 per day.[71] By the time of the trial, he "employ[ed] many men, at good pay." Asked about his labor policy, he explained that he planned "to employ still more men, to spread the benefits of this industrial system to the greatest possible number, to help them build up their lives and their homes."[72]

Reasoned the court, Henry Ford must be pursuing these policies out of altruism — and altruism was bad. The Dodge brothers had argued that Ford "deliberately proposed . . . to continue the corporation henceforth as a semi-eleemosynary [charitable] institution and not as a business institution."[73] And so the court held: Henry Ford had decided that "the Ford Motor Company has made too much money, has had too large profits, and that, although large profits might still be earned, a sharing of them with the public, by reducing the price of the output of the company, ought to be undertaken."[74]

Such beneficence the court refused to tolerate. As CEO, Henry Ford served as agent of the Ford Motor Company and its shareholders. He may have owned a majority stake in the firm, but he did not own it all — and those other shareholders had hired him as their fiduciary. The principles followed the basic agency rules of Chapter 1, and their application to partnerships in Chapter 2; Brigid O'Shaughnessy had retained Sam Spade to promote her best interests; the Ringling brothers had pooled their investments with each other on the condition that they each promote their collective best interests.

In turn, the Dodge brothers and their fellow minority shareholders had hired Henry Ford to promote their collective best interests as well. Having agreed to act on their behalf, Henry Ford now owed them his best efforts. They had not hired

---

[69] 170 N.W. at 683.

[70] *Id.*

[71] Gary J. Miller, *Managerial Dilemmas: The Political Economy of Hierarchy* 1, 68 (Cambridge U. Press 1992).

[72] 170 N.W. at 683.

[73] *Id.*

[74] *Id.* at 683-684.

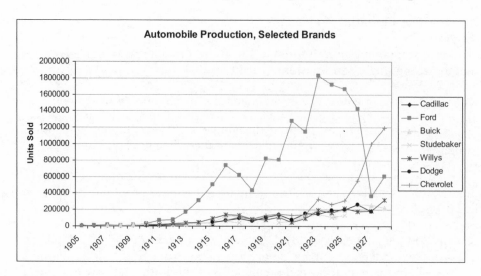

Figure 3-2

Source: U.S. Automobile Production Figures, Wikipedia, http://en.wikipedia.org/wiki/U.S._Automobile_Production_Figures (accessed Feb. 17, 2012).

him to run a charity on their dollar. They had hired him to make money. Declared the court:

> [I]t is not within the lawful powers of a board of directors to shape and conduct the affairs of a corporation for the merely incidental benefit of shareholders and for the primary purpose of benefiting others, and no one will contend that, if the avowed purpose of the defendant directors was to sacrifice the interests of share-holders, it would not be the duty of the courts to intervene.[75]

3. Complications

Yes, of course. But believing that Henry Ford ran a charity is a bit like believing that Brigid O'Shaughnessy was (as she pleadingly assured Spade in the novel and movie) looking for her lovesick younger sister, or that the Ringling brothers would never (as Alf T assured his readers) "touch a dishonest dollar." Sam Spade, at least, never believed O'Shaughnessy. "We didn't exactly believe your story," he assured O'Shaughnessy. "We believed your two hundred dollars. . . . [Y]ou paid us more than if you had been telling us the truth, and enough more to make it all right."[76]

Henry Ford told a tale of charity and generosity, but it was a tale that sold spectacularly well. During years when the sales of most brands stayed flat, Ford sales soared (see Figure 3-2). In 1920, Dodge sold 106,000 vehicles, and Chevrolet sold 146,000. Ford had sold 70,000 in 1911, but by 1920 sold 806,000.

---

[75] Id. at 684.
[76] Dashiell Hammett, *The Maltese Falcon, The Thin Man, Red Harvest* 35 (Alfred A. Knopf 2000).

III. Shareholders and Corporate Purpose

Henry Ford made money spectacularly. In suggesting that lower prices would lower profits, the court assumed constant sales. As everyone learns in the first week of microeconomics, however, posit some monopoly power and demand curves will slope down: Lower prices, and quantity will rise—and the price that maximizes profit depends entirely on the slope of that curve. If a 10 percent cut in price brings only a few additional buyers, the cut may cause a firm to lose money. If it causes hundreds of thousands to switch from Chevrolets and Dodges to Fords, it can cause the firm to make millions. Ford's price cuts caused hundreds of thousands to switch. Ford cut his prices because cutting prices made money for the firm.

As commanding a lead as the Ford Motor Company may have held, however, it was precarious—as Henry Ford realized. Ford rightly understood that his firm could lose its lead at any time. The Dodge brothers had suggested that he controlled a monopoly:

> [If] Henry Ford is permitted to continue the policy . . . of increasing production, reducing the price of cars, and increasing the capital investments . . . , the necessary result will be the destruction of competition on the sale of [low-priced cars] and the creation of a complete monopoly in the manufacture and sale of such cars. . . . [77]

Not so. Ford may indeed have had some monopoly power, but it faced competitive constraints. From 1916 to 1918, Ford sales fell more than 40 percent from 735,000 to 436,000—while Chevrolet sales climbed 25 percent. Shortly after the court published its decision, Ford sales plummeted further, and Chevrolet took the lead (Figure 3-2).

Ford hiked wages for reasons no more charitable than the reasons for which he cut prices. At $2.34 per day, his employees worked in a price-clearing market. "Changing jobs was relatively costless," Professor Gary Miller observes, "because the market-clearing competitive wage guaranteed that [the workers] would neither have to take a cut in wage nor have to stand in line for a new job." A visitor to a Ford plant captured the dynamic: A worker could "quit his job in the morning and find employment in another factory at noon."[78] Chaos on the assembly line ensued. With a turnover in 1913 of 370 percent, Ford hired 52,000 workers for a workforce of 13,600. In any given day, 10 percent of the workers stayed home, and those who arrived shirked as they could.

By contrast, at $5.00 per day, a job at Ford was a prize. By 1915, turnover had nearly disappeared. Productivity climbed by 50 percent, and workers queued for a job. Declared Henry Ford to a journalist: "I have a thousand men who if I say 'Be at the northeast corner of the building at four A.M.' will be there at four A.M. That's what we want—obedience."[79] At $5.00 per day, workers were delighted to obey.

---

[77] Dodge v. Ford Motor Co., 170 N.W. 668 (Mich. 1919) (as reproduced in Lexis).
[78] Miller, *supra* note 71, at 66.
[79] *Id.* at 66-71.

4.   The Proud CEO

At root, Henry Ford lost the case because he was too proud. Had he been willing to live with the robber-baron reputation of Cornelius Vanderbilt or John D. Rockefeller (or later, Armand Hammer), he could have won. He was not. He wanted to be a man of the people, a man who would not give "five cents for all the art in the world."[80] To the *Detroit News,* he declared:

> And let me say right here, that I do not believe that we should make such an awful profit on our cars. A reasonable profit is right, but not too much. So it has been my policy to force the price of the car down as fast as production would permit, and give the benefits to users and laborers, with surprisingly enormous benefits to ourselves.[81]

At trial, the attorneys for the Dodge brothers played pit bull with the quotation:

> Counsel for Dodge: [D]o you still think that those profits were awful profits?
> Ford: Well, I guess I do, yes.
> Counsel: And for that reason you were not satisfied to continue to make such awful profits?
> Ford: We don't seem to be able to keep the profits down.
> Counsel: . . . Are you trying to keep them down? What is the Ford Motor Company organized for except profits, will you tell me, Mr. Ford?
> Ford: Organized to do as much good as we can, everywhere, for everybody concerned. . . . And incidentally to make money.
> Counsel: Incidentally make money?
> Ford: Yes, sir.
> Counsel: But your controlling feature . . . is to employ a great army of men at high wages, to reduce the selling price of your car . . . and give everyone a car that wants one.
> Ford: If you give all that, the money will fall into your hands. You can't get out of it.[82]

Recall the otherwise puzzling language of the Michigan Supreme Court:

> [I]t is not within the lawful powers of a board of directors to shape and conduct the affairs of a corporation for the merely *incidental* benefit of shareholders . . . , and no one will contend that, if the *avowed purpose* of the defendant directors was to sacrifice the interests of shareholders, it would not be the duty of the courts to intervene.[83]

---

[80] Quoted in Henderson, *supra* note 67, at 50.
[81] Quoted in A. Nevins & F. Hill, *Ford: Expansion and Challenge, 1915-1933,* at 97 (Scribner 1957).
[82] *Id.* at 99-100.
[83] 170 N.W. at 684 (italics added).

III. Shareholders and Corporate Purpose

Henry Ford had insisted in court that the firm made money only "incidentally." And although one might otherwise wonder what director would ever "avow" the purpose of sacrificing shareholder interests, on the stand Henry Ford had done exactly that.

5. Why They Sued

The Dodge brothers sued to enjoin Henry Ford's River Rouge plans precisely because those plans were good plans. Skilled machinists, the brothers had once negotiated an exclusive contract to build engines and transmissions for Ford.[84] They had each bought a 5 percent interest in his firm and had each joined the board of directors. In 1913, however, they formed their own company. When Henry Ford tried to buy their factory, they refused to sell.[85] They resigned from the Ford board and focused on building competing cars.

The Dodge brothers probably did not need Ford's dividends. Professor Todd Henderson observes that from 1915 to 1919, Dodge sales climbed from $11 million to $120 million. By 1919, it earned profits of more than $24 million.[86] Probably, the Dodge brothers had the cash they needed.

But the Dodge brothers did not want Ford building a new, efficient factory. They competed with Ford directly. Never mind Chevrolet. Every Ford sale was a potential Dodge sale foregone. Although the brothers held 10 percent of the stock of Ford, they held a larger interest in Dodge. Any loss at Ford plausibly generated offsetting gains at Dodge.

Had the Dodge brothers owed the Ford firm a fiduciary duty, they would have violated it by using litigation to stall Henry Ford's plans for River Rouge. But the brothers did not owe Ford a fiduciary duty. They had resigned from the board. Although they owned stock, they did not hold a controlling interest. Legally, they could litigate to sabotage — and that is exactly what they did.

6. Why Dividends Mattered

The River Rouge plant, yes, but why would the Dodge brothers and Henry Ford fight dividend policy all the way to the state supreme court? Ford wanted to invest the profits in the new factory, but if the court ordered him to pay dividends, he could raise the money he needed by issuing more stock. As majority owner, he would pay 58 percent of the money to himself anyway. With the dividends he received, he could just buy new Ford shares. For the remaining 42 percent, the firm could issue more stock to other investors.

Conversely, suppose (contrary to the discussion above) that the Dodge brothers did want the Ford dividends for their own firm. If the Ford Motor

[84] Henderson, *supra* note 67, at 47.
[85] Miller, *supra* note 71, at 7-8.
[86] Henderson, *supra* note 67, at 56.

Company refused to issue dividends, they could simply sell some of their Ford stock. The value of the stock would have risen by the amount of any undistributed earnings. If they preferred cash to a larger stock portfolio, they could sell a few of their shares. They would own a smaller percentage of Ford, but (given Henry Ford's 58 percent stake) they did not own enough to make a difference anyway.

The reason for the dispute comes in two parts. First, Ford shares were not publicly traded. As a result, the Dodge brothers could not readily sell their stock. Earlier, they had tried to sell their shares to Henry Ford, but Ford had refused. Given his majority stake, anyone who bought their stock would merely have bought a fight with Ford.[87]

Second, shareholders paid taxes on dividends. In 1913, marginal income tax rates still peaked at 7 percent. The following year, World War I began, and with it came massive federal expenses. By the time the Michigan Supreme Court ordered the Ford firm to pay the dividends in 1919, the war had pushed the top marginal rate to 73 percent.[88] For every dollar the company paid to Henry Ford (or the Dodge brothers), nearly three-quarters went directly to the federal government.

D.   Using Corporations to Promote Religious Beliefs

Ford is a famous case but an odd one. In part it is odd because it is so famous, but it is also famous because it is odd. The Michigan Supreme Court declared that courts had a "duty . . . to intervene" when directors announced an "avowed purpose . . . to sacrifice the interests of shareholders." Fine and good. Coach a client well, and all but the most dense and intransigent will avoid avowing charitable goals. Given *Ford*'s fame, the issue should no longer arise.

But suppose a CEO insists that he wants to govern according to his personal religious beliefs. Does *Ford* prevent him from following goals — ethical goals, religious goals, political goals — other than profit maximization? *Shlensky* suggests not.[89] The case concerned the Cubs. Chicago is a religious town, and through the 1970s and 1980s, Chicagoans held few religious beliefs more passionately than their beliefs about whether the Cubs should install lights in Wrigley field.

Philip Wrigley ran the Cubs. He owned 80 percent of the stock and worked as president of the firm. Owners of the chewing gum empire, his family had run the Cubs since 1920. At one time, all baseball clubs had held their games during the day. With the advent of modern lighting, however, most major league teams had switched to night games. Most baseball fans work for a living, and those who do

---

[87] Henderson, *supra* note 67.

[88] Tax Foundation, *U.S. Federal Individual Income Tax Rates History, 1913-2010* (Sept. 9, 2011), *available at* http://www.taxfoundation.org/publications/show/151.html. In fact, matters were more complicated than this. Salary income was subject to the standard graduated rates, but dividend income was not. Instead, dividends were subject to only a "surtax." That surtax, however, brought high marginal rates as well.

[89] Shlensky v. Wrigley, 237 N.E.2d 776 (Ill. App. 1968).

III. Shareholders and Corporate Purpose

cannot attend ball games in the afternoon. They attend them in the evening, or they attend them not at all. Only the trust-fund set like Wrigley or summer associates at Sidley, Kirkland, or Mayer Brown take off midday to watch the Cubs.

Eyeing the low attendance figures, minority shareholder William Shlensky sued (derivatively) to force the Cubs to install lights in Wrigley field. Philip Wrigley refused. Lights would potentially damage the neighborhood, he explained, and anyway "baseball was a daytime sport." Ford refused to pay large dividends because (said he) he wanted to pay his employees well and thought every garage deserved a good car. Wrigley refused to install lights because he wanted to care for his neighbors and thought electrically lit baseball games a moral travesty. But where Ford lost, Wrigley won.

The *Shlensky* court worked hard to explain with a straight face why Wrigley's plan *might* help shareholders — how the Cubs might make more money holding its games when no one but the trust-fund set and summer associates could attend. But in the end, it did not matter. Wrigley had studied the issue and thought carefully about it. Not owning a bigger stake in the competing White Sox, he faced no conflict of interest. Shlensky could identify no fraud, illegality, conflict of interest, negligence, or waste, so the business judgment rule applied.

Perhaps courts also recognize that many of the people with the most lucrative business plans discover those plans because they love what they do. They do not work to make money. They work to have fun or do good. When their sense of fun or good coincides with consumer demands — think Steve Jobs or Bill Gates — they earn spectacular returns. Some of the most wildly creative and profitable ideas in business, in other words, come from men and women who do not self-consciously try to maximize their profits.

Perhaps courts recognize that *Ford* does no one much good. They could (as the *Ford* court does) require officers and directors to repeat the mantras of profit maximization. But why? Henry Ford would not take coaching from his attorney, but most CEOs will. When sued, their attorneys will tell them to testify that they want to make money. And so they will testify.

But why bother? Very few real-life CEOs try to give away more than modest amounts of the firm's money anyway, and very few take wildly irrational positions. Philip Wrigley did, but he is unusual. If excessively altruistic (eleemosynary?) CEOs are not a real problem, why worry? Hammer created a disaster at Occidental, but not one that resulted from excessive generosity. He created it from his massive conflict of interest. Modern courts recognize that most CEOs who refuse to repeat platitudes about profit maximization are probably still trying to make money.

In 1981, the Wrigley family sold the Cubs to the *Chicago Tribune*. The *Tribune* tried to install lights, encountered opposition from the field's neighbors, but installed them in 1988 anyway. At their first Wrigley field night game in 1988, the Cubs were ahead at the top of the fourth inning, 3 to 1. The "heavens opened," and a rainstorm shut out the game. The gods had spoken, apparently. Night baseball was a moral travesty.

IV. SHAREHOLDERS AND CORPORATE LIABILITY

A. *Introduction*

When investors incorporate a firm, they form a new legal organization — an entity separate from the people who created it, who act on its behalf, or who own equity stakes in it. This independent entity can incur obligations toward others and can obtain rights against them. To say that its shareholders enjoy "limited liability" is merely to say that it is from them a separate beast.

Complications arise when people try to use these new legal lines either to externalize the cost of doing business or to cheat those with whom they deal. Noticing that Desmond no longer much uses her Isotta-Fraschini, suppose Gillis convinces her to let him rent it for use at high school proms. To protect Desmond's other assets, they form a new corporation, Sunset Rentals, Inc. Together, they invest $10,000 and take all of its stock. The firm then rents Desmond's Isotta from her on a weekly basis, and re-lets it by the hour to high school lovers.

Suppose that Desmond and Gillis decide the Isotta-Fraschini needs extensive repairs. On the one hand, they realize that the restoration work will be expensive. Isotta parts have long since disappeared, so most will need to be fabricated by hand. On the other, they also understand that the limousine enterprise involves high risks. The high school prom night market is glutted, and cars that win the Pebble Beach Concours can still lose among middle-class high school seniors. Rather than contract for the repairs from Vintage Automobiles, Inc., in her own name, Desmond arranges for Sunset Rentals to contract with Vintage for the repairs directly.

Now posit two outcomes. First, two high school lovers overdose on OxyContin in the back of Desmond's car. They survive after emergency room attendants pump their stomachs, but incur $200,000 in health costs along the way. They claim that Vintage should have known they would take dangerous drugs in the backseat of the car — and breached its duty of care under state tort law. Second, Sunset Rental obtains $300,000 in repairs from Vintage, only to find that it cannot make money in the prom-night market after all. Desmond sells her car at Pebble Beach for several million dollars. Should either the lovers or Vintage Automobiles be able to "pierce the corporate veil" and collect from Desmond herself? The cases that follow explore that question in more detail.

B. *In Tort*

1. *Walkovszky*

William Carlton adopted the Desmond–Gillis approach to corporate structure, but without the Isotta-Fraschini. Instead, he ran a fleet of 20 (presumably dilapidated) Caprices (or Fords). He operated the fleet in New York City. The state required that he buy $10,000 liability coverage, so he bought $10,000 coverage. He took his 20 cars, and placed them 2-to-a-firm in 10 companies. He put the garage in an eleventh company. As the firms made money, he "milked out" (the plaintiff's words) the profits to himself through dividends.

When one of Carlton's drivers, Baldo Marchese, hit pedestrian John Walkovszky, Walkovszky sued Marchese, the firm (Seon Cab) that owned Marchese's cab, all of the other corporations, and shareholder Carlton.[90] From Seon's insurance, Walkovszky of course could collect the $10,000 coverage. When he tried to collect the rest from the other defendants, the court faced the question of Carlton's liability. From time to time, firms that transport high school seniors to proms will carry passengers who "do drugs" in the backseat. Such is the law of probability applied to U.S. high schools. From time to time, firms that operate cabs in New York City will run down pedestrians. That, too, is the law of probability, but applied to the streets of New York. Cabs owned by largely asset-less corporations with $10,000 insurance coverage will then impose one of the predictable costs of the cab business on pedestrians: They will externalize the cost of doing business. Should the law let them do this?

2. Fraud and Capitalization

To hold shareholder Carlton liable for the damages left uncovered by Seon's insurance, Walkovszky first claimed fraud. Unfortunately for him, Carlton had not done anything particularly fraudulent. He had simply taken a series of legal steps that—in combination—let him avoid the predictable costs of his trade. The dissent tried to make something of the undercapitalization of Carlton's firms. But again, the law did not impose a minimum capitalization standard that Carlton failed to meet.

Despite their many references to the concept, courts never explain what "undercapitalization" means anyway. Plaintiffs do not sue the shareholders of corporations that can pay their liabilities. They sue shareholders when the corporations do not have the funds to pay. If a corporation were undercapitalized whenever it could not pay its bills, then all veil-piercing cases would involve undercapitalized firms. And if an inability to pay debts justified piercing that corporate veil, then every insolvent firm would find its veil pierced. Limited liability would protect shareholders only when they did not need the protection.

3. Agency

Instead of either fraud or inadequate capitalization, the court suggested the plaintiff Walkovszky prove "agency." To see what agency might have to do with any of this, suppose Desmond and Gillis decide to run an ice cream truck business. They form a corporation, but do not hold a shareholders' meeting. Desmond buys

---

[90] Walkovszky v. Carlton, 223 N.E.2d 6 (N.Y. 1966).

a truck and sends her butler, von Mayerling, into Holmby Hills. She tells him to play the ice cream truck jingle, stop every block, and sell ice cream bars to the children playing on the sidewalks. Von Mayerling goes to Holmby Hills, but hits a little girl who runs in front of the truck.

Can the girl's parents sue Desmond personally? Desmond told von Mayerling where to go and what to do. Because the firm did not hold a shareholders' meeting (see Appendix I), it had no directors. With no directors, it had no officers. Desmond owned stock in the firm, but that stock did not give her legal authority to tell von Mayerling what to do. Stockholders cannot run the firm; they can only elect directors to run it.

Necessarily, then, when Desmond told von Mayerling where to go and what to do, she acted in her individual capacity. If von Mayerling obeyed her instructions, he presumably agreed to act on her behalf and subject to her control (see Chapter 1). He went to the suburb as her personal "servant." And if he committed a tort (hit a little girl), he did so in the course of serving Desmond, his master. Necessarily, Desmond is liable for von Mayerling's torts under agency law.

Now suppose that upon incorporating the ice cream truck firm, Desmond and Gillis held a shareholders' meeting. At the meeting, they—as the two shareholders—elected themselves (and three neighbors) to the board. Upon adjourning the shareholders' meeting, they convened a board meeting and elected Desmond president of the firm. Desmond then told von Mayerling to sell ice cream in Holmby Hills.

As senselessly formalistic as the distinction between the two accounts may seem, it makes all the legal difference. When Desmond in the second account tells von Mayerling to go to Holmby Hills, she gives those instructions pursuant to her authority as an agent (the president) of the firm. Because she acts within the scope of her authority in giving the instructions, von Mayerling acts on behalf of the corporation in following them. He agrees to act under her control—but control she exercises on behalf of the corporation. Necessarily, the corporation is liable for von Mayerling's torts, and Desmond is not.

The apparent obsession in veil-piercing cases with "corporate formalities" lies here: If a shareholder has ignored those formalities, he lacked the legal authority to run the corporation. If the employees obeyed him anyway, they must have obeyed him in his individual (not corporate) capacity. And if they obeyed him in his individual capacity, they acted as his personal "servant." As their "master," he then becomes liable for their torts under respondeat superior.

In fact, most real-world judges decide veil-piercing cases by a "scumbag rule." And any reader who took this analysis of corporate formalities and agency seriously would miss the point of a half century of legal realism. Judges do not check corporate formalities and then hold shareholders liable if the firm ignores them and absolve them if instead it follows the rules. They ask whether the shareholder is a scumbag. If he is not, they absolve him. If he is, they scour corporate documentation for evidence of missed formalities. If they find a missed formality, they hold him liable. If they cannot find a missing formality—well, usually they can. But in the rare case (like *Walkovskzy*) where they cannot, sometimes they swallow hard and let the shareholder go.

116

4. Enterprise Liability

The *Walkovszky* court asked only if shareholder Carlton were liable on driver Marchese's accident — whether Seon Cab was "a 'dummy' for [Carlton who was] in reality carrying on the business in [his] personal capacities for purely personal rather than corporate ends." Given the facts presented, Seon was not a dummy, and Carlton was not liable. The court did not discuss whether the other nine cab companies or the garage company were liable — what it termed the "quite another" question whether Seon was "a fragment of a larger corporate combine which actually conducts the business."[91]

The New York courts instead faced that "quite another" question in *Mangan v. Terminal Transportation System.*[92] The plaintiff in *Mangan* had been hit by a Terminal cab, but could not remember which. The Terminal taxi empire divided its cabs among four firms and placed its dispatch apparatus in a fifth. That fifth firm also housed the books, the payroll records, and the garage. A separate holding company held all of the stock of the dispatch-garage firm and 60 percent of the stock of each of the cab firms. Two men held the other 40 percent. Unable to recall anything about the cab that hit him beyond the Terminal logo on its side, the plaintiff did not know which of the four firms to sue. He faced a classic law-school logic puzzle: He could readily show that a Terminal cab "more likely than not" had hit him; at most, however, he could show only a 25 percent chance that a cab from any specific Terminal company had hit him.

The plaintiff threw up his hands and sued everyone: all four cab companies and the dispatch-garage firm besides. The court declared the general rule: "When one corporation controls another, and uses it as the means, agency and instrumentality by which the former carries out and performs its business, it is liable for the torts of the other."[93] It applied the rule to the facts and found the dispatch-garage firm liable. The dispatch-garage firm hired the drivers, supervised all employees, kept the books, and serviced the cars:

> We hold that the four operating companies were the agents and instrumentalities through which the [dispatch-garage firm] carried on its business, that their operation was controlled by the [dispatch-garage firm], and that [the dispatch-garage firm] is liable for the negligence of the driver of the cab involved.[94]

The question again turned on agency. Shareholder Carlton was liable for driver Marchese's torts if Marchese drove the car as servant for Carlton personally rather than as servant for Seon. The dispatch firm in *Mangan* was liable for the torts of the drivers in the other four companies if the drivers drove their cars as servant for that firm rather than their own operating companies. In theory, a firm should

---

[91] *Id.* at 8.
[92] 284 N.Y.S. 183 (Sup. Ct. 1935), *aff'd*, 247 A.D. 853 (App. Div. 1936).
[93] 284 N.Y.S. at 188.
[94] *Id.* at 191.

be able to offer dispatch and garage services by contract to a taxi firm without becoming liable for the torts of the drivers. Unfortunately, it was a theory the *Mangan* court did not much explore. Instead, the court simply declared the dispatch-garage firm liable.

C. In Contract

1. Introduction

Courts most readily pierce the corporate veil in tort. After all, tort plaintiffs seldom choose to do business with a firm deliberately. They suffer an injury and then find the person who caused their injury insulated by a corporate veil. They plead with the courts to pierce that veil and let them collect.

Suppose again that Desmond and Gillis form Sunset Rentals and lease Desmond's car. As Sunset president, Desmond contracts on the firm's behalf for repair services from Vintage Autos, Inc. Unable to compete in the high school prom market, Sunset defaults on its $300,000 restoration bill from Vintage. Should Vintage be able to collect from Desmond personally?

Absent fraud by Desmond or Sunset, Vintage lacks a very compelling claim. After all, it chose to extend the credit — $300,000's worth of credit — to Sunset Rentals. It could have required Sunset to pay an advance deposit, but did not. It could have demanded progress payments, but did not. It could have required Desmond personally to guarantee Sunset's performance, but did not. Instead, it extended very risky credit to Sunset, presumably because — one way or another — Sunset made it worth its while.

A court that lets creditors like Vintage pierce the corporate veil without showing fraud gives them a guarantee that they could have negotiated but did not. People do not give guarantees for free. Vintage could have obtained a guarantee from Desmond, but if it had, then Desmond and Sunset would have insisted on a lower price. Vintage opted not to demand a guarantee and presumably charged a higher price instead. A court that holds Desmond as shareholder liable anyway effectively lets Vintage as creditor collect twice — once through a higher price while the credit remained outstanding and once through a shareholder guarantee that it could have negotiated but chose to do without instead.

2. Kinney Shoe

The fact that contract creditors do not present very sympathetic claims for veil piercing does not mean courts never order it. Take *Kinney Shoe Corp. v. Polan.*[95] Lincoln M. Polan owned Industrial Realty, and Industrial leased property from Kinney. Industrial defaulted on the lease. As Industrial had no assets, Kinney sued Polan.

[95] 939 F.2d 209 (4th Cir. 1991).

IV. Shareholders and Corporate Liability

The court held Polan personally liable. For a test, it offered a typical veil-piercing formula:

> First, is the unity of interest and ownership such that the separate personalities of the corporation and the individual shareholder no longer exist; and second, would an inequitable result occur if the acts were treated as those of the corporation alone.[96]

It observed that Industrial "had no paid in capital. Polan had put nothing into this corporation, and it did not observe any corporate formalities."[97] It then held this enough to hold Polan liable: "This corporation was no more than a shell—a transparent shell. When nothing is invested in the corporation, the corporation provides no protection to its owner; nothing in, nothing out, no protection."[98]

The court had to stretch the law to reach this result. Past courts had generally held contract creditors to the deals they cut:

> When, under the circumstances, it would be reasonable for . . . a party entering into a contract with the corporation . . . to conduct an investigation of the credit of the corporation prior to entering into the contract, such party will be charged with the knowledge that a reasonable credit investigation would disclose.[99]

Kinney did not claim fraud. It did not argue that Polan hid anything from it. It had its corps of lawyers and could understand that it was making a highly contingent contract. Probably, it wanted to unload the real estate and, toward that end, agreed to a lease that generated rent if and only if the lessee (Industrial) made money on the property.[100] Industrial made no money, so Kinney collected no rent. At that point, it then sued for a shareholder-level guarantee that it could have negotiated at the outset but did not.

3. Sea-Land

For the most part, contract claimants present a compelling case only when a shareholder deceives them—only when the shareholder manipulates the firm to which the claimant lent money in order to enable the firm to renege on its debt. As an example, consider the *Sea-Land* case.[101] The Pepper Source firm shipped Jamaican sweet peppers with the Sea-Land firm and defaulted on the freight bill. Because Pepper Source lacked any assets, Sea-Land sued its shareholder Gerald J. Marchese and several of his other wholly owned corporations. Later, it added the Tie-Net firm, which Marchese jointly owned with one George Andre.

---

[96] *Id.* at 211.
[97] *Id.* at 212.
[98] *Id.* at 213.
[99] Laya v. Erin Homes, Inc., 352 S.E.2d 93, 100 (W. Va. 1986).
[100] I am indebted to Reinier Kraakman for this observation.
[101] Sea-Land Servs. v. Pepper Source, 941 F.2d 519 (7th Cir. 1991).

To explain what the Sea-Land firm needed to show to recover against Pepper Source's shareholder Marchese, the Seventh Circuit quoted a formula much like that in *Kinney Shoe*:

> [A] corporate entity will be disregarded and the veil of limited liability pierced when two requirements are met: First, there must be such unity of interest and ownership that the separate personalities of the corporation and the individual [or other corporation] no longer exist; and second, circumstances must be such that adherence to the fiction of separate corporate existence would sanction a fraud or promote injustice.[102]

To decide whether the plaintiff had met the unity-of-interest test, the court said it would consider

> (1) the failure to maintain adequate corporate records or to comply with corporate formalities, (2) the commingling of funds or assets, (3) undercapitalization, and (4) one corporation treating the assets of another corporation as its own.[103]

In *Sea-Land* itself, the court found the unity-of-interest test met. Marchese seldom followed corporate formalities. He routinely paid personal bills with corporate funds. And he rarely distinguished among his finances and those of his corporations.

On the record, however, the court did not find the "fraud or injustice" required by the second part of its test. To be sure, Sea-Land could not pay its bills, but an unsatisfied judgment alone did not show injustice. If it did, every veil-piercing case would meet the test. After all, creditors try to pierce the corporate veil only when corporations cannot pay.

Instead, suggested the court, to meet the fraud-or-injustice test a plaintiff should show "some 'wrong' beyond a creditor's inability to collect." Perhaps, for example, "a party would be unjustly enriched." Perhaps "a parent corporation that caused a sub's liabilities and its inability to pay for them would escape those liabilities," or a shareholder would succeed in an "an intentional scheme to squirrel assets into a liability-free corporation while heaping liabilities upon an asset-free corporation."[104]

The fraud-or-injustice requirement matters because sensible courts would not—and real-world courts do not—pierce corporate veils merely because a shareholder missed some corporate formalities. Too many firms miss them for innocuous reasons. As Judge Richard Posner explained elsewhere:

> [T]he second part of the [*Sea-Land*] test is as important as the first. [Lack of proper formalities is], after all, typical of start-up companies. They often are scantily

---

[102] Van Dorn Co. v. Future Chem. & Oil Corp., 753 F.2d 565, 569-570 (7th Cir. 1985) (citations omitted; quoting Illinois precedent; bracketed material is in *Sea-Land*).

[103] *Id.* at 570 (citations omitted).

[104] *Sea-Land Servs.*, 941 F.2d at 524.

capitalized. Their staffs are small and do not have time for elaborate bookkeeping and minute-keeping. . . . It [is] natural if somewhat irregular for [a shareholder] to finance the operations of the fledgling enterprise out of the assets of his other corporations without creating a meticulous paper record of intercorporate transfers.[105]

In *Sea-Land*, the district court on remand cited two reasons to hold Marchese liable anyway. First, in shifting assets about among his corporations, he committed tax fraud: "To allow Marchese to enjoy the continuing benefit of limited corporate liability in the face of his years of flagrant disregard for the federal and state tax laws concerning the treatment of corporate funds would clearly promote injustice."[106]

Second, he had promised Sea-Land that Pepper Source would pay, even as he manipulated funds to ensure that it would not. On reappeal from the remand, the Seventh Circuit approved the veil piercing on this ground: "Since Marchese was enriched unjustly by his intentional manipulation and diversion of funds from his corporate entities, to allow him to use these same entities to avoid liability 'would be to sanction an injustice.'"[107]

To justify holding Marchese liable, the second of the district court's reasons (asset shuffling) makes sense; the first (tax fraud) does not. The second addresses the way Marchese deliberately tricked and cheated Sea-Land; the first captures the way he cheated someone else. The asset shuffling goes to whether Sea-Land could intelligently decide whether to extend credit to Pepper Source without Marchese's personal guarantee; the tax fraud does not. Again, Judge Posner:

> If you decide to risk selling to . . . a corporation that may not have sufficient assets to satisfy a claim arising from its breach of the sales contract, you can hardly complain if the risk materializes and your judgment against the other party cannot be satisfied.[108]

But if your contract partner's shareholder fraudulently induces you to think the firm a better risk than it is, the fraud matters:

> On the other hand, if the other party . . . deceive[s] you into thinking that you are dealing with a substantial enterprise, and not a mere shell, then the fiction of separate corporate existence does become an engine of fraud, and you can pierce the veil.[109]

Take Armand Hammer again.[110] On the one hand, while at Occidental, he parked laundered cash in secret Swiss accounts. Had Occidental gone insolvent, those accounts might have proven relevant to his personal liability toward its

---

[105] Torco Oil Co. v. Innovative Thermal Corp., 763 F. Supp. 1445, 1451 (N.D. Ill. 1991) (Posner, J., sitting by designation).
[106] 1992 U.S. Dist. LEXIS 9763, at 8 (N.D. Ill.).
[107] 993 F.2d 1309, 1312 (7th Cir. 1993).
[108] *Torco Oil Co.*, 763 F. Supp. at 1451 (Posner, J., sitting by designation).
[109] *Id.*
[110] Epstein, *supra* note 2, at 138 (Faberge stamps), 270 (Swiss accounts).

contract creditors. After all, he (perhaps) contributed to Occidental's inability to pay its bills by taking what had been its money and hiding it in secret accounts to which (perhaps) only he had access. On the other hand, when importing Romanoff "treasures," Hammer brought "with him from Russia a set of the signature stamps of the Faberge workshops, so he could doctor unsigned items in the back room of his New York office." This was fraud, too, of course. But like Marchese's tax fraud, it did not affect the ability of a contract creditor to know whether to extend credit to Hammer's firm.

4. Related Questions

(a) Why Fraud or Injustice?

Sea-Land raises several other issues. First, why does the formula turn on "fraud *or injustice*"? What does "injustice" add beyond fraud?

The formula includes injustice because claimants will find it hard to show fraud on summary judgment. Fraud is always unjust, but not all injustice is fraudulent. Of the two terms, *injustice* captures a broader range of depredations. Yet fraud is an intentional act, and intent is a question of fact. As a result, claimants will usually need a jury trial to show fraud. Whether to pierce the veil, however, generally arises at pretrial. Adding "injustice" to "fraud" lets courts resolve the question without impaneling a jury.

(b) Reverse Piercing

Second, if Sea-Land obtains a judgment against Marchese, can it reach the assets of the other firms he owns? As Marchese's judgment-creditor, Sea-Land can levy against his assets. Those assets include his stock in the other corporations. Why should it "reverse-pierce" the corporate veil and obtain a judgment against these other corporations as well?

The answer goes to Sea-Land's priority in bankruptcy. If Sea-Land takes Marchese's interests in the stock of the other corporations, it becomes an equity claimant to them. Among the claimants to those corporations, it will stand last in line. If it can become a judgment creditor, it gains a higher priority. Note that the possibility of "reverse piercing" does complicate the monitoring a creditor must do. A creditor to one of Marchese's firms (for example) will need not just to monitor rival claimants to the firm. It will need also to monitor the claimants against the other legally distinct firms Marchese owns—because, if those claimants pierce the corporate veil, they could become creditors to Marchese's other firms as well.

(c) Tie-Net

Last, should Sea-Land be able to "reverse-pierce" the corporate veil against Tie-Net? In this firm, Marchese held only a 50 percent interest; Andre owned the rest.

IV. Shareholders and Corporate Liability

Despite Andre's stake, Marchese routinely stole from this firm too. As a result, by the four-part unity-of-interest inquiry, Sea-Land met the test: Marchese routinely shuttled assets between Tie-Net and the other firms. Yet by the commonsense meaning of "unity of interest," he did not have it: A 50 percent owner never has a "unity of interest" with the firm in which he has his half interest. By letting Sea-Land collect against Tie-Net, the court's logic simply collapses into this: The fact that Marchese stole from Andre in the past justifies the court's taking even more from Andre now.

D. Conglomerates

1. The Case

Of course, judges do not always "get it." In the silicone breast implant litigation, Judge Sam Pointer of the Alabama federal court did not "get it" at all. Instead, he "got" the connection between fraud and the tort-contract distinction entirely wrong.[111] Bristol-Myers Squibb (BMS) owned all of the stock of Medical Engineering Corporation (MEC), and MEC sold silicone breast implants. Implant users filed products liability claims against MEC and then sought to pierce the corporate veil against BMS. BMS moved to dismiss on the ground that the users could not show fraud.

Judge Pointer refused BMS's motion. Fraud, he reasoned, mattered in contract but not in tort (the logic appears in section C immediately above). Products liability cases lay in tort. Therefore, the plaintiffs in the products liability implant cases did not need to show fraud.

While the first two propositions are true enough, the conclusion misses the underlying logic. Fraud matters in a contractual relationship because it prevents a creditor from pricing credit accurately and from deciding intelligently whether to demand a guarantee. It does not matter in tort because tort claimants rarely pick their defendants. Sea-Land chose to extend credit to Pepper Source because Marchese lied to it. Walkovszky did not step in front of a Seon cab because Carlton cheated on his balance sheet.

The claimants in the BMS litigation bought their implants from MEC voluntarily, by contract. They did not need to buy implants. Instead, they chose to buy them deliberately. Given their choice to buy implants, they did not need to buy them from MEC. Instead, they chose MEC's implants deliberately. But having decided to buy MEC implants, they could have demanded a guarantee from BMS. Again, they chose not to do so. For a court to hold BMS liable for MEC's debts after the fact without requiring the plaintiffs to show fraud necessarily gives the claimants a contractual term they could have negotiated but did not.

In following instead the syllogism that he did, Judge Pointer relied on the fact that we law professors teach products liability in our torts classes. Tort cases involve nonwaivable legal rules, and products liability is a decidedly nonwaivable rule. Yet judges do not impose nonwaivable rules in products liability cases because the cases

---

[111] In re Silicone Gel Breast Implants Prods. Liab. Litig., 887 F. Supp. 1447 (N.D. Ala. 1995).

involve torts; instead, the cases involve contractual disputes over defective products. Rather, judges (and law professors) group products liability disputes with tort because they want to impose a nonwaivable rule. Judges (and law professors) mostly realize the inefficiency involved in imposing nonwaivable terms on contractual deals between consenting adults. They impose them in products liability cases anyway and catalog the cases in tort to disguise what they do.

It is no answer to say BMS would not have granted a guarantee. If its customers valued a guarantee highly enough to pay for it, BMS could have made money offering it (think of the elaborate warranties automobile manufacturers voluntarily offer). That it offered no guarantee merely reflects the fact that buyers did not want it badly enough to pay for it.

Neither is it an answer to say patients lacked the sophistication to demand a guarantee from BMS. Patients did not buy the implants. They retained physicians, and these physicians chose the implants for them. The patients hired sophisticated agents, in other words, to make the purchases on their behalf. In turn, those sophisticated agents had every incentive to choose wisely. Cosmetic surgery is a ruthlessly competitive market. Doctors in the field do not become rich recommending defective implants from judgment-proof sellers.

2. Denouement

The implant wars were an embarrassment all around — except for the lawyers. The litigation began in the 1970s.[112] Over the ensuing years, attorneys filed an increasing number of suits and sometimes won spectacular verdicts. Courts consolidated the claims into a class, and Judge Pointer approved the final class settlement in 1994. By the middle of the next year, more than 400,000 women had registered in the settlement.

Scientists, however, never thought the silicone implants caused the diseases attributed to them (many of the symptoms plaintiffs cited sounded much like the flu). Over time, the evidence against the plaintiffs mounted. The *New England Journal of Medicine* published a Mayo Clinic study finding no connection between the implants and disease in 1994. It published a "Harvard nurses" study finding no connection in 1995 (the year of Pointer's piercing-the-corporate-veil opinion). By late 1998, Judge Pointer himself chaired a scientific committee that found no evidence that implants caused the diseases claimed. The prestigious Institute of Medicine of the National Academy of Sciences concluded the same in 1999.[113]

---

[112] For a summary of the dispute, see PBS, *Frontline: Breast Implants on Trial,* "Chronology of Silicone Breast Implants," http://www.pbs.org/wgbh/pages/frontline/implants/cron.html (accessed Feb. 18, 2012).

[113] *Summary of Report of National Science Panel* (Pointer Report), *available at* http://www.fjc.gov/BREIMLIT/SCIENCE/summary.htm (accessed Feb. 18, 2012); Institute of Medicine, *Safety of Silicone Breast Implants* (Consensus Report) (June 1, 1999).

Scientists determined that the implants caused none of the diseases claimed. Never mind—Dow Corning and BMS left the market in 1992. The case became a classic example of "junk science in the courtroom." Destroyed by the litigation, Dow eventually went bankrupt.

V. CONCLUSIONS

Incorporate a firm, and several legal consequences follow. The new creature is a distinct beast. It can suffer losses and, when it does, sometimes obtain legal rights. Should a firm suffer a loss, its investors themselves will usually suffer a loss too — but they cannot sue. They suffer only a derivative loss. To obtain compensation, they must instead induce their corporation to sue. For a corporation, however, whether to sue on a claim is a business decision entrusted to the board. Absent a conflict of interest, courts generally defer to whatever decision the board reaches. Sometimes they defer even with a conflict of interest: When shareholders fought Armand Hammer over the $100 million he took from his firm to house his art collection, the court ignored the board's conflict and deferred to it anyway.

To run their new legal entity, investors hire agents: directors and officers. When these agents make decisions the investors do not like, sometimes the investors sue. In adjudicating the resulting disputes, courts try to defer to the agents. If the investors dislike the choices their agents make, the courts explain, they should hire new agents. When courts cannot avoid adjudicating the dispute, though, they typically explain that the agents must try to make money for the firm. In practice, they still give those agents a wide berth.

This new firm can also incur obligations. As an entity distinct from its investors, usually the firm's investors will not be liable for its debts. They will become liable on its debts only when they agree to do so. Yet once in a while, courts hold them liable on a firm's debts anyway. Typically, they do so only when the investors ignore the separate legal boundaries to the firm and treat its assets as their own.

APPENDIX I

Incorporating the Firm

You take a job as an associate at a Los Angeles law firm. During your second week, a partner calls you into his or her office. The son of the CEO of a major client wants to open a Santa Monica dealership for used Lamborghinis. Other associates will handle the regulatory clearance and tax filings, the partner tells you. You are to incorporate the dealership. What do you do?

You will first decide the state in which to incorporate. In theory, you could choose any of the states. In practice, you will choose either your local state (California) or Delaware.

You will then contact the CT Corporation. You could call them by phone, but probably you will use their Web address. You will tell them the state where you want to incorporate — let us posit that you choose Delaware. CT will then provide a form "articles of incorporation" for that state.

You could draft the articles of incorporation from scratch, but that would be silly. Law firms never reward associates for creativity along these lines. Instead, you will fill in the blanks on the CT form. Typically, the form will come on one 8-1/2'' by 14'' sheet, two-sided.

On this document, you will give the following:

- The firm's name.
- The firm's registered agent in the state of incorporation. If Delaware, your law firm will probably have a firm that it uses for this service.
- The "purposes" of the firm. You will simply write: "To engage in any lawful act or activity for which a corporation may be organized under the General Corporation Law of Delaware." You will write this because anything narrower will leave your client open to a claim that something it did was "ultra vires" — beyond the scope of allowed activity.
- The number of shares authorized. You will probably enter a number greater than what you plan to issue. This will let the firm issue more shares later without amending the articles. Some states (though not Delaware) will

require that you specify the "par value" of shares — the price below which the firm may not originally sell the stock. Note (i) that the firm may freely issue the stock at a price above par value and (ii) that par value does not govern the resale price of the stock. In short, par value is an amount that directors simply "make up" at the outset.

- The names of the "incorporators." Typically, you will list yourself, the partner who assigned you the job, and perhaps someone else. You might list the client, but you could also just add a paralegal at the firm. Alternatively, you could list the firm's first directors in the document.
- If you plan to issue more than one class of stock, you will specify the details in the articles.

You will submit these articles of incorporation to CT along with any necessary fees. CT will send the material to the secretary of state for the jurisdiction you choose. In time, that state will return a "certificate of incorporation."

While waiting for the certificate of incorporation, you will obtain a copy of the model "bylaws" that your law firm uses. This document, too, will have blanks that you will fill in. For the most part, you will do nothing more than fill in the blanks.

Much longer than the articles, the bylaws will cover a broad range of items: for example, the number and tenure of the directors, the officer positions at the firm, the time and place for the firm's annual meetings, the time and place for the board meetings, the requisite notice for the meetings, any modification to quorum rules, and so forth.

Once the state notifies you that it has incorporated the firm, you will contact the other incorporators. In person (or possibly by mail — called "unanimous consent"), you will hold an "organizational meeting" at which you will elect the first board of directors and adopt the bylaws you drafted. Those directors will then hold the initial board meeting. They will elect the officers of the firm and sell stock. The firm will then be operational.

Henceforth, the firm will hold a shareholders' meeting once a year. At it, the shareholders will elect a board of directors. A majority of the outstanding shares will constitute a quorum, though the firm could specify a different number in its articles or bylaws (though not less than one-third in Delaware; Del. Gen. Corp. L. §211(b)). As necessary (typically for merging the firm or liquidating it), the board may call other "special meetings" of the shareholders (§211(b)).

To run the firm on a daily basis, the board of directors will hire officers. It will then monitor their work. Toward that end, it will hold a board meeting as often as necessary. Most boards include at least three people, though Delaware law requires only one (§141(b)). Unless the firm specifies otherwise in its bylaws (with a minimum of one-third), a majority of the directors will constitute a quorum (§141(b)).

The firm may amend its bylaws through *either* the shareholders or the directors (§109(a)). Amendments to the articles require a majority vote of *both* the directors and the shareholders (a majority of all shares entitled to vote, not just a majority of shares voting at the meeting; §242(b)(1)).

APPENDIX II
Race for the Bottom

In 1974, Columbia law professor and former SEC commissioner William Cary published a manifesto against Delaware.[114] (See more on Cary in Chapter 5.) Delaware, he argued, led a race among states toward a corporate legal regime that helped managers steal (in effect) from investors. The argument proceeded in three steps. First, states wanted firms to incorporate under their laws. Given that they made money from incorporation fees, they competed for incorporations.

Second, managers choose the state in which to incorporate. Shareholders invested money, but had no say in the place of incorporation. Instead, managers chose.

Hence, concluded Cary, states attracted corporations by offering statutes that let managers exploit shareholders. Public firms incorporated in Delaware because its law let managers take advantage of the shareholders who had parked their money with them. Among the 50 states, Delaware was leading a "race for the bottom."

Superficially beguiling, the argument does not work — as Second Circuit judge and Yale law professor Ralph Winter quickly explained.[115] Managers cannot manage without funds. They can obtain those funds only in ruthlessly competitive capital markets. Should state A fail to protect investors from their managers as scrupulously as state B, investors will favor B firms over A firms. Should an entrepreneur incorporate in A anyway, he will attract investors only if he can promise credibly a higher return than others.

Put otherwise, the inadequate shareholder protection in state A raises the cost of capital for firms incorporated there. In turn, that capital market penalty places them at a disadvantage in the product, service, and labor markets. Over time, firms that choose the suboptimal state A will tend to disappear. As Professor Roberta Romano puts it: "Cary had overlooked the many markets in which firms operate — the capital,

---

[114] William L. Cary, *Federalism and Corporate Law: Reflections upon Delaware,* 88 Yale L.J. 663 (1974).

[115] Ralph K. Winter, *State Law, Shareholder Protection, and the Theory of the Corporation,* 6 J. Legal Stud. 251 (1977).

128

product, and corporate control markets—and that constrain managers from choosing a legal regime detrimental to the shareholders' interest."[116] As a result:

> [F]irms operating under a legal regime that did not maximize firm value would be outperformed by firms operating under a legal regime that did and the former would therefore have lower stock prices. A lower stock price could subject a firm's managers to either employment termination, as the firm is driven out of business because of a higher cost of capital than that of competitors operating under a value-maximizing regime, or replacement by a successful takeover bidder that could increase a firm's value by reincorporating. . . . Winter concluded that this threat of job displacement would lead managers to demand a value-maximizing regime for their shareholders and that states would provide it. . . . [117]

According to Winter and Romano, Delaware does not attract investors by offering bad law. It attracts them by offering good law. Delaware does not lead a "race for the bottom." It leads a "race for the top." Its virtues do not lie just in having a good statute. They also lie in its courts: In its corps of able judges who effectively specialize in corporate law and quickly issue usually sensible and almost always predictable decisions.

The Cary–Winter debate generated an enormous literature over a vast set of topics. Some scholars, for example, asked "why Delaware?" rather than some other state. Why did Delaware attract incorporating firms? They concluded that its small size probably represented part of the answer: Its resulting dependence on corporate filing revenues enabled it more credibly (than a bigger state) to commit to maintaining good law.[118] Other scholars explored the constraints that federal law imposes (or does not impose) on the interstate competition in corporate law.[119] Still others examined the types of questions on which state competition would most likely yield improvements.[120]

Empiricists continue to debate the extent of the evidence for the Delaware advantage.[121] Just how much of an advantage Delaware offers firms is unclear. Exactly where that advantage lies is also unclear. What is unambiguously certain, however, is that Cary was wrong: Delaware does not lead a race for the bottom and never did.

---

[116] Roberta Romano, *The Genius of American Corporate Law* 15 (AEI Press 1993).

[117] *Id.*

[118] Romano, *supra* note 116; *see also* Jonathan Macey & Geoffrey Miller, *Toward an Interest-Group Theory of Delaware Corporate Law*, 65 Tex. L. Rev. 469 (1987).

[119] In alphabetical order, e.g., Lucian A. Bebchuk & Assaf Hamdani, *Federal Corporate Law: Lessons from History*, 106 Colum. L. Rev. 1793 (2006); Mark J. Roe, *Delaware's Competition*, 117 Harv. L. Rev. 588 (2003); Mark J. Roe, *Delaware's Politics*, 118 Harv. L. Rev. 2491 (2005).

[120] E.g., Lucian A. Bebchuk, Oren Bar-Gill & Michal Barzuza, *The Market for Corporate Law*, 162 J. Instit. & Theoretical Econ. 134 (2006).

[121] In alphabetical order, e.g., Lucian A. Bebchuk, *Federalism and the Corporation: The Desirable Limits on State Competition in Corporate Law*, 105 Harv. L. Rev. 1435 (1992); Robert Daines, *Does Delaware Incorporation Improve Firm Value?*, 62 J. Fin. Econ. 525 (2001); Marcel Kahan & Ehud Kamar, *The Myth of State Competition in Corporate Law*, 55 Stan. L. Rev. 679 (2002); Roberta Romano, *Law as Product: Some Pieces of the Incorporation Puzzle*, 1 J.L. Econ. & Org. 225 (1985).

APPENDIX III

Dividends

A. LAW...

Corporations need not pay dividends. Instead, the law entrusts the decision about whether to issue them to the board of directors. This "optional" character to dividends constitutes one of the central differences between dividends (on stock) and interest (on loans).

Should a firm issue "preferred stock," it must first pay dividends on the "preferred" shares before paying any on the "common." Such is what it means for stock to be "preferred." Should the firm decide not to issue any dividends at all or dividends only on the preferred, however, that decision too is one the law entrusts to the board.

Directors do not have the discretion to pay dividends utterly whenever they please. They cannot incorporate a firm, borrow money, distribute the cash from the loan to the shareholders, and then default. Exactly what constraints the law places on dividends vary by state. In Delaware, however, the statute provides (§170(a)):

> The directors of every corporation ... may declare and pay dividends upon the shares of its capital stock ... either (1) out of its surplus, as defined in and computed in accordance with §154 ..., or (2) in case there shall be no such surplus, out of its net profits for the fiscal year in which the dividend is declared and/or the preceding fiscal year.

In other words, directors may pay dividends if the firm meets one of two tests. First, they may pay dividends if the firm has a large enough "surplus." "Surplus" is the difference between the firm's "net assets" and "legal capital." "Net assets" are the difference between its total assets and total liabilities. "Legal capital" is (a) for shares with par value (see Appendix I above), the number of shares outstanding times the per-share par value; and (b) for shares that do not have par value,

130

whatever portion of the cash received on the issuance of the stock the board decides to designate as "legal capital" (§154). As with par value more generally, legal capital is an amount that directors largely "make up" as they please.

Second, directors may pay dividends out of profits — either the current fiscal year or the preceding one.

From time to time, lawyers (and law students) claim that a firm's decision to pay dividends signals its profitability. Given the enormous latitude the law gives a firm about whether to pay them, the claim is obviously untrue. In fact, a firm's decision about dividends conveys almost no serious information.

B.   . . . AND ECONOMICS

Several years ago, economists Franco Modigliani and Merton Miller won the Nobel Prize for (in part) their "dividend irrelevance" theorem. At many large firms, dividends simply do not matter — and Modigliani and Miller explained why.[122] Fischer Black (himself coauthor on a study that earned a Nobel Prize) summarized their theorem this way:

> Suppose you are offered the following choice. You may have $2 today and a 50–50 chance of $54 or $50 tomorrow. Or you may have nothing today and a 50–50 chance of $56 or $52 tomorrow. Would you prefer one of these gambles to the other?[123]
>
> Probably, you would not. Ignoring such factors as the cost of holding $2 and one day's interest on $2, you would be indifferent between these two gambles.
>
> The choice between a common stock that pays a dividend and a stock that pays no dividend is similar, at least if we ignore such things as transaction costs and taxes. The price of the dividend-paying stock drops on the ex-dividend date by about the amount of the dividend. The dividend just drops the whole range of possible stock prices by that amount. The investor who gets a $2 dividend finds himself with shares worth about $2 less than they would have been worth if the dividend hadn't been paid, in all possible circumstances.
>
> This, in essence, is the Miller–Modigliani theorem.

The intuition is simple. On the one hand, when a firm pays a dividend, the price of the stock will fall. After all, there will now be less cash left in the firm. The shareholder, though, will have the cash in his pocket. If he would prefer to have the cash invested in the firm, he can use the cash to buy more stock. On the other hand,

---

[122] Merton H. Miller & Franco Modigliani, *Dividend Policy, Growth, and the Valuation of Shares*, 34 J. Bus. 411 (1961).

[123] Fischer Black, *The Dividend Puzzle*, 2 J. Portfolio Mgmt. 5 (1976), *reprinted in* Richard A. Posner & Kenneth E. Scott, *Economics of Corporation Law and Securities Regulation* 307 (Little, Brown 1980).

if the firm does not pay the dividend, the price of the stock will stay high. If a shareholder wants cash instead, he can sell some of his shares.

The discussion obviously ignores taxes. And it ignores the question of whether shareholders can trust the managers to pursue good projects.[124] The intuition, however, is simple — but crucial: In a world with trustworthy managers and no taxes, shareholders of a publicly traded firm will not care whether it pays dividends.

---

[124] Frank H. Easterbrook, *Two Agency-Cost Explanations of Dividends*, 74 Am. Econ. Rev. 650 (1984).

CHAPTER 4

Corporate Fiduciary Duties

We were someplace around Barstow on the edge of the desert when the drugs began to take hold. I remember saying something like "I feel a bit lightheaded; maybe you should drive. . . ." And suddenly there was a terrible roar all around us and the sky was full of what looked like huge bats, all swooping and screeching and diving around the car, which was going about a hundred miles an hour with the top down to Las Vegas. And a voice was screaming: "Holy Jesus! What are these god-damn animals?"

There are opening lines. And then there are opening lines. Jane Austen had her truth-universally-acknowledged. Tolstoy had his happy-families-are-all-alike. And Zonker Harris's "Uncle Duke" Thompson had the drugs taking hold on the edge of the desert.[1]

Hunter Thompson first hit flamboyant success with his 1966 book on the Hells Angels.[2] Random House published the hardback, Penguin the paperback. With the opening lines to *Fear and Loathing in Las Vegas* in 1971, he showed he could do brilliance all over again.

But Thompson could also miss deadlines. He could turn incoherent. He could arrive at book signings stone drunk. Or high. "I don't advocate drugs and whiskey and violence and rock and roll," he explained, "but they've always been good for me."[3] And the Washington *Post* once quoted him musing, "I don't know why people get so upset about my stuff — three-quarters of what I write I just make up."[4]

---

[1] Hunter S. Thompson, *Fear and Loathing in Las Vegas: A Savage Journey to the Heart of the American Dream* 3 (Random House 1971).

[2] Hunter S. Thompson, *Hell's Angels: The Strange and Terrible Saga of the Outlaw Motorcycle Gangs* (Random House 1966).

[3] Anita Thompson, ed., *Ancient Gonzo Wisdom: Interviews with Hunter S. Thompson* 381 (De Capo Press 2009).

[4] Quoted in Jann S. Wenner & Corey Seymour, *Gonzo: The Life of Hunter S. Thompson* 198-199 (Little, Brown 2007). Clinton administration lawyer and Harvard Law School graduate Sandy

Figure 4-1
The 53rd Hostage

Source: Garry Trudeau, *Doonesbury* (Jan. 27, 1981).

Suppose you edited *Rolling Stone* in the early 1980s. Hunter Thompson asks for a large advance for an article on the real cause of the Iranian hostage crisis—an exclusive interview, he promises, with the "53rd hostage" (see Figure 4-1). Do you pay it? You know that when Thompson is good, he is brilliant. Newsstands cannot keep your magazine in stock. When bad, Thompson pockets the advance and delivers nothing. And Thompson is bad often. Never mind whether you would appoint him manager to the Washington Redskins, governor of the American Samoa, or K-Street lobbyist for Greater Berzerkistan. Do you pay him an advance for an article?

Suppose you pay the advance and Thompson never writes the article. Or makes something up. A shareholder sues you. He argues that you knew Thompson would probably never deliver and demands that you repay the advance to the firm. How a court would respond turns on the "business judgment rule" discussed in Chapter 3, and the fiduciary duties first introduced in Chapter 1. This chapter explores the permutations to those fiduciary duties in the world of corporations. After a short summary of the issues involved (section I), it turns to the duty of care (section II) and the duty of loyalty (section III).

Berger recalled a conversation with Thompson about suing the *Post* over the statement. "Well, I don't think those suits would be successful, Hunter," said Berger. Thompson asked why. "Well, first of all, truth is an absolute defense in defamation," explained Berger. Thompson hung up. *Id.* Recalled Sonny Barger, founder of the Hells Angels, "I read the book, *Hell's Angels: A Strange and Terrible Saga,* when it came out in 1967. It was junk. . . . There was a lot of writer's exaggeration along with a writer's dream-and-drug-induced commentary. . . ." Ralph "Sonny" Barger, Keith Zimmerman & Kent Zimmerman, *Hell's Angel: The Life and Times of Sonny Barger and the Hell's Angels Motorcycle Club* 127 (Harper 2001).

I.   INTRODUCTION

A.   *The Business Judgment Rule*

Judges do not like to second-guess boards. Hence the "business judgment rule" of Chapter 3, so fundamental to the field:

> Absent evidence of fraud, illegality, conflict of interest, negligence, or waste, courts will defer to the business judgment of the board.

The courts would not tell Wrigley to play baseball at a time when the fans could watch (Chapter 3, section III.D). Neither would they tell Hammer to pay for his mausoleum himself (Chapter 3, Introduction). Despite the shareholders' claim that you knew Thompson would not deliver, courts will rule in your favor anyway. They realize the business question was not whether Thompson would probably deliver. It was whether the expected returns from a successful Thompson performance were high enough to offset the high odds that he probably would not perform. Such a question is hard enough to answer *ex ante*. On their better days, most judges realize they cannot hope to answer it *ex post*. The business judgment rule merely formalizes their eminently sensible reluctance to intervene.

B.   *The Business Judgment Rule and Risk*

Take a project that amounts to a lottery ticket. You run an investment company, and Thompson's sidekick Honey Huan approaches you with a proposal: Invest $10,000 in a high-risk stem-cell trafficking firm. She gives you 1 percent odds that your interest will be worth $10 million a year from now, but admits to a 99 percent chance it will flop. Everything is honest and legal, she assures you, and (perhaps against your better judgment) you believe her. Should you take her offer?

The answer is yes. Huan's investment has a present value of $10 million × .01 = $100,000. At $10,000, it is a steal (and, given the personalities involved, probably too good to be true — but that is another matter). It is a steal even though it will be worthless 99 times out of 100. Were a judge to evaluate the wisdom of failed corporate policies after the fact, he would need to gauge both the expected odds *ex ante* that the policy would pay out and the amount it would have paid if — counterfactually — it had succeeded. At root, judges realize that they cannot reliably distinguish the failure that followed a risky but wise investment from the failure that followed a risky but foolish one.

Note that the risk itself is not the problem. Sensible investors take risks, and to deal with the risk, they diversify. They do not invest in only one firm. They do not invest in only one industry. They diversify — across firms, across industries. As one of the standard texts on corporate finance explains it:

> Most stocks are substantially more variable than the market portfolio and only a handful are less variable. This raises an important question: "The market portfolio

is made up of individual stocks, so why doesn't its variability reflect the average variability of its components?" The answer is that diversification reduces variability. . . . [D]iversification can almost halve the variability of returns.

A shrewd investor can accomplish the diversification with but a few shares. The text continues:

> [Y]ou can get most of this benefit with relatively few stocks: the improvement is slight when the number of securities is increased beyond, say, 10. Diversification works because prices of different stocks do not move exactly together. Statisticians make the same point when they say that stock price changes are imperfectly correlated.[5]

Rational investors happily take risk. They simply insist that the investment sell for a price that accurately reflects the odds.

C. The Business Judgment Rule and Fiduciary Duties

Despite (in fact, by the terms of) the business judgment rule, courts do evaluate the process by which officers and directors reach their decisions. Those officers and directors act as agents for the corporation and owe the fiduciary duties so basic to agency (Chapter 1, section IV). Accordingly, courts ask whether the officers and directors followed proper process: Did they sleep on the job (negligence) or steal from the firm (conflict of interest)? If they did neither, they approve the decision reached. When a plaintiff cannot show negligence, a conflict of interest, fraud, illegality, or waste, courts invoke the business judgment rule and defer.

As explained in Chapter 3 (section II.B.2), the reference to "negligence" in the formula for the business judgment rule refers to the "duty of care." In one common definition, the test is whether the board exercised the care of an ordinarily prudent man:

> [T]hat amount of care which ordinarily careful and prudent men would use in similar circumstances.[6]

Although courts call a violation of the duty "negligence," the standard's substance is closer to "gross negligence." Delaware courts sometimes make the point explicitly:

> Director liability for breaching the duty of care "is predicated upon concepts of gross negligence."[7]

---

[5] Richard Brealey & Stewart Myers, *Principles of Corporate Finance* 124-125 (2d ed., McGraw Hill Intl. 1984).

[6] Graham v. Allis-Chalmers Mfg. Co., 188 A.2d 125, 130 (Del. 1963).

[7] McMullin v. Beran, 765 A.2d 910, 921 (Del. 2000).

II. Duty of Care

Rare is the court that holds directors or officers liable for conduct no worse than negligent.

Again, as explained in Chapter 3 (section II.D), the reference to "conflict of interest" in the business judgment rule taps the "duty of loyalty." A director or officer who secretly deals with his own firm breaches his duty of loyalty. The corporation can ratify the conflict, as discussed below (section III.B). But if it does not, it can void the transaction, sue him for damages, and demand that he disgorge his profits.

Return to your tenure at *Rolling Stone*. You pay Thompson an advance for an interview with the 53rd hostage, but Thompson does not deliver. A shareholder sues. A court will ask whether you gathered sufficient information about Thompson in advance and devoted sufficient thought to the question (with "sufficiency" depending on the size of the advance). It will ask whether you faced a conflict of interest (e.g., did you owe him $10,000 for cocaine purchases that he offered to forgive?). If you took enough care and faced no conflict, the court will apply the business judgment rule. You will win.

II. DUTY OF CARE

A. *The Basic Rule*

1. Introduction

To explore the contours of the duty of care more closely, begin with two contrasting cases. In one, shareholders challenge a preposterous board decision. Ignoring the conflict of interest that led the board to do what it did, the court asks whether the board met its duty of care. Finding that it met that duty, the court approves the decision. In the other, creditors sue a bedridden widow who failed to stop her duplicitous sons from stealing the firm's assets. The court holds that she did violate her duty of care and holds her liable for their theft.

2. *Kamin v. American Express Co.*[8]

(a) *The Facts*

Before founding the Yale Management School and running the SEC, William S. Donaldson helped organize Donaldson, Lufkind & Jenrette. In 1970, it became the first member of the New York Stock Exchange to sell its shares to the public. The next year, Lufkind left the firm to head the Connecticut Environmental Protection Commission, and in 1973 Donaldson became undersecretary of state.

---

[8] 383 N.Y.S.2d 807, aff'd, 387 N.Y.S.2d 993 (App. Div. 1st Dept. 1976).

The Lufkind and Donaldson departures left Richard Jenrette to run the firm. They were bleak days to be in charge. The Arab oil embargo had slaughtered the bond market, and the end of fixed commissions had brought fiercely competitive discount brokers to Wall Street. Shares that DLJ had issued at $15 per share in 1970 fell to $1.75 by 1975.

In 1972, American Express had bought a quarter stake in DLJ for $30 million. By 1975, that quarter interest had plummeted to $4 million. To cut its losses, the American Express board decided to jettison its stake in the firm. "That was my lowest day," Jenrette recalled. "American Express made us feel like orphans and it seemed like the end of the world to me."[9]

Four of the American Express directors worked full time for the firm and earned a salary keyed explicitly to the firm's earnings. "Earnings" are an accounting concept and by the accounting rules of the time did not reflect fluctuations in the value of a firm's assets. Instead, they reflected changes in an asset's value only if and when the company sold it. If American Express held stock that had risen in value, its earnings did not rise unless it sold the stock. If it held stock that had fallen, its earnings did not fall unless it sold it.

Given the dive in the value of the DLJ stock, the four "inside" directors could protect their compensation while divesting the firm of the stock only by avoiding a sale. American Express could have sold the stock, but the board decided not to do so. Instead, it distributed the DLJ stock to its shareholders as a "dividend in kind." By doing so, it rid American Express of the DLJ stake and did so without taking a hit to its accounting earnings.

(b)   Taxes

For the combined firm-shareholder tax bill, the distinction between selling the stock and distributing it in kind mattered enormously. Suppose first (as happened) that American Express distributed its DLJ shares as a "dividend in kind." Upon doing so, it "recognized" (under tax law) no gain or loss on the shares. It rid itself of the depreciated DLJ shares, but (just as it took no hit to its accounting earnings) it generated no loss on its tax return.

Upon receiving the stock as a dividend, American Express shareholders recognized ordinary income equal to the fair market value of the stock (subject to American Express's having adequate "earnings and profits"): $4 million. Because they then took the shares with an "adjusted basis" equal to that amount, if they immediately sold the stock they recognized capital gain income equal to $4 million (amount realized) — $4 million (adjusted basis) = $0 (capital gain).

Now suppose (counterfactually) that American Express sold the shares and distributed the cash. Recall that it paid $30 million for the shares but could sell them for only $4 million. Upon the sale, it would recognize a loss of $4 million (amount realized) — $30 million (adjusted basis) = –$26 million. Provided it had

[9] Leslie Wayne, *Forging the Equitable Connection: Richard H. Jenrette*, N.Y. Times F5 (Nov. 18, 1984).

138

II. Duty of Care

sufficient other income, this loss would reduce the taxes it would otherwise pay. The plaintiffs plausibly valued this tax benefit at $8 million.

When American Express then paid the $4 million cash (the amount it received on the sale of the shares) as a dividend, the shareholders would have recognized taxable income of $4 million (subject again to the firm's having sufficient "earnings and profits"). Whether the firm paid the dividend in kind or in cash, the shareholders recognized the same $4 million in taxable income. When the firm first sold the shares and paid the dividend in cash, it reduced its other taxable income by about $26 million — and saved about $8 million in taxes. When it paid its dividend in kind, it abandoned that $8 million savings entirely.[10]

issue in dispute

(c) Stock Prices

After noting the obvious point that a stock sale would have generated an accounting loss, American Express argued that this accounting entry would have caused the price of its stock to fall. Consider, however, a hypothetical. Suppose you form a real estate investment firm in 2005 and invest $30 million. You pick a tony metropolitan suburb and use the money to buy six houses. You hold the houses in the corporation. By 2010, the houses have fallen in value to $666,000 each, or $4 million total. Facing an expensive divorce, you decide to sell the firm.

Your buyer will not reason that you paid $30 million for the houses in 2005 and offer you $30 million for the firm's stock. Instead, he will research the current value of the homes. Upon finding them worth a total of $4 million, he will offer you $4 million. He will pay you the fair market value of the houses your firm owns, and no more.

So, too, the DLJ stock that American Express held. American Express's quarter interest in DLJ was no secret. Neither was the disastrous fall in the value of DLJ. In deciding how much to pay for American Express's own shares, analysts would not have valued the DLJ stock by the price American Express paid for it a few years earlier. They would have checked the current market price of the DLJ shares and bought and sold American Express stock at a price that reflected that current DLJ market value.

This is not something subtle. Wall Street analysts in late 2008 may have mis-valued complex credit-default swaps. They do not find it hard to value publicly traded stock. To price American Express shares, they would value the DLJ shares that American Express owned. To do so, in 1975 they would have turned to the back pages of the *Wall Street Journal*. Today, they would aim their browser at the *Journal*'s MarketWatch (http://www.marketwatch.com). In less time than it takes to drink a cup of coffee, they could calculate the value of American Express's stake in DLJ.

The point: If American Express had sold the DLJ shares and posted the loss on the firm's books, the price of its own stock would not have fallen. Instead, it would have remained unchanged. It would have stayed unchanged for a simple reason: It had fallen to a price that reflected the market value of DLJ long before.

reasoning D &O have bad argument

---

[10] See generally Boris I. Bittker & James S. Eustice, *Federal Income Taxation of Corporations and Shareholders* ¶¶7.20-7.23 (5th ed., Little, Brown 1987).

(d) The Court Decision

American Express shareholders brought a derivative suit to challenge the board's decision to distribute the DLJ shares as a dividend in kind. The suit presented the court with the issue above: The shareholders argued that the firm's strategy cost it $8 million in taxes it could avoid only if it sold the shares first; the board replied that a sale would generate an accounting loss that would cause its stock price to plummet.

The court did not want to referee the dispute. To avoid it, however, it needed to invoke the business judgment rule. And to invoke the rule, it needed first to find no conflict of interest. In fact, the board faced a major conflict. Inside directors often outmaneuver the outside directors so popular among commentators. Precisely because they are outsiders, the outside directors know very little about how the firm actually works. The insiders do, and they dominate the board. Here, the insiders earned compensation keyed to accounting earnings. Recognize the loss on the DLJ shares that American Express held, and they took a pay cut. To avoid slashing their own salaries, they caused the board to distribute the shares in kind — even though the strategy cost the firm $8 million.

The court ignored the conflict. It first noted the problem:

> [Four] of the 20 directors were officers and employees of American Express and members of its executive incentive compensation plan. Hence, it is suggested, by virtue of the action taken earnings may have been overstated and their compensation affected thereby.

Promptly, it dismissed the conflict as "speculative":

> Such a claim is highly speculative and standing alone can hardly be regarded as sufficient to support an inference of self-dealing. There is no claim or showing that the four company directors dominated and controlled the sixteen outside members of the board.[11]

Much the same phenomenon had happened at Occidental Petroleum, of course (see Chapter 3). The quintessential insider Armand Hammer had dominated the board. He convinced it to use company funds to build a museum in his honor. In response, the board assembled a special "independent" committee chaired by Albert Gore Sr. The committee rubber-stamped the transaction, and the court blessed it with the business judgment rule.

The *American Express* court ignored the conflict of interest and asked whether the board met its duty of care:

> [T]he objections raised by the plaintiffs to the proposed dividend action were carefully considered and unanimously rejected by the board at a special meeting called precisely for that purpose at the plaintiffs' request. The minutes of the

---

[11] 383 N.Y.S.2d at 812.

II. Duty of Care

> special meeting indicate that the defendants were fully aware that a sale rather than
> a distribution of the DLJ shares might result in the realization of a substantial
> income tax saving. Nevertheless, they concluded that there were countervailing
> considerations. . . .[12]

The board had called a meeting. It had heard both sides of the argument. It had
made a decision. Necessarily, it had met its duty of care.

Hence the result: The court ignored the board's flagrant conflict of interest; it
found no negligence in the process by which the board reached its decision; with
no conflict of interest or negligence on record, it cited the business judgment rule
and approved the board's decision — preposterous as it was.

3. *Francis v. United Jersey Bank*[13]

(a) *Introduction*

By way of contrast, consider a case where the court did hold a director liable
for losses it claimed she caused by violating her duty of care. In the mid-1940s,
Charles Pritchard Sr. and George Baird created what would become the Pritchard & Baird reinsurance firm. They began it as a partnership. In time, they transformed it into a network of corporations. Pritchard owned 75 percent of each firm,
and Baird 25 percent. When Baird retired in 1964, Charles Sr. bought his quarter
interest. He retired four years later and died in 1973.

(b) *Reinsurance*

Reinsurance brokerage firms regularly take money in trust. When one insurer
agrees to accept part of a risk that another firm finds too large, the broker forwards
a share of the premium from the original insurer to the reinsurer. If and when the
insured client suffers a loss, the broker then forwards a share of the insurance
payment from the reinsurer back to the original insurer.

For example, insurer A might insure a client against a catastrophe too large for
it (insurer A) to fit readily within its portfolio. Insurer B would then agree to bear
the risk of a fraction of A's potential liability in exchange for a fraction of the
premium that the client paid A. If and when the client incurred the insured
loss, B would pay to A a portion of the amount owed. On both occasions, P&B
as the intermediary would handle the cash transferred — and would handle it "in
trust" for A and B as a fiduciary.

---

[12] *Id.* at 811.

[13] 432 A.2d 814 (N.J. 1981). I take the details of the case from Reinier Kraakman & Jay Kesten, *The Story of* Francis v. United Jersey Bank: *When a Good Story Makes Bad Law*, in *Corporate Law Stories* 163 (J. Mark Ramseyer ed., Foundation Press 2009); Jonathan Kwitny, *Brother Act: Hundreds of Insurers Search for Remnants of Missing Millions*, Wall St. J. 1 (Oct. 12, 1976).

For much of the mid-twentieth century, a small group of firms dominated the American reinsurance industry. They dealt with each other informally and extended credit on the basis of personal reputation. P&B kept its books by idiosyncratic accounting rules, but given Charles Sr.'s probity no one cared. P&B thrived and in time grew to more than 100 employees.

(c) The Dispute

Upon Charles Sr.'s death, control over P&B passed to his sons Charles Jr. and William. Charles Sr. had raised his sons in a moneyed world, on estates near Jacqueline Onassis's home where — in the words of the *Wall Street Journal* — "the countryside open[ed] up into broad estates and people actually put on red coats and [rode] to the hounds."[14] He did not raise them into probity. He raised them as cads and thieves.

Accustomed to limitless accounts, Charles Jr. and William found themselves broke when their investments tanked and their ex-wives sued. To make ends meet, they "borrowed" large sums from the funds they held in trust. By the time their creditors discovered what they had done, they had stolen $70 million in what the *Journal* called the largest fraud in the history of New Jersey.[15] The criminal charges did not stick: Prosecutors accused the two of embezzlement and fraud, but the juries acquitted.

For the creditors, P&B's bankruptcy trustee then sued the two sons' mother in a civil suit. Mother Lillian Pritchard had long served on the board of P&B and had continued to serve after her husband's death. Sick, alcoholic, and bedridden, she had not actually done anything. The trustee sued on the theory that her sons were able to steal precisely because she had done nothing. She also inherited her husband's estate, of course. By suing her, the trustee gained access to the funds that her husband had amassed over the course of his own P&B career.[16]

Because mother Lillian died during the trial, daughter Lillian Overcash testified on her behalf. Mother had served her family tirelessly, she insisted. She had been "a wonderful cook and a wonderful baker." She had "loved her kitchen and . . . spent most of her years cooking for my father and for all of us."[17] Nine months after the trustee filed suit, mother Lillian had also transferred most of her assets to daughter Lillian in an *inter vivos* trust.

(d) The Court

The court held mother Lillian's estate liable. First, it reiterated what Reinier Kraakman and Jay Kesten describe as "the traditional majority view in American law": The rule "that all directors are subject to a minimum, objective duty of

---

[14] Kwitny, *supra* note 13, at 1.
[15] Kraakman & Kesten, *supra* note 13, at 164.
[16] *Id.* at 188.
[17] As quoted in *id.* at 181-182.

II. Duty of Care

attentiveness, which they must attempt to fulfill in good faith."[18] The bedridden, alcoholic mother Lillian could not possibly have accomplished the job of a director. That did not matter. Courts will not lower the standard because a director is sick or alcoholic. Investors rely on directors to protect their interests. If those directors cannot do the job, they need to resign.

Second, the court observed that in two contexts directors owe their fiduciary duties to creditors rather than (or in addition to) shareholders. When a firm receives money in trust (as reinsurance brokers routinely did), board members serve as fiduciaries for the people entrusting the funds. Additionally, when a firm becomes insolvent (as P&B was), board members owe fiduciary duties to creditors. When times are good, board members owe shareholders a fiduciary duty because the latter stand as the firm's residual claimants. When times go bad, the creditors effectively replace the shareholders as residual claimants.

Third, the court insisted that board members must monitor a firm regularly. They need not conduct "a detailed inspection of day-to-day activities." They should, though, "keep informed about the activities of the corporation" and maintain "a general monitoring of corporate affairs."[19]

Fourth, the court noted that board members, unless on notice of misbehavior, may rely on accounting statements prepared by a reputable accounting firm. If they have reason to suspect misbehavior, they must not rely. But absent that notice, they can turn to the New Jersey statute:

> [Directors are not liable if in good faith] they rely . . . upon written reports setting forth financial data concerning the corporation and prepared by an independent public accountant. . . .[20]

Last, should directors learn of misconduct, the court held that they must do what they can to stop it. At this point, reason Kraakman and Kesten, the court made a "real break with traditional doctrine." No director could have stopped the Pritchard boys. P&B's bankruptcy trustee "almost certainly failed to carry the burden of proving that Mrs. Pritchard could have halted her sons' misconduct." As a result, write Kraakman and Kesten, the case is simply "wrongly decided, both by traditional standards and by the standards of good corporate law policy."[21]

Could mother Lillian have stopped her sons? Kraakman and Kesten suggest not; the court claims yes. According to the court, if directors see their peers embezzling at the level of Charles Jr. and William, they should dissent from corporate decisions. They should insist that the minutes record their dissent. They should consult an attorney. They should sue the miscreants. They should take, in other words, whatever escalating series of steps prove necessary to stop the misbehavior.

---

[18] *Id.* at 164.
[19] 432 A.2d at 822.
[20] N.J. Stat. Ann. §14A:6-14.
[21] Kraakman & Kesten, *supra* note 13, at 185-186.

B. *The Modern Extension*

1. Introduction

Suppose Thompson and Huan operate an aggressive private equity fund that specializes in acquiring firms. Several years ago, they successfully bought and operated a medical school in Haiti that targeted the U.S. health-care market. With that background in the education industry, they now hope to expand into educational publishing. On behalf of their firm, they approach Wolters Kluwer CEO Nancy McKinstry about acquiring its law school publications line, Aspen Publishers. According to Wolters Kluwer, in 2008 "[b]ook products lines . . . declined 4% as a result of the weak economic environment." The firm reported "[s]trong performance in legal textbooks for the student market,"[22] however, and Thompson and Huan hope to capitalize on that success.

Suppose McKinstry reports the Thompson–Huan overture to the board (and suppose Delaware law applies). Must she give board members the details of the offer in advance? Must she hire an outside financial analyst to value the Aspen brand? How much time and how many meetings must she devote to the Thompson–Huan proposal? Must she research what Thompson and Huan did to the firms they bought in the past?

Put another way, how much flexibility does the duty of care incorporate?

2. *Smith v. Van Gorkom*[23]

Van Gorkom suggests "not much."

Trans Union owned railroad tank cars and "investment tax credits" (ITCs). Once part of Rockefeller's Standard Oil empire (and called Union Tank Car), it had held the tank cars that Rockefeller used to ship his oil. By the late 1970s, it also held a substantial stock of ITCs — amounts it could use to offset its tax liability, if only it had one. Because the railroad cars generated large depreciation allowances, Trans Union did not have a net positive income — and, without a positive income, did not have a net tax liability. Without that tax liability, it had no use for the ITCs. Because an ITC potentially reduced a firm's tax liability dollar for dollar, however, Trans Union's stock of ITCs offered substantial value to the right owner. Alas for Trans Union, it could not sell ITCs.

To obtain value for these ITCs, Trans Union needed to merge with a firm that had taxable income. In September 1980, CEO Jerome Van Gorkom threw a party to celebrate the new Lyric Opera season. It promised to be a star-studded year, with recitals by Luciano Pavarotti, Leontyne Price, and Renata Scotto. At his party, Van

---

[22] Wolters Kluwer, *2009 Annual Report* 36 (Mar. 18, 2010), *available at* http://www.wolterskluwer.com/2009annualreport/content/.

[23] 488 A.2d 858 (Del. Sup. Ct. 1985); *see generally* Stephen M. Bainbridge, *The Story of* Smith v. Van Gorkom, *Corporate Law Stories* 197 (J. Mark Ramseyer ed., Foundation Press 2009).

II. Duty of Care

Gorkom approached Jay Pritzker. Pritzker owned firms that made money. He ran the Hyatt hotel chain and held a large portfolio of businesses. The two men served on boards together. They skied in Vail together.

Van Gorkom suggested that Pritzker buy Trans Union for $55 per share. Given that Trans Union currently sold for about $38 per share, the $55 price represented a premium of 45 percent over market. Using internal Trans Union figures, Van Gorkom showed Pritzker that he could use Trans Union revenue to cover most of the cost of the acquisition within five years.

Pritzker agreed to pay $55, but declared that he wanted the Trans Union board to approve the sale within three days. He would not play "stalking horse" for Trans Union while it looked for a higher, rival bid. Van Gorkom complied and convened the Trans Union board. After a two-hour session, the directors approved the gist of the Van Gorkom–Pritzker deal. They did retain the right to shop for rival bids over the course of the next three months, but none materialized. In February, Trans Union shareholders approved the merger. Seventy percent voted in favor, and 7 percent against.

Dissatisfied shareholders sued, and the Delaware Supreme Court held that the Trans Union board members had breached their duty of care. They had acted too hastily and had not tried hard enough to obtain a higher price. The court explained:

> The directors (1) did not adequately inform themselves as to Van Gorkom's role in forcing the "sale" of the Company and in establishing the per share purchase price; (2) were uninformed as to the intrinsic value of the Company; and (3) given these circumstances, at a minimum, were grossly negligent in approving the "sale" of the company upon two hours' consideration, without prior notice, and without the exigency of a crisis or an emergency.[24]

Having violated their fiduciary duty, they owed the firm the difference between its "fair value" and $55 per share.

3. Legislative Response

Yet for most publicly traded Delaware firms, *Van Gorkom* is not the law. Instead, most firms have "opted out." They wanted nothing to do with the opinion.

The *Van Gorkom* decision shocked the business and legal communities. The Trans Union board members were experienced and sophisticated directors. They knew the company. An acquirer had offered 45 percent over market; the board members understood (as the court apparently did not) that firms have no "intrinsic value" apart from the price a buyer will pay. The acquirer had demanded a decision within three days; the board members had realized (as the court apparently did not) that they faced an exigency. They studied the lucrative offer,

---

[24] 488 A.2d at 874.

discussed it, and accepted it. The court now held them personally liable for not having obtained an offer more lucrative still.

Faced with the nearest thing to "outrage" one sees at Lyric Opera galas, the Delaware legislature passed §102(b)(7). Under the provision, firms could include in their articles of incorporation

> [a] provision eliminating or limiting the personal liability of a director to the corporation or its stockholders for monetary damages for breach of fiduciary duty as a director, provided that such provision shall not eliminate or limit the liability of a director: (i) For any breach of the director's duty of loyalty to the corporation or its stockholders; (ii) for acts or omissions not in good faith or which involve intentional misconduct or a knowing violation of law. . . .

 In effect, the legislature decided to let firms opt out of *Van Gorkom*. And firms did — massively. For their boards, they wanted experienced, sophisticated, senior men and women. Facing decisions like *Van Gorkom*, however, many of the best board candidates decided they did not need the work. To woo them back to the boards, firms adopted §102(b)(7) clauses. Among public firms the clauses are "nearly universal," writes Professor Bainbridge. After *Van Gorkom*, "[m]ost public corporations have amended their charters to include such provisions."[25]

4. Indemnification

 To attract the best business executives, many firms offer them protection that goes further still. By §145(c) of the Delaware code, all firms must indemnify their directors against expenses they incur in defending themselves — successfully — in suits over their work at the firm.

> To the extent that a present or former director or officer of a corporation has been successful on the merits or otherwise in defense of any action . . . such person shall be indemnified against expenses (including attorneys' fees). . . .

But §145 gives firms the option of doing more. Should they choose, they may indemnify directors and officers even if they lose, provided that they "acted in good faith." Section 145(a) provides:

> A corporation shall have power to indemnify any person who was or is a party . . . to any threatened, pending or completed action . . . (other than an action by or in the right of the corporation) by reason of the fact that the person is or was a director [or officer] . . . against expenses (including attorneys' fees), judgments, fines and amounts paid in settlement . . . if the person acted in good faith. . . .

---

[25] Bainbridge, *supra* note 23, at 198.

II. Duty of Care

Under §145(b), firms can sometimes indemnify directors and officers even in derivative suits — actions "in the right of the corporation." Should a director lose a derivative suit, he would owe the money to the firm. If the firm then indemnified him for the amount he paid, the money obviously would travel in a circle. Under §145(b), a firm may pay his expenses if he acts in good faith and does not lose the suit. If a court does hold him liable, the firm may still indemnify him if a court approves.

5. Good Faith?

(a) The Possibilities

And yet, a corporation might reasonably want to go further. Take American Express. On its 2010 board, it included people like Richard Levin, president of Yale University. Men and women like Levin do not plan to act in "bad faith," American Express does not expect him to act in "bad faith," and neither would anyone else. By the time some men and women reach late middle age they have built massive, public reputations — reputations solid enough that one can reasonably guess that their choice set excludes judicially recognized "bad faith."

By §145(b) and (c), however, firms can indemnify men and women like Levin only if they show "good faith" or obtain court approval. The question of good faith is fact specific and, like many such inquiries, will consume substantial resources in court. To recover indemnification, even people like Levin will spend large amounts in court litigating their good faith.

So consider §145(f). The section provides:

> The indemnification . . . provided by . . . the other subsections of this section shall not be deemed exclusive of any other rights to which those seeking indemnification . . . may be entitled under any bylaw [or] agreement. . . .

If a firm wants to skip the costly "good faith" showing required under subsections (b) and (c), does §145(f) let it indemnify its directors or officers without it?

(b) Waltuch:[26] The Case

Conticommodity Services included just such a provision in its articles of incorporation:

> The Corporation shall indemnify . . . each of its incumbent or former directors [and] officers . . . against expenses actually and necessarily incurred by him in connection with the defense of any action . . . in which he is made a party, by reason of his serving in . . . such position . . . , except in relation to matters as to

---

[26] Waltuch v. Conticommodity Servs., 88 F.3d 87 (2d Cir. 1996).

which he shall be adjudged in such action . . . to be liable for negligence or misconduct in the performance of duty.[27]

Unless a court held a director or officer liable for "negligence or misconduct," Conti would pay his expenses — good faith or no.

Norton Waltuch had traded silver as Conti vice president. According to civil plaintiffs and the Commodity Futures Trading Commission (CFTC), in 1979 he and Bunker and Herbert Hunt illegally "manipulated" — that is, ramped or cornered — the price of silver. The Hunt brothers had owned an oil field in pre-Gaddafi Libya. But where Armand Hammer had managed to retain much of Occidental Petroleum's interest under Gaddafi, Bunker Hunt had not. Instead, Gaddafi expropriated his field.[28] Stung, the Hunts turned to silver.

(c)   Pump and Dump

Making money by ramping stocks or other assets on markets with many traders is no simple feat. The Hunt brothers may (or may not) have ramped the price of silver, but they did not make money. They went bankrupt. Waltuch made money, but he claimed not to have ramped prices.

Consider the simple economics, without the complicating futures contracts involved in the actual case. Suppose Duke plans to "pump and dump" Microsoft stock. He believes he can raise the Microsoft stock price by buying large amounts. If his purchases cause the price to rise, they will do so because other investors believe he knows something they do not — that he holds nonpublic, positive information. In the case of investment assets like silver, other investors would reason that he holds nonpublic information about the future demand for those assets. If he knows enough to invest his own cash, they reason, perhaps the assets are worth more than they thought.

If Duke cannot convince others that he holds nonpublic information about Microsoft, the price of Microsoft shares will not rise. Suppose Microsoft sells for $50 per share. If Duke offers $51, everyone will sell to him. After all, investors buy stocks to fit in a diversified portfolio. For that portfolio, they do not need a given stock. Instead, they need a stock with a given set of qualities, and many firms have shares that provide those qualities.

As a result, if Duke starts to buy large quantities of a stock but everyone knows he has no inside information, they will simply sell. The price will not rise. As Professors Daniel Fischel and David Ross put it, the "availability of close substitutes means that an investor seeking to purchase a particular security should be able to

---

[27] *Id.* at 89.
[28] Daniel Yergin, *The Prize: The Epic Quest for Oil, Money, and Power* 584-585 (Simon & Schuster 1991); Jeffrey Williams, *Manipulation on Trial: Economic Analysis and the Hunt Silver Case* 20 (Cambridge University Press 1995).

convince current holders to sell the security at current market price."[29] Duke will buy — but sellers will sell at that current market price. Despite his purchases, prices will not rise.

This is not the way house prices move, of course. If suburban Boston software firms begin to hire, engineers will move to the area. Given the finite number of homes near their employers, those engineers who value location most highly will bid for the closest homes. Current residents indifferent to location may sell for a small premium. But many residents are not indifferent. They like where they live. To induce them to sell, the arriving engineers will need to offer high prices. As they do, home prices will rise. Stocks (and most investment assets) move by a different dynamic because they serve as close substitutes for each other. Being all about location, homes do not.

Judge Frank Easterbrook nicely explains the logic in *West v. Prudential Securities*:

> [I]nvestors do not want Jefferson Savings *stock* (as if they sought to paper their walls with beautiful certificates); they want monetary returns (at given risk levels), returns that are available from many financial instruments. One fundamental attribute of efficient markets is that *information*, not demand in the abstract, determines stock prices. . . . There are so many substitutes for any one firm's stock that the effective demand curve is horizontal. It may shift up or down with new information but is not sloped like the demand curve for physical products. That is why institutional purchases (which can be large in relation to normal trading volume) do not elevate prices, while relatively small trades by insiders can have substantial effects; the latter trades convey information, and the former do not.[30]

All this makes it hard to earn profits ramping the price of a stock (or other investment assets — though delivery on futures contracts can complicate matters). As Fischel and Ross put it, "a manipulator who is able to convince market participants that he is informed at the time of purchase must do the opposite at the time of sale."[31] To make money on his scheme, Duke will need to unload his Microsoft shares at the high, ramped price. Yet if he successfully raised Microsoft prices at the outset, he did so only by convincing other buyers that he had inside information about the future. If he now sells, those same buyers will conclude that he has inside information that the price will fall. Immediately, they will bid prices down — and on many of his shares Duke will have bought high and sold low.

The point is not that an investor can never make money "pumping and dumping" stock; the point is that he will find it very hard. For example, Tokyo investors tell the possibly apocryphal story of a South Korean investor who began buying and selling stock at several Tokyo brokerage houses. He always paid his bills. Eventually, brokers began letting him buy stock on several days' credit. One day, at brokerage

---

[29] Daniel R. Fischel & David J. Ross, *Should the Law Prohibit "Manipulation" in Financial Markets?*, 105 Harv. L. Rev. 503, 514 (1991).

[30] 282 F.3d 935, 939 (7th Cir. 2002).

[31] Fischel & Ross, *supra* note 29, at 518.

house A he began cornering the stock of one company. He bought massive amounts on credit. As other investors began to suspect that someone had positive inside information, the price of the stock soared.

At brokerage house B, the South Korean investor then sold the shares he had just bought and pocketed the cash. The price fell, of course, but he did not lose money—because he had bought the stock at brokerage house A on credit. He took his sales proceeds from brokerage house B and—before the bill came due on his purchases at house A—flew to Korea and disappeared. He made money by manipulating stock prices, but only because he bought on credit and vanished.

(d) The Law

Over the course of several months in 1979 and 1980, the Hunt brothers bought enormous quantities of silver. Prices rose. Once they tried to sell, prices plummeted. On much of their investment, they bought high and sold low.

Norton Waltuch played the game differently. While the Hunt brothers were still bidding up the price of silver, he sold his stake and pocketed a $20 million profit. After the price collapsed, private plaintiffs and the CFTC both sued him for price manipulation. Waltuch paid his lawyers $1.2 million in the litigation against the private plaintiffs. Those cases settled with a payment to the plaintiffs from Conti. Waltuch paid his lawyers $1 million in the litigation against the CFTC. That case ended when he paid a $100,000 fine.

From Conti, Waltuch collected the $1.2 million attorneys' fees he paid in the private litigation. Because the firm had paid the plaintiffs, the court had dismissed the claim against him. He was "successful" and, by the terms of §145(c), entitled to indemnity from Conti.

By contrast, the court did not let Waltuch collect the $1 million he paid his attorneys in the CFTC litigation. If he could have shown "good faith," §145(a) would have allowed Conti to indemnify him. And even absent that showing, the Conti charter had promised that the firm would pay him the amount. For unspecified strategic reasons, however, Waltuch had agreed to "forgo trial on the issue of [his] 'good faith.'" Interpreting Delaware law, the Second Circuit declared that Waltuch could not collect unless he proved good faith. Notwithstanding subsection (f), subsection (a) allowed firms to indemnify its officers and directors only if they proved "good faith."

C. Passive Negligence

1. Introduction

Consider another hypothetical. Suppose one young college graduate named Ben Braddock takes the advice he received from a family friend and goes into the plastics industry. He moves to Leominster, Massachusetts—self-described "injection-molding capital of the world" and home to John Waters's pink flamingo lawn ornaments — and takes a position as vice president for human relations. A friend of his parents, Mrs. Anne Bancroft Robinson, applies for a job.

From personal experience, Braddock knows Robinson to be a manipulative alcoholic. He hesitates to hire her. "I suppose you don't find me particularly desirable," she asks. "Oh no," he replies. "I think — I think you're the most attractive woman of all my parents' friends. I mean that."[32] In time, he relents, offers her a job, and within a month she steals $50,000 from the firm.

Did Braddock violate his duty of care? Or did he just make a bad decision? How carefully must he deliberate, and how much information must he gather? Given what he knew of Mrs. Robinson, was he under a special obligation to monitor her work with more than the usual level of care?

2. Allis-Chalmers[33]

In Delaware, the answer to these questions has changed over the past half century. The story begins in the 1950s. Throughout the decade, a handful of firms had sold electrical equipment to public utilities. They sold their equipment through closed-bid auctions. To obtain higher prices, they needed to decide in advance who would win the bid and the price at which it would win.

Two or three times a month, the electrical equipment firms met. They carefully kept a table of who had taken which contract in recent weeks. At their meetings, they then checked the table and decided who would obtain the next one. Simultaneously, they decided the price at which that firm would win the contract.[34] The other firms would then enter higher (losing) bids.

If the firms did not want their customers to discover their scheme, they obviously needed to vary the losing bids. Apparently, they forgot. The Tennessee Valley Authority discovered that the losers all happened — just happened — to bid identical prices.[35] It called the Justice Department, Justice investigated, and the scheme unraveled. The firms paid $1.9 million in fines, and several officers went to prison. It was, *Fortune* magazine declared, "the biggest criminal case in the history of the Sherman Act."[36]

One of the criminal defendants had been Allis-Chalmers. In the wake of the scandal, its shareholders brought a derivative suit against its directors and senior managers. Those directors and officers, they argued, should have prevented the crime. The directors and officers, in turn, replied that they knew nothing of it. The plaintiffs argued that they should have monitored the firm in a way that would let them discover the crimes — that they "should have put into effect a system of

[32] Charles Webb, *The Graduate* 50 (Signet 1963).
[33] Graham v. Allis-Chalmers Mfg. Co., 188 A.2d 125 (Del. Ch. 1963); *see generally* Richard Austin Smith, *The Incredible Electrical Conspiracy*, Fortune 132 (Apr. 1961); 161 (May 1961).
[34] Smith, *supra* note 33, Apr. 1961, at 137.
[35] Smith, *supra* note 33, May 1961, at 162.
[36] Smith, *supra* note 33, Apr. 1961, at 132-133.

watchfulness which would have brought such misconduct to their attention in ample time to have brought it to an end."[37]

The federal judge who presided over the criminal trials seems to have brought similar instincts. He thought the senior officers clearly guilty:

> One would be most naive indeed to believe that these violations of the law, so long persisted in, affecting so large a segment of the industry and finally involving so many millions upon millions of dollars, were facts unknown to those responsible for the corporation and its conduct.[38]

He acquitted them only because the government did not introduce the evidence necessary to let him do anything else.

Not so the Delaware court in the derivative suit. Absent a reason to suspect misbehavior, it explained, "directors were not required to install a corporate system of espionage to ferret out wrongdoing." If they learn that their officers might be breaking the law, they should investigate. Absent that notice, they have no reason to look. They are "entitled to rely on the honesty and integrity of their subordinates until something occurs to put them on suspicion that something is wrong."[39]

The implication — logically, a bit odd — is that one of the decisions protected by the business judgment rule may be a decision that a risk is small enough not to worry much about it. Directors have only so much time. Perhaps at some small corporations they should watch corporate officers closely. At a large multinational firm, however, they may reasonably decide to focus only on larger questions of strategy. The risk of petty crime at the regional office is someone else's problem. If they ignore the risk, *Allis-Chalmers* implies, that decision to ignore may itself be protected by the business judgment rule.

3.   *In re Caremark*[40]

Much of this apparently changed in 1997. That year, the Delaware Chancery Court faced a derivative suit against the health-care giant Caremark. Caremark billed the federal government for its work, and federal law banned it from paying kickbacks to physicians who referred patients to it. Caremark did not pay kickbacks, but it did hire referring physicians under consulting contracts. Some observers and prosecutors argued that the contracts constituted kickbacks. Caremark steadfastly denied that they did.

---

[37] 188 A.2d at 130.

[38] Smith, *supra* note 33, Apr. 1961, at 133.

[39] 188 A.2d at 130.

[40] In re Caremark Intl. Derivative Litig., 698 A.2d 959 (Del. Ch. 1996); *see generally* Jennifer Arlen, *The Story of* Allis-Chalmers, Caremark, *and* Stone: *Directors' Evolving Duty to Monitor,* in *Corporate Law Stories* 323 (J. Mark Ramseyer ed., Foundation Press 2009).

II. Duty of Care

Nonetheless, several entities connected with Caremark pled guilty in criminal prosecutions. One doctor associated with Caremark also pled guilty, and another was convicted at jury trial (though the judge threw out the conviction when he found that the jurors had learned of the case outside of trial). And Caremark itself pled guilty to mail fraud and paid $250 million to settle the various claims against it.

Shareholders brought a derivative suit to recover Caremark's losses from the directors. They settled, and in reviewing the agreement then-judge (now NYU professor and corporate casebook editor) William Allen announced a principle quite different from *Allis-Chalmers*. First, he explicitly declared *Allis-Chalmers* bad law:

> Can it be said today that, absent some ground giving rise to suspicion of violation of law, corporate directors have no duty to assure that a corporate information gathering and reporting system exists which represents a good faith attempt to provide senior management and the Board with information respecting material acts, events or conditions within the corporation, including compliance with applicable statutes and regulations? I certainly do not believe so.[41]

Second, Allen observed that in 1991 the federal government had passed a set of sentencing guidelines. These guidelines made two changes of note: They raised the penalties for corporate crime and introduced discounts on those penalties for firms with a corporate compliance system. If only to trade on the penalty discount, Allen implied, the board needed a compliance system:

> Thus, I am of the view that a director's obligation includes a duty to attempt in good faith to assure that a corporate information and reporting system, which the board concludes is adequate, exists, and that failure to do so under some circumstances may, in theory at least, render a director liable for losses caused by non-compliance with applicable legal standards.[42]

After announcing the need for a compliance system, Allen approved the settlement. Under the settlement, the firm obtained virtually nothing—but Allen approved it anyway on the ground that the defendants had done nothing wrong:

> The proposed settlement provides very modest benefits. . . . Nonetheless, given the weakness of the plaintiffs' claims the proposed settlement appears to be an adequate, reasonable, and beneficial outcome for all of the parties.[43]

The changes promised in the settlement "do not impress one as very significant," noted Allen, but the claims against the defendant "find no substantial evidentiary support in the record and quite likely were susceptible to a motion to dismiss in all events."[44]

---

[41] 698 A.2d at 969.
[42] *Id.* at 970.
[43] *Id.* at 972.
[44] *Id.* at 970-971.

It was the *Hammer* litigation all over again, of course. The settlement gave Caremark shareholders nothing of moment, but the firm promised the plaintiffs' attorneys $1,025,000 anyway. The court cut that fee to $869,000 and approved the payoff: "the time expended at normal hourly rates plus a premium of 15% of that amount to reflect the limited degree of real contingency."[45]

Consider the result: The attorneys file a fundamentally meritless suit. To induce them to go away, the firm promises them $1 million. One might have thought a court would dismiss the extortionate claims, fine the plaintiffs' attorneys for abusing the judicial process, and perhaps even recommend criminal prosecution. Instead, it cut the fee to $869,000 and approved it. The attorneys walked away to file again another day.

4. Avoiding Caremark?

Enter *Stone v. Ritter.*[46] AmSouth owned a bank that faced charges of violating bank secrecy and money laundering laws. Mind you, prosecutors did not claim that the bank itself had laundered funds. Instead, they argued that it had not reported "suspicious" conduct among its customers. When AmSouth paid $50 million to resolve the charges, shareholders filed a derivative suit against the board for failing to monitor its employees.

Crucially, AmSouth had adopted an "exculpatory" provision under §102(b)(7). Recall the furor caused by *Van Gorkom* (see section II.B.2 above). The court had held directors liable for violating their duty of care in approving a merger at "only" 145 percent of the firm's market price. When seasoned executives started to blanche at taking board seats, Delaware offered firms §102(b)(7): To induce good executives to serve, they could agree not to hold them liable for duty of care violations.

In the process, §107(b)(2) also made *Caremark* optional. *Caremark* concerned monitoring, and monitoring went to the duty of care. If §102(b)(7) made the duty of care optional, it made *Caremark* optional too. Mind you, making *Caremark* optional might be eminently good policy. Monitoring systems consume valuable corporate resources, demoralize honest employees, and only haphazardly (at best) prevent misbehavior. A board that wanted to promote shareholder welfare might reasonably decide not to install a monitoring system. Should it opt to do so, §102(b)(7) would—sensibly—let the firm shield the directors from liability.

With *Stone*, the Delaware court took away the option: *Caremark*, it insisted, was mandatory. Given the language of §102(b)(7), the court could not do this straightforwardly, of course. Instead, it needed to shift *Caremark*—a duty of care decision—either to the duty of loyalty or to an independent "duty to act in good faith." The *Stone* court did both. First, it declared that a refusal to install *Caremark* monitoring constituted "bad faith." If plaintiffs could show "a sustained or

---

[45] *Id.* at 972.
[46] 911 A.2d 362 (Del. 2006).

systematic failure of the board to exercise oversight," then they showed bad faith.[47] Second, it announced that if plaintiffs showed bad faith, they also showed a duty of loyalty violation:

> The failure to act in good faith may result in liability because the requirement to act in good faith "is a subsidiary element[,] i.e., a condition, of the fundamental duty of loyalty."[48]

Call it a syllogism or call it a sleight of hand: §102(b)(7) lets firms exculpate their directors against duty of care claims but not against bad faith behavior or duty of loyalty claims; to refuse to install *Caremark* monitoring shows bad faith; to act in bad faith is to breach the duty of loyalty; hence firms cannot use §102(b)(7) to insulate their directors against *Caremark* claims.

III. DUTY OF LOYALTY

A. *The Basic Rule*

1. Introduction

Recall the beautiful young "singer" Susan Alexander (from Snoopy's favorite movie). She finds herself drawn into an affair with a newspaper mogul named Charlie Kane. Kane is married to the niece of the U.S. president. One night, Alexander confides to Kane that her mother had always wanted her to sing opera. The pillow talk meanders, but Kane is entranced. Using the newspaper's funds, he diversifies into the entertainment industry. He builds an opera house. He hires Bernard Herrmann to compose a new opera, *Rosebud*. He casts Alexander as lead soprano and induces his newspaper's critic Jedediah Leland to write a favorable review.[49]

Before considering the claims a shareholder might bring, take a simpler case.

2. A Straightforward Case[50]

Verne Hayes served as CEO and 23 percent shareholder of Coast Oyster. He also owned 25 percent of the rival Hayes Oyster. When Coast Oyster fell short of

---

[47] *Id.* at 364 (quoting *Caremark*, 698 A.2d at 971).

[48] *Id.* at 369-370.

[49] Susan Alexander's disastrous performance of the Bernard Herrmann aria appears at http://www.youtube.com/watch?v=iUaNLRAaNj8 (accessed Mar. 4, 2012). Kiri te Kanawa's performance of the aria as it "should" be sung appears at http://www.youtube.com/watch?v=OzWX59Nvimw (accessed Feb. 28, 2012). Herrmann is perhaps best known for the scores he wrote for Hitchcock.

[50] State ex rel. Hayes Oyster Co. v. Keypoint Oyster Co., 391 P.2d 979 (Wash. 1964).

cash, Hayes suggested that it sell some of its oyster beds on credit to a new firm, Keypoint Oyster. Unbeknownst to Coast, Hayes Oyster owned half of Keypoint. Both the board and the shareholders of Coast approved the sale to Keypoint.

When Coast discovered Verne Hayes's role in Keypoint, it sued to recover his profits. It did not want to rescind the contract itself; it was happy with the contract. Instead, it simply wanted him to disgorge his profits. Recall the principle in *Reading* and *Tarnowski* (Chapter 1, section IV.C): Agents may not keep secret profits they earn through their agency. As CEO, Hayes had served as agent to Coast, his principal. If he profited from a transaction with Coast in which he did not disclose his role, by the *Reading–Tarnowski* rule he owed his profits to the firm.

The *Hayes Oyster* court applied the logic straightforwardly:

> Directors and other officers of a private corporation cannot directly or indirectly acquire a profit for themselves or acquire any other personal advantage in dealings with others on behalf of the corporation.[51]

Whether Verne Hayes treated Coast fairly was not the issue. Whether he profited secretly was:

> Actual injury is not the principle upon which the law proceeds in condemning such contracts. Fidelity in the agent is what is aimed at, and as a means of securing it, the law will not permit the agent to place himself in a situation in which he may be tempted by his own private interest to disregard that of his principal.[52]

Hayes kept his role secret and may have made money on the deal. If he did, he owned his profits to Coast.

3. The Mogul and the Soprano[53]

Chemical industry mogul Camille Dreyfus married his soprano. With brother Henry, Camille Dreyfus had pioneered the development of cellulose acetate and the creation of the synthetic fiber industry. The brothers had begun with fabric used to coat World War I planes. They then moved into consumer products and named their creation "Celanese."

The mogul's soprano was one Jean Tennyson. A regular at the Met, she was not a Susan Alexander. Occasionally, she recorded with the likes of Rise Stevens or Mario Lanza. Occasionally she even sang with La Scala or the San Francisco Opera.[54] But only occasionally, and she had her detractors too. "She is as far as I can tell the Florence Foster Jenkins of radio," complains one blogger. "Her voice wobbles, it's flat & has a very unpleasant scooping effect." Like much on the Web,

[51] *Id.* at 983.
[52] *Id.* at 985 (quoting Lycette v. Green River Gorge, Inc., 153 P.2d 873 (Wash. 1944)).
[53] Bayer v. Beran, 49 N.Y.S.2d 2 (Sup. Ct. 1944).
[54] *Jean Tennyson Dies; Singer and Patron*, 86, N.Y. Times (Mar. 19, 1991).

III.   Duty of Loyalty

the point is unfair. Tennyson was no Tibaldi or Callas, but neither was she Florence Foster Jenkins.[55]

In 1937, the Federal Trade Commission (FTC) warned the Dreyfus brothers' firm that it would need to call its rayon "rayon." Deceptive advertising being what it is, the firm could not distinguish its rayon from other rayon by calling it "Celanese." Senior managers worried. To differentiate their synthetic from its more plebian rivals, they decided to associate it with "a dignified program of fine music." If rayon wearers listened to Bing Crosby, Celanese wearers would listen to the Metropolitan Opera. Toward that end, in 1942 they recruited singers from the Met and sponsored them on a *Celanese Hour* radio show.

In promoting this product-differentiation strategy, CEO Camille Dreyfus erred in two ways. First, initially he failed to tell the board that the show would feature his wife. Although the court trivializes her pay, the firm paid her substantial amounts: over 1942 and 1943, $44,500. In 2010 dollars, that comes to about $570,000. Classical music is not a lucrative field. Even today, the Met pays top stars like Renee Fleming barely $15,000 per performance, and Tennyson was no Fleming.[56] In Europe, opera companies pay their most popular singers $20,000 per night. The rest they pay as little as $1,300.[57]

That Dreyfus hired his wife without telling the board introduced several risks. Most obviously, the firm may have paid her more than she deserved. If either her husband or an employee who answered to him set her pay, he may have set it too high. But Tennyson may also have been the wrong singer. To seal its product-differentiation strategy, perhaps the firm should have moved further up market: Perhaps it should have hired a diva like Tibaldi rather than the second-string Tennyson. Alternatively, perhaps it could have implemented the strategy more cheaply down market: Perhaps it should have made do with a second-tier company rather than the Met. And maybe the firm should have skipped opera entirely and sponsored *The Lone Ranger*.[58] Given that Tennyson's husband made the calls without disclosing his conflict, the firm would never know.

Second, Dreyfus skipped a formal meeting and convinced board members on the fly. According to the court, he kept "a close, working directorate."[59] He and the board members were "in daily association with one another and their full time [was] devoted to the business" of the firm. He met with them regularly, talked about the advertising campaign, and built a consensus.

---

[55] Compare Tennyson's duet with Lanza, http://www.youtube.com/watch?v=1irQ-8qCpBo, with Jenkins's infamous *Queen of the Night* performance, http://www.youtube.com/watch?v=MM6qntPpyZ0 (accessed Feb. 28, 2012).

[56] *Who Makes How Much*, N.Y. Mag., http://nymag.com/guides/salary/14497/index3.html (accessed Feb. 28, 2012).

[57] *L'argent des stars de l'opera*, Le Figaro (Oct. 15, 2009); *How Much Do Opera Singers Earn*, Intermezzo (Oct. 11, 2009).

[58] Fran Striker, *Actual First Script of the Lone Ranger*, YouTube, http://www.youtube.com/watch?v=6nlB99fX7z8 (accessed Mar. 4, 2012).

[59] 49 N.Y.S.2d at 11.

That Dreyfus skipped the meeting is unfortunate. As the court noted, formal meetings are not just so much "red tape." A director might harbor misgivings about Tennyson's strategy. Buttonholed by Dreyfus in the hall, he might agree to the strategy anyway. In a meeting with the rest of the board, however, he might mention his concerns. If other directors share them, the board might collectively decide to abandon the Dreyfus–Tennyson plan entirely. Formality can make a difference.

To the court, both problems justified skirting the business judgment rule. Although the problems did not necessarily justify holding the board liable, they did warrant telling Dreyfus to prove the advertising strategy fair and reasonable. Explained the court:

> [I]t is not improper to appoint relatives of officers or directors to responsible positions in a company. But where a close relative of the chief executive officer of a corporation . . . takes a position closely associated with a new and expensive field of activity, the motives of the directors are likely to be questioned.

It concluded:

> That being so, the entire transaction, if challenged in the courts, must be subjected to the most rigorous scrutiny to determine whether the action of the directors was intended or calculated "to subserve some outside purpose. . . ."[60]

Rather than defer to the business judgment of the board, the court subjected the decision to "the most rigorous scrutiny."

Having held the business judgment rule inapposite, the court reviewed the advertising policy, and found it appropriate anyway:

> After such careful scrutiny I have concluded that, up to the present, there has been no breach of fiduciary duty on the part of the directors. . . . The other directors did not know [that the CEO's wife would perform on the program] until they had approved the campaign of radio advertising and the general type of radio program. . . .
>
> [But the fact that] her participation in the program may have enhanced her prestige as a singer is no ground for subjecting the directors to liability, as long as the advertising served a legitimate and a useful corporate purpose and the company received the full benefit thereof.[61]

The company received the full benefit of the advertising, so the radio campaign stood. Why the court did not apply the *Hayes Oyster–Reading–Tarnowski* rule and hold Dreyfus liable anyway, it never said.

---

[60] *Id.* at 9.
[61] *Id.* at 10.

III. Duty of Loyalty

B. *Ratification*

1. Introduction

Suppose, however, that Coast Oyster had wanted to avoid its contract with Keypoint. What would Verne Hayes have needed to do *ex ante* to prevent it from doing so? What should Dreyfus have done to avoid the need to prove the propriety of the advertising campaign?

2. The Statute

To shield a contract from later attack, directors and officers like Verne Hayes and Dreyfus need §144(a) of the Delaware corporate code. Subsection (a)(1) provides that if a director discloses his conflict of interest, the board can ratify the terms of the transaction. Subsection (a)(2) provides that the shareholders can ratify it. And subsection (a)(3) provides that if the director fails to disclose the conflict, he still can enforce the transaction if he can prove that it is "fair as to the corporation":

> (a) No contract or transaction between a corporation and one or more of its directors or officers . . . shall be void or voidable solely for this reason . . . if:
> (1) The material facts as to the director's or officer's relationship . . . are disclosed or are known to the board of directors or the committee, and the board or committee in good faith authorizes the contract or transaction by the affirmative votes of a majority of the disinterested directors, even though the disinterested directors be less than a quorum; or
> (2) The material facts as to the director's or officer's relationship . . . are disclosed or are known to the shareholders entitled to vote thereon, and the contract or transaction is specifically approved in good faith by vote of the shareholders; or
> (3) The contract or transaction is fair as to the corporation as of the time it is authorized, approved or ratified, by the board of directors, a committee or the shareholders.
> (b) Common or interested directors may be counted in determining the presence of a quorum at a meeting of the board of directors or of a committee which authorizes the contract or transaction.

3. What the Sentence Implies

If ever there were an odd sentence (and subsection (a) does seem to be one sentence), this was it. Modern courts read (a)(1) to say: "A corporation may not void a contract with a director if the director disclosed his involvement to the other board members and they approved it anyway." Unfortunately, that is hardly what (a)(1) says. Instead, it says: "A corporation may not void a contract with a director *solely because of his involvement* if the director disclosed that involvement and the other board members approved it."

Logically and grammatically, the sentence puzzles. To say that a corporation may not contest a contract solely for reason A implies that it could contest it on other grounds. What is more, it implies that it could contest it even for reason A if it had other reasons for contesting it besides. What might those other reasons be? And if a firm does have other reasons for attacking a contract, what benefit does it gain from adding reason A?

Those questions are reasonable ones to ask — reasonable, but wrong. The key to the sentence lies neither in grammar nor in logic. It lies in history.[62] In the late nineteenth century, shareholders could indeed void a corporation's contract with a director solely because it was with a director. It mattered not whether the contract was fair to the firm. It mattered not whether directors or shareholders had ratified it. If a shareholder sued to void the contract, he could void it — solely because of the director's involvement. Legislators drafted §144 to reverse that rule.

Already by the early twentieth century, courts had begun to change the rule. At the outset, they held that firms could not void contracts that were both ratified and fair. They could void unratified contracts, and they could void unfair contracts, but they could not void contracts both ratified and fair. With §144, courts let directors rely on contracts with their firms if the contract was either ratified or fair. If other directors ((a)(1)) or shareholders ((a)(2)) ratified the contract, the firm could not void it. If the director showed that the contract was fair, the firm could not void it.

This §144 approach does not improve matters unambiguously.[63] Under the late nineteenth-century rule, corporations could not transact with their officers or directors. The law constituted a flat ban and cut the risk that an insider might steal from the firm. Simultaneously, however, it increased the odds that the firm would lose the advantageous deals that its officers and directors might otherwise have brought. Under the modern approach, firms less often lose those advantageous transactions, but more often find themselves victimized by duplicitous insiders.

The incidence of the trade-off probably varies by type of firm.[64] If the late nineteenth-century ban fit any company, it fit the large publicly traded firm. Shareholders at public firms seldom police their insiders. Instead, any shareholder who doubts their integrity sells his shares and moves on. What is more, the large public firms rarely suffer for lack of transactional opportunities. If a big firm needs real estate, brokers will offer land. If it needs money, banks will offer credit.

By contrast, if the modern rule fits any firm, it fits the small closely held firm. Here, shareholders do monitor the insiders. Lest unscrupulous directors steal from the firm, they watch corporate transactions closely. At the same time, small firms

---

[62] *See generally* Robert C. Clark, *Corporate Law* 160-166 (Little, Brown 1986).
[63] *See generally id.*
[64] *See generally id.*

often find that insiders offer them the best transactional opportunities. If a firm needs real estate, insiders may know best where to find it. If it needs credit, insiders are sometimes most willing to lend on acceptable terms.

4. What a Firm Must Do

Section 144 details the terms a firm must meet to ratify a transaction with an insider. First, the insider (an officer or director) must disclose his conflict of interest. If he turns to the other directors for ratification, he will need to disclose his conflict to the board. If he turns to the shareholders, he will need to disclose his interests to them.

Second, if the insider hopes for board ratification, he will need the vote of a majority of the disinterested directors. The statute helpfully notes that the disinterested directors can ratify the transaction even if they be less than a quorum. If he turns to the shareholders for ratification, he will need a vote of the majority. The statute says nothing about a quorum and nothing about the need for a vote specifically by the disinterested shareholders.

To protect his firm's contract with Tennyson, Dreyfus had two options. He could disclose Tennyson's role to the other directors and (if they did not know it already) explain that she was his wife. If they approved the contract, it would stand. Alternatively, he could disclose her role and his relationship to the other shareholders. If they approved the contract, again it would stand.

But in any shareholder vote on the Tennyson contract, could Dreyfus vote his own shares? Section 144(a)(2) does not limit the vote to disinterested shareholders, and (a)(1) indicates that the drafters understood the distinction between interested and disinterested votes. Suppose, however, that a court did not limit the (a)(2) vote to disinterested shareholders, and suppose that Dreyfus held 51 percent of the stock. In effect, as CEO he could apparently negotiate a contract with Tennyson that paid her double her market wage, and then as shareholder vote to insulate that contract from later attack. *Fleigler v. Lawrence*[65] addresses that possibility.

5. The Requisite Share Vote

John C. Lawrence served as president of the silver and gold mining firm Agau (a combination, presumably, of the chemical symbols Ag and Au). In 1969, he individually acquired rights to some antimony mines. American firms use antimony primarily as a fire retardant in plastics and obtain most of the material from China. Lawrence found a source for the mineral in Montana. To exploit these new mines, he formed the U.S. Antimony Corporation (USAC).

---

[65] 361 A.2d 218 (Del. 1976).

Lawrence first offered the antimony mines to Agau. When the board decided that it lacked the resources to exploit them, Lawrence transferred them to USAC. For Agau, however, he retained an option to buy USAC stock in exchange for 800,000 shares of Agau.

In 1970, the Agau board voted to exercise the option. Shareholders approved the exercise by majority vote. Both shareholders with a concurrent interest in USAC and those without that interest voted. Unfortunately, the tally was such that the court could not tell *ex post* whether the disinterested shareholders voted to approve the exercise.

In a derivative suit, a shareholder contested Agau's decision to acquire USAC. The defendants (the Agau officers and directors) replied that the shareholders had ratified the transaction by §144(a)(2) (the court does not address (a)(1)). As a result, the suit presented exactly the question noted in section 4 above: Does shareholder ratification under (a)(2) require approval by a majority of the disinterested shareholders?

By any ordinary canon of statutory construction, among directors only those without a conflict can vote to ratify a contract, but among shareholders everyone can vote. The drafters obviously thought about conflicts of interest and knew how to write a clause that excluded conflicted voters. If they restricted the board vote to disinterested directors but did not limit the shareholder vote to those without a conflict, then the restriction must not apply to shareholders.

That would, however, make little sense. Directors can steal from a firm, but so can controlling shareholders. To allow conflicted shareholders to ratify their own transaction with the firm would allow them to ratify their own theft. Faced squarely with the question, common corporate transactional sense trumped common statutory interpretive sense: The Delaware court declared that only disinterested shareholders could vote to ratify.

6.   Summary

In effect, ratification eliminates a conflict of interest (see Table 4-1).

- Suppose a transaction involves no conflict of interest, fraud, illegality, or negligence. If a shareholder challenges the transaction, the court will invoke the business judgment rule. The shareholder will prevail only if he can show waste.
- Suppose a transaction does involve an undisclosed conflict of interest. If a shareholder challenges the transaction, the business judgment rule will not apply. The corporation can void the transaction unless the insider can show that the contract treats the firm fairly. Even if the contract is fair, a court may still require the insider to disgorge his profits to the firm.
- Suppose a transaction involves a conflict of interest, but the board or shareholders ratify the conflict after full disclosure by a majority of the disinterested votes. A court will invoke the business judgment rule. A shareholder contesting the transaction will win only if he can show waste.

III. Duty of Loyalty

For special rules governing mergers and acquisitions, see Chapter 8, section II.

Table 4-1
The Effect of Ratification

Conflict	Ratification	BOP	Standard
No		Plaintiff	Waste
Yes	No	Defendant	Fair & reasonable
Yes	Yes	Plaintiff	Waste

As with much of corporate law, these rules follow straightforwardly from the agency principles discussed in Chapter 1. If an agent contracts with his principal while hiding his involvement, the law lets the principal rescind the contract (Chapter 1, section IV). If the agent tells the principal about his involvement and the principal replies that he does not mind, the law will not let the principal rescind. The corporate rules merely restate these obvious points.

C. Dominant Shareholders

1. Introduction

In taking their job, directors and officers explicitly agree to serve as agent for the firm (and its shareholders). They make that agency central to their appointment. As agents, they agree to work for the firm both loyally and carefully.

Shareholders agree to nothing of the sort. They buy stock in the company to get rich. Although directors and officers hope to get rich, too, the firm pays them their salary for their service as agents. The firm does not pay shareholders to serve as anyone's agent. It pays them for the use of their money.

Because shareholders work as no one's agent, they owe no one a fiduciary duty. And yet, sometimes shareholders can structure corporate transactions to redistribute wealth from other shareholders to themselves. Broadly, they can do this in two ways. First, sometimes they control the board. Nominally, directors serve as agents for the firm (and its shareholders) as a whole. Where one shareholder (or one group) dominates the firm, however, the directors serve at his whim. If he orders them explicitly or implicitly to redistribute wealth to him, they refuse at the cost of their job.

Second, sometimes shareholders themselves take actions with redistributive consequences. To merge one firm with another, for example, both directors and shareholders must approve the transaction. Skew the terms of the merger in his favor, and a controlling shareholder can pocket money at his colleagues' expense.

Typically, courts police this misbehavior by declaring that controlling shareholders owe other shareholders a fiduciary duty. Unlike directors, shareholders do not owe the duty from any agency. After all, they never agreed to serve as anyone's agent. Courts nonetheless impose the duty because they have no straightforward way of preventing opportunistic tactics that might otherwise deter people from investing in the firm.

That a controlling shareholder owes other investors a fiduciary duty does not, of course, clarify what constitutes "control." A majority stake almost always gives control. But where shareholdings are broadly dispersed, even a much smaller stake may give control effectively. Alas, courts seldom do much to clarify where the line might lie.

2. *Sinclair Oil Corp. v. Levien*[66]

(a) *Political Risk*

To illustrate the standards to which courts hold controlling shareholders, consider *Sinclair*. Sinclair Oil drilled in a wide variety of countries. As with all such firms, this made it enormously vulnerable. Crude oil does not come easily, and it does not come cheaply. To extract it, a firm will need first to invest large sums. It will need to drill for years. At most of the holes, it will strike nothing. And when it finally does locate oil, it will need to install costly, nonremovable equipment before the oil will start to flow.

These large upfront costs leave firms like Sinclair susceptible to political extortion. A firm may buy a judicially enforceable property right in a deposit. It may negotiate a contractual right to drill (a "concession") from a government. But once it sinks its initial investment, even a regime nominally committed to the "rule of law" may raise taxes to near-confiscatory levels. It may threaten to impose "environmental" controls or pollution fees. It may desist only if the firm agrees to its demands along other dimensions.

In the politically volatile Third World, oil firms find themselves more vulnerable still. Even a stable regime can renege on its promises. Successor regimes regularly declare their predecessors corrupt and void the "odious" concessions they distributed. Gaddafi expropriated Bunker Hunt's oil fields in Libya. The Mexican government nationalized foreign-owned petroleum facilities as well.[67]

(b) *Venezuela*

In 1960s Venezuela, foreign firms owned many wells that dated from the 1920s. They had obtained their concessions from the widely hated tyrant, Juan Vicente Gomez. Gomez died in 1935 and left the country unstable. For foreign firms, this instability did not augur well. In 1945, young military officers joined forces with the populist Romulo Betancourt and staged a coup. Betancourt had led the Costa Rican Communist Party in the 1930s and, as head of the new Venezuelan

---

[66] 280 A.2d 717 (Del. 1971); *see* Robert B. Thompson, *Mapping Judicial Review:* Sinclair v. Levien, in *The Iconic Cases in Corporate Law* 79 (Jonathan R. Macey ed., Thompson/West 2008).

[67] Yergin, *supra* note 28, at 276.

government, raised the tax on foreign oil to an effective rate of 50 percent on profits.

Betancourt did not last either. In 1948, Marcos Perez Jimenez toppled his regime in another coup. Like Gomez, Perez Jimenez aggressively promoted the oil industry, and like Gomez became extremely unpopular.[68] But Perez Jimenez lasted only until yet another junta ousted him in 1958. This government promptly hiked the tax on oil from 52 percent to 65 percent and brought back Betancourt. For foreign firms, this was again bad news. Betancourt was a man with a reputation as "a passionate critic of the international oil companies."[69]

Betancourt declared nationalization a central goal. Gomez had run "one of the most primitive despotisms that any people of Latin America has suffered," he wrote in 1956. His rule had reeked of despotism that "did nothing to inhibit the continuing dance of oil concessions" and the "scandalous profiteering" by the "governing clique."[70] Instead:

> In view of the explosive mixture of oil and diplomacy, the most favorable solution for a country such as ours would be to nationalize the industry. Let the state take control of oil production after indemnifying the concessionaires, thus freeing the country from the presence of these aggressive economic and political forces from abroad.[71]

Betancourt immediately announced an end to new oil concessions. He established a state-owned oil company. And when his term ended in 1963, he passed his control to Raul Leoni in his own party. Leoni then kept nationalization of the foreign oil firms near the heart of his government's ultimate goals.[72]

(c) Dividends

During the Betancourt–Leoni years, Sinclair (a New York corporation) operated in Venezuela through Sinclair Venezuela (a Delaware corporation, Sinven). Although Sinven listed its shares on the American Stock Exchange, by the time of the dispute at issue Sinclair owned 97 percent. Of the remaining 120,000 shares, the plaintiff Francis Levien owned 3,000. Sinven had once held properties outside of the country, but by 1959 it limited its focus to Venezuela.[73]

Levien filed a derivative suit against Sinclair. The firm had caused Sinven, he argued, to pay too much in dividends. He did not claim that the dividends violated any statutory cap. Instead, he argued that they left Sinven starved of the resources it needed to exploit its opportunities.

---

[68] *Id.* at 433-437.

[69] Franklin Tugwell, *The Politics of Oil in Venezuela* 51, 53 (Stanford University Press 1975).

[70] Romulo Betancourt, *Venezuela: Oil and Politics* 17, 29 (Houghton Mifflin 1979) (translation by Everett Bauman of Spanish volume first published in 1956).

[71] *Id.* at 359.

[72] Yergin, *supra* note 28, at 510.

[73] Levien v. Sinclair Oil Corp., 261 A.2d 911 (Del. Ch. 1969).

The claim is implausible on its face, and the Delaware Supreme Court denied it. If Sinven had held good business opportunities, the high dividends would not have stopped it from exploiting them. If it lacked the funds it needed, it could have issued new stock. It could have issued bonds. Or it could have borrowed from a bank.

The court, however, held for Sinclair on other grounds. As controlling share-holder, it explained, Sinclair did owe Levien a fiduciary duty. But it bore the burden of proving the "inherent fairness" of a move only if the transactional structure allowed "self-dealing." Where Sinclair paid equal dividends on all shares, the structure permitted no self-dealing: Sinclair and Levien earned exactly the same dividend on each share of Sinven stock. Absent any risk of self-dealing, the business judgment rule applied, and Sinclair won.

(d) Expropriation

The opinion does not allude to the issue, but Sinven had good reason to repatriate as much of its asset base as it could. Typically, oil companies invest heavily in their wells at the outset and then earn returns on those investments over the remaining years of their concession. In Venezuela, Sinven had made its investments decades earlier and was now earning that return.

With Betancourt and Leoni in power, it made no sense for any foreign oil firm to invest in Venezuela. Instead, rational firms repatriated their assets as fast as possible. Mexico had already nationalized its foreign-owned wells and plants. Betancourt and Leoni threatened to do the same in Venezuela.

If Sinclair paid its high dividends because it feared nationalization, it feared correctly. The Delaware Supreme Court denied Levien's dividend claim in 1971. That very year, the Venezuelan government announced the "law of reversion": Foreign firms would forfeit their concessions to the government with minimal compensation at the end of their terms. In 1972, it raised the tax rate on foreign oil to 96 percent and asserted nearly total control over the industry. And in 1976, it replaced the law of reversion with immediate nationalization. Sinclair was right to dividend Sinven's assets. Five years after the Delaware opinion, Venezuela confiscated everything that was left.[74]

(e) Corporate Opportunities

Like many multinational firms, Sinclair coordinated its international operations through country-specific subsidiaries. U.S. federal and state laws do not require firms to do so. But foreign law does sometimes encourage it, and country-specific subsidiaries often facilitate internal administration anyway. Like many of its peers, Sinclair kept Venezuelan business — but only Venezuelan business — in a specific firm.

---

[74] Yergin, *supra* note 28, at 650.

III. Duty of Loyalty

Levien argued that Sinclair should have offered other business opportunities to Sinven. Levien had "struck it rich" (the *New York Times*'s words) litigating the first pivotal corporate opportunity case.[75] Now he argued that Sinclair breached its fiduciary duty to Sinven when it placed business opportunities with its 100 percent subsidiaries rather than the 97 percent Sinven.

The Delaware Supreme Court disagreed. Sinclair had not received Venezuelan opportunities, it explained. The Betancourt–Leoni governments were threatening to expropriate; they were hardly inviting new business. Instead, Sinclair had received opportunities to invest in places like Alaska, Canada, and Paraguay.

Effectively though not explicitly, the court declared that multinational enterprises could safely partition their global operations through country-specific subsidiaries: They could maintain a series of subsidiaries that each invested only in one country. Because the law does not mandate the structure, Sinclair legally could have assigned its business opportunities to any of a dozen or more subsidiaries. Obviously, it had selfish reasons to put the most profitable opportunities in its 100 percent subsidiaries rather than the 97 percent–owned Sinven.

The court simply ignored this conflict of interest. It might have explored Sinclair's selfish incentive to route business away from Sinven. It did not. Instead, it noted that Sinclair had not received Venezuelan business opportunities, and let the matter rest.

(f) Contractual Breach

Last, Levien argued that Sinclair caused its 100 percent–owned Sinclair International to breach the contracts it had with the 97 percent–owned Sinven. By doing so, of course, Sinclair transferred wealth from Sinven to International — and hence from Sinven's minority shareholders like Levien to itself. The court agreed. Sinclair owed Sinven a fiduciary duty; in causing International to breach its contracts with Sinven, it violated that duty; hence, it was liable.

That International should pay was clear enough. It had contracted with Sinven and violated the terms. What is less clear is why Sinclair should pay. Sinclair did not breach a contract. Sinclair International did. When a firm breaches a contract, generally its controlling shareholder is liable only if the court has reason to "pierce the corporate veil" (Chapter 3, section IV). Courts pierce veils only exceptionally, and only on proof of a variety of factors never raised here. International was properly liable, but why Sinclair might be liable the court never explained.

[75] Wolfgang Saxon, *Francis Levien, 90, Industrialist Known for Conglomerates*, N.Y. Times (June 15, 1995). The case was Guth v. Loft, 5 A.2d 503 (Del. 1939).

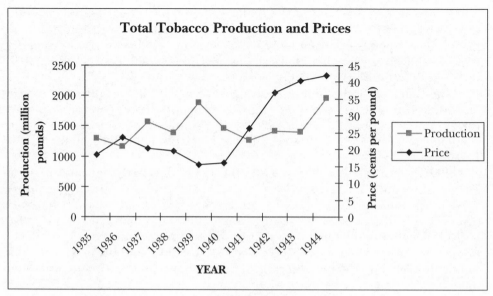

Figure 4-2
Tobacco Production and Prices

Source: U.S. Dept. of Agriculture, *Annual Report on Tobacco Statistics* (various years).

3.   *Zahn v. Transamerica Corp.*[76]

(a)   The Industry

A much more complicated case involved Transamerica's stake in Axton-Fisher. "Spud" Hughes had sold cigarettes out of the back of his car. Having learned how to lace them with menthol, he distributed them himself. Axton-Fisher had sold a regional cigarette brand called "Clown." In 1926, it bought the "Spud" name and menthol technology from Hughes and added Spud to its portfolio.

By 1943, A. P. Giannini's Transamerica held large stakes in Axton-Fisher. Of Axton's Class B stock, it owned 80 percent, and of its Class A stock, another 66 percent. Giannini had built his immigrant-oriented Bank of Italy into the Bank of America and used Transamerica for his insurance operations. Through the latter, he also invested in Axton-Fisher.

Axton-Fisher owned a large stock of tobacco that had massively appreciated in value. In 1943, the leaf stock for which it had paid $6.4 million sold for $20 million. The reason was simple: war. Cigarette companies could no longer import tobacco from abroad. Tobacco worth 16 cents per pound in 1940 had climbed by 1942 to 37 cents per pound (see Figure 4-2).

---

[76] 162 F.2d 36 (3d Cir. 1947).

III. Duty of Loyalty

In turn, federal price caps gave low-end tobacco firms an incentive to divert their stock to their higher-priced rivals. The Office of Price Administration (OPA) began suppressing cigarette prices in 1942. No longer able to obtain the market price for their cigarettes, manufacturers responded by degrading quality instead. If the OPA capped the prices of both the low-end Clowns and the cigarettes of tobacconist-to-the-crown Philip Morris, Axton-Fisher could sell its Clown tobacco to Philip Morris and liquidate. Philip Morris could then stuff the cheap tobacco in its own cigarettes and sell them at OPA-approved higher prices.

Axton-Fisher did exactly that. In April 1943, it sold the bulk of its tobacco to Philip Morris and liquidated. Class A shareholders Philip Zahn and Jack Friedman then filed a class action.

(b)   The Capital Structure

In 1943, Axton-Fisher had three classes of stock outstanding: preferred shares, Class A "common" shares; and Class B common. Firms can call stock what they want, but by function the preferred shares were "senior preferred," and the Class A common were "junior preferred" (on preferred stock, see Chapter 3, Appendix III). The true "common" was the Class B. The dispute at hand concerned the relative rights of the As and Bs; the nominal "preferred" shares do not figure in it.

The Axton-Fisher charter contained three provisions relevant here:

(I)   *Redemption:* The board could call (i.e., redeem) the Class A shares at $60 per share plus accrued unpaid dividends (for a total, by 1943, of $80.80) upon 60-days' notice;

(II) *Conversion:* The holders of the Class A stock could convert their shares to Class B at any time on a one-to-one basis; and

(III) *Liquidation:* Upon liquidation, Axton-Fisher would distribute to the Class A shares twice the amount it distributed to the Class B shares.

On July 1, 1943, Transamerica used its control over the Axton-Fisher board to call the A shares at $60 plus accrued dividends ($80.80; option (I) above), and liquidate. Upon receiving the redemption notice, some Axton-Fisher shareholders converted their A stock to B (option (II) above). Others simply took the $60 plus dividends. At liquidation, the B shareholders apparently received at least $120 per share (the plaintiffs claimed they would have received $240 if they had been allowed to hold their A stock and take double the Bs — option (III) above).

(c)   The Opinion

Consider how the *Sinclair* court might have decided the case. Because Transamerica controlled Axton-Fisher, it owed Axton (and its minority shareholders) a fiduciary duty. If it caused Axton to redeem the A shares (option (I)), it paid A shareholders $80.80 per share. If it liquidated Axton without redeeming them, it paid them much more (option (III)): twice what it paid the B shareholders.

Transamerica owned 80 percent of the B shares but less of the As. Because calling the A shares transferred money from the A shareholders to itself, the transaction apparently embodied what the *Sinclair* court called self-dealing. Unless Transamerica could show that the deal was "intrinsically fair" (and how could it do that?), it lost.

That was exactly what the Third Circuit in *Zahn* initially did. But suppose Axton-Fisher had had no controlling shareholder. What would an independent board have done? As agents, directors owe fiduciary duties to the corporation — but that mantra hardly helps. Whether they call the A shareholders or liquidate without calling them, the value of the firm remains unchanged. The fraction of firm value that the As and Bs each receive changes, but not the total. Courts sometimes tell directors they owe fiduciary duties to their shareholders — but this mantra does no better. The board owes a fiduciary duty to both classes.

(d) The Original Deal

Given the interplay among options (I), (II), and (III), the Axton-Fisher board probably added the Class A shares when the firm was doing badly. To attract new money, it invented the Class A shares and promised its owners extra protection so long as the firm remained unprofitable. Once the firm recovered, it expected the As to convert to Bs and share equally.

To see this dynamic, take a much simpler version of the actual numbers in the opinion (Table 4-2). Suppose the firm has 100 shares of Class A stock and 100 shares of Class B. It has no preferred shares, no debt, and no unpaid dividends. Now suppose (I explain why below) that the board decides to maximize the returns to the B shareholders.

Table 4-2
Hypothetical Corporate Strategies Under Three Firm Values

	A	B	C
Firm value:	$6,000	$10,000	$30,000
A receives:	$40	$60	$150
B receives:	$20	$40	$150
Call?	No	Yes	Yes
Convert?	No	No	Yes

Suppose first that the firm has assets worth $6,000 and plans to liquidate. If it liquidates without calling the As (option (I)), the As will receive twice the per-share value of the Bs (option (III)). Because the firm has 100 shares of each, the As will receive $40 per share, and the Bs will receive $20. After all, 100 A shares at $40 equals $4,000, 100 B shares at $20 equals $2,000, and $4,000 plus $2,000 totals $6,000 — the hypothesized value of the firm.

In this situation, a board determined to maximize the returns to the Bs will not call the As (option (I)). If it did, the As would receive $60 per share. Since

$60 × 100 = $6,000, this would leave nothing for the Bs. Neither would the As convert to Bs (option (II)). If they all did, the 200 resulting Class B shares would share equally, giving them $6,000/200 = $30 per share. The As do better taking the $40 they receive by not converting.

Suppose next that the firm liquidates with assets worth $10,000. If it liquidates without calling the As, the As will receive $66 per share, and the Bs will take half that amount, $66.66 × 100 + $33.33 × 100 = 10,000. In this world, a board that answers to the Bs will call the As at $60 per share and leave the Bs $40. The As, however, still will not convert. If they did, the 200 resulting Class Bs would receive $50 each. Rather than obtain $50, they will opt for the $60 offered by the board upon redemption.

Last, suppose that the firm liquidates with $30,000. If it did so without calling the As, the As would receive $200 and the Bs $100 (option (III)). Rather than pay $200, the board will call the As for $60 (option (I)). The As will not take the $60, however. Instead, they will convert (option (II)). Provided they all do so, they will receive $30,000/200 = $150.

Table 4-2 summarizes this discussion and illustrates how the corporate structure gives the As a set of protections that disappears as the firm turns increasingly profitable. So long as the firm is unsuccessful, the A shareholders receive on liquidation twice as much as the B shareholders. As the firm becomes modestly profitable, the A shareholders no longer take twice what the Bs receive, but still receive more — namely, $60. And when the firm thrives, it calls the As at $60, and that call induces the As to convert. When the firm is profitable, in short, the call is simply a device to induce the As to take B shares.

(e)   Remand

In its first opinion, the Third Circuit applied (what amounts to) the *Sinclair* logic and gave the As twice what the Bs obtained. Upon remand, the district court asked what a disinterested board would have done. As Axton-Fisher was a Kentucky corporation, it certified the question to the Kentucky Supreme Court. That court then articulated the simple principle: *Facing multiple tiers of securities, a disinterested board should adopt those strategies that maximize the returns to the junior-most security.* The "junior-most" security is the residual claimant, the security paid last.

In this case, Axton-Fisher was in the analytic equivalent of the $30,000 example (the third column of Table 4-2), and the junior-most security was the B stock. According to the Kentucky court, a disinterested board would have maximized the returns to the B shareholders. Given the finances, it would have called the As at $60 plus accrued dividends, and the As would have responded by converting to Bs.

This maximize-the-returns-to-the-junior-security rule is both generally enforced and a waivable default. Courts enforce it for convenience: It marks a clear way out of an otherwise intractable dilemma. Because investors know the rule, however, they price the different securities according to it. And because everyone buys his security at prices that reflect the rule, everyone obtains his just desserts. The rule remains one of convenience, though: Should investors for any reason want a different rule ex ante, they can freely opt out of it by charter.

(f) The Resolution

Although Axton-Fisher's position was equivalent to the third column, some A shareholders did not convert. Instead, they took the much lower $80.80 offered at redemption. Upon receiving the "call," the A shareholders needed to know whether they were in the second column of Table 4-2 or the third. Given that the firm called the stock, they knew they were not in the first. But to decide whether to take the $80.80 or to convert, they needed to know which of the other columns they were in. For that decision, they needed to know the value of Axton-Fisher's tobacco. Some (those who converted to Bs) apparently did. Others (those who took the $80.80) did not.

In turn, that some shareholders did not convert suggests that the Axton-Fisher directors redeemed the stock without disclosing the value of the tobacco. By doing so, they breached their fiduciary duty. After all, if they (as agents) caused the firm to transact (redeem stock) with the A shareholders (their principals), they (as agents) had to disclose what the shareholders (their principals) needed to know. If they caused Axton-Fisher to redeem the As without giving that information, under state law they breached their fiduciary duties to the As. Under federal law, they arguably breached the general antifraud provisions of the securities law (Rule 10b-5, discussed in Chapter 5 and cited by the district court as Rule X-10-b-5).

Note what this analysis does to the A shareholders' damages. The Third Circuit initially gave them the difference between (i) double the amount the Bs received and (ii) $80.80. Upon appeal from the remand, the court reasoned that a disinterested board would have called the As. If it had properly disclosed the value of the tobacco, the A shareholders would have known they were in the third column of Table 4-2 and would have converted their A shares into B shares. Accordingly, it instead awarded them the difference between (i) the amount the Bs received and (ii) $80.80.

D. Executive Compensation

1. Introduction

Directors monitor the firm. In the course of monitoring, they hire, supervise, and occasionally fire its senior officers. In the course of supervising the officers, they also set their pay. If loyal to the firm, they will not pay the officers more than necessary to attract and motivate people with the requisite talent and expertise. Neither will they pay them less.

To be sure, markets limit how wildly boards can ignore what a firm needs. If directors underpay their officers, the firm will lose essential leaders. It will find itself at a disadvantage in the product and service markets and less able to raise funds. If directors overpay their officers, they throw away the firm's money. Again, it will find itself crippled on the product, service, and capital markets.

But markets do not constrain directors perfectly. Some directors follow their CEO to a fault. They may know him and the other senior officers socially. They may think they owe their seat on the board to him. Deliberately or not, they may pay him and his colleagues more than they should.

To the courts, a dispute over executive compensation differs little from a dispute over any other decision by the board. A court will ask whether the board faced a conflict of interest. It will ask whether it studied and deliberated about the question. It will ask whether the salary it offered was legal or so large as to constitute waste. Absent a conflict of interest, gross negligence, fraud, illegality, or waste, it will apply the business judgment rule. Absent a fiduciary duty violation, it will leave questions of compensation to the shareholders' meeting and the market. If a shareholder dislikes what his board pays its officers, he can take one of two steps: elect new directors or sell his stock.

Questions of executive compensation can concern not just salary but perquisites too. After the death of John Ringling (see Chapter 2, section I), control over the circus (by now a Delaware corporation) passed to his two nephews, John Ringling North and Henry North. Every summer, the two traveled through Europe to recruit new talent. And travel they did. According to the *New Yorker*:

> The Norths en route through Europe have evoked memories of Edward VII, whose trips on the Continent established high-water marks of conviviality. They take a custom-built Cadillac over with them, and, landing at Le Havre, pick up their French chauffeur Henri, and their European agent, Umberto Bedini. . . .
>
> The Norths' first stop of importance is Paris, where they put up at the Ritz. The journey around Europe is exhausting, and John, a determined gourmet, likes to store up energy by eating rich foods before setting out. He visits, in turn, Maxim's, Larue, Fouquet's, L'Escargot, Le Relais de la Belle Aurore, and La Tour d'Argent, and then tries some of the smaller places, in side streets. By this time, he is beginning to have premonitions of acute indigestion, and he heads for a Turkish bath.[77]

Extravagant, perhaps, but not nearly so as the Michaels Ovitz and Eisner. And to the Delaware court, the Michaels still fell within the business judgment rule.

2.   *In re Walt Disney*[78]

Made in heaven or no, theirs was a match — one rich Michael against another rich Michael. Michael Ovitz lived on the telephone, ignored anything of detail, charged the company $90,000 for parties, and spent several million to renovate his office.[79] Michael Eisner hired Ovitz and then did everything he could to

---

[77] As quoted in Robert Lewis Taylor, *Center Ring* 36-37 (Doubleday 1956).

[78] In re The Walt Disney Co. Derivative Litig., 906 A.2d 27 (Del. 2006).

[79] Kim Masters, *Deposed: The Strange Hiring and Firing of Michael Ovitz*, Slate (Aug. 16, 2004), http://www.slate.com/articles/news_and_politics/low_concept/2004/08/deposed.html.

undermine him. Even the Delaware courts were not impressed. Faced with a share-holder derivative suit over Michael v. Michael, the court declared:

> By virtue of his Machiavellian (and imperial) nature as CEO, and his control over Ovitz's hiring in particular, Eisner to a large extent is responsible for the failings in process that infected and handicapped the board's decision-making abilities. Eisner stacked his (and I intentionally write "his" as opposed to "the Company's") board of directors with friends and other acquaintances who, though not necessarily beholden to him in a legal sense, were certainly more willing to accede to his wishes and support him unconditionally than truly independent directors.[80]

But then, this is the entertainment industry, after all — what Hunter "Uncle Duke" Thompson called the "cruel and shallow money trench . . . , a long plastic hallway where thieves and pimps run free and good men die like dogs, for no good reason."[81]

Machiavellian or imperial, cruel or shallow, CEO Michael Eisner did run Disney. In August 1995, he caused the board to offer Ovitz a five-year contract as president. Ovitz started work in October, but brought a style that did not fit. Within a year, Eisner decided he had to go. He asked general counsel Sanford Litvak whether he had "cause" to fire Ovitz. Litvak said no, so Eisner and the board fired him anyway. Given the terms of his employment contract, they now owed him $130 million to make him go away.

Milberg Weiss (see Chapter 3, Introduction) promptly sued Ovitz and the board in a derivative suit. The suit put Disney in a bind. As *New York* magazine put it, it had to argue that

> [h]iring Ovitz was entirely prudent . . . but on the other hand so was firing him after only a year, because he sucked . . . but on the other hand, so was paying him $140 million in severance, because even though he sucked, he wasn't so terrible that he could have been fired for cause.[82]

The Delaware Supreme Court dismissed the Milberg Weiss suit. It proceeded in several logical steps. First, Ovitz did not breach his duty of loyalty in negotiating a lucrative contract for himself. He negotiated the terms before he accepted the job. At that time, he did not work for Disney. He worked for himself and owed duties to no one but himself.

Second, the board did not breach a duty of care in negotiating the extravagant severance package. It delegated the contractual work to a committee, but boards may properly delegate to committees. The committee then consulted the compensation consulting firm Graef Crystal, studied the contract, and understood its

---

[80] In re The Walt Disney Co. Derivative Litig., 907 A.2d 693, 760 (Del. Ch. 2005), *aff'd*, 906 A.2d 27 (Del. 2006).

[81] Hunter S. Thompson, *Generation of Swine: Tales of Shame and Degradation in the '80s* 43 (Summit Books 1988).

[82] Kurt Andersen, *Ovitz and Eisner: A Kids' Story*, New York (May 21, 2005).

terms. It approved an extravagant contract, but it approved the extravagance after excruciatingly thoughtful deliberation.

Third, the extravagance did not rise (or perhaps fall) to the level of "waste." Although $130 million is a lot to pay a substandard employee to leave, in hiring him, Disney had made him abandon his spot in the premier movie talent agency. From it, Ovitz had earned $20 to $25 million a year. When Disney asked him to leave that job, he understandably insisted on "downside protection." It offered him the severance because he would not otherwise come.

Fourth, the board did not breach a duty of care in firing Ovitz without cause. Had it found "cause," it could have avoided the large severance payment. But Eisner had consulted Litvak, and Litvak did not think Ovitz had given Disney "cause" to fire him. Disney needed him gone, and only by paying him could it rid itself of him. By the inimitable elegance of the *New York* magazine, it was prudent to fire him "because he sucked, but so was paying him $130 million in severance, because even though he sucked, he wasn't so terrible that he could have been fired for cause."

Last, the board did not act in "bad faith." As in *Stone v. Ritter* (section II.C.4 above), the issue arose because of §102(b)(7). Disney had waived its claims against its directors for duty of care violations, but §102(b)(7) limited the scope of the waiver to directors who had acted in "good faith." The court found no violation of the good faith standard.

Note that in dismissing the bad faith claims, the court construed the phrase in a way (as in *Stone*) that potentially swept many due care violations into "bad faith." Bad faith, it explained, involved an "intentional dereliction of duty, a conscious disregard for one's responsibilities." As the chancellor had put it, a director or officer acted in bad faith:

[i]   where the fiduciary intentionally acts with a purpose other than that of advancing the best interests of the corporation,

[ii]   where the fiduciary acts with the intent to violate applicable positive law, or

[iii] where the fiduciary intentionally fails to act in the face of a known duty to act, demonstrating conscious disregard of his duties.[83]

When a director or officer acts in such a fashion, the "misconduct is properly treated as a non-exculpable, non-indemnifiable violation of the fiduciary duty to act in good faith."[84]

Once upon a time, things were clear — sort of. At the end of Chapter 1, agents owed their principals a duty of care and a duty of loyalty. They were to act in good faith too, of course, but mostly the command went without saying. Post-*Stone* and (now) *Disney*, in Delaware it no longer goes without saying. Instead, the court imposes a sort-of-separate duty of good faith. Through that duty, it

[83] 907 A.2d at 755.
[84] Brehm v. Eisner, 906 A.2d 27, 66 (Del. 2006).

captures some of what once passed as the duty of care. It captures some of what still fits better in the duty of loyalty. And sometimes it recites the duty as an entirely separate third prong: "the triads of their fiduciary duty," it declares, "good faith, loyalty, or due care."[85] It is easy to sympathize with the anonymous blogger who complained that

> [t]hese fine distinctions are matters that the DE Supreme Court rightly considers, I suppose, as they must have something useful to do, but as a practical matter to the average litigator, you either have some kind of strong evidence that the directors are crooks, or you do not. Slicing and dicing their basic duty into sub-duties accomplishes — what?[86]

The answer: The "slicing and dicing" accomplishes the dismantling of Sections 102(b)(7) and 145. In the wake of *Van Gorkom* (see section II.B.2 above), firms found it hard to recruit good directors. In response, Delaware legislators let them insulate their directors from duty of care claims. Delaware judges blanched. They were the ones who had written *Van Gorkom* in the first place, and they took back what the legislators had offered.

As judges, the judges could not formally take back the statute. So they took it back by interpretation. The statute did not let firms waive (or indemnify) bad faith behavior. Fine — they simply defined bad faith to include the duty of care violations that they did not want firms to waive (or indemnify against).

E.   Corporate Opportunities

1.   Introduction

(a)   Simple Cases

Recall Cardozo, Meinhard, Salmon, and Gerry (Chapter 2, section IV.B). Salmon ran a joint venture with Meinhard to exploit a lease from Gerry. Near the end of the term, Gerry invited Salmon to invest in a new lease that would replace the expiring one. Salmon accepted, Meinhard sued, and Cardozo declared that Salmon breached his duty of loyalty to Meinhard. The new lease was an "opportunity" of the joint venture. Had the two operated a corporation rather than a joint venture, Cardozo might have called it a "corporate opportunity." Salmon could not "take" the opportunity for himself without first offering it to their firm.

---

[85] Cede & Co. v. Technicolor, Inc., 634 A.2d 345, 361 (Del. 1993).

[86] The Conglomerate Blog, http://www.theconglomerate.org/2007/01/good_faith_care.html (Jan. 5, 2007).

III. Duty of Loyalty

Recall Agau, USAC, and Lawrence (section III.C.5 above). Lawrence ran Agau, which mined for silver and gold. Through his work for the company, he acquired several antimony mines. Lest minority shareholders claim that the antimony mines were "corporate opportunities" to Agau, he did not immediately exploit them in his own firm USAC. Instead, he "offered" them to Agau. Only after the Agau board "rejected" his offer did he develop them himself.

(b) Thompson

What of Hunter Thompson and the Hells Angels? For almost a year, Thompson rode with the Angels. He drank with them, popped pills with them, partied with them. On the basis of that year, he wrote an article for the *Nation* and then a book. The book sold wildly and catapulted him to premier gonzo-journalist status and the infamous fame that attracted groupies and cartoonists like flies.

Could Thompson keep the royalties? Or did he owe them to the Angels? Was the chance to write a book about the motorcycle club an "opportunity" of the club itself—a "corporate opportunity," given the incorporated character of the club? Some of the Angels thought so. His rides with the Angels ended in 1966 when "four or five Angels," explained Thompson, "seemed to feel I was taking advantage of them."[87]

"I'd finished the book," Thompson explained. "I was showing the Angels the cover [see Figure 4-3]. They hated it. And I said, 'Hey, I agree with you.'" But the cover also had the price: $4.95. "And the Angels said, 'Jesus, $4.95! What's our share? We should get half.' And I said, 'Come on.' I was getting careless, see. I said, 'It takes a long time to write a book. Nothing—that's your share.'"[88] Then it happened:

> The first blow was launched with no hint of warning and I thought for a moment that it was just one of those drunken accidents that a man has to live with in this league. But within seconds I was clubbed from behind by the Angel I'd been talking to just a moment earlier. Then I was swarmed in a general flail.[89]

"So here I was, suddenly rolling around on the rocks of that Godforsaken beach in a swarm of stoned, crazy-drunk bikers," Thompson recalled. "[T]here were people kicking me in the chest and one of the bastards was trying to bash my head in with a tremendous rock. . . . I don't know how long it went on, but just about the time I knew I was going to die, [my friend] Tiny suddenly showed up and said 'That's it, stop it,' and they stopped as fast as they started, for no reason."[90]

---

[87] H. Thompson, *supra* note 2, at 272.
[88] Quoted in A. Thompson, *supra* note 3, at 155.
[89] H. Thompson, *supra* note 2, at 272.
[90] Quoted in A. Thompson, *supra* note 3, at 40.

Figure 4-3
The *Hell's Angels* Cover

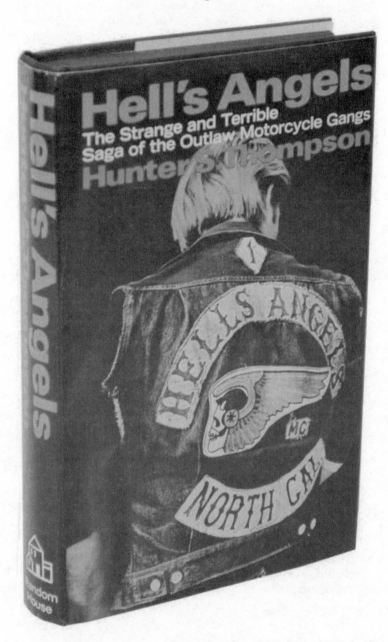

Book Cover, copyright © 1966, 1967 by Random House, Inc., from HELL'S ANGELS by
Hunter S. Thompson. Used by permission of Random House, Inc.

III. Duty of Loyalty

Thompson was an unemployed writer. He did not work for the Angels, serve as a director, or hold any position with them. Not being an "agent" of the club, he owed it no fiduciary duty. If he obtained a contract for a book about the club, he obtained it for himself.

But take Ralph "Sonny" Barger. Now more than 70 years old, Barger founded the pivotal Oakland chapter of the Angels and served for decades as its president. Probably, he also holds an office with the apparently legitimately incorporated Hells Angels Motorcycle Corporation.[91] Barger had little use for Thompson:

> I actually liked the way [the *Nation* article] was written, even though some of the facts were exaggerated. . . . But as time went by, Hunter turned out to be a real weenie and a stone fucking coward. . . . He's all show and no go. . . . I ended up not liking him at all, a tall, skinny, typical hillbilly from Kentucky. He was a total fake.[92]

So Barger wrote his own book — *Hell's Angel: The Life and Times of Sonny Barger and the Hell's Angels Motorcycle Club*. As president of the Oakland chapter and (probably) officer of the corporation, Barger owed both a duty of loyalty. In writing the book himself, did he take an "opportunity" more properly held by the chapter or the firm?

(c) The ALI Formula: What Is a Corporate Opportunity?

As "corporate opportunity" law can vary a bit from court to court, take the American Law Institute's (authors of the *Restatements*) summary. In the process, note that the black-letter law itself follows straightforwardly from standard duty of loyalty principles. The ALI defines a "corporate opportunity" as one of three types of business opportunities:

> (1) Any opportunity to engage in a business activity of which a director or senior executive becomes aware, either:
>> (A) In connection with the performance of functions as a director or senior executive, or under circumstances that should reasonably lead the director or senior executive to believe that the person offering the opportunity expects it to be offered to the corporation; or
>> (B) Through the use of corporate information or property . . . ; or
> (2) Any opportunity to engage in a business activity of which a senior executive becomes aware and knows is closely related to a business in which the corporation is engaged. . . .[93]

---

[91] According to its Web site: Hells Angels Motorcycle Club World, http://www.hells-angels.com (accessed Feb. 28, 2012).

[92] Barger, Zimmerman & Zimmerman, *supra* note 4, at 125.

[93] American Law Institute, *Principles of Corporate Governance: Analysis and Recommendations* §5.05(b) (ALI 1992). Here and throughout the book, the material from *Principles of Corporate Governance: Analysis and Recommendations*, © 1994 by The American Law Institute. Reproduced with permission. All rights reserved.

If Gerry approaches Salmon as president of Meinhard-Salmon Real Estate, Inc., and offers a new lease, the lease is a corporate opportunity by test (1)(A). If a broker approaches Lawrence as president of Agau and offers an antimony mine, the mine is a corporate opportunity by test (1)(A). If through Agau's geological studies, Lawrence learns that some local real estate may contain antimony, an option to buy that property is a corporate opportunity by test (1)(B).

Because a new lease on the Meinhard-Salmon hotel is closely related to the current hotel, if Gerry offers Salmon a new lease, the lease is also a corporate opportunity under test (2). If antimony mining is "closely related" (a variation on the sometimes-used "line of business" test) to silver or gold mining, the mine is a corporate opportunity under test (2).

Note that Thompson's book contract fits none of these categories. He was a freelance writer. He was not a director. He was not a senior executive. He did not receive the contract because of any status at the club. He did not learn of the contract through club information. And the writing of books is not "closely related" to anything club members did — indeed, according to Thompson, neither is the reading of books.

By contrast, Barger was an officer with the club (and, presumably, the corporation). He did not learn of the book contract through the use of club information (test (1)(B)) and book writing is not "closely related" to club activity (test (2)). But if he learned of the chance to write the book in "connection with the performance of" his role at the club (test (1)(A)), then the book might — only might — have been a corporate opportunity.

Note that tests (1)(A) and (B) apply to both officers and directors, but test (2) applies only to officers. Officers typically work full time for a firm, while directors work part time and may serve on the boards of several firms in the same industry. As a result, applying the "closely related" test (2) to directors raises several problems. Suppose aging pharmaceutical lawyer Joanie Caucus retires from firm A. Pharmaceutical start-ups B and C ask her to serve on their boards. They need a day or two of her time each month and pay a modest fee. Were the clause (2) "closely related" test to apply to Caucus, she could easily lose money on the directorships. As a retired star lawyer, she can reasonably anticipate multiple attractive investment opportunities in the pharmaceutical industry. Should she take the board positions, however, those opportunities would become corporate opportunities. She could no longer keep them for herself. What is more, because B and C are both in the pharmaceutical industry, the new opportunities might be equally "closely related" to each. Caucus would find herself in the unhappy position of knowing the opportunity was not hers, but not knowing whose it really was.

Given these considerations, the ALI explains:

> Because of the importance of encouraging persons who are not employees of the corporation to serve as directors, and the likelihood that many such persons will be engaged in multiple business activities, under Sec. 5.05 directors who are not

senior executives have no obligation to offer an opportunity to the corporation simply because the opportunity is closely related to the corporation's business.[94]

(d) What Should One Do with a Corporate Opportunity?

If a director or an officer receives a "corporate opportunity," he will need to offer it to the firm. Only if the firm then rejects it can he exploit it for himself:

> A director or senior executive may not take advantage of a corporate opportunity unless:
>> (1) The director or senior executive first offers the corporate opportunity to the corporation and makes full disclosure concerning the conflict of interest and the corporate opportunity;
>> (2) The corporate opportunity is rejected by the corporation; and
>> (3) Either:
>>> (A) The rejection of the opportunity is fair to the corporation;
>>> (B) The opportunity is rejected in advance, following such disclosure, by disinterested directors . . . ; or
>>> (C) The rejection is authorized in advance or ratified, following such disclosure, by disinterested shareholders. . . .[95]

The ALI then adds a clarification:

> A party who challenges the taking of a corporate opportunity has the burden of proof, except that if such party establishes that the requirements of Subsection (a)(3)(B) or (C) are not met, the director or senior executive has the burden of proving that the rejection and the taking of the opportunity were fair to the corporation.[96]

Suppose a director or officer learns of a business opportunity that falls within the scope of a "corporate opportunity." Before he can exploit it himself, he will need to offer it to the corporation. If disinterested directors or shareholders decline the opportunity on behalf of the corporation, he can take it. If neither disinterested directors nor disinterested shareholders reject it, he will need to be prepared to prove he treated the firm fairly in taking it for himself.

Suppose Gerry approaches Salmon about a new lease on the Meinhard-Salmon property. Salmon may bid for the lease only if he offers it to the firm first. Suppose Lawrence learns of an antimony mine. He may develop it within USAC only if disinterested Agau directors or shareholders reject the opportunity. And suppose a publisher approaches Barger about a book on the Hells Angels. If the offer constitutes a corporate opportunity — only an "if" — Barger will need to offer the contract to the firm before he writes the book himself.

---

[94] *Id.* at 287.
[95] *Id.* at §5.05(a).
[96] *Id.* at §5.05(c).

2. *Broz v. Cellular Information Systems, Inc.*[97]

Take two "corporate opportunity" disputes, one straightforward and one not. Robert Broz owned all the stock of RFB Cellular, Inc. (RFBC) and served on the board of the publicly traded Cellular Information Systems, Inc. (CIS). In April 1994, Mackinac Cellular Corp. contacted a broker to find a buyer for a Michigan cellular license it hoped to sell. The broker called Broz to offer the license to RFBC. The broker did not offer it to CIS.

Over the summer of 1994, Broz discussed the possibility of buying Mackinac's license with the CIS CEO and two other CIS directors. After they each replied that CIS did not want the license, Broz bid for it himself. Meanwhile, PriCellular was bidding for both CIS and the Mackinac license. Broz outbid PriCellular on the Mackinac license, but PriCellular acquired CIS and then sued Broz for the license

Broz did not take a CIS corporate opportunity, the Delaware Supreme Court held. First, he did not learn of the Mackinac license through CIS. Instead, Mackinac offered it to him for RFBC. Second, CIS did not have the money to exploit the license. Third, although the license was within CIS's "line of business," it was a line — cellular licenses — that CIS was trying to divest. Last, Broz did not compete for the Mackinac license against CIS. He competed against PriCellular and owed no fiduciary duties to PriCellular. Only after Broz bought the license did PriCellular acquire CIS (to which Broz did owe a duty).

Broz avoided liability even though he never formally offered the Mackinac license to the CIS board. The court observed that if he had done so, he would have obtained "a kind of 'safe harbor.'" Because he did not formally offer the license, he enjoyed no safe harbor. But the lack of a safe harbor did not generate liability. Formal offer or no, Broz did not take a CIS opportunity and was not liable. Throughout the process, he "comported himself in a manner that was wholly in accord with his obligations to CIS."[98]

3. *In re eBay, Inc. Shareholders Litigation*[99]

Pierre M. Omidyar and Jeffrey Skoll founded eBay in 1995. Three years later, they sold its stock to the public. Goldman Sachs handled that "initial public offering" (IPO), and over the next several years would handle several other deals for eBay as well.

Goldman underwrote IPOs for other firms, too, of course. In connection with those jobs, it sometimes acquired the right to buy the new stock at a price below the level at which it would trade after the offering. Several times, it offered these low-priced IPO allocations to Omidyar, Skoll, and other eBay officers and directors. From these arrangements, they each earned several million dollars.

[97] 673 A.2d 148 (Del. 1996).
[98] *Id.* at 157.
[99] 2004 WL 253521 (Del. Ch.) (memorandum opinion).

III. Duty of Loyalty

The practice eventually generated a congressional investigation. According to the *Wall Street Journal* in 2002:

> Prominent executives at 21 U.S. companies personally received hot IPO shares from Goldman Sachs Group Inc., which pocketed lucrative investment-banking fees from those companies during the stock market's extraordinary rise in the 1990s.[100]

The executives who obtained the low-priced IPO allocations included not just people at eBay, but Yahoo founder Jerry Yang, John Legere and Leo Hindery at Global Crossing, and the infamous Enron CEO Kenneth Lay and Tyco CEO Dennis Kozlowski.[101]

The plaintiffs sued on the ground that the low-priced allocations were corporate opportunities that the eBay officers should have offered to the company. The court agreed. eBay regularly invested in securities and had the money to buy these shares too. Although the allocations might have involved more risk than eBay would have chosen to take, the defendants never gave it the chance to choose.

In essence, the plaintiffs argued that Goldman Sachs paid the officers to steer eBay's securities work to Goldman. If true, the officers were simply taking bribes. By contrast, the quintessential "corporate opportunity" is a profitable business opportunity that an officer or a director takes for himself. As the court described the allegations:

> The conduct challenged here involved a large investment bank that regularly did business with a company steering highly lucrative IPO allocations to select insider directors and officers at that company, allegedly both to reward them for past business and to induce them to direct future business to that investment bank.[102]

Whether bribery or corporate opportunity, the actions violated the duty of loyalty:

> [E]ven if one assumes that IPO allocations like those in question here do not constitute a corporate opportunity, a cognizable claim is nevertheless stated on the common law ground that an agent is under a duty to account for profits obtained personally in connection with transactions related to his or her company.[103]

Think *Reading* from Chapter 1: If a British sergeant in Cairo collects money for riding in a smuggler's truck in his army uniform, he owes his earnings to the crown. If senior eBay managers collect money for routing firm business to Goldman Sachs, they owe their earnings to their firm.

---

[100] Randall Smith, *Goldman Gave Hot IPO Shares to Top Executives of Its Clients*, Wall St. J. (Oct. 3, 2002).

[101] *Id.*

[102] 2004 WL 253521.

[103] *Id.*

IV. CONCLUSION

Fear and Loathing had its fans. Some of them wrote to Thompson.

> Dear Mr. Thompson,
>   I just finished *Fear and Loathing in Las Vegas* and it is undoubtedly the funniest, driest, book I have ever read. I have since decided to quit school and attempt to recreate the entire novel with a friend.[104]

Hell's Angels had its fans too. I was mesmerized by it in ninth grade. Never mind high school. I spent the next three years fixing and riding motorcycles.

And because Thompson had his fans, should you — as *Rolling Stone* editor — have opted to hire him, courts would have protected you by the business judgment rule. So long as you devoted sufficient time and effort (with "sufficiency" commensurate with the money at stake), you met your duty of care. So long as you faced no conflict of interest, you met your duty of loyalty. And so long as you acted in good faith, *Rolling Stone* could waive most duty of care violations and indemnify you against your litigation expenses.

---

[104] Quoted in Jay Cowan, *Hunter S. Thompson: An Insider's View of Deranged, Depraved, Drugged Out Brilliance* 111 (Lyons Press 2009).

CHAPTER 5

Insider Trading

Well, in my book, you either do it right or you get eliminated. In the last seven deals that I've been involved with, there were 2.5 million stockholders who have made a pretax profit of 12 billion dollars. . . . I am not a destroyer of companies. I am a liberator of them!

The point is, ladies and gentlemen, that greed — for lack of a better word — is good. Greed is right. Greed works. Greed clarifies, cuts through, and captures the essence of the evolutionary spirit. Greed, in all of its forms — greed for life, for money, for love, knowledge — has marked the upward surge of mankind.

And greed — you mark my words — will not only save Teldar Paper, but that other malfunctioning corporation called the USA.[1]

Slicked hair, white collar on blue shirt, suspenders, cigars, Armani suit — Gordon Gekko (Michael Douglas in *Wall Street*) had the look. In fact, Gordon Gekko *made* the look. It was his.

He also made the speech, perhaps the most famous shareholder speech of all time. It helped to have Oliver Stone write it, of course. Stone borrowed the speech from one Manhattan arbitrageur Ivan Boesky, but Boesky brought less class. It was not just that Douglas was better looking. In 1986, Boesky had told the commencement audience at Berkeley's business school: "I think greed is healthy. You can be greedy and still feel good about yourself."[2]

"Feel good about yourself?" No class at all.

To his credit, Stone had the economics right (see Chapter 8, section III.B). Given his political priors, he probably did not believe much of it, and assigning the speech to a character he named after a lizard is not a subtle clue. But some

---

[1] Excerpt from "WALL STREET" ©1987 Courtesy of Twentieth Century Fox. Written by Stanley Weiser & Oliver Stone. All rights reserved.

[2] Quoted in *Wall Street's Gekko: 1980s–2010*, The Pop History Dig, http://www.pophistorydig.com/?tag = ivan-boesky-history (accessed Mar. 1, 2012).

companies are indeed badly run. Some are overstaffed. Some pay their employees too much. Some invest in bad ideas. Some are stuck in declining industries. Badly run, their stock trades at a discount.

In the face of these wastefully run firms, men and women like Gekko do everyone a service by buying them. To acquire control, they pay a premium for the stock. They then recover that premium by improving the firm's performance. They slash the extra workers. They cut the excess pay. They sell the inefficiently used equipment. They drop the unproductive lines. They rehabilitate the under-performing firms, the stock price rises, and they sell the firms at a profit. In time (and with transitional costs to be sure), workers shift to firms that better use their skills; asset title moves to firms that exploit the equipment more productively; and the bad ideas die an ignominious death.

Men and women like Gekko invite attacks. Because they improve firm performance by firing substandard managers, managers attack them with a vengeance. Politicians from the districts where the managers vote join the chorus. Politically driven filmmakers anoint them villains of the year. At root, however, men and women like Gekko attract the attacks they do precisely because of the good they do: because they move assets to more efficient uses and shift employees to jobs that better exploit their talents.

Not only do the Gekkos of the world fix badly run firms after the fact, by threatening to fix them, they induce managers to run them more efficiently from the start (Chapter 8, section III.B). Gekko cannot make money buying a well-run firm. He would be buying target stock only at a premium (otherwise, investors will not sell), and he can make money only if he sells the stock for more than he paid. If incumbent managers run a firm well, he will not be able to raise stock prices above what he pays. He makes money only when he can buy low, improve performance, and sell high. If incumbents run a firm well, he cannot buy low — and will not buy. To avoid a takeover, managers need simply to keep stock prices high by running their firms well from the start.

In a world where the Gekkos compete with each other to buy badly run firms, investors with good information about prospective acquisitions can make money. If you know Gekko plans to take over Teldar Paper, you can profitably buy its stock. If he has announced an acquisition but you know that funding constraints will cause him to abandon it, you can avoid a loss (or earn a profit) by selling (or buying an option to sell) Teldar immediately.

That shrewd investors make big gains by trading on nonpublic information in hostile acquisitions evokes tirades from the editorial pages, from Congress, and — sometimes — from Hollywood. But for many years it was not clear that the trades were illegal. They are illegal now, and this chapter explores the legal questions involved.

Section I describes some of the environments that give rise to insider trading. Section II outlines attempts to control the trades through state law. Section III explains how the U.S. Congress in 1934 thought it would control insider trading. And section IV turns to the way courts and prosecutors now handle trades on inside information.

I. INTRODUCTION

When a firm is "in play," stock prices reflect what investors think an acquirer will pay for the firm. The stock may currently sell for $50 per share, but if they think Gekko will offer $70, they will bid up the price to a point near $70. If they conclude Gekko will not buy it after all, they will bid the price back down.

When no one is threatening an acquisition, stock prices reflect the present value of the expected net cash flows to a firm. A share of stock represents a stake in a business. When successful, the business generates a stream of cash. Because a share of stock represents a stake in that stream of cash, it sells at the present value of the net cash stream.[3]

As a result, the price of a stock will reflect the consensus among investors about the value of its future net cash flow stream. It will reflect their estimates of the amount of the cash, the odds that the cash flow will continue into the future, and its probable variability (its riskiness). Because investors will form these estimates with the information available to them, the price of the stock will incorporate all public information.

When economists call the stock market "efficient," they capture this "informational efficiency." They mean that market prices incorporate the information available about future cash flows. They may quarrel about the details: about just how quickly and how accurately the market impounds how much information.[4] But their quarrels disguise their more basic consensus: Market prices generally reflect the information available to investors about the size and variability of a firm's cash flow.

If stock prices reflect public information, then an investor with information not yet available to others stands to make money.

Suppose a Blue Star Airlines plane crashes. The Federal Aviation Administration (FAA) investigates whether faulty maintenance contributed to the accident. If the FAA clears the firm of misconduct, Blue Star will recover its reputation and skirt additional compliance costs. If the FAA blames the firm for the accident, Blue Star will need to invest heavily in new maintenance and will likely see a drop in reservations. If Gekko learns early that the agency will clear the firm, he can profitably buy stock before its price rises. If he learns it will censure the firm, he can either sell or "go short" with options to sell. If he buys the options, then once the price falls he can earn a profit equal to the difference between the now lower market price (at which he can buy the stock) and the higher option price (at which he can contractually sell it).

---

[3] The intuition is simple. Suppose a bank account pays 5 percent interest each year. An account with a $1,000 deposit will pay $1,000 × 0.05 = $50 per year. Conversely, if the market interest rate is 5 percent, then a bank account that pays $50 per year will have a present value of $50/0.05 = $1,000.

[4] For summaries of the debate, see, e.g., Stephen J. Choi & A. C. Pritchard, *Securities Regulation: The Essentials* 28-29 (Aspen 2008); William A. Klein & John C. Coffee Jr., *Business Organization and Finance: Legal and Economic Principles* 417-425 (9th ed., Foundation Press 2004); Ronald Gilson & Reinier Kraakman, *The Mechanisms of Market Efficiency*, 70 Va. L. Rev. 549 (1984).

II.   STATE LAW

rule (Officers are fiduciaries,) and agency law bans fiduciaries from earning secret profits in trades with their principals. Does it ban them from trading on inside information on the stock market? To explore the question, take *Goodwin v. Agassiz.*[5]

The Cliff Mining Company operated mines in northern Michigan. Two directors (one of them its president) learned of a geological theory that the firm might have copper on its land. They did not know that the land in fact contained copper, but they knew of a theory suggesting it did. They trusted the theory enough to buy more land for CMC, and they trusted it enough to buy more CMC stock for themselves.

Recall the agency law in Chapter 1. Suppose Brigid O'Shaughnessy holds a bronze avian statuette. She offers it for auction at Sotheby's. Art collector Armand Hammer—a stranger to O'Shaughnessy—buys it at high bid. He may know a "theory" that the statuette hides jewels under its enamel, but contract law imposes no duty on him to disclose the theory.[6] Through his private art historian, he may even know to a certainty that the statuette is covered with jewels. He still need not disclose his information.

Under agency law, Hammer (who is not an agent) may not lie, but he need not disclose. Even though he is not O'Shaughnessy's agent, he may not lie. He who lies commits a fraud—whether he owes a fiduciary duty or not. But if Hammer is not an agent, he need (not) speak at all. Unlike the always-fraudulent lie, silence becomes fraudulent only when a person has a duty to speak. Absent a fiduciary duty, Hammer has no duty to disclose, and absent that duty his silence is not a fraud.

Sam Spade serves as O'Shaughnessy's private detective. He works as her agent and owes her a duty of loyalty. To buy the statuette from her, he must disclose both his role in the purchase and any potentially relevant information he holds. He owes this duty whether he buys the statuette in person or through the anonymity of a Sotheby's auction.

The CMC directors worked for the firm. They owed it a fiduciary duty. They could not have bought land from it without disclosing their identity as the buyers. Neither could they have bought the land without disclosing information about copper deposits.

If the CMC directors owed a fiduciary duty to their firm's shareholders, they could not secretly buy stock from them either. But did they owe the shareholders a fiduciary duty? The *Goodwin* court thought not:

> The contention that directors also occupy the position of trustee toward individual stockholders in the corporation is plainly contrary to repeated decisions of this court and cannot be supported.[7]

---

[5] 186 N.E. 659 (Mass. 1933). On the legality of insider trading under state law, see generally Stephen M. Bainbridge, *Corporate Law* 274-280 (2d ed., Foundation Press 2009).

[6] Laidlaw v. Organ, 15 U.S. (2 Wheat.) 178 (1817).

[7] 186 N.E. at 660.

II.   State Law

The directors owed the firm a fiduciary duty, but not individual shareholders. If they owed those shareholders no duty of loyalty, they owed no duty to disclose. If they had no duty to disclose, they committed no fraud in secretly buying the stock.

In fact, though, not all courts held that officers and directors owed their shareholders no fiduciary duty. Some state courts did follow *Goodwin* and found a fiduciary duty only toward the corporation. Others did not. The *Zahn* court (Chapter 4, section III.C.3), for example, forthrightly declared that "a director represents all the stockholders in the capacity of trustee for them."[8]

Even if directors do owe their shareholders a fiduciary duty, they do not breach it when they sell their stock to an outside investor. Because the investor becomes a shareholder only upon the sale, the director assumes a fiduciary duty to the buyer only *after* the consummation of the transaction. It is not a pleasant distinction. Learned Hand disavowed it: "[I]t would be a sorry distinction to allow [a director or an officer] to use the advantage of his position to induce the buyer into the position of a beneficiary although he was forbidden to do so once the buyer had become one."[9] That, however, is what the law implies. At the time of the sale, the buyer is an unrelated third party. The director may know that the price of the stock will fall, but — absent Learned Hand's wishing it so — the director has no duty to say so.

And yet, even if the CMC directors do owe a fiduciary duty only to their firm, they still may not keep the profits they make.[10] Suppose they profit from undisclosed information about CMC. Even if the trade involves someone to whom they are not a fiduciary, they capture a gain they would not have earned absent their fiduciary responsibility. Recall the discussion in Chapter 1 (section IV.C): The British sergeant in Cairo did not profit from trades with the crown, but he made profits he could not have earned without his job. The court ordered him to pay the crown his earnings. The *Tarnowski* sales agent did not profit from trades with his employer the juke box renter, but he made profits he could not have earned without his job. The court ordered him to pay his employer his earnings.

By the same logic (a logic not raised in *Goodwin*), if the CMC directors earn profits by trading on information they learn from their principal, CMC, they owe their profits to it. They owe CMC the profits even if they earn them in trades with people to whom they have no fiduciary duty. As the Restatement (Second) of Agency put it:

> [If a director] has "inside" information . . . profits made by him in stock transactions undertaken because of his knowledge are held in constructive trust for the principal. He is also liable for profits made by selling constructive information to third persons, even though the principal is not adversely affected.[11]

---

[8] Zahn v. Transamerica Corp., 162 F.2d 36, 44 (3d Cir. 1947).

[9] Gratz v. Claughton, 187 F.2d 46, 49 (2d Cir.), *cert. denied,* 341 U.S. 920 (1951).

[10] A point nicely explained by Robert C. Clark, *Corporate Law* 306-309 (Little, Brown 1986).

[11] Restatement (Second) of Agency §389 cmt. c (1958). Restatement, Second, Agency, ©1958 by The American Law Institute. Reproduced with permission. All rights reserved.

189

Given that the CMC directors had no duty to disclose, they did not act fraudulently. By the logic of *Reading* and *Tarnowski* (Chapter 1, section IV.C), though, they still owed their profits to their employer.

III.   SECURITIES LAW

A.   *Introduction*

In modern courts, the action over insider trading no longer involves state agency law. Instead, it concerns federal securities law. When Congress passed this legislation in the 1930s, it intended the litigation over insider trading to turn on derivative suits to recover the trading profits to the firm. Although plaintiffs do still bring these suits, the focus of modern litigation no longer lies here either. Instead, it lies where Congress never intended: in criminal and civil suits brought under the antifraud rules.

The securities statutes require firms to disclose a host of information, and this section begins by examining those more general information disclosure requirements (section B): what the process entails (subsection 1), which stocks are subject to the rules (subsections 2-4), and what penalties flow from violating them (subsection 5). It then turns to the rules Congress designed to stop insider trading: §16(b) (section C). Section IV concludes with the very different rule that has since become the principal deterrent to insider trading in its stead: Rule 10b-5.

B.   *Registration*

1.   Introduction

With the country mired in depression but a landslide majority in Congress, Franklin D. Roosevelt took office. He immediately set about passing what would become the Securities Act of 1933 and the Securities Exchange Act of 1934. The 1933 Act mandated the disclosure (called "registration") of an elaborate array of information in the primary market for stocks and bonds (the market for securities issued directly by the company). The 1934 Exchange Act required even more stringent disclosure of the big firms that listed their shares on national exchanges, instituted a variety of other rules for the secondary market (the resale market), and created the Securities and Exchange Commission (SEC) to enforce it all (Chapter 6, sections I.C and D; Chapter 7, appendices I-II; Chapter 8, section III.C).

Scholars sometimes justify this regime by invoking market "failures" like the Dutch tulip "mania" of the seventeenth century or the South Sea "bubble" of the eighteenth. In fact, that these events occurred anything like the way historians describe them is dubious enough.[12] That rules like those imposed by the 1933 and

---

[12] Peter M. Garber, *Famous First Bubbles: The Fundamentals of Early Manias* (MIT Press 2000).

III. Securities Law

1934 Acts would have prevented either — or the 1929 crash and the ensuing depression — is unlikelier still.

As a result, eight decades after their enactment the question of how much the two securities statutes benefit investors (other than lawyers and accountants) remains open.[13] Note first that the optimal amount of fraud and other misconduct in any field — including the securities industry — is not zero. It is positive. Reducing crime and misconduct to levels near zero would entail massive policing costs and cause people to avoid a wide range of harmless activities for fear of erroneous prosecution. As the level of crime and misconduct approaches zero, these enforcement costs overwhelm the benefit from any additional frauds prevented. Consequently, scandals like Enron and Madoff do not show that anything is amiss. In any optimally policed society, some people will kill, and some people will rob. That Skilling and Madoff robbed might reflect a regulatory lapse, but not necessarily. Even under an optimal regulatory environment, some fraud and misconduct would remain.

Second, even without mandatory disclosure, firms will disclose a wide range of information about themselves. Firms must compete for funds, and investors appreciate (cost-justified) information. To attract investors and their money, firms will disclose information. Even if the news is bad, they will disclose it, lest the investors assume the even-worse worst. And if investors find the news not credible, the firms will hire independent auditors to certify it. They will do this — and before 1933 did do this — even if the law does not require it.

Third, the current securities law regime actually reduces the amount of some information firms disclose. At the same time that the regime mandates the disclosure of some information, it prohibits the disclosure of others. It bans statements that the SEC thinks too speculative, for example, or too uncertain. And by effectively requiring firms to clear their disclosures with the SEC in advance (see subsection 2 below), it delays the disclosure even of information it mandates. In fact, of course, investors want and need speculative information as well as certain information, and they want all of this information immediately.

Given these principles, the question posed by the mandatory disclosure regime is not whether investors should have access to information, or even to information checked by outside auditors. Investors will have that access even if the law does not require it. The question is whether the law should require firms to disclose information they otherwise would not disclose. Disclosure is not free, and shareholders pay its cost. Recall, however, that rational firms in competitive markets will (in order to raise funds) generally disclose all the

---

[13] The scholarly debate began with George J. Stigler, *Public Regulation of the Securities Market*, 37 J. Bus. 117 (1964). Important contributions include George Benston, *Required Disclosure and the Stock Market: An Evaluation of the Securities Exchange Act of 1934*, 63 Am. Econ. Rev. 132 (1973); Carol Simon, *The Effect of the 1933 Securities Act on Investor Information and the Performance of New Issues*, 79 Am. Econ. Rev. 295 (1989); Merritt Fox, *Retaining Mandatory Securities Disclosure: Why Issuer Choice Is Not Investor Empowerment*, 85 Va. L. Rev. 1371 (1999); Allen Ferrell, *Mandated Disclosure and Stock Returns: Evidence from the Over-the-Counter Market*, 36 J. Legal Stud. 1 (2007).

191

information that shareholders find cost-justified. The question is whether the law should require firms to disclose more.

2.   The 1933 Act Disclosure Regime

In theory, the 1933 Act does not limit a firm's ability to issue stock. It merely requires the firm to give investors the information they need to decide whether to buy the stock. In theory, it does not limit the universe of options available to investors. It merely clarifies the nature of the alternatives they face.

Put otherwise, the idealized 1933 Act is not like the bar exam; it is like the movie ratings system. The bar exam reduces competition in the legal services industry by limiting entry to the market through a set of criteria loosely tied to performance. The movie ratings purport not to limit the quality or quantity of sex and gore offered. Instead, they index that quality and quantity and help consumers pick the sex and gore they want. At least in theory, the idealized 1933 Act does for stock what the ratings do for movies. It does not stop any firm from selling its stock. Instead, it requires firms to disclose the type and level of risk involved in the stocks and lets investors pick the risk they want.

Table the debates about whether bar exams or movie ratings really do any of this. The material required by the 1933 Act may help investors pick stock (though they would have had access to much of the information without the Act anyway), but not the way this description implies. Although the Act requires firms to disclose material, it requires material that no "average" investor would ever understand. Not even sophisticated lawyers, law professors, and law students will understand it. Instead, the Act mandates material that only industry specialist securities analysts could possibly comprehend.

And yet, that is exactly the material that average investors need. "Average" investors (or lawyers, law professors, law students) benefit from information even if they can make no sense of it. If the industry specialists at the brokerage firms understand it, those specialists will buy and sell on the basis of the information. As they do, they will drive the price of the stock to levels that incorporate the information. At that point, all other investors (whether "ordinary" or otherwise) will buy and sell at prices that reflect the information disclosed. Buying at prices that reflect the information, they will be buying at prices that (ex ante) earn them a normal market return.

3.   Exemptions Under the 1933 Act

(a)   The §5 Requirement

Because the disclosure mandated by the 1933 Act costs such an enormous amount, people avoid it when they can. Were Edith, Aubrey, and John Ringling and their creditors (see Chapter 2, Introduction) to incorporate their circus today, they would not "register" the stock (i.e., file a disclosure document) with the SEC.

Instead, they would avoid it. To understand how they would avoid it, begin with §5 of the 1933 Act:

> (a) Unless a registration statement is in effect as to a security, it shall be unlawful for any person . . . :
>> (1) . . . to sell such security through the use or medium of any prospectus or otherwise. . . .
> (b) It shall be unlawful for any person, directly or indirectly —
>> (1) . . . to carry or transmit any prospectus relating to any security . . . unless such prospectus meets the requirements of [this Act]. . . .
> (c) It shall be unlawful for any person . . . to offer to sell or offer to buy . . . any security, unless a registration statement has been filed as to such security. . . .

Suppose the Ringlings incorporate the circus. They violate §5 if they offer the stock to anyone (including each other) before filing a registration statement (the disclosure document) with the SEC (subsection (c)). They violate §5 if they consummate a sale to anyone (including each other) before the filing takes effect (subsection (a)). And they violate §5 if their sales material (the prospectus) violates the terms of the Act (subsection (b)).

Substantively but not formally, the SEC holds a veto over registration statements submitted to it. According to §8(a), a registration statement automatically takes effect 20 days after a firm files it with the SEC. Formally, the Act thus gives the SEC no veto. Instead, it merely provides a 20-day waiting period. During that time, the firm can woo potential buyers. After 20 days, it can sell.

In fact, however, a firm must include in its registration statement the price at which it plans to sell the stock. Firms cannot realistically set that price 20 days in advance. By the end of the 20-day waiting period, they would need to change it — and amend the document to incorporate the new price. That amendment would start the 20-day waiting period all over again (§8(a)).

To avoid this conundrum, firms negotiate with the SEC. They file their registration statement. The SEC reviews it. It demands changes, they negotiate, and eventually they reach a mutually acceptable agreement. At that point, the Commission waives the waiting period for the amendment. The firm inserts the new, amended price, and sells the stock.

(b) The §2 "Security"

The Ringlings would not be able to avoid registration on the ground that the ownership stakes they give each other are not "securities." The 1933 Act (the 1934 Act includes a similar definition) defines a "security" in §2(a)(1):

> The term "security" means any note, stock, treasury stock, security future, bond, debenture, evidence of indebtedness, . . . investment contract, . . . any put, call, straddle, option, or privilege on any security, . . . or, in general, any interest or instrument commonly known as a "security." . . .

A share of "stock" is a security. A "bond" is a security. And — the catchall — an "investment contract" is a security. According to the Supreme Court, an investment contract is

> [any] contract, transaction or scheme whereby a person invests his money in a common enterprise and is led to expect profits solely from the efforts of a . . . third party.[14]

Given that limited partners cannot exercise control (Chapter 2, appendix I), they earn their returns "solely from the efforts" of other people. As a result, limited partnership interests are always "investment contracts" and always "securities." From time to time, courts have even swept pyramid-sales scams and horse-breeding schemes into the "investment contract" category. Given that general partners always share control (Chapter 2, section I.A), they do not earn their returns "solely" from the work of others. As a result, general partnership interests are never "securities."

(c) §2 and Limited Liability Companies

LLCs vary. In some, investors share control over the firm's operation. In others, they do not. As the Fourth Circuit put it in *Robinson v. Glynn*:

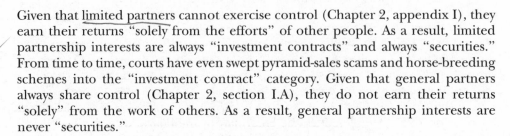

> LLCs are particularly difficult to categorize under the securities laws . . . because they are hybrid business entities that combine features of corporations, general partnerships, and limited partnerships.[15]

Obviously, this variability complicates the question of whether the organizers of an LLC need to register the equity interests with the SEC.

Consider the facts of *Robinson*. Thomas Glynn of GeoPhone Corporation approached investor James Robinson for funds. Soon, GeoPhone Company, LLC, would inherit the business of GeoPhone Corporation. Glynn assured Robinson that the firm would implement his new "Convolutional Ambiguity Multiple Access" technology. In fact, it did not. Without knowing that it did not, Robinson loaned the LLC $1 million and then agreed to convert the $1 million into equity along with another $14 million and later to invest $10 million more besides.

Upon learning that GeoPhone never implemented CAMA technology, Robinson sued in federal court for securities fraud. He also brought fraud claims under state law, but the court's jurisdiction depended on whether Robinson had a valid federal claim. In turn, whether he had a federal claim depended on whether his stake in the LLC constituted a "security."

---

[14] SEC v. W. J. Howey Co., 328 U.S. 293, 298-299 (1946).
[15] 349 F.3d 166, 174 (4th Cir. 2003).

III. Securities Law

GeoPhone called the equity stakes "shares" and "securities." Notwithstanding the last clause of §2(a)(1) quoted earlier, the court did not care:

> While this may be persuasive evidence that Robinson and Glenn believed the securities laws to apply, it does not indicate that their understanding was well-founded. Just as agreements cannot evade the securities laws by reserving powers to members unable to exercise them, neither can agreements invoke those same laws simply by labeling commercial ventures as securities.[16]

To the court, GeoPhone's equity interests were "securities" only if they were "investment contracts." Following the Supreme Court (language quoted in subsection (b) above), the Fourth Circuit asked whether Robinson expected to exercise some control over GeoPhone. If he could protect himself through that control, he did not hold a security. If his investment left him at the mercy of the others, he did.

Robinson had negotiated elaborate controls. He controlled two seats on the GeoPhone board, he served as vice chairman of the board, he participated in a four-person executive committee, and he worked as GeoPhone treasurer. Given his power at the firm, the court reasoned that he did not hold an "investment contract." Accordingly, he had not bought securities and could not now assert a securities fraud claim. Equity stakes in some LLCs might be securities, the court suggested, but not here.

(d) The §4 Exemptions

Rather than argue that their stakes in the firm were not securities, the Ringlings would have avoided registration through §4 of the 1933 Act. The section gives two exemptions relevant here:

> The provisions of section 5 shall not apply to:
> (1) transactions by any person other than an issuer, underwriter, or dealer.
> (2) transactions by an issuer not involving any public offering.

Suppose again that the Ringling partners incorporate the circus. They offer and sell stock only to one another and to the few men who have lent the firm money. Because they offer the stock only to a small group, they have not offered it to the public. Accordingly, §4(2) exempts their sale from the registration requirement of §5. Note that the provision does not exempt the security itself. Instead, it exempts only a particular transaction — the sale of stock from the circus (the "issuer") to the Ringlings and their creditors.

Suppose that Edith Ringling retires from the circus and gives her stock to son Robert. Given that §4(2) applies only to "transactions by an issuer," it would not exempt this transfer to Robert. After all, the firm is the issuer — not Edith. Because

---

[16] *Id.* at 172.

Edith is not an underwriter or dealer either, however, her transfer to Robert falls within §4(1).

That said, only the ill-advised would ever rely on the statutory language of §4. Planning to attend her tenth high school reunion, suppose Aubrey Haley (part of the Ringling family) decides to buy some circus stock to sell to her classmates. If she bought the shares "with a view to . . . [its] distribution" to her classmates, she could be an "underwriter" (see §2(a)(11)). She could no longer claim the §4(1) exemption when she does sell the stock to her classmates.

The unfortunate consequences of issuing stock to an "underwriter," however, go much further. The size of a firm's initial offering includes not just the people to whom the firm's organizers offer the stock, but the people to whom any underwriters offer it too. As a result, the size of the circus's own initial offering would include not just the Ringlings and the creditors. It would include all the classmates to whom Aubrey (as underwriter) later offered the stock. If that total were sufficiently large, then the entire distribution would constitute a "public offering" — and be ineligible for the §4(2) exemption. Through her later sale, Aubrey would have disqualified the circus even from an exemption on its initial issue to the Ringling family and its creditors.

Because of these risks, well-advised closely held corporations issue their shares only through elaborate "safe harbors." These safe harbors appear at length in regulations and rules under the 1933 Act and form the heart of the securities regulation course in law school.[17] Typically, the SEC keys the safe harbors to the size of the firm, the number of people offered the stock, and the wealth and sophistication of the people contacted. It traditionally looked at

> (1) the number of offerees; (2) the relationship of the offerees to each other and to the issuer; (3) the size of the offering [i.e., the amount of money raised]; (4) the number of units [i.e., shares, in the case of stock] offered; and (5) the manner of the offering [i.e., the type and quantity of advertising].[18]

As the Supreme Court explained in *SEC v. Ralston Purina Co.*,[19] whether to call an offering a private placement turns in part on whether the investors offered the stock can "fend for themselves." If a firm offers only a few shares for a few dollars to a few people, those factors militate toward finding a private placement. They do not, however, end the inquiry. The question also turns on "whether the particular class of persons affected need[s] the protection of the Act." To that question, the Fifth Circuit returned in the *Doran* case (see subsection 4(b) below).

---

[17] For a careful exposition of the safe harbors, see Choi & Pritchard, *supra* note 4; William A. Klein, John C. Coffee Jr. & Frank Partnoy, *Business Organization and Finance* 452-454 (11th ed., Foundation Press 2010).

[18] Choi & Pritchard, *supra* note 4, at 301, summarizing Securities Act Release No. 285 (Jan. 24, 1935).

[19] 346 U.S. 119, 124 (1953).

III. Securities Law

4. Penalties

(a) The Statutory Structure

When business executives or firms violate the securities statutes, they face harsh liabilities. Consider three provisions: §§11, 12, and 10(b). The three sections cover overlapping (but not identical) transactions, require different elements of proof, and impose different consequences.

Section 11. Section 11 of the 1933 Act provides:

> (a) In case any part of the registration statement . . . contained an untrue statement of a material fact or omitted to state a material fact required to be stated therein or necessary to make the statements therein not misleading, any person acquiring such security (unless it is proved that at the time of such acquisition he knew of such untruth or omission) may . . . sue —
>
>> (1) every person who signed the registration statement;
>>
>> (2) every person who was a director . . . ;
>>
>> (4) every accountant, engineer, or appraiser . . . who has with his consent been named as having prepared or certified any part of the registration statement . . . , with respect to the statement in such registration statement . . . which purports to have been prepared or certified by him;
>>
>> (5) every underwriter. . . .
>
> (e) The suit . . . may be to recover . . . the difference between the amount paid for the security . . . and (1) the value thereof as of the time such suit was brought, or (2) the price at which such security shall have been disposed of in the market before suit, or (3) the price at which such security shall have been disposed of after suit but before judgment if such damages shall be less than [subsection (1)]: *Provided,* That if the defendant proves that any portion . . . of such damages represents other than the depreciation in value of such security resulting from such part of the registration statement . . . not being true . . . , such portion of or all such damages shall not be recoverable. . . .

Note several characteristics of a §11 claim. (a) Plaintiffs must show a misstatement (or material omission) in a registration statement. They need not show that they read the statement (much less that they relied on it), but they may not sue over oral misstatements or over private placements exempted from the registration requirement. (b) A defendant may defend by showing that the plaintiff knew that the statement was untrue. (c) Plaintiffs need not show privity. They may sue the issuer (the issuer signs the registration statement under subsection (a)(1)), the directors, those experts (like accountants) who misstated something in the portion of the registration statement they certified, and the underwriters. (d) Plaintiffs may recover the fall in the price of the security, but defendants may defend by showing that the price fell for other reasons.

Section 12. Section 12 provides an overlapping but quite different recovery regime:

> (a) In general. — Any person who —
> (1) offers or sells a security in violation of section 5, or
> (2) offers or sells a security . . . by means of a prospectus or oral communication, which includes an untrue statement of a material fact or omits to state a material fact necessary in order to make the statements . . . not misleading (the purchaser not knowing of such untruth or omission), and who shall not sustain the burden of proof that he did not know, and in the exercise of reasonable care could not have known, of such untruth or omission,
> shall be liable . . . to the person purchasing such security from him, who may sue . . . to recover the consideration paid for such security . . . , or for damages if he no longer owns the security.
> (b) Loss causation. — In an action described in subsection (a)(2), if the person who offered or sold such security proves that any portion or all of the amount recoverable under subsection (a)(2) represents other than the depreciation in value of the subject security resulting from such part of the prospectus or oral communication . . . not being true or omitting to state a material fact required to be stated therein or necessary to make the statement not misleading, then such portion . . . shall not be recoverable.

Consider several ways in which this §12 differs from §11. (a) A plaintiff may sue the person who sold a security to him if the seller did not register it and did not have an exemption (subsection (a)(1)). (b) A plaintiff may sue the person who sold him a security if the person either used an untrue sales document, said something untrue, or misleadingly omitted to say something. (c) A defendant may defend by showing that he did not know that the statement was untrue and could not reasonably have known. (d) A plaintiff may sue for rescission. If he already sold the stock, he may sue for damages. (e) The defendant may defend by showing that the stock price fell for reasons unrelated to the misstatement.

Section 10(b). Last, consider §10(b) of the 1934 Act:

> It shall be unlawful for any person . . . To use or employ . . . any manipulative or deceptive device or contrivance in contravention of such rules and regulations as the Commission may prescribe. . . .

The section obviously is not self-enforcing. Instead, it turns on the rules the SEC writes. The most important of those rules is Rule 10b-5:

> It shall be unlawful for any person . . .
> (a) To employ any device, scheme, or artifice to defraud,
> (b) To make any untrue statement of a material fact or to omit to state a material fact necessary in order to make the statements made . . . not misleading, or

> (c) To engage in any act, practice, or course of business which operates . . . as a fraud or deceit . . . ,
>
> in connection with the purchase or sale of any security.

Rule 10b-5 bans fraud. As such, it gives rise to criminal sanctions, but courts have also implied private causes of action.[20] Even in those private suits, however, a plaintiff will need to show scienter (the defendant's state of mind).[21] Nevertheless, sometimes a plaintiff will find a suit under Rule 10b-5 more advantageous than one under §11 or 12.

Note that a Rule 10b-5 plaintiff must actually have bought or sold a security. He cannot claim he would have bought a share but for the misstatement.[22] An investor who planned to buy stock but decided not to do so because of the defendant's statement cannot sue. The rule covers all securities, whether registered or not.

And a plaintiff must assert deception (a point that recurs in the *O'Hagen* case, see section IV.F.3 below). He cannot claim simply that the defendant engineered an unfair transaction.[23] An investor who loses money when a director manipulates the corporate process might have a claim under state law. He will have a claim under Rule 10b-5 only if deception was part of the scheme.

(b) Section 12 — Doran v. Petroleum Management Corp.[24]

William Doran invested in Petroleum Management Corp., a California limited partnership drilling for oil. For his stake, he paid $25,000 down and guaranteed a $114,000 note from PMC. Under the terms of the note, PMC would pay the installments due out of its production payments. In fact, however, PMC overproduced its wells, and regulators closed it for a year. PMC defaulted, and the creditor sued Doran. In turn, Doran sued to rescind his purchase of the firm's securities under §12 on the grounds that PMC had not registered them.

Doran's claim turned on the argument that PMC should have registered his limited partnership interest. He did not claim lack of sophistication on his own part. He did not argue that anyone misrepresented anything when he bought. He did not suggest that PMC violated the partnership agreement by overproducing the wells. He claimed merely that it should have registered the offering.

Given that limited partnership interests are securities, the question turned on whether the limited partnership issue constituted a public offering. It raised only modest funds and involved little advertising. Although few parties bought the securities, the test goes to the number of people offered them. The court found eight and concluded that the number was small enough to qualify as a private placement.

---

[20] Superintendent of Ins. v. Bankers Life & Cas. Co., 404 U.S. 6, 13 n.9 (1971).

[21] Ernst & Ernst v. Hochfelder, 425 U.S. 185 (1976).

[22] Blue Chip Stamps v. Manor Drug Stores, 421 U.S. 721 (1975).

[23] Santa Fe Indus. v. Green, 430 U.S. 462 (1977).

[24] 545 F.2d 893 (5th Cir. 1977).

The court remanded, however, on the question of whether the other offerees had the information they needed to evaluate the security. "Even [Doran's] 20-20 vision with respect to the facts underlying the security would not save the exemption if any one of his fellow offerees was in a blind."[25] It noted that all the offerees were sophisticated enough. The question was whether they had the information they needed:

> [T]here must be sufficient basis of accurate information upon which the sophisticated investor may exercise his skills. Just as a scientist cannot be without his specimens, so the shrewdest investor's acuity will be blunted without specifications about the issuer.[26]

(c)   Section 11 — Escott v. BarChris Construction Corp.[27]

BarChris made bowling alleys. During the bowling boom of the late 1950s, it grew exponentially. When the boom collapsed, it found itself short of funds. It issued debentures (unsecured bonds) in 1961, but filed for bankruptcy and defaulted in 1962.

Investors who bought the debentures sued under §11 on the grounds that the registration statement hid the firm's precarious financial straits. Several of the defendants then pleaded "due diligence" defenses — yes we missed the inaccuracies, but we had diligently checked it for mistakes. These defenses arise under §11(b) (paragraphs added and indentation altered):

> Notwithstanding the provisions of subsection (a) of this section no person, other than the issuer, shall be liable . . . who shall sustain the burden of proof . . . (3) that
>
> (A) as regards any part of the registration statement not purporting to be made on the authority of an expert, . . . he had, after reasonable investigation, reasonable ground to believe and did believe . . . that the statements therein were true and that there was no omission to state a material fact . . . necessary to make the statements therein not misleading; and
>
> (B) as regards any part of the registration statement purporting to be made upon his authority as an expert . . . ,
>
> (i) he had, after reasonable investigation, reasonable ground to believe and did believe . . . that the statements therein were true and that there was no omission to state a material fact . . . necessary to make the statements therein not misleading, or
>
> (ii) such part of the registration statement did not fairly represent his statement as an expert . . . ; and
>
> (C) as regards any part of the registration statement purporting to be made on the authority of an expert (other than himself) . . . , he had no reasonable ground to believe and did not believe . . . that the statements therein were

---

[25] *Id.* at 902.
[26] *Id.* at 903.
[27] 283 F. Supp. 643 (S.D.N.Y. 1968).

III. Securities Law

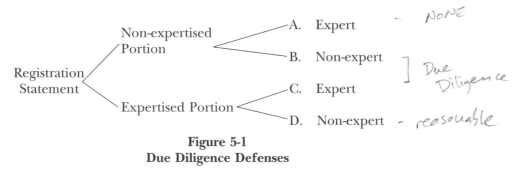

Figure 5-1
Due Diligence Defenses

untrue or that there was an omission to state a material fact . . . necessary to make the statements therein not misleading. . . .

It helps to divide the registration statement into halves: the half drafted in the name of the professional experts and the half drafted in the name of the nonprofessional directors. Outside accountants are the most common experts, but engineers and other professionals appear occasionally too. The accountants audit the financial statements. Other experts certify various professional reports.

The division of the registration statement into halves generates four sets of due diligence defenses (see Figure 5-1).

1. *Zone A:* With respect to the "non-expertised" portion of the statement ("expertise" is a verb in the world of the 1933 Act), the experts are not liable. By §11(a)(4), they are liable only on the portions they certify.
2. *Zone B:* With respect to the non-expertised parts, the non-experts can avoid liability for misstatements if they exercise "due diligence": if, "after reasonable investigation, [they had] reasonable grounds to believe and did believe . . . that the statements therein were true" (§11(b)(3)(A)).
3. *Zone C:* With respect to the expertised portion of the registration statement, the experts face the same due diligence standard that the non-experts faced on the non-expertised portion: "[A]fter reasonable investigation, [they had] reasonable grounds to believe and did believe . . . that the statements therein were true" (§11(b)(3)(B)).
4. *Zone D:* With respect to expertised parts, the non-experts can avoid liability by meeting an easier standard: They "had no reasonable ground to believe and did not believe . . . that the statements therein were untrue" (§11(b)(3)(C)).

The investors sued several defendants. First, they sued the issuer BarChris. Section 11(b) gives the issuer no due diligence defenses, but BarChris had no money. Whether it had a defense made no difference. Second, the investors sued BarChris's president and vice president—two gentlemen by the names of

Vitolo and Pugliese. The two men argued that with their limited education they had no idea what the registration statement said. The court suggested that they lied and that their education made no difference anyway. As the court in *Francis* (Chapter 4, section II.A.3) noted, directors face an objective minimum standard. If they cannot meet it, they should not serve. Third, the investors sued various board members. They each asserted a due diligence defense, but the court held they had not investigated the firm aggressively enough: They asked some questions, received cursory replies, and let the matters drop. Fourth, they sued the accounting firm. The accountant, too, the court noted, had not checked the material given him carefully enough. The court added that he was liable only on the numbers he certified; about the data he did not claim to audit, he was not responsible.

Fifth, the investors sued Grant, of the Perkins, Daniels, McCormick & Collins law firm. BarChris was Perkins Daniels's client, and Grant was a partner. He drafted the registration statement, but the investors did not sue over any malpractice in drafting. Instead, they sued him as a director. He too claimed his due diligence defense, and his too the court rejected: He did not check what the BarChris officers told him aggressively enough. Indeed, the court held him to a higher standard than the other directors. Because he was corporate counsel, "more was required of him in the way of reasonable investigation than could fairly be expected of a director who had no connection with this work."[28]

That the lawyer could not rely on what the BarChris officers told him goes to why some law firms prohibit their partners from serving on client boards. Clients retain the men and women as lawyers because they value their judgment and expertise. For just that reason, sometimes they also want them on their boards. Should a partner agree, however, by the terms of §11 he will sometimes need to refuse to take a client at his word. Rather than place their partners in that extremely uncomfortable position, some firms simply ban them from serving on client boards.

C. Short-Swing Profits

1. The Statute

When Congress passed the Securities Exchange Act in 1934, it addressed insider trading directly.[29] The provision was §16(b):

> For the purpose of preventing the unfair use of information which may have been obtained by such beneficial owner, director, or officer . . . , any profit realized by him from any purchase and sale, or any sale and purchase, of any equity security . . . within any period of less than six months, . . . shall inure to and be recoverable by the issuer. . . .

[28] *Id.* at 690.
[29] *See generally* Donald C. Cook & Myer Feldman, *Insider Trading Under the Securities Exchange Act*, 66 Harv. L. Rev. 385 (1953).

III.   Securities Law

> This subsection shall not be construed to cover any transaction where such beneficial owner was not such both at the time of the purchase and sale, or the sale and purchase, of the security. . . .

In turn, by "such beneficial owner" Congress referred to §16(a), which defined him as a person who owned:

> more than 10 per centum of any class of any equity security . . . which is registered pursuant to section 12 of [the 1934 Securities Exchange Act].

The basic rule then is simple: If any officer, director, or 10 percent shareholder buys low and sells high within six months, he owes his profits to the firm. The logic behind the rule is also simple: identify a class of transactions likely to involve insider trading and require people who engage in those transactions to pay their gains to the firm. By the agency principles of *Reading* and *Tarnowski* (Chapter 1, section IV.C), fiduciaries owe any profits they earn from opportunities they obtain through their positions to their employer. If corporate officers earn profits from inside information, they owe their profits to their firm.

2.   The Philosophy

With that short summary, however, any philosophical discussion of §16(b) ends—for the section does not concern philosophy. It concerns mechanics. Think "rule against perpetuities" for the corporate bar. In §16(b), form almost always triumphs over substance. Courts treat the section as a prophylactic statute, and lawyers and law students do best by ignoring any "conceptual jurisprudence" and applying a few ruthlessly mechanical rules.

William O. Douglas explained why §16(b) takes this approach. Douglas has entered U.S. legal history for his years on the Supreme Court—for reflexively voting left on virtually any case it heard, for offering legal standing to trees,[30] even for his flamboyantly young third and fourth wives. But Douglas had started at the preeminently stuffed-shirt Cravath firm. After a short stint in the Pacific Northwest, he joined the Columbia faculty and from there moved to Yale. The quintessential young man in a hurry, he soon became commissioner to the new SEC and in 1937 became chairman. He knew the 1933 and 1934 Acts and cared about them. In a 1973 dissent, he explained the reason for the mechanical approach:

> The purpose of §16(b) is stated in its preamble: "preventing the unfair use of information which may have been obtained by such beneficial owner, director, or officer by reason of his relationship to the issuer. . . ." The congressional investigations that led to the enactment of the Securities Exchange Act revealed widespread use of confidential information by corporate insiders to gain an unfair

---

[30] *Sierra Club v. Morton*, 405 U.S. 727 (1972) (Douglas, J., dissenting).

advantage in trading their corporations' securities. . . . Unlike other remedial provisions of the Act, . . . Congress drafted §16 (b) as an objective rule, designed to have a clearly "prophylactic" effect. . . . As Thomas Corcoran, a principal draftsman of the Act, explained to Congress: "You hold the director, irrespective of any intention or expectation to sell the security within 6 months after, because it will be absolutely impossible to prove the existence of such intention or expectation, and you have to have this crude rule of thumb, because you cannot undertake the burden of having to prove that the director intended, at the time he bought, to get out on a short swing."[31]

3. The Mechanics

The principal rules to applying §16(b) follow.

(a) Companies

The section covers those and only those firms that register their securities under the 1934 Act. These are the very largest companies (those with at least $10 million in assets and 500 shareholders) and those companies that trade their securities on national exchanges.[32] This is a subset of the firms that register under the 1933 Act. By contrast, note that the antifraud Rule 10b-5 applies to any corporation (even if not registered under the 1933 Act) and even to limited partnerships.

Parenthetically, note the different sweep of the various securities law provisions: (a) Start with all investment interests in a firm. (b) Of those investment interests, some (but only some) qualify as "securities" — corporate stock is a security, a general partnership interest is not. If a "security," the investment interest is subject to the antifraud provisions of Rule 10b-5. (c) Among all securities, some are subject to the registration requirements of the 1933 Act. This Act provides the various remedies discussed in *Doran* and *BarChris* above. (d) Among the securities registered under the 1933 Act, some (those of the largest firms and of firms listed on national exchanges) must also be registered under the 1934 Act. (e) And of the securities registered under the 1934 Act, "equity securities" (see below) are subject to §16(b).

(b) Equity Securities

Section 16(b) applies only to trades in equity securities: stock, convertible debt, and options to buy and sell stock and convertible debt. By contrast, the 1933 Act and Rule 10b-5 cover both equity and debt securities.

---

[31] Kern County Land Co. v. Occidental Petro. Corp., 411 U.S. 582, 608-609 (1973) (Douglas, J., dissenting).

[32] 1934 Act, §12(g); Rule 12g-1.

III. **Securities Law**

(c) Recovery to the Firm

Traders disgorge their profits to the firm — not to the government and not to the investor from or to whom they bought or sold the securities. If a corporation will not sue to recover §16(b) profits, shareholders may file a derivative suit on its behalf. For filing the suits, lawyers may collect attorneys' fees.[33]

(d) Six-Month Window

Firms may recover only those gains on matching pairs of purchases and sales that occur within six months. The logic behind the six-month window apparently lay in the fact that taxpayers in 1934 paid a tax on capital gains at lower rates if they held an asset for six months or more. Hence, anyone who sold within six months must have had — so the logic went — inside information. In fact, of course, traders without inside information may sell stock immediately if they need cash; traders who bought on inside information may hold the stock indefinitely if it fits within their portfolio.

(e) Purchase and Sale, Sale and Purchase

The section does not just cover low-priced purchases followed by higher-priced sales. As the language of the statute implies, it covers cases where an investor sells stock high and then, within six months, buys it back low.

(f) Specified Insiders

The section applies only to three statutorily defined categories of insiders: directors, officers, and holders of more than 10 percent of the firm's stock. The scope of "director" is generally clear enough: members of the board. For the most part, "officer" is clear too: the firm's "president, principal financial officer, principal accounting officer . . . , any vice-president . . . in charge of a principal business unit, division, or function . . . , and other officer who performs a policy-making function."[34] The 10 percent ownership test is more complex, as *Reliance Electric* and *Foremost-McKesson* (subsection 4 below) illustrate.

Officers and directors fall within the scope of the section if they are such at the time of the first of the paired transactions, even if they resign or are fired by the time of their second.[35] If anyone is an officer or a director, he is of course subject to §16(b) even if he holds less than 10 percent of the stock.

[33] *See* Gilson v. Chock Full O'Nuts Corp., 326 F.2d 246 (2d Cir. 1964); Smolowe v. Delendo Corp., 136 F.2d 231, 241 (2d Cir.), *cert. denied,* 320 U.S. 751 (1943).
[34] Rule 16a-1(f).
[35] *See* Rule 16a-2.

(g) Stock Classes

To determine the percentage of stock that a shareholder owns, courts examine each class of equity security separately. If an investor holds more than 10 percent of any one class, he is then liable on matching transactions within any (including any other) class. Suppose an investor owns 15 percent of Class A. If he now buys Class B shares and resells them at a higher price within a six-month window, he is liable for the difference under §16(b).

Note that courts do not match purchases and sales across classes. An investor can buy Class A stock at $10 per share and sell Class B stock at $20 per share. The two transactions do not generate §16(b) liability.

(h) Matching Transactions

To calculate a trader's liability under §16(b), courts pair whichever transactions (in a given stock class) within a six-month window maximize the amount he owes.[36] For example, suppose a corporate officer engages in the following transactions:

Jan. 1: Buy 10 shares at $30/share.
Jan. 2: Buy 10 shares at $5/share.
Jan. 3: Buy 10 shares at $60/share.
Jan. 4: Sell 15 shares at $40/share.
Jan. 5: Sell 15 shares at $1/share.

What, if anything, does the officer owe? If courts followed "first-in, first-out" (FIFO) accounting principles, the officer would have sold on January 4 the 10 shares he bought on January 1 and 5 of the shares he bought on January 2. He would owe ($40 − $30) × 10 + ($40 − $5) × 5 = $275.

If courts followed "last-in, first-out" (LIFO) principles, the officer would have sold on January 4 the 10 shares he bought on January 3 plus 5 of the shares he bought on January 2. He lost money on the January 3 shares. Because §16(b) allows no offset for losses, he would simply owe ($40 − $5) × 5 = $175.

Suppose the officer placed the stock certificates he received on January 1, 2, and 3 in different file folders. To sell on January 4, he deliberately picked 10 of the January 3 shares and 5 of the January 1 shares. If §16(b) allowed him to pick the shares used to calculate the firm's recovery, he would owe only ($40 − $30) × 5 = $50.

But courts do not — not — use any of these rules. Harsh and unprincipled as it may seem, they instead match whatever purchases and sales will generate the largest liability. In this case, they would deem the officer to have sold on January 4 the 10 shares he bought on January 2 and 5 of the shares he bought on January 1. His §16(b) liability would thus be ($40 − $5) × 10 + ($40 − $30) × 5 = $400. They would ignore his January 3 purchases because they cannot match them

---

[36] Smolowe v. Delendo Corp., 136 F.2d 231 (2d Cir.), cert. denied, 320 U.S. 751 (1943).

with a higher-priced sale. They would ignore his January 5 sales because they cannot match them to a lower-priced purchase.

Note that the officer lost money over the period: $[(\$40 \times 15) + (\$1 \times 15)] - [(\$60 \times 10) + (\$5 \times 10) + (\$30 \times 10)] = \$615 - \$950 = -\$335$. That does not matter. In calculating §16(b) liability, courts ignore whether the investor lost money over the period as a whole.

(i) Options

For many years, courts took the §16(b) law of options from the Supreme Court's decision in *Kern County*.[37] The case involved a failed takeover attempt, a defensive merger, and an option contract negotiated as part of the eventual settlement. The question for the Court was whether the merger, the option acquisition, and the option exercise qualified as purchases or sales under §16(b). To decide it, the Court asked whether the investor involved (i) had had a choice about the transaction, (ii) had had access to confidential information, or (iii) could have influenced the shape and timing of the transaction. Sensible questions all, but they decidedly do not reflect the prophylactic tradition of §16(b). By asking them, the Court seemed to signal a reprieve from the relentless formalism that otherwise characterized §16(b) jurisprudence.

Although *Kern* still stands for the principle that substance can sometimes (on rare occasions) triumph over form in §16(b), it no longer gives the rule for options. Instead, in 1991 the SEC issued rules that take a different approach. Under these rules, the acquisition of an option to buy or sell has the same effect as the purchase or sale of the underlying stock. In calculating §16(b) liability, courts thus can pair the purchase of an option to buy with either a matching sale of the stock itself or an offsetting option to sell. Explained the SEC:

> [H]olding derivative securities is functionally equivalent to holding the underlying equity securities for purposes of section 16, since the value of the derivative securities is a function of or related to the value of the underlying equity security. . . . Just as an insider's opportunity to profit commences when he purchases or sells the issuer's common stock, so too the opportunity to profit commences when the insider engages in transactions in options or other derivative securities that provide an opportunity to obtain or dispose of the stock at a fixed price. . . . The functional equivalence of derivative securities and their underlying equity securities for section 16 purposes requires that the acquisition of the derivative security be deemed the significant event, not the exercise.[38]

[37] Kern County Land Co. v. Occidental Petro. Corp., 411 U.S. 582 (1973).
[38] SEC Rel. No. 34-28869 (Feb. 21, 1991).

Accordingly, the SEC's Rule 16a-4(a) now provides:

> For purposes of Section 16 of the Act, both derivative securities and the underlying securities to which they relate shall be deemed to be the same class of equity securities. . . .

4. Litigation

The litigation over the scope of the 10 percent ownership threshold illustrates the (almost) relentless formalism of §16(b). Take Emerson Electric. It bought 13.2 percent of the stock of Dodge Manufacturing through a tender offer (Chapter 8, section III), and Dodge then negotiated a defensive merger into its ally, Reliance Electric.[39] Faced with the prospect of becoming a minority shareholder in a firm it could not control, Emerson negotiated a pair of sales: one that took its holdings barely below 10 percent and another that disposed of the rest.

Emerson argued that it was not a 10 percent shareholder at the time of its second sale, and the Supreme Court agreed. That it had planned the two sales as an integrated package did not matter. It owned more than 10 percent when it sold its first block. It owned less than 10 percent when it sold the second. It was subject to §16(b) rules only on the first sale.

But should Emerson have had any §16(b) liability at all? Immediately before its tender offer, it had owned no stock in Dodge. If it did not own more than 10 percent when it bought the 13.2 percent, then it had no purchase within the ambit of §16(b) to match against even its first sale. Emerson won on this ground at the trial court, but—apparently leery of looking too greedy—did not make the argument at the Supreme Court.

Provident Securities took up where Emerson feared to tread.[40] Provident owned securities, but wanted to liquidate. Foremost agreed to buy its securities. For them, it would give Provident cash and convertible debt ("equity securities" for §16(b) purposes). Because the convertible debt, if converted, would have constituted more than 10 percent of Foremost stock, this transaction made Provident a "beneficial owner" under §16(b). Provident then distributed the debt and cash to its shareholders and liquidated.

Provident was not subject to §16(b). Although it became a "beneficial owner" covered by the section after it acquired the Foremost debt, it did not own a 10 percent stake immediately before the acquisition. The test, the Court explained, was whether Provident owned the stake "before the purchase." It did not—and accordingly was not liable under §16(b).

---

[39] Reliance Elec. Co. v. Emerson Elec. Co., 404 U.S. 418 (1972).
[40] Foremost-McKesson, Inc. v. Provident Secs. Co., 423 U.S. 232 (1976).

III. Securities Law

5. Examples

To illustrate these principles, consider some simple examples.

(a) Gekko

Gordon Gekko hires aspiring stockbroker Bud Fox. Fox's father is a mechanic at Blue Star Airlines. Blue Star had an accident, but Fox's father has learned that the FAA will clear the airline of misconduct.

(1) Fox's father tells his son the news, his son tells Gekko, and Gekko buys.

No liability under §16(b). Gekko is not an officer or a director of Blue Star. Immediately before buying the Blue Star stock, neither was he a 10 percent share-holder. Note that there was no matching sale within six months anyway.

(2) Same as (1), but Gekko carries out the following transactions:
Jan. 1: Buys 6 percent stake in Blue Star at $10 per share.
Jan. 2: Buys 8 percent stake in Blue Star at $15 per share.
Jan. 3: Buys 10 percent stake in Blue Star at $50 per share.
Jan. 4: Sells all of his Blue Star stock at $30 per share.

No liability.
Immediately before buying the January 1 stock, Gekko owned no Blue Star stock. Hence, the initial 6 percent purchase is not subject to §16(b).
Immediately before buying the January 2 stock, Gekko owned only 6 percent of Blue Star. The 8 percent he bought that day put him over the 10 percent line, but — under *Foremost-McKesson* — the question is whether he had 10 percent immediately before the transaction. Thus, the 8 percent purchase is not subject to §16(b) either.
Immediately before buying the January 3 stock, Gekko owned more than 10 percent of Blue Star. Hence, this purchase is subject to §16(b). Immediately before selling his stock on January 4, Gekko owned 24 percent, so this sale is subject to §16(b) as well. However, Gekko bought his January 3 stock at $50 per share and sold it on January 4 at $30 per share. Given that he sold the shares for less than he paid, he owes nothing under §16(b).

(b) Boesky

Securities arbitrageur Ivan Boesky bribes Michael Levine, employee at the securities firm Drexel Burnham Lambert, to tell him about takeovers planned by Drexel customers. He then buys (in one transaction for each target firm) the target stock in advance.
No liability. Boesky was not an officer, a director, or a 10 percent shareholder of the target firms before the purchase. Neither was there a matching sale within six months.

(c) Hammer

Armand Hammer is CEO of Occidental Petroleum, which in turn is traded on the New York Stock Exchange. Consider the following hypothetical trades.

(1) In January of 1981, Hammer buys ten shares of Occidental at $50 per share. By late March, the stock has climbed to $70 per share. Hammer knows that the firm plans to disclose negative information that will cause the stock to plummet to $20. On March 31, he sells ten shares at $70 per share.

Hammer owes Occidental ($70 − $50) × 10 = $200.

Note that Hammer avoided a $70 − $20 = $50 fall per share. That calculation is irrelevant to his §16(b) liability. Under §16(b), he simply owes the price he received less the price he paid. Given that Hammer is CEO, the percentage of shares he owns is also irrelevant.

(2) Same as (1), but Hammer has no information about an impending price drop.

Hammer still owes the $70 − $50 = $20 per share gain.

(3) Hammer sells 10 shares at $70 in April and buys back 10 shares in May at $50.

Hammer owes $70 − $50 = $20 per share, or $200 total. He owes the same amount whether he buys low and sells high or sells high and buys back low.

(4) Hammer buys ten shares at $10 in January, ten shares at $20 in February, and fifty shares at $70 in March. He sells all his shares at $30 in April.

Note first that Hammer lost money over the four months. To buy the 70 shares, he paid ($10 × 10) + ($20 × 10) + ($70 × 50) = $3,800. He sold all 70 shares at $30, giving him $2,100. Hence, he lost $1,700 on the series of transactions.

Nonetheless, Hammer is still liable under §16(b). The court simply ignores the losses and imposes liability on those transactions it can pair to generate a gain. Hammer owes [($30 − $10) × 10] + [($30 − $20) × 10] = $300.

(5) Hammer buys 10 shares at $10 in January, 10 shares at $20 in February, and 50 shares at $70 in March. He sells 15 shares at $30 in April.

Hammer owes [($30 − $10) × 10] + [($30 − $20) × 5] = $250. The court matches those purchases and sales that generate the largest §16(b) liability.

IV.   RULE 10b-5

A.   *Introduction*

William O. Douglas was an odd justice, and his §16(b) is an odd statute. The section declares itself against insider trading, but makes no attempt to determine whether a trader has inside information. It catches many who trade on no inside information and misses many who trade on much. It demands that an unsuccessful defendant disgorge his earnings, but requires nothing else.

For insider trading, state law offers just as odd a framework. Some states let those who trade with an insider sue. Other states let only the corporation sue. And still others let investors sue, but only if the insider traded with that investor in person. And if insider trading constitutes criminal fraud, state prosecutors seem not to notice.

Given this apparent "problem,"[41] the SEC might have lobbied for a new statute; instead, in 1961 John Kennedy appointed Columbia law professor William Cary (later of "the states are racing for the bottom so let's federalize corporate law" fame; Chapter 3, appendix II) as head of the SEC. To Cary and his supporters, the SEC needed to radically change. "It was imperative that the markets *should* change," recalled one colleague. "They were in trouble. Collapse of self-regulation on the American Stock Exchange had highlighted the abuses rampant in an overheated stock market."[42] Never mind what an "overheated" stock market might be. Cary and his colleagues thought they knew it when they saw it. The markets needed to change, and to change the markets the SEC needed to change.

Rather than obtain new legislation, Cary manipulated an otherwise ignored 1942 antifraud rule: Rule 10b-5. The rule said nothing about insider trading. It did ban fraud, so the trick for Cary was to declare insider trading fraudulent. He did it in an administrative opinion in an uncontested settlement, *In re Cady, Roberts.*[43] By that sleight-of-hand, a colleague recalled, he "converted an obscure SEC antifraud rule into a potent weapon for striking down the shady stock market dealings of corporate insiders."[44] Put less generously—but at least as accurately—he took a rule designed for one purpose and used it against an activity for which Congress had designed another rule entirely.

Cady, Roberts involved a trader with nonpublic information, and Cary—writing the SEC opinion—announced that his trades violated Rule 10b-5:

> An affirmative duty to disclose material information has been traditionally imposed on corporate "insiders," particularly officers, directors, or controlling

---

[41] Only "apparent" problem. The normative case for banning all insider trading (rather than allowing firms to opt out of any ban) is far from clear. *See generally* Henry Manne, *Insider Trading and the Stock Market* (Free Press 1966); Stephen M. Bainbridge, *Insider Trading Regulation: The Path Dependent Choice Between Property Rights and Securities Fraud*, 52 SMU L. Rev. 1589 (1999); Dennis W. Carlton & Daniel R. Fischel, *The Regulation of Insider Trading*, 35 Stan. L. Rev. 857 (1983).

[42] Walter Werner, *Bill Cary and the SEC*, 84 Colum. L. Rev. 767, 767 (1984) (italics in original).

[43] In re Cady, Roberts & Co., 40 S.E.C. 907 (1961).

[44] Werner, *supra* note 42, at 767.

stockholders. We, and the courts, have consistently held that insiders must disclose material facts which are known to them by virtue of their position but which are not known to persons with whom they deal and which, if known, would affect their investment judgment.[45]

As legal history, the statement was preposterous — and preposterous in a way that Cary would have known full well. The SEC had taken no such position, and neither had the courts. Cary was moving the SEC into an entirely new field and praying that the courts would follow.[46]

B. The Beginning — Texas Gulf Sulphur

1. The Case

And the courts did follow.

After publishing his uncontested settlement opinion in *In re Cady, Roberts*, Cary turned to Texas Gulf Sulphur.[47] In late 1963, the mining company was exploring lands in northern Ontario for ore. Near Timmins, it recovered ore samples that suggested it might have found a rich deposit. In order to buy the surrounding land cheaply, it ordered its employees to keep quiet.

"The Sunday morning after [the engineer] took his sample," *Life* magazine reported, "Kenneth H. Darke, the firm's field geologist in the area, sloshed out to the site. Samples of core brought up that morning looked even more promising, and Darke quickly realized he had a big problem on his hands. The hole had been drilled in the corner of a small, square 160-acre plot, owned by Texas Gulf, that was completely surrounded by land belonging to others."

TGS needed to buy the surrounding land and needed to buy it quickly before its neighbors realized how much the land was worth. To avoid suspicion, it mailed its ore samples from the post office in the neighboring town. Even the telephones were risky. "One of Timmins' telephone operators caught a snatch of talk about the assay report," reported *Life*. "Rumors began to spread."[48]

Note the free-wheeling deception: TGS knew that the land probably contained an extraordinarily valuable deposit of ore. Its neighbors did not. If it disclosed the deposit to those neighbors, they would demand a high price for their land. Rather than pay the high price, TGS bought the land without disclosing the deposit. It did not lie to the owners. But neither did it give them the information they needed (and it held) to value the land appropriately.

---

[45] 40 S.E.C. at 911.

[46] Donald C. Cook & Myer Feldman, *Insider Trading Under the Securities Exchange Act*, 66 Harv. L. Rev. 385, 408 (1953).

[47] SEC v. Texas Gulf Sulphur Co., 401 F.2d 833 (2d Cir. 1968) (en banc), *cert. denied sub nom.* Coates v. SEC, 394 U.S. 976 (1969); *see generally* Kenneth G. Patrick, *Perpetual Jeopardy: The Texas Gulf Sulphur Affair — A Chronicle of Achievement and Misadventure* (Macmillan 1972).

[48] Chris Welles, SEC vs. Texas Gulf *Raises Sticky Questions: Bonanza Trouble*, Life 29 (Aug. 6, 1965).

IV. Rule 10b-5

In hiding its ore strike, TGS acted within the law. John Marshall (in a classic contracts case) assured Laidlaw & Company that it did not need to tell the sellers of the tobacco it bought about the 1815 peace treaty with England — even though the treaty changed the value of the tobacco.[49] By the same logic, a mining company that discovered a hidden vein of ore did not need to tell its neighbors what it knew and they did not. The law does not let people lie about what they know, but neither does it require them to volunteer it. They can keep what they know to themselves — and buy land cheap.

But could TGS officers buy stock from shareholders without disclosing the information? Several of them did, particularly corporate vice president Charles Fogarty. If the officers served as agents to their shareholders, they owed a duty (as fiduciaries) to disclose both their identity and any important relevant information they held. If they bought without disclosing, they committed a fraud. Under the new logic Cary had outlined in the *Cady, Roberts* settlement, they violated Rule 10b-5.

Recall that not all courts held that corporate officers owed fiduciary duties to their shareholders. The officers served as agents for the firm, and some courts (like *Goodwin*) argued that they owed no duties to the shareholders. If officers traded on private information they acquired through their agency, some (not all) courts followed the *Tarnowski–Reading* logic to require them to pay their profits to the firm. But given that the officers owed no duty to the person with whom they traded, they committed no fraud when they traded on the undisclosed information.

2. Insider Trading

Cary's SEC ignored this common law entirely, and the Second Circuit happily did the same. It prominently declared Cary's *Cady, Roberts* settlement the law:

> The essence of the Rule [10b-5] is that anyone who, trading for his own account in the securities of a corporation, has "access, directly or indirectly, to information intended to be available only for a corporate purpose and not for the personal benefit of anyone" may not take "advantage of such information knowing it is unavailable to those with whom he is dealing," i.e., the investing public. Matter of Cady, Roberts & Co., 40 SEC 907, 912 (1961).[50]

It then transformed Cary's declaration into the famous duty to "abstain or disclose":

> Thus, anyone in possession of material inside information must either disclose it to the investing public, or, if he is disabled from disclosing it in order to protect corporate confidence, or he chooses not to do so, must abstain from trading in or recommending the securities concerned while such inside information remains undisclosed.[51]

---

[49] Laidlaw v. Organ, 15 U.S. (2 Wheat.) 178 (1817).
[50] *Texas Gulf Sulphur*, 401 F.2d at 848.
[51] *Id.*

213

The court did not base the outcome on any fiduciary duty. It did not derive its duty to abstain or disclose from any relationship between the insider and the investor. Instead, it located the duty in the securities market itself:

> The core of Rule 10b-5 is the implementation of the Congressional purpose that all investors should have equal access to the rewards of participation in securities transactions. It was the intent of Congress that all members of the investing public should be subject to identical market risks — which market risks include, of course the risk that one's evaluative capacity or one's capital available to put at risk may exceed another's capacity or capital. The insiders here were not trading on an equal footing with the outside investors.[52]

This "intent of Congress" is not anything Congress expressed in §10(b). Instead, in §10(b) it simply banned fraud, and nondisclosure is only fraudulent if someone has a duty to disclose. The question of whether an officer owes a fiduciary duty to his shareholders matters precisely because the officer would have a duty to disclose only if he owed that duty. Section 10(b) bans only fraud, and a corporate officer who trades on inside information acts fraudulently only if some *other* law (like the agency law of fiduciary duties) imposes a duty to disclose the inside information.

Nonetheless, the Second Circuit declared its newfound duty to abstain or disclose an intrinsic part of the securities market. Buyers and sellers in other markets have no duty to disclose private information. TGS, the Second Circuit assured its readers, could quite properly buy the land from its neighbors without telling them about the minerals it contained:

> We do not suggest that material facts must be disclosed immediately; the timing of disclosure is a matter for the business judgment of the corporate officers entrusted with the management of the corporation within the affirmative disclosure requirements promulgated by the exchanges and by the SEC. Here, a valuable corporate purpose was served by delaying the publication of the [mineral] discovery.[53]

But to the Second Circuit, real estate markets were different from stock markets. TGS could buy the land without disclosing the discovery, but TGS officers could not buy stock without doing so. Through *Cady, Roberts* and now *TGS*, explained one observer, William Cary had "creat[ed] an insider trading prohibition where none had been before."[54]

3. Materiality

Even under *TGS*, insiders did not need to disclose all nonpublic information. Instead, they needed to disclose only "material" information. Matters contingent

---

[52] *Id.* at 851-852.
[53] *Id.* at 850 n.12.
[54] Jerry W. Markham, *A Financial History of Modern U.S. Corporate Scandals* 378 (M. E. Sharpe 2006).

or minor enough not to rise to that level they could safely ignore. In fact, however, under the court's test any information important enough to matter to the insider was important enough to be "material."

Formally, the court set the standard for materiality by the "reasonable man":

> "The basic test of materiality . . . is whether a *reasonable* man would attach impor-
> tance . . . in determining his choice of action in the transaction in question. . . ." . . .
> This, of course, encompasses any fact ". . . which in reasonable and objective con-
> templation *might* affect the value of the corporation's stock or securities. . . ." . . .
> The speculators and chartists of Wall and Bay Streets are also "reasonable" investors
> entitled to the same legal protection afforded conservative traders.[55]

Effectively, though, if an insider cares about a piece of information, it is material. Materiality turns on what an insider does with the information. If he thinks it important enough to trade on it, it is material. If he finds it trivial or dubious enough to ignore, it may be immaterial:

> [A] major factor in determining whether the [mineral] discovery was a material
> fact is the importance attached to the drilling results by those who knew about it.[56]

Sensible as the test may seem, it eliminates "materiality" as an issue in real-world litigation. If an insider trades on a piece of information, it is material. If he does not trade on it, it may have been immaterial. But given that he did not trade, he will not be sued, and the case will not appear in court. The test resembles nothing so much as the medieval trial by ordeal: Throw the witch in the water; if she swims to shore, the water rejected her, so the community will burn her at the stake; if she drowns, the water accepted her, and she must have been innocent, but — alas — she is also dead.[57] So, too, here: If an insider trades on the information, it is material and he goes to jail; if he does not trade, it may have been immaterial, but because he did not trade, he also made no money.

4.   The Press Release

TGS also expands the scope of activities "in connection with" the purchase or sale of a security. Recall that Rule 10b-5 bans fraud only "in connection with" such a purchase or sale. In *TGS*, the company issued a cryptic press release denying the rumors. It claimed that some of the rumors "exaggerate[d]" the scope of the find, but admitted that the Timmins hole might have scored a hit.

Although the company issued the press release, it neither bought nor sold any stock. Arguably, it did not issue the statement "in connection with" a purchase or

---

[55] 401 F.2d at 849.

[56] *Id.* at 851.

[57] *See generally* John H. Langbein, Renee Lettow Lerner & Bruce P. Smith, *History of the Common Law* 44 (Wolters Kluwer 2009).

sale. Not so. If it issued a statement that was of the "sort that would cause reasonable investors to rely" on it, then — according to the court — it issued a statement in connection with a purchase or sale.

5.   Conclusion

As its name implied, the TGS firm had begun its business in Texas. By the mid-1970s, it conducted the bulk of its activities in Canada. A Canadian firm eventually bought a 30 percent stake in it, and by 1980 the firm could boast George H. W. Bush on its board. In 1981, a French firm took control.

Fogarty himself thrived. If the firm thought his stock purchases a breach of duty, his career does not show it. By 1968, he was president of TGS, and by 1973, the CEO. "Fogarty was the driving force and the major instrument in achieving [the] expansion in products" that made TGS "a diversified natural resources company," reported one biographer.[58] Rather than his downfall, the Timmins find was a crucial accomplishment: "Perhaps the crowning achievement of the exploration effort was the discovery of the ore body in Timmins, Ontario, one of the most important mines in North America." His professional peers did not consider his insider trading problematic either. In 1976, they elected him to the National Academy of Engineering.

C.   Chiarella

1.   The Case

TGS left a basic issue unresolved. On the one hand, the case purported to apply Rule 10b-5. The rule bans "fraud," and nondisclosure was fraudulent at common law only if a person had a duty to disclose. On the other hand, the case declared insider trading a violation of Rule 10b-5 without looking for such a duty. It announced simply that "[i]t was the intent of Congress that all members of the investing public should be subject to identical market risks." The question left unresolved was whether courts would follow the common law of fraud or the expansive and untethered language of *TGS*.

In 1980, the Justice Powell pushed the Supreme Court to stay with the common law.[59] Vincent Chiarella had worked as a "mark-up man" for one of the major financial printers, Pandick Press. Pandick handled the disclosure documents required under securities law, and those documents included the material filed in tender offers (Chapter 8, section III).

Take (the fictional) Gordon Gekko. Suppose he plans a hostile takeover of Larry Wildman's Anacott Steel. To comply with the tender offer rules, he will need

---

[58] Albert P. Gagnebin, *Charles Franklin Fogarty*, in *Memorial Tributes: National Academy of Engineering* vol. 2, 83, 84 (NAE 1984).

[59] Chiarella v. United States, 445 U.S. 222 (1980); *see After the Fall*, Wall St. J. 1 (Nov. 18, 1987).

to submit an elaborate document to the SEC. To assemble the material, representatives from his firm and his investment bank will meet during the day with their lawyers. They will discuss their strategy, the target's possible defenses, and how best to describe it all in the SEC filing. At the end of the day (at least through the 1970s and 1980s), the law firm associate assigned to the case will take the draft they produce to Pandick and hand it to Chiarella. While the associate naps, eats, or runs on a treadmill, Chiarella will incorporate the day's notes into the document. The associate will proofread the draft, return to the law firm, drink coffee, change into a fresh shirt, and start the day all over again.

Each evening, the associate will bring a marked-up copy of the document to Chiarella, and each night Chiarella will incorporate the changes. To ensure that news of the planned takeover not leak to the target, the lawyers will not name the firms in the document. Instead, they will refer to them pseudonymously. In the 1975 Emhart Corporation tender offer for USM Corporation stock, for example, the lawyers handed Chiarella documents that discussed "Arabia Corp.'s" tender offer for "USA Corp."[60] Only on the night before the acquirer announces the takeover will the associate identify the acquirer and target and ask Chiarella to swap the pseudonyms for the firms' true names.

Necessarily, however, the lawyers will include a wide variety of information about the firms in the document. Even if they do not name the firms, they will describe their industries, give their financials, and report their stock prices. Rather than sleep, Chiarella apparently spent his days at the New York Public Library and used public documents to identify the targets. He then bought their stock. Over the course of 1975 and 1976, he traded on five acquisitions and made $30,000.

2. The Law

At trial, Chiarella found himself convicted of criminal Rule 10b-5 violations. In his defense, he argued that "because he was not an insider of the target corporations . . . , he did not owe a fiduciary duty to target shareholders who sold before the tender offer was announced." He worked for the acquirer, after all, not the target. If he owed a fiduciary duty to anyone, he owed it to the acquirer. Yet he bought the stock of the target. Owing target shareholders no fiduciary duty, he owned them no duty to disclose. He "was not subject to the 'disclose or abstain' rule of *Texas Gulf Sulphur*," and if not under a duty to disclose he did not violate Rule 10b-5 in buying their stock.[61]

Writing for the Second Circuit, Judge Irving Kaufman (of *Flying Tiger* fame; Chapter 3, section II.E.2) repeated the broad *TGS* rule: Insider trading is wrong because it violates the integrity of the market. It is "apodictic" (huh?) "that betting

---

[60] United States v. Chiarella, 588 F.2d 1358, 1363 (2d Cir. 1978), *rev'd*, 445 U.S. 222 (1980).
[61] *Chiarella*, 588 F.2d at 1365.

on a 'sure thing' [is] anathema to the ideal of 'fair and honest markets,'" and if it is anathema to the ideal, it is fraud to the law:

> In enacting the securities laws, Congress did not limit itself to protecting share-holders from the peculations of their officers and directors. A major purpose of the antifraud provisions was to "protect the integrity of the marketplace in which securities are traded." . . . Anyone, corporate insider or not, who regularly receives material nonpublic information may not use that information to trade in securities without incurring an affirmative duty to disclose.[62]

As with Cary's *Cady, Roberts*, this is fictional history. "Congress" did no such thing. To police insider trading, it enacted only §16(b). And given that Congress said no such thing, the Supreme Court (Justice Powell) reversed:

> At common law, misrepresentation made for the purpose of inducing reliance upon the false statement is fraudulent. But *one who fails to disclose material information prior to the consummation of a transaction commits fraud only when he is under a duty to do so.* And the duty to disclose arises when one party has information "that the other [party] is entitled to know because of a fiduciary or other similar relation of trust and confidence between them."[63]

Chiarella owed no duty to disclose because he stood in no relationship of trust and confidence to the target shareholders:

> [T]he element required to make silence fraudulent—a duty to disclose—is absent in this case. No duty could arise from [Chiarella's] relationship with the sellers of the target company's securities, for [Chiarella] had no prior dealings with them. *He was not their agent, he was not a fiduciary, he was not a person in whom the sellers had placed their trust and confidence.* He was, in fact, a complete stranger who dealt with the sellers only through impersonal market transactions.[64]

Through his job at Pandick, Chiarella may have owed a fiduciary duty to the acquirer, but he did not buy the acquirer's stock. He bought the target's stock, and neither he nor anyone for whom he worked owed any duty to those target share-holders. Absent a duty, he committed no fraud when he bought their shares without telling them what he knew.

3. The Dissent

Justice Burger dissented. In buying the target's stock, he reasoned, Chiarella "misappropriated" information about the takeover. Chiarella worked for Pandick,

---

[62] *Id.*
[63] *Chiarella*, 445 U.S. at 227-228 (italics added).
[64] *Id.* at 232 (italics added).

and Pandick had posted prominent signs banning employees from trading on any information they acquired. When Chiarella traded anyway, he broke Pandick rules. He "misappropriated" the information and committed a fraud on Pandick and its clients. In turn, this fraud constituted a Rule 10b-5 violation: "a person who has misappropriated nonpublic information has an absolute duty to disclose that information or to refrain from trading."[65] To Burger, Rule 10b-5 transformed Pandick's ban from an in-house infraction to a federal crime.

The Burger dissent raised several points. First, as Powell noted in his response to Burger, the logic came too late. Chiarella was convicted by jury, but the prosecution did not present Burger's misappropriation theory to the jury. An appellate court may not affirm on legal theory B a conviction obtained under theory A.

Second, if the legality of insider trading (under Rule 10b-5) turned on the Pandick's house rule, then Pandick itself could change the scope of the insider trading ban. If Gekko wanted to pay lower salaries, he could invite his staff to buy target stock instead. If he wanted to pay his financial printer less, he could invite it (and its mark-up men) to buy target stock too.

Third, Pandick banned the trades only because the SEC told it to ban the trades. It did not post the signs banning the trades voluntarily. It posted them because the SEC was claiming that the trades were a crime and prosecuting printers who made them.[66] To reason that the trades were a crime because Pandick posted the signs gives circularity a bad name.

D. Tippee Liability

1. The Equity Funding Firm

Suppose an insider does not trade. Suppose instead that he (as tipper) passes the information to a friend (tippee) who trades. The opinion in *Dirks v. SEC*[67] (again by Powell) traces the law involved. The story begins with Raymond Dirks, a stock analyst with a broker-dealer firm who specialized in the insurance industry. In March 1973, he took a phone call from one Ronald Secrist. Secrist had worked for the California life insurance firm of Equity Funding. He had just been fired, and he was unhappy—very unhappy.

The firm was a monumental fraud, declared Secrist. He described "forgery parties," "girls" closeted for days in windowless offices popping pills, ties to the mob. In short order, he made what the Justice Department later called "a series of

---

[65] *Id.* at 240 (Burger, J., dissenting).

[66] *Chiarella*, 588 F.2d at 1369.

[67] Dirks v. SEC, 463 U.S. 646 (1983); *see generally* Amicus Curiae Brief of the U.S. in Support of Reversal, Dirks v. SEC (Dec. 30, 1982); Raymond L. Dirks & Leonard Gross, *The Great Wall Street Scandal* (McGraw-Hill 1974); Ronald L. Soble & Robert E. Dallos, *The Impossible Dream: The Equity Funding Story: The Fraud of the Century* (G. P. Putnam's Sons 1975); Brian Trumbore, *Ray Dirks and the Equity Funding Scandal*, StockandNews.com (Feb. 6, 2004), *available at* http://www.buyandhold.com/bh/en/education/history/2004/ray_dirks.html.

detailed but nearly incredible allegations." By his account, "the company had produced large numbers of spurious insurance policies to inflate its sales revenues." It "threaten[ed] the lives of employees who objected to the fabrications." And it could credibly threaten them because "its top officers had Mafia connections."[68]

Given that his clients held large stakes in Equity Funding, Dirks flew to Los Angeles. Through "two weeks of concerted effort, at times resembling something from detective fiction," wrote the Court of Appeals, he "investigated and confirmed rumors of massive fraud." Secrist had wanted Dirks to tell his clients, and he did. He wanted those clients to dump their Equity Funding stock, and they did. As the Justice Department put it, he wanted to trigger "large-volume securities sales that would lead to a full investigation: 'by jarring the stock, he would jar the . . . corporate officers.'" He "would . . . rattle the Wall Street financial community" and "someone would take action very quickly."[69]

Secrist would later explain his tactic as a last resort. Employees had tried to report the fraud before, he reported. When they did (in the Justice Department's words), they had been "brushed aside with a comment that that's a ridiculous story." Worse, sometimes they had "found . . . the information . . . relayed back to Equity Funding." This then "placed [them] in personal jeopardy" — recall the mob connections — "as a result of having gone there."[70]

Employees had tried the SEC, and they had tried insurance regulators. Both had ignored the reports. Again, the Justice Department:

> As early as 1971, the SEC had received allegations of fraudulent accounting practices at Equity Funding, [and] on March 9, 1973, an official of the California Insurance Department informed the SEC's regional office in Los Angeles of Secrist's charges of fraud. . . . The SEC's staff attorney "stated that similar allegations had been made about Equity Funding before by disgruntled employees." He nonetheless recommended "delaying any type of inspection of the Equity Funding operations until next year . . . absent further corroboration."[71]

Employees could not stop the fraud by going to the regulators, but Secrist did stop it by going to Dirks. "Largely thanks to Dirks one of the most infamous frauds in recent memory was uncovered and exposed," concluded the Court of Appeals.[72] Of the firm's 99,000 life insurance policies, 56,000 were fake. Of its $117 million in loan receivables, $62 million were fake.[73]

It was bizarrely complex fraud. The "actual creation of a phony life insurance policy file was a time-consuming process," explained one account. It "included construction of an individual's personal and medical history — in short, the same

[68] Amicus Curiae Brief of the U.S., *supra* note 67.
[69] *Id.*
[70] *Id.*
[71] *Id.*
[72] 681 F.2d 824, 829 (D.C. Cir. 1982).
[73] Soble & Dallos, *supra* note 67, at 12-13.

detailed information found on a real insurance policy." To do this work, Equity Funding maintained "the infamous Maple Drive Gang, a group known only to the handful of Equity Funding individuals who were in on the fraud scheme."[74]

The Gang — the "girls" — worked out of a windowless office in a separate building. When insurance auditors demanded sample contracts to examine, they went to work. "Starting from scratch, [they] would use a manual that gave them choices for answers to the dozens of policy application questions." It took time. "On a very good day we could manufacture between fifteen and twenty policies," recalled one employee. "It was like an assembly line."

And as suddenly as it started, it would stop. The auditors would leave, and the work would disappear. "We either had to have one hundred policies out in a week or there was nothing to do for months," complained the employee.

> To liven things up in that drab, windowless office where the air conditioning constantly broke down and the roof leaked, [workers] would hold parties at the drop of a hat. . . . Pills also were popular at Maple Drive, especially the pill called Quaalude, a sedative, which . . . made the girls "relaxed" at the Maple Drive happenings.[75]

2. The Law

Perhaps Dirks thought he deserved a medal. Equity Funding had run a massive scam. He had shut it down. But hell hath no fury like a bureaucrat scorned. The SEC came not to praise Dirks but to bury him, and for tipping his clients, they censured him under Rule 10b-5.

Dirks sued to clear his name. As Powell set up the problem, Secrist (as insider) was the tipper, Dirks was the tippee, and his clients (who traded on the information) were the secondary tippees. Tippees and secondary tippees violate Rule 10b-5, Powell reasoned, when a tipper breaches a fiduciary duty in tipping the information and the tippee knows or has reason to know of the breach.

> [A] tippee assumes a fiduciary duty to the shareholders of a corporation not to trade on material nonpublic information only when the insider has breached his fiduciary duty to the shareholders by disclosing the information to the tippee and the tippee knows or should know that there has been a breach.[76]

Applied here, the principle exonerated Dirks: (i) Secrist tipped Dirks because he wanted to stop the fraud; (ii) stopping fraud is a good thing; (iii) thus, Secrist breached no fiduciary duty in tipping Dirks; and (iv) if Secrist the tipper breached no duty, then Dirks and his clients could freely trade.

---

[74] *Id.* at 138.
[75] *Id.* at 139-140.
[76] 463 U.S at 660.

Unfortunately, Powell did not leave well enough alone. He decided to elaborate instead, and in elaborating introduced a bizarrely cramped notion of fiduciary duty:

> [T]he test is whether the insider personally will benefit, directly or indirectly, from his disclosure. Absent some personal gain, there has been no breach of duty to stockholders. And absent a breach by the insider, there is no derivative breach.[77]

The test is not whether the tippee gains; it is whether the tipper does. Dirks and his clients gained, but that did not matter. Secrist did not gain, so Dirks and his clients could freely trade.

In fact, of course, agents do not owe their principals one fiduciary duty — they owe two: a duty of loyalty and a duty of care. They do indeed breach their duty when they earn for themselves a secret profit. But they also breach it when they act carelessly. Take an example. A law firm shares its office building with an investment bank. Returning home late one night, an associate takes an elevator down. At the investment bank's floor, two employees join him. They continue their conversation in the elevator, and by the time it reaches the ground floor the associate has learned of a planned tender offer.

May the associate trade on this information? Employees should not discuss confidential material in public elevators. When they do, they breach their duty of care. Because they did not "gain" from their carelessness, however, their breach does not "count" under *Dirks*. The tippers (the investment bank employees) did not gain, so the tippee (the associate) may freely trade.

3.   Additional Observations

In the course of the opinion, Powell makes several other unrelated points of note. First — and most basically — an investor does not violate Rule 10b-5 simply by trading on an informational advantage. Market specialists will always have an informational advantage, and so they should. Only by trading on that advantage will they cause market prices to reflect the information about the firm. And only if market prices reflect that information can uninformed investors trade at prices that reflect the consensus estimate (among specialists) of the firm's anticipated performance. Ban trades on an informational advantage and the market's informational efficiency falls:

> Imposing a duty to disclose or abstain solely because a person knowingly receives material nonpublic information from an insider and trades on it could have an inhibiting influence on the role of market analysts, which the SEC itself recognizes is necessary to the preservation of a healthy market.[78]

The broad language in *TGS* about "identical market risks" is not the law.

Second, for purposes of the legal formula *Dirks* articulates, a firm's lawyers and accountants are insiders rather than tippees. Suppose Gekko runs a publicly traded

---

[77] *Id.* at 662.
[78] *Id.* at 658.

firm. He retains a lawyer on behalf of the firm and tells him about his plans. The lawyer buys stock in Gekko's firm for his personal account. Gekko does not breach a fiduciary duty in telling the lawyer about his plans for the firm. If Gekko were the "tipper" and the lawyer the "tippee," then under *Dirks* the lawyer could freely trade.

According to Powell's formula in footnote 14 of *Dirks*, the lawyer instead is an insider. More precisely, he is what has come to be called a "temporary insider":

> Under certain circumstances, such as where corporate information is revealed legitimately to an underwriter, accountant, lawyer, or consultant working for the corporation, these outsiders may become fiduciaries of the shareholders.[79]

Last, an outsider becomes a "temporary insider" only if he accepts an appointment with a firm. Suppose Armand Hammer asks Gekko for funds. Occidental is embarking on a Venezuelan oil project, and Hammer would like to exploit it through a joint venture with Gekko's firm. Gekko asks why Hammer thinks the venture will succeed. Hammer explains that the Venezuelan government has promised him a lucrative oil concession. Gekko declines Hammer's invitation, but reasons that Occidental will make money from concession and buys Occidental stock. May he do so?

Powell answers the question — yes, Gekko may — in footnote 22. There, he cites with apparent approval a case involving just that question:

> [T]he defendant investment banking firm . . . investigated another corporation that was a possible target of a takeover bid by its client. In the course of negotiations the investment banking firm was given, on a confidential basis, unpublished material information. Subsequently, after the proposed takeover was abandoned, the firm was charged with relying on the information when it traded in the target corporation's stock. . . . In the absence of any fiduciary relationship, the Court of Appeals found no basis for imposing tippee liability on the investment firm.[80]

Because Gekko refused Hammer's invitation, he does not become a temporary insider. One becomes an agent only if he agrees to the agency, and Gekko does not agree. He does not become a fiduciary to Occidental, and Hammer breaches no fiduciary duty in giving him the information — so Gekko may freely trade (but see subsection 5 below).

4. Look-Alike Facts

Dirks is a 1983 opinion, and in 1984 the Oklahoma federal court heard a case involving an investor who claimed to have overheard a tip at a track meet.[81] As the investor told the story, he was basking in the sun on the bleachers behind

---

[79] *Id.* at 655 n.14.
[80] *Id.* at 662 n.22.
[81] SEC v. Switzer, 590 F. Supp. 756 (W.D. Okla. 1984).

a CEO and his wife. He had been to New York, the CEO told his wife, and had talked with Morgan Stanley about his firm's impending merger. What is more, he added, several potential acquirers had bid for his firm. None of this news was public. The sunbathing investor bought stock in the CEO's firm, the firm announced the merger at a high price, and the investor pocketed a profit.

The SEC sued the investor for violating Rule 10b-5, and the court acquitted. It reasoned from *Dirks*: The CEO was the tipper, the investor was the tippee, and tippees violate Rule 10b-5 by trading on nonpublic information only when the tipper breaches a fiduciary duty by tipping them the information. The tipper breaches that duty, in turn, only if he earns a "personal gain" by giving the tip.

Here, the CEO merely explained his plans to his wife. He had just returned from meetings in New York, his wife was herself about to leave town for a week, and the track meet gave the two a rare chance to synchronize their calendars. Other than a domestic armistice, he earned no "personal gain" from telling his wife his business affairs. He may well have breached his duty of care by discussing his plans in public, but under *Dirks* duty of care violations did not count. Only duty of loyalty violations that earn the tipper a gain mattered.

The story of the inadvertent tip fits *Dirks*—indeed, it fits the *Dirks* template almost too well. Consider the identities of the people involved. The sunbathing investor was Barry Switzer, head coach of the University of Oklahoma Sooners football team. Switzer was nothing if not successful. He had amassed one of the "winning-est" college records in history, had coached three national university championship teams, and would soon take the Dallas Cowboys to a Super Bowl victory.

But Switzer would also resign from the university in disgrace. He would not resign because of insider trading. He would resign because the league would put the Sooners on probation. Among other things, five of his players would be arrested for serious felonies—including soliciting cocaine, rape, and a shooting.

And the tipping CEO was not a random spectator. He was, in the court's words, "a supporter of Oklahoma University football." He collected Switzer's autographs for his children. His firm sponsored "Switzer's football show, 'Play Back.'" He held season tickets to Sooners games, and Switzer routinely upgraded them.

Did Switzer's story fit *Dirks* too well? One account of the case fairly oozes with suspicion:

> At the time, Switzer was the head football coach at the University of Oklahoma and Phoenix [the target firm] was the sponsor of Switzer's television show. Its CEO, George Platt, was a prominent Oklahoma booster, a season ticket holder, and a personal acquaintance of Switzer. He also was the source of Switzer's inside information. Sounds like a classic case of tipping. But Switzer won.
>
> What was his defense? Switzer testified that he ran into Mr. Platt at an Oklahoma track meet. They spoke to one another, and then Switzer laid [*sic*] down on a row of bleachers behind Platt in order to sunbathe. While sunbathing, Switzer overheard Platt talking to his wife about Phoenix's pending transaction. Shortly

thereafter, Switzer bought Phoenix stock based on what he had overheard. Nobody contradicted this story, and the court dismissed the SEC's complaint.[82]

5. Footnotes 14 and 22

Nor could courts keep footnotes 14 and 22 straight.[83] Lavere Gilbert Lund was CEO of Verit, and Horowitz was CEO of P&F. On behalf of P&F, Horowitz negotiated a joint venture with a casino. He then called Lund and asked him to invest Verit's funds in the venture. Before replying, Lund bought stock in P&F.

These are footnote 22 facts. Horowitz approaches Lund as an outsider and asks him to invest in P&F; Lund does not accept; but on the basis of Horowitz's information, Lund buys stock in P&F. Horowitz the tipper breaches no fiduciary duty in giving Lund the information, and Lund the tippee agrees to no agency relationship with P&F. By footnote 22 and the logic of *Dirks*, Lund may trade.

In fact, the court cited footnote 14 instead. "Lund was a temporary P&F insider when he traded on the basis of the information concerning the [casino] project."[84] As Chapter 1 makes clear, however, one becomes an agent only when one agrees to become an agent—and Lund had not agreed. He received inside information, but had not accepted an agency. Notwithstanding the law, the court applied footnote 14 and ruled that Lund violated Rule 10b-5.

E. *Misappropriation*

1. The *Chiarella* Progeny

(a) *Introduction*

Through its *Chiarella* opinion, the Supreme Court snubbed both the SEC and the Second Circuit. Neither took it well. The SEC responded by drafting a rule under §14(e) of the 1934 Act that would (if upheld) let it do what the Court would not let it do under §10(b). The Second Circuit responded by ignoring the majority opinion entirely and following Burger's dissent.

(b) *Rule 14e-3*

To the SEC, insider trading was wrong whether the insider served as a fiduciary to his trading partner or not. When Cary wrote *In re Cady, Roberts* in 1961, he had not hinged his new insider trading ban on any fiduciary duty. When the SEC argued *TGS* a few years later, it did not hinge Cary's ban on any such duty.

---

[82] Brad Foster, Securities Litigation E-Alert: The SEC, Insider Trading, and Dallas Sports, Andrews Kurth, LLP (Nov. 25, 2008), http://www.andrewskurth.com/pressroom-publications-592.html.

[83] SEC v. Lund, 570 F. Supp. 1397 (C.D. Cal. 1983).

[84] *Id.* at 1403.

When it attacked insider trading in the increasingly common tender offers, it did not worry about any such duty. And now, Powell had declared that the SEC could attack the phenomenon only if the insider did owe his trading partner a fiduciary duty. TGS vice president Fogarty may have owed (by the agency law of some states) such a fiduciary duty to TGS shareholders. But Chiarella had worked for the acquirer rather than the target whose shares he was buying, and the Supreme Court had acquitted Chiarella. No longer, Powell explained, could the SEC prosecute investors who buy target stock on information acquired through ties to an acquirer.

Because most insiders who trade on tender offers do buy target stock on the basis of information obtained from acquirers, *Chiarella* seemed to stop the SEC from using Rule 10b-5 to police tender offer insider trading. It needed a new rule, the SEC reasoned, and turned to §14(e) of the 1934 Act. The section banned "fraud" in tender offers and invited the Commission to write some rules:

> It shall be unlawful for any person . . . to engage in any fraudulent, deceptive, or manipulative acts or practices, in connection with any tender offer. . . . The Commission shall . . . by rules and regulations define, and prescribe means reasonably designed to prevent, such acts and practices as are fraudulent, deceptive, or manipulative.

To implement this section, the SEC now wrote Rule 14e-3:

> a. If any person has taken a substantial step or steps to commence . . . a tender offer . . . , it shall constitute a fraudulent, deceptive or manipulative act or practice within the meaning of section 14(e) of the Act for any other person who is in possession of material information relating to such tender offer which information he knows or has reason to know is nonpublic and which he knows or has reason to know has been acquired directly or indirectly from:
>   1. The [acquirer],
>   2. The [target], or
>   3. Any officer, director, partner or employee or any other person acting on behalf of the [acquirer] or [target],
>   to purchase or sell . . . any of such securities. . . .

In effect, the SEC hoped to overrule the Supreme Court through its rule-making authority. But §§10(b) and 14(e) both banned "fraud." The Court had held that fraud under §10(b) required a fiduciary relationship between the trading partners. In Rule 14e-3, the SEC defined "fraud" under §14(e) without such a requirement. The obvious question: Could the SEC do this?

(c) *Newman*[85]

Equally snubbed by the Supreme Court in *Chiarella*, the Second Circuit decided to ignore the majority opinion and follow Burger's dissent instead. The

---

[85] United States v. Newman, 664 F.2d 12 (2d Cir. 1981).

majority had not expressly rejected Burger's "misappropriation" theory. It did not need to address it at all. Burger had invented the theory on appeal, and appellate courts cannot affirm convictions on theories not presented to the jury. Given that Burger's ruminations were out of order, the majority could properly ignore them. But if the majority did not reject them, then the Second Circuit could plausibly structure its jurisprudence around them.

The year after *Chiarella*, the Second Circuit heard a case involving employees at the Morgan Stanley and Kuhn Loeb investment banks. The two firms had been retained by acquirers in hostile takeovers, and the employees had tipped investors who bought stock in the targets. Because no one in the buyer's information chain owed a fiduciary duty to target shareholders, by *Chiarella* the tippees should have been free to trade. Following Burger's *Chiarella* dissent, the Second Circuit convicted them instead.

(d)   Musella[86]

In 1984, the New York federal courts faced a case against the officer manager of Sullivan & Cromwell. The firm had been retained by acquirers, and the office manager had apparently tipped information about their acquisitions to several traders who then bought target stock. Again, by *Chiarella* the manager and the traders should have been free to trade. Alluding to Burger's dissent, the Southern District of New York declared that they violated Rule 10b-5.

(e)   Materia[87]

And once more in 1984, the Second Circuit faced *Chiarella* all over again. Anthony Materia worked at a financial printer. Like Vincent Chiarella, he used the information in the rough drafts of the disclosure documents to deduce the identity of the targets. He bought their stock and found himself sued. On exactly the same facts, the Supreme Court had acquitted Chiarella. The Second Circuit held Materia liable, and the Supreme Court denied certiorari.

(f)   Willis[88]

United States v. Willis offered a more amusing set of facts. Robert Willis was a prominent Manhattan psychiatrist who included among his patients Joan Weill, wife of the ever-ambitious Sanford I. Weill. Sanford had served as CEO of Shearson Loeb Rhodes until 1981, when he became president of American Express. He wanted to run Bank of America. Toward that end, he obtained a commitment from Shearson to invest $1 billion in Bank of America if he succeeded. All this

---

[86] SEC v. Musella, 578 F. Supp. 425 (S.D.N.Y. 1984).

[87] SEC v. Materia, 745 F.2d 197 (2d Cir. 1984), *cert. denied*, 471 U.S. 1053 (1985).

[88] United States v. Willis, 737 F. Supp. 269 (S.D.N.Y. 1990); *see* Credit Markets; *Psychiatrist Is Sentenced*, N.Y. Times (Jan. 8, 1992).

ambition apparently disrupted family life because Joan discussed Sanford's plans with Willis.

Ambition should be made of sterner stuff, but Willis simply responded by buying Bank of America stock. He owed no fiduciary duty to the bank shareholders, after all. Sanford probably breached no fiduciary duty in discussing his office life with Joan and certainly earned no "personal gain" under *Dirks*. Joan was not an insider or a temporary insider, and anyway did nothing wrong in discussing her husband's ambitions with her psychiatrist. Under *Chiarella* and *Dirks*, Willis could not have violated Rule 10b-5.

The Southern District of New York convicted Willis anyway. Although he owed no fiduciary duty to bank shareholders, as a physician he owed a duty of confidentiality to his patients. To the Southern District, his violation of that duty transformed his purchase of bank stock into fraud under Rule 10b-5:

> The underlying rationale of the misappropriation theory is that a person who receives secret business information from another because of an established relationship of trust and confidence between them has a duty to keep that information confidential. By breaching that duty and appropriating the confidential information for his own advantage, the fiduciary is defrauding the confider who was entitled to rely on the fiduciary's tacit representation of confidentiality.[89]

The court sentenced Willis to five years' probation and community service, and restitution, fine, and penalties of about $290,000.

If the person Willis wronged through his trading was Joan rather than the bank shareholder whose stock he bought, then presumably Joan could have authorized his purchases. She could have told him: "Sanford has walked out. He's closed our accounts and canceled my cards. I can't pay you. But how's this? Instead of paying you your hourly charge, suppose I tell you Sanford's plans for the Bank of America?"

Could Joan have done this? And if she did, could Willis have traded? *Chiarella–Dirks* would not have prevented it. Logically, neither should the Second Circuit's misappropriation logic have stopped it. But of course Joan did not do this. Instead, when she learned that Willis had traded on what she told him, she sued him for $5 million. They settled for an undisclosed amount.[90]

2.   Gordon Gekko

(a)   Blue Star: The (Fictitious) Story

Return to the saga of Bud Fox and Gordon Gekko. Bud Fox's father Carl worked as a union official at Blue Star Airlines. After a plane crash, the

---

[89] 737 F. Supp. at 274.
[90] Monica Langley, *Tearing Down the Walls* 108 (Simon & Schuster 2003).

IV. Rule 10b-5

FAA launched an investigation into Blue Star's maintenance practices and tested the workers for drugs. One day, Bud met his father after work for a beer. Work was tough, Dad recounted, but at least the FAA had cleared Blue Star of the accident. The airline would be able to buy new plans and fly new routes.

Later that week, Bud met with investment banker Gekko to solicit his brokerage business. Gekko taunted Bud to tell him something he didn't know. After all, it was his birthday. Bud passed on his father's news about Blue Star and the FAA.

Gekko took Bud's tip, made a profit, and hired him. He paid Bud lavishly and entrusted him with $500,000. The two agreed that the information had been "inside information" and that the trade was illegal. Was it?

The law. As a senior employee and union official at Blue Star, Carl owed the firm a fiduciary duty. He himself could not have traded on the information.

But Carl did not trade. Instead, he told his son the news in the course of a routine paternal lecture. Perhaps he breached his duty of care in telling his son, but only perhaps. Under *Dirks*, however, whether he did does not matter. Rule 10b-5 does not turn on duty of care violations. Instead, it turns on whether Carl earned a "personal gain" by telling his son, and the answer is (almost surely) no — paternal bonding does not count as a gain.

Blue Star did not try to appoint Bud a temporary insider, and Bud did not try to obtain such an appointment. Footnote 14 does not apply.

Would "misappropriation" have mandated a different outcome in the Second Circuit? Misappropriation allows a court to stop an insider who breaches a duty to someone other than the person with whom he trades, but the *Dirks* requirement of a "personal gain" remains. Carl did not gain. Is it enough if Bud violates Carl's unstated request that he keep the information confidential?

Because the transaction did not involve a tender offer, Rule 14e-3 does not apply.

Hence the possible conclusion: The initial tipper (Carl) earned no gain in tipping the information to the tippee (Bud), so perhaps Oliver Stone was simply wrong. If so, then in 1985, the tippee (Bud) and secondary tippee (Gekko) still could have bought Blue Star stock without violating Rule 10b-5.

(b) Larry Wildman: The (Again Fictitious) Story

Several years earlier, Gekko had fought Larry Wildman for control of a pharmaceutical firm. Gekko had lost and nursed a grudge ever since. An eminent U.K. industrialist, Wildman held a British peerage but had recently acquired U.S. citizenship and returned to New York.

Gekko sneered about "Sir" Larry Wildman. Find out his plans, he told Fox. Learn where he goes, whom he meets, and figure out what he's buying. Fox hesitated. After all, he reminded Gekko, they could go to jail.

Could they?

The law. Where Wildman eats lunch is public information. If he takes a table in the middle of the restaurant, then whom he eats with is public too. The office buildings he enters are public information. Anyone could collect this information if they wanted. Fox and Gekko did not break the law by gathering it.

Fox and Gekko made money on this information, but not because they had better information than anyone else. They made money because they had better analysis. They collected public data (where Wildman went, whom he saw) and from it drew better conclusions than their competitors. Conceptually, what they did is no different from what any good stock analyst does. They took public information and analyzed it. They did not make money because they traded on inside information. They made money because they were smart.

Readers with a cinematic memory will complain, of course. At a crucial point in the movie, Bud Fox sees Wildman board a private plane. He needs to know where the plane will go. He tells the airport mechanic that his boss had asked him to deliver a package to Wildman and asks him where the plane was headed. Erie, Pennsylvania, the mechanic replies.

With this last crucial clue, Bud and Gekko were able to deduce — correctly — that Wildman was about to announce a tender offer for Anacott Steel. They then bought Anacott shares.

Does this lie make a difference? Under *Chiarella–Dirks*, Fox and Wildman do not violate Rule 10b-5. They owe no duty to Anacott shareholders and, absent that duty, do not violate the rule.

Under Burger's "misappropriation" theory, Fox and Gekko arguably misappropriated — stole — the information. If so, then arguably they violated Rule 10b-5, though the lie to the mechanic seems a minor sin on which to hang a federal crime.

Until the lie to the mechanic, Fox and Gekko had not violated Rule 14e-3 either. The rule bans only trades on nonpublic information, and Fox and Gekko had no nonpublic information. After the lie, they do have nonpublic information: the destination of the private plane. Arguably, they violated Rule 14e-3, though again the lie seems a trivial basis for a federal crime.

3. Ivan Boesky: The (True) Story

In the mid-1980s, Ivan Boesky worked as an arbitrageur: He bought and sold the stock of tender offer targets, making money by playing the odds that an offer would succeed or fail. Boesky did well (so well that Berkeley invited him to give a commencement address), but he did well in part by buying inside information. In particular, he had a deal with Dennis Levine. Levine worked at the investment banking firm Drexel Bernham Lambert. Because Drexel routinely bankrolled acquirers, Levine had access to information about which firms the acquirers were targeting, which offers were most likely to succeed, and which were (over problems like financing) most likely to fail. Levine would pass the information to Boesky, and Boesky would share with him a portion of the profits he made.

The law. The U.S. Attorney's Office shut down Boesky's operation in 1986, but consider the law. First, under *Chiarella–Dirks*, Boesky broke no law. He obtained his information from Levine, Levine worked for Drexel, and Drexel represented the acquirer. With that information, Boesky traded on target stock. Neither Boesky nor anyone in his chain of information owed any fiduciary duty to target shareholders.

As a result, Boesky did not owe the people with whom he traded any duty to disclose. Absent a duty to disclose, he did not commit a fraud and, absent fraud, did not violate Rule 10b-5.

Second, under Burger's approach, Boesky did violate Rule 10b-5 — if misappropriation were good law. Drexel worked as agent to the acquirer, and Levine worked for Drexel. For a financial payoff, he tipped information to Boesky. Levine misappropriated — stole — information from the acquirer, and Boesky traded on it. By Burger's logic, he violated Rule 10b-5.

Last, Boesky straightforwardly violated Rule 14e-3 as well — again, if 14e-3 were good law. He traded on target stock based on nonpublic information he obtained from the acquirer. By the terms of the rule, he broke the law.[91]

4. Armand Hammer: The (Strange but Still True) Story

In the late 1980s, I taught as a junior professor at UCLA, and my wife worked as a resident in internal medicine at the UCLA Medical Center. Armand Hammer (Chapter 3, Introduction) lived in Holmby Hills, but just barely. He was very old, and he was desperately ill. Regularly, his handlers moved him in and out of the hospital for the critical care he so badly needed.

One day, my wife came home with some news. One of her friends in the residency had noticed that every time Hammer checked into the Medical Center, the price of Occidental Petroleum stock jumped. At every bit of news that their CEO might die, shareholders bid up the price of their stock.

The law. I never tried to confirm the story, and — rest assured — I never acted on it. But suppose I had. Suppose my wife comes home and announces that Hammer has checked into the emergency room. Exhausted, she falls asleep on the couch, and I call my broker to buy 10 shares of Occidental.

Preliminarily, note that I do not violate Rule 14e-3. The rule applies only to tender offers, and this piece of news does not concern a tender offer.

Turn to Rule 10b-5. Suppose first that my wife spent all night working with the cardiologist on Hammer's heart, that she came home and told me the news, and that she urged me to buy the stock. Under the majority approach in *Chiarella–Dirks*, she can trade. She is not an Occidental insider who owes a fiduciary duty to its shareholders; as Hammer's personal doctor, she is not a temporary insider at Occidental; and Hammer has not himself breached any fiduciary duty in checking into the emergency room.

---

[91] Can a criminal trade on information about his own prosecution? The SEC apparently decided he could. "[T]he plea agreement negotiated by [Boesky's lawyer] permitted Boesky to sell his stock before the public announcement of his arrest. That inside information allowed Boesky to avoid the sharp drop in stock values for that stock that occurred after the announcement." Markham, *supra* note 54, at 384.

In contrast, under Burger's misappropriation theory, she replicates *Willis* and may not trade. By trading on confidential patient information, she violates Rule 10b-5.

Suppose second that my wife worked on Hammer's heart, but did not expect me to buy Occidental stock. She (the tipper) does not violate patient confidences by telling her husband (the tippee) what she did at work. Whether under the majority or dissenting opinion in *Chiarella*, I can trade.

Suppose third that my wife did not herself care for Hammer. Instead, she simply noticed the paramedics wheeling him down the hall on a stretcher. Under the majority approach in *Chiarella–Dirks*, she and I can again trade.

Under Burger's misappropriation theory, the question is harder. Because Hammer was not her patient, she did not owe him an obligation to protect his confidences. *Willis* thus does not directly apply. Instead, the question turns on the employment rules at the UCLA Medical Center. If the hospital explicitly bans doctors from trading on information they learn at the hospital, then she misappropriates the information if she trades. She also misappropriates it if she tips me and asks me to trade. But if she merely tells me the news in a routine "What did you do at work today?" conversation, then (given the absence of personal gain to her under *Dirks*) possibly I can trade.

F. The Supreme Court and Misappropriation — Rule 14e-3

1. Introduction

The 1980s were a strange time to teach corporate law.

On the one hand, the Supreme Court had declared that an investor could violate Rule 10b-5 only if he owed a fiduciary duty to the person with whom he traded. On the other, the principal federal appellate court in securities law was following a Supreme Court dissent and sending investors to prison who had owed no such duty.

On the one hand, the Supreme Court had declared that insider trading was "fraudulent" within the meaning of §10 of the 1934 Act only when the trader owed a fiduciary duty to the person with whom he traded. On the other, the SEC was enforcing a rule that defined insider trading as "fraudulent" within the meaning of §14 of that Act even when the trader owed no such duty.

Whatever one might call the situation, it did not seem like an equilibrium.

2. Winans

By 1987, the end to this three-way standoff seemed near. R. Foster Winans and his lover David Carpenter had worked at the *Wall Street Journal*.[92] Winans wrote a

---

[92] Carpenter v. United States, 484 U.S. 19 (1987), *aff'g* 791 F.2d 1024 (2d Cir. 1986), *aff'g* 612 F. Supp. 827 (S.D.N.Y. 1985).

IV. Rule 10b-5

"Heard on the Street" column for the paper, and Carpenter was a news clerk. In the column, Winans touted various stocks, but not on the basis of "corporate inside information." According to the Southern District of New York, he simply wrote "a daily market gossip feature." Through the column he apparently had "an impact on the market," the court concluded, and it was "certainly obvious that the defendants believed that the column had such an impact."[93]

Peter Brant and Kenneth Felis worked as stockbrokers at Kidder, Peabody. Brant was the star of the pair, "the number one broker at Kidder Peabody," and a man with "phenomenal market success" and a "flamboyant lifestyle."[94] Winans met Brant in connection with a story. According to Winans, Brant observed that "if I knew beforehand what was going to be in the column, we could make a lot of money."[95] In time, they cut a deal: Winans would let Brant know what was going to be in the column, Brant would trade on the information, and Brant would share with Winans his profits. Felis and Carpenter played subsidiary roles.

Kidder, Peabody noticed the trades in Brant's account. The SEC investigated, the group quarreled, and Winans and Carpenter talked. The Justice Department prosecuted, the Southern District of New York convicted, the Second Circuit affirmed, and the Supreme Court granted certiorari.

Under *Chiarella–Dirks*, none of the conspirators violated Rule 10b-5. No one at the *Journal* owed any fiduciary duty to any of the firms Winans named in his columns, and without a duty to the people with whom the conspirators traded, they did not violate the rule. As the Southern District explained:

> To find *Dirks* controlling would be to find no securities violation here, since Winans was not a temporary insider, did not owe any duty to the corporations he wrote about, and was not a tippee of any corporate inside information. In terms of the securities law, neither Winans nor the Wall Street Journal owed any duties at all to the corporations that were the subject of *Heard* columns or to the shareholders of those corporations.[96]

The Southern District instead decided that *Chiarella* and *Dirks* did not control. Rather, Burger's dissent to *Chiarella* controlled. The *Journal* prohibited Winans from trading on the information about his columns, but Winans did anyway. He thus "misappropriated" the information:

> As to the securities counts, Winans and Felis employed devices, schemes and artifices to defraud and engaged in acts, practices and a course of business which operated as a fraud and deceit on the Wall Street Journal and Dow Jones & Co., Inc.[97]

---

[93] *Carpenter*, 612 F. Supp. at 830 & n.2.
[94] *Id.* at 832.
[95] *Id.*
[96] *Id.* at 841.
[97] *Id.* at 849.

As a result, the case turned on the *Journal's* internal rule. It did not have to maintain this rule. Had it wanted to do so, it could itself have traded on the information about its columns. The Second Circuit made the point explicitly:

> [I]n the present case the *Wall Street Journal* or its parent, Dow Jones Company, might perhaps lawfully disregard its own confidentiality policy by trading in the stock of companies to be discussed in forthcoming articles.[98]

No law prohibited the *Journal* from trading on information about those firms in forthcoming articles, but it banned its employees from doing so. Winans violated that rule, and in the Second Circuit, that made his conduct a federal crime.

The case gave the Supreme Court a chance to clarify whether *Chiarella* and *Dirks* did control, but it was a chance the Court did not take. Powell had quit, and Kennedy had not yet joined the Court. The remaining justices split four to four on misappropriation. By Court practice, evenly split votes result in an affirmance, but without precedential value. For another decade, the Second Circuit would continue to follow a Supreme Court dissent.

3. O'Hagen

(a) The Case

Eventually clarity did come, but not until 1997 — nearly two decades after *Chiarella*.[99] James Herman O'Hagen was a partner at the Minneapolis law firm of Dorsey & Whitney. His firm had been retained by Grand Met, which planned to announce a tender offer for Pillsbury. Having embezzled funds from a client, O'Hagen needed cash. Buying Pillsbury stock and options on Pillsbury stock, he netted $4.3 million. The SEC noticed, and prosecutors indicted him for violating both Rule 14e-3 and Rule 10b-5. The District Court convicted him, but the Eighth Circuit reversed: Rule 14e-3 was invalid, and misappropriation was bad law.

Recall the weakness to Rule 14e-3. Both §§10(b) and 14(e) of the 1934 Act ban fraud, and both invite the SEC to issue rules implementing the ban. In *Chiarella* the Supreme Court held that for insider trading to be "fraudulent" under §10(b), the trader must owe a fiduciary duty to the person with whom he trades. Rule 14e-3 bans insider trading as "fraudulent" under §14(e), but does not require that fiduciary duty.

Not to worry, wrote the Supreme Court. The SEC has broad rule-making authority. In Rule 14e-3 it wrote a ban "reasonably designed to prevent" fraud related to tender offers. The rule may "encompass[] more than the core activity

---

[98] *Carpenter*, 791 F.2d at 1033.
[99] United States v. O'Hagen, 521 U.S. 642 (1997).

prohibited" by the section, but so be it. It is a prophylactic rule, and a "prophylactic measure" often sweeps broadly.[100] Rule 14e-3 is good law.

Recall "misappropriation." O'Hagen practiced with a law firm representing the acquirer and used information from the acquirer to buy stock in the target. He owed no fiduciary duty to target shareholders and, under *Chiarella*, thus could not violate Rule 10b-5.

Not to worry, the Court again explained. Misappropriators deceive, and Rule 10b-5 bans deceptive conduct. The *TGS* insiders deceived the shareholders of the firm at which they worked. O'Hagen deceived Grand Met for which he worked. By deceiving the acquirer, he committed a fraud. Misappropriation is good law too.

(b) Odds and Ends

But again the Court was not about to leave well enough alone. Suppose, it asked, that O'Hagen had called Grand Met and told it he would be buying Pillsbury stock. Grand Met objected, but he bought the stock anyway. Suppose he were a disloyal agent, in other words, but not a dishonest one:

> [F]ull disclosure forecloses liability under the misappropriation theory: Because the deception essential to the misappropriation theory involves feigning fidelity to the source of information, if the fiduciary discloses to the source that he plans to trade on the nonpublic information, there is no "deceptive device" and thus no §10(b) violation — although the fiduciary-turned-trader may remain liable under state law for breach of a duty of loyalty.[101]

The Court had earlier held that Rule 10b-5 banned only "deceptive" fiduciary duty breaches.[102] Once O'Hagen told his principal that he would steal its information, he was a thief but not a deceptive one. He violated state law, but not Rule 10b-5.

In fact, the amusing unreality to this opinion went farther still. Was it enough for O'Hagen to call Grand Met, the Court asked? No, it answered, he also needed to call his partners at Dorsey & Whitney:

> Where . . . a person trading on the basis of material, nonpublic information owes a duty of loyalty and confidentiality to two entities or persons — for example, a law firm and its client — but makes disclosure to only one, the trader may still be liable under the misappropriation theory.[103]

If O'Hagen told Grand Met and Dorsey he would trade, if Grand Met and Dorsey told him to stop, and if he then traded anyway, was he really free under Rule 10b-5? Indeed, explained the Court, he was free.

[100] *Id.* at 672-673.
[101] *Id.* at 655.
[102] Santa Fe Indus. v. Green, 430 U.S. 462 (1977).
[103] 521 U.S. at 655 n.7.

[T]he textual requirement of deception precludes §10(b) liability when a person trading on the basis of nonpublic information has disclosed his trading plans to . . . the principal — even though such conduct may affect the securities markets in the same manner as conduct reached by the misappropriation theory. . . . [O]nce a disloyal agent discloses his imminent breach of duty, his principal may seek appropriate equitable relief under state law.[104]

But suppose Grand Met instead took pity on O'Hagen and told him he could trade?

[I]n the context of a tender offer, the principal who authorizes an agent's trading on confidential information may, in the Commission's view, incur liability for an Exchange Act violation under Rule 14e-3(a).[105]

Suppose you serve as CEO. One of the partners from your law firm calls, explains that he embezzled from a different client and would like to trade on your impending tender offer to recoup the money he stole. "Do you mind?" he asks. You should mind, the Court carefully explains. You would violate Rule 14e-3 if you authorized his trades.

4.   Husbands and Wives

Dirks created another problem. Nancy McKinstry is CEO of Wolters Kluwer (and the firm trades its stock on the New York Stock Exchange). Suppose she learns that the firm is about to launch a blockbuster product. If she buys stock in anticipation of the launch, she violates Rule 10b-5 under *TGS*. But suppose, when she comes home one evening, her husband asks her, "What did you do at the office today, honey?" Suppose she replies, "We're getting ready to launch a blockbuster new product." And suppose the two keep their assets separate and that he then buys Wolters Kluwer stock for his personal account?

Nancy's husband is not a Wolters Kluwer insider. He is not a footnote 14 "temporary insider." And (per *Switzer*) Nancy does not breach a fiduciary duty in a way that generates a "personal benefit" when she tells her husband what happened at the office. One might have thought that her husband "misappropriated" the information when he used what she told him to buy stock, but in 1991 the Second Circuit declared (to the shock of most married couples) that husbands and wives do not owe each other fiduciary duties.[106]

For the SEC, the result was an obvious nightmare. To trade on inside information, a CEO need simply place the trade in his or her spouse's account. When the SEC comes calling, the two can then invent a "What did you do at the office today, honey?" conversation. So long as neither wants to put the other in prison, they are both home free.

---

[104] *Id.* at 659 n.9.

[105] *Id.*

[106] United States v. Chestman, 947 F.2d 551 (2d Cir. 1991), *cert. denied*, 503 U.S. 1004 (1992).

IV. Rule 10b-5

To address the problem, in 2000 the SEC adopted Rule 10b5-2:

> This rule provides a non-exclusive definition of circumstances in which a person has a duty of trust and confidence for purposes of the "misappropriation" theory of insider trading. . . .
>
>> (b) For purposes of this section, a "duty of trust or confidence" exists . . . :
>>
>>> (1) Whenever a person agrees to maintain information in confidence;
>>>
>>> (2) Whenever the person communicating the material nonpublic information and the person to whom it is communicated have a history . . . of sharing confidences, such that the recipient of the information knows or reasonably should know that the person communicating the material nonpublic information expects that the recipient will maintain its confidentiality; or
>>>
>>> (3) Whenever a person receives or obtains material nonpublic information from his or her spouse, parent, child, or sibling. . . .

If Nancy's husband trades on information she gives him, he misappropriates the information under Rule 10b5-2(b)(3).

5. Examples Again

(a) Blue Star

Flash forward to the twenty-first century and consider again the Blue Star episode. Father Carl tells Fox about the FAA clearance, Bud tells Gekko, and Gekko trades.

Bud owes Carl a "duty of trust and confidence" under Rule 10b5-2(b)(3). Should he trade on the information, he misappropriates. Should he tip Gekko in exchange for a payment, he and Gekko both violate Rule 10b-5 under a combination of "misappropriation" and the *Dirks* tipping analysis.

(b) Wildman

Fox tails Wildman and learns whom he sees. He follows Wildman to the airport and lies to the mechanic to discover where Wildman is going. He and Gekko deduce that Wildman is about to bid for Anacott Steel. Gekko buys Anacott.

Misappropriation and Rule 14e-3 are good law. If the lie to the airport mechanic is a crucial part of the analysis, then Fox and Gekko breach both Rule 10b-5 and Rule 14e-3.

(c) Boesky

Acquirers retain Drexel, Levine works for Drexel, and Levine tips Boesky about impending tender offers in exchange for a payment. Boesky trades.

Boesky straightforwardly violates Rule 14e-3, and the rule is good law. Through a combination of "misappropriation" and *Dirks*, Boesky also violates Rule 10b-5.

(d) Hammer

Ramseyer's wife returns from the UCLA Medical Center to report that she saw Hammer being rushed to the emergency room. She emphatically tells Ramseyer not to trade and not to tell anyone.

If Ramseyer buys Occidental stock, he violates Rule 10b-5 through misappropriation based on Rule 10b5-2.

Badly needing a boost in his student evaluations, Ramseyer reports Hammer's illness to his 8:00 A.M. corporate law class. If a student buys Occidental stock, Ramseyer and the student both violate Rule 10b-5 through a combination of misappropriation, Rule 10b5-2, and *Dirks*.

(e) Willis

Sanford Weill details his business plans to wife Joan, and Joan tells her psychiatrist Willis.

If Willis trades, he violates Rule 10b-5 under misappropriation.

But suppose, counterfactually, that Willis agrees not to charge Joan for her counseling sessions if she gives him a tip about Sanford's business plans. Can Willis trade?

Joan owes Sanford a "duty of trust and confidence" under Rule 10b5-2. She misappropriates the information in violation of that rule if she tips Willis in exchange for free sessions. Both she and Willis violate Rule 10b-5.

V.   CONCLUSIONS

You have to wonder.

Anytime the outcome to a criminal prosecution turns on section (b)(3) of the second sub-rule to the fifth rule implementing subsection (b) of §10 of a statute, you have to wonder. The outcome may well be sensible.[107] But might there not have been a simpler way to reach it?

Lewis Powell thought so. "The SEC," he once suggested, "should have gone to Congress long ago" instead of inventing "expansive rules" that pushed the "vague language" of §10(b) "to the edge of rationality."[108] But it was a road the Commission did not take. It pushed the "vague language" of Rule 10b-5, and there matters stayed.

---

[107] Or maybe not. *See generally* Manne, *supra* note 41; Carlton & Fischel, *supra* note 41; Bainbridge, *supra* note 41.

[108] Quoted in Kurt A. Hohenstein, *Fair to All People: The SEC and the Regulation of Insider Trading*, Virtual Museum & Archive of the History of Financial Regulation, http://www.sechistorical.org/museum/galleries/it (accessed Mar. 2, 2012).

V. Conclusions

Congress in the early Roosevelt years passed a statute mandating extensive disclosure. It added a prophylactic provision ostensibly designed to catch insider trading. But the "action" in the past half century has not turned on that provision. It has instead turned on a much "vaguer" antifraud rule drafted by the SEC in 1942. Insider trading today is usually illegal — and illegal because of that Rule 10b-5.

CHAPTER 6

Corporate Control (I)

It was a dark and stormy night.

Or so it seemed to Marion Crane, as she left the highway and pulled into the motel parking lot. She had met her boyfriend over the lunch hour that Friday. When she returned to work, a client had arrived with $40,000 in cash. It being the start of the weekend, her boss asked her to take it to the bank.

Marion did not go to the bank. Instead, she bought herself a used car and skipped town. She had worried that an officer in a patrol car had noticed something untoward, but he had said nothing. He had merely watched her leave.

Marion drove. The sun set, and the rain poured, but Marion kept driving. Exhausted, she pulled up to a seemingly deserted motel. She asked the attendant for a room, and he gave her "Cabin One." A friendly young man named Norman, he struck up a conversation. His mother owned the motel, he explained, but she was not well. He managed the operation and would inherit it on her death. It was not a busy job, but he did not mind. The free time gave him a chance to pursue his taxidermic hobby.

After Marion checked into her room, Norman returned with a warm dinner. He had cooked it himself, he said. Mother had long since stopped working in the kitchen.

So Hitchcock tells us. But suppose that Marion liked the motel. She liked the stuffed-bird taxidermic decorating motif. She liked Norman's cooking. She liked the tastefully appointed showers. Halfway through an MBA program from the University of Phoenix, she thought the motel had franchising potential.

Suppose, Marion asked Norman, they franchised the motel's formula? They could form a corporation, with 50 percent of the stock for each of them. Alternatively, perhaps Norman's mother would like to buy an equal share too? Prospective motel operators would build their own buildings, but according to specifications that Norman and Marion would detail in their franchising rules. Operators would use the name of Norman's original motel — the "Bates Motel." They would decorate their motels according to the style of the original. And they would buy the more important decorative items like shower fixtures and stuffed-bird wall ornaments directly from the franchisor corporation.

Privately, Marion anticipated a couple of potential problems. First, she cared with whom she did business. She pegged Norman as a wimp whom she could easily manipulate. She could happily do business with him. His mother she had not met, and what Norman told her about his mother she did not like. If Norman died intestate and his interest passed to his mother, she would find herself locked into a firm with this woman, and — if Mother perhaps now had a two-thirds interest — routinely outvoted. That she did not want.

Second, Marion needed a way to liquidate her interest in the firm. She was on the run, after all. She had stolen $40,000, and the police were looking for her. She needed a way to cash out her interest quickly, and at a price close to its fair market value.

In this chapter and the next, I explore how people like Marion and Norman — directly or indirectly — control and manage the firms in which they invest. Marion and Norman (and perhaps his mother) may buy the firm's stock, but they probably will not run it in their capacity as shareholders. Instead, they will elect a board of directors, and that board will then hire executive officers. Those officers will run the firm.

In section I, I ask how shareholders select their board. As investors, Marion and Norman might choose nonstandard ways to exercise their control. In section II, I outline some of their options. Given the risk that they might try to exploit each other, I detail some of the protective devices they could choose. Most of these devices are ones courts approve. In section III, I explore options that courts sometimes reject.

I. CHOOSING THE TEAM THAT RUNS THE FIRM

A. *The Mechanics*

1. The Allocation Between Managers and Investors

Consider how managers and investors might allocate control.

Sometimes, investors themselves run the firm. Sometimes — but not usually. Investors bring funds that the firm needs, but do not necessarily know how best to run it. For that, they hire professional managers. In turn, managers rarely have the funds that the firm needs. For that, they recruit investors. Managers bring business plans and professional expertise; investors bring money. Together, they assemble a firm.

Sometimes, investors and managers will negotiate a deal of limited duration. Investors will entrust their funds to their managers for a stated period. At the end, the managers agree to return the money. In exchange for the use of the money, they add a fee besides. Through the deal, the two groups negotiate a loan: The managers obtain the use of the borrowed money for a stated term and repay the investors (called creditors) the principal with interest. Except when a firm is close to insolvency, the groups will not negotiate a deal that gives much control to such investors (see *Cargill* at Chapter 1, section I.B, and *KNK* at Chapter 2, section I.C)

Sometimes, managers may not want to repay the funds advanced, and investors may want to entrust their funds long term. To compensate investors for the use of their money, managers now agree to pay themselves a fixed amount (denominated salaries) and let the investors keep the rest. Those investors, in turn, agree to split that remainder (their equity stake) among themselves in proportion to the amounts they each advanced. Provided the managers have filed incorporation papers with the secretary of state (see Chapter 3, appendix I), the investors have bought shares of stock in the firm.

Having entrusted their funds for the indefinite future, shareholders will want some control over the long-term direction of the firm. In turn, to induce investors to entrust their funds long term, managers will give them that control. Most shareholders still will not have the plans or expertise to run the firm day to day. As a result, most will not want day-to-day control. What is more, even if any one shareholder wanted a say, he may not want any of his shareholding colleagues to have day-to-day control. Neither in most cases will managers want to give shareholders quotidian control. The managers will give shareholders power, but only over long-term matters. They will give shareholders power only (a) over the selection of the people who will monitor the managers and (b) over transactions that go to the survival of the firm itself.

Providing as it does a set of waivable default governance terms for investors and managers, corporate law reflects these common preferences. Shareholders do not run the firm. Instead, they elect directors who hire officers to run it. As the Delaware statute puts it: The "business and affairs of every corporation . . . shall be managed by or under the direction of a board of directors" — and not the shareholders.[1] Officers do not repay shareholder investments with interest. Instead, shareholders invest for the life of the firm. The firm returns money to them only if the board decides either to redeem the stock or to pay a dividend (neither of which it need do).

And waivable defaults that they are, these terms are ones that shareholders and officers can and do sometimes waive. Sometimes they do want the shareholders to manage, and they can so agree — as Marion and Norman might reasonably agree. By the terms of the "close corporation statutes" in many states, they can assign managerial powers to shareholders, subject to assorted requirements and limits (section II below). Should they want the right to sell their stock to the firm or to their co-shareholders on certain occasions at certain prices, they can negotiate such provisions. Should they want the right to buy the stock of their co-investors, they can cut that deal too. Again, Marion and Norman might reasonably negotiate these terms. I return to their plight at section II.A below and Chapter 7, section I.A.

---

[1] Del. Gen. Corp. L. §141(a).

2. The Process

The law provides (because many parties would otherwise demand something similar anyway) that shareholders vote once a year to elect the members of the board of directors (Chapter 3, section I.B). Those directors then monitor, hire, and fire the officers who run the firm day in and day out. The law also gives shareholders a vote on transactions involving the life of the firm—mergers, for example, or liquidations and sales of substantially all the corporate assets (Chapter 8, section I.A).

Often, shareholders vote at the annual meeting by proxy. They could personally attend if they wanted, but many do not want. At large publicly traded firms, they almost never attend. At small closely held companies, they might or might not.

If shareholders do skip the meeting, they vote by appointing someone there to vote in their stead as their agent. In the language of the law, they appoint that someone their proxy. In the language of practice, the document by which they appoint a voting agent is called a "proxy card." The process by which rival board candidates solicit shareholder support is known as a "proxy fight." And the federal rules that govern the content of their solicitation material are known as the "proxy rules."

B. An Example

Suppose you own a substantial minority block of shares in a publicly traded Hollywood studio. Last year, it released a cheap black-and-white slasher about a psychopathic attendant at a nondescript, deserted motel. The film was a hit. Having made such a huge profit, the studio's officers now want to make another. You read news of their plans. Enough is enough, you respond. They should focus on edifying films like *Doctor Zhivago*. To force them to change their plans, how might you respond?

First, you could make a "tender offer" for the firm's stock (that is, you could "offer" to buy any stock "tendered" to you; described in Chapter 8, section III). If successful, you would then own the firm and (by voting your friends onto the board) could tell the officers to make whatever movies you wanted. Inevitably, however, you would pay a large premium for the shares. You would buy them anyway, only if you believed that switching from slasher to edifying films would increase the market value of the firm (and hence the price of the stock). You do some investigation. You count the number of films on the life of Mother Theresa and compare it to the number of films on the life (so-called) of Freddie Krueger. Increase market value? Not likely.

Second, you could file a derivative suit against the board (see Chapter 3, section II). In your complaint, you would argue that by supporting the decision of the firm's officers to produce a series of slasher films, the board violated its fiduciary duty to the studio. Recall, however, the business judgment rule (Chapter 4). You have no evidence of any conflict of interest. You will need to show that the board acted with gross negligence. Win the suit? Even less likely.

I. Choosing the Team That Runs the Firm

Finally, you could launch a proxy fight. To do so, you would not propose to your shareholders a motion in favor of edifying movies. Because such a motion would concern the "business and affairs" of the firm, it would violate the corporate statute (subsection A.1 above) delegating such matters to the "board of directors." The officer chairing the shareholders meeting would rule your motion out of order. Should you challenge his decision in court, the judge would rule the same.

Instead, you would nominate yourself and your friends to the board. You would urge your fellow shareholders to back your slate and ask them to appoint you their proxy for voting at the shareholders' annual meeting. Should you obtain the support of a majority of the shares represented at the meeting, your slate would become the new board. You and your friends could then take the firm's movie portfolio to a higher plane.

C. Paying for the Proxies

1. Introduction

You will not find the proxy fight cheap. You will need to learn who the other shareholders are. You will need to mail them your material. You will want to telephone some of them. You will want to take those with the largest blocks of stock to dinner. Your opponents currently control the board, and they will want to do the same.

Consider two questions. First, who pays for all this? Can the incumbents charge the firm for their expenses? Can you? Does it matter whether you win or lose? Second, how will you discover who owns the stock? Your opponents hold the shareholder list, so they know. Must they give you a copy? The courts deal with the first of these questions in *Levin* and *Rosenfeld*. They address the second in *Crane*, *Sadler*, and *Pillsbury*.

2. *Levin v. MGM*[2]

On the use of corporate funds to solicit proxies, *Levin v. MGM* announces half the rule: *In contests over policy, the incumbent board may charge the firm for reasonable proxy solicitation expenses.*

Robert H. O'Brien became MGM president in 1963. A University of Chicago Law School graduate, he had worked briefly as an SEC commissioner before taking a job with Paramount in 1944. He moved to MGM's parent company in 1957. "I'm no mogul," he once confided to the *New York Times*, and reporters agreed. They saw his appointment to MGM as "a sign that a corporate culture was coming to the once-colorful movie industry."[3]

---

[2] Levin v. Metro-Goldwyn-Mayer, Inc., 264 F. Supp. 797 (S.D.N.Y. 1967).

[3] Leslie Eaton, *Robert H. O'Brien, 93, MGM President in 60's*, N.Y. Times (Oct. 11, 1997).

Although MGM lost $32 million in 1963, O'Brien gave the studio its share of hits. In fact, he gave it some of its most profitable films ever: David Lean's 1965 *Doctor Zhivago,* grossing $112 million ($912 million in 2010 dollars) and winning five Academy Awards; the 1967 *Dirty Dozen,* grossing $45 million; and Stanley Kubrick's 1968 *2001: A Space Odyssey,* grossing $57 million and winning an Academy Award.

Still, MGM could lose as well as make money, and for its erratic performance O'Brien acquired detractors. Philip Levin was among them. Perhaps a mogul might have been a match for Levin, but O'Brien was no mogul. Levin owned MGM stock and did not like O'Brien. He had made more than $100 million in real estate. Much of it he had made in Florida, and some of it he had made through friends in the syndicate. Some telephone records traced him to "Lucky" Luciano and his Genovese family. Other connections tied him to mob boss Meyer Lansky.[4]

In both 1966 and 1967, Levin launched proxy fights to oust O'Brien — at a private cost of at least $800,000.[5] According to the 1967 District Court opinion, he owned 553,000 shares, and his allies another 127,000. According to *Time* magazine, he would eventually control 720,000 shares, 14.3 percent of the total. In court, he argued that MGM should double the films it produced and license them to television only slowly. O'Brien replied that it should produce fewer, but license them sooner.

The Levin group and the MGM incumbents both solicited proxies for the February 1967 annual meeting. Levin then sued to enjoin the incumbents from using corporate facilities in the effort. Specifically, he argued that MGM should not use corporate funds to hire lawyers or proxy solicitation specialists.

The court disagreed. It first noted that:

> [T]he differences . . . are much more than mere personality conflicts. . . . There are definite business policies advocated by each group, so divergent that reconciliation does not seem possible.[6]

It then observed that the incumbents did not spend an unreasonable amount of money on the solicitation and that they had disclosed what they were doing. Accordingly, concluded the court, they could properly charge the firm for the costs of soliciting proxies.

O'Brien won the proxy fights, won the litigation, and lost the war. At the 1967 shareholders' meeting, Levin assured the audience that he would not sell his shares for "the foreseeable future," which, he explained, "means the next ten or 15 years."[7] Later that same year, he sold them to *Time* and the Seagram liquor firm's Edgar Bronfman for a $19 million profit.[8] Bronfman quickly lost patience with O'Brien and expelled him within two years.

---

[4] *Investment: Newest Life of Leo the Lion,* Time (Sept. 1, 1967); Gus Russo, *Supermob* 340 (Bloomsbury 2006).

[5] *Investment: Newest Life, supra* note 4.

[6] 264 F. Supp. at 801.

[7] *Management: Fight in the Lion's Den,* Time (Mar. 3, 1967).

[8] Stephen Fox, *Blood and Power* 24-25 (William Morrow 1989); *Investment: Newest Life, supra* note 4.

I. Choosing the Team That Runs the Firm

3. *Rosenfeld v. Fairchild*[9]

On the use of corporate funds to solicit proxies, *Rosenfeld v. Fairchild* announces the other half of the rule: *In contests over policy, the insurgent candidates may charge the firm for their proxy solicitation expenses, provided the amounts are reasonable, the insurgents win, and the shareholders approve the expenditure.*

Sherman M. Fairchild had founded the Fairchild Engine & Airplane firm. With a father who cofounded IBM, he came from inventive stock.[10] In time, Sherman himself would invent a wide variety of products in a wide range of industries: in photography, for example, aviation, and semiconductors. Eventually, his Fairchild Semiconductor would play a key role in creating Silicon Valley itself.

In 1940, Sherman Fairchild hired J. Carlton Ward to run his aircraft firm. Ward led the firm successfully through the war — but it did not take much talent to lead an airplane company through World War II. The government bought as many planes as a firm could produce. Hard times came instead with the peace, and Ward did not do well in peace. Rather than retool the firm for the consumer market, he lobbied the government for more subsidies. He pleaded with it (successfully) for a contract to explore an atomic-powered plane. Pity the people on the ground if the plane ever crashed, but research on the plane — and the Thorium-based atomic energy that would power it — continued for more than a decade out of laboratories in Lexington, Massachusetts, and elsewhere.[11]

Fairchild objected to the direction in which Ward led the firm. Fairchild chaired the board and owned the largest block of stock, but by 1946 Ward had stacked the board with his friends. Fairchild lost his fight within the board, resigned, and solicited support from other shareholders. By 1949, he was ready. He campaigned to oust Ward, he won, and Ward resigned.[12]

While still in office, Ward and his allies spent $106,000 in corporate funds to solicit proxies. After Fairchild retook control, the firm paid the Ward group another $28,000. And after the shareholders had approved the payment, the Fairchild group charged the firm $127,000 for their own proxy solicitation expenses.

In a derivative suit challenging these expenses, the New York Court of Appeals laid out the rule it would apply:

> In a contest over policy, as compared to a purely personal power contest, corporate directors have the right to make reasonable and proper expenditures, subject to

---

[9] Rosenfeld v. Fairchild Engine & Airplane Corp., 128 N.E.2d 291 (N.Y. 1955).

[10] Donald M. Pattillo, *Pushing the Envelope* 53 (U. Mich. Press 1998); Udayan Gupta, *Done Deals* 141 (Harvard Business School Press 2000).

[11] Frank Kofsky, *Harry S. Truman and the War Scare of 1948*, at 25 (St. Martin's 1993) (Ward's peacetime performance); Donald M. Pattillo, *Pushing the Envelope* 182 (U. Mich. Press 2001) (Ward lobbies government); Robert Pool, *Beyond Engineering* 72 (Oxford University Press 1995) (atomic-powered plane); Alvin Martin Weinberg, *The First Nuclear Era* 97 (AIP Press, 1994) (Lexington research).

[12] Pattillo, *supra* note 10, at 183; Ralph Sanders, ed., *J. Carlton Ward, Jr.: The Life and Thought of an Industrial Statesman* 24 et seq. (Industrial College of the Armed Forces 1988).

the scrutiny of the courts when duly challenged, from the corporate treasury for the purpose of persuading the stockholders of the correctness of their position and soliciting their support for policies which the directors believe, in all good faith, are in the best interests of the corporation. The stockholders, moreover, have the right to reimburse successful contestants for the reasonable and bona fide expenses incurred by them in any such policy contest, subject to like court scrutiny.[13]

4. Questions

Together with *Levin, Rosenfeld* details the two halves of the rule: *Assume the contest concerns policy* (more below) *and that the adversaries incur only reasonable expenses. Incumbents may charge their expenses to the firm. They may charge them whether they win* (Levin) *or lose* (Rosenfeld). *Insurgents may charge their expenses to the firm only if they win and only if the shareholders approve the expenditure* (Rosenfeld).

Straightforward as the rule may seem, it does hide a couple of complications. First, as the dissent to *Rosenfeld* observed, all disputes involve policy. No insurgent would solicit proxies without criticizing the incumbents' policies. What would he proclaim: "I think the present CEO is doing a fine job and I have no new policies to suggest, but I'd like his post anyway"? Were an insurgent ever to do this, however, apparently neither he nor the incumbent could charge their costs to the firm.

Second, if successful insurgents needed unanimous shareholder approval to charge their expenses to the firm (as the *Rosenfeld* dissent urged), they would never be able to charge them. The former incumbents will almost always hold at least some stock. If they can use it to veto money to their successors, they will veto the money. Few of them would support a motion to pay their successors the cost of evicting them from their jobs.

The rule obviously stacks the contest in the incumbents' favor. If insurgents fund their own costs, why not require the same of the incumbents? What is more, the incumbents work as agents for the firm and its shareholders. Why should a principal pay the cost his agent incurs to convince him that he (the agent) does a good job?

Yet the rule stacks the contest in a way most shareholders would favor. Any other rule would simply make it too hard to recruit good directors. Proxy contests are expensive, and outside directors (those not also serving as officers) do not collect large paychecks for their efforts. Faced with the prospect of funding a proxy fight themselves, most would simply resign. They would resign regardless of whether the insurgents brought any expertise or honesty to the job. Shareholders would find their sophisticated and honest directors quitting whenever a random set of insurgents decided they wanted their jobs.

Note, however, the inevitable conflict of interest. The *Levin–Rosenfeld* rule lets directors use corporate funds to fight to keep their private salaries. In theory, the rule generates as clear a conflict of interest as any. In practice, the conflict is one

---

[13] *Rosenfeld*, 128 N.E.2d at 293.

that courts simply ignore. They ignore it because doing anything else would wreak havoc at the boards.

D. Contacting the Shareholders

1. Introduction

Return to your plight as an aesthetically offended shareholder. You own stock in a movie studio that plans to produce a series of slasher films about demented attendants in dilapidated motels. You own a substantial minority block of stock. To turn the studio toward more edifying fare, you assemble a slate of like-minded right-thinking investors. How will your team contact the other shareholders in the studio?

If the studio is subject to the proxy rules (the rules apply to the same group of firms as §16(b); see Chapter 5, section III.C), those rules give it a choice: It can either mail your proxy materials for you or give you the shareholder list. If the studio mails your material for you, it can charge you for its costs. Because you would like to see the list yourself, the studio will opt to mail your materials directly.

You would like to see the list because all shareholders are not created equal. Some hold 2 shares and others hold 10,000. You do not care about the former. They do not own enough stock to affect the vote outcome. You want to know who owns the big blocks. You want to contact those shareholders, plead with them, buy them dinner at the Four Seasons. Precisely because you want to contact them, the firm will prefer to keep the list secret and mail your material to them itself.

Should the studio opt to mail your material directly, the federal proxy rules do not give you a right to demand the shareholder list. Instead, you will need to turn to state corporate law. Generally, that state law will give you a right to the list. Often, it will give you a right to some other corporate documents too. *Crane, Sadler,* and *Pillsbury* illustrate these state statutes.

2. *Crane Co. v. Anaconda Co.*[14]

Distant relative to the industrialist and one-time Treasury Secretary Andrew Mellon, Thomas Mellon Evans bought the Crane Company in 1959.[15] In time, Gordon Gekko would immortalize greed-is-good (Chapter 5, Introduction), but decades before him, Evans had already built a career around buying and fixing mismanaged firms:

> Long before Drexel's Michael Milken became a household name in the eighties by facilitating the use of junk bonds to finance hostile corporate takeovers [see

---

[14] 346 N.E.2d 507 (N.Y. 1976).
[15] *Corporations: Heirloom Collector,* Time (May 11, 1959).

generally Chapter 8], Tom Evans had used debt, cash, and the tax code to seize control of more than eighty American companies, small and large. Long before giant pension funds and other institutional investors began to lobby for "shareholder rights," Tom Evans was demanding that public companies operate only for their shareholders. . . . [16]

By the 1970s, Anaconda was dying—and dying fast. It had started its life as a Montana mining firm, first for silver, then for copper. It diversified and went international. In the early 1950s, the young Che Guevara would ride his Norton 500 past its Chilean mines and bewail the "lives of the poor unsung heroes . . . who die miserable deaths in one of the thousand traps nature sets to defend its treasures, when all they want is to earn their daily bread."[17]

But by the 1970s, Anaconda had reached the end of the road. In 1971, Salvador Allende nationalized its mines in Chile. Luis Echeverria Alvarez confiscated its mines in Mexico. And in 1975, Thomas Evans looked to buy a minority stake. Anaconda management interpreted his interest as a hostile acquisition and moved to block him. It hired Joe Flom of the Skadden, Arps firm (see Chapter 8, section III.F) to coordinate its defense and bought a valve company (the Walworth Corporation) that competed with some of Crane's business to introduce an antitrust problem into Evans's plans.[18]

For reasons unclear, Evans wanted a 23 percent stake. Toward that end, he proposed a tender offer: For every share of Anaconda stock tendered to him up to 23 percent, he offered Crane bonds worth $25. Why would anyone prefer Crane bonds to Anaconda stock? No one would necessarily prefer them, of course. Rational investors do not prefer bonds to stock. But Anaconda stock traded for $15 per share. For stock trading at $15, a bond that a holder can immediately resell for $25 is always a good deal.

To implement his tender offer, Evans wanted to contact the shareholders. Anaconda refused to make matters easy. He asked for the shareholder list, it refused, and he then sued in New York. Although Anaconda was a Montana corporation, it did business in New York, and New York law let its residents demand a shareholders' list from an out-of-state firm if they met one of two conditions: (1) They had owned the company's stock for at least six months or (2) they owned at least 5 percent of the stock.[19] Crane owned 11 percent of Anaconda, so it met the second of the two conditions.

Anaconda declared that Evans wanted the list for the wrong reasons and refused. The statute let a firm deny the list if a stockholder wanted it "for a purpose which is in the interest of a business or object other than the business of the foreign corporation." Anaconda's business was mining. Crane did not want the list for the

[16] Diana B. Henriques, *The White Sharks of Wall Street: Thomas Mellon Evans and the Original Corporate Raiders* 14 (Scribner 2000).
[17] Ernesto Che Guevara, *The Motorcycle Diaries: A Journey Around South America* 62 (Ann Wright trans., Verso 1995) (Anaconda's Chuquicamata mines).
[18] Henriques, *supra* note 16, at 273. For a discussion of tender offers and Joe Flom, see Chapter 8.
[19] N.Y. Bus. Corp. L. §1315.

business of mining. It wanted the list because it planned to buy Anaconda stock. Crane wanted the list for a purpose other than Anaconda's business, reasoned Anaconda, and so it did not need to give Crane the list. As the court put it, Anaconda argued

> that inspection should not be compelled where the stockholder desires to obtain the identity of the other stockholders to convince them to sell their stock, since this does not involve the business of the corporation.[20]

Anaconda was too clever by half. The "statute should be liberally construed in favor of the stockholder," reasoned the court. Anaconda's claim to the contrary was "myopic," and it needed to disclose the shareholders' list.[21]

Anaconda lost the battle and won the war — sort of. If it could not block Crane from contacting its shareholders, it would adopt other tactics:

> After trying the usual defenses — Skadden Arps's barrage of lawsuits, congressional hearings, and acquisition of one of Crane's competitors — Anaconda tried to rebuff Evans by merging with Tenneco, in a swap of stock that Evans considered a very bad deal.[22]

Evans refused to sell to Tenneco. Instead, he induced Arco to buy Anaconda at an even higher price. Arco did, and Evans made $58 million.[23]

Arco found itself with a nightmare. Soon, the price of copper fell, and Anaconda's domestic mines turned unprofitable. By 1980, Anaconda had closed the Montana mines.[24] Worse, a century's worth of mining had taken its toll on the neighborhood. Anaconda had laced the land with arsenic, copper, cadmium, and lead. The Environmental Protection Agency declared it a "superfund site," and Arco (along with its parent corporation, BP) stood liable for the cleanup.

3. *Sadler v. NCR Corp.*[25]

In 1991, the Second Circuit expanded on *Crane*. There, the New York Court of Appeals had required a target firm to give its shareholders' list to a tender offeror who owned at least 5 percent of its stock. In *Sadler*, the Second Circuit told the target to disclose the actual (beneficial) owners of those shares as well.

In the middle of a tender offer for NCR, ATT demanded that NCR tell it who actually owned its stock. Because brokerage firms handle transactions for

---

[20] 346 N.E.2d at 512.

[21] *Id.*

[22] Henriques, *supra* note 16, at 274.

[23] *Id.*

[24] Anaconda Co. Shut Down 30 Years Ago, Great Falls Tribune, Sept. 29, 2010, at http://www.greatfallstribune.com/article/20100929/NEWS01/9290302/Anaconda-Co-shut-down-30-years-ago.

[25] 928 F.2d 48 (2d Cir. 1991).

thousands of clients, they may not bother reporting their client purchases and sales to the firms themselves. Instead, they simply hold enough stock in their own name to cover their clients' needs. When clients buy and sell orders, they then enter the ownership changes on their own books. In turn, the shares themselves they entrust to "depository firms."

Because of these tiered arrangements, a given firm may list on its shareholders' records only the name of the depository institution. The depository holds the stock for the brokerage firm, and the brokerage holds it for the client. A "CEDE" list (the Depository Trust Company uses the name Cede & Company for shares it holds on behalf of the brokerage firms) identifies the brokerage houses; the "NOBO" (non-objecting beneficial owner) list identifies those brokerage firm clients who did not ask that their names be kept confidential.[26] ATT wanted the CEDE and NOBO lists.

The *Sadler* court ordered NCR to disclose both lists. The CEDE list was no big deal. NCR could produce it quickly. The NOBO list, however, would take about ten days. Delaware courts had declined to order firms to produce NOBO lists they did not have ready. Not to worry, the Second Circuit declared. This was New York law, and New York would order firms to produce NOBO lists.

4. State ex rel. Pillsbury v. Honeywell, Inc.[27]

Great-grandson of the doughboy founder, Charles A. Pillsbury came from Minnesotan privilege. Honeywell was the local employer, and Charles's parents played tennis with its CEO. Charles himself prepped at St. Paul's and then went to Yale in 1968. It was a wild year to enter Yale. It was the year of the Tet offensive and the My Lai massacre, the Robert Kennedy and Martin Luther King assassinations. It was the year that students shut down the city of Paris, closed Columbia University, and wreaked havoc at the Chicago Democratic Convention. It was the year that the Soviets invaded Czechoslovakia. And it was the year Americans elected Richard Nixon president.

Pillsbury entered Yale with Republican sympathies and the nickname "Doone." The term was St. Paul's slang for "clueless." But Yale was not a place for Republicans in 1968. The draft was in force, a war was raging, and nothing focuses the mind like the prospect of getting shot. In the dormitory, Pillsbury roomed with another St. Paul's alumnus, a left-wing aspiring graphic artist named Garretson Trudeau. Trudeau took to sketching pictures of his roommate, and the clueless Charles "Doone" Pillsbury started to find his likeness in the student newspaper. He also converted to the antiwar cause (see Figure 6-1).[28]

---

[26] *See generally* Robert C. Clark, *Corporate Law* 359-360 (Little, Brown 1986).

[27] 191 N.W.2d 406 (Minn. 1971).

[28] As Trudeau did not syndicate his comic strip until late 1970, this strip apparently appeared sometime after 1970. Johnson, however, had already decided in 1968 not to seek reelection, and Nixon became president in 1969.

I. Choosing the Team That Runs the Firm

Figure 6-1

DOONESBURY © 1971 G. B. Trudeau. Reprinted with permission of UNIVERSAL UCLICK. All rights reserved.

In court, Pillsbury would explain that at a 1969 meeting of the "Honeywell Project" he had been "shocked" to learn "that Honeywell had a large government contract to produce anti-personnel fragmentation bombs."[29] Sure, he was shocked. And Capt. Renault was shocked to find all that gambling at Rick's Casablanca café. If Pillsbury was shocked in 1969 to learn that Honeywell made shrapnel, he was nearly the last person in the country to know. I was in eighth grade in 1968, and I knew. Everyone knew. Dow Chemical made napalm. And Honeywell made shrapnel. For shrapnel it was. According to the *New York Times*:

> The bombs, about the size of baseballs, are filled with steel pellets. They explode above the ground, spraying a path about 300 yards wide and 1,000 yards long. The fragments are not big enough to tear through a wall, but they do injure and kill humans.[30]

Members of the "Honeywell Project" opposed the firm's role in producing the shrapnel. They were nothing if not emphatic:

> The producers of this weaponry, who maneuver among themselves for the lucrative contracts of its production but who unite among themselves and with others to keep war policies and profits going, are surely the greatest war criminals mankind has ever known.[31]

Not only was Pillsbury the model for Michael Doonesbury, his first wife, Mary Pearl, apparently served as the model for Joanie Caucus. *See Doonesbury: Drawing and Quartering for Fun and Profit*, Time (Feb. 9, 1976).

[29] 191 N.W.2d at 408 (court's words).

[30] *War Foes Adopt Business Tactic*, N.Y. Times 60 (Dec. 28, 1969).

[31] Quoted in Alain Jaubert, *Zapping the Viet Cong by Computer*, New Scientist 685, 688 (Mar. 30, 1972).

Pillsbury bought 100 shares of Honeywell stock. From the "greatest war criminals mankind has ever known," he then demanded the firm's shareholder list. He also demanded "all corporate records dealing with weapons and munitions manufacture."[32]

Honeywell refused. Headquartered in Minneapolis, it was incorporated in Delaware, and Delaware law allowed it to refuse the shareholders' list if it could show that Pillsbury wanted it "for an improper purpose."[33] It could refuse the business records unless Pillsbury could himself prove that he wanted them "for a proper purpose."

The Minnesota Supreme Court denied Pillsbury's claim. Charles Pillsbury "had utterly no interest in the affairs of Honeywell before he learned of Honeywell's production of fragmentation bombs," it reasoned. "But for his opposition to Honeywell's policy," he "probably would not have bought Honeywell stock, would not be interested in Honeywell's profits and would not desire to communicate with Honeywell's shareholders." As a result, he lacked a proper purpose: "Such a motivation can hardly be deemed a proper purpose germane to his economic interest as a shareholder."[34]

The court explained further. Pillsbury might have won, it wrote, if he had tied his left-wing politics to claims about profits:

> We do not mean to imply that a shareholder with a bona fide investment interest could not bring this suit if motivated by concern with the long- or short-term economic effects on Honeywell resulting from the production of war munitions.[35]

Conversely, right-wing shareholders could ask for lists if they thought a firm's opposition to a war hurt its profits:

> Similarly, this suit might be appropriate when a shareholder has a bona fide concern about the adverse effects of abstention from profitable war contracts on his investment in Honeywell.[36]

But Pillsbury never claimed to care about profits at all:

> [P]etitioner was not interested in even the long-term well-being of Honeywell or the enhancement of the value of his shares. His sole purpose was to persuade the company to adopt his social and political concerns, irrespective of any economic benefit to himself or Honeywell.[37]

---

[32] 191 N.W.2d at 409.
[33] Del. Code. Ann. tit. 8, §220.
[34] 191 N.W.2d at 411.
[35] *Id.* at 412.
[36] *Id.*
[37] *Id.*

Pillsbury went to the 1971 shareholders' meeting anyway and lost. Alluding to the German industrialist who built Hitler's military machine, he taunted his parents' tennis partner and Honeywell CEO James Binger: "How does it feel to be the Krupp of Minneapolis?"[38] Honeywell had the proxies, though. Binger controlled 83 percent of the votes. Obviously, he won. As the *New York Times* reported, the "stockholders overwhelmingly re-elected present directors."[39]

Not that Honeywell shareholders would have shared Pillsbury's politics anyway. By 1971, support for the war was fading fast. A large swath of the U.S. electorate wanted the military out of Vietnam, and they would have wanted Honeywell out of munitions. But they would not have owned Honeywell stock. Given how public Honeywell's role had become, those investors who shared Pillsbury's politics would have sold their stock long ago. Only those happy to invest in a munitions firm would still have held their shares.

Notwithstanding the court's rhetoric, its approach does not sort shareholders by the propriety of their "purpose" anyway. It sorts them by whether they will lie. Pillsbury ingenuously told the court he cared only about the morality of the war. To win, all he had to do was to fake an interest in stock prices. Lie a little — tell the court he worried about the effect of shrapnel production on the long-run value of Honeywell's brand name — and he could have had the documents. Henry Ford could have avoided a dividend if he had told the judge he wanted to get rich (Chapter 3, section III.C.1). Charles Pillsbury could have obtained the shareholders' list if he had done the same.

Upon graduation, Pillsbury went to law school. He settled in New Haven and ran for Congress under the Green Party in 2002. He ran again in 2010 and teaches at the Quinnipiac law school.[40]

II. ALLOCATING CONTROL IN THE CLOSE CORPORATION

A. *The Possibilities*

1. Introduction

Suppose Marion and Norman decide to franchise their motel formula. They will incorporate their firm as the Bates Motel, Inc., and they and Norman's mother

---

[38] Funding Universe, *Honeywell, Inc.*, http://www.fundinguniverse.com/company-histories/ Honeywell-Inc-company-history.html (accessed Mar. 12, 2012).

[39] *Honeywell Holders Defeat Dissidents' Slate Soundly*, N.Y. Times 51 (May 11, 1971); *Corporations: Proxies for Protestors*, Time (Jan. 26, 1970); *War Foes Adopt Business Tactic*, N.Y. Times 60 (Dec. 28, 1969).

[40] Thomas MacMillan, *Pillsbury Seeks 1% Against DeLauro*, New Haven Independent (Aug. 31, 2010), http://newhavenindependent.org/index.php/archives/entry/green_challenger_returns_ for_delauro/.

will each take a third of the stock. Suppose further that the trio decide to recruit an experienced manager to run the firm. Through a national search, they identify a young advertising executive named Roger O. Thornhill. Holding as he does a stable and lucrative job at an established firm, Thornhill hesitates to gamble his career on an unproven start-up. Although Marion and Norman have sold him on their idea for a franchise, he wants some control over the firm before he moves. He worries that he will quit his established position, bet everything on the new firm, and find himself outvoted by three people he does not know well.

Marion, Norman, and Mother are eager to recruit Thornhill. They want to give him control over the firm during his tenure as CEO. Consider some of the alternatives available to them.

2. Stock

The trio could sell Thornhill a majority stake in the firm. For this, of course, he would need to invest more than half the capital of the firm. Unless he has the requisite funds, this option will not work.

If Thornhill does buy a majority stake in the firm, several other issues will come to the fore. For example, the original trio may be happy to have Norman as majority shareholder, but not necessarily anyone else. If so, they will want to limit his ability to sell his stock — raising issues discussed more fully in Chapter 7, sections IV and V. In turn, Thornhill may agree to buy a majority stake only if he has a way to sell his stake to the trio when he quits — again, raising issues discussed in Chapter 7, section III.

3. Vote Classes

The trio could also sell Thornhill "stock" that votes but does not entitle him to dividends or a liquidation distribution. In other words, they could sell him stock that gives him a controlling vote at the shareholders' meetings, but not much (if anything) else. Investors do not use this arrangement often (probably because other options work just as well), but the Illinois Supreme Court approved it in *Stroh v. Blackhawk Holding Corp.*[41] To avoid giving Thornhill permanent control, the trio could demand a contractual right to buy (or have the firm redeem) his stock when his employment ends.

A more common alternative involves nonvoting stock. Where the *Stroh* stock had a vote but nothing else, the usual arrangement uses stock that has everything else but not a vote. If investors want to give one investor a larger vote than his investment would otherwise warrant, obviously they can usually

---

[41] 272 N.E.2d 1 (Ill. 1971). The Delaware courts approved it in Lehrman v. Cohen, 222 A.2d 800 (Del. Sup. Ct. 1966).

reach that goal either way: They can issue ordinary stock to everyone, but add *Stroh*-style stock to the investor who will run the firm, or sell the controlling investor ordinary (i.e., voting) stock, and everyone else a mix of voting and nonvoting shares. Although some jurisdictions have prohibited nonvoting stock from time to time, most states allow it. Delaware, for example, allows firms to "issue one or more classes of stock" with "such voting powers, full or limited, or no voting powers . . . as shall be stated . . . in the certificate of incorporation."[42]

Investors can accomplish a variety of other goals through stock classes as well. As noted, they can mix voting and nonvoting stock classes. But if Thornhill wants to receive dividend income before the others, the corporation can issue him "preferred stock" (see also Chapter 3, appendix III). If he wants a veto over any merger, the corporation can sell him 100 percent of a given "class" of stock and then specify in the corporate charter that a merger requires a majority vote in each stock class. If he wants the ability to pick three directors to the board, the corporation can specify in the charter that his class elects three.[43]

4. Cumulative Voting

Sometimes, investors can use "cumulative voting" to ensure that a minority investor has a place on the board.[44] If Thornhill buys no stock, cumulative voting will not ease his plight. Even if he does buy stock, it will not give him control. But where a minority shareholder wants to ensure that he at least keeps a place on the board, cumulative voting may accomplish that much.

Start with the usual "straight voting." Under this approach, shareholders vote for "slates." For example, suppose that Marion, Norman, Mother, and Thornhill each own a quarter of the 100 outstanding shares of Bates Motel, Inc. Suppose that the firm has five directors, elected to one-year terms, and suppose that Marion, Norman, and Mother form a block. Under straight voting, the trio

---

[42] Del. Gen. Corp. L. §151(a).

Blackhawk issued the special stock that had a vote but nothing else because the Illinois Constitution at that time did not allow nonvoting stock. Ill. Const. art. XI, §3 (1870) (repealed); *see* People ex rel. Watseka Tel. Co. v. Emmerson, 134 N.E. 707 (Ill. 1922). It paired ordinary stock with vote-only stock to accomplish what it probably would otherwise have done by pairing ordinary stock with nonvoting stock.

[43] *See* William A. Klein, John C. Coffee Jr. & Frank Partnoy, *Business Organization and Finance* 129, 293 (11th ed., Foundation Press 2010); Clark, *supra* note 26, at 780. On multiple classes under Delaware law, see Del. Gen. Corp. L. §151(a).

[44] Some state constitutions have required cumulative voting—including the former Illinois Constitution behind *Stroh* that banned nonvoting stock. *See* Harry G. Henn & John R. Alexander, *Laws of Corporations* 42, 495 (3d ed., West 1983). In other states, like California, it is statutorily required of some corporations. Cal. Corp. Code §§708, 301.5.

will nominate one slate of five directors: presumably, Marion, Norman, Mother, and two friends. Thornhill will nominate a rival slate of five. The trio's slate will obtain the votes of 75 shares, and the Thornhill slate will have the votes of his 25. The trio's slate will be elected, and Thornhill's will have no representatives on the board.

Under cumulative voting, investors can "cumulate" their votes and allocate them to a few candidates (i.e., less than a full slate). Given that the shareholders will fill five seats, each shareholder will have five votes per share of stock.[45] With his 25 shares, Thornhill will have $25 \times 5 = 125$ votes. Suppose he wants to ensure that he has a place on the board. He will nominate himself and vote all 125 votes for himself. The trio will have $75 \times 5 = 375$ votes. If they try to elect all five of their candidates, each will receive $375/5 = 75$ votes. Because Thornhill received 125, they will not be able to keep him off the board. Now suppose that Thornhill wants to elect two representatives to the board. If he splits his 125 votes between them, one will have 63 votes and the other 62. Obviously, the trio can ensure that he not receive two spots.

More generally, cumulative voting allows a minority shareholder with a substantial block of stock to obtain board representation roughly proportional to his fractional interest in the firm.[46] If he owns a third of the stock, he will pick about a third of the board.[47] If he owns half of the stock, he will pick half the board. If he owns a tenth of the stock, he will be able to elect a tenth of the board — if ten seats are up for election. Should the board have ten seats but be divided into two panels of five directors serving two-year terms (called a "staggered" or "classified" board), the owner of the one-tenth interest will not be able to elect a representative.[48]

---

[45] This is customary, but obviously does not affect the outcome. Treating each share as entitled to one vote rather than five does not make a difference.

[46] The general formula giving the relation between the number of shares a shareholder owns and the number of directors he can elect is given in Clark, *supra* note 26, at 363; Henn & Alexander, *supra* note 44, at 495; Robert W. Hamilton, *The Law of Corporations* 267 (West 2000).

[47] Suppose the board has three members. Shareholder X has 33 of the 100 outstanding shares. If X cumulates his $33 \times 3 = 99$ votes on one board candidate, the others will not be able to outvote his candidate. They will have $67 \times 3 = 201$ votes. Divided three ways, that allows only 67 votes per candidate — which will not outvote X with his 99 votes.

Suppose the board has five members. Shareholder X has 33 of the 100 outstanding shares, or $33 \times 5 = 165$ votes. The others have $67 \times 5 = 335$ votes. Since $335/5 = 67$, they cannot elect five directors and prevent X from taking a seat. But can X obtain two seats? Split his 165 votes two ways, and one candidate will take 83 votes while the other takes 82. To prevent X from electing two directors, the others will need to elect four. If they divide their 335 four ways, three candidates will have 83 votes and one 84. Hence, X's second candidate (with 82 seats) will lose.

[48] Suppose X has 10 of the 100 outstanding shares. If five of the directors are up for election, X will have 50 votes. The others will have $90 \times 5 = 450$ votes. If they divide their votes among five candidates, each will have 90 votes. With only 50 votes, X's representative will lose.

II. Allocating Control in the Close Corporation

5. Voting Trusts

Traditionally, the Marion–Norman–Mother trio might have satisfied Thornhill's concerns through a "voting trust." Under this arrangement, the trio would create a trust and assign their stock to it. By naming themselves its beneficiaries, they would keep the economic incidents of the stock for themselves. As trustee for the trust, however, they would name either Thornhill himself or someone else whom they would tell to vote the stock according to Thornhill's instructions. As Professor Robert Clark put it:

> The shareholders become beneficial or equitable owners of the shares. They retain the right to receive dividends and other asset distributions, and normally receive transferable voting trust certificates evidencing their interests.[49]

Through the trust, in other words, the trio would separate the economic incidents of stock ownership from the vote. The former they would keep for themselves. The latter they would assign to Thornhill. They would then arrange for the trust to dissolve when Thornhill quit his job.

As one of the earliest arrangements to separate a share's vote from the other perquisites of stock ownership, voting trusts encountered some skepticism from judges and legislators. In many states, legislators subjected them to a variety of restrictions. In Delaware, for example, investors must create the trust in writing and file a copy of the trust document with the secretary of state.[50] In many states (though no longer Delaware), they cannot create a trust that lasts longer than ten years.[51]

6. Vote Pooling Agreements

The Marion–Norman–Mother trio could also satisfy Thornhill simply by agreeing to vote their stock as he directs. Rather than create a new legal entity (a trust), they would just agree to pool their stock and vote it as he wished. At first, judges were skeptical. Voting trusts were subject to limits like ten-year maximum terms. Should investors be able, they asked, to draft agreements that accomplished what trusts would accomplish while avoiding the statutory restrictions? When investors negotiated contracts that did exactly that, courts sometimes voided the agreements as failed trusts.[52] More recently, courts have come to enforce the

---

[49] Clark, *supra* note 26, at 777.

[50] Del. Gen. Corp. L. §218(a).

[51] Rev. Model Bus. Corp. Act §7.30(c). Delaware law did at one time limit voting trusts to ten years, as discussed in Ringling Bros.-Barnum & Bailey Combined Shows v. Ringling, 53 A.2d 441 (Del. 1947).

[52] *See* the discussion of *Ringling*, section B below; Stephen M. Bainbridge, *Corporation Law and Economics* 801 (Foundation Press 2002); Clark, *supra* note 26, at 778-779. The Model Bus. Corp. Act

agreements,[53] and many statutes now authorize them explicitly.[54] Note that investors can also facilitate enforcement by assigning proxies on their shares to a third party (see subsection 7 below).[55]

The *Ringling* case, discussed in section B below, illustrates some of the historical evolution. The circus owners initially used a voting trust. Delaware law allowed voting trusts, and had they stayed with the trust the litigation would not have become the mess that it did. When the trust expired, two of the owners (Edith Ringing and Aubrey Haley) turned to a vote pooling agreement. Such agreements were new — and left the Delaware courts uneasy. In the end, the Supreme Court did not invalidate the agreement as a failed voting trust (though it addressed that possibility), but it did declare it unenforceable.

7. Irrevocable Proxies

The trio could also give Thornhill voting control by assigning him a proxy to vote a given number of their shares. In general, shareholders can revoke their proxies at will. To assuage Thornhill, the trio would need to promise not to revoke the proxies for a given period — perhaps, for example, as long as he works for the firm.

As with vote pooling agreements, early courts viewed agreements not to revoke proxies skeptically. They enforced them only when the shareholder coupled the proxy "with an interest." Less cryptically, they treated a proxy as irrevocable only when the person taking the right to vote had another "interest" in the firm. Under Delaware law, for example:

> A duly executed proxy shall be irrevocable if it states that it is irrevocable and if, and only as long as, it is coupled with an interest sufficient in law to support an irrevocable power.[56]

 The Delaware statute itself does not specify what "interest" might support irrevocability. Usually, however, if a person (like Thornhill) works at the firm, his job counts as an "interest." If he has lent money to the firm, the loan counts as an

---

§7.31(a) explicitly rejects this approach. *See also* Abercrombie v. Davies, 130 A.2d 338 (Del. 1957) (invalidating a vote pooling agreement as a failed trust).

[53] Lehrman v. Cohn, 222 A.2d 1 (Del. 1981); *see* Bainbridge, *supra* note 52, at 801; Clark, *supra* note 26, at 778-779.

[54] Del. Gen. Corp. L. §218(c); *see also* Model Bus. Corp. Act §7.31(b). The Official Comment to the section notes that this "avoids the result reached in Ringling Bros. . . . , where the court held that the appropriate remedy to enforce a pooling agreement was to refuse to permit any voting of the breaching party's shares."

[55] Note that Bainbridge, *supra* note 52, at 446, argues that assigning an irrevocable proxy to enforce a vote pooling agreement will increase the odds that a court recharacterizes it as a failed voting trust.

[56] Del. Gen. Corp. L. §212(e).

"interest." And if he has negotiated a vote pooling agreement that he uses the proxy to enforce, that agreement counts as an "interest."[57]

8. The Logic

Investors may litigate ex post, but they negotiate ex ante. It is in the nature of things that they bring their arrangements into court only after they can no longer work together. By contrast, they negotiate them at the start of their relationship when they still enjoy each other's company. Note that they do negotiate them as consenting adults: They give each other these unusual voting rights if, but only if, they think the total contractual package (of which these rights form a component) enhances their welfare.

Typically, investors negotiate these odd arrangements when one of them has agreed either to work at the firm or to lend it large amounts. Like Thornhill, one of them may have left a stable, high-paying job to come work at a start-up. Before gambling his career on the firm, he wants some control. Others may be lending large sums to an unproven management team (or worse, a team at a firm like KNK or Warren Elevator that has proven itself unreliable). Before risking good money, they want control. In any event, the parties adopt the arrangements for good and rational reasons. As odd as they may look after the fact, the arrangements make sense when the parties initially adopt them.

The law gives investors the multiple avenues to accomplish the same goals (subsections 1-7 above) precisely because the arrangements looked so odd after the fact. The parties brought the arrangements to court ex post — when they looked odd. The courts then refused to enforce them (as did the Delaware Supreme Court in *Ringling*, section B below). But the parties had negotiated the arrangements for good reason. If courts blocked one type of arrangement, parties invented another. Eventually, the courts realized the logic to the arrangements ex ante and started enforcing all of them. When they did, the parties found themselves with the panoply of heavily overlapping options that they enjoy today.

B. *Ringling*[58]

1. Introduction

Return to the Ringling brothers of Chapter 2. In their fratricidal disputes of the 1930s and '40s (see Table 6-1), the heirs to the original brothers manipulated

---

[57] N.Y. Bus. Corp. L. §§609(f)(4) (employment), 609(f)(3) (loan), 609(f)(5) (pooling agreement).

[58] Ringling Bros.-Barnum & Bailey Combined Shows v. Ringling, 53 A.2d 441 (Del. 1947). Adapted from J. Mark Ramseyer, *The Story of* Ringling Bros. v. Ringling: *Nepotism and Cycling at the Circus*, in *Corporate Law Stories* 135 (J. Mark Ramseyer ed., Foundation Press 2009). © The Foundation Press 2009, used with permission of Thomson Reuters.

Table 6-1
The Ringling Family

(Relevant Members and Information Only)

Alfred (Alf T) (d. 1919)
   m. Della Andrews --------------- Richard (d. 1931)
                  m. Aubrey Black
                     m. James Haley (m. 1943)

Charles (d. 1926)
   m. Edith Conway --------------- Hester (b. 1893)
                     Robert (b. 1897)
John (d. 1936)
Ida (d. 1950)
   m. Henry North ----------------- John Ringling North (b. 1903)
               ----------------Henry Ringling North (b. 1909)

several devices discussed in section A. Earlier, they had run the circus as a partnership (Chapter 2, Introduction). Facing pressure from their creditors, they incorporated it in 1932 (Chapter 2, section VII). Under this new arrangement, the circus was a Delaware corporation. Its creditors held one-tenth of the stock. Edith Ringling, Aubrey Ringling (soon to be Haley), and John Ringling each held a third of the rest. John Ringling then secured the $1,017,000 remaining debt (assumed by the corporation) with his personal assets.[59]

At the first shareholders' meeting, the creditors took control. Although the shareholders elected John president, they made it clear they named him only to a titular post. The representative of the creditors would run the firm as general manager, and Edith and Aubrey would serve as vice presidents. John Ringling suffered coronary thrombosis and died four years later.

2. John Ringling North

The youngest of the Ringling siblings had been a daughter, Ida (b. 1874). She bore two sons: John Ringling North (she named him after brother John) and Henry North. John North saw his own future in the circus,

---

[59] *See generally* Ernest J. Albrecht, *A Ringling by Any Other Name: The Story of John Ringling North and His Circus* 29 (Scarecrow Press 1989); David Lewis Hammarstrom, *Big Top Boss: John Ringling North and the Circus* 29-31 (U. Ill. Press 1992); Henry Ringling North & Alden Hatch, *The Circus Kings: Our Ringling Family Story* 207, 218-219 (U. Press of Fla. 1960); Richard Thomas, *John Ringling* 210 (Pageant Press 1960); David C. Weeks, *Ringling: The Florida Years, 1911-1936*, at 217-219, 234 (U. Press of Fla. 1993). For the details of the various transactions, see Am. Circus Joint Venture v. Commr., 39 B.T.A. 605 (1939); *see also* In re New York Investors, Inc., 79 F.2d 182 (2d Cir. 1935); In re Allied Owners Corp., 79 F.2d 187 (2d Cir. 1935).

and after time at Yale (funded by Uncle John) he returned to work for his uncle.

John Ringling had named John and Ida North the executors to his estate, and John and Henry North his trustees. Not only did this give John North a sizeable executor's fee when his uncle died in 1936, but it also gave him control over the estate's assets. And those assets included a 30 percent stake in the circus's stock.

To eliminate the circus's meddlesome creditors, John North decided to buy them out. Because the circus still owed $850,000, he needed cash.[60] He approached the Manufacturers Trust Bank, and both its president and its attorney were favorably disposed. As a condition for the loan, they insisted that he himself run the circus: no control to North, no loan, and no reprieve from the creditors. Enter the first of the section A devices above: To give North that control, Edith and Aubrey agreed to put their stock in a voting trust.

Provided they did not exceed ten years, even in the 1930s voting trusts were good under Delaware law. In the case of the Ringlings, the trust would last no longer than the debt itself. Pay off the Manufacturers Trust, and Edith and Aubrey would recover their shares. What is more, the trust did not disenfranchise the two women. It simply gave them three of the seven directors. John North controlled another three, and the Manufacturers Trust installed its vice president William Dunn as the seventh.[61]

By most accounts, John North was as good as his uncle. Under the management of John and Henry North, the circus thrived. John hired Igor Stravinsky to compose a polka for his elephants. He dressed the elephants in tutus and hired George Balanchine to choreograph their dance. By 1940, he had ushered in the best year since 1929, and by 1942 — when 4 million people saw the show — he had repaid the note.[62]

3. The "Ladies' Agreement"

Edith and Aubrey were not pleased. Edith had not been happy with John Ringling's (profitable) management in the 1920s, and she was not happy with John North's (profitable) management in the 1930s. She wanted her son Robert to run it. In time, Aubrey would marry the accountant James Haley hired to untangle the John Ringling estate, and she wanted him to run it too. Trouble was, neither

---

[60] *See* Hammarstrom, *supra* note 59, at 37; North & Hatch, *supra* note 59, at 252-253.

[61] Rev. Code Del. 1935, §18. The ten-year limit is now gone; *see* Del. Gen. Corp. L. §218. *See* Henry S. Cohn & David Bollier, *The Great Hartford Circus Fire* 19 (Yale U. Press 1991); see North & Hatch, *supra* note 59, at 255; Albrecht, *supra* note 59, at 47.

[62] Ringling Bros.-Barnum & Bailey Combined Shows Inc. v. Ringling, 29 Del. Ch. 610 (1947); *see* Robert Lewis Taylor, *Center Ring* 34 (Doubleday 1956); Hammarstrom, *supra* note 59, at 75, 495.

Robert nor James was a "circus man." If James kept the books, Robert mostly sang baritone at the opera.[63]

Nevertheless, to place their men in management, in 1941 Edith and Aubrey signed a "vote pooling agreement" (known in the dispute as the "Ladies' Agreement"):

> 2. In exercising any voting rights . . . , each party will consult and confer with the other and the parties will act jointly in exercising such voting rights in accordance with such agreement as they may reach. . . .
> 3. In the event the parties fail to agree . . . , the question in disagreement shall be submitted to Karl D. Loos, of Washington, D.C., as arbitrator and his decision thereon shall be binding upon the parties hereto.[64]

They signed it to retake control from the North brothers, and retake it they did.

4. The War

Canvas burns, patrons smoke, and crowds attract arsonists. With cigarettes, cooking fires, flammable tents, and arsonists, circus fires were a constant risk. Fireproofing was not an option. The technology did exist in 1944, but by wartime exigencies the government had arrogated the materials to itself. Under John and Henry North, the early 1940s circus had combined three more primitive strategies instead. On the big top, it applied a "fire-resistant" treatment. It then placed fire extinguishers under the bleachers and surrounded the tent with a ring of pumping trucks, engines running and fully manned.[65]

Unfortunately, these strategies presented other problems. Fire-resistant canvas leaked—it kept out some fire, but let in some rain. Surrounding the tent with manned pumping trucks required a large staff—but with the country at war, young men were scarce. In most years, the Ringling circus had employed 1,600; in 1942 it made do with 1,200.[66]

As the new year opened in 1943, John and Henry North decided to wait out the war. Chronically shorthanded, the circus presented too serious a risk of fire. But it was not just fire. The government regulated the railroads in ways that complicated

[63] *Robert E. Ringling, Circus Chairman*, N.Y. Times (Jan. 3, 1950); *see* North & Hatch, *supra* note 59, at 250.
[64] Ringling Bros.-Barnum & Bailey Combined Shows Inc. v. Ringling, 29 Del. Ch. 610 (1947); Ringling v. Ringling Bros.-Barnum & Bailey Combined Shows, 29 Del. Ch. 318, 322-323 (1946); *see* North & Hatch, *supra* note 59, at 321; Hammarstrom, *supra* note 59, at 98.
[65] *See* North & Hatch, *supra* note 59, at 317, 327; Don Massey & Rick Davey, *A Matter of Degree* 26 (Willow Book Press 2001); Cohn & Bollier, *supra* note 61, at 7.
[66] *See* Massey & Davey, *supra* note 65, at 37; Cohn & Bollier, *supra* note 61, at 7 (staff of 424 doing work of 1,000).

any move from town to town. And it levied taxes at rates that made it hard to keep any profits they made anyway.

At the January 1943 board meeting, John North outlined two options. Convert to a nonprofit basis for the duration of the war and perform for the government at military installations and USOs. Possibly, the government would then give the circus the priority it needed in transportation, fireproofing supplies, and personnel. Alternatively, shut down and wait for peace.[67] By January 1943, the tide had already turned. The Soviets had repelled the Nazis and launched their counteroffensive. The Americans had won at Midway and were firebombing Tokyo.

John North presented the choice to a board of seven. Henry and circus treasurer George Woods voted with him to shut down the circus. Edith, Robert, and Aubrey voted to continue as is. Representing the Manufacturers Trust, Dunn voted with the women — and the circus continued as is.[68]

John promptly resigned as president, and the board elected Robert in his stead. A shareholders' meeting followed in April, and (as explained above) Edith and Aubrey used the "Ladies' Agreement" to name a majority of the seven directors.

5. The Fire

But it was all over in minutes. According to the American Red Cross:

> The performance was well under way. The wild-animal acts had just been concluded. The aerialists were taking their positions on the platform for the next act. Suddenly a small flame appeared along the side wall near the main entrance. At first there was no panic, only haste and anxiety, as people started to leave for the exits. Pandemonium soon broke loose, however, for the canvas, soaked in gasoline and paraffin to repel water, blazed high like burning celluloid.
>
> Within a few minutes, the entire tent was a flaming mass[, and the temperature within soared to 1,600 degrees].[69] . . . Within an hour, all that remained of the "Greatest Show on Earth" were twisted metal poles which had fallen one by one as the supporting guy ropes burned away, the metal animal runways and exhibition cages, and the charred bleacher seats.[70]

The fire in the Ringling tent on July 6, 1944, killed at least 168 people. Given the condition of the bodies, the death toll was never more than an estimate. Of the dead, 56 were under ten years old (see photo, "Ringling Tent Fire, July 6, 1944").[71]

---

[67] *See* North & Hatch, *supra* note 59, at 322; Hammarstrom, *supra* note 59, at 98; Albrecht, *supra* note 59, at 142; Taylor, *supra* note 62, at 34.

[68] *See* North & Hatch, *supra* note 59, at 323. The voting trust would terminate in a few months.

[69] *See* Davey & Massey, *supra* note 65, at 63.

[70] Am. Natl. Cross, *Hartford Circus Fire, July 6, 1944*, at 2-3 (Am. Natl. Red Cross 1946).

[71] *See id.* at 10; North & Hatch, *supra* note 59, at 329; Cohn & Bollier, *supra* note 61, at 14.

Figure 6-2
Ringling Tent Fire, July 6, 1944

Whatever the immediate cause of the fire, the Hartford police quickly attacked circus management. Because the North brothers' fire-retardant canvas leaked in the rain, Robert had abandoned the technology and resurrected the old water-proofing method — dissolve melted paraffin in gasoline, as the Red Cross explained, and sweep it into the canvas. Touch a flame, and the canvas ignited violently, raining burning paraffin like napalm on the crowd below. Robert also ignored the manpower shortage. Badly overextended, his workers had left the fire extinguishers undistributed, the water pumping trucks unmanned, and two of the exits blocked.[72] The audience never had a chance.

Given this scope to the malfeasance, prosecutors went for involuntary manslaughter. At a New York dentist on the day of the fire, Robert escaped prosecution.

[72] *See Report of Commissioner of State Police as State Fire Marshal to State's Attorney for Hartford County Concerning the Fire in Hartford on July 6, 1944,* at 8-13 (unpublished); North & Hatch, *supra* note 59, at 318, 326; Albrecht, *supra* note 59, at 150; Hammarstrom, *supra* note 59, at 107-109; Cohn & Bollier, *supra* note 61, at 98-99; Karen Goldberg, *The Hartford Circus Fire of 1944,* Concord Rev. 35, 38 (1990); Davey & Massey, *supra* note 65, at 45, 26, 103.

II. Allocating Control in the Close Corporation

Not so James. Along with five other senior circus officials, he pleaded nolo contendere and the judge sentenced him to a year and a day.[73]

James Haley's prison term gave John North the opening he needed. Robert Ringling walked, while James Haley served time. Worse, Robert did not fight for Haley at the trial, did not visit Haley in prison, did not even write.[74] Haley had taken the fall for Robert's catastrophic mismanagement, and Robert refused to acknowledge it.

In truth, James Haley did not like John North either, but North saw the chance to divide his enemies. Toward that end, he tried repeatedly to visit Haley in prison. Initially, Haley refused even to see him. Eventually, he relented. No one observed what the two men discussed. Everyone would soon see what Haley decided to do.[75]

6. The Litigation

On Christmas Eve, 1945, James Haley walked. He had served 8 months 17 days, released early for good behavior.[76] The shareholders would next meet in April 1946. Aubrey Haley was bound by the "Ladies' Agreement" to vote as agreed with Edith Ringling or — if they could not agree — as dictated by the attorney who drafted the agreement for them, Karl Loos.

Edith Ringling and Aubrey Haley each held 315 shares. They had owned 300 shares from the circus's incorporation in 1933 and had bought another 15 from the creditors when the circus repaid its debt in 1937. John North bought the other 70 shares held by the creditors and voted 300 shares as executor of the John Ringling estate.[77]

Under the terms of the Ringling corporate charter, the shareholders elected the seven directors by cumulative voting. Edith and Aubrey each could cast $315 \times 7 = 2,205$ votes (as explained in subsection A.4 above). North cast $370 \times 7 = 2,590$.

Shunned by Robert Ringling despite serving prison time for Robert's mismanagement, James Haley sided with the North brothers, and so did his wife Aubrey. Obviously, Edith and Aubrey could no longer agree how to vote. Their disagreement threw the decision to Loos. Placed in an impossible situation, he told the women to stay with the original purpose behind their agreement: minimize John North's seats on the board.

---

[73] See Albrecht, *supra* note 59, at 152; Stewart O'Nan, *The Circus Fire* 295 (Doubleday 2000). On the responsibility of the municipal authorities, see *Report of the Municipal Board of Inquiry on the Circus Disaster* (Nov. 1944) (unpublished).

[74] See O'Nan, *supra* note 73, at 300; Cohn & Bollier, *supra* note 61, at 58-59; Albrecht, *supra* note 59, at 153-154.

[75] See O'Nan, *supra* note 73, at 300; Albrecht, *supra* note 59, at 153-154.

[76] See O'Nan, *supra* note 73, at 301; Albrecht, *supra* note 59, at 156; Hammarstrom, *supra* note 59, at 111.

[77] See North & Hatch, *supra* note 59, at 254; Albrecht, *supra* note 59, at 49.

Table 6-2
Stockholder Votes at the Ringling Annual Meeting

A. As Directed by Loos:

	Votes		
Candidates	Edith	Aubrey	Total
Edith R	882		882
Robert R	882		882
Aubrey H		882	882
James H		882	882
Dunn	441	441	882
Griffin			
North			
Wood			
Total:	2205	2205	4410

B. As Actually Cast:

	Votes			
Candidates	Edith	Aubrey	North	Total
Edith R	882			882
Robert R	882			882
Aubrey H		1103		1103
James H		1102		1103
Dunn	441			441
Griffin			864	864
North			863	863
Wood			863	863
Total:	2205	2205	2590	7000

James attended the meeting in Aubrey's stead. With James siding with John, Edith moved to adjourn. As arbitrator under the "Ladies' Agreement," Loos ordered James to vote to adjourn. James refused, the motion to adjourn failed, and the meeting continued. Loos then ordered Edith and James to cast their votes as given in Panel A of Table 6-2. Had they voted as Loos ordered, Edith would have controlled a faction of three on the seven-member board: Edith, her son Robert, and their ally Dunn. The opposing faction elected Aubrey, her husband James, John North, and his ally Griffin.

James again refused to follow Loos's instructions and voted as given in Panel B. Dunn now had the lowest vote total of the eight candidates. He lost, and Wood won a seat on the board. John and James counted James's votes as legally cast, held a meeting of the directors so elected, and replaced Robert with James as Ringling president. John and James had cut a deal: James would serve for one year and then resign in favor of John.

II. Allocating Control in the Close Corporation

The parties contested the agreement at trial. Had Edith and Aubrey stayed with a voting trust, the litigation would have been simple: The court would have enforced the terms of the trust. But the two had tried a vote pooling agreement, and such agreements were still novel. The agreement left the Delaware Supreme Court obviously troubled—and it ultimately held the agreement legal but unenforceable. The agreement contained, the court explained, "no express delegation or grant of power" to Loos (like an irrevocable proxy) to enforce his orders. Never mind that the agreement provided that Loos's "decision thereon shall be binding upon the parties hereto." As they did not delegate, the court would not enforce their agreement. It was still legal, however, and James had flouted it. As he had not voted his wife's shares legally, he had not voted them at all. They simply did not count. Edith had elected three directors (Edith, Robert, Dunn), John had elected three (John, Griffin, Wood), and James had elected none.

7. Denouement

In fact, the Haley–North alliance was unraveling anyway. James Haley had defected from the "Ladies' Agreement" in exchange for John North's promise to let him become the first president. John had agreed to James's presidency in exchange for his promise to resign after one year. With the year almost up, James decided he liked his job too much to quit.[78]

John North then shifted strategy. So what if James Haley would not resign the presidency? John North would simply buy control. He first bought the stock that John Ringling had left through his estate for the state of Florida. With the purchase, he owned—not just voted, but owned—37 percent.[79] He then turned to Edith Ringling. Robert had never been a healthy man, but after a stroke in the summer of 1947 he lost his enthusiasm for family feuds. What is more, John was suing him for mismanagement. Although duty of care suits are hard to win, John could point to the criminal convictions and millions in civil damages. By mid-1947, he had won at trial. Robert appealed the verdict, but John offered to drop the suit if Edith would vote her stock as he (John) instructed.[80] Edith agreed.

John North now had voting control, and Aubrey and James promptly capitulated. They sold 140 of their shares to John, and 175 to Robert. Thereby, John acquired 51 percent of the firm.

---

[78] See Cohn & Bollier, *supra* note 61, at 60; Albrecht, *supra* note 59, at 160.

[79] Time (May 12, 1952); *see* North & Hatch, *supra* note 59, at 341; Albrecht, *supra* note 59, at 161.

[80] See Cohn & Bollier, *supra* note 61, at 60; O'Nan, *supra* note 73, at 310; North & Hatch, *supra* note 59, at 336-337.

8.   Why Litigate?

Why did James Haley ignore Karl Loos's instructions (even had he complied, he and John North would have controlled four of the seven seats)? Why did Edith Ringling contest the election (she lacked a majority either way)? And having lost at trial, why did Aubrey Haley appeal (why was four of the seven not good enough)? Whether or not Aubrey (and James) could ignore Loos, Edith took a minority of board seats. If Loos could bind Aubrey, Edith obtained three of seven (Edith, Robert, Dunn). If he could not, she obtained two (Edith, Robert). Either way, she lost any vote at the board. Why did Edith and Aubrey care?

They probably did *not* care. But the day's proceedings had not stopped with the shareholders' meeting. They had continued to a meeting of the new board. There, the board had turned to the selection of "officers and the election of an executive committee and the fixing of salaries" — and fired Robert. Edith denominated her suit not just as a challenge to the shareholders' meeting but also to the selection of the "officers of the corporation" and sued everyone "whose title to office is brought into question by this proceeding.[81] The president collected a salary. He enjoyed an elaborate array of perquisites. And he decided when, where, and what the circus performed. Since 1943, Robert Ringling had held the job. Edith Ringling wanted him to keep it, Aubrey Haley wanted it for James, and John North wanted it for himself.

As intensely as Edith Ringling and Aubrey Haley cared about the presidency, however, legally they could not include it in the "Ladies' Agreement."[82] By a long line of cases (see *McQuade, Clark,* and *Galler* immediately below), courts banned nonunanimous agreements among shareholders about who served in which office at what pay. Unable to include it, they promised instead to negotiate. Presumably, they negotiated not just about how to vote their stock, but about whom to appoint as president. Although neither could enforce any agreement they negotiated in court, so long as they reached a mutually advantageous arrangement, they would not need court enforcement.

Come 1946, Edith and Aubrey fundamentally disagreed about who should run the circus. As president, Robert had killed 168 people, incurred millions in projected liabilities, and sent James to prison. He wanted to keep the job anyway, and Edith wanted him to want it. James and John wanted it for themselves.

As the annual meeting opened, Edith and Aubrey still disagreed: Would it be Robert, or would it be James? They had fought the night before until nearly midnight.[83] Loos now made a last-ditch attempt to reopen the talks. Adjourn the meeting, he ordered. Return to the negotiations.

---

[81] *Ringling v. Ringling Bros.*, 29 Del. Ch. at 320, 324.

[82] Though in fact the parties may have treated it as binding their votes as directors as well. A biographer to John North reports that Loos also arbitrated disagreements between Edith and Aubrey at a 1947 board meeting. *See* Hammarstrom, *supra* note 59, at 119. In their agreement, the parties recited that they intended "to continue to act jointly in all matters relating to their . . . interest" in the circus. *Ringling v. Ringling Bros.*, 29 Del. Ch. at 322.

[83] *Ringling v. Ringling Bros.*, 29 Del. Ch. at 322.

But Aubrey and James Haley no longer needed Edith. Once John North offered to vote James president for a year, they did not need her votes. Blithely, they ignored Loos's instructions to vote for adjournment. They ignored his instructions to vote for Dunn. And in the board meeting that followed, they fired Robert and appointed James.

Edith sued. Although the court focused (as do most corporate law classes) on the board seats, her suit went to the presidency itself. If Loos could bind Aubrey, the shareholders' meeting never happened; instead, the shareholders adjourned it at the outset. If the shareholders' meeting never happened, the directors never held the board meeting that followed, they never ousted Robert—and James had no claim (other than in quantum meruit) to what by the time of the Supreme Court decision was a year's worth of salary, a year's worth of elaborate perquisites, and a year's worth of changes to circus management.[84]

9.   The Moral

Agreements among shareholders to restrict their ability to vote as they please left courts uneasy. After the fact, the agreements looked odd. The Ringling family had initially used a voting trust. Delaware law allowed the trusts, and, had they stayed with a trust, the court would have enforced it readily. But Edith and Aubrey did not want to use a trust and prevailed on their lawyer to draft them something new. To keep his clients happy, he gave them a vote pooling agreement. This, however, left the court uneasy all over again. In the end, the Delaware Supreme Court did not invalidate the agreement as a failed trust—as some courts did. But it did not enforce it either.

It is the kind of opinion that pushes the corporate bar back to its perennial default: If it ain't broke, don't fix it.

III.   RESTRICTIONS ON THE POWER OF THE BOARD

A.   *Introduction*

Suppose Marion, Norman, and Thornhill continue their talks about a motel franchising company. After elaborate negotiations, Thornhill decides to stay with his advertising firm. Marion and Norman agree to run the motel franchising operation themselves. Marion will serve as president and operate it on a daily basis. Norman will work as vice president for artistic development. He will spend his time

---

[84] *See* Hammarstrom, *supra* note 59, at 119; Albrecht, *supra* note 59, at 161. Stephen Bainbridge notes that a majority of four would not be sufficient to insulate any vote electing John or James president from conflict of interest claims since the four include John and James themselves. *See* Bainbridge, *supra* note 52, at 804 n.19, applying Del. Gen. Corp. L. §144.

designing new taxidermic wall ornaments and shower fixtures. Marion and Norman agree that they will each take a $50,000 annual salary for their work.

Mother is not pleased. She convinces Norman that the agreement is a bad deal. At the next shareholders' meeting, Norman and his mother vote their stock to elect a board slate that excludes Marion (the firm did not have cumulative voting or stock classes). That board then fires Marion from her job as president and appoints Norman's mother. Marion sues.

To explore the law that would govern the litigation, consider in turn *McQuade*, *Clark*, and *Galler*.

B.   McQuade v. Stoneham[85]

> Nick Carraway wondered who he was. He turned to Gatsby:
> "Who is he anyhow — an actor?"
> "No."
> "A dentist?"
> "Meyer Wolfshiem? No, he's a gambler." Gatsby hesitated, then added coolly:
> "He's the man who fixed the World's Series back in 1919."
> "Fixed the World's Series?" . . .
> "Why isn't he in jail?"
> "They can't get him, old sport. He's a smart man."[86]

1.   The Case

In May 1919, Charles Stoneham, John McGraw, and Francis McQuade bought a majority interest in the National Exhibition Company. The NEC owned the New York Giants. Stoneham bought 1,166 of its shares; the other two bought 70 shares apiece for $50,338.10. As part of the deal, the three agreed that they would each work at the firm:

> The parties hereto will use their best endeavors for the purpose of continuing as directors of said Company and as officers thereof the following:
> Directors:
>
>> Charles A. Stoneham
>> John J. McGraw
>> Francis X. McQuade
>
> —with the right to the party of the first part [Stoneham] to name all additional directors as he sees fit:

---

[85] 189 N.E. 234 (N.Y. 1934).
[86] F. Scott Fitzgerald, *The Great Gatsby* 77-78 (Scribner 1995) (originally published 1925).

III. Restrictions on the Power of the Board

Officers:

> Charles A. Stoneham, President
> John J. McGraw, Vice-President
> Francis X. McQuade, Treasurer

No salaries are to be paid to any of the above officers or directors, except as follows:

President $45,000
Vice-President 7,500
Treasurer .... 7,500[87]

The trio continued the arrangement for several years. In 1925, they raised McQuade's salary to $10,000, but three years later the board replaced McQuade with Leo J. Bondy. Stoneham and McGraw abstained, and the other board members (who answered to Stoneham) voted to replace McQuade.

McQuade sued for his job and back pay. Stoneham and McGraw argued that their agreement jeopardized the interests of the other shareholders — those shareholders not party to their three-way contract. They (Stoneham and McGraw) held their board positions in trust for the corporation and its other shareholders. Were they to agree in advance about what they would do on the board, explained Stoneham and McGraw, they would violate the fiduciary duties they owed to those other investors.

The New York Court of Appeals agreed with Stoneham and McGraw:

> [T]he stockholders may not, by agreement among themselves, control the directors in the exercise of the judgment vested in them by virtue of their office to elect officers and fix salaries. . . . Directors may not by agreements entered into as stockholders abrogate their independent judgment.[88]

The court noted that shareholders could agree about how they would vote their stock. Shareholders act for themselves; they are not agents of anyone else. They can properly agree about whom they will elect to the board. What they cannot do is to agree about what actions those directors will take once elected. Directors are agents for the corporation and owe a legal duty to promote the interests of all shareholders — including shareholders not party to any agreement. For one group of shareholders to try to control how the directors vote would prevent those directors from fulfilling the fiduciary duties they (as directors) owed the firm and the other shareholders. Here, Stoneham, McGraw, and McQuade tried to do exactly that, and the court held their agreement void.

The court added a second reason for favoring Stoneham and McGraw. McQuade was a city magistrate. That position was a full-time one, and New York law banned magistrates from holding other jobs. As McQuade's position at the

---

[87] 189 N.E. at 235.
[88] *Id.* at 236.

NEC violated that law, the court cited it as another reason to void his agreement with Stoneham and McGraw.

2. The Story

Stoneham was a stockbroker, and a crooked one at that. From outside the doors of the New York Stock Exchange, he ran what journalists of the time called a "bucket-shop" operation. Clients placed orders, and sometimes he executed them. Sometimes he did not. Running the office this way was illegal, but as long as he paid his clients what they would have earned if he had placed the orders, no one should have cared. Clients did care because Stoneham did not always pay. In 1921, he dissolved his operation and shifted their accounts to other firms. Within two years, two of those firms collapsed. Apparently, Stoneham had simply stolen their money.[89]

John McGraw had been the Giants' manager since 1902.[90] He had begun his career with the Orioles. There, he had compiled a career on-base percentage of 0.466 — shy only of the all-time records eventually set by Ted Williams and Babe Ruth. As Giants manager, he then took the team to ten National League pennants and three World Series victories. Of course, he also cheated. He played at a time when the game had only one umpire. When the umpire looked elsewhere, McGraw sometimes blocked runners. Other times, he simply tripped them.[91]

And McQuade? McQuade was a magistrate, a lower court judge in the New York state court system.

But *McQuade v. Stoneham* is not just about these three men. It is also about a fourth, whose name never appears in the opinion: Arnold Rothstein (see photo). From about 1910 until his death in 1928 (gunned down, probably over a gambling debt), Rothstein ran the New York mob. From his table at Lindy's Restaurant on Broadway and 49th, he controlled a vast network of casinos, gambling houses, horse races, and pool halls. When prohibition began in 1920, he imported whiskey from Canada and Europe. From whiskey, he moved into narcotics. Meyer Lansky, associate to the MGM dissident shareholder Philip Levin, learned his trade from Arnold Rothstein. Lucky Luciano claimed that the relentlessly dapper Rothstein had "taught me how to dress." Indeed, he mused, if Rothstein had only "lived a little longer, he could've made me pretty elegant." And at the behest of Rothstein (the obvious model for Fitzgerald's Meyer Wolfshiem), in the fall of 1919, Eddie Cicotte, Shoeless Joe Jackson, and their Black Sox cohorts threw the World Series.

On January 19, 1919, a police squad raided Rothstein's crap game on West 57th Street. Before they made it into the house, Rothstein gunned them down. Through the door, he hit and wounded three. It was he who fired the shots; even

---

[89] Stoneham was prosecuted for these transactions. At trial, he was represented by Arnold Rothstein's attorney William Fallon and acquitted. Lyle Spatz & Steve Steinberg, *1921: The Yankees, the Giants and the Battle for Baseball Supremacy in New York* 20-21 (U. Neb. Press 2010).

[90] Spatz & Steinberg, *supra* note 89, at 17.

[91] *Giants' Owners Buy Track*, N.Y. Times (Oct. 18, 1919).

III. Restrictions on the Power of the Board

Figure 6-3
Arnold Rothstein, 1928

Transcendental Graphics/Getty Images Sport/Getty Images

his lawyer's biographer would later recall that it had been he.[92] Rothstein's lawyer stalled as best he could, but eventually prosecutors filed charges against all 21 men in the place. On June 5, the twenty men other than Rothstein appeared before magistrate Francis X. McQuade.[93] McQuade dismissed the charges against them all. No evidence, he explained. The district attorney then filed charges against Rothstein himself. The grand jury duly indicted him, and Rothstein appeared before a judge on June 25. Once McQuade had dismissed the cases against the other twenty men, however, all testimony against Rothstein vanished. Given that Rothstein had shot the police from behind the door, the only men who saw it were the twenty in the room. With the cases against them dismissed, none had any reason to cooperate with the prosecutor:

> Q: Do you know who did the shooting?
> A: No.
> Q: Did you see Rothstein have a gun, or did you see him do the shooting?
> A: No.

[92] Gene Fowler, *The Great Mouthpiece: A Life Story of William J. Fallon* 203 (Blue Ribbon 1931); Leo Katcher, *The Big Bankroll: The Life and Times of Arnold Rothstein* 156-164 (Harper 1959).
[93] David Pietrusza, *Rothstein: The Life, Times, and Murder of the Criminal Genius Who Fixed the 1919 World Series* 143 (Carroll & Graf 2003).

Q: Well, who in your opinion did the shooting? Give us your best opinion.
A: From reading the papers, my opinion is that it was Rothstein.[94]

The judge excoriated the prosecutors:

> This appears to be the only evidence that in any way relates to Rothstein. Under our system of jurisprudence, fortunately, a surmise, a conjecture, or a guess can have no place as evidentiary of the commission of a crime. Why the Grand Jury ordered an indictment in this case is incomprehensible. It should not have been voted. It was idle to do so. The motion to dismiss is granted.[95]

For his "perjury" before the grand jury in testifying against Rothstein, prosecutors then turned to the hapless police inspector Dominiq Henry. Henry had ordered his men to raid the game and urged the state to prosecute Rothstein for shooting them. For his efforts, he found himself tried for perjury.[96]

On May 21, 1919—15 days before the state arraigned the twenty witnesses before McQuade—Rothstein brokered the sale of the New York Giants to Stoneham, McGraw, and McQuade. The news surprised and mystified fans. The team had been for sale, but the principal candidates for the purchase had always been the Loft candy company's George Loft, entertainer George M. Cohan, and Harry Sinclair of the Sinclair oil firm.[97] At a time when federal judges made $6,000,[98] state judge McQuade found more than $50,000 to pay for his stake. Nor was this the trio's only purchase. At the same time they bought the Giants, they also bought—in partnership with Rothstein—a casino and racetrack in Havana.[99]

Why Stoneham and McQuade eventually quarreled is obscure, but quarrel they did. McQuade first sued Stoneham for stealing from the firm: From 1919 to 1925, claimed McQuade, Stoneham had borrowed $410,000 from the NEC for the "Cuban-American Jockey Club."[100] Stoneham and McGraw then sued McQuade for "willfully and maliciously" trying to "wreck and destroy" the firm. They also fired McQuade and hired Bondy—but McQuade then sued for back pay. It was a mess, and McQuade's lawyer admitted as much. Stoneham, McGraw, and his client McQuade were all "of the same ilk and none was an angel," he explained to the court. "They were all drinking men, all cursing men, all fighting men."[101]

---

[94] Quoted in *id.* at 143-144.
[95] Quoted in *id.* at 144.
[96] Katcher, *supra* note 92, at 156-164; Pietrusza, *supra* note 93, at 143-145.
[97] Noel Hynd, *The Giants of the Polo Grounds* 210-211 (Doubleday 1988).
[98] Evans v. Gore, 253 U.S. 245, 264 (1920) (Holmes, J., dissenting).
[99] Katcher, *supra* note 92, at 193; Herbert Mitgang, *The Man Who Rode the Tiger: The Life and Times of Judge Samuel Seabury* 189-190 (Fordham U. Press 1996); Steven A. Riess, *Touching Base: Professional Baseball and American Culture in the Progressive Era* 88, 188 (U. Ill. Press 1999); David L. Porter, *Biographical Dictionary of American Sports* 1487 (Greenwood Press 2000). For details on the Havana casino, see Craig Thompson & Allen Raymond, *Gang Rule in New York* 194-195 (Dial 1940) (giving the date of casino purchase as 1920); Harold Seymour, *Baseball: The Golden Age* 140 (Oxford U. Press 1971).
[100] Henn & Alexander, *supra* note 46, at 297.
[101] Quoted in *id.* at 303.

III. Restrictions on the Power of the Board

The Court of Appeals noted that McQuade resigned his job as magistrate in December 1930. McQuade did resign, but not to spend time running baseball teams. He resigned because a special commission headed by one Justice Samuel Seabury had been appointed to investigate the corruption among New York City magistrates. McQuade was near the top of Seabury's list. He resigned—and thereby "obviat[ed]," as the commission put it, "the necessity for a trial."[102]

In their Court of Appeals opinion, the justices never mention Arnold Rothstein. But they read newspapers. They knew Seabury; after all, he had himself served on the Court of Appeals. They also knew Stoneham. They knew he had bought the team through Rothstein. They knew he had robbed his bucket-shop investors. They knew the state had prosecuted him for that theft and that Rothstein's lawyer had won him an acquittal in the case (and that Rothstein's attorney was "notorious for bribing jurors").[103]

And they knew McQuade too. They knew Rothstein had shot three policemen. They knew McQuade had protected him by dismissing the charges against anyone who might have testified. They knew that he had dismissed the charges 15 days after Rothstein had obtained for him an interest in the Giants. They knew that no honest magistrate would have had $50,000 to invest in a baseball team. And they knew he had resigned his position because the Seabury Commission was about to prosecute him for corruption.

The justices did not like Stoneham, but they probably liked McQuade even less. They did not expect bucket-shop operators to be honest. They did expect judges to be. In McQuade, they had a state judge who went into business with a hopelessly corrupt business partner. That business partner had stolen the bribe that the leading New York mob boss had paid the judge to keep him out of prison for shooting three policemen. And the judge had now sued that business partner to get his bribe back.

The judge lost.

But then, sometimes cases are "overdetermined."

C. *Clark v. Dodge*[104]

Together David Clark and John Dodge owned two pharmaceutical firms: Bell & Company and Hollings-Smith. In each, Dodge owned a 75 percent interest and Clark, 25 percent. Dodge owned the majority of the stock; Clark ran the firms. The two companies produced their drugs by "secret formulae," and those "formulae and methods of manufacture . . . were known to [Clark] alone."[105]

---

[102] Quoted in Mitgang, *supra* note 99, at 189.

[103] Seymour, *supra* note 99, at 309. McQuade was part of the Tammany Hall Democratic machine. The Court of Appeals justices, by contrast, were known either as Republicans, as men who had been jointly endorsed by the Republicans and Democrats, or (like Chief Justice Pound) endorsed by the Republicans and Progressives. Note that Fiorello LaGuardia was elected mayor of New York on an anti-Tammany reform platform in late 1933.

[104] 199 N.E. 641 (N.Y. 1936).

[105] 199 N.E. at 641.

Worried that only Clark knew how to produce the pharmaceuticals so key to the firm, Dodge asked him to teach his son. In return, he promised to use his three-quarter interest in the firm to keep Clark on the board, to keep Clark as general manager as long as Clark was "faithful, efficient and competent," and to ensure that Clark received a quarter of the firms' net income. Once Clark had told his son the secret formulae, Dodge fired Clark.

Clark sued for his job and back pay. To the New York Court of Appeals, the question was "whether the contract is illegal as against public policy within the decision in *McQuade v. Stoneham*."[106] Crucially, the *McQuade* trio had not owned all the stock, whereas Clark and Dodge had. Reasoned the court:

> If the enforcement of a particular contract damages nobody — not even, in any perceptible degree, the public — one sees no reason for holding it illegal, even though it impinges slightly upon the broad provision of section 27 ["The business of a corporation shall be managed by its board of directors."]. . . . Where the directors are the sole stockholders, there seems to be no objection to enforcing an agreement among them to vote for certain people as officers.[107]

Consider the logic at stake. Shareholders elect directors to serve as fiduciaries and run the firm to maximize their (shareholders') interests. Suppose, however, that a subset of shareholders can effectively pick the directors that they want and agree in advance about what those directors will do once elected to the board. If bound by that agreement, the directors will not have full discretion to promote the interests of all shareholders. Instead, they will be acting only on behalf of a subset.

Now suppose that all of the shareholders are party to the agreement. The directors will still face restrictions on their ability to promote shareholder interests — but they will face restrictions to which all the shareholders have agreed. The only people who might otherwise suffer from the agreement, in other words, have voluntarily agreed to it.

Stoneham cheated McQuade. Nonetheless, the Court of Appeals refused to force Stoneham to abide by his agreement. Were it to do so, it explained, those shareholders not party to the agreement would lose the full benefit (such as it was) of Stoneham's and McQuade's services.

Dodge cheated Clark too. Here, though, the parties to the agreement held all the stock. The agreement restricted the range of discretion that Dodge and Clark could exercise, but those restrictions could harm only Dodge and Clark themselves. Given that they had voluntarily agreed to the terms, the court duly enforced them against Dodge.

The Court of Appeals' 1936 opinion leaves discreetly unsaid any detail about the pharmaceuticals (see photo). The box describes the medicine as "A Nerve Tonic and Stimulant for the treatment of Mental and Physical Exhaustion, Depression, Insomnia, Neuralgia, etc."

---

[106] *Id.* at 642.
[107] *Id.*

III. Restrictions on the Power of the Board

Figure 6-4
Bell Pharmaceuticals

The label lists the ingredients: strychnine and marijuana.[108]

D. *Galler v. Galler*[109]

Together, the brothers Benjamin and Isadore Galler owned all of the shares of the Galler Drug Company (an Illinois corporation) — 110 shares apiece. In 1945, they each sold 6 shares to an employee named Mandel Rosenberg. Isadore repurchased those 12 shares in 1961.

In March 1954, the two brothers decided to draft an agreement that would protect their families when they died. Before they could finalize its terms, Benjamin suffered two heart attacks. Isadore asked his accountant to finish the contract and bring it to Benjamin's home. The accountant did, and in July 1955 the two brothers and their wives signed it. Benjamin died in December 1957.

---

[108] By the early 1930s, the movement to ban the medicinal use of marijuana was rapidly gathering support (the film *Reefer Madness* appeared in 1936), and the Marijuana Tax Act makes the use of marijuana prohibitively expensive in 1937.

[109] 203 N.E.2d 577 (Ill. 1964).

Under the terms of the contract, (a) all four parties to the agreement (Benjamin and his wife Emma, Isadore and his wife Rose) would serve on the board; (b) if either brother died, his wife would name his replacement to the board; (c) the firm would pay a minimum dividend (subject to appropriate limits); and (d) if either brother died, the firm would pay double the amount of his salary to his wife over a five-year period.

Benjamin died, Isadore and his son refused to follow the agreement, and Emma sued. The court enforced the contract by its terms:

> Where, as . . . here, no injury to a minority interest appears, no fraud or apparent injury to the public or creditors is present, and no clearly prohibitory statutory language is violated, we can see no valid reason for precluding the parties from reaching any arrangements concerning the management of the corporation which are agreeable to all.[110]

By the logic of *McQuade*, the agreement was void. It was a <u>nonunanimous</u> agreement among shareholders that bound what they could do as directors. By the logic of *Clark*, the agreement would have been valid if the two brothers had held all the stock. The question was whether Rosenberg's 12 shares moved the case from *Clark* to *McQuade*. On the ground that Rosenberg did not complain about the agreement, the court applied *Clark* and enforced the promise.

On the one hand, the agreement served much the same purpose as a life insurance contract. The firm could have bought life insurance contracts for their officers. It promised to pay the benefits itself instead.

As articulated by the court, however, the rule in the opinion creates an incentive for people to lie. Whether the court will enforce an agreement turns on whether the other shareholder complains about it. That shareholder — Rosenberg — can choose whether to complain (or not), and the other parties to the case can make it worth his while to complain (or not). If Isadore can avoid his liability to Emma if Rosenberg complains, Isadore can ensure that Rosenberg complains.

What is more, by the time the parties finally signed the contract, it served no corporate purpose. Investors could rationally want to offer a contract like this to someone they want to attract to or retain at the firm. If Hollings-Smith offered Benjamin an attractive job designing new marijuana cocktails, Galler Drug might counter with an attractive salary continuation agreement payable to his wife.

By the time the parties signed the contract, though, no one was offering Benjamin a rival job. Having suffered two heart attacks, he was too ill to work for anyone. In return for the salary continuation agreement, Benjamin could not offer the firm more or better service. The agreement was nothing but a gift.

[110] 203 N.E.2d at 585.

III. Restrictions on the Power of the Board

To nonparty shareholders like Rosenberg, the contract was a sheer loss. In exchange for the contract, Rosenberg obtained nothing of value — no product, no service. The money was to go to Benjamin's wife, Emma, but Benjamin was not about to do any more work. Rosenberg paid a tenth of the cost of the agreement. In return, he took nothing.

E. *Ramos v. Estrada*[111]

On shareholder agreements that bind the board, *McQuade–Clark–Galler* define the contour of the law. But if the law seems clear, the clarity can mislead. *Ramos* illustrates some of the problems that can arise in its application.

Two groups competed for a license from the Federal Communications Commission for a Spanish-language television station in Ventura County, California. One was "Ventura 41," the other the "Broadcast Group." Leopoldo Ramos and his wife owned half of Broadcast. Five other couples owned the other half. Tila Estrada and her husband were among that other half.

Ventura 41 and Broadcast decided to cooperate. They would form a new corporation, Television, Inc., and assign the license to it. Ventura would take one-half of Television, and Broadcast the other. Within that half interest, members of Broadcast would each take Television shares proportional to their stake in Broadcast. During the first eight months, the Broadcast members would pick four of the eight Television directors. Thereafter, they would pick five of the nine.

The Broadcast members agreed to vote their Television shares together. They would consult with each other and hold a vote among themselves to decide how to vote their Television stock. Once they had decided by majority vote, they would all abide by it. Should anyone deviate from this agreement, he would sell his Television shares to the other Broadcast members at cost plus 8 percent per year.

Ramos became president of Television, and Estrada one of the directors. For reasons the court does not disclose, in 1988 Estrada — in her capacity as director — voted with the Ventura group to fire Ramos as president. When the Broadcast members later met to determine how to vote their Television shares, they decided to nominate a board slate without either Estrada. In response, the Estradas repudiated the stockholders' agreement, and the others sued to buy their Television shares.

When Tila Estrada voted to fire Ramos as president, she did not violate the stockholders' agreement. The Broadcast members made no agreement about whom they would elect president. Neither could they legally have done so. To include such an agreement would have been to constrain what they each could do as director, and — by *McQuade–Clark–Galler* — such an agreement was valid only if unanimous. The Broadcast members owned only half of the Television shares.

Instead, Estrada violated the stockholders' agreement when she repudiated it. She had repudiated it because the others had dropped her from their slate. And they had dropped her from the slate because she had voted to fire Ramos.

---

[111] 10 Cal. Rptr. 2d 833 (Ct. App. 1992).

The Broadcast members could not directly have agreed to elect Ramos and then agree that anyone who breached the agreement would forfeit his or her stock. But what the members could not do directly, they here did indirectly. As Television director, Estrada voted to drop Ramos as president. She violated no formal agreement in so voting, but Broadcast dropped her from their slate anyway. In response, she declared the agreement void — and by doing so forfeited her stock. The court duly held the agreement enforceable against Estrada.

In short, the Ramos block used a formally valid shareholder agreement to accomplish indirectly something it could not legally do directly — and the court complied. The members of the block could not formally bind one another in their capacity as directors, so they bound one another informally — but just as effectively — instead. When Estrada violated the informal agreement, they used the formally valid shareholder agreement to punish her. When she complained, they invoked the penalty clause and declared her stock forfeit. The court, in turn, duly enforced what they did.

F. Close Corporation Statutes

People do not form new corporations, invest their money, and then — and only then — decide who will run the firm and what it will produce. They assemble the people. They pick the product. They form a business plan. And only then do they agree to invest.

In the real world, people will not buy stock in a new corporation unless they know who will run it and what they will make. Giving directors the discretion to run the company as they see fit has a nice ring. In the real world with new corporations, it does not work. In the real world, people do not invest in a new firm unless they can eliminate that discretion.

Norman would like Marion to invest her $40,000 in their motel franchising operation. Marion trusts Norman. She does not trust his mother. She will not put $40,000 in the firm and then wait to see whom the board hires to run the firm. She will negotiate the details first and only invest her money second.

For the most part, states provide statutes that let investors do exactly what Norman and Marion would like to do. For the most part, they codify the outcome of *McQuade* and *Clark*. Take the California Corporations Code. First, the California code entrusts management to the board:

> [T]he business and affairs of the corporation shall be managed and all corporate powers shall be exercised by or under the direction of the board.[112]

Second, the code lets shareholders agree among themselves about how they will vote their shares (Cal. Corp. Code §706(a); this is of course exactly what Edith

---

[112] Cal. Corp. Code §300(a).

IV. Conclusions

Ringling and Aubrey Haley did). At the time of *Ramos*, the section applied only to statutory "close corporations" (see below), but today it applies to any firm:

> [A]n agreement between two or more shareholders of a corporation, if in writing and signed by the parties thereto, may provide that in exercising any voting rights the shares held by them shall be voted as provided by the agreement. . . .

Third, subject to several specific conditions, the code lets shareholders agree not just about whom they will elect to the board, but also about what they will do once they become directors. Section 300(b) specifies the rule:

> [N]o shareholders' agreement, which relates to any phase of the affairs of a close corporation . . . shall be invalid as between the parties thereto on the ground that it so relates to the conduct of the affairs of the corporation as to interfere with the discretion of the board. . . .

Consider the several conditions. First, the firm must be a "close corporation" (§300(b)). By California law, it must have no more than 35 shareholders and must elect (under §158) to be treated as a statutory "close corporation."

Second, §186 defines a "shareholders' agreement" to include only unanimous deals:

> "Shareholders' agreement" means a written agreement among all of the shareholders of a close corporation. . . .

Third, the shareholders must take responsibility for the fiduciary duties that directors would otherwise owe. Given that they are making decisions as shareholders that directors would otherwise make, they owe the duties that directors would owe were they to make the decisions (§301(d)):

> An agreement of the type referred to in subdivision (b) shall, to the extent . . . the discretion or powers of the board in its management of corporate affairs is controlled by such agreement, impose upon each shareholder who is a party thereto liability for managerial acts performed or omitted by such person . . . that is otherwise imposed by this division upon directors. . . .

IV. CONCLUSIONS

Quintessentially, shareholders elect directors to manage the firm. The directors then act as agents for the firm and its shareholders. As agents, they owe duties of loyalty and care. Often, investors and managers will follow the quintessential arrangement, but not always. Sometimes, they will want to modify it. Should shareholders agree with one another about how they will vote their stock, modern courts will enforce the deal they cut. Should they agree about what they will do when they elect one another directors, the courts will sometimes enforce this agreement as well — but sometimes not. Generally, they ask whether the agreement included all shareholders to the firm. Where a subset of less than all shareholders tries to cabin the discretion of the board, the courts often refuse to enforce the deal they make. It poses, they reason, too large a risk to the interests of the omitted shareholders.

CHAPTER 7

Corporate Control (II)

"A grown man, and you're still at home?" Marion Crane[1] could hear the old woman in the Victorian next door taunting her son Norman. "You've got no gumption."

> "That's the real reason you're still sitting over here on this side road, isn't it, Norman? Because the truth is that you haven't any gumption. *Never* had any gumption, did you, boy?
>
>   "Never had the gumption to leave home. Never had the gumption to go out and get yourself a job, or join the army, or even find yourself a girl—"[2]

Marion had checked into Cabin One at the Bates Motel. What she could hear of Norman Bates's mother, she did not like. But she did like the shy and ingenuous young Norman. Suppose the two of them talked business (see Chapter 6). Marion had arrived at the motel with $40,000 in cash. Suppose she now considered investing it in a firm (a new firm) that would franchise the motel's operating formula. Suppose Norman promised to invest $40,000 too, and so did his mother. They would each buy a third of the stock.

Marion liked the motel and thought the franchising idea promising. Still, she worried about investing her cash in a business where she might be outvoted by Norman and his mother. She gave Norman the benefit of the doubt, but not his mother. To be sure, she had not met his mother. But what she heard of the quarrels between mother and son did not suggest to Marion that she would agree with Norman's mother about business strategy—or much of anything else.

Suppose Mother were able to influence Norman, Marion mused. The two of them could outvote her routinely. They could keep her off the board. They could appoint themselves the firm's exclusive officers and pay themselves whatever salaries they wanted.

---

[1] "Marion" in the movie; "Mary" in the original novel.
[2] Robert Bloch, *Psycho* 8 (Philipp Reclam 2000) (originally published in 1959).

Figure 7-1
Norman, Next to Mother's Victorian Home

© Underwood & Underwood/Corbis

What is more, Norman might die. You never know what Mother might do, worried Marion. She did not want to find herself locked in a firm where Mother owned two-thirds of the shares. If Norman died, could she stop his mother from inheriting his stock?

And what if she needed her cash quickly, continued Marion? After all, she was on the lam. Could she make Norman and his mother repurchase her stock when she wanted the money? If she could, what price should she charge?

In this chapter, I explore how Marion might address these questions. I first outline the scope of the problem (section I.A) and some of the ways modern courts address it (sections I.B–D). I describe several statutory responses (section II) and discuss the contractual approaches Marion and Norman might take (section III). Finally, I turn to limits on the ability of shareholders to transfer their stock (sections IV and V).

I. THE FREEZE-OUT

A. *The Problem*

1. Dividends

Suppose Norman, Marion, and Mother form the franchising firm. In time, the relations between Norman and his mother improve, while those between him and Marion deteriorate. At the firm's annual meeting, he and his mother (Mother does not actually attend the meeting, but she gives Norman her proxy) propose a board slate that includes the two of them and several of their friends, but excludes

I. The Freeze-Out

Marion. With two-thirds of the shares, they elect their favored slate. As board members, they appoint each other officers. They ask their nominally independent friends on the board to approve the salaries they pay themselves. In the face of these tactics, Marion does not have a spot on the board, does not have a job as officer, and does not receive a salary.

If Norman and his mother act strategically, Marion may not receive dividends either. As the Delaware court illustrated in *Kamin* (Chapter 4, section II.A.2), firms with sufficient resources may pay dividends if they wish — but need not wish. The elaborate language in *Dodge v. Ford* to the contrary notwithstanding (Chapter 3, section III.C.1), a profitable firm that does not want to pay dividends need never do so.

Firms have good tax reasons not to pay dividends. Should a firm choose to pay dividends, it will pay them out of after-tax income. It cannot deduct the amount of the dividend from its taxable income, in other words, but its shareholders will pay tax on the dividend when they receive it. Famously (or infamously), dividends are thus taxed twice: first at the corporate level and then at the shareholder's.[3]

2. Dividends and the Publicly Traded Firm

Should firms pay dividends? Take a publicly traded firm in a tax-less world. Suppose the firm pays a dividend. It will have less cash, but its investors will have more. The price of its stock will fall by the amount of the cash the investor receives. If the investor wants the cash, he can keep it. If he prefers to stay invested instead, he can use the cash to buy more stock.

Now suppose the firm does not pay the dividend. Necessarily, its stock price will reflect the amount of cash it chose (by not paying dividends) to retain. Its investors will hold stock whose price is higher by exactly the amount of cash it could have distributed but did not. If they want to stay invested, they can sit tight. If they prefer to hold cash instead, they can sell some of their shares.

This is the intuition of the famous "Dividend Irrelevance Theorem" summarized in Chapter 3, Appendix III. Franco Modigliani and Merton Miller won a Nobel Prize (in part) for making it, and if the point seems obvious in retrospect, rest assured it did not seem obvious at the time.[4] Absent tax and various other complications, Modigliani and Miller pointed out that investors will not care whether a firm pays dividends. If it does pay a dividend, they will receive cash exactly offset by the decline in the price of their stock. If it does not pay a dividend, they receive no cash, but hold stock worth correspondingly more. Dividend or no dividend, they stay whole.

Real firms do not operate in a tax-less world, of course, and tax law militates in favor of no dividends.[5] Earnings repatriated as dividends are taxed twice, but those

---

[3] *See* Marvin A. Chirelstein, *Federal Income Taxation* 76-79 (11th ed., Foundation Press 2009).

[4] Merton Miller & Franco Modigliani, *Dividend Policy, Growth, and the Valuation of Shares*, 34 J. Bus. 411 (1961).

[5] The puzzle then becomes why firms ever issue dividends at all. *See* Frank H. Easterbrook, *Two Agency Cost Explanations of Dividends*, 74 Am. Econ. Rev. 650 (1984).

retained at the firm are taxed only once. True, investors will need eventually to cash out their investment, but "eventually" need not come anytime soon. When "eventually" does arrive, they can sell their stock for the cash they want — and recover their earnings at the often-lower capital gains tax rate. If they die, their heirs will take the stock with an "adjusted basis" equal to its fair market value at the time of inheritance — and avoid the investor-level income tax completely.[6]

3. Dividends and the Closely Held Firm

In a closely held firm like the Bates Motel chain, matters become more complex. Should Marion buy a one-third interest in the firm, she buys stock without an organized market. If and when she decides to sell the stock, she may find no one willing to buy it — at any price. For her, the question of how to turn her investment into cash will not be a matter of any Nobel Prize–winning "indifference" theorem. Notwithstanding Modigliani and Miller, she may want dividends desperately.

Suppose, however, that Norman, Marion, and Mother each work for the firm. As employees, they can now regularly liquidate parts of their investment without declaring dividends. Instead, they can simply pay themselves salaries. To liquidate firm earnings, moreover, they can pay themselves more than their services are worth.

The generous-salary ploy has a tax angle. Suppose the trio pay themselves 20 percent more than their market worth. In effect, they pay themselves a market salary plus a dividend (disguised as salary) equal to another fifth. Firms can properly deduct salaries from corporate income. They cannot deduct dividends. By disguising dividends as salary, the trio obtains a tax deduction to which they would not otherwise be entitled.

To the Treasury, this disguise-dividends-as-salary ploy is obvious. It tries regularly to police it. But it polices in a legal world with considerable play. Sometimes it does not notice the excessive pay. Sometimes it cannot prove the pay excessive. And sometimes courts uphold even egregious violations. Hoping for error, taxpayers regularly play the game.

The Bates Motel trio can play the disguised-dividend game and treat each other fairly, however, only if they each hold paid jobs at the firm. Dividends go to all investors, in proportion (usually) to the number of shares they hold. Salaries go to all workers, in proportion to the market value of their services. If all three investors work at the motel chain, the motel can add a disguised dividend to each of their salaries. If fewer than all three work, the firm will be paying dividends to some of the three but not all.

---

[6] *See* Chirelstein, *supra* note 3, at §4.01(b).

I. The Freeze-Out

B. The Massachusetts Story

1. Donahue

(a) Introduction

It is this risk that the firm will pay disguised dividends to some but not all of the shareholders that so often lies behind the excruciating pain of the "freeze-out." And it is at the firm where some but not all of the shareholders work for pay that the risk most commonly becomes real. In theory, controlling-shareholder fiduciary duties should mitigate that risk. Unfortunately, state courts do not always understand the law.

Thinking they need new rules to handle close corporation freeze-outs, some courts instead invent new law. One of the best-known examples of this occurred in Massachusetts, and the process began with *Donahue v. Rodd Electrotype.*[7] Unlike most freeze-out cases, *Donahue* did not involve dividends. Instead, it involved redemptions.

Joseph Donahue worked at Rodd Electrotype. As of the late 1950s, he owned 20 percent of the stock. Harry Rodd, the company president, owned the other 80. Nearing the end of his life, Rodd decided to distribute the bulk of his stock to his children and to sell the rest to the firm for cash. Consisting of Harry's two sons and a lawyer, the board agreed to redeem his stock at $800 a share.

When Joseph Donahue and his wife, Euphemia, learned of the transaction, they asked the firm to buy Joseph's stock for $800 a share too. The board refused. Over the course of the next several years, it offered the couple prices ranging from $40 to $200 per share. The Donahues wanted more. Once Joseph died, Euphemia sued on the grounds that the Rodds violated their fiduciary duty to the firm when they redeemed Harry Rodd's stock at $800 per share.

(b) The Decision

The Massachusetts court sided with Euphemia. Minority shareholders in close corporations run a risk, it observed. If unscrupulous, the majority can refuse to pay them dividends, refuse to pay them a salary, refuse to repurchase their shares — and effectively freeze them out. Were they to sue for a fiduciary breach, they would "find difficulty in challenging dividend or employment policies" because courts relegate those decisions to "the judgment of the directors."[8]

Had the Rodds and Donahues formed a partnership, the court continued, the Donahues would not have faced this problem. If a partner "feels abused by his fellow partners," he "may cause dissolution by his 'express will . . . at any time.'" In the process, he can "recover his share of partnership assets and accumulated profits."[9]

---

[7] 328 N.E.2d 505 (Mass. 1975).
[8] *Id.* at 513.
[9] *Id.* at 514.

A shareholder has no such luck. He cannot dissolve the firm on his own. He cannot force the firm to buy his stock. But because the typical close corporation and partnership face similar business exigencies, their owners (said the court) need similar legal protection:

> Because of the fundamental resemblance of the close corporation to the partnership, the trust and confidence which are essential to this scale and manner of enterprise, and the inherent danger to minority interests in the close corporation, we hold that stockholders in the close corporation owe one another substantially the same fiduciary duty in the operation of the enterprise that partners owe to one another.[10]

Close corporation shareholders and partners owe each other, the court declared, the same fiduciary duties.

Close corporation shareholders often serve as directors, of course, and directors owe shareholders fiduciary duties — but this was different, insisted the court:

> We contrast this strict good faith standard with the somewhat less stringent standard of fiduciary duty to which directors and stockholders of all corporations must adhere in the discharge of their corporate responsibilities.[11]

Given the fiduciary duty that the Rodds (as shareholders) owed the Donahues (as shareholders), the Rodds should have offered to buy Euphemia's stock:

> [I]f the stockholder whose shares were purchased was a member of the controlling group, the controlling stockholders must cause the corporation to offer each stockholder an equal opportunity to sell a ratable number of his shares to the corporation at an identical price.[12]

The Rodds refused to buy her stock. Accordingly, explained the Supreme Judicial Court, the trial judge should either require Harry's heirs to repay his purchase price to the firm or require the firm to buy Euphemia's shares on the same terms.

(c) Implications

The *Donahue* opinion is odd on multiple dimensions at once. First, the Rodd sons served on the board. As directors, they owed the firm a fiduciary duty. In voting to redeem their dying father's shares, they faced a conflict of interest. Under traditional law, they could safely redeem his stock at $800 per share only if they could prove that the purchase was "fair and reasonable" to the firm (Chapter 4, section III.A).

---

[10] *Id.* at 515.
[11] *Id.* at 515-516.
[12] *Id.* at 518.

I. The Freeze-Out

Second, the Rodd sons dominated the firm as controlling shareholders. As such, they again owed shareholders like Euphemia a fiduciary duty. When they caused the firm to redeem Harry's but not Joseph's stock, they engaged in a classic self-dealing transaction under *Sinclair* (Chapter 4, section III.C.2). Again, they could safely redeem Harry's only if they could prove that the deal was fair.

Harry's sons would not have found it easy to prove they acted fairly. They redeemed their father's stock at $800 and refused Joseph's on the same terms. The court justified its new rule on the ground that under traditional corporate law the courts would have deferred to the board. "[D]ividend or employment policies," it wrote, fell "within the judgment of the directors."[13] The court was wrong, of course. The business judgment rule applies to redemptions only when a board faces no conflict of interest. Both as directors and as controlling shareholders, the Rodd sons faced serious conflicts.

Third, the court describes the partnership fiduciary duty (which it declares that it is now importing into the law of close corporations) as a duty higher than that owed by corporate directors. Again, the court is wrong. Partners did not owe fiduciary duties higher than directors. They did owe higher duties than noncontrolling shareholders — because such shareholders owed no fiduciary duties at all. But what partners owed, so, too, did directors and controlling shareholders: All (other than controlling shareholders) were agents, and all owed the fiduciary duties standard to agency.

2. Wilkes

(a) The Firm

The Massachusetts high court was wrong in *Donahue*, but rather than retreat, in *Wilkes v. Springside Nursing Home*[14] it embroidered its mistake with more detail. *Wilkes* concerned a quartet of businessmen in the small town of Pittsfield.[15] Stanley Wilkes was a community regular, the son of immigrant farmers. He quit school after eighth grade and, over time, built a contracting business in roofing and siding; he also cultivated a knack for making money in real estate.

Leon L. Riche was his friend, an outgoing life insurance salesman. He asked Wilkes to keep him in mind when next he saw a promising real estate opportunity. Wilkes found an option to buy a small, privately owned hospital in 1951 and contacted Riche. Riche asked to participate and brought along T. Edward Quinn and Hubert A. Pipkin. The following year the four bought the property across the street and, in 1956, acquired the Pittsfield tuberculosis sanitarium.

---

[13] *Id.* at 513.

[14] 353 N.E.2d 657 (Mass. 1976).

[15] The details not in the court opinion come from a conference at the Western New England College School of Law in the fall of 2010 and in particular from a presentation by Professor Eric Gouvin. See Eric J. Gouvin, *Wilkes v. Springside Nursing Home, Inc.: The Backstory*, 33 W. New Eng. L. Rev. 269 (2011).

Table 7-1
Nursing Homes

	1960	1963	1964	1967	1969	1971	1973
Total nursing home beds	N.A.	510,180	556,600	765,148	879,091	944,697	1,107,358
Total residents	469,700	N.A.	554,000	N.A.	815,100	N.A.	1,075,800*
Expenditure ($ millions)	480	N.A.	N.A.	1,271**	N.A.	3,818#	7,450##

* 1973-74
** 1965
#1970
##1974

Sources: Burton David Dunlop, *The Growth of Nursing Home Care* 8 tbl. 2-1 (D. C. Heath 1979); Paul L. Grimaldi, *Medicaire Reimbursement of Nursing-Home Care* 10 tbl. 2, 16 tbl. 5 (Am. Enter. Inst. 1982).

On the advice of a lawyer, the four incorporated their operation as the Springside Nursing Home. Each man took a quarter stake in the firm and served on the corporate board. Each worked for the firm and received a salary. Wilkes served as janitor.

Although initially the four may have thought that they were investing in real estate, they quickly focused on the nursing home industry. They chose the right time (see Table 7-1). From 1954 to 1963, the number of Americans living in nursing homes nearly doubled, and spending on nursing home care quintupled. With the 1965 passage of Medicaid and Medicare, spending jumped yet again.[16]

Pipkin was a physician. The other three seem to have thought he would provide referrals, but he did not. When he retired to Florida, they pressured him to sell his stake to a local banker named Laurence Connor.

Quinn had both political connections and (as a podiatrist) the medical license the group needed to run the home. The political connections suggested trouble. Years earlier, he had served on the liquor license board — and by local rumor had allocated the licenses on extralegal grounds (the details are murky). At the nursing home, the group had been buying laundry services from an outside provider. When Wilkes tried to bring the work in-house, he discovered that the provider had been paying Quinn a kickback.

[16] The numbers are estimates — as the fluctuation among sources discloses. *See, e.g.,* John Wright. *The New York Times Almanac 2002,* at 369 (Penguin Putnam 2001); Douglas L. Anderton, Richard Edward Barrett & Donald Joseph Bogue, *The Population of the United States* 326 tbl. 7-26 (3d ed., Simon & Schuster 1997); Paul L. Grimaldi, *Medicaid Reimbursement of Nursing-Home Care* 10 tbl. 2 (Am. Enter. Inst. 1982); R. A. Cohen & J. F. Van Nostrand, *Trends in the Health of Older Americans* 280 tbl. 1 (U.S. Dept. Health & Human Servs. 1995); Karen Stevenson, 1950-1970: Nursing Home Population and Costs, ElderWeb, http://www.elderweb.com/node/2842 (accessed Mar. 4, 2012).

Figure 7-2
Springside Nursing Home

Photograph courtesy of Professor Eric Gouvin, Western New England College of Law. Printed with permission from The Berkshire Eagle.

In 1966, Quinn announced that he wanted to buy some of Springside's real estate. He offered $12,000. That seemed low, and Wilkes countered with an offer to buy it at $25,000. Quinn now found himself forced to match the $25,000 bid. He resented Wilkes's interference, retaliated, and induced the others to drop Wilkes from the corporate board and fire him as janitor.

(b)   The Economics

Suppose Springside paid its four officers market wages and distributed its profits as dividends. If it fired Wilkes, he would no longer collect pay for janitorial services from the firm. He could work as a janitor elsewhere, though, and collect the market value of his services there. Such is what it means for a wage to be a "market wage." Because the firm distributed its earnings as dividends, moreover, he would continue to collect his share of the profits.

In fact, Springside did not pay dividends and did not pay market wages. Instead, it avoided the double tax on distributed earnings by disguising its nondeductible dividends as deductible wages. The nursing home itself seems to have been profitable, and interior photographs like the one included here do not suggest the firm reinvested any substantial earnings. The wards are as stark as they come.

Starting in 1955, Springside paid its four officers a "salary" of $100 per week, $5,200 a year. The median family at the time (1950) earned an income of $3,216, and the median schoolteacher made $2,987.[17] Janitors do not make more than teachers — in 2010, the median schoolteacher made $40,000 to $45,000, and janitors collected barely $20,000 to $32,000. Janitor Wilkes made 75 percent more than the median teacher.

So long as they each worked at the home, all four shareholders gained from this petty tax fraud. But when his three co-investors fired him, Wilkes did not just lose his janitorial wage — that he could replace at another job. He also lost his share of the profits — the dividend distributions that the four had been hiding in their salaries. Because the others still worked at Springside, they continued to receive their share of the corporate profits. Wilkes did not.

(c)   The Court Formula

When Wilkes sued, the Massachusetts Supreme Judicial Court declared that the three had breached their new *Donahue* duties to him. The quartet had together invested in a close corporation; hence, they owed each other a duty of "utmost good faith and management." Because controlling groups need flexibility to manage effectively, the three could avoid liability by demonstrating "a legitimate business purpose" for what they did. Should they show that purpose, Wilkes could counter that they could have met their "objective . . . through an alternative course of action less harmful to the minority's interest."[18]

Assert, rebut, surrebut — the court's three-part elaboration on its new *Donahue* rule is nothing if not classically "judicial." Yet why this intermediate position, not quite a partnership and not quite a corporation? The foursome started as a partnership. If they had stayed a partnership, the court would have imposed on them a strict duty of good faith. It would not have offered the majority an out by showing a "legitimate business purpose." If corporate investors need the flexibility that the "business purpose" clause gives them, why not partners? If partners need strict fiduciary duties with no business purpose out, why not shareholders?

Alternatively, a court might have asked whether it should not try to expand the choice-set available to investors. Toward that end, it could refuse to impose on corporate investors any shareholder-level fiduciary duty at all. Investors who wanted investor-level duties could form a partnership. Those who did not could

---

[17] Bureau of Labor Statistics, *100 Years of U.S. Consumer Spending: Data for the Nation, New York City, and Boston* (May 2006), *available at* http://www.bls.gov/opub/uscs/; Aubrey L. Berry & Ruth G. Boynton, *Economic, Social, and Legal Status of the Elementary- and Secondary-School Teacher*, 22 Rev. Educ. Res. 212 (June 1952), http://www.jstor.org/pss/1168570.

[18] 353 N.E.2d at 663.

form a corporation. And those who wanted intermediate duties could specify them by contract. By imposing on all close corporation shareholders intermediate duties instead, the court narrowed the scope for value-enhancing bargains.

For all the reasons discussed with *Donahue*, however, the court's rule was superfluous anyway. The majority trio were directors — and owed the firm a fiduciary duty as directors. They were controlling shareholders — and owed Wilkes a fiduciary duty under the logic the Delaware court articulated in *Sinclair*. When the three paid one another more than the market value of their services but excluded Wilkes from the tax scam, they faced a straightforward conflict of interest. The business judgment rule did not protect them. Instead, both as directors and as controlling shareholders they breached their fiduciary duties.

3.   Atlantic Properties

(a)   The Decision

If the rule that the Massachusetts courts created was unnecessary in *Donahue* and *Wilkes*, in *Smith v. Atlantic Properties, Inc.*[19] it was plain pernicious. The case involved a real estate venture between Boston-area physician Louis Wolfson and three other investors.[20] Each of the four bought a quarter of the firm's stock, and the firm itself bought rental real estate. Because each of the investors worried about what the other three might do (never a good sign in a new firm), each kept a veto. Toward that end, in the firm's charter and bylaws they inserted a rule that the firm could act only on a "vote of eighty (80%) per cent of the capital stock."

In time, the four quarreled. Wolfson thought the firm should reinvest its earnings and fix its deteriorating buildings. The other three thought it should distribute those earnings as dividends. Wolfson asked to transfer his shares to his private charity. The others said no.

Each faction had a plan about what to do with the firm's cash. One side wanted to reinvest the money. The other side wanted to distribute it. Each vetoed the other's plan, and the profits accumulated.

Under 1960s law, in accumulating its profits the firm incurred a penalty tax. With the top marginal personal income tax rate at 91 percent, 1960s shareholders in close corporations had a strong incentive to keep their profits in corporate solution. Rather than declare a dividend and pay 91 percent to the government, they did best to keep the money in the firm. If and when they needed the cash, they could sell their shares and pay a tax at the lower capital gains rate. If they died before they needed the cash, they could bequeath their shares to their children. They in turn would take an "adjusted basis" in the stock equal to its market value at the time of their parents' death and avoid the investor-level income tax entirely.

---

[19] 422 N.E.2d 798 (Mass. 1981).

[20] Not the securities felon Louis E. Wolfson who destroyed the career of Justice Abe Fortas; instead, the otorhinolaryngologist (i.e., ear, nose, and throat specialist) Louis E. Wolfson, associated with the Tufts Medical Center.

To induce high-bracket investors not to do this, Congress imposed an accumulated earnings tax. The AET penalty applied to firms that accumulated their earnings. It did not apply to those that distributed those earnings. Neither did it apply to those that reinvested their earnings. Had Atlantic Properties paid the dividends that the threesome had proposed, it would have avoided the AET. Had it used its earnings to make the improvements that Wolfson had proposed, it would have avoided the AET. Having done neither, it owed the tax.

The Massachusetts court purported to decide the quarrel between the two sides according to *Wilkes*. All four investors owed each other duties of utmost good faith, it explained. When Wolfson vetoed the dividends that the other three advocated, "he recklessly ran serious and unjustified risks of precisely the penalty taxes eventually assessed." He acted, the court explained, in a manner "inconsistent with any reasonable interpretation of a duty of 'utmost good faith and loyalty.' "[21] Accordingly, he owed the others damages equal to the amount of the AET penalty.

(b) The Logic

At best, this is silly. At best.

If Wolfson caused the firm to incur the AET by vetoing the dividends, the threesome caused it to incur the AET by vetoing the improvements. Either all four violated the duties they owed each other, or none of the four did. Determined to have their way, each of the four played brinksmanship to the end. None of the four wavered, and — to mix a few metaphors — together they plunged into the abyss.

The court cites *Wilkes*, but *Wilkes* adds nothing of value to the case law. Under the traditional approach that Delaware would soon articulate in *Sinclair*, all four were controlling shareholders. As such, all four owed each other a duty of loyalty. But because all four took equal shares of any dividend, profit, or AET, the situation presented no self-dealing. None of them violated his *Sinclair* duty, so no one owed money to the others. Instead, they should each pay (indirectly, through their stake in the firm) a quarter of the AET.

Each of the four was also (presumably) on the board. In that capacity, each owed the others a duty of care and loyalty. The case involved no self-dealing, but the brinksmanship might have violated a duty of care. Because they each played the same brinksmanship, either all of them violated the duty of care or none of them did. If all of them violated the duty, then they each paid a quarter of the AET to the firm. If none of them violated the duty, then they each shared (through their stake in the firm) a quarter of the loss. Either way, the results are the same.

(c) Taxes

The source of the disagreement lay in the differing tax regimes that the four men faced. Wolfson was rich and paid taxes at a high marginal rate. At least two of

---

[21] 422 N.E.2d at 803.

I. The Freeze-Out

Table 7-2
Taxable Income of Atlantic Properties Shareholders

Stockholder	1965	1966	1967	1968
Paul T. Smith	$ 45,111.58	$ 65,929.81	($ 36,039.35)	($ 14,966.23)
William H. Burke Jr.	11,904.39	10,601.76	10,665.50	8,518.54
Abraham Zimble	20,659.00	59,406.00	60,755.00	42,123.00
Louis Zimble	87,319.00	159,607.00	104,215.00	139,283.00
Louis E. Wolfson	152,586.58	133,656.59	263,375.00	65,649.00

Source: Atlantic Props. v. Commissioner, 62 T.C. 644, 648 (1974).

the others were poorer and paid taxes at a much lower rate. This rate difference, in turn, drove a wedge between the return that any improvement to the firm's real estate needed to earn to satisfy the two groups.

The logic proceeds in three steps. First, the firm's buildings needed repair. By the 1960s, they had deteriorated so badly that the firm was losing tenants:

> Many of petitioner's buildings were vacant, not rented or untenable, resulting in petitioner's foregoing income as a result of diminished rents and removal by tenants to other space.[22]

To determine where to start, Wolfson had hired an engineer:

> Dr. Wolfson was influenced in his decision to refrain from the payment of dividends in favor of reinvestment . . . by his prior experience in real estate and by the report of an engineering firm . . . recommending that extensive repairs, replacements, and capital improvements be made to petitioner's property. Dr. Wolfson estimated the cost of the repairs, replacements, and improvements . . . to be approximately $250,000 as of 1968.[23]

Second, the four investors paid taxes at very different rates. Table 7-2 gives their taxable income over several years; married couples filing joint returns in 1967 paid taxes at marginal rates ranging from 0 to 70 percent. Smith had a tax loss: He could earn up to $36,000 in dividends without paying any taxes at all. Burke would have paid taxes on any dividends at 22 percent. Abraham Zimble paid taxes at 53 percent, and Louis Zimble at 62 percent. Louis Wolfson would have paid tax on his dividends at 70 percent.[24]

---

[22] Atlantic Props. v. Commr., 62 T.C. 644, 647 (1974), *aff'd*, 519 F.2d 1233 (1st Cir. 1975).

[23] 62 T.C. at 647-648.

[24] *U.S. Federal Individual Income Tax Rates History, 1913-2010*, Tax Foundation (Sept. 9, 2011), *available at* http://www.taxfoundation.org/publications/show/151.html. Presumably, if the others had let Wolfson transfer his shares to his family foundation, he could have avoided this tax.

Third, these marginal tax rates determined the rate of return that Atlantic needed to earn on its repairs for an investor to consider them worthwhile. If Atlantic paid Smith a $100 dividend, he kept it all. If he invested the dividend personally, he kept any of the return it earned. By contrast, if Atlantic paid Wolfson a $100 dividend, he kept only $30. If he invested that $30, he kept only 30 percent of anything he earned.

Wolfson supported the firm-level improvements and opposed the dividends because he was rich. His other income put him in a tax bracket where he kept very little of any money distributed to him — far better, to him, to invest the money at the firm level and keep the earnings in corporate solution. The others opposed the firm-level improvements and supported the dividends because they were poorer. Their other income put them in brackets where they kept more of what they made. Both were equally rational, and both were equally selfish. Either they all breached their fiduciary duties or none did.

4.   Brodie

(a)   The Opinion

Brodie v. Jordan[25] provides a more recent variation on *Wilkes*. Walter Brodie had helped start a ball bearing firm called Malden and took one-third of the equity. By 1988, he had retired from the business and begun to disagree with the other owners. Four years later, the others voted him off the board and fired him from the presidency. Walter had negotiated no right to "put" his shares to the others or to the corporation, and when he asked them to buy his stock, they refused. As in *Wilkes*, the firm paid no dividends, but the other investors continued to draw salaries. Walter died in 1992.

Walter's widow, Mary, inherited his stock and sued the other investors for a fiduciary duty breach. Sympathetic, the trial court ordered them to buy her shares. On appeal, the Supreme Judicial Court applied *Wilkes*. It agreed that the majority owed Mary fiduciary duties under *Wilkes* and agreed that the majority had wronged her.

Yet the appellate court ordered the trial judge to find a different remedy. Mary and Walter knew they were investing in a corporation. Accordingly, reasoned the court, neither of them could have expected the firm to repurchase their shares. By ordering the others to buy their stock, the trial court effectively placed Mary in a better position than she would have been without the defendants' misconduct. Find, the court told the judge below, a remedy that better matched Walter's and Mary's "reasonable expectations."

And what might those "reasonable expectations" have been? An investor in a close corporation could negotiate a right to "put" the stock to the others — but (as the court reasoned) absent that negotiated clause he will not have such a right. He

---

[25] 857 N.E.2d 1076 (Mass. 2006).

could negotiate a clause requiring the firm to pay him dividends (in certain circumstances) — but absent that clause he will not be entitled to dividends. He could
negotiate a contract giving him a seat on the board — but absent such a contract he
could not necessarily expect a seat. He could (subject to cases like *Stoneham*, Chapter 6, section III.B) negotiate a deal that guaranteed him a job with the firm — but
absent that deal he would hold his position at will. Brodie's widow could not
reasonably expect the others to buy her stock. But neither could she reasonably
expect much of anything else.

(b) The Outcome

The law is subtle — but sometimes subtlety is neither here nor there. The
lower court had decided the case in favor of Mary, and the Supreme Judicial
Court had purported to reverse that judgment. When I telephoned the lawyers
for the two sides, however, both dismissed any suggestion that Mary had lost. She
had won, they insisted. The trial judge had made it obvious that she favored Mary,
and on remand the case went back to her.

Faced with a congenitally sympathetic judge, Mary's lawyer made it clear that
he would "get really ugly." Through discovery, he would comb the firm's business
records. The defendants had overpaid themselves, he argued. He would recon-
struct the firm's balance sheets as if they had taken more appropriate payments and
demand Mary's share of the difference. That amount would represent the damage
that the others caused through their duty of loyalty breach.

Rather than relitigate the case before a hostile judge, the defendants settled.
The trial court had earlier awarded Mary $94,500.[26] The Supreme Judicial Court
had vacated the award as beyond her "reasonable expectations." Sent back to the
pro-Mary trial judge, the defendants settled out of court for even more than the
original award.[27]

C. Beyond Massachusetts

1. Delaware

The Massachusetts state supreme court thought it took corporate law in a new
direction with *Wilkes*. About that direction, courts that understood corporate law
were less enthusiastic. The Massachusetts court had invented the *Wilkes* rule to
solve the freeze-out problem, but it had not needed a new doctrine to solve
freeze-outs. The appellate court had applied it beyond freeze-outs in *Atlantic Properties*, but the effect was not good. The court had applied it in *Brodie*, and the plaintiff
used it to extort a settlement even larger than its sympathetic judge originally
awarded in court.

---

[26] Brodie v. Jordan, 66 Mass. App. Ct. 371 (2006).
[27] The account is based on conversations with some of the lawyers involved.

Delaware courts take a different approach. In 1993 in *Nixon v. Blackwell*,[28] investors with nonvoting stock faced a board dominated by present and past employees with voting stock. The board had adopted several mechanisms to enable employees to sell their stock, but refused to apply them to the nonvoting non-employee plaintiffs. Those nonemployee plaintiffs then sued.

The court refused to require the board to buy the plaintiffs' shares. The board had adopted policies that provided liquidity to employees but not to other investors. Given the employee representation on the board, the policies constituted self-dealing. Under *Sinclair*, the board had to show that the policies were fair. Concluded the court, it did: A board could rationally take steps that facilitated stock ownership among employees but only among employees.

In the end, explained the court, it was all a matter of contract. The employees had contracted for policies that would enhance the liquidity of their investments. The plaintiffs had not:

> The tools of good corporate practice are designed to give a purchasing minority stockholder the opportunity to bargain for protection before parting with consideration. It would do violence to normal corporate practice and our corporation law to fashion an ad hoc ruling which would result in a court imposed stockholder buy-out for which the parties had not contracted.[29]

Three years later, the court explicitly declared *Wilkes* not the law of Delaware. In *Nagy v. Riblet Products Corp.*,[30] Seventh Circuit Judge Frank Easterbrook faced a question involving Delaware law in a case much like *Wilkes*. Did Delaware apply the *Wilkes* doctrine? Easterbrook certified the question to the Delaware Supreme Court, and the court replied no: If a firm fires a stockholder-employee, he may have a claim under his employment contract but not through his investment. *Wilkes*, it explained, "has not been adopted as Delaware law."[31]

2. New York

In *Ingle v. Glamore Motor Sales*,[32] the New York Court of Appeals took much the same tack as Delaware. Philip Ingle owned a minority interest in Glamore Motor Sales, and James Glamore and his sons owned the rest. Ingle had worked as a sales manager since 1964. Each of the shareholders held their stock subject to the following agreement:

> In the event that any Stockholder shall cease to be an employee of the Corporation for any reason, Glamore shall have the option for a period of 30 days after such

---

[28] 626 A.2d 1366 (Del. 1993).
[29] *Id.* at 1380.
[30] 79 F.3d 572 (7th Cir. 1996).
[31] Riblet Prods. Corp. v. Nagy, 683 A.2d 37, 39 (Del. 1996).
[32] 535 N.E.2d 1311 (N.Y. 1989).

I. The Freeze-Out

termination of employment, to purchase all of the shares of the stock then owned by such Shareholder.[33]

In 1983, the Glamores fired Ingle and caused the firm to buy his stock. Although Ingle had worked under an at-will contract, he claimed that his status as minority shareholder protected him against discharge. His "employment status," he argued, "should not be governed by the employment at-will doctrine but, rather, that as a minority shareholder in a close corporation he should be treated as a co-owner, equivalent to a partner, whose employment rights flow from a special duty of loyalty and good faith."[34]

Not so, said the court. The matter was simple:

> A minority shareholder in a close corporation, by that status alone, who contractually agrees to the repurchase of his shares upon termination of his employment for any reason, acquires no right from the corporation or majority shareholders against at-will discharge.[35]

Apparently, the New York courts have not adopted *Wilkes* either.

D. *Jordan v. Duff & Phelps*[36]

1. Introduction

The *Ingle* court thought the problem simple, but not everyone has found it so. Consider the quarrel between Judge Frank Easterbrook and Judge Richard Posner (both of the Seventh Circuit and the University of Chicago Law School faculty) in *Jordan v. Duff & Phelps*.[37] As in *Ingle*, the difficulty arose from the disjunction between the terms of the plaintiff's employment contract and the terms of the fiduciary duty that the directors (arguably) owed him as a shareholder. An employee may work at the firm on an at-will contract (as Philip Ingle did), but if he also owns stock, the firm's board will owe him a fiduciary duty. The issue in *Jordan* was the issue in *Ingle*: Does the shareholder-level fiduciary duty shape the terms of the employment contract (as *Wilkes* seemed to suggest), or does the at-will employment eliminate any shareholder-level protection the board would otherwise owe (as *Ingle* implied)?

---

[33] *Id.* at 1312 (italics in original removed)

[34] *Id.* at 1313.

[35] *Id.*

[36] The material below is adapted from J. Mark Ramseyer, *Not-So-Ordinary Judges in Ordinary Courts: Teaching* Jordan v. Duff & Phelps, 120 Harv. L. Rev. 1199 (2007).

[37] 815 F.2d 429 (7th Cir. 1987), *cert. denied*, 485 U.S. 901 (1988).

2. The Facts

Jordan worked as a securities analyst at Duff & Phelps. In taking the job, he signed no employment contract. By Duff & Phelps policy, however, he could regularly invest in the closely held firm's stock. By late 1983, he owned a 1 percent stake.

When buying the stock, Jordan signed a shareholders' agreement and a stock purchase agreement. Through the latter, he acknowledged that "nothing herein contained [would] confer on [him] any right to be continued in the employment of the Corporation."[38] If he left the firm for any reason, he agreed to resell the stock to the firm for its book value at the end of the previous calendar year. Note that during the early 1980s, the board had adopted a resolution letting a fired employee keep his or her stock for five years. (CEO Claire Hansen had had an affair with Carol Franchik, and after the firm fired Franchik, she threatened to sue. In response, the board adopted a resolution letting anyone fired keep his or her stock.)

Not unlike many other in-law pairs, Jordan's wife and mother despised each other. To placate his wife, Jordan decided to look for work elsewhere. In November 1983, he obtained an offer from Underwood Neuhaus in Houston. He took the job and tendered his resignation to Hansen. Hansen accepted it, but let Jordan work until the end of the year to obtain a higher book value for his stock — $23,000.

On January 10, 1984, Duff & Phelps announced a merger with Security Pacific at a price that would have let Jordan clear at least $450,000 for his stock, and possibly as much as $650,000. What is more, the firm explained that Hansen had preliminarily tried to negotiate a merger the previous summer. Those initial talks had collapsed, but Hansen had renewed negotiations in December and this time finalized the deal's price and structure.

Rather than cash his $23,000 check from Duff & Phelps, Jordan sued. While the suit was pending the merger collapsed (again), this time because the Federal Reserve placed on it conditions too onerous. In December 1985, however, Duff & Phelps's senior managers decided to buy the firm themselves in a leveraged buyout. Had he stayed at Duff & Phelps and sold his stock to them, Jordan claimed he would have grossed $500,000.

Jordan argued that Hansen violated Rule 10b-5. When he tendered his resignation, explained Jordan, Hansen should have told him about the summer merger talks. If Hansen had done so, he never would have resigned (so he said). Instead, he would have stayed through 1985 and sold his stock for $500,000. In repurchasing his stock on the firm's behalf at book value without disclosing the talks, Hansen violated the "abstain or disclose" rule at the heart of 10b-5.

3. Easterbrook

Simple the case was not meant to be. Writing for the majority, Easterbrook proceeded through several steps. First, the merger talks were material to Jordan.

---

[38] 815 F.2d at 446.

I. The Freeze-Out

He had to decide whether to sell his stock to Hansen, and for that the possibility of a high-priced merger mattered. True, the merger collapsed, but if the firm was worth a premium to Security Pacific, it was probably worth a premium to someone else. Jordan might reasonably conclude that another high-priced offer would follow.

Second, although Jordan could not hold his stock if he quit, he did not need to quit. Instead, he could choose to stay at Duff & Phelps and keep his stock. Had he known about the Security Pacific negotiations, he might have done just that. He might have surmised that another firm would soon offer a premium — and stayed.

Third, although Jordan had no *right* to stay at the Duff & Phelps, Duff & Phelps showed no inclination to fire him. What is more, it could not have fired him just to increase the senior management's gains in a buyout anyway (what Easterbrook calls an "opportunistic" firing). It could not, as Easterbrook inimitably put it, have told him that "even if you hadn't resigned, we would have fired you, the better to engross the profits of the merger for ourselves. So long, sucker."[39]

Hence the conclusion: Jordan could have chosen to stay at Duff & Phelps and keep his stock; to decide whether to stay, he needed information Hansen had but did not disclose; Hansen stood in a fiduciary relation to Jordan as shareholder; and in repurchasing Jordan's stock without disclosing the information Jordan needed to decide whether to keep his stock (and stay) or sell it (and go), Hansen violated the abstain or disclose rule of Rule 10b-5.

4. Posner

We judges should be "thankful," Posner replied, "that our opinions are not subject to Rule 10b-5."[40] As an at-will employee, Jordan had no legal right to stay at Duff & Phelps. If he had no right to stay, he had no right to keep his stock. Rule 10b-5 mandates disclosure, but only when an investor can use the information. Without a right to hold stock, Jordan lacked a right to respond to any news of a merger that Hansen might give him. He had no right to use the information, so Hansen had no duty to disclose it.

Second, although Duff & Phelps showed no inclination to fire Jordan, the law should not penalize firms for being nice. It could have fired him, and for any reason or no reason. If it had, Jordan could not have kept his stock and could not have sold it at the higher buyout price.

Last, although directors owe fiduciary duties to minority shareholders, Jordan waived them. Through the stock purchase agreement, he specifically agreed that "nothing herein" would "confer on [him] any right to be continued in the employment of the Corporation."[41] He had a right to the information only if he had a right to stay at Duff & Phelps; as an at-will employee, he had such a right only if he

[39] *Id.* at 437.
[40] *Id.* at 448.
[41] *Id.* at 446.

obtained it as an adjunct to any right he might acquire as a minority shareholder; and through the shareholders' agreement he waived any such right.

But what of the resolution the board adopted after firing Carol Franchik? Suppose Jordan wanted to stay and refused to quit. To induce him to leave, the firm would have needed to fire him. Yet if it fired him, by the terms of the resolution, he acquired a legal right to keep his stock. Would that not destroy Posner's argument? Apparently, the requirement that departing employees sell their stock stemmed from the shareholders' agreement, and the agreement was subject to change only by unanimous shareholder vote. The board had not obtained that vote — so the "Franchik Resolution" was void on its face.

And opportunism — "the possibility that corporations will exploit their junior executives"? That, wrote Posner, "may well be the least urgent problem facing our nation."[42]

II.   STATUTORY DISSOLUTION

A.   *Introduction*

Consider again the hypothetical Bates triangle. Marion, Norman, and Mother buy one-third interests in a firm that will design and offer a new motel franchising formula. Locally, they will also pave the parking lot, renovate the motel's bathrooms, and dredge the adjacent swamp.

Suppose that they operate as a partnership. If Marion finds Mother an impossible business partner, she can liquidate her investment whenever she wants. As a partner, she can dissolve and wind up the firm as she pleases.

Suppose instead that they operate as a corporation. Marion has no right to force anyone to buy her stock. Neither can she liquidate the firm. Instead, corporations dissolve only upon the majority vote of the directors and shareholders (e.g., Del. Gen. Corp. L. §275).

Investors will not necessarily want the right to dissolve the firm on a whim. They might each want the right themselves (why not, after all?). But they will not necessarily want their co-investors to have the right. Take Marion. Suppose she finally ditches the boyfriend she left in Phoenix. He kept promising to divorce his wife, after all, but never quite found the time to file the papers. Instead, she decides to marry Norman. Does she want to give her incensed (and possibly psychotic) mother-in-law the right to dissolve their new business?

Not always, but sometimes. Sometimes, investors will want to give each other the right to dissolve the firm. To do so, they can operate as a partnership. The virtues of limited liability being what they are, however, sometimes they will want to incorporate. For such shareholders — those who want to combine a dissolution right with limited liability — some corporate law statutes sometimes give shareholders of close corporations the right to dissolve the firm.

---

[42] *Id.* at 449.

B. *Stuparich v. Harbor Furniture Manufacturing*[43]

Take the Californian approach. A brother and his two sisters owned the Harbor Furniture Manufacturing firm. As its name implied, the firm made furniture, but it also ran a trailer park in southern California. The brother held 52 percent of the voting stock of the firm, and his sisters owned the rest. In the minds of his sisters, he ran it as he pleased. They received regular dividends, but felt ignored.[44] They sued to dissolve.

Under California corporate law (currently Cal. Corp. Code §1800), minority shareholders in a close corporation can dissolve it whenever "liquidation is reasonably necessary for the protection of the rights or interests of the complaining shareholder or shareholders." To claim the benefit of the statute, the minority shareholders must recruit either half of the directors or shareholders holding a third of the stock (§1800(a)). Then, they need to show one of several reasons for dissolution.

First, the dissolving shareholders could rely on §1800(b)(3):

> (b)(3): There is internal dissension and two or more factions of shareholders in the corporation are so deadlocked that its business can no longer be conducted with advantage to its shareholders. . . .

Apply §1800(b)(3) for a moment to a case we already know, *Smith v. Atlantic Properties, Inc.*[45] Assume, counterfactually, that Atlantic Properties had been a California firm. Louis Wolfson, because he did not control half of the Atlantic Properties board or own a third of the stock, could not have met the preliminary §1800(a) filing requirements. Had he met them, though, the deadlock would have given him a plausible claim under (b)(3).

Second, the dissolving shareholders could turn to §1800(b)(4) and (b)(5):

> (b)(4) Those in control of the corporation have been guilty of . . . pervasive fraud, mismanagement or abuse of authority or persistent unfairness toward any shareholders. . . .
>
> (b)(5) In the case of any corporation with 35 or fewer shareholders . . . , liquidation is reasonably necessary for the protection of the rights or interests of the complaining shareholder. . . .

Imagine the Springside Nursing Home had been a California firm.[46] Stanley Wilkes would not have met the §1800(a) requirements either, of course. But if he had met them, he would have had a reasonable claim under either (b)(4) or (b)(5).

---

[43] 100 Cal. Rptr. 2d 313 (Ct. App. 2000).

[44] The firm had elected "S corporation" status under the tax code, which made the shareholders liable on undistributed firm earnings. The sisters claimed that the dividends were not large enough to cover their resulting tax liability. Harbor Furniture Mfg. v. Tuttleton, 2007 Cal. App. LEXIS 3886 (May 15, 2007).

[45] 422 N.E.2d 798 (Mass. 1981).

[46] Wilkes v. Springside Nursing Home, 353 N.E.2d 657 (Mass. 1976).

The Harbor Furniture sisters sued under subsection (b)(5). The court suggested that "the grounds for dissolution under subdivision (b)(5) [were] considerably broader than those in subdivision (b)(4),"[47] but still rejected their claim. The sisters cited an

> inability to play a meaningful role in the operation of the corporation, the complete breakdown of their relationship with their brother, and the continuing losses incurred by the furniture manufacturing operation.[48]

Their brother treated them, they claimed, as "second-class" shareholders. That was not enough, replied the court. The sisters received "significant dividends" and were "not entitled to substitute their business judgment for their brother's" anyway.[49] If he ignored their opinions, that did not give them grounds to dissolve the firm. Dissolution was a "drastic remedy," and they did not show reasons that justified so drastic a measure.

C. *Alaska Plastics v. Coppock*[50]

Three friends formed a corporation named Alaska Plastics and took a one-third interest each. They also served as officers and directors. They never voted dividends on the stock, but did pay each other salaries and directors' fees. One of them divorced and gave his ex-wife, Patricia Muir, half his stock.

In 1974, the three friends offered Muir $15,000 for her stock. She refused and hired an accountant who valued the stock at $23,000 to $40,000. She offered to sell at $40,000; the three countered with $20,000, and she sued.

At the time, the Alaska statute gave a close corporation shareholder the right to liquidate his firm if he could show either that "the acts of the directors or those in control of the corporation [were] illegal, oppressive or fraudulent" or that the "corporate assets [were] being misapplied or wasted."[51] The Alaska Supreme Court hesitated to liquidate the firm. "Liquidation is an extreme remedy," it explained.

> In a sense, forced dissolution allows minority shareholders to exercise retaliatory oppression against the majority. Absent compelling circumstances, courts often are reluctant to order involuntary dissolution.[52]

Instead, the Supreme Court remanded the case. The trial court had ordered the friends and the corporation to buy Muir's stock for $32,000, and

---

[47] 100 Cal. Rptr. 2d at 318.

[48] *Id.* at 319.

[49] *Id.* at 319-320.

[50] 621 P.2d 270 (Alaska 1980).

[51] Dissolution is now governed by Alaska Stat. §10.06.628, which tracks the Cal. Corp. Code §1800 discussed in *Harbor Furniture.*

[52] 621 P.2d at 274.

the Supreme Court applauded the order "as an equitable remedy less drastic than liquidation." If she hoped to enforce the order, however, she would need to show "that the acts of [the three friends] were 'illegal, oppressive or fraudulent'" or "a waste or misapplication of corporate assets."[53] She did, and the trial court (again) ordered the firm to buy Muir's stock at its fair value — which it (again) pegged at $32,000.

D. How "Drastic" Is Dissolution?

1. Introduction

In *Harbor Furniture* and *Alaska Plastic*, the courts hesitated to let disaffected shareholders dissolve the firm. Dissolution, they implied, was simply too "drastic."

But why? Judges (and readers more generally) often worry that dissolution will cause profitable going concerns to disappear. The new Bates Motel franchisor may have 20 franchised motels in the Southwest that send it a steady stream of payments. Were Marion to dissolve the firm unilaterally, she would eliminate the thriving business.

Does a dissolution right promote this? Generally, no.

2. Going Concern

Take California's §1800. The *Harbor Furniture* court understood that well-run firms have a "going-concern value." It realized that most firms are worth more alive than dead, worth more as operating entities than as fire-sale assets. If the court let someone like Marion liquidate a firm, it worried that she would burn that going-concern value.

In fact, Marion would not destroy any going-concern value. As Professors Michael Dooley and John Hetherington explained several decades ago, when shareholders sue to dissolve positive going-concern-value firms, they seldom actually dissolve them.[54] Anyone who did would not just burn the other shareholders' money. He would burn his own too. Although investors do sometimes burn their money out of spite, they burn it more often in movies than in real life.

Instead, the dissolution right lets a shareholder like Marion force her co-investors to the bargaining table. Rather than let her liquidate Bates Motel, Inc. (and burn its going-concern value), Norman and his mother will offer to buy her stock. Given that she will obtain her pro rata share of the fire-sale price if she liquidates the firm, Norman and Mother will offer her at least that much. In effect, the liquidation right sets a floor on the amount that the others will offer her.

---

[53] *Id.* at 275.

[54] Michael P. Dooley & John A. C. Hetherington, *Illiquidity and Exploitation: A Proposed Statutory Solution to the Remaining Close Corporation Problem*, 63 Va. L. Rev. 1 (1977).

Marion owns a one-third interest in Bates Motel, Inc. Suppose that the firm is worth $180,000 as a going concern, but would fetch only $120,000 at fire-sale auction. Norman and his mother refuse to let Marion participate in management, pay themselves generous salaries, and declare no dividends.

Suppose Marion has no right to dissolve the firm. If she asks Norman and Mother to buy her stock directly, they can refuse. If she asks the firm to redeem her stock, Norman and Mother as a majority of the directors can refuse. If she asks someone unrelated to the firm to buy her stock, he will offer no more than a trivial amount. After all, the shares pay no dividend and entitle the owner to no salary. Why pay any more? In effect, Marion holds shares that earn her nothing and that she cannot sell.

Now suppose Marion has a right to dissolve Bates Motel, Inc. If the firm goes into dissolution, she will obtain $120,000/3 = $40,000. In effect, she will have destroyed the firm's $180,000 − $120,000 = $60,000 going-concern value. Rather than let her do this, Norman and his mother will offer to buy (or to have the firm redeem) her stock at some price greater than $40,000.

Unfortunately, the dissolution right does not determine the actual price that Norman and his mother will offer. $180,000/3 = $60,000 may seem intuitively most "fair." But given that Marion does better to settle for $40,001 than to insist on dissolution, she might agree to less than $60,000. And because Norman and his mother would take only $120,000 × 2/3 = $80,000 in dissolution, they can profitably offer her any price up to $180,000−$80,001 = $99,999.

If Marion can dissolve the firm, in other words, she might sell her shares for as little as $40,001 or as much as $99,999. Locked as the two sides are in a "bilateral monopoly," the price at which they will settle the dispute is indeterminate. That both sides do better not to dissolve, however, is not.

3. Opportunism

A statute that offers disaffected shareholders the right to dissolve the firm is indeed problematic, but not because it destroys going-concern value. After all, it does not. Instead, the statute is problematic because it encourages shareholders to extort side payments from each other through opportunistic games. It encourages Marion to pick a time when the others cannot readily buy her out and sue to dissolve. She can then offer to withdraw her suit if (for example) they let her live in Mother's Victorian at the top of the hill. It encourages Norman's mother to sue to dissolve and offer to withdraw the suit if (for example) Norman and Marion agree not to marry.

As Judge Frank Easterbrook and Professor Daniel Fischel put it, the logic is that the right to dissolve generates "more deadlocks, more claims of oppression." In turn, "[t]he threat to create a deadlock (or claim oppression) may be used to induce the other party to hand over more of the firm's profits." Investors will anticipate this, of course, and fear the risk of this behavior. Unfortunately, argue Easterbrook and Fischel, the "anticipation of opportunistic behavior of this sort will make the entire business transaction less attractive at the outset."[55]

III. BUYOUT AGREEMENTS

A. *Introduction*

Under standard corporate law, shareholders have no right to liquidate their shares; as a result, they risk a freeze-out. Under special close corporation statutes shareholders may have an easy right to dissolve the firm; as a result, they risk opportunistic claims. Shareholders who anticipate these (and other) problems, however, can negotiate their own contractual provisions. Tailored to the details of their own peculiar situation, these privately negotiated terms can potentially improve on both default terms.

Return to Marion, Norman, and Mother. Suppose that after several successful seasons, they decide to expand from low-end motels into high-end mountainside resorts they will call "Shinings." To help design an appropriate franchising formula, they recruit a middle-aged widower named Jack Torrance. Jack brings extensive experience running the lavish Colorado resort, the Overlook Hotel. There, he doubled as off-season caretaker. Tragically, he lost his wife and son in a series of unfortunate events one winter several years ago.

Marion explains to Jack that they have not yet located any potential franchisees for their resort hotels. As a result, his job may include long periods with little work. Jack replies that he does not mind. He has brought his own typewriter and is writing a treatise for Aspen on the legal status of Native American burial grounds. He is happy for the spare time.

Jack urges the trio to consider planting hedge mazes next to the hotels. "Really popular with tots," he mumbles.

To induce Jack to devote himself to the new venture, Marion and Norman want him to buy stock in their firm. Jack is happy to invest, but has two concerns:

> Concern (1): He wants a way to liquidate his investment. If the resort hotel venture does not perform as well as the four of them hope, he wants a way to convert his shareholding into cash.
> Concern (2): Norman's mother is not well. Should she go to be with her maker, Jack worries that her shares might pass to an inappropriate investor. He has no objections to Norman's inheriting his mother's stock. But should Norman decide to sell the stock, he wants some say over the identity of the buyer.

Consider the range of issues the quartet will negotiate.

---

[55] Frank H. Easterbrook & Daniel R. Fischel, *The Economic Structure of Corporate Law* 239 (Harvard U. Press 1991).

B.   The Agreements

1.   Liquidity

(a)   Introduction

With a bit of planning, Marion, Norman, Mother, and Jack can skirt some of the dilemmas that vexed courts from *Wilkes* through *Alaska Plastics*. They will negotiate tailored "buyout agreements." Begin with Jack's Concern (1): his need for a way to liquidate his investment.

(b)   The Purchase

The quartet can draft an agreement that gives them each the right to sell their shares under designated circumstances. This might be the right to sell to the others upon the occurrence of given events, or it might be the right to have their shares redeemed by the corporation. If they include all four of them as the buyers under the former formula, then the distinction between the sale and redemption will not much matter. If they involve fewer than all investors, it could matter greatly.

The four can also agree to the inverse: They can agree to give the rest of the group (or the firm) the right to buy their shares upon the occurrence of given events. Because of the problems inherent in dissolution rights (see section II above), they probably will not give each other the right to dissolve the firm.

(c)   Triggers

To lower the risk that anyone uses the agreement opportunistically, the four can specify the events that trigger the buyout provisions. Jack will not, for instance, want to give the others the right to play Posner's Claire Hansen: fire him and buy his stock at a price far below its market value. Neither will the investors want to give Mother the right to choose a time when they are short of cash, demand that they redeem her stock, then offer to withdraw her demand on condition that Norman not marry Marion.

Often, investors provide a buyout triggered upon death. Heirs typically need cash to pay taxes and divide the estate. Unless they fear that Mother or Jack might choose to die strategically, the four may want to draft a "put" triggered by death.

Senior executives at closely held firms frequently want to sell their stock when they quit. As a result, the four may want to draft a "put" triggered by termination of employment.

Conversely, investors in closely held firms also may want to prevent stock from falling into the wrong hands. The four might give the firm the right to redeem the stock upon the death of any one of them. They might give it the right to redeem the stock should any of them quit. But as *Jordan* illustrates, they will also want to avoid drafting an agreement that could induce the others to fire them.

The triggers that the investors actually choose will vary from firm to firm. They will depend on the constraints that the product and capital markets impose on the firm. And they will depend on the concerns that those constraints create for the investors.

(d) Price

Norman, Marion, Mother, and Jack will need to decide the price at which they will transfer the shares. They might reasonably want to transfer them at market value, but they have no market. After all, that absence of a market is precisely why they need a buyout agreement at all. Had they a market where they could readily sell the stock, they could skip these negotiations.

Consider four basic pricing mechanisms.

(1) Appraisal. The four could agree to transfer the stock at an appraised price. Stanley Wilkes notified the other three that he intended to sell them his shares at their "appraised price." Alas, he had not negotiated any right to force them to buy his stock, appraised or no. Patricia Muir hired an accountant to appraise her Alaska Plastics shares. Neither had she negotiated a right to force the others to buy them.

Note that the four resort hotel investors will need to pick an appraiser. Although they can select from among an entire industry dedicated to valuing closely held firms, they will need in advance to agree how they will select. By the time their relations have so soured that one of them wants to sell, they probably will not agree about much at all. To avoid a deadlock, they could pick the appraisal firm ex ante — though the firm might disappear by the time they quarrel. Alternatively, they could agree that they will each pick one appraiser and that those two appraisers (if there are two sides to the dispute) will pick a tie-breaking third. The strategy avoids a deadlock, but obviously trebles the cost.

(2) Formula. The four could also agree to transfer the stock at a formula-determined price. Typically, they would negotiate a formula that approximated the present value of the firm's expected net revenue stream. At the most basic level, the concept is straight algebra. Suppose Harry meets Sally and offers to sell her a bank account paying $500 annual interest. What should Sally pay? She would first investigate what banks offered on comparable accounts. If they paid 4 percent a year, she would offer $500/0.04 = $12,500. Because $12,500 × 0.04 = $500, an account paying $500 in a market where comparable deposits pay 4 percent is worth (i.e., has a "present value" of) $12,500.

If the basic concept is simple, the real-world details are not. To implement the formula, the four will need to agree on two numbers: The net revenue stream (the $500 in the Harry-Meets-Sally example) and the interest rate (the 4 percent). For the net revenue, they could use the firm's taxable income — but probably would not want to do so. Their accountant calculates "taxable income" by Internal

Revenue Code rules, but Congress drafted those rules with many objectives in mind — only one of which was to approximate market value. Alternatively, they could calculate revenue by "generally accepted accounting principles" (GAAP). Yet the accounting profession established GAAP to stop entrepreneurs from exaggerating their prospects when they approached potential investors — and thus incorporates a conservative bias.

If agreeing on a sensible definition of revenue seems daunting, even more so is the prospect of agreeing on the interest rate (the "discount rate") to use in present-valuing that revenue stream. The riskier the firm, the higher the interest rate the four will want to use (federally insured savings accounts pay a trivial interest because they are so safe; only riskier investments pay more). In practice, investors use a wide variety of market measures. They might, for example, sensibly consider the capital structure of the firm, its competitive position in the industry, and the characteristics of the industry itself.

(3) Book value. The four could also negotiate a transfer at book value. Readers with accounting backgrounds will blanch at the following. Stripped of complications, however, the book value of an asset equals its purchase price less any depreciation taken. The book value of a firm equals the total book value of its assets, less liabilities. And the book value of a share of stock equals the book value of the firm, divided by the number of shares outstanding. Book value is how the parties valued their stakes in *G&S Investments* (Chapter 2, section VI.C.3) and *Duff & Phelps* (section I.D above).

Only by accident will the book value of a firm ever equal its market value. If other entrepreneurs built a competing nursing home near Springside, Springside's market value might fall below its book value. If AARP declared Pittsfield a top-ten place to retire, its market value might climb above it. If Holiday Inn located a new franchise a mile from the Bates Motel, the motel's market value might fall. If the state built an exit off the interstate near the motel, its market value might climb. And if a famous director made a movie about the Bates Motel — well, if he made a movie about it, it all depends on what happened in the movie.

(4) Buy-sell agreement. And the four might negotiate a "buy-sell agreement." This provision will not guarantee liquidity to a frustrated investor, but it does let quarreling investors divorce. The intuition is easy enough to explain. Suppose Norman and Marion marry and have two sons. Norman buys them a piece of cake. He knows they regularly quarrel, so he asks Marion how he should slice it. "Don't slice it," she replies. "Let one of them slice it. Then let the other one pick the piece he wants."

That, in essence, is the buy-sell agreement. Suppose Harry and Sally form a corporation, invest equal amounts, and acquire a Bates Motel franchise. In their shareholders' agreement, they insert a simple buy-sell clause. After several years, Harry wants out. To sever his investing relationship with Sally, he will announce that he is triggering the buy-sell clause. He will then declare his estimate of the value of a half interest in their firm. In response, Sally has a choice: She can either buy Harry's share at that price or sell him hers at the same price.

The virtue of the buy-sell agreement lies in the incentive it gives people to declare the true value of their stock. Even when they would find it hard to prove the valuation in court, the investors themselves often know (and agree about) what a company is worth. Suppose Harry and Sally agree that their motel is worth about $1 million. Suppose further that Harry thinks he would like to buy Sally's stake on the cheap and names a price that he knows is less than the value of her stock — say, $400,000. Rather than sell Harry her stock at the price, Sally will buy his at the $100,000 discount. Suppose Harry thinks he would like to sell Sally his stock at an inflated price — and names $600,000. Rather than buy Harry's stock at that price, she will sell him her shares at the $100,000 premium.

Buy-sell agreements work best when two parties do not care whether they buy or sell and face no liquidity constraints. They work less well when the parties are not indifferent between buying and selling, when one of the parties is occasionally cash-constrained, or when they involve more than two investors.

2. Identity

(a) Introduction

Turn to Jack's Concern (2): controlling the identity of the people with whom he does business. In a closely held corporation, a co-shareholder is not just someone who has invested in the firm. Often, he is someone with whom one must collaborate. Norman may find Marion easy to work with, but suspect that she will die and bequeath her stock to her estranged boyfriend. Mother may find Jack a delight, but worry that he will transfer his stock to unsavory associates from his long winters at the Overlook Hotel.

The quartet may have other reasons to monitor stock transfers as well. For example, they may have elected to be governed by the state's close corporation statute. Generally, those statutes limit the number of investors who may hold the stock. The four will not want one of them jeopardizing their election by selling his stock to too many buyers.

Second, the four investors did not register their stock offering under the 1933 Securities Act. They avoided the registration requirement by issuing their stock in a "private placement." That exemption, however, protects them only if none of them offers the stock to too many of the wrong kind of investors too soon (Chapter 5, section III). To preserve the exemption, they will want to forestall any such disqualifying offering.

Third, the four may have elected to be taxed as an "S Corporation" (i.e., taxed under Subchapter S of the Internal Revenue Code; Chapter 2, appendix I). By doing so, they avoid the corporate tax and instead report a proportionate share of the corporate income on their personal returns. The S election is available only to firms with — again — no more than a specified number and kind of shareholders.

(b) Consent

The Bates Motel investors could solve many of these problems by each retaining the right to consent to any sale of stock. In effect, they would each hold a veto over any new shareholders. Had they formed a partnership, absent an agreement to the contrary, new partners would have been admitted only upon the unanimous vote of the existing partners (Chapter 2, section III.A). By retaining for themselves the right to consent to new shareholders, the Bates four can accomplish the same result with a corporation.

(c) Right of First Refusal

Through a right of first refusal, the Bates investors can retain control over transfers but avoid some of the problems that vetoes (like consents) create. An investor with a veto can play a variety of opportunistic games. Suppose Marion comes to hate Norman. Norman has decided to leave for film school and wants to sell his interest in the firm to pay tuition. If Marion holds a consent right, she can veto any attempted sales. To be sure, the quartet could try to mitigate this risk by providing that the consent "shall not unreasonably be withheld." Given the vicissitudes of the U.S. judiciary, however, investors always do well not to stake their future on any judicial interpretation of reasonableness.

Marion could also use her consent to obtain a collateral advantage. Suppose Jack still owns an Aspen condominium from his days at the Overlook Hotel. Marion wants the apartment. If Jack decided to sell some of his Bates Motel shares, Marion could refuse to consent—and offer to retract her veto only if he sold her the condominium.

The right of first refusal mitigates these problems. If the investors each hold a right of first refusal, they can each stop the other investors from selling their stock, but only if they buy it on the same terms. If Norman finds a buyer for his shares, he can be sure of a sale—one way or the other. If Marion does not like the buyer he found, he may not sell to that buyer—but he will be selling to Marion on the same terms. One way or the other, he will be able to liquidate his investment and go to film school.

The right of first refusal is not a perfect solution. Faced with a right of first refusal, an exiting investor will find it harder to locate a prospective buyer. After all, to decide whether to buy stock in a close corporation, an investor will need to research the firm. He will need to devote time (and money) deciding whether (and, if yes, for how much) to buy. Should another investor have a right of first refusal, a prospective transferee may invest resources valuing the firm only to find it bought by someone else at the price he named. Given this risk, he will be less eager to invest his resources in valuing the firm, and the original investor will find it harder to obtain the initial outside offer.

3. Exclusive Damages

In negotiating their buyout agreement, the Bates four might have analogized their deal to a liquidated damages clause. They agreed to do business with each other. They promised to treat each other fairly. But they realized that concepts like *fairly* are hard to prove in court. Rather than specify the detail, they opted instead to give each other the right to exit the relationship on more readily demonstrable terms.

In other words, the four might have thought that the buyout agreement specified the amount they would recover should they "divorce." At least one court, however, has interpreted the agreement as giving not the exact amount that the parties would recover but the minimum. In *Pedro v. Pedro*,[56] the Minnesota Supreme Court faced a dispute among three brothers who together owned a leather goods company. The three quarreled, and two of them fired the third. The third sued.

The three maintained a buyout agreement, and the court awarded the fired brother the $767,000 specified. It also found, however, that the other two had breached the fiduciary duties that they—as controlling shareholders—owed him. For that breach, it awarded the fired brother another $563,000—the difference between the fair market value of his one-third stake and the $767,000 owed him under the buyout agreement.

IV.   CONTROL BLOCK SALES

A.   *Introduction*

In addition to his work with the Overlook and Bates hotels, Jack Torrence owned a major stake in the Hotel Dolphin at 1408 W. 61st Street in New York. Mike Enslin wrote travelogues. While writing a collection of essays on haunted hotels, Enslin learned that Torrence was selling the Dolphin at a discount. Apparently, a series of mishaps in one of the rooms had caused travelers to shun the hotel. The resulting revenue loss pushed the firm into insolvency. Enslin decided to buy the hotel and then follow the Plaza Hotel model and convert most of the building into condominiums.

The hotel's shares traded on the over-the-counter market at about $13 per share. Torrence owned about 15 percent of the stock. Given the dispersed ownership of the other shares, that 15 percent gave Torrence effective control.

Because he expected to increase building value, Enslin decided he could profitably pay substantially more than market. If the stock currently traded for $13 per share, he calculated that he could profitably pay up to $20. He realized, however, that if he began to amass the stock through small orders, sellers would suspect that someone had a plan to renovate the hotel. They would then start demanding higher prices.

When Torrence offered his 15 percent block to Enslin at a premium over market, Enslin agreed. Although individual shares sold for $13, Enslin realized

---

[56] 489 N.W.2d 798 (Minn. App. 1992).

he would never be able to amass a control block at that price. Given that he could profitably pay up to $20 per share, he agreed to buy Torrence's stock at a premium.

More generally, when an investor holds enough stock to control a firm, his shares will often sell for more (on a per-share basis) than the other shares. They will sell for more because they give the buyer control. Should the buyer know of a way to increase profitability, the control block will give him the power to accomplish that transformation. And the buyer will pay the premium because he knows he might not be able to amass such a block at the market price of the noncontrol shares.

And yet, when controlling shareholders did sell their blocks at a premium, some courts blanched. Eventually, they came to allow the control premiums — and do today. They arrived at that permissive approach, however, only after considerable hesitation. *Perlman* exemplifies the early skepticism. *Zetlin* and *Frandsen* show the modern approach.

B. *Perlman v. Feldmann*[57]

1. The Facts

A buyer might pay a premium for a controlling stake in a firm for two reasons: He might plan to increase value, or he might plan to steal. Enslin planned to increase value. Courts typically let people like him pay a premium for their shares: If plaintiffs cannot tell a plausible story about how a buyer plans to steal, they ask, why stop the transaction? Better to let the buyer pay the premium and run the firm. If he improves value, so much the better. If he steals, they can hold him liable after the fact.

In *Perlman*, the plaintiffs had an at-least-superficially-plausible story about how the buyer might loot the firm. C. Russell Feldmann was a wild and crazy inventor. One of the first to develop a radio that worked in a car, he controlled the Detrola firm and sold a variety of radios to firms that then resold them under their house brands. He owned the Eureka vacuum cleaner firm. And in the late 1950s, he invented the Henny Kilowatt electric car. It went 60 miles at 60 mph on a single charge — though Feldmann never sold more than 47 (see photo).

With his family, Feldmann also owned 37 percent of the small steelmaker Newport. During the Korean War, the U.S. government needed steel for its tanks and ships. Demand spiked, but to avoid bad publicity, steelmakers kept prices low. A shortage ensued, of course. To raise effective prices while keeping nominal prices low, Feldmann as CEO then imposed what the industry came to call the "Feldmann Plan."

Under this plan, any firm that wanted to buy Newport steel loaned it money on an interest-free basis. Feldmann claimed to need the money to improve the firm's facilities, but whether he needed the money is beside the point. If he needed it,

---

[57] 219 F.2d 173 (2d Cir.), *cert. denied*, 349 U.S. 952 (1955).

Figure 7-3
The Work of C. Russell Feldmann

The 1960 Henney Kilowatt, a project pioneered by C. Russell Feldmann. The car used 12 sequential 6-volt batteries and had a 60 mph top speed and a 60-mile range.

then the loan saved Newport the interest it would otherwise have paid a bank. If he did not need it, Newport could simply invest the funds and pocket the return. In effect, Feldmann used mandatory interest-free loans to bring Newport's effective steel prices closer to the market prices that (given public pressure) it could not formally charge.

In this market, several of Newport's customers organized the Wilport Company. Through it, they bought the Feldmann family's 37 percent at $20 per share when the market price of the stock stood at $12. For selling their control block at a premium, the family found themselves sued by other Newport shareholders on a breach of fiduciary duty claim. Although the court found "no fraud, no misuse of confidential information, no outright looting of a helpless corporation," it held the Feldmanns liable anyway. They were, it explained, "siphoning off for personal gain corporate advantages to be derived from a favorable market situation."[58]

---

[58] 219 F.2d at 176.

2. Innocuous Reasons

Just what did the Feldmann family do wrong? If anyone tried to assemble a 37 percent stake in a publicly traded firm, he would not acquire it for 37 times the price of a 1 percent interest. Once he started buying the stock, sellers would begin to suspect that a buyer—some buyer, they typically would not know who—was trying to take control. Necessarily, they would reason, he must know a way to increase the value of the firm.

Once buyers in the market conclude that someone has a plan to increase firm value, they will demand a higher price. Inevitably, the buyer will be unable to assemble his control block at the market price. Buyers who buy preassembled control blocks at a premium are simply compensating the seller for the cost of assembling the block.

Buyers pay this premium if, but only if, they can extract that value from the firm. Suppose, for example, that the Wilport crew think they can raise Newport's value by more than the premium. The stock may sell for $12 a share, but if Wilport thinks it can raise firm value by more than 67 percent, it may offer $20.

When a court bans control-block premiums, it simply increases the cost of these value-enhancing transactions. When it requires control-block sellers (like Feldmann) to negotiate higher prices for all the other shareholders (the "take me along provisions"), it increases the cost of executing value-enhancing deals. Minority shareholders may receive higher prices in those value-enhancing transactions that still occur. But they will experience fewer such transactions on which to capture the higher prices.

3. Nefarious Reasons

Wilport might have been planning to increase the value of Newport, or it may have been planning to steal. Under the Feldmann plan, Wilport could buy Newport steel only if it loaned money interest-free. Once it controlled Newport, it could buy the steel without that loan. Formally, it would buy the steel at the same price as everyone else. In substance, however, it would pay a lower price. Because everyone else bought the steel at the formal-price-plus-interest-free-loan, if Wilport bought it at the flat formal price it bought it at a submarket price. In substance, Wilport would be looting the firm.

4. A Test

As plausible as the looting hypothesis may seem, according to Frank Easterbrook and Daniel Fischel, it did not happen. Easterbrook and Fischel first identify the problem:

The Wilport syndicate paid two-thirds more than the going price and thus could not profit from the deal unless (a) the sale of control resulted in an increase in the value of Newport, or (b) Wilport's control of Newport denuded it of a business advantage (the advances), the equivalent of looting.[59]

They then outline a test. Suppose, they write, Wilport planned to loot the firm:

> Newport has 100 shares, and Wilport pays $20 for each of 37 shares. The market price of shares is $12, and hence the premium over the market price is $8 × 37 = $296. Wilport must get more than $296 from Newport in order to profit; this comes at the expense of the other 63 shares, which must drop approximately $4.75 each, to $7.25. So . . . [u]nless the price of Newport's outstanding shares plummeted, the Wilport syndicate could not be extracting enough to profit.[60]

To perform this test, Easterbrook and Fischel ask which direction the stock price moved after Wilport bought control: "In fact, however, the value of Newport's shares . . . appreciated. The data refute the court's proposition that Wilport appropriated a corporate opportunity of Newport."[61]

If Wilport stole, Newport stock would have fallen. If Wilport improved firm efficiency, it would have risen. In fact, it rose. Easterbrook and Fischel conclude: "Wilport installed a better group of managers and, in addition, furnished Newport with a more stable market for its products."[62]

Even in *Perlman*, the acquirer apparently did not loot from the company. In the more common case, the plaintiffs who contest a control premium cannot even invent a plausible argument about looting. In *Perlman*, the plaintiff could at least claim that Wilport would buy the firm's product at an effectively submarket price. In the ordinary case, he cannot do even that. And if a controlling shareholder did try to buy the firm's product at a submarket price, it would straightforwardly violate its fiduciary duty. When it tried, the plaintiff could sue and the court would hold the controlling shareholder liable.

C. *Zetlin v. Hanson Holdings*[63]

For these reasons, modern courts routinely reject control premium claims. Star structural engineer Lev Zetlin formed Lev Zetlin & Associates in 1956. He had invented the cable-suspension roof and, over the course of a long career, would build a wide variety of structurally innovative buildings. He sold his firm to Gable in 1973, and Gable sold it to Thornton-Tomasetti in 1975. By the late 1970s, Zetlin owned 2 percent of Gable, and Hanson Holdings and the Sylvestri family owned 44.4 percent. Gable stock went for $7.38, but Hanson-Sylvestri sold their block to Flintkote Company for $15.00 per share.

---

[59] Easterbrook & Fischel, *supra* note 55, at 128.
[60] *Id.*
[61] *Id.* at 128-129.
[62] *Id.* at 129.
[63] 397 N.E.2d 387 (N.Y. 1979).

Figure 7-4
First Bank of Grantsburg

Zetlin sued. He argued that he should be able to share in the premium that Hanson-Sylvestri negotiated. In essence, he claimed that controlling shareholders owe a duty to the minority to negotiate take-me-along provisions on their behalf. The New York Court of Appeals roundly rejected the assertion:

> [A]bsent looting of corporate assets, conversion of a corporate opportunity, fraud or other acts of bad faith, a controlling stockholder is free to sell, and a purchaser is free to buy, that controlling interest at a premium price. . . . [64]

D. *Frandsen v. Jensen-Sundquist*[65]

The *Frandsen* case illustrates how the modern approach works under a more subtle set of facts. The Jensen family owned 52 percent of the Jensen-Sundquist insurance agency, and Jensen-Sundquist owned a majority interest in the First Bank of Grantsburg (see photo). Walter Jensen controlled both: He had served as president of the bank and had formed the Jensen-Sundquist insurance agency in 1945. Dennis Frandsen held an 8 percent interest in Jensen-Sundquist.

Frandsen had an agreement with the Jensen family. As Richard Posner described it:

> By a stockholder agreement drafted by [Walter] Jensen and a lawyer representing the [First Bank of Grantsburg] and Jensen's family, the majority bloc [i.e., the

---

[64] *Id.* at 388.
[65] 802 F.2d 941 (7th Cir. 1986).

IV. Control Block Sales

Jensen family] agreed "that should they at any time offer to sell their stock in Jensen-Sundquist, Inc., . . . they will first offer their stock to [Frandsen and six other minority shareholders who had negotiated for this provision] at the same price as may be offered to [the majority bloc] . . . and . . . they will not sell their stock to any other person, firm, or organization without first offering said stock" to these minority shareholders "at the same price and upon the same terms." The majority bloc also agreed not to "sell any of their shares to anyone without at the same time offering to purchase all the shares of" these minority shareholders "at the same price."[66]

Like many contracts, the language can seem a bit obscure. The gist of the agreement involves two clauses which, paraphrased, might read:

> *Clause I.* Should the Jensen family offer to sell their stock to anyone, they will first offer it to Frandsen at the same price.
> *Clause II.* Should Frandsen not wish to buy the stock offered to him under Clause I, the Jensen family will offer to buy Frandsen's stock at the same price.

First Wisconsin Corporation (FWC) wanted to buy the First Bank of Grantsburg (FBG). If FWC had bought FBG directly from Jensen-Sundquist, it would not have triggered the agreement. After all, Clause I applied only when the family offered to sell their Jensen-Sundquist stock. It said nothing about Jensen-Sundquist offering to sell the Grantsburg bank. For unspecified reasons, however, FWC and Jensen-Sundquist did not structure their initial transaction as a transfer of the bank.

Instead, FWC proposed a cash-out merger: Jensen-Sundquist would merge into FWC, former Jensen-Sundquist shareholders would receive cash, and FWC would merge the Grantsburg bank into another FWC subsidiary. In turn, Frandsen responded by announcing that he would exercise his Clause I right and buy the Jensen family shares at the cash-out merger price. The Jensen family refused and restructured the transaction as a purchase of FBG stock by FWC. Under the new transaction, FWC would pay cash to Jensen-Sundquist, and Jensen-Sundquist would distribute the cash in liquidation.

Frandsen sued to enforce his Clause I rights, and Posner replied that he did have any that applied. A sale of stock is not a merger, explained Posner, even when the two accomplish the same result. Frandsen had negotiated an agreement triggered by an offer to sell. He could have negotiated an agreement triggered by a merger, but he did not. Having contracted for an agreement triggered by A, he cannot enforce it when the others engage in B.

Posner then turned to the obvious interpretive question: Could Frandsen have rationally wanted a contract triggered only by offers to sell rather than mergers; or is inadvertence the only plausible explanation for the contract he obtained? To understand Posner's analysis, consider a third clause that Frandsen and the Jensen family might have negotiated but did not:

---

[66] *Id.* at 942-943.

Clause III. Should the Jensen family negotiate a merger of Jensen-Sundquist into another firm, Frandsen shall have the right to enjoin the merger and buy the family's stock at the effective price of the merger.

Now consider what motives might have driven Frandsen. In effect, Posner identified three possible motivations:

Reason A. Control premium. Perhaps Frandsen wanted to share in any "control premium" that the Jensen family negotiated. Frandsen did not have control, but the Jensen family did. If they obtained a premium for their control block, Frandsen wanted his proportionate share.

Reason B. Majority identity. Perhaps Frandsen did not want to work with majority shareholders he did not trust. Frandsen knew the Jensen family and was willing to invest in a firm they ran. But he knew that the Jensen family might someday sell. When they did, he wanted a veto over any buyers they might choose.

Reason C. Bidding war. Perhaps Frandsen wanted to buy the First Bank of Grantsburg, but wanted to avoid a bidding war with another buyer. At the time he negotiated the shareholders' agreement, the Jensen family still refused to sell. He thought they might change their mind and wanted the chance to buy the bank when they did.

If Frandsen cared about Reason A, then he needed Clause II but not Clause III. Under a statutory merger, a controlling shareholder obtained no premium. Instead, everyone would (and in the case at hand, everyone did) obtain the same price. If Reason A lay behind the shareholders' agreement, the court did not need to enforce the right of first refusal that Frandsen asserted.

If Frandsen cared about Reason B, then he needed Clauses I and II but — again — not Clause III. Suppose the Jensen family decided to sell their block. If Frandsen did not want to work with the prospective buyer, Clause I gave him the right to buy the family's block himself. If he could not afford it, then Clause II gave him the right to sell his stock at the same price. He did not necessarily need a Clause III because under many statutory mergers (and crucially, under the cash-out merger in the case at hand), he would not work with the purchasing shareholder. If Reason B lay behind the shareholders' agreement, the court did not need to enforce the right of first refusal Frandsen asserted.

If Frandsen cared about Reason C, then he did need both Clauses I and III. If the family wanted to sell the bank, they could transfer it by selling the Jensen-Sundquist stock, but they could also transfer it by merging Jensen-Sundquist into a buyer. Crucially, any lawyer would have realized this. Indeed, had Frandsen cared about Reason C, he would also have needed a Clause IV:

Clause IV. Should the Jensen-Sundquist Agency negotiate a sale of the First Bank of Grantsburg, it will first offer the Bank to Frandsen.

Hence Posner's conclusion: Frandsen did not negotiate a Clause III because — probably — he did not care about Reason C. Frandsen might have worried about Reason A or B. If so, he would have negotiated Clauses I and II — which he did. If he had worried about Reason A or B, he would not have needed

Clause III — and he did not negotiate Clause III. True, if he had worried about Reason C he should have negotiated Clause III — but not having done so, he is simply stuck. As Posner put it:

> It is true that he was not represented by a lawyer in connection with the stockholder agreement, but when an experienced businessman deliberately eschews legal assistance in making a contract he cannot by doing so obtain a legal advantage over a represented party should a dispute arise.[67]

Ironically, Reason C may be precisely what lay behind Frandsen's clauses: He wanted the bank. Frandsen had started his business career years earlier, straight out of high school. When he heard of a 200-acre forest for sale in Minnesota, he negotiated a contract to buy it. Unfortunately, he had no money. He asked his local bank for a loan, but it turned him down. By sheer luck, he found the First Bank of Grantsburg. FBG loaned him the money, and he bought the forest. He cut the trees, sold the lumber, and launched what would become an enormously successful career.[68]

Over the course of his life, Frandsen bought and sold a wide variety of businesses, but apparently retained an affection for the bank that had lent him money when everyone else said no. There never was much to Grantsburg — the entire county has a population of 1,328. There was never much to the First Bank of Grantsburg either — as the earlier photograph shows. For Frandsen, however, the bank was apparently always a special place.[69]

V. BOARD SEAT SALES

A. *Introduction*

Return to Jack Torrence. Suppose he owns 15 percent of the Dolphin Hotel stock and negotiates a sale of his block to Enslin. Because Enslin hopes to reconfigure the hotel immediately, he wants to place himself on the board. Currently, the board includes Torrence and his friends from his days at the Overlook. Like most corporate charters, the Dolphin charter provides that vacancies on the board are filled by the other board members.

Enslin suggests that Torrence and his friends resign (one at a time) and replace themselves with Enslin and his friends. To be sure, Enslin will acquire control in time anyway and stack the board with his friends. But he wants to hurry the process along.

---

[67] *Id.* at 944-945.

[68] *The Frandsen Story*, Frandsen Corp., http://www.frandsencorporation.com/asp_pages/frandsen_corp_frandsen_story.asp (accessed Mar. 5, 2012).

[69] *Why Jensen-Sundquist?*, Jensen-Sundquist Insurance Agency, http://www.jensen-sundquist.com/Pages/why_jensen.html (accessed Mar. 5, 2012).

May Enslin do this? Board members do not answer only to a 15 percent shareholder. Instead, they owe a fiduciary duty to all shareholders of the firm. *Harris v. Carter* takes an easy case and gives a clear answer. *Essex v. Yates* examines a harder version and gives no answer at all.

B. *Harris v. Carter*[70]

In *Harris*, a controlling shareholder (he held a 52 percent interest) sold his stock to a fraudulent operator who then looted the company. The Delaware chancellor noted "the principle that a shareholder has a right to sell his or her stock and in the ordinary case owes no duty in that connection to other shareholders when acting in good faith."[71] Yet the chancellor also observed that a controlling shareholder did owe fiduciary duties to the others:

> [W]hen a shareholder presumes to exercise control over a corporation, . . . that shareholder assumes a fiduciary duty of the same kind as that owed by a director to the corporation. . . .[72]

The point follows straightforwardly from *Sinclair* (Chapter 4, section III.C.2).

In addition to selling his stock, the *Harris* shareholder arranged to swap the buyer's designees for the incumbent board. But the buyer was dishonest — and flagrantly so. Given the obvious dishonesty, held the court, the seller was on notice under the *Allis-Chalmers* (Chapter 4, section II.C.2) and *Francis* (Chapter 4, section II.A.3) logic:

> [W]hile a person who transfers corporate control to another is surely not a surety for his buyer, when the circumstances would alert a reasonably prudent person to a risk that his buyer is dishonest . . . , a duty devolves upon the seller to make such inquiry as a reasonably prudent person would make. . . ."[73]

The seller sold his stock and transferred control to an obvious thief. In doing so, he breached the duty he owed the other shareholders.

C. *Essex Universal Corp. v. Yates*[74]

Most cases lack the in-your-face fraud of *Harris*. In most cases, the buyer is not a flagrant thief. The question posed by situations like the Enslin-Torrence deal is

---

[70] 582 A.2d 222 (Del. Ch. 1990).
[71] *Id.* at 234.
[72] *Id.*
[73] *Id.* at 235.
[74] 305 F.2d 572 (2d Cir. 1962).

V. Board Seat Sales

whether the seller can stack the board with the buyer's designees in such transactions. Unfortunately, cases like *Essex* do not answer the question.

Herbert J. Yates founded Republic Pictures in 1935. Over the course of his career, he would promote a variety of actors who would go on to become Hollywood stars: John Wayne, Gene Autry, Roy Rogers. He would also promote the career of his decidedly less talented second wife, Vera Ralston. Primarily, he would produce the low-budget "B-movies" that theaters paired as double features with blockbusters from other studios. Yates owned 28 percent of Republic and served as president. By 1957, he was nearing the close of his career. He was making the *Beginning of the End*—and would feature in it a cataclysmic war between the heroic U.S. Air Force and giant killer mutant grasshoppers.[75]

To cap his career, Yates agreed to sell Essex the bulk of his stock at $2 above market. This stake would give Essex control. Essex, however, wanted more. Like Mike Enslin at the Dolphin Hotel, it wanted its own designees on the board. Yates agreed. He promised to hold a special meeting of the board and to have each director resign, while the rest of the directors replaced him with an Essex nominee. After all, the Republic bylaws did give the board the power to fill vacancies.

In September, Essex arrived at the scheduled closing prepared to buy the shares. Yates refused to sell. "Well, there can be no deal," he explained. "We can't close it."[76] Apparently, the price of Republic stock had risen, and he wanted more money. A bit like Stoneham reneging on his contract with McQuade (Chapter 6, section III.B), Yates argued that the contract violated the fiduciary duties he owed the other Republic shareholders.

The parties litigated in the Southern District of New York and, on appeal, faced a panel of three. Judge Edward Lumbard noted that it was "illegal to sell corporate office or management control by itself."[77] Because Republic maintained a staggered board (three classes of three, each with a three-year term), Essex would not have acquired complete control for some time. Lumbard explained that he would have approved the contract if Essex had been buying a majority stake, but found the case problematic given that it was buying only 28 percent.

In fact, of course, even if Essex had bought 51 percent, it would not have acquired control immediately. State statutes generally stop shareholders from removing directors on staggered boards without cause. After all, firms adopt staggered boards precisely to delay changes in control. In Delaware, for example, §141(k) provides:

> Any director or the entire board of directors may be removed, with or without cause, by the holders of a majority of the shares then entitled to vote at an election of directors, except as follows:
> (1) Unless the certificate of incorporation otherwise provides, in the case of a corporation whose board is classified . . . shareholders may effect such removal only for cause. . . .

---

[75] The trailer is available on YouTube, http://www.youtube.com/watch?v=uqVL8blr-rw (accessed Mar. 4, 2012)

[76] 305 F.2d at 574.

[77] *Id.* at 575.

The second judge, Henry Friendly, thought the provision

> violative of public policy save when it was entirely plain that a new election would be a mere formality—i.e., when the seller owned more than 50% of the stock.... Moreover, in view of the perhaps unexpected character of such a holding, I doubt that I would give it retrospective effect.[78]

And the third judge? Charles Clark (one-time dean of the Yale Law School) declared it impossible to decide the case without more facts.

VI. SUMMARY

Corporate law imposes on those who would run a firm a duty to run it in the interests of those who invest their money. They serve as agents, in short, for those who provide the funds. Sometimes, the principle implicates transactions they negotiate outside the firm at the shareholder level.

For an investor, the most vexing of these shareholder-level transactions involve closely held corporations. Because the stock is not publicly traded, they (as investors) cannot readily exit the firm. That leaves them vulnerable to their co-investors. This chapter illustrates some of the ways the courts stop investors from trying to exploit that vulnerability, and some of the ways investors anticipate the problem by contract.

---

[78] *Id.* at 581.

APPENDIX I

Private Actions for Federal Proxy Violations

Section 14 of the 1934 Securities Exchange Act regulates proxy solicitation. Although it does not explicitly authorize private suits to enforce its terms, in the 1960s the Supreme Court did just that. The J. I. Case Company[79] had made farm equipment for decades and, by the middle of the twentieth century, was a major tractor manufacturer. Despite its name, the American Tractor Corporation (ATC) was not. Instead, mostly it made a backhoe attachment. In 1962, Case merged the ATC into itself. Unfortunately, it later discovered that some investors had manipulated the price of ATC stock. Because the firms had set the merger exchange ratio (the number of shares of one firm exchanged for one share of the other) by relative stock prices, the manipulation potentially skewed the terms of the merger itself.

The issue before the Supreme Court was not whether anyone had committed fraud. Neither was it what remedy might be appropriate. Instead, it was whether a shareholder of a firm in which a merger had been approved through fraudulent proxy solicitation material had a cause of action under the 1934 Securities Exchange Act. The Court held that he did.

So a shareholder can sue under §14. What causation must he show? As in *J. I. Case*, the shareholder in *Mills v. Electric Auto-Lite Co.*[80] argued that his company had been merged into another through a shareholder vote accomplished through misleading proxy solicitation material. Realistically, however, he could not prove that the thousands of other shareholders had each relied on the misstatements.

The Supreme Court held that the *Mills* plaintiff needed to show two things. First, he needed to show that any misstatement or omission in the proxy solicitation process was "material." He needed to show, in other words, that the misstatement or omission was of the sort that a reasonable shareholder would think important in deciding how to vote. Second, he needed to show that the proxy solicitation was an important link in the process of accomplishing the merger.

---

[79] J. I. Case Co. v. Borak, 377 U.S. 426 (1964), *aff'g* 317 F.2d 838 (7th Cir. 1963).
[80] 396 U.S. 375 (1970).

And what procedures were important links in the merger process? If a firm needs to solicit proxies to accomplish the merger, the solicitation is a crucial link. Yet sometimes firms solicit shareholder votes that — strictly speaking — they do not need to solicit. Where corporation A owns a majority of corporation B's stock, for example, A can merge B into wholly owned C without bothering to obtain proxies from the other B shareholders. If corporation A does solicit proxies from those other B shareholders (perhaps to obtain disinterested "ratification"), can a plaintiff contest the accuracy of the solicitation material that A distributes? Do any misstatements in that material fit within the chain of causation described in *Mills?*

In *Virginia Bankshares, Inc. v. Sandberg*,[81] the Supreme Court said no. In *Virginia Bankshares*, a parent corporation owned 85 percent of a subsidiary's shares. It merged the subsidiary in a cash-out merger. It could have pushed through the merger without proxies, but it solicited them anyway. The plaintiffs claimed that the solicitation materials were misleading. Given that the parent did not need the proxies to accomplish the merger, the Court denied their claim.

[81] 501 U.S. 1083 (1991).

APPENDIX II

Shareholder Proposals

Suppose you own some stock and want to change the way the firm does business. You might telephone the officers and chat with them. You might take them out to lunch. If they seem reluctant to change, you might solicit proxies and install yourself and your friends on the board. But given that corporate statutes delegate firm management to the board, you could not — as a shareholder — force the firm to change direction. Should you introduce a motion at the shareholders' meeting to change the way the firm does business, the chairman will rule it out of order. And properly so.

Nonetheless, the SEC's shareholder proposal rules under the 1934 Act seem to encourage such shareholder involvement. "Seem to" is the operative phrase. For despite their superficial appearance, the SEC rules do not change corporate law and practice. Instead, they primarily just impose a modest administrative cost on a corporation.

These rules probably do not promote shareholder welfare. Firms raise their funds on competitive capital markets. If a given rule increased shareholder welfare, many firms would adopt it voluntarily. They would adopt it because it improved their ability to raise money. If instead they shun a rule — if they adopt it only because the SEC requires them to adopt it — they probably shun it because shareholders do not want it.

Shareholder welfare or no, the SEC has made the shareholder proposal provisions the law. According to its rules (under §14 of the 1934 Securities Exchange Act), shareholders may ask a firm to include their proposals in its proxy material. The firm may exclude a proposal only if it can cite one of several approved reasons, which appear in Rule 14a-8:

> (1) If the proposal is not a proper subject for action by shareholders. . . .
> (2) If the proposal would, if implemented, cause the company to violate any state, federal, or foreign law. . . .
> (3) If the proposal or supporting statement is contrary to any of the Commission's proxy rules, including Rule 14a-9, which prohibits materially false or misleading statements. . . .
> (4) If the proposal relates to the redress of a personal claim or grievance. . . .

(5) If the proposal relates to operations which account for less than 5 percent of the company's total assets at the end of its most recent fiscal year, and for less than 5 percent of its net earnings and gross sales for its most recent fiscal year, and is not otherwise significantly related to the company's business;

(6) If the company would lack the power or authority to implement the proposal;

(7) If the proposal deals with a matter relating to the company's ordinary business operations;

(8) If the proposal relates to an election for membership on the company's board of directors or analogous governing body; . . .

(12) If the proposal deals with substantially the same subject matter as another proposal . . . that has . . . been previously included in the company's proxy materials within the preceding 5 calendar years, a company may exclude it from its proxy materials for any meeting held within 3 calendar years of the last time it was included if the proposal received:

(i) Less than 3% of the vote if proposed once within the preceding 5 calendar years;

(ii) Less than 6% of the vote on its last submission to shareholders if proposed twice previously within the preceding 5 calendar years; or

(iii) Less than 10% on its last submission to shareholders if proposed three times or more previously within the preceding 5 calendar years. . . .

To see how the process works, take several hypothetical proposals:

Proposal A: Wolters Kluwer shall publish books by author X rather than Ramseyer (or that Wolters Kluwer shall negotiate the purchase of the Gilberts outline series or shall buy paper imported from Canada rather than Indonesia).

Wolters Kluwer can exclude any such proposal for at least two reasons. First, it concerns the firm's ordinary business operations (Reason (7)). Second, precisely because it concerns the firm's business operations, it concerns a matter that corporate law entrusts to the board. As a result, it is not a "proper subject for action by shareholders" (Reason (1)).

Proposal B: Wolters Kluwer shall promote democratic reform in Burma (or support moves to slow global warming or oppose capital punishment).

Wolters Kluwer can exclude this proposal under Reason (6): It lacks the power to implement the proposal. Arguably, it can also exclude the proposal under Reason (5): Unless it trades extensively with Burma, the proposal does not substantially touch on any business the firm conducts.

Proposal C: Because the recent federal financial reporting rules threaten the liberty at the heart of the Madisonian vision, Wolters Kluwer shall refuse to comply.

Wolters Kluwer can exclude the proposal under Reason (2).

Appendix II   Shareholder Proposals

Proposal D: Because of [insert false claim], Wolters Kluwer shall take [desired action].

Wolters Kluwer can exclude the proposal under Reason (3).

Proposal E: Wolters Kluwer shall rehire Ramseyer as vice president for strategic planning.

That the proposal is a transparently bad idea is not an acceptable reason to exclude it. However, Reason (4) is. And if the proposal concerned board membership, Reason (8) would be as well.

What, however, is one to make of Reason (5)?

(5) If the proposal relates to operations which account for less than 5 percent of the company's total assets at the end of its most recent fiscal year, and for less than 5 percent of its net earnings and gross sales for its most recent fiscal year, and is not otherwise significantly related to the company's business. . . .

What type of proposal would "significantly" relate to a company's business, yet account for less than 5 percent of its assets, earnings, and sales?

Take the Dodge Viper. In 2009, the Chrysler Group (which includes Dodge) sold 482 Vipers. It sold 932,000 vehicles of all models that year in the United States. Vipers were a trivial part of its business. Under the Reason (5) numerical cutoffs, Chrysler could exclude any proposal relating to the Viper (also Reasons (1) and (7), of course). Arguably, however, Viper production was indeed "otherwise significantly related" to Chrysler's business.

Here is the argument: Disproportionately, fathers purchase the family car. Assigned to buy a minivan, Dad heads out on Saturday morning. Having just turned 40, he does not want a minivan. He wants a Porsche 911. But he has no money for a 911, and anyway the 911 will not carry his three children and the groceries. Between the Dodge minivan and the Ford minivan, he could not care less. He does not want either. But if the Dodge showroom carries the Viper, he will head for the Dodge dealership rather than the Ford.

The Dodge salesman has seen his type before. He sees them every Saturday. He probably will not let Dad drive the Viper around the block. But he will let Dad ogle it all he wants. He will let Dad sit in it. He will let Dad dream about the life he might live, if only he had not succumbed to the lures of domesticity. And after he lets Dad finish dreaming, he will sell him a minivan.

Put otherwise, the Viper is arguably "significantly related" to the firm's business because of the positive externalities it brings to the firm. The Viper's importance to Dodge does not lie in Viper sales. It lies (if successful) in the additional minivan sales it generates by luring suburban dads into the dealership.

Arguably, the inverse dynamic may have applied to 1968 Honeywell (Chapter 6, section I.D.4). Honeywell may or may not have sold enough shrapnel to hit the 5 percent cutoffs. Even if sold very little shrapnel, however, the public so closely identified Honeywell with the use of shrapnel in Vietnam that the shrapnel business

331

may have reduced Honeywell's thermostat sales. If the Viper created positive externalities for Dodge, the shrapnel may have generated negative externalities for Honeywell. So badly might shrapnel have tarnished the firm's brand name that even if shrapnel sales missed the 5 percent cutoff, they may have been "otherwise significantly related to the company's business."

A very different—and very odd—interpretation of Reason (5) appears in *Lovenheim v. Iroquois Brands, Ltd.*[82] Food distributor Iroquois Brands imported paté de foie gras. Lawyer-journalist Peter C. Lovenheim objected to the way farmers produce the paté—by force-feeding geese. Under the shareholder proposal rules, he introduced a resolution that Iroquois Brands

> form a committee to study the methods by which its French supplier produces paté de foie gras, and report to the shareholders its findings and opinions, based on expert consultation, on whether this production method causes undue distress, pain or suffering to the animals involved and, if so, whether further distribution of this product should be discontinued until a more humane production method is developed.[83]

It is hard not to believe Lovenheim is being disingenuous here. This is the man, after all, who wrote a book called *Portrait of a Burger as a Young Calf.*[84] It is a fair bet that he did not need a committee of experts to find out whether paté production caused geese "undue distress." He knew it did. It is also a fair bet that he did not want Iroquois Brands to form a committee to study paté production. He wanted it to stop importing paté.

Consider what drove Lovenheim to propose the resolution he did. If he had proposed that the company stop importing paté, the company could have excluded the proposal under Reasons (1) and (7). Instead, Lovenheim proposed that the company form a committee to study paté production. That subject still goes to the "ordinary business operations" of the company, but the SEC tends not to let firms exclude proposals that the company form a committee to study aspects of its ordinary business operations. By phrasing the resolution as he did, Lovenheim avoided Reasons (1) and (7). Necessarily, of course, he also lost the ability to bind the company. Even if the proposal passed, the board could decide not to call the committee. And even if the committee recommended that the firm drop paté imports, the board could decide to import it anyway.

Iroquois Brands excluded the proposal under Reason (5). Because the firm imported only trivial paté, the imports easily failed the numerical cutoffs. Because few people identified the brand with paté, the imports also implicated no substantial Honeywell-style negative externalities.

Yet the federal district judge held that the ethical issues involved precluded exclusion. The proposal, he explained, raised issues of "ethical and social

---

[82] 618 F. Supp. 554 (D.D.C. 1985).

[83] *Id.* at 556.

[84] Peter Lovenheim, *Portrait of a Burger as a Young Calf: The True Story of One Man, Two Cows, and the Feeding of a Nation* (Harmony 2002).

significance."[85] If a proposal raises ethical issues of "significance," apparently, a firm cannot cite Reason (5) to exclude it—no matter how trivial its relation to the company. If that is what the SEC intended to say in Reason (5), it chose an odd way to say it.

Many proposals do not come to a vote at all. From 2000 to 2006, 1,067 firms received 6,743 shareholder proposals. Of these, 2,939 were not presented to a vote. Some were dropped because they failed one of the reasons given above. Others were dropped because the proponents cut a deal with management.[86] Of the proposals that did go to a vote during this period, 30 percent related to the structure of the board, 20 percent to compensation, 18 percent to social and economic issues, 16 percent to nonboard governance-related issues, and 12 percent to environmental and health-related issues.[87] Of the proposals actually presented to the shareholders, about 19 percent passed.[88]

---

[85] 618 F. Supp. at 561.

[86] Bonnie Buchanan, Jeffrey N. Netter, and Tina Yang, *Proxy Rules and Proxy Practices: An Empirical Study of US and UK Shareholder Proposals*, SSRN 1474062, at 14 (Aug. 28, 2009).

[87] *Id.* at tbl. 3.

[88] *Id.* at 19.

CHAPTER 8

Mergers and Acquisitions

It had been a tough December for Mary Bailey. Her husband George ran the local bank, the Bailey Building & Loan, Inc. (BBL). Its business was not good. He also ran a local real estate firm, Bailey Park, Inc. (BPI). Its business was no better. The local Potterville economy was down, their neighbors were out of work, and no one was borrowing money or buying houses. Increasingly, George yelled at Mary and their children, and increasingly, he drank too much. All too often, he left for the bars after dinner and returned sometime in the early morning hours.

It was on one of those all-night binges that George met and fell under the sway of a mystic named Clarence Odbody. With a Svengali-like smoothness and an effortless facility with religious turns of phrase, Clarence acquired almost hypnotic control over George. George asked him for advice about the bank. He asked him about Bailey Park. He asked him about Mary.

Suppose, at this point, that Mary declared it all over. It was as though she were married not just to George but to a Gollum-ish shadow besides. By the end of January, she was through. It was hard enough enduring an abusive alcoholic. She would not tolerate a wacky spiritualist too. Suppose she hired a lawyer, sued for divorce, and settled for a block of stock in the BBL and BPI.

Mary then approached George's brother Harry. Recently returned from four years at Princeton, Harry had hoped to modernize and rationalize BBL and BPI. Alas, he found high school–educated George implacably opposed. Together, Mary and Harry reasoned that their shares in the two firms might give them the control Harry needed. Toward that end, they placed their shares in a newly formed Bailey Family Trust, Inc. They would exercise their stock together, take control, and rationalize the firms.

In this chapter, I explore some of the legal and business issues that men and women like Mary and Harry face in ousting incumbents from control. Section I outlines the main legal structures they can manipulate (mergers, asset sales) and some of the legal implications (dissenters' rights) that follow from the choice. Section II then explains how they might use mergers to eliminate minority shareholders. Finally, Section III explores the mechanics of specifically hostile acquisitions and the legality of the defenses incumbents adopt, and Section IV discusses the statutes various states have adopted to limit such acquisitions.

I. MERGERS

A. Introduction

1. The Project

Suppose a local businessman named Henry Potter specialized in buying and rationalizing badly run companies. Typically, he took control, jettisoned a firm's least profitable divisions, and expanded and modernized the rest. Through it all, he fired mediocre managers, created new jobs for the community, and raised returns to the shareholders.

Seeing BBL in trouble, suppose Potter turned to Mary and Harry Bailey. Suppose, he suggested, they combined BBL with his own larger and better-run Potter State Bank, Inc. (PSB). Mary and Harry agreed. The three consulted the firm's lawyer. He explained that they could combine the two banks in several ways. The tax consequences would vary substantially, but the differences in the business law consequences were minor.

2. The Merger

(a) Small into Large

As their lawyer put it, Potter and the Baileys could merge BBL into PSB (Del. Gen. Corp. L. §251(a)). BBL would disappear as an independent entity, but PSB would continue its business and assume its rights and liabilities. In exchange for their BBL stock, the former BBL shareholders would receive PSB shares (though the boards could negotiate other compensation if they wanted).

The merger would proceed through several prescribed steps. First, the executives of PSB and BBL would cut a deal — a merger agreement. Second, the boards of the two companies would approve the agreement (e.g.,§251(b)). Third, the shareholders of the two corporations would approve the merger by (in Delaware) majority vote (§251(c)).

(b) Large into Small

But Potter and the Baileys would not need to merge BBL into PSB, their lawyer continued. Even if they intended effectively to have the PSB run BBL's business, they could merge PSB into BBL instead. That would leave BBL as the surviving corporation, of course. But it would include all the business of PSB, and Potter and the Baileys could rename it the "Potter State Bank, Inc.," anyway. The end result: a firm called PSB that continued the combined businesses of PSB and BBL and assumed the rights and liabilities of both.

This merger would proceed through the same steps. The executives of the two firms would negotiate a merger agreement. The two boards would approve it. And the shareholders of the two firms would approve it as well. The shareholders would then rename the firm "PSB."

(c) Other Mergers

Mergers do not all require shareholder approval. The exact rules vary by state, of course. But suppose a (relatively) small firm merged into a much larger firm. Under §251(f) of the Delaware corporate code, both the board and the shareholders of the small disappearing firm would vote on the merger. At the larger surviving firm, only the board would vote. A merger qualifies for this abbreviated procedure if the amount of stock issued by the surviving firm to the shareholders of the disappearing firm constitutes less than 20 percent of the surviving firm's outstanding stock at the outset.

Suppose a parent firm merged a subsidiary into itself. Under Delaware law (it defines a subsidiary as a firm owned at least 90 percent by another; see §253), the parent board must approve the merger agreement. Presumably because the merger just reshuffles assets already under the firm's control, the shareholders of the parent need not vote. And presumably because it would not matter, "[n]either the subsidiary's board nor its minority shareholders have any say" either.[1]

Or suppose the firms negotiated a merger in which the shareholders of the disappearing firm received only cash. Although students often assume shareholders receive stock in a merger, they need not do so. Firms can compensate shareholders of a disappearing firm with cash or other property if they want. If shareholders receive only cash or property, they obviously will not trigger the 20 percent stock threshold in §251(f) — and, at the surviving firm, will not have a vote on the merger.

(d) Asset Sales

To combine PSB and BBL, Potter and the Baileys would not need to negotiate a merger at all. Instead, they could just sell the assets of the one firm to the other. Structure it appropriately, and an asset sale would closely mimic a merger.[2]

---

[1] Stephen M. Bainbridge, *Corporate Law* 343 (2d ed., Foundation Press 2009); *see* Del. Gen. Corp. L. §253.

[2] One significant area of difference concerns the creditors of the selling corporation. In this hypothetical, the selling corporation would probably liquidate and distribute the cash (or other assets) to its shareholders. In general, creditors will be repaid before any liquidation distribution is made to the shareholders. Creditors whose claims were unknown at the time of liquidation, however, raise

To implement the transaction, they would need a majority vote among the share-holders of the selling corporation but not the buying firm.

Suppose Potter and the Baileys decided to combine their two firms, decided that PSB would continue the business of the combined companies, and decided that BBL shareholders would continue as shareholders of the combined entity. Suppose further that they decided to combine the firms through an asset sale. Much as with a merger, the officers of the two firms would first negotiate an agreement that specified the terms of the transaction. Second, the boards of the two firms would approve the agreement.

Third, BBL (the selling firm) shareholders would approve the transaction by majority vote. The Delaware requirement appears in Del. Gen. Corp. L. §271(a):

> Every corporation may at any meeting of its board of directors . . . sell . . . all or substantially all of its property . . . upon such terms and conditions . . . as its board of directors . . . deems expedient and for the best interests of the corporation, when and as authorized by a resolution adopted by the holders of a majority of the outstanding stock of the corporation entitled to vote thereon. . . .

Note that PSB (the buying firm) shareholders do not vote on the transaction. BBL falls within the ambit of §271 because it sells "all or substantially all" of its assets. Because PSB buys all or substantially all of the assets of another firm, §271 does not apply.

Fourth, BBL would liquidate. In exchange for BBL's assets, PSB could have paid BBL whatever the two firms negotiated. It might have paid cash, but — by the terms of this hypothetical — here it paid with PSB stock. As a result, after the sale BBL would hold only PSB shares. To complete the transaction, the firm would liquidate and distribute those PSB shares to its stockholders. That liquidation will require a vote of both the BBL board and BBL stockholders (Del. Gen. Corp. L. §275).

"All or substantially all" is not as clear as one might think. In the 1981 Delaware case of *Katz v. Bergman*,[3] for example, Plant Industries sold a subsidiary that accounted for 51 percent of its assets and 45 percent of its sales. The court reasoned that the subsidiary operated what had been "historically the principal business" of Plant. As a result, even though the subsidiary represented only half of Plant, the transaction fell within §271 and Plant shareholders had a vote.

Query (as we law professors like to say) if *Katz* is still the law. Query if it ever was. By 2004,[4] Vice Chancellor Leo Strine held that newspapers constituting 56 to 57 percent of the value of a publications empire did not constitute "substantially all." Asked Strine, "[h]as the judiciary transmogrified the words 'substantially all' . . . into the words 'approximately half'?" No, he answered. "A fair and succinct equivalent to the term 'substantially all' would . . . be 'essentially

---

more difficult questions. *See generally* Franklin A. Gevurtz, *Corporation Law* 695-699 (2d ed., West 2010); Bainbridge, *supra* note 1, at 347.

[3] 431 A.2d 1274 (Del. Ch. 1981).

[4] Hollinger, Inc. v. Hollinger Intl., 858 A.2d 342 (Del. Ch. 2004).

everything.' "[5] And the Model Business Corporations Act specifies that even three quarters is not "substantially all." According to §12.02(a):

> A sale . . . of assets . . . requires approval of the corporation's shareholders if the disposition would leave the corporation without a significant continuing business activity. If a corporation retains a business activity that represented at least 25 percent of total assets . . . and 25 percent of either income . . . or revenues . . . , . . . the corporation will conclusively be deemed to have retained a significant continuing activity.

B. *Appraisal and De Facto Mergers*

1. Introduction

As their lawyer explained to Mary and Harry Bailey, the combinations in section A do not yield identical results. They do not generate identical tax consequences. And despite their similarity, neither do they quite generate identical corporate consequences. Most obviously, some combinations give rise to "appraisal rights," while others do not.

Also known as "dissenter's rights," appraisal rights give a shareholder who objects to certain transactions the right to "dissent" from the transaction and obtain the "appraised" value of his shares. Suppose Harry and Mary Bailey vote to merge BBL into PSB. George owns a minority stake in BBL and objects. Under the law of most states, he can force the firm to pay him the appraised value of his stake. Typically, the case and statutory law require an amount that approximates the value of the shares before the contested transaction.

Appraisal rights had their genesis in a nineteenth-century legislative bargain.[6] At the time, mergers typically proceeded only on a unanimous vote of all shareholders. This obviously gave each shareholder an incentive to threaten to veto the transaction. In exchange for a suitable side payment, he could then change his mind and vote yes. Because each shareholder had an incentive to threaten to "hold up" the firm, entrepreneurs found value-maximizing mergers stalled. In due course, states dropped the unanimity requirement. In exchange, they gave shareholders who objected to a merger the right simply to obtain the "appraised value" of their shares.

Corporate officers do not like to pay appraisal rights. For the most part, they do not dislike appraisal because they hope otherwise to cheat their shareholders. They dislike it because it complicates planning. Typically, they want to know before a transaction how much cash they need to prepare. Unfortunately, they will not know how much they need to pay in "appraisal" until after they complete a transaction. Only then will they know how many shareholders dissent. And only when they know how many dissent will they know how much cash they need to pay.

---

[5] *Id.* at 377.
[6] Robert C. Clark, *Corporate Law* 443-444 (Little, Brown 1986).

Because appraisal makes merger planning so hard, some observers argue that states should provide the remedy only for closely held firms. Section 262(b)(1) of the Delaware code states that:

> [N]o appraisal rights . . . shall be available for the shares of any class or series of stock, which . . . were . . . listed on a national securities exchange. . . .

If a shareholder of a listed firm objects to a merger, commentators reason that he can simply sell his stock. Giving him the right to demand appraisal burdens the firm's officers without an offsetting benefit — because the shareholder can obtain fair value on the market anyway. The logic is not entirely right, of course. If the merger harmed the firm, the shareholder would sell his stock at a price that reflected the harm. He would be made whole only with a right that gave him the value of his shares before anyone announced the merger.

2.   Farris

Given the complications that appraisal imposes, firms sometimes structure their transactions to avoid it. When they do, sometimes the courts try to prevent them. The doctrine they use goes by the name of de facto merger. Consider the Pennsylvania case of *Farris v. Glen Alden.*[7]

List (a large Delaware corporation) owned 38 percent of Glen Alden (a smaller Pennsylvania corporation). The boards of the two firms decided to combine them. Because both Delaware and Pennsylvania law gave merged shareholders appraisal rights, they could not avoid appraisal rights if they merged.

To avoid those rights, the boards instead arranged (i) for List to sell its assets to Glen Alden, (ii) for Glen Alden to pay for the assets with its stock, (iii) for List to liquidate and distribute the Glen Alden stock to its shareholders, and (iv) for Glen Alden to rename itself List-Alden. The resulting List-Alden firm would hold all the assets of the two constituent corporations and be owned by the shareholders of the two firms.

Presumably, the deal was fair all around. The court complains about a mismatch in book value, but book value does not matter. It is just an accounting entry. What does matter — what shareholders care about — is market value: What would a disinterested third party pay for the firm? As explained in Chapter 7 (section III. B), only by random chance would book value ever coincide with market value.

Shareholders approved the transaction at both firms. The List shareholders voted because their firm sold all of its assets — and state law gives shareholders a vote on a sale of "all or substantially all" of a firm's assets (section I.A.2.(d) above). By contrast, state law does not give shareholders a vote on a decision to buy all of another firm's assets. In order to pay List for the assets, though, Glen Alden needed

---

[7] 143 A.2d 25 (Pa. 1958).

to issue more stock than authorized by its charter. As a result, it needed to amend its charter — and charter amendments require a shareholder vote. Not to worry, Glen Alden shareholders duly approved the transaction.

Under Delaware law (§262(b)), shareholders of a firm that sells its assets do not have appraisal rights. Consequently, List shareholders could not demand appraisal. Conversely, Pennsylvania law explicitly stated that shareholders of a firm that bought all the assets of another firm did not have appraisal rights. The Pennsylvania courts had awarded appraisal rights in such cases in the past, and the legislature had overruled them.

Never mind, declared the *Farris* court. The sale was a de facto merger. "[W]e will not blind our eyes to the realities of the transaction. Despite the designation of the parties and the form employed, Glen Alden does not in fact acquire List, rather, List acquires Glen Alden," wrote the court. Hence, "the right of dissent would remain with the shareholders of Glen Alden."[8]

Faced with an intransigent Supreme Court in *Farris*, the Pennsylvania legislature once again declared (with Horton) that it meant what it said and it said what it meant. De facto mergers were not the law, even 0 percent. In *Terry v. Penn Central Corp.*,[9] the Third Circuit finally declared what the Pennsylvania Supreme Court would not: The de facto merger doctrine was not the law of Pennsylvania.[10]

3. Hariton

Farris may not be the law of Pennsylvania; it certainly is not the law of Delaware. In *Hariton v. Arco Electronics, Inc.*,[11] Arco sold its assets to Loral in exchange for Loral shares and then distributed the Loral stock in liquidation. An Arco shareholder sued for appraisal rights, and the court refused. The merger and asset sale provisions of the Delaware General Corporation Law were "of equal dignity."[12]

Curious as its circumlocution may seem, the court meant that neither statutory section trumped the other. If a corporate board chose to structure a transaction through the asset sale section of the law, the court would not recharacterize it by the merger section. Boards could apply the statutory provisions they wanted, and the courts would respect their choice. Under Delaware law, some corporate combinations granted dissenters appraisal rights. Others did not. Effectively, the court declared appraisal an optional remedy.

---

[8] *Id.* at 31.

[9] 668 F.2d 188 (3d Cir. 1981).

[10] Bizarrely, in In re Jones & Laughlin Steel Corp., 412 A.2d 1099, 1104 (Pa. 1980), the Pennsylvania Supreme Court describes *Glen Alden* as an "attempted merger . . . where merger was structured so as to defraud dissenting shareholders of their right to an appraisal."

[11] 188 A.2d 123 (Del. 1963).

[12] *Id.* at 125.

4. Rauch

(a) The Case

A court faced the inverse of sorts to de facto mergers in *Rauch v. RCA Corp.*[13] Suppose two firms negotiate a cash-out merger. Should a court recharacterize it as something else? General Electric decided to merge RCA into a subsidiary. RCA had two classes of stock, common and preferred. General Electric agreed to pay the common $66 per share and the preferred $40. The RCA charter provided, however, that the company could redeem the preferred at $100 per share.

Holding preferred stock, the plaintiff argued that the court should recharacterize the transaction as a redemption of the preferred at $100. Applying Delaware law, the court refused. The merger and redemption provisions were "of equal dignity." RCA knew how to merge, and it knew how to redeem. It chose to merge, and the law entitled it to make that choice. The court would not now recharacterize the merger as a redemption after the fact.

(b) Incentives

Consider, however, whether the preferred would have exercised any right to obtain $100 in a merger anyway. When a preferred shareholder claimed that the charter gave preferred shareholders the right to have their shares redeemed at $100 in a merger, he misstated its terms. It did not. Instead, the charter gave the firm the right to redeem their shares at $100:

> The First Preferred Stock at any time outstanding may be redeemed by the Corporation, in whole or in part, at its election . . . at the price of one hundred dollars ($100) per share and all dividends accrued or in arrears. . . .[14]

RCA had a right to "call" the preferred; the preferred did not have a right to "put" their stock to RCA.

And yet, even if the charter had given the preferred the right to have their shares redeemed at $100 in a merger, they would have waived the right. To see why, take a simplified variation on the firm. Suppose it had 100 common shares and 100 preferred. Suppose further that because of their different rights to the firm's earnings, the two classes traded (as they usually do) at different prices. The common sold for $61 per share, and the preferred at $35. At 100 shares each, the firm was worth a total of $(100 \times \$61) + (100 \times \$35) = \$9,600$.

Now suppose that GE thought that it could increase the value of the firm by about 10 percent, or $1,000. For all the outstanding shares of RCA, it was willing to pay $\$9,600 + \$1,000 = \$10,600$. Crucially, even if the preferred stockholders had a

---

[13] 861 F.2d 29 (2d Cir. 1988).
[14] *Id.* at 30 n.2 (italics in original).

contractual right to receive $100 per share in a merger, under these numbers they would have waived the right. If they insisted on $100, they would have left $600 for the common — $6 per share. The common obviously would reject the merger, and the preferred would find themselves stuck with stock worth $35.

What the preferred want is a share of GE's 10 percent premium. If they can split the premium with the common, then both classes can benefit from the merger, both classes will vote to approve the merger, and the preferred will receive more than their current $35. Suppose, for example, that they split the $1,000 premium equally. The common would receive $66 per share in the merger, and the preferred would receive $40.

Put otherwise, the choice facing the preferred was not $40 or $100. Even if (counterfactually) they had had a right to put their stock to the firm at $100 in a merger, they would not have received $100. Instead, the common would have voted down the merger and the preferred would have found themselves left with shares worth $35. Only by waiving their right to the $100 would they have obtained any of the 10 percent premium at all.

II. FREEZE-OUT MERGERS

A. *Introduction*

1. Why

The fiduciary duty that controlling shareholders owe the minority under cases like *Sinclair* (see Chapter 4, section III. C.2) can cause trouble. Suppose (purely for the sake of this illustration) that Mary and Harry Bailey's Bailey Family Trust (BFT) owned 80 percent of BBL and 60 percent of the BPI construction firm. Suppose further that BBL regularly supplied trade credit financing to the construction firm.

If the trust owned 100 percent of the bank and firm, Mary and Harry would not worry about the terms that the bank charged the firm. After all, the financing just shifted money from one of its pockets to another. But the BFT did not own all the stock of either firm. It owned 80 percent of the bank and 60 percent of the construction firm. Because the risk entailed in trade credit depends on a borrower's financial health and the state of its industry, it does not have a clear "market price." Unfortunately, if the BBL charges a price that is arguably "too high," the BPI shareholders will sue under *Sinclair*. If it charges a price that is too low, the BBL shareholders will complain.

Although Mary and Harry can avoid this headache by eliminating the minority shareholders in the two firms, they cannot eliminate the shareholders just by offering to buy their stock. Knowing how badly Mary and Harry want the stock, sleazeball Clarence will advise George (a minority shareholder) not to sell. "Why settle for market?" he will ask. "Hold up your ungrateful ex- and brother, and demand more."

2. How

The "freeze-out merger" (sometimes known as a "cash-out merger") solves the hold-up problem Clarence creates. To "freeze out" George, Harry and Mary will form two corporations of which they will own 100 percent. They will then merge BBL and BPI into those firms. As compensation, they will distribute cash (some acquirers use stock) to the BBL and BPI minority shareholders (like George).

To accomplish these mergers, both the directors and the shareholders of the firms will need to approve the transaction. For reasons discussed below (section C), Harry and Mary would like to see a majority of the minority shareholders approve the merger too (though in this particular case, George and Clarence may refuse). Provided that the controlling shareholder pays them at least the market value of their stock, however, a majority of the minority usually will approve the merger. After all, minority shareholders do not gain by blocking value-increasing mergers.

B. Singer and Tanzer

Despite this innocuous rationale, freeze-out mergers make courts uneasy. Necessarily, the controlling shareholder dictates the terms and necessarily has an incentive to underpay the others. If the shares are publicly traded, a court can easily ensure that the minority obtains a fair price. Unfortunately, many freeze-out transactions involve shares without a market.

In 1977, the Delaware Supreme Court decided *Singer v. Magnavox Co.*[15] Magnavox had introduced the first home videogame console in 1972. A few years later, TMC bought 84 percent of its stock in a tender offer at $9 per share and merged the remaining 16 percent into a subsidiary through a $9 per share cash-out merger. Given the risk of self-dealing, said the court (it did not explain how there could be self-dealing when the cash-out merger proceeded at the same price as the public tender offer), TMC would need to show a "business purpose" for the merger.

Later the same year, the court elaborated on its new rules. In *Tanzer*,[16] it faced a merger where the parent corporation had a business purpose for engineering a freeze-out merger of its subsidiary, but the purpose did not relate to the subsidiary's business. Instead, the purpose went to the parent's. That sufficed, explained the court.

C. Weinberger

In 1983, the Delaware Supreme Court abandoned this business purpose requirement. The case — *Weinberger*[17] — involved Signal's acquisition of UOP. Signal was

---

[15] 380 A.2d 969 (Del. 1977).

[16] Tanzer v. Intl. Gen. Indus., 379 A.2d 1121 (Del. 1977).

[17] Weinberger v. UOP, Inc., 457 A.2d 701 (Del. 1983) (en banc).

an aerospace and automotive firm eventually acquired by Honeywell; UOP was an oil company formed by one Jesse Dubbs and his son named (I kid you not) Carbon Petroleum Dubbs. Signal had bought 50.5 percent of UOP at $21 per share in a tender offer. Three years later, it decided to acquire the rest in a freeze-out merger.

To determine the price it would pay, Signal assigned two of its officers, Charles Arledge and Andrew Chitea, to study UOP. The men examined the firm's business and finances and decided that Signal could profitably pay up to $24 per share. Were that the whole story, Signal probably would not have needed to disclose its $24 reservation price. A parent may owe a fiduciary duty to the minority shareholders of its subsidiary, but that duty does not include a general obligation to disclose its reservation price.

But that was not the whole story. Arledge and Chitea were not just Signal officers. They were UOP directors. To determine Signal's reservation price, they had used confidential UOP documents to which they had had access only because of their positions on its board.

When Signal announced to UOP that it would freeze out the minority, it negotiated with the non-Signal UOP directors. Those directors then hired the Lehman Brothers investment bank to advise them. For no reason other than strategic game playing, however, Signal gave Lehman only three days to value the firm.

Signal declared it would pay $21, Lehman advised UOP to accept the offer, and UOP minority shareholders overwhelmingly approved it. A disgruntled minority shareholder sued to challenge the merger and then discovered Arledge and Chitea's conflict of interest.

The court held for the plaintiff. Given a minority shareholder who could allege some misbehavior, the court explained, Signal as the controlling shareholder bore the burden of proving the entire fairness of the transaction. Had a majority of the minority shareholders approved the merger's terms after full disclosure, the burden would have shifted to the plaintiff. He would not (later cases would clarify) have needed to show that the transaction constituted waste, but he would at least have needed to show that it was unfair. Because Signal did not disclose that Arledge and Chitea used confidential UOP information, here the ratification did not shift any burden. Instead, Signal retained the burden of proving the merger's fairness.

To meet that burden, continued the court, Signal needed to show both that the price was fair and that the procedures followed were fair. For the most part, shareholders who receive a fair price in a merger will not care whether controlling shareholders manipulate process. Investors do not buy stock to revel in process. They buy stock to make money.

Usually, though, Delaware judges realize that they lack a comparative advantage in valuing stock — as crucial as value is. They are not investment advisers and do not know much about valuing firms. They are lawyers and do know how to structure procedure. If a fairer procedure can help ensure a fairer price, then by policing procedure they can push prices toward fairer levels.

What the Delaware court did not do was to require a business purpose. Six years after introducing the requirement in *Singer*, it jettisoned it in *Weinberger*. The court did not say so, but two facts seem obvious. First, controlling shareholders always have a business purpose for their freeze-out mergers. They do not invest in firms for the fun of it. They invest for business reasons. When they restructure their investments they plan those restructurings for business reasons too — always.

Second, if a controlling shareholder knows he will need to show a business purpose, he can introduce several off-the-rack reasons anyway. For example, a less-than-100-percent shareholder will face minority investors to whom he owes fiduciary duties. Those duties, in turn, will complicate his job and his ability to respond to market exigencies. The less-than-100-percent shareholder will also need to implement costly disclosure and auditing procedures. And precisely because he owns less than all the stock, the less-than-100-percent shareholder faces lower incentives to run his firm efficiently.

As long as he knows a court will require him to show a business purpose, a controlling shareholder will rarely have trouble proving several. Implied the court in *Weinberger*, why bother?

D.   *Coggins*

Yet if the Delaware court eventually "got it right" in *Weinberger*, *Coggins v. New England Patriots Football Club, Inc.*,[18] illustrates how badly courts can confuse the issues. In 1959, "Billy" Sullivan paid $25,000 for the eighth and last franchise in what was then the American Football League. He contributed the franchise to a new corporation, nine others contributed $25,000 in cash, and each of the ten took 10,000 shares in the firm. They apparently had a winning corporate strategy. Four months after they acquired their voting stock at $2.50 per share, they successfully sold 120,000 shares of nonvoting stock to the general public at $5.00. It was the first football team to offer stock to the public.

Although Sullivan initially ran the firm, in 1974 the other voting shareholders ousted him from the board. To retake the firm, he began buying their 90,000 shares. By 1975, he had acquired all the voting stock. He booted the others from office and took control.

To pay for the stock, Sullivan had to borrow $5 million, and the bank insisted that he structure team finances to devote its revenue stream toward the loan repayment. In effect, the bank wanted Sullivan to secure his loan with the football team. Had he owned all the stock, Sullivan could have done that legally. Unfortunately for him, he did not. As long as any minority shareholders remained, he violated his fiduciary duties to them if he secured a personal loan with firm property.

As a condition of the loan, Sullivan thus had to eliminate the other shareholders. To freeze them out, he formed a new corporation of which he owned 100 percent. He then merged the old Patriots firm into his new firm and paid the nonvoting shareholders $15 per share. An ardent Patriots fan, David Coggins,

---

[18] 492 N.E.2d 1112 (Mass. 1986); Frank Litsky, *Billy Sullivan, 86, Founder of Football Patriots, Dies*, N.Y. Times (Feb. 24, 1998).

owned 10 of the nonvoting shares. He owned them for the sheer pleasure of investing in his favorite team. Incensed that Sullivan would make him sell, he sued.

The Court noted that Sullivan as controlling shareholder owed the other shareholders a fiduciary duty under *Wilkes* (Chapter 7, section I.B.2). It also noted that Delaware had imposed a business purpose requirement on freeze-out mergers in 1977. It realized that Delaware had abandoned the requirement six years later, but declared that it liked the requirement anyway. Henceforth, it held, Massachusetts would require controlling shareholders to show a business purpose for any freeze-out merger.

Sullivan had not shown a business purpose. Why would he, after all? That had not been a requirement. He did explain that the National Football League was discouraging teams from selling shares to the public, but the court dismissed the point. On the grounds that he had not shown a business purpose, it declared the merger illegal.

In fact, of course, Sullivan had frozen out the minority shareholders because the bank would not otherwise lend him the money he needed to buy the stock. He had a business purpose for what he as a shareholder did; it simply was not a purpose of the corporation. Yet even before they abandoned the business purpose requirement in *Weinberger*, the Delaware courts recognized shareholder-level business purposes as sufficient. That was the point of *Tanzer*. Effectively, the Massachusetts court adopted *Singer* without *Tanzer* and held Sullivan's purpose inadequate.

The court would not undo the merger. Sullivan had frozen out the minority in 1976, but the court did not decide *Coggins* until 1986. A decade later, too much had happened to return the team to the premerger days. Instead, Coggins would receive the value that his shares would have reached if Sullivan had let him hold them.

Under Sullivan's control, the Patriots had thrived. From 1968 to 1976, the Patriots went a desultory 28–78. Over the next decade, they would go 96–63 and go to the Super Bowl besides.

Winning teams make money. By 1986, Coggins's shares were worth $80 per share. The team had prospered because of Sullivan's leadership, Sullivan had been able to lead because the bank had lent him funds, and the bank had lent the money on condition that he freeze out the minority. After the fact, the court let the minority pretend that this had not happened and free-ride on his work.

For Sullivan, the case was a disaster. To pay the former nonvoting stockholders what the court ordered, he needed money he did not have. To raise it, he tried to sell stock back to the public. Yet if the Court had earlier declared the NFL's opposition to public ownership a smokescreen, the NFL did not think so. When Sullivan tried to sell stock to the public, the league blocked him. Desperate, Sullivan abandoned his team to Victor Kiam (netting $5 million).[19]

[19] Timothy W. Smith, *Foxboro Follies: Kiam and Patriots Need Styptic Pencil*, N.Y. Times B5 (Nov. 11, 1991).

347

Sullivan then sued the NFL for damages. By blocking him from selling the stock to the public, he claimed, it violated the Sherman Act.[20] The jury awarded him $114 million, the judge slashed it to $51 million, and the appellate court dismissed his claim entirely.[21] In the end, he settled with the league for $11.5 million.[22]

III. HOSTILE ACQUISITIONS

A. *Introduction*

Return to George Bailey. Suppose Gower Pharmaceuticals is a major employer in Potterville. Because of products liability claims stemming from negligent manufacturing processes for one of its drugs, its stock trades at an extremely low price. Aging motel-chain executive Marion Crane hopes to acquire control of the firm. So does Henry Potter. The Gower board would prefer to deal with Crane.

In a tender offer, a would-be acquirer tries to buy a controlling stake in a firm. Suppose Potter wanted to acquire Gower. Suppose further that Gower currently trades at $100 per share. Potter would announce that he stands willing to buy Gower shares at (for example) $150 per share. More specifically, he would "offer" to buy any Gower share "tendered" to him at $150.

In their tender offer statements, acquirers will include a variety of detail. For example, Potter might not have the money. He might be planning to ask investment banker Gordon Gekko to raise the funds for him. If so, his offer to buy the Gower stock would be conditional on his obtaining that financing. Gower might have in place a "poison pill" defense (see section F below). Potter would make his offer conditional on the board's removing the pill. Potter will specify how long he will keep the offer open (federal law sets a minimum — see section C below). He will specify how much stock he will buy. He might want as much as he can obtain (an "any and all" offer), or he might want only a certain number of shares. And he will specify which stock brokerage firm will serve as his agent for accepting tendered stock.

In the rest of this section III, I turn first to the economics of tender offers (section B). I summarize their federal regulation (section C). I then discuss a series of defensive tactics: greenmail (section D), self-tenders (section E), and poison pills (section F). I conclude with an outline of more recent Delaware opinions (section G), and special rules on the shareholder franchise (section H). In section IV, I turn to state anti-takeover statutes.

---

[20] William M. Bulkeley, *Antitrust Suit Could Rewrite NFL Playbook*, Wall St. J. B4 (Nov. 17, 1991).

[21] Sullivan v. NFL, 34 F.3d 1091 (1st Cir. 1994), *cert. denied*, 513 U.S. 1190 (1995).

[22] Gerald Eskenazi, *Patriots' History Is Colorful, if Checkered*, N.Y. Times C14 (Jan. 12, 1997).

III. Hostile Acquisitions

B. *The Economics*

The modern analysis of tender offers began with a 1965 article by a lawyer (later professor and dean) named Henry Manne.[23] Manne would go on to play a crucial role in the development of "law and economics," but his scholarly career started with his study of tender offers.

Manne suggested that hostile acquisitions took place within a "market for corporate control." Formally, of course, they take place in a market for stock. But through tender offers, acquirers use the stock market to buy the right to control a firm. They buy that control, observed Manne, when "an existing company is poorly managed." Badly run, it will have stock whose price declines "relative to the shares of other companies in the same industry or relative to the market as a whole." In turn, that low price signals an opportunity:

> The lower the stock price, relative to what it could be with more efficient management, the more attractive the take-over becomes to those who believe that they can manage the company more efficiently.[24]

As a result, explain Logan Beirne and Professor Jonathan Macey more recently:

> [A] properly functioning market for corporate control clearly provides benefits for the shareholders of companies whose shares are purchased by the outside bidder. Such shareholders receive a substantial premium, generally around fifty percent of the price at which the target firm's shares had been trading before the bid.[25]

Note two crucial points. First, acquirers do not make money buying well-run firms. They make money only if they can buy low and sell high, and they can accomplish that feat only if they can run a firm better than the incumbents do. Second, acquirers do not make money "busting up" well-run firms. A well-run firm will have "going concern" value — it will be worth more than the sum of its parts. An acquirer can make money selling off a firm's component parts only if the incumbents are doing so bad a job that the going-concern value is negative — that the firm is worth more dead than alive.

What is more, a corporate control market provides benefits that go beyond those gains to incumbent shareholders to shareholders more generally. Again, as Beirne and Macey put it:[26]

> When a company is open to the threat of a takeover, management and directors' best defense against losing their positions due to a hostile takeover is to keep share prices high, thereby making the company more expensive for the acquirer. . . . In this way, an efficient market for corporate control . . . allows shareholders to keep their agents in check.

---

[23] Henry G. Manne, *Mergers and the Market for Corporate Control*, 73 J. Pol. Econ. 110 (1965).

[24] *Id.* at 113.

[25] Logan Beirne & Jonathan Macey, *Out with the Bathwater: Erosion of Shareholders' Takeover Power*, in *The Iconic Cases in Corporate Law* 209, 211 (Jonathan R. Macey ed., Thomson West 2008).

[26] *Id.* at 212.

C.   The Federal Statutory Framework

1.   The Genesis

Tender offers improve operating efficiency; they throw mediocre managers out of work. Investors hold their stock in a diversified portfolio; managers earn a large fraction of their livelihood in salary from their employer. And investors lie scattered across 50 states and hundreds of electoral districts; managers live in the one or two electoral districts that include and surround their corporate headquarters.

These facts do not make for an electoral formula that promotes investor welfare. Instead, they point to an unfortunate political truth: Although tender offers help investors earn higher returns by putting resources to better use, they do not help politicians win elections. As a result, both federal and state legislatures have passed statutes that impede tender offers. The net effect on economic welfare has been unambiguously negative.

At the federal government, the architect of the regulatory legislation was one Harrison Williams, Democratic senator from New Jersey. Williams would go to prison in 1982 for taking bribes, but in 1968 he was still a powerful senator.[27] That year, he masterminded the set of amendments to the 1934 Securities Exchange Act that would take his name.

Before the Williams Act, most bidders moved fast. If they could buy control within a few days, they could deny the target board the time necessary to launch defenses. And to induce shareholders to tender quickly, they would take stock tendered on a first-come, first-served basis. The result was simple, beneficial, and clear: Bidders would acquire firms more cheaply, more bids would be profitable, and the corporate control market would more sharply discipline incumbent managers. After the popular handbag handguns for the all-night partying set in crime-ridden 1960s New York, critics called the fast-paced bids "Saturday night specials."[28]

> A hostile cash tender offer would be announced, usually over a weekend, at a modest premium over market price. The offer would be limited to a certain percentage of the company's outstanding shares, sufficient to give the bidder control of the target. All shares tendered up to that percentage would be bought on a first-come, first-served basis, typically in the early part of the following week. Shares tendered too late, or not at all, would not be bought, and faced a squeeze out merger after the bidder took control of the company. . . .

The Williams Act changed all this. Because of the act (along with state anti-takeover statutes (section IV) and court jurisprudence (sections D-G)), it became "easier for target firm management to entrench themselves." In effect, the act gave

---

[27] Joseph Fried, *Williams Is Guilty on All Nine Counts in Abscam Inquiry*, N.Y. Times, (May 2, 1981).
[28] Andrew Moore, *The Birth of Unocal*, 31 Del. J. Corp. L. 866, 866-867 (2006).

III. Hostile Acquisitions

"them 'earlier warning' about an outside bid, and more time to react."[29] But the result was not just that managers could more strongly entrench themselves. It was that they increased their power to extract for themselves some (or much) of the efficiency gains that the acquirer would bring.

To see this, suppose an acquirer can improve firm performance by 30 percent. Suppose further that the incumbent managers (the source of the present inefficiency) can prevent the acquirer from gaining control. The two have an obvious deal to make: The incumbents will agree to a "friendly" transaction and transfer control to the acquirer, and the acquirer will share some of the resulting efficiency gains with the departing managers. Obviously, the incumbents breach their fiduciary duties to the shareholders when they do this: They are extracting a bribe to leave and make room for better managers. But a little cynicism goes a long way: Just as obviously, if the two parties couch the payoffs as a "consulting contract" where the departing managers promise to "share their expertise" with their successors, it is a fiduciary breach no court will ever stop.

2. The Statute

Not only did Harrison Williams stop the fast bids, he imposed a variety of other rules that made tender offers more costly and harder to implement as well.[30] In general, the rules applied to firms registered under the 1934 Act (the §16(b) companies; see Chapter 5, section III.C). They fell within six broad categories.

(a) Disclosure of 5 Percent Threshold

Should anyone (or any group of people or firms) acquire more than 5 percent of the stock of a firm, he must disclose his identity and plans to the SEC and the firm within ten days. He can continue buying stock past the 5 percent threshold, but he must file a disclosure statement within ten days of crossing the line. Effectively, the rule prevents "creeping tender offers" — acquisitions where the bidder tries to obtain a solid base in the target's stock before anyone learns his plans (1934 Act, §13(d)(1), (3); this was Maremont's tactic in *Cheff* below).

(b) Disclosure of Offeror Identity

Should anyone initiate a tender offer, he must file an elaborate document with the SEC (1934 Act, §§13(d), 14(d)). In it, he must disclose his "background and identity," his "source and amount of the funds," the number of shares he already owns, and his plans for the target's business. The rule illustrates the point of the Williams Act. Despite the routine incantations of "shareholder protection," the Act

---

[29] Beirne & Macey, *supra* note 25, at 214.
[30] For a general discussion of the act, see Franklin A. Gevurtz, *Corporation Law* 736-750 (2d ed., West 2000).

is not about protecting investors — investors who sell their stock for cash do not care what a buyer plans to do with a firm. It is about making tender offers more expensive.

(c) Minimum Offer Window

An acquirer must keep his offer open for at least 20 business days (Rule 14e-1(a)). No more "Saturday night specials." The additional time obviously gives incumbent managers more chance to mount a defense that will prevent the acquirer from buying control. Necessarily, it also reduces the ability of shareholders to sell their stock at a premium.

To be sure, the extra time also gives incumbents more time to locate a "white knight" (Forstmann, in *Revlon*, section F below) who will make a competing bid. The ensuing auction may raise the price target shareholders eventually receive. By raising the ultimate cost of successful bids, however, it lowers the returns to launching takeovers in the first place. The result: Fewer hostile bids and less of the disciplining effect Manne identified in the market for corporate control.

(d) Withdrawal of Tendered Stock

Investors who tender shares to an acquirer may withdraw them at any time during the course of the tender offer (Rule 14d-7(a)(1)).

(e) Pro Rata Acceptance

If investors tender more shares than an acquirer wants to buy, he must take them pro rata from each investor. In order to induce investors to tender early, acquirers would prefer to take them first come, first served. This they may not do (Rule 14d-8).

(f) Uniform Pricing

An acquirer must pay the same price for all shares. If during the course of an offer he raises the price he is willing to pay, he must pay the higher price not just to those who tender under the new, higher price. He must also pay the higher price to those who already tendered under the earlier, lower price (1934 Act, §14(d)(7)).

D. Greenmail

1. Introduction

Return to the George and Clarence's nemesis Henry Potter and his ruthlessly efficient financial empire. Suppose Potter launches a bid for Gower Pharmaceuticals. He buys a substantial minority stake and demands a place on the board. The incumbent Gower managers do not want him there. Because he owns less than a majority, they can plausibly refuse his demand.

III. Hostile Acquisitions

Still, Gower managers realize that Potter owns enough stock to cause trouble. He can ask other shareholders for their proxy, and they may listen. He can talk to newspaper reporters, and they may listen. He can talk to Gower's suppliers and buyers. Rather than fight him at every turn, they want him gone. If Potter offers to sell his Gower stock to the firm at a premium, can they cause it to buy the stock? Remember: They owe a fiduciary duty to all shareholders but would be paying a premium to one that they would not pay to the others. And they would be paying that premium to protect their jobs.

Known as greenmail, these stock redemptions at above-market prices almost inevitably hurt the other shareholders. Suppose a firm has 10,000 shares outstanding, and each sells for $100. Suppose further that the firm redeems 3,000 of the shares for $150. Where the firm had been worth $100 \times 10,000 = \$1$ million, it will now have only $1 million $- (\$150 \times 3,000) = \$550,000$. Given that the firm has 7,000 shares left, each will be worth $550,000/7,000 = \$78.60$. As a result of greenmail, the value of the shares will have fallen from $100 to $78.60.

2. Holland Furnace: The Opinion

Under Delaware law, the legality of greenmail turns on *Cheff v. Mathes*.[31] Headquartered in southern Michigan, the Holland Furnace Company had made and sold furnaces for private homes. Primarily, it had sold them through door-to-door salesmen. It could have sold them through independent retailers, but when the firm began at the turn of the last century it encountered problems caused by improper installation. Rather than continue through retail outlets, it decided to sell through its own experienced employees.

In 1957, Holland Furnace officers noticed that someone seemed to be assembling a large position in its stock (they feared a "creeping tender offer," now banned by the Williams Act; section C.2. a above). In June, that someone identified himself as Arnold Maremont. He demanded a place on the board. Holland CEO P.T. Cheff refused. Maremont acquiesced and withdrew.

When Holland officers investigated Maremont, they found someone with a reputation something like the Lord High Executioner for southern Michigan. He bought firms, sold their assets piece by piece, and liquidated them. For incumbent managers (see sections B, E), this is as damning an endorsement as any: The firm is actually worth more when disassembled than when run as a going concern.

Despite his assurances to the contrary, Maremont reappeared. I want a say in the firm, he insisted. I will leave only if you buy my stock at a premium. Eager to be rid of him, Cheff's wife, Katherine, considered buying his shares through her family trust. Even with this tactic, she would have invited fiduciary claims. After all, she was buying Maremont's stock to save her husband's job and perquisites.

But ultimately, Katherine Cheff did not use her family's money. She persuaded the board to buy Maremont's stock with Holland Furnace's money instead.

---

[31] 199 A.2d 548 (Del. Ch. 1964).

The principle is simple: When paying too much for something, use someone else's money rather than one's own. Holland stock was selling for $10 per share, and Maremont wanted $14. On every share bought, she would be losing $4. Necessarily, she did better to lose the $4 per share from the company treasury than from her own portfolio.

Shareholders challenged the board's decision to buy Maremont's shares and lost. Firms can buy back their shares, the Delaware court observed. To be sure, if a CEO causes a firm to repurchase the stock to preserve his job, he faces a conflict of interest. Even outside directors may have something of a conflict. Even they may feel their board seats threatened by the acquirer. "The directors are of necessity confronted with a conflict of interest," the court observed, "and an objective decision is difficult."[32] That said, for the outside directors the conflict is more minor than for a corporate officer who would lose a full-time position.

When challenged by shareholders, the court announced, outside directors who adopt defensive tactics in a hostile acquisition must show "reasonable grounds to believe [that there existed] a danger to corporate policy and effectiveness."[33] The court continued: "It is important to remember that the directors satisfy their burden by showing good faith and reasonable investigation; the directors will not be penalized for an honest mistake of judgment, if the judgment appeared reasonable at the time the decision was made."[34] The standard is thus intermediate: Outside directors cannot rely on the business judgment rule, but neither must they prove the "inherent fairness" of what they did.

3. Holland Furnace: The Firm[35]

The Holland board located the "threat to corporate policy" in Maremont's plans to fire the firm's sales staff. Maremont made no attempt to hide his plans. He did indeed intend to fire the salesmen. The firm should sell its furnaces, he explained, "like mufflers, in a retail way."

By the time of Arnold Maremont, the Holland sales force was famous — the stuff of legend. As one author put it:

> Holland's standard sales technique was to send a representative to a private home who would claim to be an inspector from the gas company. Once inside, he would dismantle the heater as part of his "inspection" and then flatly refuse to put it back together, claiming there was grave danger of explosion. In the middle of the family

---

[32] *Id.* at 554 (quoting Bennett v. Propp, 187 A.2d 405, 409 (Del. 1962)).

[33] *Id.* at 555.

[34] *Id.*

[35] *See* William H. Boer, *The Holland Furnace Company Tragedy: An Insider's Lament* (privately printed 1995); Donald L. van Reken & Randall P. Vande Water, *Holland Furnace Company, 1906-1966* (privately printed 1993); Christopher D. Stone, *Where the Law Ends: The Social Control of Corporate Behavior* (Harper & Row 1975).

crisis that inevitably ensued, a solution would present itself magically at the door in the form of a Holland furnace salesman, who would make a quick sale.[36]

Cheff might as well have modeled his personal career on something out of a comic book too. Holland Furnace had been founded by J.P. Kolla and A.G. Landwehr, but their heir-apparent (Landwehr's son Paul) had died in a boating accident in 1928. Landwehr then spiraled into a depression and checked himself into a mental hospital; Kolla died in 1933. A foreman in the foundry and Kolla's personal chauffeur, Cheff used the crisis to charm and woo Kolla's divorced daughter Katherine. He married her in 1931 and joined the board as soon as Kolla died. He climbed to vice president and production manager, and soon the complaints about salesmen disassembling furnaces began to plague Midwestern Better Business Bureaus. Cheff continued his climb and by 1946 was president and chairman of the board.

At root, Holland sold products no one wanted to buy. By the middle of the twentieth century, consumers wanted air-conditioning units; Holland had none, or at least none anyone wanted. They wanted furnaces that ran on oil or natural gas; Holland sold furnaces burning coal. Although the law did eventually catch up with P.T. Cheff, it took two decades. The complaints about Holland Furnace started in the early 1940s. Not until the 1960s did the scam end. The firm paid a $100,000 fine, Cheff went to prison, and the company disappeared.

E. Self-Tender

1. The Two-Tiered Offer

(a) The Problem with Any-and-All

George Bailey was a man behind the times. He never went to college, never even left town. He ran the Bailey Building & Loan, but ran it as an anachronism. When brother Harry tried to introduce modern finance, George promptly threw him out.

Suppose Harry Bailey decided to move BBL into the twenty-first century. He organized a local campaign to urge George to resign. He distributed T-shirts with the slogan, "Jump, George Bailey, jump." To no avail. George refused to quit. In order to take control, Harry pooled his stock with the shares that George's ex-wife Mary owned. That did give him control over a substantial block. Unfortunately, the rest of the shares remained publicly traded.

Suppose Harry announces a tender offer for the BBL. To keep things simple (and contrary to the hypothetical above), suppose that no one (even Harry and Mary) owns a large block of BBL stock (see Table 8-1). Instead, the shares are publicly held by thousands of investors and trade at $100 per share. Harry knows that he can dramatically improve firm performance. Even if he pays $140 per

---

[36] James W. Coleman, *The Criminal Elite: Understanding White-Collar Crime* 25-26 (Worth 2002).

Table 8-1
Any-and-All Offer

	Tender offer	
	Succeeds	Fails
Tender	140	100
Not tender	140+	100

Hypothetical payoffs to shareholder; conditions given in text.

share, he can make money. So suppose Harry offers $140 per share. Will he acquire the firm? To be sure, the investors would rather sell for $140 in cash than hold the stock under George's anachronistic management. But will they tender?

Why, the investors will ask themselves, does Harry offer $140? Harry went to Princeton. He is no fool. If he offers $140, he must calculate that he can raise the price of the stock above $140. Why then should we tender? True, if the tender offer fails, we will find ourselves with shares trading for $100. But if the tender offer succeeds, we do best if hold on to our stock. Rather than $140 in cash, we will find ourselves with stock worth even more. In effect, by keeping our shares we can "free-ride" on Harry's efforts to transform the firm.

If any one of the investors held enough stock to determine whether the tender offer succeeded, he might tender. Better to tender for $140 in cash than be left with stock worth $100. But if thousands of shareholders hold the stock in small lots, no one will own enough to affect the outcome. Whether any one investor tenders will have no appreciable effect on the offer's success.

And if all the shareholders make these calculations, then the tender offer will fail. Even though Harry has a cannot-lose plan to transform the bank, even though every investor would like to see him win control — every shareholder will reason that his own decision (whether to tender) will not affect the outcome of the offer (whether it succeeds). Between $140 in cash and an even higher valued share, he will take the higher valued share. Everyone will prefer that the offer succeeds, but no one will tender, and the offer will fail.

(b)   The Two-Tiered Solution

To overcome this coordination problem among shareholders, acquirers in the 1980s turned to the "two-tiered tender offer." Suppose again that Harry wants to buy the BBL and is willing to pay $140 per share for all outstanding stock. Rather than make an "any and all" offer, he will announce a two-tiered bid. He will first buy exactly half of the outstanding shares in a tender offer. Once he obtains that stock, he will cashout the remaining shareholders in a freeze-out merger of BBL into one of his own wholly owned firms. He will buy the stocks in the first tier (the tender offer) at $160. He will cash out the rest in the merger at $120.

III. Hostile Acquisitions

Now, note several aspects of this transaction:

(i) Everyone has an incentive to tender. If an investor tenders his stock and the offer succeeds, then (if everyone else also tenders) he will find half his stock purchased at $160 and half at $120. If he does not tender but the offer succeeds, he will find all his stock bought at $120. If the tender offer fails, he holds stock worth $100 whether he tenders or no. If the tender offer succeeds, he does better to tender than not to tender; if it fails, it makes no difference what he does. As a result, everyone will tender, and the offer will succeed. Investors no longer have the option of free-riding on Harry Bailey's efforts to improve the firm.

(ii) Harry pays the same total price as in the one-tiered offer. In an any-and-all offer, Harry buys all the shares at $140 per share. In a two-tiered offer, he buys half the stock at $160 and half at $120. Under either scheme, he pays an average of $140 per share.

(iii) Even the back-end merger takes place at a generous price. Although Harry Bailey pays less per share in the cash-out merger ($120) than in the front-end ($160), he still pays a premium over the market price ($100) of the stock. Under no plausibly sensible definition of "fair price" is he paying an unfairly low amount.

From time to time, courts and commentators complained that the two-tiered offers "coerced" investors into tendering. Would that we all could be so coerced. The offers "coerce" investors only by coupling an extravagantly generous front-end price with a reasonably generous back-end price. They "coerce" investors into tendering only because investors prefer "extravagantly generous" to "reasonably generous."

2. Unocal and the Self-Tender Defense

Unocal[37] presented the Delaware Supreme Court with both a two-tiered bid and a "self-tender" defense. The court found the two-tiered bid "coercive." It found the self-tender a reasonable response.

Unocal was an oil company, and one that in the early 1980s found itself with an enormous amount of cash.[38] More relevantly, it found itself with more cash than good projects. As a result, for several years incumbent managers had invested its funds at low returns. For its CEO, the firm had Fred Hartley—a "crusty, hard-bitten, oilman" not given to public relations. When one of the firm's oil rigs blew up off the coast of Santa Barbara and laid an 800-square-mile slick, Hartley declared himself "amazed at the publicity for the loss of a few birds" (see photo).[39]

---

[37] Unocal Corp. v. Mesa Petro. Co., 493 A.2d 946 (Del. 1985).

[38] For a discussion of why oil firms had this cash in the early 1980s, see Jeffrey N. Gordon, *The Story of* Unocal v. Mesa Petroleum: *The Core of Takeover Law,* in *Corporate Law Stories* 227, 227-228 (J. Mark Ramseyer ed., Foundation Press 2009).

[39] Andrew G. T. Moore II, *The Birth of Unocal—A Brief History,* 31 Del. J. Corp. L. 865, 877 (2006).

Figure 8-1
The Unocal Spill

© The Tribune/Photos From the Vault

T. Boone Pickens was an oilman too, and a financier besides. He ran Mesa Petroleum and ran it well. By 2011, he found himself worth $1.4 billion. In his personal life, he ran things less well. He devoured a succession of wives and left at least one of his sons mired in alcohol, drugs, and financial scandal. All this was the stuff of legend, of course. He made, as one writer eventually observed, "an unlikely combination of King Lear, Lazarus, Robin Hood, and Amarillo Slim."[40]

---

[40] Harry Hurt III, *Fortune Hunter*, Portfolio.com (Apr. 16, 2007), http://www.portfolio.com/executives/features/2007/03/29/Fortune-Hunter/index1.html.

III. Hostile Acquisitions

Pickens wanted Unocal. Incumbent managers were throwing good cash at bad projects, and he reasoned he could do better. Through Mesa he already owned 13 percent of the stock. He wanted the rest. To obtain it, he announced a two-tiered bid. In the front-end tender offer, he would buy 37 percent at $54 per share — just enough to tip him over the 50 percent line.[41] Then, he would cash out the rest through a merger giving investors bonds worth $54.

For reasons explained earlier (section E.1.), the bonds were almost certainly worth less than $54. The two-tiered offer induces shareholders to tender by paying them more in the front than at the back. If the back-end bonds were worth exactly the front-end cash, then shareholders would be indifferent between tendering and not tendering. If they wanted cash, after all, they could sell the bonds for exactly $54 in cash. And if they could not sell the bonds for $54, then by definition the bonds were not "worth" $54. Given that Pickens knew what he was doing, he would have offered bonds actually worth less than $54.

The court contemptuously dismissed the bonds as junk bonds, but the term is a cheap shot. Like any other investment, junk bonds are worth whatever a buyer will pay. The derogatory name simply reflects the unpopularity among the business elite (incumbent managers) of the people who used the bonds (the acquirers). Bidders in takeovers sometimes funded their acquisitions with borrowed money. Typically, they borrowed from the public and subordinated their claims to other borrowers. Because of that subordination, their bonds were riskier than other bonds and paid higher returns.

As maligned as they were, junk bonds were never riskier than stock. They were subordinate to other (so-called senior) bonds, but stock was always junior to (and riskier than) them. Target managers called the subordinated bonds "junk" only because they did not like the men who were using them to buy their firms and take their jobs. Newspapers and politicians called them "junk" because they listened to target managers.

Unocal managers did not like Pickens. To justify their efforts to ward him off, they hired the investment banking firm of Goldman Sachs. Goldman duly opined that Pickens's offer was "inadequate." Simply by liquidating Unocal, Goldman could fetch more than $60 per share. Unocal managers needed Goldman to say this because an "inadequate" bid justified their opposition. If Pickens offered shareholders too little, they could legitimately oppose his efforts. Goldman's valuation gave them the excuse they needed.

As excuses go, it is as embarrassing as they come. Or at least it *ought* to have been embarrassing. In late 1984, Unocal stock sold for about $38: Outside investors valued Unocal under Hartley's management at $38 per share.[42] Goldman claimed that it could sell Unocal's assets piecemeal and obtain $60 per share. In effect, Goldman declared that Unocal's assets would be worth over 50 percent more

---

[41] Michael C. Jensen, *When Unocal Won over Pickens, Shareholders and Society Lost*, Financier 50 (Nov. 1985).

[42] Chevron, *Unocal IR Archive*, http://www.chevron.com/investors/archives/unocalirarchive/ (accessed Mar. 7, 2012).

under the control of someone else than they were under the control of Hartley. Were Hartley managing the firm in the interests of its shareholders, he would sell the assets to those more able outsiders, distribute the cash to his shareholders, and fall on his sword.

Hartley did not fall on his sword, of course. Instead, he announced a self-tender for $72 per share. The offer was conditional. If — but only if — Mesa purchased 37 percent, Unocal would buy the rest with bonds paying $72 per share.

The defense was clever, but possibly too clever by half. Consider the incentives that an Unocal shareholder now faced. He held too few shares to affect the outcome of the tender offer. Before Unocal announced its self-tender, he had an incentive to tender to Mesa. Under its current managers, Unocal stock sold for $38 per share, but Mesa offered $54 cash for the first 37 percent tendered and bonds worth something less than $54 for the rest. Rather than swap all his shares for the sub-$54 bonds, he did better to tender and take $54 in cash for at least part of his stock.

Unocal's self-tender flipped those incentives. If an Unocal shareholder tendered to Mesa and the tender offer succeeded, he received a mix of $54 in cash and bonds worth something less. If he tendered to Unocal and the Mesa offer succeeded, he received bonds paying $72. If the Mesa offer failed, his stock would trade for $38. Obviously, a Unocal shareholder would want the Mesa offer to succeed, but just as obviously he would want the other shareholders to tender to Mesa (for $54) while he tendered to Unocal (for $72).

If any one Unocal shareholder owned too few shares to affect whether Mesa's offer succeeded, he did best by tendering to Unocal. Although each shareholder would prefer that Mesa bought the firm, each did best by tendering to Unocal. Because everyone would tender to Unocal, no one would tender to Mesa. Mesa would never obtain its 37 percent, and Unocal's conditional offer would never take effect. No one would obtain $54 from Mesa, no one would obtain $72 from Unocal, and everyone would find himself with stock worth $38 in a company run by Hartley.

The shareholders were livid. Under pressure, the Unocal board relented and agreed to buy back (i.e., redeem) 29 percent of the stock at $72 regardless of whether Mesa obtained 37 percent.[43] Mesa then demanded that Unocal buy a proportional share of its stock too. Unocal refused, and Mesa sued.

Mesa wanted to participate in Unocal's self-tender because otherwise the rest of the stockholders would receive an effective dividend in which it did not share. Take a simplified version of the story. Unocal had about 173 million shares outstanding. Before the tender offer, Mesa owned 22 million of those shares. At $38 per share, the firm was worth $38 × 173 million = $6.6 billion, and Mesa's 22 million shares were worth ($6.6 billion × 22 million)/173 million = $840 million. If Unocal redeemed 50 million shares at $72, the firm would be

---

[43] Jeffrey Gordon argues that arbitrageurs held much of the Unocal stock by this point. Because of their relatively small number, they could have agreed among themselves to tender enough shares to Mesa to make sure that it obtained its requisite 37 percent and tendered the rest to Unocal. Had they been able thus to overcome their coordination problem, Unocal would have had to redeem the shares even under the earlier conditional offer. *See* Gordon, *supra* note 38, at 238-239.

worth only \$6.6 billion $-(\$72 \times 50$ million) $= \$3$ billion. Mesa now owned a 22 million/123 million stake in this \$3 billion firm—a stake worth \$540 million. Through Unocal's self-tender, Mesa would lose \$840 million − \$540 million = \$300 million.

Unocal could legally exclude Mesa. The Delaware court cited *Cheff v. Mathes* (section D above) for the proposition that to justify its defensive measures, target directors "must show that they had reasonable grounds for believing that a danger to corporate policy and effectiveness existed." They satisfied that burden if they showed "good faith and reasonable investigation." The court explained that a board would find it easier to meet this standard if a majority of its members were not full-time officers. It noted that the board's defensive measures "must be reasonable in relation to the threat posed." And it added that in considering its options, the board could consider the impact of the hostile bid "on 'constituencies' other than shareholders (i.e., creditors, customers, employees, and perhaps even the community generally)."[44]

Applied to this case, the court explained that Mesa had presented the threat of "a grossly inadequate two-tier coercive tender offer coupled with the threat of greenmail."[45] Its "grossly inadequate" bid had been an offer to buy Unocal shares at a 42 percent premium over market. Its "coercive" bid had combined \$54 in cash with bonds worth somewhat less. And its "threat of greenmail" reflected the fact that Pickens would leave if the firm agreed to pay him to leave. For offering shareholders a 42 percent premium, the court let the Unocal board fine Pickens \$300 million.

F. Poison Pills

1. Introduction

Suppose Harry Bailey decided that his time had come. He would launch a takeover bid for BBL. He approached Gordon Gekko, and Gekko agreed to help him raise the funds. He recommended that Harry retain Joseph Flom at the Skadden firm, and Flom recommended a two-tiered offer of the sort Pickens used in *Unocal.*

Faced with a two-tiered bid, George Bailey and Clarence Odbody retained Martin Lipton at the Wachtell firm. Lipton suggested that they adopt what he called a Preferred Share Purchase Rights Plan. As described:

> [The] Plan provides that [BBL] common stockholders are entitled to the issuance of one Right per common share under certain triggering conditions. There are two triggering events that can activate the Rights. The first is the announcement of a tender offer for 30 percent of [BBL] shares ("30% trigger") and the second is the acquisition of 20 percent of [BBL] shares by any single entity or group ("20% trigger").

---

[44] 493 A.2d at 955.
[45] *Id.* at 956.

If an announcement of a tender offer for 30 percent of [BBL] shares is made, the Rights are issued and are immediately exercisable to purchase 1/100 share of new preferred stock for $100 and are redeemable by the Board for $.50 per Right. If 20 percent of [BBL] shares are acquired by anyone, the Rights are issued and become non-redeemable and are exercisable to purchase 1/100 of a share of preferred. If a Right is not exercised for preferred, and thereafter, a merger or consolidation occurs, the Rights holder can exercise each Right to purchase $200 of the common stock of the tender offeror for $100.[46]

The plan was an example of what the legal press calls a "poison pill." Note three crucial facets of the plan:

(a) The defensive tactic (the "pill") is triggered by the announcement by a hostile bidder of plans to buy at least 30 percent of BBL.
(b) Initially, the BBL board can redeem these "pills" at 50 cents each.
(c) If the bidder actually buys a 20 percent stake in the firm, the board can no longer redeem the pills.
(d) If the acquirer merges the firm into another firm (effectively, if the acquirer pushes through the cash-out merger at the back-end of a two-tiered offer), then BBL shareholders obtain a right to buy acquirer stock at half price.

If no one tries to buy BBL, the pill has no effect (part (a)). If an acquirer implements a two-tiered bid (or tries any merger after a tender offer), target shareholders can buy the acquirer's stock at a fire-sale price; in the process, the pill imposes a correspondingly large cost on acquirer shareholders (part (d)). But the target board can make it all disappear; if the acquirer cuts a deal with the target directors before he buys 20 percent, they can redeem the pill at a trivial cost (part (b)).

In *Moran v. Household International, Inc.*,[47] the Delaware Supreme Court faced a challenge to exactly this pill. The Household board had adopted it before a hostile bidder had actually materialized. The court held that the board had the statutory authority to adopt the pill; that the pill did not completely preclude hostile bids; and that the pill was less onerous than many other defensive tactics. It cited *Unocal*, and asked whether the directors could show "reasonable grounds for believing that a danger to corporate policy and effectiveness existed." It noted that they satisfied the requirement if they could show "good faith and reasonable investigation," and that the pill was "reasonable in relation to the threat posed."[48]

The *Moran* board thought their stock undervalued.[49] As a result, they feared someone might want to buy the firm. To the court, that sufficed.

---

[46] Moran v. Household Intl., Inc., 500 A.2d 1346, 1348-1349 (Del. 1985).

[47] 500 A.2d 1346 (Del. 1985).

[48] *Id.* at 1356.

[49] What CEO and board did not think their stock underpriced? Law firm partners always think their participation interest too small, law students always think their grades too low, law professors always think their teaching evaluations too low—and CEOs and boards always think their stock underpriced.

III. Hostile Acquisitions

2. Revlon[50]

(a) Introduction

Ronald Perelman ran Pantry Pride, and Michel Bergerac ran Revlon. Having bought a grocery store chain, Perelman decided he wanted a cosmetics firm too. He talked with Bergerac, but Bergerac refused to sell. Perelman asked his board to let him make a tender offer. Revlon had been trading for about $36 per share. In response to Perelman's request, the Pantry Pride board authorized him to pay $45 per share. Perelman hired Drexel Burnham Lambert to raise the funds he needed and Skadden Arps to coordinate his legal moves.

The Revlon board declared Perelman's bid too low and initiated its defense. It hired Lazard Freres to value the firm, and Lazard opined that Revlon would yield $60 to $70 per share if sold in parts. Revlon retained Wachtell Lipton on the law.

(b) The Players

Perelman and Bergerac. Charles Revson founded Revlon in 1932 as a middle-tier cosmetics firm. During the 1960s, he began to move his firm into the health-care products market. Under his successor Bergerac, the shift accelerated. Perelman had initially hoped to keep Bergerac in place — but as Bergerac despised Perelman, that collaboration was not to be. Perelman planned to jettison Revlon's health-care business and return the firm to its core cosmetics industry.

Milken and Drexel. A southern-California boy from the San Fernando Valley, Michael Milken went north to college at Berkeley and east to Wharton, the business school at Penn. At Wharton, he studied the market for high-risk, high-return bonds (*Unocal*'s "junk bonds"). In the process, he discovered that a portfolio of the bonds would outperform lower-risk investment-grade securities.

After graduation, Milken joined the investment banking firm that would become Drexel Burnham Lambert. From its office in New York and later Beverly Hills, he built a thriving business in the high-yield bonds. High-yield because high-risk, and high-risk because heavily subordinated, the bonds became the principal means by which he raised funds for acquirers like Perelman.

Through his Drexel office, Milken funded acquirers — and out of that office Dennis Levine tipped Ivan Boesky (Chapter 5, section IV.E.3). Working as U.S. attorney for the Southern District of New York, Rudy Giuliani launched an investigation. Although Levine did indeed tip Boesky, Giuliani never introduced serious evidence that Milken traded on inside information. Giuliani's office indicted Milken under the federal racketeering statute anyway (it was one of the first times the government used RICO against someone unrelated to the mob) and indicted his younger brother Lowell. Rather than place his brother at risk, Milken pled guilty in 1990. He served 22 months in prison and paid $1 billion in fines and "compensation."

---

[50] Revlon, Inc. v. MacAndrews & Forbes Holdings, Inc., 506 A.2d 173 (Del. 1986).

The efficiency gains in the corporate sector during the 1980s owed much to the financing that Milken made possible. Wrote the *Economist* magazine in 2010:

Drexel's ability quickly to raise hundreds of millions of dollars in "mezzanine" debt (so called because it ranks between secure bank loans and at-risk equity in the capital structure) made the threat of buy-outs credible and forced many big companies to slim costs and increase returns to shareholders to stave off the threat of takeover.[51]

The former editor of the *Harvard Business Review* explained the process in more detail:

Milken's real contribution was far greater than simply to sell portfolios of bonds. His real contribution was to get investors to understand that the stock and bond markets were not really separate markets. Milken created a tremendous pool of liquidity and guided its use with surgical precision. He did it in a way that took an often bloated and ailing American economy and made it lean, mean and resilient. Much of the strength and resilience of the economy today — including its ability to rebound in times of adversity — is due to the way people using Milken's financing vehicles remade ailing companies or put their entrepreneurial zeal to work.[52]

Rohatyn and Lazard. Felix Rohatyn was a partner at the Lazard Freres investment bank, but not just any partner. Among his clients, he counted Harold Geneen at ITT and Steve Ross at Time-Warner. In time, he would become a senior advisor to the Democratic Party, ambassador to France, a commander in the French Legion of Honor — and a star of the New York society pages. He was, as the *Huffington Post* put it, "friends with, well, nearly everyone" — certainly everyone who mattered. In his autobiography, Rohatyn would claim to talk movies with Woody Allen at the über-high-gloss "Elaine's restaurant."[53] "In his spare time," continued the *Huffington Post*, "he regularly opined on economic and fiscal matters for The New York Times and New York Review of Books."[54]

Forstmann. Theodore Forstmann helped managers in the 1980s buy their own firms with borrowed money. True to form, in *Revlon* he played the part of the "white knight" — the incumbent managers' ally. People called his tactics "leveraged buy-outs" (LBOs) if they focused on the source of the funds. They called them "management buy-outs" (MBOs) if they focused on the identity of the buyers.

The second son of a troubled but rich family, Forstmann started at Phillips Andover. He went to Yale, became a straight-C student and goalie on the hockey team, and proceeded to Columbia Law School (this in the days when C-students

---

[51] *Stars of the Junkyard*, Economist (Oct. 21, 2010).

[52] Joel Kurtzman, *How the Markets Really Work* (Crown 2002).

[53] Felix G. Rohatyn, *Dealings: A Political and Financial Life* 151 (Simon & Schuster 2010).

[54] Robert Teitelman, *Felix Rohatyn's "Dealings,"* Huffington Post (Oct. 21, 2010), http://www.huffingtonpost.com/robert-teitelman/felix-rohatyns-dealings_b_772119.html.

III. Hostile Acquisitions

from Yale could still go to a good law school). After graduating, he shifted to finance and started Forstmann Little.

One-time *Vanity Fair* and *New Yorker* editor Tina Brown would have it that Forstmann dated Princess Diana (young enough to be his daughter) too. "It's a true story," she recalls him claiming."Diana had the idea that we should get married, that I should run for president and she would be First Lady." But in the end, alas, he was but a crying shoulder: "I used to get calls from her on Christmas Eve and she was alone," said Forstmann. "She was unhappy about Camilla. There was this war with the Royal Family, and she had to do this or that about it."[55]

And by 2010, he was worth over $1 billion.

Flom and Lipton. The Skadden and Wachtell firms owed their rise in part to the anti-Semitism at the "WASP" firms. By the 1960s, 60 percent of New York lawyers were Jewish, but a majority of the largest firms remained white and Protestant. Even if they hired Jewish lawyers as associates, they rarely promoted them to partnership. Like Paul Weiss and Cleary Gottlieb before them, Skadden (led by Joseph Flom) and Wachtell (by Martin Lipton) grew within this world by promoting Protestant and Jewish lawyers alike.

Outside the central legal elite, Skadden and Wachtell embraced work that the others shunned. Takeovers were part of that portfolio. If "gentlemen" bankers did not work on tender offers, then neither would their WASP law firms. Into those deliberately ignored assignments, Skadden and Wachtell invested their talent.[56]

Lipton and Wachtell focused on takeover defenses. In the 1980s, they invented the poison pill. Lipton argued for his tactics in the legal press. He argued for his clients. And throughout it all, he led his firm carefully, grew it slowly, and maintained astonishing levels of profitability.

Flom and Skadden took a different tack. Where Lipton focused on targets, Flom represented acquirers too. Where Lipton grew Wachtell slowly, Flom grew Skadden exponentially. And where Lipton could seem respectable, Flom almost deliberately cultivated a street-fighting persona. One source recounted:

> Proxy fights were down and dirty and winners of the contest were determined in the counting room, more colloquially called the snake pit. [In his history of the Skadden firm, Lincoln] Caplan writes: "The event was often informal, contentious, and unruly. Adversaries were sometimes in T-shirts, eating watermelon or sharing a bottle of scotch (sic)." These fights for corporate control matched Flom's personality. . . .
>
> Flom built Skadden Arps in his own image. Like Flom, . . . the firm prided itself on its lack of pedigree: "In addition to its cast-offs, the firm consisted of late bloomers and, if not misfits, then not quite smooth fits. Performance counted. Birthright was irrelevant. . . ." . . .
>
> One senior Wall Street lawyer told Caplan about a conversation he had with an investment banker: "I remember getting a call from a crusty investment banker.

[55] Tina Brown, *The Diana Chronicles* 372, 374 (Random House 2007); *see* Bryan Burrough & John Helyar, *The Jeremiah of Junk Bonds*, New York 34 (Jan. 29, 1990).
[56] Eli Wald, *The Rise and Fall of the WASP and Jewish Law Firms*, 60 Stan. L. Rev. 1803 (2008).

Figure 8-2
Joseph Flom

Printed with permission of Edward Sorel.

III. Hostile Acquisitions

> They called up and said, 'Our client is going after someone else. We want you to represent us. We know you'd rather represent the company, but we're bringing Flom in for that. We feel we need a sewer rat—someone who will fight dirty and win at any cost.' "[57]

(c) The Poison Pill

Revlon retained Lipton, and Lipton recommended a poison pill. Called the "Note Purchase Rights Plan," the pill gave each shareholder a right to exchange one share of stock for a $65 Revlon note (debt) payable in one year. The pill took effect if and when someone acquired 20 percent or more of Revlon stock at a price below $65. The acquirer had no rights under the pill, and the Revlon board could redeem it for 10 cents apiece. In effect, if any hostile acquirer obtained a 20 percent foothold and did not cut a deal with incumbent Revlon managers, the firm paid the other shareholders $65 per share (in one year).

(d) The Initial Offer

The fight formally began on August 23. Pantry Pride announced a tender offer for "any and all" Revlon shares at $47.50 per share. It made its offer conditional on the Revlon board's redeeming the pill.

(e) The Selective Repurchase

Six days later, the Revlon board responded with its own offer: Revlon would redeem 10 million shares of its stock for $47.50 in notes, payable 1995, plus one-tenth of a share of preferred stock (nominally worth $100 per share). The notes contained covenants (contractual agreements) that limited the firm's ability to incur more debt. Those covenants also, however, gave the firm's independent (outside) directors the power to revoke the covenants if they chose.

Consider the arithmetic. Ten million shares constituted about one-third of Revlon's outstanding stock. At a time when its shares traded for $36, Revlon repurchased one-third of the stock at about $57. Suppose all shareholders tendered their stock to Revlon. Revlon would take a third of the shares from each. In effect, it would shrink the company through a massive dividend distribution.

At a crude level, if everyone tendered his shares, then no one gained and no one lost. As a result of the effective dividend (the $21 per share premium over market), the price of the stock left outstanding would fall. In turn, that fall would be exactly offset by the accompanying cash distribution.

The point is the same as the point in sections D and E above. If Revlon's 30 million shares traded at $36 per share, outside investors must have valued the company at $36 × 30 million = $1,080 million. Suppose the firm redeems 10 million shares at $57 per share. It will distribute to shareholders $57 × 10 million

---

[57] Jean Fergus, *The Law According to Joseph Flom*, Intl. Fin. L. Rev. (Feb. 1994).

= $570 million. That will leave the firm with $1,080 million − $570 million = $510 million. With 20 million shares outstanding, the price of the stock will fall to $510 million/20 million = $26.

Now consider one subtlety: Taxes. The distribution is what tax professors call a "recognition event." Potentially, it brought a tax liability. Particularly for those investors who had bought their Revlon stock decades ago at a low price and now lay on their deathbed (who planned for their heirs to obtain a "step-up" in basis when they inherited the stock), the distribution imposed costs.

And consider another subtlety, too: Even if everyone tendered his shares, whether shareholders gained or lost depended on whether the firm had good use for the money. If the firm had more attractive investment opportunities than its shareholders, then the distribution caused a loss — it had good business prospects that now it could not (without raising money again) pursue. If the shareholders had the better opportunities, then the distribution caused a gain — it puts the cash in the hands of the party (the shareholders) who can make better use of it.

Yet not everyone tendered his stock to Revlon. Any rational investor who heard the news would have tendered, of course. But Revlon is a big place. Not all shareholders are rational, not all receive their mail, and not all read the mail they do receive. The $21 per share premium to those who tender causes a drop in the price of the remaining shares. Those who tender their stock and receive their portion of the premium will be made whole (other than the complications mentioned above). Those who do not tender, simply lose money. According to the opinion, 13 percent of the Revlon shares were not tendered.

(f)   The LBO

Pantry Pride made its offers, Revlon fought back, and Pantry Pride raised its bids. Then, in September the incumbent Revlon managers decided to buy the firm for themselves. With Forstmann Little's help, they would borrow large sums (hence, an LBO or MBO). Probably, Forstmann would invest some of its own funds as equity, and the incumbent managers would invest their money too.

Bizarrely — or outrageously, perhaps — Bergerac and his colleagues planned to obtain the equity they would invest through their "golden parachutes." These "parachutes" represent a second-best approach to mediocre managers. In a first-best world, managers generally maximize profits. When managers try anything else, a better set of managers buys control. Recognizing their own mediocrity, the incumbent managers go quietly into the night.

Investors do not live in a first-best world and they know it. They live in a world where some managers do well, some do poorly, and those who do poorly fight fiercely to keep their jobs. Recognizing that mediocre incumbents will fight any takeover bid, many potential acquirers do not even bother trying to take over badly run firms. Investors, however, want those hostile bids. Acquirers pay a premium in the bids because they believe can improve a firm's management, and investors want the premium because it represents a large capital gain. To encourage potential acquirers to launch such takeovers, investors sometimes offer their managers golden parachute contracts that will dissuade them from fighting any acquirers who might launch takeover bids.

With golden parachute contracts, in other words, shareholders bribe their managers not to fight a hostile bid. The parachute is no more than a simple contract. Through it, the firm promises to pay its officers a large sum if anyone buys the firm and discharges them. In the year before Perelman's offer, Bergerac received total pay of $1.3 million. Through his golden parachute, he stood to collect $35 million.[58] Absent a parachute, a mediocre manager might fight to keep his job. With a $35 million exit bonus, he might be willing to pocket the money and leave. Or so goes the logic. Obviously, it does not always work, and it did not work with Bergerac.

At Revlon, the LBO itself apparently triggered the golden parachute payments. Note the madness. Shareholders offer parachutes to induce their managers to leave when *outsiders* bid for the firm. Through an LBO, these incumbent Revlon managers hoped to buy the firm for themselves. No honest and intelligent corporate counsel would have drafted a parachute contract in which shareholders paid their managers a bonus for the managers to use to buy the firm. The point of the contract is to pay managers to leave when someone *else* offers a premium. Apparently, however, Revlon's corporate counsel "blew it." Apparently, he drafted a golden parachute contract that paid cash to Bergerac and his friends if they themselves bought the firm.

At this point, the notes (the debt contracts) that Revlon had issued in its initial buy-back presented a problem. Recall that the notes included covenants (contractual promises) that limited Revlon's ability to borrow. Being debt financed, the planned LBO would have raised Revlon's debt to levels beyond those covenants. To accomplish the LBO, the incumbent officers needed the covenants waived, and the outside directors duly obliged.

The note holders were apoplectic. The firm had included the covenants to protect the note holders — in particular, to protect them from the risks associated with higher leverage. To facilitate their buying the firm for themselves, Bergerac and his friends had prevailed on the nominally independent directors to waive those contractual protections. The opinion does not detail the terms of the covenants, but the note holders apparently thought that the waiver violated the terms. They sued.

(g) The Revised Plan

The LBO never happened. Instead, Forstmann Little offered to buy Revlon at $57.25. It promised to maintain the value of the notes but demanded several conditions. It wanted a right to buy two of Revlon's health-care product divisions for $525 million (a "lockup"). It wanted a $25 million "cancellation fee" if it did not ultimately acquire the firm. And it wanted Revlon to promise not to look for other buyers (a "no-shop" agreement).

---

[58] *Business Notes: Nov. 18, 1985,* Time (Apr. 18, 2005), http://www.time.com/time/magazine/article/0,9171,1050588,00.html

The conditions highlight several points. First, at $525 million, Forstmann negotiated a lockup price substantially below market. We know it was below market because otherwise Perelman would not have cared. The lockup gave Forstmann the right to buy two divisions for $525 million. Between $525 million's worth of assets and $525 million in cash, Perelman and Forstmann would have been indifferent. They were not indifferent. Forstmann must have obtained something he could not obtain on the market.

Second, although Forstmann's lockup price was not $100 to $175 million below market, it was $100 to $175 million below the price Rohatyn put on the divisions at the outset. The price Rohatyn originally quoted was the number Bergerac paid him to name in order to justify his opposition to Pantry Pride. Given that Perelman had offered a generous premium over market, Bergerac needed Rohatyn to exaggerate massively the value of Revlon's assets. When now he tried to sell those very assets to his ally Forstmann at a huge discount, he found himself (like Rosencrantz and Guildenstern) hoist with his own petard.

Third, lockups and cancellation fees do not necessarily harm shareholders. They often do. They may have harmed them here. But they do not harm shareholders always. They do usually stop the bidding. As the court observed, they had a "destructive effect on the auction process." Should anyone successfully have bought control of Revlon, he would have found himself obliged to transfer an enormous set of assets and cash to Forstmann. Once Forstmann obtained the lockup and cancellation fee, no one would outbid it for Revlon.

But that a tactic ends the bidding does not necessarily hurt shareholders. Absent the lockup and cancellation fee, Forstmann might never have raised the bid as far as he did. Forstmann bid $57.25, and the lockup and cancellation fee stopped the bidding from going further. But had Forstmann not obtained those rights, he might not have bid $57.25. The shareholders might instead have walked away with less.

In the end, Bergerac tried to jettison exactly the divisions Perelman wanted jettisoned anyway. Charles Revson had founded a cosmetics firm. Late in life, he started to diversify it into health-care products, and his successor, Bergerac, pushed the strategy further.[59] Perelman wanted to return Revlon to its core cosmetics business.[60] When Bergerac finally tried his LBO, he outlined a series of transactions that did what Perelman had urged all along — split cosmetics from health care. Bergerac would have sold the cosmetics line for about $900 million, some of the health-care divisions for $350 million, and kept only some of the other health-care units.[61]

(h) The Opinion

The *Revlon* court turned first to the poison pill and the 10 million share buy-back. It found that the incumbent board had "reasonably concluded" that Pantry

---

[59] *Id.*

[60] Anthony Ramirez, *The Raider Who Runs Revlon*, Fortune (Sept. 14, 1987).

[61] *See* Charles P. Alexaner & Jeanne McDowell, *Jousting for the Top Brands*, Time (Oct. 14, 1985).

III. Hostile Acquisitions

Pride's initial $45 per share offer (at 25 percent over market) "was grossly inadequate." It noted that Lazard had told the board that Perelman planned a "bust-up" takeover (he would jettison the firm's health-care products divisions and return it to its core cosmetics business).[62] Given these threats, the board "acted in good faith and upon reasonable investigation." It adopted tactics that were not "unreasonable, considering the threat posed."[63] It faced the *Unocal* standards, in short, and met them.

The court then turned to the lockup, the cancellation fee, and the no-shop agreement. These it found illegal:

> [W]hen Pantry Pride increased its offer to $50 per share, and then to $53, it became apparent to all that the break-up of the company was inevitable. . . . The duty of the board had thus changed from the preservation of Revlon as a corporate entity to the maximization of the company's value at a sale for the stockholders' benefit. This significantly altered the board's responsibilities under the *Unocal* standards. . . . The directors' role changed from defenders of the corporate bastion to auctioneers charged with getting the best price for the stockholders at a sale of the company.[64]

These tactics did not facilitate an auction. Instead they stopped it. Never mind that the price might otherwise never have reached $57.25. In adopting tactics that stopped the auction at $57.25, the board violated its fiduciary duty to its shareholders.

Recall that the Revlon board claimed to favor Forstmann in part because it promised to protect the note holders. Doing so, the board explained, followed from its right under *Unocal* to protect "other constituencies." In rejecting the board's claim, the *Revlon* court explained:

> Here, the rights of the noteholders were fixed by agreement, and there is nothing of substance to suggest that any of those terms were violated. . . . Thus, nothing remained for Revlon to legitimately protect, and no rationally related benefit thereby accrued to the stockholders.[65]

The court's analysis is odd. The note holders either had a legitimate claim or they did not. Suppose they had a legitimate one. The court could hardly mean that the board had an obligation to ignore its contractual promises to the note holders. Boards owe fiduciary duties to shareholders, but those duties do not extend to breaking contracts with their creditors. Alternatively, suppose the note holders had no legitimate claim. Boards regularly manage litigation. They face some suits that raise legitimate claims and some that do not, but they do not always fight the "bogus" claims. Some are too expensive to litigate, even when the boards are sure

---

[62] 506 A.2d at 180.
[63] *Id.* at 181.
[64] *Id.* at 182.
[65] *Id.* at 182-183.

they will win. Some entail too high a reputational cost to contest. Realizing these complications, courts delegate litigation-related questions to the business judgment of the board (see Chapter 3, section II). That Revlon's board could not legitimately consider the note holders' claims seemingly violates that more basic principle.

G. Delaware Developments

1. Introduction

All this leaves the fictional Gower Pharmaceuticals directors at something of a loss. They face a hostile takeover bid from Henry Potter, but would prefer to deal with Marion Crane. Both are likely to bid for the firm.

Were a lawyer to tell the Gower directors that they owe a fiduciary duty to their shareholders, they would understand the principle. Were a lawyer to tell them that they can fight unsolicited bids if they can show that they exercise "good faith and reasonable investigation" and that their tactics are "reasonable in relation to the threat posed," they would understand the formula. They might wonder how fighting high-priced bids fits their fiduciary duty to their shareholders, but at least the statement tells them what they need to pretend to do to keep their jobs.

But now suppose a lawyer tells the Gower directors that somewhere in the fight for corporate control their role will change from being "defenders of the corporate bastion to [being] auctioneers charged with getting the best price for the stockholders at a sale of the company."[66] We owe our shareholders a fiduciary duty, they will reply. Why would that not *always* obligate us to "get the best price for the stockholders"? If at the outset of a takeover we do not owe that obligation, at what point does it start? Were a lawyer to tell them that it starts when "the break-up of the company [became] inevitable,"[67] they will ask why a breakup would trigger a change in the duty they owed their shareholders.

And so people asked. And over the next two decades, the Delaware judges tried to explain.

2. *Paramount Communications v. Time, Inc.*[68]

In 1989, Time negotiated a merger agreement with Warner Communications on terms advantageous to Warner shareholders. Necessarily, the terms were disadvantageous to Time. Time shares had traded for about $126.

Suddenly, Paramount announced a $175 per share any-and-all cash tender offer for Time, provided Time directors cancelled the Warner merger. The Time

---

[66] *Revlon*, 506 A.2d at 182.
[67] *Id.*
[68] 571 A.2d 1140 (Del. 1989).

directors and senior officers had spent years cultivating Warner. They did not want the transaction jeopardized, and neither did they want their stock owned by Paramount. Worried (reasonably) that their shareholders would prefer the lucrative Paramount premium to the disadvantageous Warner merger, they restructured the transaction. If they acquired Warner through a merger, they would need to submit the deal to a shareholder vote. If they bought Warner for cash, they could avoid that shareholder vote. Rather than risk a vote they might lose, they decided to buy Warner for cash. Paramount responded by raising its offer to $200.

Time shareholders sued their directors on a *Revlon* claim: Having effectively offered Time for sale through the Warner merger, they bore an obligation to obtain the highest price possible. Here, that pointed to the Paramount offer. In turn, Paramount sued on a *Unocal* claim: Having made an extremely high-priced any-and-all bid, its offer was neither inadequate nor coercive, and the Time board could not validly oppose it.

The Delaware Supreme Court rejected both claims. Bergerac had decided to break up Revlon, but the Time board planned to keep the firm intact. Hence, *Revlon* did not apply. As generous as the Paramount offer may have been, the Time directors could reasonably worry "that Time shareholders might elect to tender into Paramount's cash offer in ignorance . . . of the strategic benefit which a business combination with Warner might produce." Hence, the risk of shareholder confusion justified their opposition under *Unocal.*

The shareholders and Paramount lost in court, and Time shares plummeted to $93 per share.

3. *Paramount Communications v. QVC Network*[69]

Five years later, the Delaware court faced the question — in effect — of whether it really meant what it said in *Time.* Maybe not, it sheepishly admitted.

After failing to obtain Time, Paramount continued to look for a suitable business partner. In 1993, it settled on Viacom. In exchange for agreeing to deal with Paramount, Viacom wanted some protection. First, it wanted Paramount to adopt a no-shop agreement and promise not to look for other options. Second, it wanted a $100 million "termination fee" (what the parties called a "cancellation fee" in *Revlon*), payable if the deal fell through.

Third, Viacom wanted the right to buy 20 percent of the outstanding Paramount shares at $69 per share, again if the deal fell through. The firms called the provision a "stock option agreement." But Viacom also wanted the right to short-circuit it and simply take the cash difference between the market price of Paramount stock and $69 (on 20 percent of the outstanding shares).

Soon, QVC entered the picture and announced a tender offer for Paramount. With Viacom's competition, QVC continued to raise its bid. Eventually it offered $90 — at which point the cost of Viacom's "stock option" came to $500 million. QVC

---

[69] 637 A.2d 34 (Del. 1994).

sued. It cited *Revlon* for the proposition that the Paramount board had an obligation to obtain the highest price possible. As that pointed to QVC's $90, Viacom's option — potentially blocking as it did the QVC offer — was illegal. Paramount replied that *Revlon* did not apply because it did not plan to break up the company.

Declared the court: *Revlon* did indeed apply. *Revlon* did not just apply when the parties planned to break up the firm. It also applied when corporate control would shift. Here, Paramount had been owned by a "fluid aggregation of unaffiliated stockholders on the market." After its merger with Viacom, it would be controlled by a single shareholder. Given that shift, *Revlon* applied:

> [W]hen a corporation undertakes a transaction which will cause: (a) a change in corporate control; or (b) a break-up of the corporate entity, the director's obligation is to seek the best value reasonably available to the stockholders.[70]

Additionally, noted the court, the Paramount board "clearly gave insufficient attention to the potential consequences of the defensive measures demanded by Viacom."[71] Those measures would hamper its ability to obtain a higher bid. Although Paramount had a chance to negotiate better terms from Viacom, it failed to do so. Paramount also needed to show that its "decision was, on balance, within a range of reasonableness,"[72] but it did not do that either.

Revlon was odd in the first place. Given that directors are agents of the shareholders, why do they not *always* have a duty to obtain the best price possible? But *QVC* simply compounds the oddness. Why should the obtain-the-best-price duty only apply when control would shift to a closely held firm?

QVC may simply be what it purports to be: an odd doctrinal permutation on an odd doctrinal statement. Alternatively, however, it may be a case of judicial damage control. In *Time*, the Delaware court let incumbent directors block an any-and-all tender offer paying a 100 percent premium. So preposterous was its opinion that it quickly became the target of massive ridicule. With *QVC*, the court may be telling the corporate bar: Yes, you're right; we were wrong in *Time*.

4. Omnicare[73]

In *Revlon*, the Delaware Supreme Court banned defenses that stopped the auction process. The board had promised Forstmann such an onerous lockup and cancellation fee that no one would outbid it. By agreeing to the lockup and cancellation fee, it violated its fiduciary duty to its shareholders.

In *Omnicare*, the court faced the same question — and gave the same answer. NCS had done badly. Competitor Omnicare had offered to buy it, but not on

---

[70] *Id.* at 48.
[71] *Id.* at 49.
[72] *Id.* at 45.
[73] Omnicare, Inc. v. NCS Healthcare, Inc., 818 A.2d 914 (Del. 2003).

generous terms. Another competitor named Genesis arrived with a better deal. Genesis had lost a bidding war to Omnicare before, however, and wanted some protection. Crucially, it wanted NCS's board chairman and CEO to agree to vote their stock in favor of its offer. Because of their large stakes, their support would ensure that the merger proceeded.

According to the Delaware Supreme Court, this contract with NCS's chairman and CEO was illegal — and hence unenforceable. The two men controlled a majority of NCS votes. If they agreed to favor the Genesis offer, Genesis won. Said the court, "the deal protection devices of the NCS board were both preclusive and coercive."[74] The court continued:

> Instead of agreeing to the absolute defense of the Genesis merger from a superior offer, . . . the NCS board was required to negotiate a fiduciary out clause to protect the NCS stockholders if the Genesis transaction became an inferior offer.[75]

Unfortunately, the opinion raises the same problem as *Revlon*. A higher offer is always nice. But the bidding may have reached the level that it did in *Revlon* and *Omnicare* only because the target offered its favored white knight the protection it wanted. Had the target not agreed to the protection, the winning bid may have been much lower. In so many words, Justice Norman Veasey made exactly that point in dissent:

> If the NCS board [did not agree to the deal protection] and if NCS had insisted on a fiduciary out, there would have been no Genesis deal! Thus, the only value-enhancing transaction available would have disappeared.[76]

5. *Kahn v. Lynch Communication Systems*[77]

In *Kahn*, the Delaware Supreme Court asked by what metric courts should judge the fairness of cash-out mergers in the corporate control market. No differently from the way they judged other freeze-out mergers, it answered. Alcatel owned 43 percent of Lynch. Through that shareholding, it had negotiated the power to name 5 of the 11 members of the Lynch board. Despite some opposition from that board, it decided to acquire the remaining Lynch shares through a freeze-out merger. The Lynch board appointed a committee to handle the negotiations. The committee recommended that the firm approve Alcatel's offer, and the board complied.

Faced with a challenge to the transaction, the court first applied *Sinclair* (Chapter 4, section III.C.2). Alcatel was a controlling shareholder. Although it owned less than a majority, it could (and did) dominate Lynch. As a result:

[74] *Id.* at 935.
[75] *Id.* at 938.
[76] *Id.* at 941.
[77] 638 A.2d 1110 (Del. 1994).

A controlling or dominating shareholder standing on both sides of a transaction, as in a parent-subsidiary context, bears the burden of proving its entire fairness.[78]

Yet this was not the simple dispute over corporate opportunities or supply contracts that the court had seen in *Sinclair*. This involved a freeze-out merger. Accordingly, the *Weinberger* variation on *Sinclair* applied (section II. C. above):

> [T]he exclusive standard of judicial review in examining the propriety of an interested cash-out merger transaction by a controlling or dominating shareholder is entire fairness. . . . The initial burden of establishing entire fairness rests upon the party who stands on both sides of the transaction.[79]

Here, the board had ratified the transaction. The impact of that ratification turned on *Lawrence* (Chapter 4, section III.B.5):

> [A]n approval of the transaction by an independent committee of directors or an informed majority of minority shareholders shifts the burden of proof on the issue of fairness from the controlling or dominating shareholder to the challenging shareholder-plaintiff.[80]

Given that the board had relied on an independent committee, the court turned to the significance of the committee's work. For it to give weight to the committee's decision, the court held, Alcatel needed to show:

> First, the majority shareholder must not [have] dictate[d] the terms of the merger. . . . Second, the special committee must have [had] real bargaining power that it [could] exercise with the majority shareholder on an arm's length basis.[81]

In the case at hand, Alcatel had indeed dictated the terms of the merger. The independent committee had thought the price too low, but Alcatel had insisted on the merger anyway. Consequently, ratification by the board had no effect—and Alcatel bore the burden of proving the "entire fairness" of the merger.

6. *In re Pure Resources, Inc., Shareholders Litigation*[82]

Suppose an acquirer thought the *Weinberger–Lynch* "entire fairness" standard too onerous. If it eliminated its minority shareholders through a tender offer rather than a merger, could it avoid that burden of proof?

---

[78] *Id.* at 1115.
[79] *Id.* at 1117.
[80] *Id.*
[81] *Id.* (quoting *Rabkin v. Olin Corp.*, 1990 WL 47648 (Del. Ch. Apr. 17, 1990)).
[82] 808 A.2d 421 (Del. Ch. 2002).

III. Hostile Acquisitions

Turnabout is fair play. After playing target in the mid-1980s, Unocal turned acquirer in 2002. It owned 65 percent of Pure Resources and wanted to eliminate the remaining shareholders. It could have merged Pure into a wholly owned subsidiary, but that would have invited a minority shareholder to claim that it bore the burden (under *Weinberger*) of proving the merger's "entire fairness." Rather than face that hurdle, it announced a tender offer for the remaining 35 percent.

Minority shareholders sued anyway. The court should not let Unocal duck the fairness standard, they argued, by structuring its takeover as a tender offer rather than a merger. The Delaware Chancellery Court did let Unocal duck the standard. In a merger, it explained, a shareholder has no choice. He loses his shares and obtains in exchange whatever the board negotiated. It matters not whether he liked the merger's terms or no. In a tender offer, a shareholder who does not like the deal's terms can simply refuse to sell.

That said, the court did not exempt all tender offers from the *Weinberger–Lynch* standard. Instead, a tender offer was exempt only if

> 1) it is subject to a non-waivable majority of the minority tender condition; 2) the controlling stockholder promises to consummate a prompt §253 merger at the same price if it obtains more than 90% of the shares; and 3) the controlling stockholder has made no retributive threats.[83]

What is more, the acquirer needed to give the target board "free rein and adequate time" to evaluate the terms of the offer. If the acquirer did all this, *Weinberger–Lynch* would not apply:

> When a tender offer is non-coercive in the sense I have identified and the independent directors of the target are permitted to make an informed recommendation and provide fair disclosure, the law should be chary about superimposing the full fiduciary requirement of entire fairness upon the statutory tender offer process.[84]

H. The Shareholder Franchise

1. *Schnell v. Chris-Craft Industries*[85]

Some defenses that target boards adopt affect the business of the firm. Others affect the way shareholders control the board itself. Delaware courts have been less willing to defer to target boards on the latter. In the modern jurisprudence, the case law begins with the early 1970s case of *Schnell v. Chris-Craft Industries*. There, the

---

[83] *Id.* at 445.
[84] *Id.* at 445-446.
[85] 285 A.2d 437 (Del. 1971).

bylaws set the annual meeting of shareholders for January 11, 1972. The board decided to move it to December 8, 1971. As the court saw it:

> [M]anagement has attempted to utilize the corporate machinery and the Delaware Law for the purpose of perpetuating itself in office; and, to that end, for the purpose of obstructing the legitimate efforts of dissident stockholders in the exercise of their rights to undertake a proxy contest against management. These are inequitable purposes, contrary to established principles of corporate democracy.[86]

Given that finding, of course, the result was overdetermined. The court held the tactic illegal.

2. *Blasius Industries v. Atlas Corp.*[87]

The case that brought to the fore this distinction between business decisions and the "shareholder franchise" was Chancellor William Allen's 1988 opinion in *Blasius.*

Blasius owned 9 percent of Atlas, but wanted the firm to change direction. Unfortunately for Blasius, the Atlas board was classified (i.e., staggered). Even if Blasius obtained the support of the other shareholders, it would need to wait several years before it could control the board. To accelerate its takeover, Blasius proposed to increase the size of the board from the current 7 to the maximum 15 allowed by the charter. If it could add 8 right-minded directors, it could shift the direction of the firm immediately.

The incumbent Atlas directors responded by increasing board size by 2 and appointing their allies. Obviously, this left Blasius without a way to obtain immediate control. Even if it increased the board to 15, it would have a block of only 6.

Allen began by distinguishing business management from what he called "the shareholder franchise":

> The shareholder franchise is the ideological underpinning upon which the legitimacy of directorial power rests. Generally, shareholders have only two protections against perceived inadequate business performance. They may sell their stock . . . , or they may vote to replace incumbent board members.[88]

Given this conceptual framework:

> [I]t is clear that [the sanctity of the shareholder franchise] is critical to the theory that legitimates the exercise of power by some (directors and officers) over vast aggregations of property that they do not own.[89]

---

[86] *Id.* at 439.
[87] 564 A.2d 651 (Del. Ch. 1988).
[88] *Id.* at 659.
[89] *Id.*

III. Hostile Acquisitions

When incumbent managers manipulate the vote to keep themselves in power, they raise "the question who, as between the principal and the agent, has authority with respect to a matter of internal corporate governance."[90] This question implicates none of the reasons that justify the deference embodied in the business judgment rule:

> A board's decision to act to prevent the shareholders from creating a majority of new board positions and filling them does not involve the exercise of the corporation's power over its property, or with respect to its rights or obligations; rather, it involves allocation, between shareholders as a class and the board, of effective power with respect to governance of the corporation. This need not be the case with respect to other forms of corporate action that may have an entrenchment effect—such as the stock buybacks present in *Unocal* [or] *Cheff*. . . .[91]

Concluded Allen:

> Action designed principally to interfere with the effectiveness of a vote inevitably involves a conflict between the board and a shareholder majority. Judicial review of such action involves a determination of the legal and equitable obligations of an agent towards his principal. This is not, in my opinion, a question that a court may leave to the agent finally to decide so long as he does so honestly and competently; that is, it may not be left to the agent's business judgment.[92]

3. *Hilton Hotels Corp. v. ITT Corp.*[93]

As another illustration of the logic in *Blasius*, consider *Hilton*—a federal district court opinion applying Nevada law that nonetheless relies heavily on Delaware jurisprudence. When Hilton announced a tender offer for ITT, the ITT board introduced a staggered (i.e., classified) board with three-year terms. Hilton challenged the move, and the court held for Hilton.

The court first distinguished between a board's control over the assets of the firm, and its control over its relations with its shareholders. The former it subjected either to the business judgment rule or to *Unocal*: It gave the board wide latitude. The latter it scrutinized closely: Because the vote was one of the few ways shareholders could challenge board control, the court would carefully review any attempt by directors to interfere with that franchise.

> [S]hareholders generally have only two protections against perceived inadequate business performance. They may sell their stock or vote to replace incumbent

---

[90] *Id.* at 660.
[91] *Id.*
[92] *Id.*
[93] 978 F. Supp. 1342 (D. Nev. 1997).

board members. For this reason, interference with the shareholder franchise is especially serious.[94]

Given this principle, the court enjoined the staggered board. Staggered boards were not normally illegal, it noted. But a "normally permissible" measure may yet be illegal "if the primary purpose is to disenfranchise the shareholders in light of a proxy contest."[95] To determine that "primary purpose," timing mattered. The ITT board had adopted the staggered board only after Hilton had launched its tender offer. The staggered arrangement was "preclusive" (see *Omnicare* above). And the board adopted it to keep itself in office.

IV.   STATE ANTI-TAKEOVER STATUTES[96]

A.   *The Earliest Statutes*

Recall Henry Manne's discussion of the market for corporate control (section III. B above). Acquirers buy firms only if they think they can make money on the transaction. They will make money only if they can sell the firm for more than they paid. And because share prices reflect the expected net cash flows to the firm, they will buy a firm only if they think they can increase that cash flow. To increase net cash flow, they will need to cut expenses, raise revenues, or both.

When an acquirer increases the net cash flows to a firm, he confers a benefit on all shareholders and imposes a cost on the mediocre managers, whom he sacks in the process. Yet shareholders of public firms do not vote locally; instead, they live across the entire country (and sometimes even the globe). By contrast, incumbent managers vote for local politicians; they live near the corporate headquarters. The Williams Act raised the cost of hostile acquisitions, but it did not eliminate them entirely. Once the corporate control market turned active during the 1980s, incumbent managers began pressuring state legislators to stop the market cold.

By 1982, 37 states had passed anti-takeover statutes.[97] Consider the Illinois variation. It applied to any corporation having specified contacts with the state, even if not incorporated there. If an acquirer announced a tender offer for a firm covered by the statute, the statute required the acquirer to sit quietly for 20 days. During that time, the target could communicate with shareholders freely; the acquirer was to stay mum. What is more, the acquirer could not proceed with its

---

[94] *Id.* at 1351.

[95] *Id.* at 1348-1349.

[96] *See generally* Daniel R. Fischel, *From MITE to CTS: State Anti-Takeover Statutes, the Williams Act, and the Commerce Clause, and Insider Trading,* 1988 Sup. Ct. Rev. 47; Roberta Romano, *The Political Economy of Takeover Statutes,* 73 Va. L. Rev. 111 (1987).

[97] Guhan Subramanian, Steven Herscovici & Brian Barbetta, *Is Delaware's Antitakeover Statute Unconstitutional? Evidence from 1988-2008,* 65 Bus. Law. 685 (2010).

tender offer unless and until an Illinois regulatory agency approved its "fairness." The agency did not need ultimately to approve an offer and faced no deadline by which to act.

The Illinois legislature went too far, declared the U.S. Supreme Court in the 1982 *Edgar v. MITE* decision.[98] The justices wrote so many separate opinions that one is hard put to unravel any coherent logic to the whole. A majority did find, however, that the statute constituted an unconstitutional burden on interstate commerce.

B. *The Next Generation*

The Indiana statute a few years later was different. It applied only to companies both incorporated in Indiana and meeting certain tests of corporate presence. If an acquirer crossed one of several stockholding thresholds (20 percent, 33 percent, 50 percent), the acquired stock lost its vote. Only on a majority vote by the other shareholders could an acquirer vote the stock. And to obtain that majority vote, an acquirer could require the firm to convene a shareholders' meeting within 50 days.

In the *Dynamics v. CTS*[99] challenge to the statute, the federal district court held the statute both preempted by the Williams Act and a violation of the Commerce Clause. Writing for the Seventh Circuit, Judge Richard Posner affirmed:

> Even if a corporation's tangible assets are immovable, the efficiency with which they are employed and the proportions in which the earnings they generate are divided between management and shareholders depends on the market for corporate control—an interstate, indeed international, market that the state of Indiana is not authorized to opt out of, as in effect it has done in this statute.[100]

The effect of the Indiana statute "on the interstate market in securities and corporate control," he explained, "is direct, intended and substantial."[101] The statute both violated the Commerce Clause and was preempted by the Williams Act.

The Supreme Court reversed.[102] To the justices, the difference between the Illinois and Indiana statutes turned on three factors. First, the Indiana statute applied only to firms incorporated in Indiana; the Illinois statute had applied to non-Illinois firms showing specified levels of contact with the state. By convention, the law of the state of incorporation governs the internal affairs of a corporation. For better or worse (recall the "race for the bottom" debate in Chapter 3, appendix II), the convention does keep things clear. The Indiana statute did not interfere with that convention; the Illinois statute had.

[98] 457 U.S. 624 (1982).
[99] Dynamics Corp. of Am. v. CTS Corp., 794 F.2d 250 (7th Cir. 1986).
[100] *Id.* at 264.
[101] *Id.*
[102] CTS Corp. v. Dynamics Corp. of Am., 481 U.S. 69 (1987).

Second, the Indiana statute set a firm deadline for the acquisition. The Williams Act requires acquirers to hold a tender offer open at least 20 days, but no more. Under the Indiana act, the acquirer would not know whether it could vote its shares until the shareholders had voted on the question, but at least it could require them to hold a meeting within 50 days. The Illinois statute had imposed no deadline at all. An acquirer would know whether its offer could proceed only when the state regulatory agency decided to announce its decision — and it could decide whenever it wanted.

Last, the Indiana statute required no regulatory approval. The Illinois regulators had retained the power to pass on the offer's fairness. The Indiana regulators did not.

The Court turned first to the claim that the Indiana statute was preempted by the Williams Act. It noted that firms could comply with both the Indiana statute and the Williams Act. The two statutes did not impose conflicting requirements. What is more, claimed the Court, the two statutes embodied similar "purposes." The "Williams Act struck a careful balance between the interests of offerors and target companies."[103] The Illinois act had upset that "balance" through its 20-day pre-commencement period, its lack of a regulatory deadline, and its fairness review; the Indiana act reflected the same balance as the Williams Act.

The Court then addressed the Commerce Clause. The Indiana act did not discriminate against out-of-state acquirers: It treated domestic and foreign acquirers the same. Because it applied only to firms incorporated in Indiana, it did not impose inconsistent regulations. And because states determined the structure of corporate governance rules anyway, it merely embodied a variation on the standard corporate statutes. Hence its conclusion: The statute did not violate the Commerce Clause.

C. The Delaware Statute

Given how many big firms incorporate in Delaware, Delaware's anti-takeover statute is the one that matters. Delaware passed its statute in 1988 — one year after *CTS*. It bans an acquirer from using a back-end merger to eliminate minority shareholders after acquiring a 15 percent stake unless it takes one of three steps. First, it can obtain the approval of the target board in advance of its acquisition. Second, it can raise its stake from 15 to 85 percent in a single tender offer. Or third, after buying its 15 percent stake it can obtain the approval of two-thirds of the other shareholders.[104]

The Delaware statute does not prevent an acquisition. It does, however, make it hard for a firm to eliminate minority shareholders after it takes control. Early on, three federal courts ruled on its constitutionality, and all upheld it.[105] Scholars

---

[103] *Id.* at 80.

[104] Del. Gen. Corp. L. §203.

[105] Subramanian, Herscovici & Barbetta, *supra* note 97.

have noted how difficult the statute can make takeovers, but the courts have called it constitutional. It has since become a model for a wide variety of other state statutes.[106]

V.   CONCLUSION

Takeovers increase operating efficiency, but do so by booting incumbent directors and officers from their jobs. Faced with a hostile bid, incumbents resist. For the most part, the courts have let them resist. From time to time, legislators have helped them resist.

Soft-touch local managers are popular in the press. Numbers-driven New Yorkers are not. Families with young children make hot chocolate and watch George Bailey and his friend Clarence every Christmas. No one watches Gordon Gekko. In the market for family movies, compassion sells better than greed every day.

But compassion does not replicate the corporate control market. It does not rationalize firms. And it does not replace underperforming officers. As a result, even the beloved George Bailey has his detractors. After all, Internet hawkers still sell those sweatshirts emblazoned, "Jump, George Bailey. Jump!"

[106] *Id.*

APPENDIX

Self-Study

I. SELECTED OBJECTIVE QUESTIONS

Problem Set A

1. Fitzwilliam Darcy Enterprises, Inc. (Darcy) decided to expand its operations in the town of Maryton. To acquire the properties it needed, it retained the real estate firm of Elizabeth Bennet, Inc. William Collins, Inc. (Collins) is another real estate firm in the Maryton area. Hearing rumors of Darcy's interest in Maryton, Collins began contracting to buy Maryton properties. Although Darcy never contacted Collins, Collins believed (correctly) that Darcy would want the properties it was purchasing. In the course of negotiating with several sellers, Collins claimed that it was acting on behalf of Darcy.

   (a) Because Collins was acting on behalf of Darcy and subject to its control, Darcy is liable on Collins's contracts by inherent agency power.
   (b) Because Collins created its own apparent authority, Darcy is liable to sellers who dealt with Collins.
   (c) If Darcy now unambiguously indicates to Collins that it wants land that Collins has contracted to buy on the terms that Collins negotiated, Darcy may be liable on Collins's contract by ratification.
   (d) None of the above is true.

2. Grendel, Inc. (Grendel), is a Delaware corporation with a single asset, oil-drilling rights in a promising sector of U.S. territorial waters in the Gulf of Mexico. Hrunting, Inc. (Hrunting), a much larger publicly traded oil company incorporated in Delaware with numerous subsidiaries around the world, holds 75 percent of Grendel's outstanding common stock.

   Hrunting has decided to eliminate Grendel's other shareholders by selling Grendel's assets to Hrunting in exchange for cash and then liquidating Grendel.

Suppose a Grendel shareholder sues, claiming that he would have been entitled to appraisal rights if Hrunting had merged Grendel into Hrunting. He should not be precluded from those rights, he argues, simply because Hrunting structured the transaction as an asset sale followed by a liquidation instead.

(a) The shareholder will be entitled to appraisal rights under the de facto merger doctrine.
(b) The shareholder will be entitled to appraisal under substance-over-form principles.
(c) The shareholder will not be entitled to appraisal rights.
(d) Both (a) and (b) are true.

Problem Set B

Philip Pirrip owns and operates an investment company called Pip Co. Estella Havisham is the CEO to Expectations, Inc. Expectations is a Delaware corporation listed on the New York Stock Exchange. To engineer the acquisition of Expectations by Pip Co. as a friendly merger, Pirrip invited Havisham to dinner at an exclusive New York restaurant. Initially, Havisham was receptive to the idea of the acquisition and provided Pirrip with a variety of information about Expectations not yet disclosed to the public. The two did not discuss confidentiality. Despite extensive negotiations, however, the two were not able to negotiate a mutually agreeable merger.

After Pirrip and Havisham broke off negotiations, suppose that the stock purchases given in the questions below were made. For each transaction, the possible answers are the same:

(a) The party is liable under Rule 14e-3.
(b) The party is liable by a straightforward application of *TGS* and *Dirks*.
(c) The party may be liable under *O'Hagan* or Rule 10b5-2.
(d) None of the above is true.

For each question, give the correct answer from among options (a) through (d) above.

1. On the basis of information disclosed by Havisham during the negotiations, Pirrip's wife (after hearing about the negotiations from her husband) buys 1,000 shares of Expectations.
   Why might the answer be ambiguous?
2. On the basis of information disclosed by Havisham during the negotiations, Pip Co. buys 1,000 shares of Expectations.
   Why might the answer be ambiguous?
3. On the basis of information disclosed by Havisham during the negotiations, an associate at the law firm retained by Expectations to handle the possible merger buys 1,000 shares of Expectations.

I. Selected Objective Questions

4. After buying the 1,000 shares for the associate mentioned in Question 3, the associate's broker buys 1,000 shares for himself. The broker did not know *why* the associate was buying the shares but reasoned that he must know *some*thing. The brokerage house clearly bans such "tag-along" transactions.

5. Pirrip goes golfing with his neighbor one Saturday (the two do not customarily discuss business matters). The neighbor notices a pile of documents in the car relating to the merger negotiations. On the basis of what he sees on the documents, the neighbor buys 1,000 shares of Expectations.

   Why might the answer be ambiguous?

6. Pirrip goes golfing with his neighbor one Saturday. Because of their involved discussion, they move slowly. One golfer in the foursome behind them on the course overhears the conversation. On the basis of what he hears, he buys 1,000 shares of Expectations.

   Why might the answer be ambiguous?

7. In the course of discussing child-care arrangements during the merger negotiations, Havisham discloses important aspects of Expectations' R&D to her husband. On that basis, her husband buys 1,000 shares of Expectations.

8. Assume that 900,000 shares of Expectations stock are outstanding. Assume further that, prior to the transactions discussed, none of the following parties owns any Expectations stock. Now assume that each of the parties buys 100,000 shares and then, at a gain, sells the shares 100 days later.

   Which of the parties below would be liable under §16(b)?

   _____ Pip Co.

   _____ Pirrip

   _____ Expectations' law firm's associate

   _____ Havisham

9. Of the four parties listed in Question 8, which would incur criminal liability under §16(b)?

Problem Set C

Avonlea, Inc., is a pharmaceutical firm incorporated in Delaware and traded on NASDAQ. Its earnings are almost entirely a function of a patent it holds on a single drug used extensively by stroke patients. The patent is due to expire in seven years.

Gilbert Blythe is a member of the board of Avonlea. He argues that the firm faces a serious risk of bankruptcy if it does not develop a successful new drug in the next seven years and notes that the odds of such a new drug are low. Accordingly, he proposes that Avonlea acquire an unrelated low-risk firm to protect shareholders from that downside contingency. The board rejects his proposal.

1. Shareholder Anne Shirley brings a derivative suit against the board for rejecting Blythe's proposal. Assume the firm has no outside directors who could staff an independent litigation committee.
   (a) Shirley will likely win if she can show that the directors (who own significant interests in Avonlea) are richer than most shareholders — for if they are richer, they will be better able to diversify their investments; and their greater ability to diversify may constitute self-interest under a duty of loyalty claim.
   (b) Shirley will likely win, as the failure to acquire the smaller firm is probably a duty of care violation.
   (c) Shirley will likely lose.
   (d) Both (a) and (b) are true.
2. Shareholder Matthew Cuthbert notes that Avonlea's research involves the use of embryonic stem cells, a practice he finds immoral. Together with several friends who share his moral opposition to embryonic stem-cell research, he organizes a slate of candidates for the board. If elected, they promise to end all research involving stem cells. At the next general meeting, he plans to contest the incumbent board with his rival slate.
   (a) Cuthbert's slate is illegal because he and his friends are opposing the incumbents on grounds other than profit maximization.
   (b) Cuthbert's slate is illegal because he and his friends have agreed not just about how they will vote their shares, but about what they will do (stop stem-cell research) if elected.
   (c) Cuthbert is free to organize a slate of insurgents who will contest the incumbent board. The concerns in (a) and (b) are not concerns that a real-world court would consider grounds for holding the slate illegal.
   (d) Both (a) and (b) are true.

Problem Set D

Dr. Kasper Gutman (Gutman) is a prominent educational administrator in Philadelphia. Recently, he learned that he was under consideration for a high-paying job at a major Boston-area firm.

1. In eager anticipation of the Boston job offer, Gutman bought a house on Cape Cod and asked the general contracting firm of Bollinger & Lee (Lee) to remodel it. Lee decided it was too busy and recommended another general contractor, Kent Clark, Inc. (Clark). In exchange for recommending its work to Gutman, Clark paid Lee $10,000.
   (a) Lee can keep the $10,000.
   (b) Lee must forfeit the $10,000 to Gutman.
   (c) Clark must forfeit its profits on the transaction to Gutman.
   (d) Both (b) and (c) are true.
2. Still in anticipation of the Boston job offer, Gutman hired real estate agent Jean Simmons & Partners (Simmons) to sell his Philadelphia mansion.

Simmons arranged for the University of Pennsylvania to buy it—but (in exchange for a $30,000 bribe from the university to Jean Simmons, the individual partner) at $300,000 less than the price Gutman would have been able to obtain from another buyer.

News of the payoff reached the *Philadelphia Inquirer* and became a minor scandal. Embarrassed, the University of Pennsylvania paid Gutman an additional $300,000. Gutman has sued Simmons (the partnership) for the $30,000 bribe.

(a) Because Gutman has already been made whole, Simmons (the partnership) need not pay him the $30,000.

(b) Because Simmons (the partnership) breached its fiduciary duties to Gutman, it must pay him the $30,000.

(c) Neither (a) nor (b) is true.

3. Although formally a partnership as the name indicates—Jean Simmons & Partners—Jean Simmons (the individual) runs a despotic shop. She makes all decisions at the firm, does not disclose the finances of the firm to the other real estate agents, and compensates them according to the properties they are able to sell. It was she who took the bribe from the University of Pennsylvania.

Because of the bribe, the state of Pennsylvania has rescinded the real estate license of the Simmons firm as a whole. This has delayed the sales of many properties that the firm had contracted to sell. Those clients sued.

(a) If the Simmons firm has inadequate assets to pay the judgments against it, Jean Simmons (the individual) is liable individually.

(b) If the Simmons firm has inadequate assets to pay the judgments against it, the real estate agents other than Jean Simmons are liable individually.

(c) Both (a) and (b) are true.

(d) Neither (a) nor (b) is true.

Problem Set E

Faced with debilitating competition in the educational market, Porcellian University (the "university") decided to take a variety of steps to shore up its income. One step involved a decision to move down market into SAT preparation centers. Ultimately, it hoped to establish a nationwide chain of franchised centers that would use the Porcellian name to sell SAT prep courses to high school students.

To facilitate its entry into the test prep industry, the university created a Massachusetts corporation, Porcellian Test-Prep Center, Inc. (PTPC). According to the university's plan, this firm would franchise independently owned test prep outlets located around the country.

The members of the board of directors of PTPC are all university faculty named by the university president. For the post of PTPC president, they recruited a recent Porcellian Law School graduate, Pamina Kaplan, granddaughter of the founder of a competing (and extremely successful) chain of test prep centers.

For the other board positions, they hired several young scholars who had recently been denied tenure at the university (of which there are always many).

The university owns all the common stock of PTPC. To give incentives to Kaplan and the other directors to devote their energies to making PTPC profitable, PTPC issued them generous amounts of preferred stock.

The PTPC board members reasoned that they could not intelligently design and manage the franchise network unless they understood the test prep industry themselves. To help them learn and monitor the industry, PTPC opened test prep centers in four target communities: Lexington, Massachusetts; White Plains, New York; Ann Arbor, Michigan; and Palo Alto, California. It owned and ran these four centers itself.

The university wanted to gauge the general profitability of the centers before it announced its entry (through PTPC) into the test prep business. Because of this concern, the university president ordered the PTPC board to operate these four directly run centers under a name that did not include "Porcellian." PTPC thus operated these four centers as Win Test Prep (WTP) centers. They were, however, wholly owned internal operations of PTPC (they were not separate corporations).

To staff the four WTP operations, Kaplan hired recent graduates of Porcellian Ph.D. programs who were unable to find university positions (of whom there were also many). They each worked 20 hours per week for WTP.

PTPC expected ultimately to pay dividends on its stock. Three years into the program, however, it still has not paid dividends.

The Lexington WTP center was run by a young mathematics Ph.D. named Louis Carroll. One evening in the spring of 2011, Carroll arrived at the Lexington WTP center drunk. He was scheduled to teach an SAT prep session. When a student complained about his drunkenness, Carroll beat him severely.

The student sued WTP for the injuries caused by Carroll. After filing suit, however, he discovered that WTP was owned and operated by PTPC. At that point he added claims against PTPC and the university.

Characterize the following statements as true or false:

1. _____ Because Carroll was not a full-time employee of WTP, he was not a "servant." Hence, WTP, PTPC, and the university are not liable.
2. _____ Because the student was not aware of the role of PTPC and the university, holding either liable would result in a windfall to the student. Accordingly, neither PTPC nor the university is liable.
3. _____ To prevail against PTPC (at least under standard agency law), the student will need to show that the instructor was "motivated at least in part by a desire to serve his master."
4. _____ To prevail against PTPC, a court will demand that the student show either that PTPC's failure to disclose its ownership of the WTC was fraudulent or that PTPC failed to follow corporate formalities.

Using information gleaned through its operation of the four WTP centers, PTPC began a national franchise network. Within a year, it had franchised 30 PTPC test prep centers.

I. Selected Objective Questions

To obtain a PTPC franchise, a local entrepreneur (typically a public school teacher looking for weekend and evening income) applied to PTPC. In exchange for the right to use the "Porcellian Test Prep Center" name, each franchisee agreed to assign PTPC textbooks, to hire only staff who met PTPC standards, and to abide by a wide variety of other quality control regulations set by PTPC. He or she paid PTPC 15 percent of his or her gross revenues.

The Miami Beach, Florida, franchisee was one Pierra Fermat. Fermat reasoned that the high cost of the materials might be discouraging potential students from signing up for her program. After all, PTPC charged students $300 a copy for each textbook. To lower the cost to her students, Fermat opened a used-book center. When a student completed the test prep course, she offered to buy back his or her textbook (if still in good condition). She then offered the used books to the next cohort of students at 33 percent off the price for new books.

Unfortunately, Fermat was also cheating her students. At the outset, she promised them ten sessions. In fact, she typically provided only seven.

Fermat now faces two lawsuits. First, PTPC has sued her for operating a used-book outlet. Although the franchise agreement is silent about such an operation, PTPC argues that the provision of used books to students deprives PTPC of royalty income. Accordingly, by operating the outlet she breaches her fiduciary duty to PTPC.

Second, the students have sued Fermat over the promised-but-not-delivered instructional sessions. In this suit, they have also named PTPC as a defendant.

Characterize the following statements as true or false:

5. ____ PTPC is not liable for Fermat's fraud because Fermat, as a part-time operator of the franchise, is not PTPC's general agent.

6. ____ If students are unable to show that Fermat acted as PTPC's agent, they may still be able to collect against PTPC by "piercing the corporate veil." This is facilitated by the way that the Porcellian president directly instructed PTPC directors about what actions to take.

7. ____ Fermat would owe a fiduciary duty to PTPC only if she is its agent, but if she is its agent, then PTPC is potentially liable for her fraud.

The Ann Arbor WTP center had been run by a young medical scholar named Don Basilio. Once the PTPC board members had decided that they had learned all that they could learn about the test prep industry from the four WTP centers, they decided to close them. They sold the facilities of the Ann Arbor WTP center to the PTPC franchisee for metropolitan Detroit and laid off the staff.

Basilio, on hearing that he would be laid off, sued PTPC.

Characterize the following statements as true or false:

8. ____ PTPC will lose unless it can establish a business purpose for closing the Ann Arbor WTP center.

9. ____ PTPC will lose unless it can show that the sale of the WTP center to the Detroit PTPC franchisee took place through fair procedures and at a fair price.

10. ____ If PTPC shows a legitimate business purpose for discharging Basilio, then Basilio (by principles of corporate law) will have the right to show that the same purpose could have been accomplished through a course of action less harmful to his interests.

Problem Set F

Ten investors decided to go into a trash removal service. They expected that their revenues would come primarily from contracts with municipalities in the area. For a variety of reasons no longer clear, (i) the trucks themselves were owned by Friends, LLC (LLC), a limited liability company; (ii) the employees (the drivers and other workers) were hired by Friends & Partners (Partners), a partnership; and (iii) Partners leased the trucks from LLC. Each of the ten investors owned a 10 percent interest in both LLC and Partners.

Two of those ten investors are Fred and George. Both men also serve as LLC officers and actively participate as partners in Partners. Through various friends in government, Fred learned that three cities for which the firms had been providing trash removal services would not be renewing their contracts. Because this was a big part of the operation's revenue, Fred predicted (correctly) that this would result in a major loss to the two firms.

Explaining that he was now 65 years old (which was true), Fred asked George to buy his 10 percent interests in LLC and Partners (the other partners promised to admit George as a partner). George agreed.

1. Upon learning that the three cities have cancelled the service contracts, George sues Fred under Rule 10b-5.
   (a) George wins on both ownership transfers.
   (b) George loses on both ownership transfers.
   (c) George may or may not win on the LLC transfer, but he loses on the partnership transfer.
   (d) George wins on the partnership transfer and loses on the LLC transfer.
2. Upon learning that the three cities have cancelled the service contracts, George sues Fred under state law.
   (a) George wins on both ownership transfers.
   (b) George loses on both ownership transfers.
   (c) George wins on the LLC transfer and loses on the partnership transfer.
   (d) George wins on the partnership transfer and loses on the LLC transfer.
3. Upon learning that the three cities have cancelled the service contracts, George sues Fred under §16(b).
   (a) George wins on both ownership transfers.
   (b) George loses on both ownership transfers.
   (c) George wins on the LLC transfer and loses on the partnership transfer.
   (d) George wins on the partnership transfer and loses on the LLC transfer.

II.   SELECTED ESSAY QUESTIONS

Problem Set A

The son of boardinghouse proprietress Mary Kane and her dissolute husband Robert, Charles Foster (Charlie) Kane was born in the small mining town of Little Salem, Colorado. There, until age 12 he lived a relatively uneventful childhood. That year, his mother discovered that a mine given her years earlier by a destitute boarder was worth a fortune.

In order to prepare young Charles for a future career, Mary Kane sent him to live in Manhattan with investment banker Walter Parks Thatcher. Thatcher already managed the Kane family's new fortune, but Mary named him Charlie's legal guardian as well. Initially, the family fortune consisted only of the mine. In time, Thatcher grew it into a diversified portfolio of a wide variety of assets. All these assets he placed in the Kane Family Trust (KFT).

The Kanes had no other children. Charlie's mother and father both died by the time he reached age 21.

Grim and humorless, Thatcher did not spend much time actually raising Charlie Kane. Instead, he sent Kane to a series of boarding schools. From those schools, the misbehaving Charlie managed to find himself serially expelled.

Under the terms of the KFT, Charlie was its sole beneficiary and Thatcher its trustee. Those terms entitled Thatcher to reasonable compensation both (a) for raising Charlie and (b) for managing the assets of the KFT. They further provided that Thatcher would use the trust assets as needed (i) to pay for Charlie's educational expenses; (ii) to pay for Charlie's reasonable room, board, and incidental expenses; and (iii) to provide Charlie with a reasonable allowance. By its terms, the KFT was to dissolve automatically on Charlie's 25th birthday. Thereupon, Charlie would come into complete possession of its assets.

Despite their occasionally strained relations, Charlie Kane continued to employ Thatcher as his financial advisor after age 25. Although the KFT dissolved as scheduled, Kane then shifted most of the assets to a new trust — the CFK Trust. He again named himself its beneficiary and Thatcher its trustee. Under the terms of this new CFK Trust, Kane could withdraw assets from it at his sole discretion, and Thatcher would receive reasonable compensation for the work involved in its management. On average, that work took about one day a week of Thatcher's time.

As trustee of the CFK Trust, Thatcher regularly bought and sold stocks, bonds, limited partnership interests, and real estate. He bought the stocks, bonds, and limited partnership interests in the name of the trust. When he bought real estate, however, he often bought the assets in his own name to preserve Kane's anonymity. He then held the land for the benefit of the CFK Trust. The terms of the CFK Trust explicitly permitted this practice.

Kane used some of the assets of the CFK Trust to buy a 51 percent interest in a New York newspaper, the *Inquirer*. The CFK Trust holds that 51 percent, and the other 49 percent is held in small lots by about 100 investors. Kane named himself the *Inquirer*'s editor in chief and his college friend Jedediah Leland its business news editor. Because of Leland's careful, deliberate approach to the news, the *Inquirer* has become one of the most trusted names in financial circles.

Soon after taking over the *Inquirer*, Kane married Emily Monroe Norton. Norton came from a prominent New York socialite family and was introduced to Kane through Thatcher. Thatcher had long managed the Norton family investments. After Norton's marriage to Kane, Thatcher continued to manage her investment portfolio independently of the CFK Trust. His work for Emily Norton took another one day per week of his time. Norton is on the board of the *Inquirer*.

1. Every Friday, the *Inquirer* publishes a column by Leland touting stocks that he thinks are a good bet. Kane notices that the price of the stocks Leland endorses often rise sharply. Leland usually submits his articles to the paper by Thursday noon. Suppose Kane reads Leland's article on Thursday afternoon and learns that Leland will tout the stock of Zabar, Inc. Zabar is listed on the New York Stock Exchange. Kane then asks Thatcher to buy (on behalf of the CFK Trust) a large quantity of Zabar stock.
   a. Has Kane violated Rule 10b-5?
   b. Kane's purchase comes to light, and the circulation figures for the *Inquirer* plummet. Assume the *Inquirer* does not have the requisite directors to staff an independent litigation committee. Can a disgruntled shareholder bring a derivative suit against Norton?
2. Suppose that Thatcher's firm does not have a seat on the New York Stock Exchange. Instead, he places all his orders for stock purchases and sales through a brokerage firm that does have such a seat. That brokerage firm bans all "tag-along" orders—under its definition, purchase (or sale) orders on behalf of one client initiated to replicate purchases (or sales) made by another client.

   Suppose further that, upon receiving Kane's order (described in Question 1), Thatcher reasons that Kane must know something important about Zabar. Accordingly, on his own initiative he buys 100 shares of Zabar stock for Emily Norton's account.
   a. Has Thatcher violated Rule 10b-5?
   b. Has Emily Norton violated Rule 10b-5?
3. Suppose that Thatcher makes the purchase described in Question 2. Suppose further that the SEC begins to investigate the transaction.

   Emily Norton panics. She recalls that she had earlier decided that she was overinvested in equities and had told Thatcher not to buy any more stock. Can she rescind the Zabar stock purchase?
4. Kane believes that much land is overvalued and tells Thatcher not to buy any more real estate without obtaining his permission first. Notwithstanding that instruction, Thatcher buys 1,000 acres of Florida real estate on behalf of the CFK Trust but in his own name. Upon visiting the site, Kane discovers that the property is undevelopable swampland. Is the CFK Trust bound by the purchase?
5. Emily Norton and Charles Kane together constitute Thatcher's largest client. In fact, however, Thatcher also handles hundreds of other investment

accounts. Several of these other clients believe Thatcher has shortchanged them. More specifically, they believe that Thatcher has routed the most lucrative investment opportunities to either Norton or Kane's accounts and given them only the remainder.

a. Discuss the legal basis for any claim they might have against Thatcher.

b. If Thatcher is liable, might Kane be liable as well?

After several years, Kane decided (for reasons not relevant here) that the CFK Trust had become unwieldy. To simplify matters (or so he intended), he dissolved the trust and transferred its assets to two organizations. The securities he transferred to a Delaware corporation, CFK, Inc. (CFKI). The real estate investments he transferred to a general partnership, Charles & Emily (C&E).

Kane and Norton hold the shares of CFKI in equal part. CFKI is solely an investment vehicle, and its assets are managed (as before) by Thatcher. Formally, Thatcher serves as CFKI president and vice president, and Kane as its secretary-treasurer. Kane, Norton, and Thatcher are the only directors of the firm. Thatcher receives a salary for his work; Kane and Norton do not.

The only partners to C&E are Charlie Kane and Emily Norton. They have equal interests in the partnership. It, too, is merely an investment vehicle, and Thatcher again manages its assets. For this he is paid by the hour.

Work on Kane's and Norton's investments (now represented by the CFKI and C&E accounts) still occupies about two days a week of Thatcher's time.

Shortly after dissolving the CFK Trust and establishing this new alternative structure, Kane began a romantic affair with one Susan Alexander. Alexander hoped to become an opera star, but unfortunately had little musical talent.

6. Thatcher's son is a prominent software engineer. He has begun a venture that shows great promise, but needs generous funding. Thatcher believes that the venture will indeed prove profitable. He would like to invest CFKI funds in it, but recognizes the conflict of interest involved.

   Suppose Thatcher writes a letter to Kane, detailing his son's venture and his reasons for recommending that CFKI invest in it. He discloses his parental conflict of interest and asks Kane to approve the purchase. To facilitate the approval, he encloses a "Permission to Invest" form for Kane to sign. The form details Thatcher's conflict of interest and authorizes Thatcher to make the investment anyway.

   Kane does not read the letter. He has entrusted his business correspondence to Mr. Bernstein, his personal confidant. Bernstein is tired of signing the many proxy solicitation letters Kane receives and tells his secretary that she should "just sign all that investment-related garbage that Mr. Kane gets from that tired old man Thatcher." Bernstein's secretary signs Thatcher's form, and Thatcher invests CFKI's funds in his son's venture.

   If the venture loses money, can CFKI rescind the investment? Can it sue Thatcher for damages?

7. For several years, Kane has run a crusade against the incumbent governor, Jim W. Gettys, in the pages of the *Inquirer*. Gettys has now discovered Kane's liaisons with Alexander.

    Suppose Gettys approaches Kane and Norton with a proposition: (a) Gettys owns a dilapidated cabin in Wisconsin worth $20,000; (b) if Kane and Norton will buy this cabin from him for $2 million, he will agree not to disclose the Kane–Alexander affair to the public; but (c) should Kane and Norton refuse the purchase, he will immediately tell the local TV and radio stations about the affair.

    Kane indignantly refuses the proposition. Later, however, and without telling Kane, Norton approaches Gettys and (acting on behalf of C&E) buys the Wisconsin cabin.

    a. Upon learning of the purchase, Kane is outraged. Can C&E rescind the purchase? Can C&E sue Norton for damages?
    b. Suppose Norton bought the cabin on behalf of CFKI. Is CFKI bound?
8. Kane and Norton both believe that Internet companies are overvalued. Accordingly, at a board meeting they tell Thatcher not to buy any more stock in Internet firms. Nevertheless, Thatcher learns of a privately held Internet company that he believes shows unusual promise and whose stock is currently available at $50 a share. He believes that this is an extremely good price and that if he is to obtain any stock at this price, he will need to act immediately. He tries to contact Norton and Kane by phone, but they do not answer.

    Thatcher quickly writes a short note on a blank sheet of paper and sends a PDF of the note to the firm from his home computer: "Please consider this letter an order to purchase 100 shares of stock in your firm, at $50 per share, in the name of CFK, Inc. Sincerely, Walter Parks Thatcher, investment advisor to CFK, Inc." Assume that no one affiliated with CFKI has had any contact with this firm and that the firm has never heard of CFKI.

    Can CFKI rescind the purchase?
9. Suppose Kane believes that he should be paid for his work as secretary-treasurer of CFKI, and Thatcher agrees. Norton objects. Can she stop CFKI from paying anything to Kane?

Problem Set B

The Cord Motor Company (Cord) has been plagued with quality control problems in the production of its flagship sedan, the Phaeton. In order to increase reliability, it has decided to take a page from Toyota and "outsource" the production of a substantial fraction of the parts used in the Phaeton. Toward that end, it now purchases a large number of customized components from other firms located near its headquarters in Oxford, Mississippi.

Cord is incorporated in Delaware; its stock is publicly traded on the New York Stock Exchange.

II. Selected Essay Questions

1. The Auburn Company produces transmissions for the Phaeton. Recently, Auburn CEO Andrew Asriel learned that Auburn will be unable to ship the transmissions it promised and has communicated that information to the Cord vice president for production, Clarissa Coulter.

   The Phaeton is a close competitor to the new Duesenberg V-12 sedan. The Phaeton transmission problems are likely to boost sales of the Duesenberg sedan.

   Suppose Asriel and Coulter each sell 1,000 shares of Cord stock and buy 1,000 shares of Duesenberg stock. Discuss the liability of each under the federal securities laws.

2. Stutz, Inc. (a Delaware firm) produces air conditioners for the Phaeton. Five years ago, Stutz suffered a cash flow crisis and convinced Cord to invest $10 million in Stutz. In return, Stutz issued Cord a 10 percent equity stake.

   During a conference at Cord headquarters regarding the production plans for the Phaeton, Stutz CEO Roger Raknison learned that Cord was desperately trying to meet the Phaeton production deadlines it had promised its investors: If all goes well, it may meet those deadlines, but if it encounters any production problems, it is likely to miss the deadlines. And if it misses the deadlines, a variety of negative collateral consequences will ensue.

   Raknison (honestly) tells Cord that Stutz will find it very hard to deliver the air conditioning units as promised. Midway through its contract with Cord, he (Raknison) demands a 30 percent increase in the price of its air conditioning units. Cord agrees (and pays the 30 percent premium), but (for reasons unrelated to Stutz) misses its production deadlines anyway.

   Suppose Cord sues Stutz for breaching its fiduciary duty to Cord. What result?

3. Hispano, Inc., produces Phaeton fuel injection units for Cord. Hispano is a Delaware company, run by CEO Sue Suizo. Cord owns 40 percent of the stock of Hispano. Six Suizo family members hold the remaining 60 percent in equal amounts. Because Hispano's production facilities are customized to producing Cord fuel injection units, Hispano would incur large costs to reengineer its plants to produce fuel injection units (or anything else) for any other buyer.

   Suppose Cord and Hispano have a three-year supply contract. Midway through the contract, Cord demands a 20 percent decrease in the price of Hispano's fuel injection units. Alternatively, suppose Cord demands the 20 percent decrease at the end of the first three-year contract, as a condition for another three-year renewal.

   Discuss Hispano's legal options.

4. Edsel, Inc., produces brake units for Cord. Edsel is a Delaware corporation whose stock is traded on the New York Stock Exchange. Dakota Blue is one of the directors of Cord. She knows that the Cord board has just voted to produce a new sports car model, and further realizes that this will dramatically increase Cord's orders for brake units from Edsel.

   a. Suppose Blue owned no stock in Edsel. Without disclosing Cord's plans, she buys a 15 percent stake in Edsel. Discuss her liability under §16(b), Rule 10b-5, Rule 14e-3, and state corporate law.

   b. Suppose Blue owned a 30 percent interest in Edsel. Without disclosing Cord's plans, she buys an additional 10 percent stake in Edsel. Discuss her liability under §16(b), Rule 10b-5, Rule 14e-3, and state corporate law.

Problem Set C

The Pacific All Risk Insurance Company (PARIC) is a Delaware corporation. It has 100,000 shares of common stock outstanding and 50,000 shares of cumulative preferred.

The preferred does not vote unless the company fails to pay dividends on the preferred for four quarters in a row; the company has regularly paid the prescribed dividends on the preferred. Preferred stockholders may convert their stock into common stock at any time on a one-to-one basis.

PARIC has five directors: Tom Dietrichson, his young second wife Phyllis Dietrichson, his daughter (by his first marriage) Lola Dietrichson, Walter Neff, and Barton Keyes. Each of the five directors holds 10,000 shares of the PARIC preferred.

Upon liquidation, PARIC preferred shares are entitled (on a per-share basis) to receive double the distribution paid to the common shares.

The common stock is held by more than 10,000 shareholders. The single largest block of the common is held by the Dietrichson Family Investments, Inc. (DFI) — which holds 30,000 shares. DFI is a Delaware corporation. It is owned by a dozen members of the Dietrichson family: Tom, his children (including Lola), and his grandchildren by his late first wife. Phyllis does not hold DFI stock.

Tom is president of DFI, but is not actively involved in management. Instead, Keyes and Neff handle DFI business. Keyes serves as vice president and handles all transactions at DFI relating to insurance and all investment-related correspondence. Neff serves as the treasurer of DFI.

Lola Dietrichson is estranged from her father Tom and (especially) her stepmother Phyllis. She lives with her boyfriend Nino Zachetti. She is so convinced that her father made a mistake in marrying Phyllis that she no longer attends any PARIC board meetings.

According to the PARIC Articles of Incorporation, the board may redeem PARIC preferred shares at any time upon 60 days' notice. The redemption price is $100 plus all unpaid, accrued dividends.

Suppose (for purposes of the next two questions) that PARIC has assets of $17 million. The PARIC board votes to redeem the preferred and liquidate the firm. Eighty-three percent of the common shareholders vote to approve the liquidation (assume, unrealistically, that all shares were voted). After the liquidation, a common shareholder sues the board for fiduciary duty breach on the ground that it did not disclose the true value of the assets at the time that it redeemed the preferred.

1. Has the board breached its fiduciary duty to the common shareholders? In any litigation, what does the common shareholder need to show?
2. Has PARIC violated Rule 10b-5?

Now suppose (for purposes of the next five questions) that PARIC has assets of $9 million. Suppose further that Neff and Phyllis fall in love. They know that Tom will be attending his Stanford college reunion on October 1 and call a board meeting for that day. At the meeting (attended by Phyllis, Neff, and Keyes), the board votes to redeem the preferred and liquidate the firm.

3. A common shareholder sues the board to challenge its decision to redeem the preferred. The shareholder argues that it is a direct rather than derivative suit. Explain the argument.
4. A common shareholder sues the board to challenge its decision to redeem the preferred. In a claim against Phyllis, Neff, and Keyes, does the common shareholder win? Why or why not?
5. A common shareholder sues the board to challenge its decision to redeem the preferred. In a claim against Lola, does the common shareholder win? Why or why not?
6. A common shareholder sues the board and DFI to challenge the board's decision to redeem the preferred. In a claim against DFI, does the common shareholder win? Why or why not?
7. Phyllis, Neff, and Keyes worry about the possibility of fiduciary duty litigation. Accordingly, before redeeming the preferred, they present the planned redemption and the liquidation to PARIC shareholders for ratification. They disclose all information relevant to the proposed transaction to the shareholders. Overwhelmingly, the shareholders ratify it. As vice president for investment-related matters, Keyes signs the proxy material on behalf of DFI ratifying the redemption.

   Have Neff, Phyllis, or Keyes violated their fiduciary duties? To whom, and in what capacity? In any ensuing litigation, what would be their burden of proof?

III. ANSWERS TO SELECTED OBJECTIVE QUESTIONS

Problem Set A

1. Answer (c) correctly states the requirements for ratification. Answer (a) is wrong (among other reasons) because Collins was not acting under Darcy's control. Answer (b) is wrong because agents can create their own apparent authority only when their statement about their agency is truthful when made. Here it was not. Chap. 1, §§II. C, F, G.

2. Delaware law does not grant dissenting shareholders appraisal rights in asset sales (*Farris*, Chapter 8). Hence answer (c) is correct. Note that the de facto merger doctrine is itself a substance-over-form doctrine. Chap. 8, §I.B.

Problem Set B

Initially, note that there is no tender offer at stake. Hence, Rule 14e-3 does not apply.

Questions 1 and 2: Although Pirrip and Havisham discussed a joint venture, they never reached agreement. Hence, although Havisham disclosed nonpublic information to Pirrip, Pirrip never agreed to serve as her or her firm's fiduciary. Absent his agreement, he cannot become her agent and cannot owe fiduciary duties.

By this logic, Pirrip would not violate Rule 10b-5 by trading — and so footnote 22 of *Dirks* implies. Note, however, two caveats. First, lower courts have not necessarily followed this footnote. *Lund,* discussed in Chapter 5, is a good example. Section IV.D.5. Second, Rule 10b5-2 indicates that Pirrip cannot trade if he "agrees" to keep the information confidential. Chap. 5, §IV.E. The question implies that he did not do so.

This analysis suggests that Pirrip probably would not violate Rule 10b-5 by trading (question 2), though the answer is ambiguous.

Rule 10b5-2 indicates that wives cannot trade on information acquired from their husbands. That would seem to suggest that (question 1) she cannot trade here. Given that Pirrip himself can (probably) trade, however, that would seem a very odd result. Chap. 5, §IV.E.

But return to question 2. The express question is not whether Pirrip can trade; it is whether his investment company Pip Co. can trade. If Pirrip does not violate Rule 10b-5 by trading, then neither would Pip Co. Yet if Pip Co. can trade, and Pip Co. is an investment company, then is this investment a "corporate opportunity" of Pip Co.? If it is, then plausibly Pirrip *cannot* buy Expectations stock. The reason, however, is not that he is Havisham's fiduciary or tippee. Rather, the reason is that the investment is a corporate opportunity to Pip Co., that he is a fiduciary to Pip Co., and that he breaches that duty when he invests in Expectations for his own account. Chap. 4, §III.E. And (to complicate matters further) if Pirrip cannot trade because the investment is Pip Co.'s corporate opportunity, then arguably Pirrip's wife cannot trade by Rule 10b5-2. Chap. 5, §IV.E.

Question 3: The associate may not trade. He is a "temporary insider" under *Dirks* footnote 14. Chapter 5, §IV.D.3.

Question 4: Given that the brokerage house bans "tag-along" transactions, the broker has "misappropriated" the information. He violates Rule 10b-5 under *O'Hagan.* Chap. 5, §IV.E.

Question 5: Suppose the neighbor had been playing golf with Havisham. If he spotted the papers in Havisham's car, he arguably received a tip. Arguably, Havisham was careless in leaving the papers in a visible place — and arguably breached a duty of care. Under *Dirks,* however, only violations of a duty of loyalty (with a gain to the tipper) generate tips on which a tippee may not trade. Hence, the neighbor would be able to trade. Chap. 5, §IV.D.

Here, the neighbor spotted the papers in Pirrip's car. Given that Pirrip did not owe Havisham or Expectations a fiduciary duty, it is hard to see why the neighbor should not be able to trade on this information.

III. Answers to Selected Objective Questions

Because the neighbor and Pirrip do not regularly swap tips, Rule 10b5-2 does not apply. Chap. 5, §IV.E.

Question 6: Same analysis as with 5, and very much like *Switzer.* Chap. 5, §IV.D.

Question 7: The husband violates Rule 10b5-2 when he trades. Chap. 5, §IV.E.

Question 8: Expectations is listed on the NYSE; hence, §16(b) potentially applies to trades in its stock. Chap. 5, §III.C.

A purchase of 100,000 of 900,000 shares puts a buyer over the 10 percent threshold, but of course the test is whether the buyer owned more than 10 percent before the purchase. We are told that none did. Chap. 5, §III.C.

Of the four buyers, only Havisham was an officer of Expectations. Given that the others did not own 10 percent before the purchase, only she is potentially liable under §16(b). Chap. 5, §III.C.

Question 9: Section 16(b) does not result in criminal liability. Chap. 5, §III.C.

Problem Set C

Question 1: Portfolio theory in finance indicates that rational shareholders will diversify by holding a balanced portfolio of stock. There is no need for any individual corporation to diversity its own business. Hence, a refusal to diversify is not a mistaken judgment — and not a violation of either a duty of care or a duty of loyalty. Answer (c) is correct; all the prose in (a) and (b) is a smokescreen. Chap. 3, §III; Chap. 4, §I.

Question 2: This is a question of "judgment" — not of legal technicality. All the plausible prose in (a) and (b) notwithstanding, the arguments are still irrelevant. The right answer is (c). Notwithstanding black-letter doctrine, real-world courts do not hold board slates illegal for reasons such as these. Chap. 3, §III; Chap. 6, §§I, III.

Problem Set D

Question 1: An agent may not earn secret profits in transactions involving his agency, but Lee never agreed to be an agent. Thus, it does not violate any fiduciary duty in keeping the referral fee. Clark did become an agent, but agents do not violate a fiduciary duty when they pay others a fee for routing business to them. Hence answer (a) is correct. Chap. 1, §IV.

Question 2: Gutman has indeed been made whole, but agents may not keep profits earned in violation of their fiduciary duty, even when the principal has suffered no harm. They must instead disgorge their earnings. Hence (b) is the correct answer. Chap. 1, §IV.C.

Question 3: Answer (c) is correct. Partners are jointly and severally liable for all amounts chargeable to the partnership. Hence, Jean Simmons is liable. Chap. 2, §II.A.

If the other real estate agents are partners in the firm, they are liable as well. Are they agents? Do they share profits and control? Whether true partners or not, they have consented to be represented to the outside world as partners. Probably, they would be liable as apparent partners even if a court were to hold them not true partners. Chap. 2, §I.D.

Problem Set E

Question 1: Principals are liable for the torts of their agents only if the agents are servants. Chap. 1, §§I.A, III. The test for "servant" is whether the principal can tell the servant how to do his job. Here the principal can — even though Carroll is not a full-time employee. However, Carroll does not work for the university. Instead, he works for WTP and the PTPC.

Classically, principals were liable for the torts of their agents only if those agents were motivated, at least in part, by the purpose of serving their master. Carroll was not. Modern courts, however, tend to ignore the doctrine and hold principals liable for the violent intentional torts of their servants. Chap. 1, §III.

Question 2: The liability of a principal for an agent's torts does not depend on whether the victim knew that the agent was an agent. Chap. 1, §III.

Question 3: The statement is true, as discussed in Chap.1,§III.E.

Question 4: The points discussed go to the question of whether a court will "pierce the corporate veil." Chap. 3 §IV. While they might apply to the liability of university for Carroll's torts, they do not apply to PTPC's liability. Chap. 1, §III.

Question 5: A principal's liability for fraud is not limited to the frauds of general agents. However, Fermat is a franchisee — and as the cases discussed in Chapter 1 illustrate, courts split on whether franchisees are agents. Chap. 1, §§I.A, III.

Question 6: The plaintiff is not trying to collect against a shareholder; rather the plaintiff is trying to collect against a franchisor. "Piercing the corporate veil" is irrelevant. Chap. 1, §§III, IV.

Question 7: True.

Question 8: The business purpose test potentially relates to mergers; it is not a test for when a firm can close an outlet. Chap. 8, §II.

Question 9: These tests, too, potentially relate to mergers; they are not tests for when a firm can close an outlet. Chap. 8, §II.

Question 10: These tests, too, potentially relate to mergers; they are not tests for when a firm can close an outlet. Chap. 8, §II.D.

Problem Set F

Question 1: Answer (c) is correct. Rule 10b-5 applies only to securities. LLC interests may or may not be securities; general partnership interests are not securities. Chap. 5, §III.

Question 2: Answer (a) is correct. As George's partner, Fred owes him a fiduciary duty. That duty includes the duty to disclose to him any private information he may have about the value of any investment interest that he is selling George. Chap. 2, §IV; Chap. 5, §II.

Question 3: Answer (b) is correct. Section 16(b) applies only to very large (generally publicly traded) corporations. Chap. 5, §III.C.

IV. ANSWERS TO SELECTED ESSAY QUESTIONS

Problem Set A

Question 1:

a. Neither Kane nor Leland is an insider at Zabar, and neither has any inside information about the firm. Instead, their inside information concerns what the *Inquirer* will publish, and they are not buying *Inquirer* stock. Moreover, they have no basis for any fiduciary duty toward Zabar.

If the *Inquirer* had a rule against stock purchases based on the content of forthcoming articles, then Kane would be misappropriating the information about Leland's article. Under *O'Hagan*, the purchase would violate Rule 10b-5. Chap. 5, §IV.E. However, the problem gives no hint of such a rule.

The only even potential fiduciary duty breach involves the duties Kane owes the other shareholders in *Inquirer*. Arguably, by trading on the news about Leland's article Kane jeopardizes the reputation (and sales) of the *Inquirer*—because readers might well think less of Leland's articles if they knew Kane was trading on them. Query, however, whether that would give rise to a 10b-5 claim.

b. Whether there is a derivative claim against Norton (not Kane) hinges on whether the board had a duty to create a monitoring program against this sort of activity. Had it been foreseeable that *Inquirer* staff members would trade on Leland's columns, and had it also been foreseeable that such trades would cause *Inquirer* sales to fall, then arguably the board had a duty to install a program to prevent it (*Caremark*). Chap. 4, §II.

Curiously perhaps, the board's liability need not turn on the legality of Kane's trades. Even if the trades were legal, if they caused a loss to the corporation, then arguably the board should have maintained a rule against them, and a monitoring system to enforce the rule.

Question 2:

a. Independent of the brokerage house rule, has Thatcher violated 10b-5? Kane is not damaged by Thatcher's tag-along transactions and has not prohibited them. Yet as a client, might he be entitled to assume that his broker would keep confidential any information about his trades? Would a tag-along trade violate that entitlement? Would it violate the entitlement if the only beneficiary were Kane's wife? And if it did, would that make the tag-along trade a 10b-5 violation? I doubt it—though I do not think the issues are clear.

Here, Thatcher routes the trades through an investment house that does ban such trades. Does that house rule now transform the otherwise (arguably) legal trade into a federal crime under Rule 10b-5? The answer is yes. Chap. 5, §IV.E.

b. Assume Thatcher has violated 10b-5. Thatcher is Norton's agent, but not her servant. A principal can be liable for the fraud of her non-servant agent. Hence, Thatcher's actions would seem potentially to give rise to Norton's liability. Criminal liability under Rule 10b-5 requires scienter, however, and here Norton has none. Chap. 5, §IV.

Question 3: Thatcher is Norton's agent. Because his purchase was unauthorized, he did not have actual authority. However, as her investment advisor who regularly buys and sells securities on her behalf, she almost certainly gave him apparent authority. If so, she cannot rescind. Chap. 1, §II.B, C.

Note: Thatcher's work for Norton does not involve continuity of service. Hence, he is not a general agent, and inherent agency power does not apply. Chap. 1, §II.F.

Question 4: Thatcher is Kane's agent, but not his servant; Kane is an undisclosed principal. If Thatcher were a general agent, then Kane is probably liable under inherent agency power. This purchase is, after all, very close to that which Thatcher is otherwise authorized to do. The fact that Thatcher's work is irregular and part time, however, militates against his being a general agent. Chap. 1, §II.F.

Because Kane is an undisclosed principal, there is no apparent authority. Chap. 1, §II.C. The CFK Trust is not bound.

Question 5:

a. Thatcher owes all his clients a fiduciary duty. What makes this case difficult is that (i) he naturally has an incentive to route his most lucrative investments to those clients for whom he does the most work; (ii) but because he performs the same services for all clients (investment advice), he has no easy way to determine what should go to whom; and (iii) he is not routing any investment to his *own* account. Given that he may still earn higher personal returns if he gives Norton and Kane the best investments, the plaintiffs may have a duty of loyalty claim against him.
b. Principals can be liable for the frauds committed by non-servant agents. That would seem to suggest that Kane should be liable (if this is fraud — which is not clear). Note that Thatcher's actions do seem to have been motivated by a desire to serve his master. Chap. 1, §III.

Question 6: Thatcher is an officer of CFKI and is using CFKI funds to invest in an opportunity in which he has a conflict of interest. The investment is voidable at the option of CFKI unless ratified by a majority of shareholders or directors, or unless Thatcher can show that it was inherently fair to the firm. Chap. 4, §III.B.

As a practical matter, given that the venture has lost money, Thatcher is unlikely to be able to show inherent fairness. Hence, the question will turn on whether there has been ratification. There has not. First, although the Delaware statute does not explicitly demand a meeting of directors or shareholders for ratification to take place, the importance generally placed on corporate formalities would seem to dictate a formal meeting. Second, Kane controls a majority of neither the disinterested board nor disinterested shares. Hence, there has been no ratification — and any negligence on the part of Kane's staff is irrelevant. Chap. 4, §III.B.

Question 7:

a. Every partner is an agent of the partnership for the purpose of carrying on apparently the usual business of the partnership. Here, Norton is a partner, and the business of the firm is real estate investment. Hence, the firm would seem to be bound. Chap. 2, §§I, II.

   That said, Norton would arguably be liable for having deliberately made a bad investment. The purpose served by buying Gettys's silence (saving Norton from embarrassment) is not a purpose of C&E.

b. No. Norton is a shareholder and director of CFKI, but not an officer. She would not have authority to make the purchase. What is more, the business of CFKI does not include real estate investments. Hence, even if she had been an officer, she probably did not have apparent authority to bind the firm.

Question 8: First, the CFKI has not made any manifestations to the firm, and Thatcher is not using anything (like stationery) that would be evidence of a general manifestation. Second, an agent cannot create his or her own apparent authority if the statement is false when made. Accordingly, there can be no apparent authority here. Chap. 1, §II.C.

Can there be inherent agency power? Making investments is the type of work that the firm relies on Thatcher to do. Accordingly, the issue turns on whether he is a general agent. The answer is unclear: On the one hand, the work he does is ongoing and does not require regular authorization; on the other, Thatcher's hours are irregular and only (on average) about one or two days a week. Chap. 1, §II.F.

Question 9: Whether to pay a corporate officer is a decision entrusted to the board. Here, the board members are Kane, Thatcher, and Norton. If they vote, Norton loses, two to one. However, if she then sues, Kane cannot claim disinterested ratification. If there is no ratification, then Kane must show that his compensation is fair and reasonable. Chap. 4, §III.B.

Problem Set B

Question 1: When Coulter (Cord VP) sells Cord stock on information about its potential production problems, she violates Rule 10b-5 by *TGS*. Chap. 5, §IV.B.

When Coulter buys Duesenberg stock, she does not violate Rule 10b-5. She owes no fiduciary duty to Duesenberg. She received no tip from any insider at Duesenberg. And Cord (apparently) had no rule (relevant to *O'Hagan*) against buying stock in its competitors. Chap. 5, §IV.

Asriel's liability for selling Cord is unclear. He owes no fiduciary duty to Cord. He might or might not have received the information about Auburn's production problems with an expectation of secrecy (hence a possible Rule 10b5-2 problem), but the point is unclear. After all, Asriel does not trade Auburn stock; he trades Cord stock. Chap. 5, §IV.E.

Asriel's purchase of Duesenberg stock raises the same issues as Coulter's purchase.

Question 2: If Cord had not bought stock in Stutz, Stutz would not owe a fiduciary duty to Cord. Any suit here would have to be brought on contractual grounds.

Given that Cord owns 10 percent of Stutz, Stutz does owe a fiduciary duty to it. However, Stutz owes a fiduciary duty to *all* its shareholders, and it furthers that duty by maximizing its profits. Here, it maximizes profits by (opportunistically) holding up Cord for a price increase. Although Cord will have to pay a higher price for the air conditioners, it will obtain a pro rata share of those increased profits — and note that the contractual dispute is unrelated to Cord's equity investment. Chap. 4, §III.

Question 3: First, note that the harm to Hispano does not depend on whether Cord makes its demands during the contract term or at the end. In either case, given Hispano's large relationship-specific investments, Cord's tactic is an "opportunistic holdup" — and highly damaging.

Second, suppose Cord did not stock in Hispano. If it demanded the price cut during the term of the contract, Hispano would have a contractual claim against it. If it demanded the price cut at renewal, it would not.

Last, suppose that Cord owns a controlling interest (as it does here) in Hispano. Cord now owes a fiduciary duty to Hispano, and the holdup would seem to violate that duty. The puzzle in this case (and the answer is indeed a puzzle) comes from the fact that Cord is not using its controlling interest to obtain the lower price; Cord's majority stake (and fiduciary duty) is unrelated to its renegotiation of the price term. Chap. 4, §III.C.

Question 4:

a. Because Edsel is a NYSE-traded company, §16(b) potentially applies. However, Blue is not an officer or director of Edsel, and she apparently held no Edsel stock before this purchase. If she did not own Edsel stock, she is not liable under §16(b). Note as well that there is no offsetting sale of the stock. Chap. 5, §III.C.

As there is no tender offer at stake, Rule 14e-3 does not apply. Chap. 5, §IV.E.

Blue uses information she acquires in connection with her work at Cord to trade on Edsel. Under *Chiarella-Dirks*, this is not a Rule 10b-5 violation. Whether it is under *O'Hagan* depends on internal Cord rules. Chap. 5, §IV.

Given that Blue is not a fiduciary at Edsel, state law insider-trading rules would not prevent her purchase. However, arguably the investment in Edsel was a corporate opportunity for Cord. If so, then Blue may have been under an obligation to offer the opportunity to Cord. Chap. 4, §III.E; Chap. 5, §II.

IV. Answers to Selected Essay Questions

b. Does the analysis under section (a) above change if Blue holds a large equity stake in Edsel? As a dominant shareholder, she would now owe the other shareholders a fiduciary duty. If she buys their stock without disclosing inside information she holds, she would seem to be violating that fiduciary duty—and hence Rule 10b-5. Chap. 4, §III.C.

This follows the language of the case law; however, it is not an approach courts seem to take. Note, too, that Blue is not trading on information she acquired through her large stake in Edsel. Instead, her inside information is entirely unrelated to her investment interest in Edsel; rather, it comes from her place on the Cord board.

Although Blue held more than 10 percent of the Edsel stock before the purchase, there is no offsetting sale that would generate §16(b) liability.

Problem Set C

Question 1: The problem covers two separate transactions: a redemption and a liquidation. Decisions to redeem are made by the board. Decisions to liquidate require votes of both the board and the shareholders.

The redemption: When the board voted to redeem the preferred, they engaged in self-dealing. After all, they owned all of the preferred. They have the burden of proving that the redemption was fair and reasonable to the firm. The standard is what a disinterested board would do, and the *Zahn* decision on remand tells us that this is to favor the junior-most security (the common). Chap. 4, §III.C.

In this problem, redeeming the preferred at $100 does favor the common. Were the company to liquidate without redeeming the preferred, the preferred would take double the amount of the common. The firm is worth $17 million. There are 100,000 common and 50,000 preferred. If the firm liquidates without redeeming the preferred, the common would get $85 and the preferred $170. (This is simple algebra with two equations and two unknowns: Let P equal the payout to the preferreds and C equal the payout to the commons; we know that $P = 2C$ and $100{,}000C + 50{,}000P = \$17{,}000{,}000$.) Hence, redeeming the preferred at $100 favors the common. Despite being dominated by the preferred, the board favored the common when it redeemed the preferred (i.e., themselves) at only $100 per share.

Another way to make the same point is to note that if the company liquidated without redeeming the preferred, the common would get half of the company, or $8.5 million. After all, there are half as many preferred shares, but they get twice as much per share. If the firm redeemed the preferred at $100, that would cost $5 million—leaving the common with $12 million.

The liquidation: What of the liquidation? Initially, the board owned only preferred. It called the preferred prior to liquidation, so at liquidation the board members would either hold cash or common (they would hold common if they converted). Accordingly, there was no self-dealing involved, and the plaintiff would have to show that the liquidation constituted waste. The plaintiff would lose.

Ratification: Given the analysis above, ratification is irrelevant because the plaintiff loses anyway—but ask yourself: Was there majority-of-minority ratification? Chap. 4, §III.B. Because 83 percent of the common approved the merger, apparently a majority of the minority shareholders did approve it. I say "apparently" because we do not know how much common the directors held. Some of the directors indirectly held a portion of the 30,000 shares of common held by DFI. Let us suppose that the directors control all 30,000 shares. If acting rationally, the directors would also have converted their preferred to common. If so, there would have been $100,000 + 50,000 = 150,000$ shares of common. Of these, DFI would have owned 30,000, and the directors would directly have owned another 50,000. If 83 percent of the common approved the merger, the votes in favor would have been $150,000 \times 0.83 = 124,500$. The no votes would have been 25,500. If we posit that all 80,000 votes controlled by the board voted in favor of the merger, that would leave 44,000 other yes votes. Hence, 44,000 of the 70,000 non-board shares voted to approve the merger.

Suppose the directors (irrationally) did not convert any of their preferred. If 83 percent of the common approved the merger, the yes votes were 83,000. The directors held a portion of the 30,000 held by DFI. That would leave 53,000 shares voted in favor by the nonboard shareholders. Again, a majority of the minority must have approved the merger.

This would seem to be majority-of-minority ratification—except that the plaintiff claims that there was not full disclosure. Absent full disclosure, ratification does not count.

Ratification may not count—but it does not matter here anyway. As the liquidation did not involve self-dealing, the business judgment rule applied. Plaintiff loses.

Question 2: When a company redeems stock, the redemption constitutes a purchase of a security covered by Rule 10b-5. Accordingly, the company must disclose any material nonpublic information it might have.

But disclose to whom? PARIC is not redeeming the common. It is redeeming only the preferred, and the board owns all of the preferred. Hence, the people who are the target of the redemption have access to full information. That would suggest that Rule 10b-5 is not a problem.

And yet, what about Lola? Because she does not attend the board meetings, she probably lacks information about the value of the firm. Is that relevant? If she has a duty to attend the board meetings but skips them, does the company have a duty to contact her and expressly tell her the value of the firm? The answer is unclear.

Question 3: The plaintiff is not complaining about a loss to the corporation; instead, the plaintiff is complaining about the allocation of value among the classes of stock. Hence, the claim is direct. Chap. 3, §II.D.

Question 4: Because the directors all own preferred stock, they face a conflict of interest. They are obligated to favor the junior-most security—and here that would entail *not* redeeming the preferred. If they liquidate without redeeming, the preferred would get $90 per share and the common $45 (by algebra). By redeeming the preferred at $100, the directors leave less for the common.

Note that Lola and Tom both also have an interest in the common through DFI. The other three directors have deliberately chosen a time when Lola and Tom will not be there to engineer this transfer to the preferred. (Note, however, as discussed in (6) below, that Lola and Tom's gains on the preferred probably outweigh their loss on their share of DFI common.)

Neff and Keyes are officers in DFI. As a result, they violate their fiduciary duty to the DFI shareholders as well. That point is not directly relevant to the question here, which involves a claim by PARIC shareholders.

Question 5: Lola violates her duty of care by not attending board meetings. In the suit at hand, causation (of the loss to the common shareholders) is of course an obvious question. Note that this problem does *not* implicate *Stone v. Ritter* and *Caremark*. Instead, this is a straightforward *Francis* problem. Chap. 4, §II.

Lola does own preferred, even if she has a stake in the common too. Thus there is a potential duty of loyalty question as well.

Question 6: DFI may be a controlling shareholder. If so, it has a fiduciary duty to the other shareholders. Given that the redemption in this problem hurts the common (see Question (4) above), however, why would DFI do this? Could it possibly have gained from a redemption? And if it could not have gained, why should it be liable?

Note that Tom and Lola have interests in DFI. We do not know how much of an interest they have in it, but they have some. They each also own 10,000 shares of the preferred. What now is the impact of the redemption on them personally?

a. Recall (from (4) above) that if the firm were to liquidate without redeeming the preferred, the common would receive $45 per share and the preferred would receive $90 per share. If the firm redeems the 50,000 shares of preferred at $100 per share, that would leave $4 million to be divided among 10,000 common shares — or $40 per share.

b. Hence, a redemption increases the distribution to the preferred by $10 per share, whereas it decreases the distribution to the common by $5 per share.

c. Tom and Lola together have 20,000 preferred shares. Their excess gain on the preferred from the liquidation is thus $200,000. Tom and Lola have some (unstated) fraction of the DFI interest of 30,000 shares of common stock. The entire loss on DFI from the redemption is $150,000.

Conclusion: Notwithstanding their interest in the common through DFI, Tom and Lola apparently earn a net gain by redeeming the preferred.

Now consider two further issues. First, although the two DFI investors on the PARIC board (Tom and Lola) do gain from the redemption (through their shares of preferred), they did not participate in the board decision. If they had no part in this, should they be liable personally? And if they personally are not liable, then by what logic would DFI (which may have earned them their places onto the board) be liable? Perhaps it simply is not liable.

Second, two of the directors who do engineer the redemption are Keyes and Neff, and they are also officers of DFI (and hence its agents). Is there a way in which DFI should be held liable for their duty of loyalty violations to PARIC? Given that DFI loses from the transaction, one would think not.

Question 7: Neff, Keyes, and Phyllis violate their fiduciary duty to PARIC (for reasons discussed above). Given that DFI holds common, Neff and Keyes also violate their fiduciary duty to DFI.

Ordinarily, ratification by the shareholders would shift the burden of proof. And here there has been full disclosure. Yet Neff, who clearly has a conflict of interest, controls the vote by the DFI shares. Ratification thus seems problematic (we are not given the actual numbers) — a point consistent with the fact that rational common stockholders would never approve the redemption.

Table of Cases

Table of Cases

Table of Cases

Index

Index

corporate opportunity, 159–162, 166–167, 176–183
dominant shareholders, 163–172
in agency, 1–2, 26–29
in derivative suits, 91–97
in partnership, 49–58, 61–64, 67–68
ratification, 159–163. See also Ratification

Easterbrook, Frank H., 35, 42, 132, 149, 287, 300–304, 308–309, 318–319
Efficient capital markets hypothesis. See informational efficiency
Enterprise liability, 117–118
Exculpatory clauses, 145–146, 154–155
Executive compensation, 172–176
Express authority. See Authority

Ferrell, Allen, 191
Fiduciary duties. See Duty of loyalty and Duty of care
Fischel, Daniel R., 148–149, 211, 308–309, 318–319, 380
Flom, Joseph, 365–367
Formalities. See Piercing the corporate veil
Forstman, Theodore, 364–365, 368–370
Fox, Merritt, 191
Franchising, 18–23, 39–40, 241–242, 255–256
Fraud
  and the business judgment rule, 87, 136
  and insider trading, 188, 199, 214. See also Insider trading
  piercing the corporate veil, 115, 119–125
Freeze-outs, 286–304
  statutory dissolution as solution, 304–309
  buy-out agreements as solution, 309–315
  freeze-out mergers, 343–348
Friendly, Henry, 25, 326

General agent, 12
Gevurtz, Franklin A., 338
Gilmore, Grant, 12
Gilson, Ronald, 187
Golden parachutes, 368–369
Good faith, 147–155, 175–176
Gordon, Jeffrey N., 357, 360
Greenmail, 352–355
Grundfest, Joseph, 96

Hammer, Armand, 79–83, 85–86, 88, 97, 121–122, 135, 148, 154, 231–232, 238
Hand, Learned, 12, 189
Henderson, M. Todd, 106, 112
Herscovici, Steven, 380
Hetherington, John A.C., 307

Implied authority. See Authority
Incorporation procedure, 126–129
Indemnification of board, 146–147
Independent contractors. See Agents
Informational efficiency of stock prices, 139–140, 148–150, 187, 190–192
Inherent agency power. See Authority
Insider trading. See also Rule 10b–5, Rule 10b5–2, Rule 14e–3, and Securities Exchange Act of 1934
  close corporations, 301–304
  fiduciary duty requirement, 189, 216–225
  level playing field theory, 212–216
  materiality, 214–215
  misappropriation theory, 218–219, 225–238
  temporary insider, 225
  tippee liability, 219–238
  under Rule 10b–5, 211–239
  under Sec. 16(b), 202–210
  under state law, 188–190
Irrelevance theorem, dividend, 131–132, 287–288
Irrevocable proxies, 260–261, 269

Jensen, Michael C., 359

Kahan, Marcel, 129
Kamar, Ehud, 129
Kaufman, Andrew L., 54
Kaufman, Irving, 98, 217
Kesten, Jay, 141, 143
Klein, William A., 36, 187, 196, 257
Kraakman, Reinier, 119, 141, 143, 187

Legal capital, 130–131
Lender liability, 7, 36–37
Level playing field theory. See Insider trading
Leveraged buy-outs, 302, 364, 368–369
Limited liability companies, 76–77
Limited liability for shareholders, 114
Limited liability limited partnerships, 75–76
Limited liability partnerships, 77
Limited partnerships, 75
Lipton, Martin, 361, 365–368
Liquidation of corporation, 169
Lockups, 369–370
Loyalty, duty of. See Duty of loyalty
Lumbard, Edward, 325

Macey, Jonathan, 129, 164, 349
Management buy-outs, 364, 368
Manne, Henry G., 211, 349, 380
Materiality. See Insider trading
McGraw, John, 272–277

419

Index